P9-DDM-104

A River
Running
West

The Life
of John Wesley Powell

Donald Worster

OXFORD
UNIVERSITY PRESS

2001

A River Running West

OXFORD
UNIVERSITY PRESS

Oxford   New York
Athens   Auckland   Bangkok   Bogotá   Buenos Aires   Calcutta
Cape Town   Chennai   Dar es Salaam   Delhi   Florence   Hong Kong   Istanbul
Karachi   Kuala Lumpur   Madrid   Melbourne   Mexico City   Mumbai
Nairobi   Paris   São Paulo   Shanghai   Singapore   Taipei   Tokyo   Toronto   Warsaw

and associated companies in
Berlin   Ibadan

Published by Oxford University Press, Inc.
198 Madison Avenue, New York, New York 10016

Oxford is a registered trademark of Oxford University Press.

Library of Congress Cataloging-in-Publication Data
Worster, Donald, 1941–
     A river running west : the life of John Wesley Powell / by Donald Worster.
        p. cm.
     Includes bibliographical references and index.
     ISBN 0-19-509991-5
     1. Powell, John Wesley, 1834–1902. 2. Explorers—United States—Biography. 3.
Conserationists—United States—Biography. 4. Colorado River
(Colo.-Mexico)—Discovery and exploration. 5. Grand Canyon (Ariz.)—Discovery
and exploration. 6. West (U.S.)—Discovery and exploration. I. Title.

F788.P88 W67 2001
333.7'2'092—dc21
[B]
                                                                    00-032623

Book design by Susan Day

9 8 7 6 5 4 3 2 1
Printed in the United States of America
on acid-free paper

TO BEV, AGAIN

Contents

Part Three: Washington, D.C.

Green River Station, 1869

In the month of May 1869 two parties gathered in America's western wilds with travel and adventure on their minds. The larger party met at Promontory Summit, Utah, to celebrate the first railroad uniting the Atlantic and Pacific oceans. The smaller party, only ten men in all, encamped a few hundred miles to the east; their leader called them the Colorado River Exploring Expedition. Together the two groups created a pivotal moment in the nation's movement west. Both were filled with hopes and dreams, but they were in many ways different hopes, different dreams.

At the time the railroad builders drew all the attention. On 10 May they met on a sun-baked, desolate plain near the Great Salt Lake to lay the last rails and drive the final spike joining the two halves of the transcontinental line, one approaching from the east, the other from the west. Former governor of California and now company president Leland Stanford represented the Central Pacific railroad, while General Grenville Dodge and T.C. Durant represented the Union Pacific; around them massed a crowd of governors, congressmen, local officials, and assorted onlookers fortified with guns and whiskey bottles. When the maul came down on the spike at 12:32 P.M. local time, it sent an electrical signal all the way to Washington: "Done." Church bells began to ring and cannon to boom in cities across the land, while orators clambered to their feet to proclaim what one newspaper writer called the marriage of "the gorgeous east and the imperial west of America, with the indisoluble seal of inter-oceanic commerce."[1]

For the first ticket-buying passengers the achievement of the railroad kings was more concrete and immediate. They could now board trains from New York to Council Bluffs, Iowa, cross the Missouri River on a ferry boat, board another train at Omaha, and—passing over vast grasslands and foothills, snow-covered ranges and alkaline basins—arrive in Sacramento where they could catch a steamer going to San Francisco Bay, end of the line. The time consumed in that cross-country trip was only seven days; the cost was about $200, beds and meals included. And the experience was little short of miraculous. They slept in Pullman Palace Car comfort as the train rocketed over the land at twenty-five to thirty miles an hour. Walnut paneling, ice water from a faucet, embossed French glass and mirrors, and forty-inch-wide berths hung with heavy curtains rivaled the accommodations of an elegant hotel. In the dining car they ate gourmet dinners and drank fine red claret.[2]

Among the stopping places along the way was the railroad town of Green River in the territory of Wyoming. The previous fall it had been a raucous construction camp populated by Irish laborers, prostitutes, and saloons. Behind the dusty town with its false-front buildings, many of which now stood empty, rose an imposing sandstone monolith, Citadel Butte. The river furnished clear mountain water to replenish the steam boilers of the locomotive, which was why the train stopped here briefly.

If they looked downstream, the passengers could make out that other group of travelers, camped on a low island. With far less national attention, the second group had come in the name of science to explore the last unmapped part of the continental United States. None of them belonged to any corporation. Although some hoped for gold or other bonanzas, none would ever grow rich. Their plan was to go down the Green to its junction with the Grand, where the Colorado River begins, and then continue down the Colorado through the Grand Canyon. In sharp contrast to the railroad passengers they would travel in small wooden boats, eat hardtack and bacon, sleep on mosquito-thick sandbars, and drink from the increasingly silt-laden river. It would take them three months of hard work, much of it spent portaging their boats around dangerous rapids, and not all of them would make it through alive.

The day after the "final spike" ceremonies at Promontory Summit, on 11 May, while the newspapers were discussing the significance of the new railroad, the leader of the Colorado River Exploring Expedition joined his men. His name was John W. Powell. A thirty-five-year-old Civil War veteran, he was short of stature and maimed in body, though his bristling auburn burnsides promised dash and energy. His waiting crew included an Indian trader, a printer, a soldier, and miscellaneous frontier knockabouts. Although no reporters were on hand to write about this gathering, and indeed there was little ceremony to witness, a story at least as compelling as the railroad's saga of torrid construction and capitalist triumph was about to commence. They launched their boats on 24 May 1869.

Which was the more significant event that spring? Public opinion then, and probably now, would say that it was the completion of the railroad. As observers correctly predicted at the time, the new railway made possible a new nation and a new West. But the small group setting off to discover the course of the Colorado River had an impact too, some of it economic, more of it cultural. Their expedition made Powell one of the most admired explorers of the century. He brought back vital knowledge of the hidden Southwest—its rivers, mountains, natural resources, and, not least, the Grand Canyon. He became one of the leading interpreters of the West, an influential voice on its land and water issues as well as its treatment of indigenous peoples, a voice often contesting that of the railroad promoters.

Today Promontory Summit has become a protected historic site, but not many tourists find their way there. In contrast, Powell's Green and Colorado rivers are among America's leading natural attractions in a nature-hungry age. Five million visitors a year visit the Grand Canyon National Park, nearly half of them from foreign countries; over twenty thousand actually float down the river where it still races through the canyon walls. And everywhere they go the tourist hordes encounter the name and image of John Wesley Powell. He has been canonized by the National Park Service and by the Bureau of Reclamation, by outdoor writers and boatmen, as one of the greatest pathfinders in American history and as a prophet of what the West might still become.

Celebrity and fame, to be sure, often obscure a more complicated reality. Powell's views of nature and technology, of economic progress, and even of railroads, were more tangled than we usually remember. He did not hesitate, for example, to use the railroad to join his exploring party. He called for building dams, for transforming the arid lands into an agricultural empire, though at the same time he extolled the wilderness and criticized ruthless corporations. To discover the man behind the celebrity, with all his ambivalence and contradiction, is to discover a more complicated America.

Powell's contemporaries, to be sure, did not make it easy for later generations to gain insight into his complexities or contradictions. After his death, one of his closest associates, the geologist Grove Karl

Gilbert, destroyed most of the personal papers he left behind.[3] One can only guess what secrets they might have revealed or insights they might have afforded. Still, much material has survived, more in fact than anyone has ever brought together before.

It has been nearly half a century since the first full-scale biographies of Powell appeared in print, and their interpretation or authority has seldom been challenged. The first biography was *Powell of the Colorado*, published in 1951 by William Culp Darrah, a geologist in private employ. The second was *Beyond the Hundredth Meridian*, published in 1954 by the acclaimed novelist Wallace Stegner. Stegner's book now ranks as one of the most influential books ever written about the West, and more than any other work its publication explains Powell's resurrection to sainthood after World War Two. Yet Stegner's biography was based on limited research into its subject or the nation's development. And it laid such strong claim to Powell as Man of the West, a prophet for the arid region, that it obscured the fact that he was, above all, an intensely nationalistic American.

Like a great river in floodtide, America in the nineteenth century flowed across the continent with more power and force, much of it destructive, than any river of nature. Powell was part of that flow. He was enthusiastic and optimistic about where that river was heading. Although he dreamed of a different and better nation, he believed in its essential goodness. The expansion of America framed his childhood experience, inspired his adult career, and even became, as it did for so many of his fellow citizens, a personal religion.

Powell's story must begin even before he was born, with his parents in England, members of an urban working class animated by evangelical faith, hopeful immigrants who came to America to rise out of obscurity, insecurity, and moral corruption. Long before the son dared to take on the formidable canyons and deserts of the West, he prepared himself in their adopted world — the back country of upper New York State, the thick green forests of Ohio, and the broad prairies of Wisconsin and Illinois. How that growing up shaped his outlook and charged him with hope and ambition is a story that has never been fully told.

Powell's life is also the story of the rising influence of the natural sciences, of rationalism contesting the faith of traditional religion, and of a new nationalism and secularism taking its place. As he was coming of age, science was rising to influence the study of nature and culture and even the making of laws. In his day science meant, above all, geology, evolution, and Darwinism. The contest of those ideas with what is now called religious fundamentalism for supremacy in the American mind is mirrored in Powell as nowhere else.

His life, moreover, is a story of a nation struggling with the troubled relations among its several races and cultures, a struggle that always threatened to spoil the promise. Powell not only explored the Colorado River, he explored the native peoples, becoming for a period the nation's foremost authority on them. His work on Indians helped bring a shift in national policy from one of warfare and removal to one of peaceful integration and assimilation, with all the ethnocentric limitations that such a shift implied. And not only Indians but African Americans figured significantly in his vision of America — from the days of chattel slavery through the Civil War to emancipation. He reflected the conscience of a nation struggling with issues of justice, cultural diversity, and man's inhumanity to man.

Powell's story is finally one of Americans confronting and learning to live with the land they came to possess. He knew as well as anyone the Colorado Plateau and its great chasm, as he knew the arid West, but he also knew much of eastern America — together, a land as physically impressive as any on earth. He became a founder of the national movement to conserve that land, to adjust settlement and economic use to its limitations, and (more muted) to preserve its beauty and diversity for future generations.

None of this, of course, could have been appreciated by those riding comfortably on the transcontinental rails in spring 1869. Even if they had paid more attention than they did, they could not have found in the man or his exploring party much to admire or explain. They could not have grasped the significance of his role in the nation and its expansion. Even today, travelers pass on their way without knowing what kind of man this was: his faults and weaknesses as well as his strengths and achievements. This book seeks to explore that intrepid pathfinder and his place in the canyons of America's past.

Part One

Northern Days

CHAPTER 1

A Mission to America

John Wesley Powell was born on 24 March 1834 in Mount Morris, New York, a tidy village of brick churches and clapboarded houses newly planted in the back country. His parents, Joseph and Mary, were immigrants from England in need of work. Their son was delivered in the Methodist parsonage where they had taken temporary shelter and named after the great hero of their lives, John Wesley, founder of the evangelical Protestant movement called Methodism. He would grow up, they prayed, to become a spiritual leader and be for America what Wesley had been for the old country, a magnetic prophet who drew sinners out of corruption.

"Train up a child in the way he should go," advised the Book of Proverbs, "and when he is old, he will not depart from it." The parents took Solomon's advice seriously. Although their outward circumstances were not impressive, they intended to train this child carefully in biblical doctrine and instill in him a strong moral character. They would teach him to put the love of God above the things of the earth and subdue his naturally selfish will. He must learn to make Jesus his lord and master and trust in the promise, "I am the light of the world: he that followeth me shall not walk in darkness, but shall have the light of life" (St. John 8:12).

Such were the hopes of this pious couple. What they did not reckon with was the competition they would have from the world outside the parsonage windows. An aggressive, self-confident, and at times intensely secular society was out there, filled with energy and purposes of its own. No parents could altogether protect their progeny from its competing influence and certainly not these parents, who had come to America to join that society and improve their material condition.

They would not find it easy to keep their family on the narrow path to righteousness or to determine how their children would grow up in such an environment.

The year John Wesley Powell (or "Wes" as he came to be called) was born, Andrew Jackson was well into his second term as president of the United States. Jackson had won two landslide victories in some of the dirtiest and most rambunctious campaigns the nation had seen thus far. As president, he wanted to sweep the native peoples from the path of the invading whites. He approved the driving of the Sauk and Fox Indians from Illinois and paraded their defeated leader, Black Hawk, as a trophy of war. He ignored the Supreme Court's decision that the Cherokees, one of the "Five Civilized Tribes" of the South, must be protected from white land-grabbers, and in the winter of 1838 his troops forced the Cherokees at bayonet point along the infamous "Trail of Tears" to the newly established Indian Territory (later named Oklahoma). By that date Jackson's policies had emptied most of the country east of the Mississippi of its remaining native inhabitants.

Jackson was also reshaping the American political system toward a modern mass democracy. Among the chief issues of the day, after the president's moral character and Indian policy, was whether a business elite would continue to control the economy or whether the president would succeed in destroying their monopolistic institution, the Bank of the United States, and in dispersing power over interest rates and the money supply among the citizenry. Jackson saw himself as the champion of the common man. Ostensibly, the country was wrangling over who should control the currency, but really it was asking how much democracy it could stand without sacrificing prosperity.

Foreign observers were awestruck by, and not a little fearful of, that rising clamor of "the People" demanding a voice in American affairs. The French traveler Michel Chevalier, touring the country the same spring that Wes was born, saw emerging the world's first true democracy. Whereas in Europe a tradition of inequality had survived half a century of revolution, in America society had become "essentially and radically a democracy, not in name merely but in deed." The egalitarian spirit suffused all national habits and customs. It fed on a widespread condition of ease made possible by high wages in a land of natural abundance. Families could buy bread, meat, sugar, or tea at cheaper prices than in France or England and earn incomes that were double or triple what they were overseas. There were no poor here, Chevalier noted — none at least in the northern states "which have protected themselves from the leprosy of slavery."[1] America's free white laborers and farmers enjoyed, in his opinion, a standard of living well above that of ordinary people in older countries. Naturally, they expected that they should have a say in the running of their institutions.

The Powells came to America wanting to share in the country's promise for commoners, not realizing that its pushy democracy and economic individualism might be incompatible with key parts of their Methodist beliefs. God's will must rule, said Wesley, not any man's. Within the human family that divine will was represented, however imperfectly, by the figure of the father. The good father must break the will of his children. He must teach them that they are "fallen spirits," not the salt of the earth, and show them that they are more ignorant, foolish, and wicked "than they can possibly conceive." In their self-seeking ambition and pride, they are "like the devil," unfit and unruly. In their "foolish desires" and "grovelling appetites" they are no better than the beasts of the field. Their nature is filled with "disease," the revered Wesley warned, and they must be purified by divine grace working through patriarchal authority. "The one thing needful," the eminent man preached, was "the renewal of our fallen nature."[2] None of that sounded quite like the noisy assertiveness of Jacksonian democracy.

Over the next few decades, as Wes passed through childhood and became an adult, the American national ethos made it harder and harder for him or anyone else to drink the pure milk of Methodist spirituality. A vast continent opened to the west, diverting his attention and that of many others from sanctifying their corrupt souls to pursuing more worldly excitements. Two years after he was born, American interlopers declared Texas to be a sovereign nation and then demanded that it be annexed as a state. In 1848 other expansionists lobbied to have California and the Southwest added to the territory of the United States, fulfilling a manifest destiny to stretch from sea to sea. An advance guard of explorers and fur trappers was already combing through those lands beyond the Mississippi River, and they in turn gave way to gold miners, cavalry officers, cattle drovers, and covered-wagon pioneers bound for the prairies of Nebraska, the towering mountains of Utah, the lush pastoral promise of Oregon's Willamette Valley. This exuberant push westward packed many Bibles in its baggage, and often the pushers invoked the name of God to sanctify their efforts, but the conquest of the West did not run easily alongside a genuine, self-abnegating piety. The conquest of the continent was preoccupied with displacing native peoples, acquiring property, asserting a right to occupancy; while evangelical religion was focused on disciplining chaotic desires, getting an unruly spirit ready for heaven.

Other national transformations were in the making, and they too made it difficult to raise a child in the way that God and his prophet Wesley said it should be done. The United States stood on the verge of large-scale industrialization in the year Wes was born. Although the population was still employed overwhelmingly in agriculture, more farmers than ever before focused on producing marketable commodities rather than growing their own sustenance. Their customers were merchants, manufacturers, clerks, shopkeepers, and millhands whose numbers were increasing exponentially. By the 1830s the new system of factory production was spreading beyond New England and Pennsylvania and was turning out a wealth of textiles, shoes, buckets, chairs, ropes, and stoves. In the year Wes became a teenager, John Deere established a factory in Illinois to produce steel plows.

So much mass production required more and better transportation to move goods to consumers. The boy grew up with the making of canals and railroads to carry commodities from farm to city, from industry back to farm. He saw the emergence of an economy based on coal, petroleum, and steel, and eventually one based on electricity and automobiles. In his lifetime the United States became the leading industrial nation on earth, surpassing Great Britain and Germany. It allowed personal fortunes to accumulate on a far greater scale than any known in President Jackson's day, or indeed in the days of kings and emperors of old.

All those economic feats testified to a love of the world, a confidence in human nature, a passion for wealth and power that was decidedly secular. How those achievements could be squared with true religion was not clearly shown by the Reverend Wesley. The Bible was explicit, firm, and uncompromising in its general principles: "If any man love the world, the love of the Father is not in him" (I John 2:15). But America of the nineteenth century was emphatically in love with the world and all its goods.

One more unforeseen obstacle to teaching this new child the way he should go was the shadow of war already looming on the American horizon. When it came — a civil war over race and national identity — it tore the country apart. What Chevalier called "the leprosy of slavery" poisoned the rising democracy nearly to its roots. A democracy for white people only could not endure its own contradictions for long. Wes gave nearly four years of his life to the cause of ending slavery and holding the nation together. In making that sacrifice, more than in any other way, he fulfilled his parents' ideals, for they took most seriously the equality of all human beings before God. But the trauma of brutal, often senseless bloodshed was not an experience that a devout religious upbringing could altogether prepare one to understand.

How little then was in the hands of those godly parents, whether they were aware of the fact or not, as they beheld their new son. They could read their Bible over his wee head. They could thumb Wesley's sermons and hymns for inspiration. They could earnestly resolve to train this boy in the way he should go. Their success, however, must be partial and unpredictable. They could not anticipate, nor control, the changing society outside the village parsonage. God had given them a child, but America helped produce a son.

The parents Mary and Joseph Powell came out of Britain's urban artisan class. They grew up in small cities where their families had acquired a degree of self-reliance based on traditional craft knowledge. Caught in the throes of change like everyone else, they enjoyed more independence and security than many below them in the social scale and, for all their piety, were eager to climb the ladder of success to higher rungs.

Mary's native place was the maritime trading center of Kingston-upon-Hull (or simply Hull). She was born on 11 November 1803 to Joseph Dean and Ann Pickering.[3] Her mother must have died soon thereafter, because local records show that her father Joseph and another woman, Mary Ann Worthy, became man and wife and in 1805 had a son also named Joseph, followed by six more children. Mary's father was described as a cabinet maker and furniture broker with his own separate auction room. Eventually, he became an "appraiser and auctioneer" in new premises on the street named Market-place—a man moving up from the labor of using planes and chisels to running a small business.[4]

The Deans lived in the parish of Sculcoates, part of the larger city located at the junction of the Hull and Humber rivers. Once an outlying agricultural village, Sculcoates was becoming an urbanized district and a favored site for industry by the time Mary was born. Hull was already five centuries old by that point. Founded by King Edward I as a base for his Scottish campaigns, the city grew into one of England's leading ports. The Humber provided easy access into the Yorkshire interior, and out of its broad estuary, some twenty miles wide where the city sits, ships sailed to London, Germany, Sweden, and Russia. The population of the city, including Sculcoates, was twenty-seven thousand in 1800 and increasing faster than the national average. "The whole town lies on a level tract of ground," wrote one observer, making "a very rich and splendid appearance."[5]

Hull's most famous resident was William Wilberforce, member of Parliament and foe of the trade in African slaves going on in the British Empire. Like other critics of that dehumanizing commerce, he came to his views through a conversion to evangelical religion, and, following his example, Hull became a center of godly benevolence. The Deans were not part of Wilberforce's movement or of the established church; they were part of the Catholic minority. But Mary eventually drifted out of the family religion and over into Methodism, converting at the age of twelve. Perhaps she was on the outs with her stepmother and half-brothers and half-sisters; only her younger sibling Joseph kept up any contact with Mary in later years, and then it was a distant one. Whatever the reason, Mary became an evangelical and an opponent of slavery.

Unlike many other converts, Mary was never rigidly doctrinaire about her adopted theology. She liked to read, and through her reading she discovered the writings of the Swedish polymathic genius, Emanuel Swedenborg, who in the eighteenth century had created a new ecumenical theology all his own. A widely respected scientist who turned to religion at middle age, he drew many followers in England and America, some of whom incorporated themselves as the Church of the New Jerusalem to spread his message. Swedenborg claimed to have received directly from Jesus Christ a deeper, more tolerant, and inclusive understanding of the Scriptures. Sectarianism, he warned, is destructive to the work of salvation. "Men of every religion are saved," provided they live a life of charity that "consists in thinking kindly of another, and . . . perceiving joy in one's self from the fact that others are saved."[6] Mary Dean may have broken with her family, but she did not do so to take up cudgels. What she sought for the rest of her life was a world united in love of Jesus, with malice toward none and kindness toward all. She merged Swedenborg with Wesley, both of them reinforcing her belief that a pious heart was more important than doctrinal correctness.

How she met the man she would marry, Joseph Powell, is a mystery. He was an auburn-haired Welshman from the other side of the country—more disputatious by nature, more commanding in appearance and voice, more determined to save souls from their many errors. Mary probably left Hull for London, where Joseph had become a licensed exhorter in the Methodist sect, or for Birmingham, where Methodism and Swedenborgianism were both strong. Somehow, across imposing gulfs of space and personality, they met and pledged their lives to one another.

Joseph's origins are a little more elusive than Mary's. His tombstone gives his age at death as sixty-six, which would make his birthdate 1805. Family memories add that he was from Shrewsbury, the county seat of Shropshire. No parish record in that city, however, nor in any other part of the county, lists his birth or baptism in 1805 or any other year.[7] A younger brother's grave in the same plot in Wheaton, Illinois, where Joseph is buried yields the names of "Geo. P. and Charlotte W." as parents. Both Christian names occurred during the first decade of the century in the town of Ludlow, some thirty miles south, but apparently not in Shrewsbury. It seems safe to say that, if Joseph was Ludlow born, he was Shrewsbury raised.

Those west-country towns began as ancient border fortresses guarding the Welsh Marches, the frontier that once separated warring England and Wales. By 1800 they were thriving market towns serving one of the country's most alluring landscapes, the green dales of Shropshire, a countryside threaded by the River Severn, which empties into the sea near Bristol. Ludlow, standing on a prominent hill, was proud of its ancient castle built to keep out the Welsh. Shrewsbury, almost an island in a horseshoe bend of the river, boasted a medieval castle too, along with a Benedictine monastery, the Abbey, long disused and in ruins. The town experienced a burst of affluence during the sixteenth and seventeenth centuries, following the Act of Union that made the two nations one, when wool from Wales began coming to the English market. Wool created here a gemstone of Tudor architecture: many black-and-white frame houses, imposing in size if never quite straight in their lines, built along the narrow, twisting streets, the homes of merchants and drapers.[8]

During the time when young Joseph Powell was prowling the local neighborhoods—the Dingle, Pride Hill, St. Alkmund's Place, Fish Street—Shrewsbury was a quiet, uneventful provincial town. The most prominent local figure was Dr. Robert Darwin, the physician son of the great scientist and poet Erasmus Darwin. Across the Welsh Bridge that led out of town and into the countryside, on the suburban meadow lands, Robert had built a large Georgian house, the

Mount, where he presided over his numerous family, patients, and debtors. In 1809, when Joseph Powell was a small lad, the Darwins gave birth to a son named Charles. That Darwin later became one of the most important thinkers of the modern age, though in his Shrewsbury youth Charles was an unimpressive child of privilege who liked to spend his leisure shooting guns, playing with dogs, and collecting beetles.

Possibly young Charles Darwin knew his slightly older fellow-townsman Joseph Powell, for Shrewsbury had a population of only fifteen thousand people, all packed closely together. The two boys may have nodded at one another along the river banks or in the narrow foot passageways called "shuts" that ran between the buildings. Or they may have thrown rocks at each other in battles between rich and poor boys. If they were at all acquainted, they were separated by a barrier wider than the Severn. At an early age Charles was sent to board at Shrewsbury School in the town center, a famous private institution that educated elite children for Oxford or Cambridge. No Powell, according to records, ever attended the school in those years. While Charles was force-fed a diet of Greek and Latin, hating every minute of it, Joseph became apprenticed to a tailor in one of the wool shops and learned a trade that he would pursue for many years.[9]

The Powells were not only working-class artisans; they were also an ethnic minority—Welshmen living in what had become an Englishman's world. That fact alone would have meant that they could not become part of the social circles in which the Darwins moved. Yet Joseph's parents were not illiterate rustics. They had at least one other child, a boy they called Walter Scott Powell, born probably in 1814 and named after the Scottish novelist who published his first novel, *Waverley*, in that same year and would go on to write two novels set in the Welsh Marches, *The Bethrothed* and *The Talisman*. Naming their son for a brilliant new writer suggests that the parents were avid but not especially religious readers. Whoever they were, or whether they even survived for long, the older Powells did not establish an enduring family bond with their sons. Perhaps, as in the case of Mary Dean, the subject of religion separated them. Joseph, at some point in his youth, became a Methodist convert. Walter meekly followed his older brother's lead, and the two of them left their family, left Shrewsbury, and eventually left Britain together.

The county of Shropshire lies sandwiched between, on the west, the mountains of Wales and, on the east, the English Midlands, hotbed of the industrial revolution. It was toward the latter center of activity that the Powell boys went, after a sojourn in London, to the city of Birmingham where they made their home for the next several years. Long a center of Puritan sympathies, Birmingham had been swept by Methodist revivals from the late eighteenth century on. Besides religion, the compelling interest of the city was making money. The French writer Alexis de Tocqueville described the place as "an immense workshop, a huge forge, a vast shop. One only sees busy people and faces brown with smoke. One hears nothing but the sound of hammers and the whistle of steam escaping from boilers."[10] At the end of the work day the citizens commonly retreated to one of the four hundred public houses in the city to wash down the smoke and grit of manufacturing. The Powell boys did not join them, but they were now part of an industrial proletariat, learning to survive in one of England's great metropolises.

Here in Birmingham on 31 January 1828, in the Anglican mother church of St. Martin's, were married "Joseph Powell, Bachelor," and "Mary Dean, Spinster," both described as "of this parish."[11] She was twenty-five, he was twenty-three years old. Both were firmly committed Methodists, but when it came to weddings they still saw themselves as part of the established Church of England. A little over nine months later they brought into the world their first child, whom they christened Martha Ann, followed a year later by a second girl, Mary Pickering—two little daughters named after the good sisters who ministered to Jesus after He raised their brother from the dead. By this point the Powells resided in Wolverhampton, a suburb of Birmingham, where Joseph was tailoring, brother Walter was learning to make and repair clocks, and wife Mary was tending the children. They were all three also beginning to think of emigrating to America.

By the time of Mary and Joseph's marriage Methodism had existed for nearly a century. Its founders, the brothers John and Charles Wesley, had been denied church pulpits, so they preached on street corners, in open fields, in barns, wherever people would listen. Altogether, John delivered some forty thousand sermons in his lifetime and traveled by coach and horseback several hundred thousand miles. In the 1730s the brothers crossed the ocean to the colony of Georgia, planting in the New World the seeds of their faith. For a long while the harvest was small, though soon after John died in 1791 (Charles died three years earlier), a new Wesleyan Methodist Church came into being, separate from the Church of England; in America it took the name Methodist Episcopal Church. A rigorously "methodical" study of scriptures and a scrupulous conduct of life must accompany the soul's awakening, the evangelist warned, or conversion would not be genuine.

Methodism became the religion not of the poorest or most desperate but of skilled or semiskilled workers who came looking for jobs in the new manufacturing and mining districts.[12] John Wesley told these workers that they were hideous wretches in the sight of God — but no worse wretches than London or Oxford swells decked out in their finery. He was a Tory who abhorred democracy; the existing social order was God's wise design. Yet he also inspired a vision of social change. When the French Revolution broke out in 1789, the followers of Wesley stayed true to their leader's example of passive obedience to Britain's ruling order. But when that tumult ceased, these non-revolutionaries went to work to make their own country over into a liberal, progressive society. They agitated against slavery and for worker rights, joining the ranks of Luddites and Chartists.[13]

Artisans, whether they spoke English or Welsh, were an aspiring lot who had tasted some of the fruits of capitalist enterprise and wanted more. They saw enormous profits being made from the new methods of factory production. They watched men no better educated nor more noble than themselves become rich, buying country estates and hiring personal valets and coachmen. Even while jeering at their parvenu employers, they thirsted like them for advancement and respect. Repeatedly, they were told that respect comes from self-discipline, hard work, and sobriety. Piety was guaranteed to bring worldly rewards of upward mobility, middle-class status, and a full larder.

But evangelical religion was as much a cry of the uprooted and alienated for community, authority, and traditional values as it was a search for respectability, security, and comfort. The movement, in short, stood in ambivalent relation to the economic changes sweeping across Great Britain and the United States in the early nineteenth century. It was a modern religion responding to modernizing forces and adopted by modern workers, yet it preached indifference, and sometimes hostility, to those same forces. It enjoined obedience to the new industrial order, while urging men and women to refuse allegiance to corrupt institutions. It was a volatile mix of subservience and rebellion, conformity and withdrawal, spirituality and worldliness — precisely the ambivalence felt by people like Mary and Joseph. That ambivalence they would hand down to their children, and not least to their fourth child, John Wesley Powell, who throughout his life exemplified the tensions within that working-class

Methodist temperament born in the throes of British social and economic change. Temperament often endures where faith and doctrine do not.

"It is a serious and solemn thing to leave the land of our birth, our home, and our friends — to travel thousands of miles over sea and land, and to be aliens in a distant and strange country." Writing in "Yr American," a pamphlet published in the Welsh language in 1840 to advise immigrants, the Reverend Benjamin Chidlaw acknowledged the heavy personal costs but rushed on to present immigration as part of a providential design to propagate the gospel in foreign lands. To be sure, it was not a mission for everyone. He was specific about those who belonged in the stay-at-home category: anyone who was well-off, hated an atmosphere of social equality, was old or disabled, a heavy drinker, lazy and irresponsible, or strongly attached to family and community should not make the effort, for they would be unhappy or useless in the new country. On the other hand, "young people, sober, industrious, and faithful; maidservants, and menservants; together with ordinary mechanics, active and skillful, are the fit persons to go to America." The Powells matched that description, and in 1830 they made a fateful decision to cut loose and leave.

Chidlaw's pamphlet was published too late to aid them, though later in New York State they would actually meet him and solicit his advice on the most fertile missionary fields. In 1821 he had emigrated with his family from Bala, Wales, to Ohio, where he served as a Presbyterian minister among Welsh settlers, and was a fount of practical knowledge about where to go and how to get on. But though the Powells could not have used this particular pamphlet, it does offer insight into the process that families like theirs, Welsh or English, went through in order to find a new home.

Start with some money in your pocket, Chidlaw advised; do not wait until you are nearly bankrupt to go. Take as much money as you can — English gold sovereigns are acceptable currency in the United States — and as little baggage. Limit your goods to sturdy cloth and linen garments, portable beds, earthenware, knives and forks, all items you will need on the ship. Take yourselves to Liverpool, where ships come and go frequently, and make your own arrangements there with a captain. Men will approach you with offers of help, but it is safer not to trust them to engage a vessel or secure food on your behalf; "all should be careful lest they be misled or deceived." Observe the cargo loading to discern when a ship is ready to sail and then try to book passage on it. The fare for steerage passengers will be four to five pounds a head, though a good, fast merchantman may charge only three pounds. Cabins cost fifteen to twenty-five pounds — a great expense, but they allow one to avoid contact with the rough, irreverent mob aboard any ship. American vessels are usually better managed than British, and they are constantly coming into port. A family will need enough food to sustain them for six to eight weeks aboard ship, so pack a standard Welsh diet of bread, oatmeal, butter, cheese, and meat, along with tea, coffee, sugar, treacle, and salt. Pack along Epsom salts or rhubarb for upset stomachs. Once underway, walk the decks regularly to avoid seasickness and other ailments. When you arrive, "be careful of your health; your character; and your success, and avoid idling, drinking and unruly company. These are what have injured hundreds of men after reaching America. There are good places for men-servants, maid-servants, and artisans, in the large cities; a better place for families is in the country or in villages."[14]

Mary added to the recommended packing list a small chest of her linens and two dozen of her books, and then they were set to go — herself, Joseph, the little girls, and sixteen-year-old Walter. Mary's own brother Joseph Dean and his wife had indicated that they were eager to come along, but they failed to show up on the docks and the boat had to leave without them. Nothing held the migrants back. They were determined to go and they would never return, even for a family visit. The wind filled their ship's sails, blowing them into the Irish Sea and away from all they had ever known.

Sailing across the Atlantic and around Sandyhook into one of the world's great harbors, New York City, the doorway to a continent, docking in the forest of masts at the foot of the island called Manhattan, the Powells faced a few challenges that no book of advice could fully prepare them to meet. Was this a godly place? Would they find acceptable work and shelter? Methodists, they would discover, were numerous here as in Britain, with many congregations established in the city's various wards. The harder question was whether two young men, neither of them masters yet of their trade, could find a decent living in this intensely aggressive city of two hundred thousand people.

By Old World standards America might be a democracy, but that did not mean that New York City presented no struggles, no inequalities, no poverty. A scale of class distinctions, though more fluid than in England, was already taking shape under the rules of laissez-faire enterprise. Millionaire capitalists such as the fur king John Jacob Astor stood at the top of that scale, while immediately beneath them ranged a number of craftsmen entrepreneurs whose workshops feverishly competed against each other for customers. At the bottom of the social heap were thousands of paupers, black and white, crawling out of squalid cellars to beg for a little food.

Without substantial capital, it would be hard for newcomers to find an independent niche in that economy. Even an industrious, capable man might have to sell his labor more or less as he did in London or Birmingham and end up working for others. Then there was the frightful prospect of getting trapped in the sweatshops that were turning out shoddy garments with exploited labor. America, at least here in the metropolis, was leaving behind its older Jeffersonian republican ideal of an independent, virtuous citizenry — a nation of small farmers and shopkeepers — to embrace dreams of acquisitive individualism and industrial growth. In a few more years waves of Irish and German immigrants began flooding the city, making a heavy sea for the job seeker who had only his labor to sell.[15] As for shelter, a family without large means had to rent a flat in the more crowded and decrepit parts of the city. The Powells were dead set against that existence. They had come to America in part to tell the Good News, in part to improve their economic condition, and not to join the desperate scramble of the hapless and miserable. In later years Mary would tell her children how they "thought it a great disgrace to live in a rented home, as they must do in N. Y. City."[16]

Gathering their belongings, they took passage up the Hudson River to Albany, looking for a more promising situation. At Albany they shifted to a packet boat on the Erie Canal, the longest man-made river in the world, a forty-foot-wide ditch completed just six years earlier. The new canal was largely responsible for making New York City the booming port it had become, and the Powells could see, as they moved with exquisite slowness through the landscape, the wheat fields, the lumber yards, the settlements that had been freshly created in this upstate region to feed the down state metropolis. Utica came into sight, where Welsh had settled in large numbers. Their handsome churches would have reassured the travelers that here was a righteous land, but they tarried only a little while before pushing on to their chosen destination, the western canal town of Palmyra.[17]

Palmyra, like other canal-side settlements, had palpitated with extravagant hopes of becoming a major center of commerce, though by this point it was being overshadowed by the flour-milling center of Rochester a short distance farther west. The Powells liked what they saw, nonetheless, and invested their savings in a house of their own. One year later, in summer 1832, Mary and Joseph had their third child whom they named William Fletcher, after the Methodist evangelist to Shropshire's iron foundry workers. That child, however, lived only two years.

Fortunately, Fletcher was the lone fatality in the Powell brood, as over the next decade and a half Mary gave birth to six more children, making a flock of eight in all. That was an average-size family for rural, back-country people in Britain or America, though it was well above average for the middle class.[18] In this aspect as others the Powells were on the cusp separating social divisions. It also appears that Mary was an uncommonly healthy woman for her time. She bore a large set of hearty children and lived to be nearly seventy years old, though she could never forget that one of her earliest tasks in America was to place in a grave the body of her first son.

The Powells had found their way to one of the most intensely evangelical districts in America. All during the building of the canal and well into the 1830s western New York was on fire with religion, as Congregationalists, Presbyterians, and Methodists vied to save souls; observers called this "the burned-over district" because of the frequent revivals that raged like forest fires through the countryside. Rochester was the persistent center of the fire. In 1830 a New England preacher, Charles Grandison Finney, with bulging blue eyes and tense, gripping voice, came to that city and for six months preached nearly every night and three times on Sunday, converting thousands.[19]

While Rochester could point to Finney and his stupendous achievements, Palmyra made its own contribution to the religious ferment, one that would eventually reverberate to the far western deserts. Palmyra was the birthplace of Mormonism. Joseph Smith, an uneducated farm boy living south of the village center, claimed to have found on a nearby drumlin, Hill Cumorah, a set of golden plates written over in strange hieroglyphics that he alone could read. Sitting behind a curtain, he translated them aloud as a new revelation from God. He then took the transcription to a local printer, who in 1830 published them as *The Book of Mormon*.

That same year, the very year the Powell family arrived, Smith formed a new Church of Jesus Christ of Latter-day Saints, which even the most enthusiastic religionists feared must be a dangerous cult.[20] For the Powells, here was another American strangeness to absorb along with Jacksonian politics, Manhattan street life, wild forest scenes, and Yankee twang. They had brought with them the true Christian faith, based on the traditional Bible, and they needed no other, certainly not one from an upstart bumpkin who said he had

Mount Morris, Livingston County, New York, circa 1830, looking westward.
The Genesee Gorge lies beyond the horizon, and the town of Castile is on the far side
of the Gorge. (From J.W. Barber and Henry Howe, *Historical Collections of the*
State of New York [1841]).

seen angels. Even had they had been interested, the Powells arrived
too late to follow the progress of Mormonism closely, for within a
year of their arrival, Smith assembled several hundred people and
departed to safer ground in Ohio.

The Powells also soon left the canal town, only three years after arriving, making the first of many removes that would long keep them
unsettled in the New World, as unsettled as they had been in the Old.
They migrated up the Genesee River to the town of Mount Morris,
named after Robert Morris, a Philadelphia merchant who had been a
member of the Continental Congress and the nation's first finance
minister. The real father of the town, however, was General William
Mills, a veteran of the Revolutionary War, who erected a substantial
log house and settled among the native peoples to make money from
grain, stock, and whiskey.

When the Powells arrived, probably in 1833, there were more than
three thousand white settlers—and no Indians. On Main Street
stood Mills's cabin (he would eventually replace it with a Federalist
mansion), several other residences, a tavern, two dry goods stores,
Percival's Hotel, and the Mechanics Hall. With increasing settlement
the manufacture and sale of booze had become a divisive issue.
Methodist newcomers had set about repressing the liquor trade, and

young church members had signed pledges not to imbibe. A leading shopkeeper, Rueben Sleeper, explained in the newspaper that he would stock "Ardent Spirits" but keep them with the poisons and "other filthy drugs for medicinal purposes only; and it is hoped [they] will never be needed by any of his customers."[21]

The drys were led by a bombastic Methodist minister, John Hudson, who claimed to have played a decisive role in reclaiming the wilderness from the ungodly natives. "I have been where the tracks of the red man of the forest were fresh," he puffed, "and the marks of the tomahawk and scalping knife were still legible on the bark of the oak and maple, while the wigwams of the natives were still standing."[22] All that was needed to render civilization complete was to abolish whiskey and construct a new church on the corner of Chapel and Stanley streets. The Powell brothers, learning that hands were needed for that work, had come straightaway from Palmyra. It was in Hudson's parsonage that John Wesley Powell was born, and in the church's graveyard that Fletcher was buried.

Earning a living in this place, however, was not easy. Already another tailor had located in the town, and Joseph, who would rather preach than cut cloth, must work hard to achieve a place here. Then there was Walter, who also required employment. A few months after Wes was born an advertisement appeared in the newspaper:

New Establishment.
W. Powell
Clock & Watchmaker,
(Late from England)

Has taken a shop
nearly opposite the
new brick Tavern, Chap-
el street, Mount Morris,
where he doubts not, but
by strict attention to the
above business, in all its branches, to ensure a share of the public patronage.

REPAIRING
Done with promptness, accuracy and des-
patch.
Mount Morris, June 1st, 1834[23]

That was from the hand of Uncle Walter, now age twenty, trying to drum up work for himself to support the household. The ad ran through mid-December, then disappeared, for the Powells were itching to move again.

West of Mt. Morris lay a vast gorge through which the Genesee flowed, a wild and noble relic of the Ice Age. On the other side beckoned a still newer frontier, Wyoming County. There a reservation had been established for the Senecas, and there the famous white woman, Mary Jemison, who had been carried into captivity and married an Indian man, lived out her last years. Lumbermen, however, were invading the Seneca lands with impunity, cutting down their thick forest of oak, chestnut, hemlock, beech, and white pine for the Rochester market. They were a hard group of notorious drinkers as well as land destroyers. Temperance forces, however, were hot on their heels, demanding abstinence and holding revivals to create a better moral order in the cutover land. An agricultural town, Castile, was founded, and by 1835 it had twenty-five hundred residents, a Baptist church, and — so the Powells learned — a new Methodist church undergoing construction here too.

So the family shifted west to Castile where they purchased a house fronted with white pillars, affording shelter and a place of business. Joseph and Walter fell to work building the church. It would seem that at last they had found what they were looking for in America: a new community taking shape, one that needed them and offered room and opportunity. In December 1836 Mary delivered another son, William Bramwell (nicknamed Bram), and in March 1838 a third daughter, Eliza Dean (or Lida).[24]

Castile, Mount Morris, indeed the whole Genesee country eventually settled down to rural stability, transformed into a landscape of maples, apple orchards, Holstein cows, and dairy farms. It added a railroad here, a highway there, a few more houses and stores but not enough to alter radically its mid-nineteenth-century character. The area's most important asset remained the Genesee gorge, renowned as one of the great natural attractions of the state. A young geologist, James Hall, showed up in 1837 to study the Devonian shales that formed the river cliffs and dig out the fossils that revealed the ancient history of western New York State long before either Indians or whites lived here.[25] Young Wesley Powell might have had a satisfying life growing up in this imposing landscape that twentieth-century tourists have called "the Grand Canyon of the East." He might have studied with James Hall and become another New York State geologist, or he might have become a farmer milking his herds every day. But he was not to have either of those chances.

When he was four, his father again grew restless, despite the comfortable life they were making, and informed the family that he now had his eye on Ohio. God was summoning to move once more. Joseph longed not merely to build churches but to preach the gospel and save souls. He had come to the New World with a mission to evangelize as well as prosper. Western New York State had plenty of preachers; Ohio did not. So, with many tearful good-byes, the family packed their clothes and portable goods and headed deeper into the nation's interior .

The society that the Powells had joined was in perpetual motion, and from the start the Powells merged into the flow. They had become used to saying good-bye in Hull and Shrewsbury, in Birmingham and Wolverhampton; clearly, being in motion was not something they had to wait to learn in the New World. Tradition, roots, community had never been very important to them, so long as they could find brothers and sisters in Christ wherever they went. Nor was the beauty of a place any draw, else the Genesee country would have won their hearts. Nor, in the final reckoning, was it merely money or security in the world's sense that mattered most at this stage of their lives. They trusted in divine power to provide all that they needed. What moved them on, and on again, was a still, small voice calling in Joseph's inner ear, and in Mary's too—a voice that said, come west and help us.

It was the Welsh who first discovered America—that is, after the Indians did, and if you believe the right authorities. An intrepid wayfarer named Madoc, possibly a bodyguard of the great prince of North Wales, Owain Gwynedd, found his way across the Atlantic in A.D. 1170, more than three centuries before Columbus. On a second voyage he brought with him a boatload of colonists, and they wandered across North America, fighting against native resistance, losing battles but surviving somewhere in the back country—a remote tribe of red-haired, blue-eyed Europeans still speaking the Welsh language.

In 1792 a young Methodist preacher out of Wales went looking for that lost tribe. He wanted to bring his wayward countrymen the new gospel of Wesley, which they had missed hearing, but apparently they had slipped away farther west and he died, unsuccessful, in New Orleans. Thomas Jefferson, himself of Welsh extraction, may have believed in the "Welsh Indians" too, but the exploring party he sent out under Lewis and Clark could find no traces of them.[26]

A more plausible and better documented story brings the Welsh to North America in modern times and tells of modest, occasionally brilliant, success. In the last years of the eighteenth century one bad harvest after another, along with the enclosures movement, drove many Welsh families nearly to starvation. Desperate, they turned to America. Some went to Utica, as noted, but the largest number headed for Philadelphia, then crossed over the mountains into the Ohio Valley.

The most flourishing of those refugee bands formed a farming community at Paddy's Run, Ohio, near Cincinnati, where Benjamin Chidlaw came to preside as their minister. In 1818 six other families set sail from Aberaeron on the west coast of Wales, their destination the Ohio River and Paddy's Run, but they bogged down along the way. Running low on provisions, they tied up their rafts near the French settlement of Gallipolis, across from present-day West Virginia. Some of the men found work building a road inland through a wooded, knobby-hilled country that reminded them of home. Why go any farther, they wondered, why not settle here? Over the next three decades hundreds more followed them, clustering together in what became southern Jackson County, Ohio, trying to keep their language and culture intact.[27]

The Reverend Chidlaw knew about these wayward settlements, but they were too far away for him to tend regularly to their souls. Although he wanted to see more of his countrymen taking up residence in Ohio and thriving as he had done, the motherland needed to send more preachers as well as farmers. Twice he journeyed back to Wales to hold a series of revivals and recruit more evangelists, and his route east took him along the Erie Canal from Buffalo to Albany.[28] According to Wes's memory, Chidlaw met father Joseph on one of those trips, and seeing that he had the call to preach, though only a lowly Methodist, urged him to settle among the Welsh in Jackson County and nourish their souls.[29]

It was, he might have added, a rich, booming place. After national independence, the Ohio Valley defined the movement west. It became the leading postcolonial frontier, the destination of land-hungry pioneers whose enterprise created new territories and new notions of what it meant to be American. Here was some of the most fertile land in the world, clearly intended by God for an agrarian civilization, and farmers from New York, Pennsylvania, and Virginia, along with various European countries, streamed in to claim that land and possess it.

Overnight it seemed, the once remote, trans-Appalachian state of Ohio grew to 1.5 million residents by 1840, making it the third largest in the nation. Its center of business and culture was Cincinnati, the "Queen City of the West," with a population of fifty thousand; though stray pigs still roamed the streets, large-scale meatpacking was fast becoming its major industry. What the Erie Canal had been a decade earlier, the nation's most important artery of commercial growth, the Ohio with its many tributaries was now becoming. Steamboats had taken over the river all the way to the Mississippi, even down to the Gulf of Mexico, and the sound of their paddles was as common as the splashing of catfish. Lumber, cotton, tobacco, wheat, and corn crowded their decks; and a polyglot people jostled each other for a place by the rail.

For the Powells, removing to Ohio involved taking a steamer across Lake Erie, then making a long canal trip south from Cleveland through Akron, Masillon, Coshocton, Newark, Columbus, getting off at the former capital of Chillicothe. Inspired by the Erie Canal's success, developers dug the Ohio Canal over three hundred miles long (going all the way to the Ohio River), with 152 locks and 16 aqueducts. When linked to the Erie Canal, it put much of the state within cheap, easy reach of New York City.

But a ride on the canal took heroic patience if you were not a bag of grain. The lowslung boats, pulled along towpaths by tired, plodding horses, moved through the water at only four miles per hour. They moved day and night. Men and boys slept in one cabin, women and girls in another, or they all slept together in one cabin with a curtain hanging down the middle. They could see the countryside well only if they clambered up on the roof, where they ran the risk of having their brains knocked out by a low bridge. The water through which they moved was stagnant—good habitat for mosquitoes—and dead animals often floated alongside the boats. Canal travel was not designed to inspire poetry or psalms but to move goods efficiently to market.[30]

A wagon and team brought the Powells the last twenty-eight miles from Chillicothe through dense, majestic forests and unglaciated hills, an altogether different landscape from the long valleys and ridges they had left. The trees made an emerald paradise of buckeye, black walnut, mulberry, tulip poplar, ash, oak, hickory, beech, sassafras, and box elder, with sycamores scattered along the rivers. They arrived in the morning at the village of Jackson, county seat of Jackson, both names honoring the hero of the Battle of New Orleans and former president. The team had to strain hard to climb to the plateau on which the village had been laid out.

The prospect at the top looked a little discouraging if they came believing all of Chidlaw's brag. This was still a raw frontier community, little more than two decades old. The county had been organized in 1816 and it now counted nearly ten thousand residents, black and white, but only three hundred of them lived in the village proper. It could not have looked so prosperous or neat as those western New York towns: a few dirt streets lined with six or eight stores, a printing office, Presbyterian, Baptist, and Methodist churches, and a cacaphony of hound dogs, chickens, and children.

It looked familiar, yet it looked different. Enthusiastic Welsh voices welcomed them as they climbed down from the wagon. Other voices, however, had a peculiarly "southern" sound. Many of the locals were Virginians, commonly Scotch-Irish from the Appalachian back country, and their open, friendly manners were partially offset, the Powells soon realized, by other characteristics that were not so pleasant. Many of them drank and chewed, many were irreligious, slovenly, and lackadaisical; most of them believed that they were infinitely superior to the free black families who had settled in their midst, people who like many of the whites had come from slaveholding states just over the river.[31]

The Welsh lived out of town, in rural enclaves where they tended to their farming. The Powells, however, chose not to move out into those environs. They were used to a more urban life, closer to the center of activity, though this village was far less urban or active than Hull, Birmingham, or even Mount Morris. For $200 they bought a town lot on Main Street between Portsmouth and Locust streets, one block from what became the courthouse square, and when a new cottage was ready for occupancy, the family moved in and the menfolk set up for business in the front rooms.[32]

Their residence was located near the edge of the plateau, and below they could see the tangled riverine forest of Little Salt Creek, which flows west to the Little Scioto, which enters the Ohio River about fifty miles away. An anonymous historian has written, "Along most of these creeks, and especially along the [Salt], is some of the most beautiful, romantic, and picturesque scenery the eye of man ever beheld."[33] But wildlife and humans had long come here looking for that very practical necessity after which the stream was called — salt. The valley offered several salt licks where bison and elk, and before them mastodons and giant bears, had congregated, sometimes leaving their bones. In 1836 geologists, while excavating salt deposits in Jackson County, unearthed the skeleton of a hairy mammoth whose tusks measured eleven feet and weighed 180 pounds each.

The not long departed Native American population was becoming part of an exotic past too. Once the Shawnees had come to the creek regularly to extract salt for trade; and on one occasion, local story-tellers said, they brought Daniel Boone as a captive, forcing him to make salt for them until he escaped, hiding in caves along the creek. The Indian method of getting salt was to dig wells in the soft bottom-lands, let them fill with brine, then boil it off to leave a thick white cake. Beginning in the 1790s Euro-Americans entered the area to take permanent possession, and they followed the same procedure as the Indians, for they too needed salt to preserve their food. They boiled brine in iron kettles and packed the surplus out for sale.[34]

The other valuable mineral in the county was bituminous coal, though only a few inhabitants were yet making use of the abundant deposits that could be mined hereabouts, part of the vast coal beds that underlay southern Ohio, Pennsylvania, eastern Kentucky, and western Virginia. The most farsighted among them was a man of sub-stantial professional credentials, William W. Mather, who settled in Jackson the same year the Powells arrived. A descendant of the Puri-tan divine Cotton Mather, he had graduated from West Point, then left the military for civilian employment as director of Ohio's first ge-ological survey. When legislators suspended the survey, he was forced to look around for other income possibilities, which he located with quick success. He purchased coal-bearing lands, dug out the coal, and used it to manufacture iron, glass, and pottery, as well as to saw marble and evaporate salt. Eventually, he would incorporate his new business as the Ohio Iron Manufacturing Company and with the profits build a mansion in town overlooking the Little Salt Creek. Mather was one of the state's first industrial entrepreneurs, mimicking what the English had been doing in Shropshire's Coalbrookdale.[35]

Joseph Powell might likewise have made a fortune in exploiting the abundant natural resources if he had taken a strong interest in them. Jackson County was part of the Hanging Rock iron ore district which extended down into Kentucky. Small forges proliferated throughout the district, turning out pig iron for bars, rods, and plates. Coming from Shropshire, Joseph had to know at least a little about the processes associated with those resources and their indus-

Joseph and Mary Powell, daguerreotypes taken late in life.
(Courtesy: Powell Memorial, Jackson County Supervisors, Jackson, Ohio)

trial uses. The Welsh he rode out to preach to every Sunday were also familiar in a general way with those uses. Though they were intently focused on cropping their rich soils, they might have been assembled into an industrial army. Joseph, moreover, had a little bonanza at his very feet. In 1842, while digging a well next to his house, he struck a vein of coal, the first ever found within the town, and it made him famous for years to come.[36] But he let all such opportunities slide, leaving others to set up coal-extracting and iron-smelting operations.

Instead of tumbling to those opportunities, what Joseph did, besides preach many sermons and cut out many waistcoats, was invest in land. The land was extraordinarily cheap and he had never owned much before. Now he began to plunge. According to Jackson County courthouse records, he filed on the deed to his house lot on 4 September 1838, a few months after arriving. Then in October he bought an interest in a four-acre lot on the south side of town and in November took sole possession of a similar outlot across Salt Lick Creek, which he soon sold for $110, making a 10 percent gain in less than four weeks. That would do him for a while. But then in the period 1841–46, after the family was securely situated, he acquired another outlot, and in nearby Liberty Township, commonly known as the Scioto Salt Reserve, he purchased two rural properties, totaling over 120 acres, enough to make an average-size farm.

He had no intention, however, of becoming a farmer. Those properties were sought primarily as investments, either for their rental income or their potential market appreciation. Where he got the money to invest in all those properties is hard to say. He could not have made much income, if he made any, serving the Welsh congregations as their circuit-riding minister, so apparently the tailoring business afforded a decent financial base in Jackson.[37] They had arrived in the village with $330 in pocket. When they left eight years later, selling all their properties, they carried away $1,700.[38]

The family grew at a regular pace with their assets. When the census taker came in 1840, he found four females and four males living in this household of "free white persons."[39] But later that same year Ellen Louella (called Nellie) was born, then Walter Henry in 1842, and, the last of the brood, Juliet Felicia, in 1844. The cottage was getting crowded by this point, with eight children and two parents packed under the same roof. Then there was Uncle Walter, who shared their quarters for a while before moving out to start his own family. Somewhere in Ohio, perhaps in Jackson, he met a woman named Ellen and decided to marry her. Their firstborn, a son named Clement, was born in 1850.

Through all these burdens of childbearing, Mary strenuously tried to fulfill the archetypal role of Victorian Christian mother. While Joseph's preaching circuit took him farther and farther away from home, as he extended beyond the Welsh community to serve Chillicothe and other towns, she was pious domesticity exemplified. Much of the time she had to manage the household all on her own. She baked, sewed, kept house, settled childish disputes, and read her Bible. There is no evidence that she hired any domestic help, though she might well have done what so many middle-class women of the period did. She was also teacher to her children, and she was a good one, mixing the King James Bible with works of British literature. It was probably Mary who taught them all to read, though Jackson, like other Ohio towns, had established a public school that the older ones attended six months in the year. She made sure, even when father had to be gone, that the family met morning and evening to pray, sing psalms, and read the words of Jesus.

Mary likely would have conveyed, in those quiet moments of family worship, a rather different idea of God than her husband's. Her God encouraged spontaneous obedience rather than demanded it like a harsh disciplinarian. He wanted His children to practice a life of daily virtue, acting with solicitude and love toward members of the family above all others, to treat one another with kindness, patience, and understanding. Wes, like the other children, was raised to be emotionally close to his brothers and sisters and especially close to his mother. Sitting at her side, he learned the Scriptures well, memorizing their stories, proverbs, and cadences, and they left a trace of antique eloquence on his adult patterns of speech, as they did on the speaking habits of other Americans of the period whose home libraries consisted mainly of the family Bible. Later in life he proudly remembered that, while still a small boy, he learned by heart the entire Four Gospels.

But as the home parlor got more congested, with so many little ones running about, Wes tried more and more to get out of the house — either to attend lessons with the schoolmaster Alexander Miller or to explore Little Salt Creek's fishing holes or to buy ginger cakes at Mrs. Sylvester's store. He and brother Bram went exploring. Then at some point Wes fell under the spell of one of the biggest men in Jackson, indeed one of the biggest men in Ohio, and the intense, close family and brotherly ties loosened considerably.

George Crookham came to Jackson from Carlisle, Pennsylvania, in 1799, at the age of twenty, the son of English-born Calvinists. One of the earliest settlers, he had thought of becoming a teacher, but the salt wells attracted him instead. He hired on to tend the kettles of boiling brine, though he liked to read a book while keeping the fires hot. He read David Hume's *History of England*, Edward Gibbon's *The Decline and Fall of the Roman Empire*, and whatever he could find of natural history. The local natural environment fascinated him, and he read eagerly to find out about the native peoples, the mysterious earthen mounds scattered around southern Ohio, the minerals buried underground, the fossils that emerged out of the creek banks, the living plants and animals. When he left the salt business, he acquired a farm north of the creek, married a woman named Sarah, and fathered sixteen children. The day the Powells pulled into town Crookham was among the greeters, offering a temporary camping place on his farm. By then he was nearly sixty years old, retired from farming but still a dominating presence in the community.[40]

One could not miss him — he weighed 350 pounds. "Big George," as he was called, liked to sit at the post office reading his favorite newspaper, the *National Era*, and having conversation with everyone in town. He took only one daily meal, a prodigious dinner at noon, but after that he was available for consultation on any question that plagued his neighbors. They recognized him as an accomplished scholar, an outstanding mathematician, a powerful memory, a walking encyclopedia.

They also knew he had strong opinions on most matters, which often they did not share. He had been a heavy tippler in his youth but then abruptly gave up whiskey and became a total prohibitionist. Alcohol, he warned, turned pioneers into barbarians. On that subject he seemed adamant and unreasonable. In politics, he was a Whig, the more conservative party of his day, and repeatedly he was a candidate for the Ohio legislature, though never elected. Whatever they thought of his views, the townsmen stood in awe of his girth and intellect. One admiring biographer called him "another Samuel Johnson, but a plant of the weeds and not of the town."[41]

Crookham's views on strong drink may have been controversial, but even more controversial were his views on slavery and African Americans. He despised the peculiar institution on which the southern economy rested. Reputedly, any help he could give a runaway slave he would give, and consider it, no matter how illegal, a moral victory for freedom and decency. Slaves who crossed the Ohio River to escape their masters came to him looking for passage on the "underground railway," the chain of people who secretly harbored and transported them north to Canada, beyond the arm of the slave law. Crookham was well known to be one of the first stops on that railway, even if no one could prove anything. His farm was a notorious hiding place for runaways. He showed them where they could conceal themselves in the caves along Little Salt Creek. He was also friendly with the free blacks who lived in and around Jackson, a despised minority in the eyes of white townspeople.

Prejudice against blacks may have been stronger in southern Ohio than in the South itself, for many settlers had come here to get away from any contact with blacks. They resented competing with them for jobs, yet accused them of lacking industry or intelligence. Blacks were not allowed to vote anywhere in the state, or testify in court against whites, or hold office, or attend the public schools.[42] Crookham, then, was a threat to the whole nasty idea and practice of racial supremacy from which many of his white neighbors took their self-esteem.

Still, the man was a prodigy, like a great talking stone in their midst that no one dared run against. Townsmen told how he had gone to

Chillicothe once to get a certificate to teach school; he was handed a newspaper to read, upside down, but fooled his examiners by proceeding to read it in that position. He was a brilliant talker, they agreed, always interesting to listen to, withering in denunciation of fools and rascals, a plain-dealing and self-made man as they all were. Then there was that remarkable school and museum he had established on his farm. In a two-room log cabin, with an open-air "dogtrot" down the middle, he set up a classroom on one side, where from time to time he took private pupils free of charge, mainly young adult men who wanted to learn how to read, and on the other side, a museum of natural curiosities—stuffed birds, discarded snake skins, unusual rocks, Indian artifacts he had collected in the vicinity. Crookham performed valuable community service, apart from his unpopular aid to slaves, and he gave Jackson a certain pride in itself.

This longtime and prominent resident saw in Mary and Joseph (whom he called "Great Britain") unostentatious but intelligent folks like himself—people who respected learning and adhered to principle. He began visiting them regularly, sitting in the kitchen for long theological debate, arguing against their Arminian doctrine of universal salvation and in favor of predestination. Undoubtedly they discussed politics, slavery, history, and ethics as well. Wes sat in their midst, listening to the often intense debates and finding his mother, still a reader of Swedenborg, to be the most sensible and persuasive of the party.

More and more, though, he was captivated by this large old man who knew so much about the outdoors, who could identify the trees along the creek, who knew the songs of birds, who was excited by rocks. Crookham was on friendly terms with William Mather, the geologist in the fine mansion, and occasionally brought him into the kitchen conversations. When Crookham and Mather went on wagon rides into the countryside to examine the lay of the land, they managed to squeeze a small, shy Wes between them.

For all his natural reticence Wes was more than a tagalong. He became the protégé of the big man, and the experience, he always believed, changed his life. From this point on he sought to become a naturalist—a lover of rivers and shells, of botany and geology, of all the branches of knowledge called natural history. His father was too busy serving two professions to pay much attention to him or any of the children. His uncle was a quiet, unimpressive sort. His mother (though he felt a bond with her above all others) had demanding chores to do most of her day. His siblings were all, in some sense, competitors for their parents' distracted affections. But Crookham, whose own offspring were all grown, was enthusiastically available for Wes's boyhood needs. He knew what to read and he had books to furnish. He offered relief from the steady religious diet. He was the missing grandfather.

The Northwest Ordinance of 1787, which established the process by which Ohio and neighboring states to the west came into the Union, prohibited slavery north of the Ohio River and east of the Mississippi. But it could not prevent the topic of slavery and race from affecting politics in the region. For a while, in the first few decades of settlement, the subject did not come up much. By the 1830s, however, slavery was becoming the dominant topic of the entire nation. Southerners were beginning to defend the institution with vehemence and determination, as though their very identity depended on it. Northerners were beginning to ask whether slavery was a moral stain on the nation's bright promise that could not be tolerated, that must be cleansed.

The Powells, when they were new to the country and intent on getting adjusted, paid little attention to the question of slavery. They may not even have seen many people of African descent until they got to Ohio. But now in Jackson they saw them regularly, met many runaway slaves, and felt a polarization developing around them about the morality of slavery. They were now living in the contested borderland that separated North from South. Having entered the state with evangelical Welshness in mind, they increasingly found their lives being refocused on debates over racial prejudice, chattel slavery, and abolition. Concerned people of intelligence, they could not avoid being drawn into the struggle to win that borderland to one side or the other.

The religious movement that they had joined in England was increasingly in danger in the United States of splitting apart over the issue of slavery. Methodism was strong in the South, and its followers there included many slaveowners who demanded that the church not interfere with their livelihood. In contrast, the northern church was more divided between, on the one side, accommodationists who did not like slavery but feared dissension even more and, on the other side, abolitionists who looked on slavery as a deep sin.

Despite this spreading crack in its foundation, Methodism was writing a tremendous success story in the new nation. Yearly, and particularly in years of economic downturn, it was gathering huge numbers of converts in the larger cities; as in England they came mainly from the middling and lower classes. Its legendary preachers on horseback, the circuit riders who traveled among crossroads storekeepers, primitive backwoods farmers, and isolated squatters without title to the land, who knew how to use their fists as well as quote texts — men such as the muscular Peter Cartwright of Kentucky ("the Lord's breaking plow")—were winning rural souls at a phenomenal rate too.[43] The years 1842–44 saw a membership growth rate of thirty percent, yielding a total of over one million members. By mid-century Methodists were the largest denomination in America, far surpassing their success in England. Methodists and Baptists together constituted two-thirds of all Protestant church members and Protestant ministers in the United States.[44] On the surface, this success produced boundless optimism. America was evidently God's chosen country, and America was soon to be won over wholly to Methodist principles. More revivals would be the means, revivals in which men and women sought personal holiness and sanctification. Any kind of political distraction, but especially the distraction of slavery and abolition, would destroy that success. Yet a number of Methodists were coming to the view that a sacralized nation under God that practiced slavery was a contradiction in terms.

Slavery was not bad in the eyes of its critics because it was inefficient or unprofitable. The case against slavery came primarily from religion. In fact, the discrediting of slavery may have been, in the terms of this world, evangelical Protestantism's greatest achievement in the eighteenth and nineteenth centuries. Long-standing criticism of slavery was fanned into a moral crusade by renowned preachers such as Charles Finney and Lyman Beecher. In 1831, as the Powells were settling in Palmyra, William Lloyd Garrison, a New England Baptist influenced by Quakers, began publishing his journal *The Liberator*, which demanded immediate emancipation of all blacks and full racial equality.

But for any staunch Methodist the most persuasive preacher against slavery had to be John Wesley himself. His essay *Thoughts upon Slavery*, first published in 1774 and reprinted often in the United States during the stormy antebellum years, was a searing indictment of the African slave trade that gave readers a positive, sympathetic impression of the African people. Wesley had spoken directly to American slaveowners about the evil imbedded in their way of life:

> The blood of thy brother (for, whether thou wilt believe it or no, such he is in the sight of Him that made him) crieth against thee

from the earth, from the ship, and from the waters. Oh, whatever it costs, put a stop to its cry before it be too late. Instantly, at any price, were it the half of your goods, deliver thyself from blood-guiltiness. Thy hands, thy bed, thy furniture, thy house, thy lands, are at present stained with blood.

"Liberty," he went on, "is the right of every human creature as soon as he breathes the vital air; and no human law can deprive him of that right, which he derives from the law of nature."[45]

Whether other American Methodists heeded their founder's plea or not, Joseph and Mary Powell must. Their British past had prepared them for all the moral arguments against slavery, and they learned, in the autumn of 1833, that Parliament, after considerable debate, had voted to free the slaves in Britain's West Indian possessions. Once more, the old tensions within the movement surfaced: an uncompromising war against sin in all its forms contending against a belief that Christians should not interfere with those whom God had placed in power. This time the Powells came down on the side of uncompromising war. When the abolitionists, failing to get their petitions heard, walked out and established a new Wesleyan Methodist church in 1843, Joseph Powell walked with them.[46]

Their first target, naturally, would have been the Methodist church sitting only a block and a half from their home. The family were regularly present in its pews, with or without the itinerant Joseph, and always ready to do good work on its behalf. In the late 1830s a battle broke out in the church, causing some members to withdraw and form their own congregation. Likely, the fight had something to do with slavery and the Powells were involved, though no records from that episode survive.[47]

Nearby Cincinnati was strategically placed to be a beachhead for abolitionists against the slaveowners' imperium. The city attracted critics of servitude, southerners and northerners, as well as critics of those critics, both proslavery diehards and more radical emancipationists. On their occasional visits to the city, the Powells may have met or heard at some point the famous Lyman Beecher who lived there as head of the Lane Theological Seminary, a Presbyterian evangelical school, and his daughter, Harriet Beecher Stowe, wife of one of the school's eminent Bible scholars and, in 1852, author of *Uncle Tom's Cabin*.

In 1834 a dispute erupted within the seminary when the students wanted to debate slavery and express more uncompromising views.

Fifty-one of them abruptly withdrew from the school, some of them going to Oberlin College near Cleveland.[48] Oberlin had opened its doors to all students, black or white, female or male — becoming the first racially integrated, coeducational institution in the nation. The famed evangelist Charles Finney was its president, and under his leadership Oberlin was a citadel of antislavery politics. Other causes joined that dominant one around the edges: women's rights; peace and disarmament; prohibition not only of liquor but of the noxious weed, tobacco, a mainstay of the slave economy. A new journal, the *Oberlin Evangelist*, promoted those causes all across the northern tier of states and carried news of worldwide missionary activity and revivals.

At least one attentive subscriber of the *Oberlin Evangelist*, and an ardent admirer of the college, lived in the down state village of Jackson: the increasingly militant abolitionist Joseph Powell. He opened his house on Main Street to visiting Oberlin faculty and students when they toured the state preaching their radical gospel. Joseph, who was probably finding it hard to stay interested in his Welsh flock by this point, came to know the Oberlin brigade as personal friends and comrades. With Crookham, Mather, and a few other townies he became part of a statewide network of "extremists" who were turning Ohio into a pivotal national battleground in the struggle against the slave power.

Some abolitionists, William Lloyd Garrison most infamously, insisted on withdrawing from any participation in conventional politics, because in their view the very act of voting would give legitimacy to a government founded on sin. Joseph did not agree. He wanted to vote, and to vote for whoever stood for abolitionism and Christian government. In 1839 he took out naturalization papers and became a U.S. citizen, with an eye to participating in the upcoming national elections.

Joseph's first presidential election turned out to be one of the most disagreeable ever for putting slogans over substance. Democrats nominated in 1840 the incumbent Martin Van Buren, a follower of Andrew Jackson who was not known for any strong religious convictions, while the Whigs picked a vacuous war hero, William Henry Harrison of Ohio (old "Tippecanoe"), whose chief qualifications seemed to be that he had whipped Indians, drunk hard cider, and lived in a log cabin. Neither man appealed to the immigrant tailor in Jackson. His candidate must be from a third party, and he found his man in James G. Birney, running on the Liberty ticket.

A well-born plantation and slave owner, Birney had come to reject slavery as wrong. Moving to Cincinnati he set up an antislavery newspaper, which was twice attacked by mobs who threw his press into the Ohio River. But he had more than publishing in mind. The country needed, he felt, a party that stood for abolitionist views and, unlike the Democrats and Whigs, included no slaveholders in it. In April 1840 he and a group of like-minded men established the new Liberty Party, with Birney as their presidential candidate. Their platform was first and foremost abolition, though they called for immediate abolition only in the District of Columbia and the western territories.[49]

Despite its gradualist approach, the Liberty Party did not do very well that year. General Harrison won the presidency, while Birney got less than 7,000 votes. In Ohio, the state where he was best known, Birney got a mere 903 votes. Undiscouraged, the party would try again in the next election and would fail again. Clearly, the Liberty Party, which Americans tended to see as more of a religious than a political organization, led by men of no practical experience or broad understanding of national affairs, was not going anywhere. Eventually, its more pragmatic members would break with Birney and form a new Free-Soil Party, which would allow slavery in the South but keep it (and blacks) out of new territories to the west. Subsequently, the Liberty party vanished altogether.[50]

As their party was failing to move the nation, the Powell family was losing ground in their community until they could no longer endure their neighbors' ill will. Son Bram, in a letter to the Jackson paper sixty years later, recalled those difficult days when the name Powell often came with a curse. Joseph, it was said, was altogether too friendly with the African lovers. His house had become a hotbed of menacing abolitionists, Oberlin miscegenationists, Birney and his Liberty zealots, indeed, all manner of strange, subversive fanatics. He was notoriously against drink in a town that liked drinking. When he stood on the courthouse steps and openly advocated the Liberty ticket, he was mobbed. "His house," wrote Bram, "was besmeared and his horse's mane and tail were cut off and the decorative art was further exercised on the body of the horse."[51]

Nor was that the end of repressive violence. One day Crookham came hustling up to the Powells's door to announce that his school-museum had been burned to the ground by vandals, which he saw as an act of retaliation against his own outspoken views. Neither of these men could depend on the law or community to protect them.

The terrorism left its effects on the children, particularly on Wes. He was the oldest son of one of the leading radicals in town, and other youngsters let him know that he was bad company and had better stay out of their way. Eventually, it became impossible for him to attend the public school where he might be pelted with rocks. Crookham, ever sympathetic to the boy, offered to take him more fully under his own tutelage, whenever he could relocate his school. Thus, Wes became a full-time private student to the elderly man, assigned to read through those dense works of Hume and Gibbon. Teacher and pupil rambled around the outdoors more than ever, concentrating on science in spite of the tense political climate. For Wes, getting out of the public school had a few advantages, for the education provided in an ungraded classroom, among students who sneered and taunted him, and at the hands of a teacher who was probably less mature and less well read than Crookham, was not worth much. Still, the mark of the outcast was upon him. He did not belong in this town, nor did any of his family.

In the fall of 1846 Joseph and Mary decided it was time to move once again, this time to Wisconsin. They had heard that the federal government had opened up new land at a cheap price in that territory, and suddenly the prospect for improving their financial estate seemed brighter that way.

Undoubtedly, the decision to migrate was only partly economic. Ohio had been on the front-line of a battle between profoundly hostile forces that were preparing to tear the nation apart. Southern Ohio had proved to be dangerous country for this evangelical couple who took the teachings of Wesley seriously. They had come to aid their Welsh brethren, but instead they had encountered Dixie, or an approximation of it, and they now knew for certain that they were not Southerners. Under fire they had become determined Yankees. Their political as well as spiritual home was in the North — and in as northern a place as they could find. Wisconsin was certifiably Yankee land, where virtually no one of southern roots or sympathies lived, and there they must go.

They sold their properties, therefore, packed their belongings, and prepared to depart, this time without Walter, who chose to stay behind with his wife, though he rejoined them later on. Crookham they also left behind, and not long after he died of a stroke at the age of seventy-seven. Despite all the controversy they had attracted, "many prominent citizens" turned up to say good-bye; the Powells were leaving not only a community of terrorists but also many good friends. "With characteristic warm Southern hearts," Bram remembered, those friends followed the Powells on the way out of town, some camping with them the first night before turning back.

The family needed two wagons, for they were carrying more children and more goods than when they had first arrived at Jackson. Joseph drove one of the wagons. The other, a broad-wheeled, double-teamed Conestoga with canvas cover was in the hands of one of those regretful friends, James Cisna. His brother William was captain of a company of would-be soldiers eager to go fight in the Mexican War. The volunteers never got beyond Portsmouth and sheepishly came back home. But the Powells did not return to Jackson, ever. They set their faces down a long road that, they hoped, would lead them permanently and safely away from violence, immorality, and the bitter pangs of conflict.

CHAPTER 2

Rising on the Prairie

A straight-line distance to the southern edge of Wisconsin, where the Powells were headed, is about four hundred miles, but their route over the land was longer: north toward Columbus, Ohio, then angling across Indiana and Illinois, skirting marshes and fording streams, swinging around low glacial moraines to save their animals' strength. They traveled a dusty, rutted road for a full month or more. Each meal they cooked over an open fire, each night they slept inside or under their wagons. They had each other for company, and no one else much of the time.

September is typically a dry month in this country, with cool, crisp nights and broad, clear skies spangled with glittering stars. Migrating birds fill the air with their wing beats and cries. As the family creaked along the beaten trails, the wide horizon stretched before them, the land flattening out into a mosaic of grasses turning sere and brown, bronze, gold, crimson, yellow. They had crossed into the "prairie archipelago," a patchy region of prairie islands interspersed among the woods. Some of the openings were twenty miles across, some were even larger, like an ocean surrounding the groves of trees. By October the country could turn black, as fires broke out and ran with the wind. No one could agree on the origins of this Midwestern environment, so different from the great forest to the east. Some argued that Indians had created it by frequent burning while others explained it by lightning or by deficient soil moisture. Scientists one day would say that it may have been the work of glaciers leaving a poorly drained landscape of bogs and marshlands in their wake or the outcome of a complicated history of climate change and pollen relicts that we cannot fully explain.

First impressions of this prairie country were often negative — too monotonous, too flat. But the prairie inspired its lovers too, among them Hamlin Garland, raised in Wisconsin, Iowa, and Dakota Territory. This self-named "son of the Middle Border" knew from personal experience how hard and discouraging it was to try to make an agricultural living from any grassland. Yet no one expressed better than he the sheer aliveness of a prairie or its appeal to the mystical in humankind.

> Nothing could be more generous, more joyous, than these natural meadows in summer. The flash and ripple and glimmer of the tall sunflowers, the myriad voices of gleeful bobolinks, the chirp and gurgle of red-winged blackbirds swaying on the willows, the meadow-larks piping from grassy bogs, the peep of the prairie chick and the wailing call of plover on the flowery green slopes of the upland made it all an ecstatic world to me. It was a wide world with a big, big sky which gave alluring hints of the still more glorious unknown wilderness beyond.[1]

What lay beyond was, of course, the West — and the prairie was an open-handed invitation to its promise.

By 1846 the prairie landscape was already being transformed into corn belt, and new split-rail fences marked off farms along the way. Then Lake Michigan hove into view, a patch of blue on their right hand, then the environs of Chicago where they could stop to rest amid the push and bustle of commerce. Shoving on, they followed the road west toward the Rock River, turned north again, then east on a track that led them into extreme southwestern Walworth County, Wisconsin. Climbing down from the wagons, they would immediately have offered a prayer of thanksgiving for a safe journey and a plea for divine guidance ahead. They had a new life to build in this country of bluestem grasses and bur oaks.

Thousands of other Americans were on the move that year, seeking like the Powells new territory and adventure. Bernard DeVoto has called 1846 the "year of decision," when the country was swept by an extravagant dream of geography. America's destiny must be continental; it must expand all the way to the Pacific, displacing whoever was in the way. One large group of citizens, armed with rifles and bayonets, was marching into what was still foreign territory to wrest part of the southwestern desert away from Mexico. On 13 May the United States declared war on that nation. At war's end Americans claimed all the land from the Rio Grande to the coastal redwoods. California was the greatest prize they sought. The rest — except for eastern Texas, a beckoning prize to the cotton kings — was merely a safe, protected corridor to its golden shore. Mexico, widely regarded as a weak and oppressive nation, indeed hardly a nation at all, had no God-given right to that prize. Now a more just, enlightened government would take California for its own uses, though precisely what uses those would be hardly anyone in the United States knew. California for most citizens was simply the port of Monterey, a few shiploads of cowhides, and nothing more — nothing more than a dream.

Squarely in the middle of that part of Mexico soon to become America was an even bigger blank spot about which there was virtually complete national ignorance — a place that would one day be called the Territory of Utah and the Colorado Plateau. It too was now becoming a destination. Early in that year of frenzied mobility, one thousand six hundred Mormons crossed the frozen Mississippi to set up temporary headquarters for an immense migration into the Great Salt Lake basin. By fall, as the Powells were getting resettled, twelve thousand more of the Mormons had gathered at Winter Quarters, near present-day Omaha, waiting for the coming spring to begin their move. Joseph Smith was dead, killed two years earlier by an angry mob in Illinois. His successor, Brigham Young, a poorly educated carpenter, had no fewer than thirty-five thousand Latter-day Saints to lead west, away from their oppressors and into Mexican territory. They were the new chosen people of God, making an exodus out of bondage. On the other side of the Rockies lay their Canaan.

Nor was this all. Thousands of "gentiles" (non-Mormons), scattered through many states and territories and lacking any common leader, had begun to feel the itch of Oregon and California. For the past five years pioneer families had been loading up their possessions in wagons like those of the Powells and finding their way across the plains and mountains to greener pastures. Driving straight through Indian country, they quickly standardized the Oregon Trail that ran along the Platte River, over South Pass, and northwest to the Columbia River. Meanwhile, more commercially minded travelers had cut another trail through the homeland of the Kansa Indians down to the Arkansas River, then bee-lined over the semiarid high plains to Santa Fe. After gold was discovered in 1848 at Sutter's Fort in the Sacramento Valley, both routes became even busier. Nearly three hundred thousand people followed the trails west from 1849 to 1860.[2]

The Powells, therefore, were neither very remarkable in their small wagon train nor very adventuresome by national standards. They did not travel far by comparison with others. They encountered no hostile Indians nor Mexican guns nor mountain snowstorms. They had plenty of water and food along the way. They were, in a strict sense, not pioneers at all. Yet they too knew what it meant to pick up and go, leaving many tender attachments behind. They nursed all the familiar aspirations for a better life. Their task ahead was daunting in its own terms: a family headed by two immigrants out of urban-industrial England, inexperienced in the arts of soil cultivation, were setting out to farm. They would try to wrest a living from a still wild, primeval prairie whose complexities they could not begin to anticipate. All their goods were stowed in a couple of wagons. All their knowledge was yet to be acquired.

The fittingly named Increase Lapham, who published the first major book on Wisconsin, a guide to its lands and economic potential, was high on Walworth County in particular as a destiny for prospective buyers. He described it as one of the territory's most auspicious agricultural counties, "possessing a rich soil, with about the proper proportion of timber and prairie land to suit the convenience and fancy of the first settlers of a new country."[3] A farmer needed timber to build fences, houses, and barns; the timber here consisted of white and bur oak, hickory, poplar, and ash, all good hardwoods. A farmer also needed prairie for crops and pasture. Walworth offered a rolling surface of heavy clay loams on its higher lands, rich alluvial deposits in the bottoms; the land was not well drained, however, and swamps and lakes took up too much space. Above all it had the attraction of location: one county over from Lake Michigan and its shipping facilities at Milwaukee, Racine, and Southport (later renamed Kenosha) and in the spreading urban shadow of Chicago.

The Powells, seeking a farm in this well-advertised place, now encountered for the first time the federal land system, at once highly complex and deceivingly simple. That system occupied Wes through much of his adult life, and it is worth trying to understand just how it functioned in terms of their lives in Wisconsin. The brainchild of Thomas Jefferson, who hoped to create a nation firmly secured in the hands of small, independent farmers, the land system began with passage of the Land Ordinance in 1785, which established a uniform survey of all land west of Pennsylvania into rectangles called townships, each six miles square. A single township contained, after completion

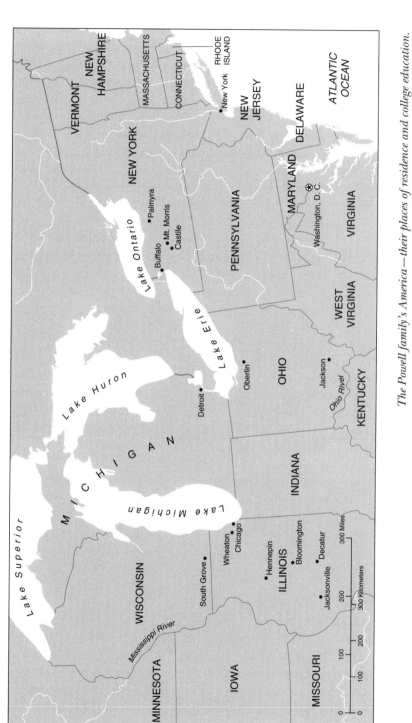

The Powell family's America—their places of residence and college education.

of a map, sixteen uniform sections of 640 acres each, and the sections could be further broken down into half-sections, quarter-sections, or quarter-of-a-quarter sections. From the base point where the Ohio River crosses the Pennsylvania state line, a series of grid lines called ranges marched westward, establishing coordinates for the whole system and enabling anyone in Washington, D.C., Jackson, Ohio, or Chicago, Illinois, to put a finger precisely on the map location of a given piece of land. The simplicity of the system was appealing to a people who had experienced all the uncertainties and irregularities of using the land's own features as boundary markers — a stream here, a hill there, a tree over there. On the other hand, the simplicity gained by ignoring the natural contours of the land levied a long-term cost on settlers, on politicians, and later on land-use planners who had to wrestle with the manifold discrepancies between a simple, rational geometry and a messy, complicated terrain.

Another kind of complexity came with the passage of more and more laws governing the disposal of the federal domain. Congress in the beginning was pleased to sell land in large parcels to rich private individuals who resold at profit to small family farmers. By the 1840s, however, the government had recognized that numerous families, lacking the money to buy, had simply squatted and farmed, waiting for the surveyors to catch up and the sheriff to evict them. For the sake of justice, they deserved a chance to compete against well-heeled speculators. Other laws gave land as "bounties" to men who had served in the military. In 1862, under pressure from agrarian reformers, the government passed the Homestead Act, which gave absolutely free to any bona fide settler a quarter-section of land, or 160 acres. Jefferson's ideal, it would seem, would finally be realized in a generous way, though eight decades late.[4]

The Powells came too early to get a free homestead. To acquire land, they had to pay out most of the money they had accumulated in Ohio. On 25 November, Joseph bought from David J. Best, a local merchant living at Best's Corners in southwestern Walworth County (an area later called South Grove), a parcel of 120 acres for the sum of $1,200. The deed read, in the official language of the federal survey, "the east half of the southwest quarter and the northwest quarter of the southwest quarter of Section 17, Township 1 north of Range 15 east." Three years later Joseph would buy an adjoining piece of land from David Larkin, justice of the peace, giving the family a close approximation of the basic 160-acre homestead.[5]

The high price of the Best land reflected several improvements that had been made, including a house, barn, and cleared cropland, along with market appreciation. Best had been among the earliest settlers, arriving in 1837, and had his pick among the sixteen townships in the county. He arrived one year after Wisconsin had separated from Michigan to become a territory in its own right, anticipating state-hood with an influx of population.[6] The federal government, follow-ing its usual practice of offering land only after surveys had been done and when the market seemed ready for it, let contracts to private sur-veying parties who went out to measure and plat the countryside. In February 1839 the survey was complete, and the regional land office in Milwaukee advertised that land was now ready for sale by public auction at a minimum price of $1.25 per acre. Best showed up at the auction, paid the minimum price, received title to a piece of Sharon township, and went home to do a little farming. He also opened a store, got himself designated postmaster, made a few boots and shoes on the side, and built a frame house. He had created the nubbin of a town, if anyone was interested.[7]

The Powells liked what they saw and bought, though they under-stood there was still much work ahead to make their property into a fully productive farm. The house, though cramped and primitive, sat at a crossroads where they could feel connected to society, living and dead (the South Grove cemetery was not far away). A Methodist con-gregation of twelve members had been meeting in private dwellings, and thus Joseph had a pulpit standing empty and ready. Behind their house, the land sloped down to a small creek, which powered a sawmill downstream, and on the far side of the creek the land rose to a low, heavily forested glacial ridge. Immediately to the west lay a wet-land of cattails, reeds, and bullfrogs, forcing the road to detour sightly, a small flaw in the otherwise square grid of roads that reticu-lated their new countryside. It was so much more orderly than Ohio or New York had been. The government had designed for them and their neighbors a model of rural efficiency, if only they could live up to it.[8]

Missing from the picture when the Powells arrived were the abo-riginal inhabitants, the Potowatomis who had once lived here. They were now removed beyond the Missouri River. In 1833 they had ceded their land, as the government tried, with a shower of gifts, ra-tions, annuities, and promises, to clear by treaty all occupancy rights that the native Americans might claim.

A few years after the Powells assumed ownership, a party of Winnebagoes came through their farm from the north, leaving an impression on a boy that would last half a century. As Wes recalled, they first passed through on their way to Chicago, "footsore and disconsolate," their horses weary too, and sank down to rest along the creek running through the Powell farm. Later they met with government officials in the city, who gave them new calico dresses, blankets, and shoes. Returning in better spirits, they camped on the farm once again without permission. Mary, her two older daughters, and Wes did not resent the intrusion but went down to the camp to visit. They found the Indians circled in canvas tents around a campfire on the north side of the creek, among a grove of bur oaks where a spring came out of the ground. This was, they explained, an old, familiar place to them, where their forefathers had often stopped to hunt, set snares in the creek, and drink the cold water. They stayed a week, dancing and feasting each night. Mary gathered from two or three Indians who could speak English that they had collected in Chicago a payment for turning over their ancient tribal rights to the government, rights that the Powells now held. "The strip of ground on which we had planted our apple orchard," Wes remembered, "had been their rabbit preserve." These were the first Indians that Wes had ever met, and so great was their impact that he would devote much of the rest of his life to studying the Native American's condition and fate.[9]

Joseph, it turned out, had no intention of turning himself to the work of a farmer. Henceforth he devoted his days exclusively to evangelism, giving up even the craft of tailoring. The patriarch's plan was that Wes, twelve years old, and his brother Bram, only ten, would take over the work of earning an income for the family on their new land. Joseph had provided the capital, they would provide the labor. They could hire temporary help from the large pool of farmless young men in the area, many of them recent German immigrants who knew well enough how to plant and harvest crops or manage livestock but lacked the capital to get a farm for themselves. They could also get help to cut trees and pull stumps, expanding the area under cultivation. But without any appeal Wes and Bram would have to put their books aside and become family breadwinners.

The challenge would have been immense even for full-grown, experienced men. The two boys had to figure out how to transform their large, abstract square on the map into a comfortable, secure livelihood for ten people, plus hired hands, with minimal parental in-

struction, and even that minimum came from parents who were as innocent and inexperienced as they. Wes was not apprenticing to an
ancient family tradition or craft nor working land that had been occupied for generations. He knew virtually nothing about the art of
farming, and this was mostly land that had never been farmed (a rabbit preserve, the Winnebagoes called it). The weather alone would
have baffled any young, unseasoned mind: the average timing of the
first frost, the unpredictability of winter blizzards, the earliest spring
date when one could safely plant, the dangers of drought, hail, and
wind. Then there were those Egyptian plagues of grasshoppers,
fungi, and cutworms about which he did not even realize he was supposed to be worried. Like so many other European immigrants who
came to the New World, the Powells entered on a life of farming casually, with neither sufficient experience nor knowledge, assuming as
they did that agriculture was simply a matter of buying land and taking its fertility to market—a primitive but easy route to wealth, one
that even untrained boys could handle. All that was needed was hard
work, and any Powell youngster ought to be well prepared for that.

Joseph managed to bring home some neighborly advice about
what to plant and what to buy. They needed wheat seed to establish a
cash crop, corn and oats to feed the animals, and the animals ought
to include at least two milk cows, four hogs, four sheep, and a flock of
chickens; all of the latter Joseph purchased and called his Noah's ark.
The horses that brought them north must do for hauling and plowing, though they may have purchased a yoke or two of oxen as well.
Mother set out her day-lily bulbs in the front yard and inside set up
school for the youngest children; there was no public school organized yet in the vicinity. Then they hunkered down to wait for spring,
harvesting the wood from an acre or two to keep warm through their
first Wisconsin winter.

In the spring Wes put his hand to the plow. Within three years they
had sixty acres under cultivation, but for now there were only fifteen
acres to get ready for seed. They planted spring wheat in the traditional way of broadcasting by hand. Most of their tools and methods
were simple, cheap, and labor-intensive. The wheat that Wes planted
was already the grain of choice in their new home, indeed in the entire region. Prairie wheat, whether the spring or winter variety, was
taking over, and soon these western producers would drive eastern
ones to the wall.[10]

How much the Powell farm contributed to that new flood of wheat
pouring out of the prairies is unclear, though given their limited

methods and labor pool, they qualified as small-scale producers — perhaps five, later no more than thirty, acres worth. Every acre that Wes and his helpers cleared and planted they had to harvest by scythe and cradle, without aid of machinery. They waited patiently until the wheat was ripe, hoping the weather was on their side, then quickly did the cutting before the seed heads shattered and fell to the ground, then gathered up the cut stems into shocks for threshing. The first year they beat the seeds out of the shocks with a flail, but later they constructed an oak threshing floor where they could drive the horses round and round over the wheat, knocking the grains from the straw. Always the grain was mixed with weeds and had to be cleaned before being bagged for market. Every part of that tiring process put a ceiling on what they could raise.

Except for a few bushels reserved for seed, the wheat had to travel to wholesale grain buyers, flour millers, and shippers, all of them located on the shores of Lake Michigan, more than fifty miles east of South Grove. Wes was put in charge once again, and in those days of wagon transport even a small producer had a heavy assignment. An outstanding yield would have produced twenty-five to thirty bushels per acre, though the norm was closer to ten or fifteen (and with continuous cropping on unfertilized soils, the yields soon fell to five). A bushel of wheat weighs sixty pounds. Wes had, therefore, anywhere from two to ten tons of grain to haul — and a single ton would have been a big load for a farm wagon drawn by horses or oxen over the typically rough roads. He faced many long trips.

Waiting until late fall or early winter when the roads were dry and free of snow, he set out again and again in a farm-to-market ritual. A trip to Southport took six days in fair weather — three days out, three days back. Thus, he had to spend much of his time after harvest alone on a wagon seat, with his family's potential income riding in the wooden box behind him, wending his way toward a city. On the way home he was supposed to bring a bag of money, along with such purchased supplies as sugar, cloth, medicines, dishware, and nails.

The production costs in this commercialized agriculture were high, and they got higher as the years went on. Besides hired labor, work animals, plows, and wagons, Wes had to earn enough to pay the taxes on the farm. He may also have paid a fee to use the new plank roads that companies built in those years from the interior to the lake shore. They sawed oaks into planks, pegged them to long beams like a wooden railway, and charged travelers two cents a mile. The roads saved time and effort, but they were an additional expense. Fortunately, the Powell farm was free of debt, a burden that was sinking many of their neighbors.

The family managed to make good money for a couple of seasons. Then they made a little less than that. Wheat in flush years might bring as much as a dollar per bushel, but beginning in 1849 and continuing for the next two years, a combination of scanty snowfall, falling yields, and failing prices—down to fifty cents a bushel—made Wisconsin wheat farming suddenly a more discouraging task. Prices would recover, even soar, but Wes was learning first-hand a sobering lesson. The lot of the farmer was a hard, uncertain one. It was not an occupation for the lazy or incompetent or inexperienced. And farmers, he was learning, were a deserving class who had a compelling case to make against exploiting money interests and power elites in the city. On a personal level he was also learning that, good year or bad, whatever he made in selling the farm's produce was not his to keep—the family took it all.

He had a few compensations in this hard round of physical toil and responsibility. The wagon box where he stored his lunch usually held a book or two, which he pulled out to read as the wagon jolted along. He liked to read histories and biographies, and he had in his box Thomas Dick's *Philosophy* (given him by Crookham, a reminder of those idyllic days spent with his tutor), along with Milton's *Paradise Lost* (his mother's recommendation). But his favorite was *The Pilgrim's Progress* by John Bunyan, a story that he never regarded as mere "fiction" but as allegorical truth that could stiffen a young man's resolve, whatever the temptations he faced.

Christian on his way through the Wilderness to the Celestial City described Wes on his way through life's difficulties. Vanity Fair lay ahead on the road. Would he escape its bawdy whores and thieves? Would the simple, homespun lad be an object of scorn and sport among more worldly, sophisticated people? Evangelist approaches Christian on the outskirts of the town: "I have sowed, and you have reaped, and the day is coming, when both he that sowed, and they that reaped shall rejoice together; that is, if you hold out; for, in due time ye shall reap, if you faint not." The growing question, however, was what exactly would he reap—always wheat and more wheat, or something more and better?

Wes met in his endless market trips another clean, upstanding young wagon driver, who like himself was often thrown into doubtful company and temptations. William Wheeler, the son of a Walworth County farmer, was a devout Congregationalist and an enthusiastic reader with some college years to his credit. It was probably he who first suggested to Wes the appeal of a good book while driving. The two began stopping to camp together and review their experiences as farmers and marketers. But William's main advice was nowhere to be found in John Bunyan's text: get a college education, however you can, and above all study the natural sciences. It was a view that Wes was coming to himself. He needed more formal education.

Even more influential than Wheeler in clinching the point was another young man, John Davis, who with his father came riding through South Grove one evening and inquired about lodging at the Powells. The Davises were farmer and son from Macon County, Illinois. The younger Davis was smitten by the oldest Powell daughter, Martha, and they were married in May 1851 in the local church.[11] John's subsequent influence over brother-in-law Wes would be hard to exaggerate. It lasted for more than four decades, it strengthened the agrarian sympathies that Wes was developing from his farming experience, and all in all it may have been the most important family influence outside that of his parents and Crookham.

There was another young man whom Wes did not have a chance to meet, but whose life followed a pattern similar to his own: John Muir of Marquette County, Wisconsin, less than a hundred miles to the northwest. Had they met, they would have had plenty to discuss. Muir's family came into the state in 1849, less than three years after the Powells, and they came straight from Dunbar, Scotland. They too went shopping for a farm on the raw edge of settlement and purchased a quarter-section near the Fox River. Muir was eleven when they arrived; nonetheless, he was put to work hauling and burning brush to prepare the way for the plow. He learned to handle (so he claimed) one of the large, clumsy breaking plows all on his own. Pulled by four or five yoke of oxen, its steel share sliced through the densely matted, deeply rooted native grasses and turned a furrow two feet wide, like cutting through a thick blanket. He planted corn, potatoes, wheat, and pumpkins in the dark soil, chopped out weeds through the warm summer days, and gathered in the fall harvest.

"No matter what the weather," Muir wrote in his memoir at age seventy, "there was always something to do. During heavy rains or snowstorms we worked in the barn, shelling corn, fanning wheat, thrashing with the flail, making ax-handles or ox-yokes, mending things, or sprouting and sorting potatoes in the cellar." The land was, for all its cruel blows, good to the Muirs, as it was to the Powells. Within a few years, the elder Muir traded one farm for another and could claim title to 320 productive acres. Yet as John Muir remembered his boyhood, this rural community worked itself far too hard—far beyond what was needed or reasonable. They "toiled and sweated and grubbed themselves into their graves years before their natural dying days, in getting a living on a quarter-section of land and vaguely trying to get rich."[12]

The two boys had more in common than learning to work hard in Wisconsin during the same span of years. Each had a father born in the British Isles who came to America wanting to evangelize. Muir's father Daniel was a Campbellite, a fundamentalist offshoot of Scottish Presbyterianism, and he too aspired to be a preacher of the gospel more than a farmer. He taught his children "grim self-denial, in season and out of season, to mortify the flesh, keep our bodies in subjection to Bible laws, and mercilessly punish ourselves for every fault imagined or committed." He refused his children any leisure time or worldly pleasures, while ironically an unbridled hunger for land took possession of his own soul. Muir's retrospective portrait of his preacher-father was bitter. Even at a late date, he all but hated this man who had set him to doing chores that were beyond the strength of a child, chores that he himself could not or would not do. Muir despised the life of a Midwestern farmer. From his experience, he found it to be a life of ruthless, unceasing conquest, a life that acknowledged none of the beauty of nature nor the right to existence of any living thing other than man. As he told it, he nearly died from that incomprehensibly brutal labor, and as soon as he was old enough he ran away from it.

The parallel with Wes Powell was striking in many aspects. Wes worked at least as hard as John Muir, and he too began to resent his father, who preached Christian virtue but seemed to exploit his own children, demanding their self-sacrifice so that he might be free to preach his doctrine. Wes never wrote a memoir of his youth to compare with Muir's, but had he done so, it would have shown a boy heading toward a breaking point, when he could no longer accept the role he had been assigned by parental authority. Yet Wes never seems to have felt anything like Muir's deep contempt for his father or his father's narrow piety. Wes never expressed in print any loathing of rural toil, nor did he ever make any indictment of farmer attitudes toward nature. Perhaps that difference explains why Muir would grow up to become one of nineteenth-century America's most radical outsiders, a lover of the wilderness and a defender of the rights of other creatures to exist, while Powell would become a more social individual, an insider and a joiner, and throughout his life a defender of the small rural community against outside forces. Both boys experienced that Wisconsin world of Protestantism, capital accumulation, and work ethic, mixed with an intimacy with the land. Both would eventually go into the far-off West to find new meanings for their lives and, indeed, would become charismatic figures in that West. Both would become prophets of the American conservation movement. But they would express different points of view about what the land, the West, and conservation should offer.

The 1850 federal census found the Powell family well settled on their farm in South Grove. Joseph and Mary were each recorded as forty-two years old, which was off by several years. Martha and Mary, though young women on the verge of marriage, were still in the household, along with Bram, now fourteen, Lida, Nellie, Walter, and Juliet, ages twelve to four, all of whom were now in attendance at public school. None of the family was "illiterate, deaf-dumb, blind, insane, idiotic, a pauper, or convict." Squarely in the middle of that family list was "Jno W, age 16, male, Farmer." He now had an adult identity, but it was not one that he would keep.

Their fourth harvest was the family's last at South Grove. In the fall of 1850, when the grain was all threshed, Wes announced that he was quitting farming and going off to find a proper education. He trudged twenty miles to Janesville to enroll in school. The town boasted that it had one of the few secondary schools in the state, though as he discovered on arrival it was a pathetic one-room affair with forty students and a poorly qualified teacher. Nonetheless, he knew he needed knowledge of mathematics, grammar, and classical languages to qualify for college admission. His parents had given him no money, so on the town's outskirts he had stop to earn his tuition before proceeding. A farmer put him to work for two weeks, splitting wood and repairing tools. The same farmer offered him room and board during his studies as payment for more labor, and after chores each evening Wes read his schoolbooks by firelight, rocking the baby's cradle with his foot.

Although Joseph and Mary had not been very helpful, they did not dispute his decision to go to school; after all, they were now ready to sell the farm. On 3 October, they signed their title over for $2,100, making a profit of $700, or 50 percent of their purchase price. But they did not mean to be done with farming. Joseph immediately went across the state line into adjoining Boone County, Illinois, to enter upon a new round of land dealings. On the eastern side of that county, an area still rather inaccessible by road, he found what he was looking for — prime agricultural potential in what was called the Bonus (Latin for "good") Prairie. On 26 June 1851 he filed in the county court house in Belvidere deeds on three separate parcels in Bonus and Boone townships, totaling 160 acres at a combined cost of $1,120, or $7 an acre. This was unimproved land, so they would have to start all over the process of wresting a working farm out of undisturbed prairie. That same summer Wes rejoined the family in their new home and helped them break sod. Later on Joseph would buy additional acreage in Boone and also McHenry counties.

By this point Joseph had become an aspiring rural capitalist, buying and selling numbered spaces on a map as though land were a commodity like any other and recruiting cheap labor to work that land for him. Like many fellow citizens, old and new, he found it hard to attach himself to any particular place in America. The prairie was not a habitat that he understood well or cared much about. Mary and he had come into one of the world's most bountiful, complex, and beautiful landscapes, where nature had worked for aeons on a lavish scale, but all that land meant to them was opportunity to acquire more capital that would appreciate in value as the population increased. They would buy it, use it for a while, sell it to another wave of land seekers, and move on. Their personal values had become an unstable, incongruous mix of otherworldly devotion to religion and worldly accumulation of wealth.

The Reverend John Wesley, especially toward the end of his life, had taught his followers that riches and piety were fundamentally incompatible goals for the Christian. "It is absolutely impossible, unless by that power to which all things are possible, that a rich man should be a Christian — to have the mind that was in Christ, and to walk as Christ walked."[13] The rich man would inevitably succumb to the sins of pride, willfulness, debauchery, even atheism. Love of money was always, as St. Paul had warned, the "root of all evil." But then Wesley had left that small opening to the rationalizing mind—"unless by that power to which all things are possible." Divine grace, a sophist might argue, could save a rich man as easily as a poor one. Who could deny that God worked in mysterious ways? With that kind of reasoning, and not a little confidence in his own virtue, Joseph could pursue his speculative dealings with a clear conscience. He was not yet a rich man in his own eyes, but if he became one, God would surely look out for his soul.

The harsher truth was that Illinois, indeed the whole United States, was making it increasingly difficult for pious men and women like the Powells to keep their affections firmly trained on God. Wesley's words were hard to hear over the excited din created by politicians and businessmen, including the popular senator from Illinois, Stephen Douglas, the Little Giant. On election to the Senate in 1847, he moved to Chicago and began investing in real estate as other men had been doing for the preceding decade and a half. It was a smart time to be arriving. The city boomed when the Illinois and Michigan Canal opened, a twin of the Erie Canal and, like it, projected to be the artery of a lavish commercial empire.

But Douglas had a more technologically advanced vision to promote: a railroad system that would run down the middle of the state, north to south, linking Chicago with Cairo, bypassing St. Louis altogether to boost his adopted home as the world's greatest mercantile center. Douglas went to work in Washington to get a federal subsidy for his ambitious scheme. Congress complied by granting free to a group of capitalists no less than 2,595,000 acres of Illinois land, making them the largest proprietors in the state. In exchange for constructing the Illinois Central railroad, the capitalists could sell that land, which their enterprise would make accessible and valuable. The railroad was completed in 1856, and it was so successful in promoting settlement that Congress would try the same approach in granting a land subsidy to the first transcontinental line a few years later.

From 1850 to 1860 Illinois laid over two thousand miles of track. Its population soared to 1.7 million, making it the fourth largest state in the union. Chicago climbed to more than one hundred thousand inhabitants, surpassing not only its competing lake shore ports but also all its competitors on the Mississippi and throughout the Midwest. Virtually the whole state became a gigantic farm raising corn, wheat, flax, hogs, and cattle. Log cabins gave way to white frame houses, scythes to mechanical reapers, wooden fences to barbed wire.

In his 1855 message to the citizens, the governor invoked the words "commerce" and "business" as though they were from Holy Scripture. He had nothing to say about the spiritual condition of his constituents, or about whether morality was on the increase, or whether good citizenship was still at the heart of the republic. Instead, he reveled in the state's material successes: "the capital and energy that is being invested among us in consequence of our advantages. . . . I think the history of the world may safely be challenged for instances of more rapid growth in the elements of wealth and prosperity than have characterized this state for the past few years."[14]

The *Oberlin Evangelist*, Joseph's favorite reading matter, now echoed that enthusiasm and even went so far as to characterize economic progress as God's strategy for regenerating the human species. "Progress is the genius of the hour," its editor wrote in 1855; "it would seem that our race have only begun to live." By means of improved grains and farm animals, labor-saving machinery and domestic comforts, God shows "glorious uses for human skills and labor — that he is preparing our world for the reign of the Prince of Peace — the 'King who shall reign in righteousness.'"[15] With both the profane and sacred press drumming the same message of economic growth into their heads, Joseph and Mary had considerable cultural support for their speculations in farm land. They had made their move to the prairie at exactly the right moment if prosperity was what they sought, and increasingly it was. A life devoted to spreading the good word was still their primary mission, but they had found ways to serve their God and have the world's goods too.

The older children were now reaching their majority, preparing to leave home. In June 1852 daughter Mary became the wife of William Wheeler and went back to Wisconsin to live as a farmer's wife, as Martha was doing in central Illinois. Then in the fall of that year Wes, with his mother's encouragement, determined to leave home and commence teaching school. Although he had been to Janesville for a season of formal schooling, he knew there was still much that he did not know. He went up into the family garret with a pile of textbooks on grammar, mathematics, and geography, and over the next six weeks he absorbed their contents day and night. When he felt ready, he went looking for a position in Jefferson County, Wisconsin, traveling by foot thirty miles over frozen roads.

He readily discovered a position, but getting it required him to visit the house of the district superintendent of schools to obtain a certificate of proficiency. Over supper, the superintendent led him to talk about himself, his family background, and his scholarly attainments. Abruptly at bedtime, much to Wes's surprise, the man signed the certificate. Wes now had secured a position at $14 a month for presiding over a one-room stone schoolhouse — his first regular, income-earning job. The new teacher was still only a teenager; some of his pupils were older than he. Despite passing the superintendent's inspection, his gaps in learning were immense. After all, his own education had consisted mostly of Crookham's idiosyncratic tutoring, his mother's benevolent guidance, and his own cram sessions. Through that first term behind the desk, he had himself to teach as much as the students.

Geography became his favorite subject. One night a week he offered lectures on it to his most advanced students, and the lectures proved so popular in this education-starved (and entertainment-starved) community that soon he was drawing a bigger audience, compelling him to work the few geography texts in his possession harder than ever. The wife of the couple he lodged with, a Mrs. Little, formerly a schoolteacher in New England, pulled books from her excellent library to help him with his platform performances. She also looked over the outlines of his talks in advance — a generous mentor who helped ease him through the transition from farmer to teacher. Thus the rural counties of the region endeavored to educate their children. Thus New England showed the Midwest the need for institutions of common schooling, while the Midwest stumbled awkwardly behind.

The Powell family's life on the land lasted only six or seven years, a period when agriculture was passing through a tremendous transition to large-scale business methods. Farming would require more and more capital for land and machinery, while the traditional rural community would wither and fade. Though the Powells had never really been part of the ancient tradition of farming, neither were they prepared for a future in agribusiness. Mary and Joseph, after a short interlude of residing in Boone County, advanced toward the fringes of Chicago. Wes, the self-identified "farmer" in the family, the one who had done the most to improve the lands they had occupied, gave up farming completely to try teaching, and Bram would follow his lead. Meanwhile, Illinois raced on toward a shimmering vision of unlimited growth, productivity, and wealth. Matter shoved spirit aside. America, which for a few decades had been caught up in the rapture of evangelical revivalism, was now more than ever a predominantly secular nation.

The *Oberlin Evangelist* approved of railroads in general, for they had been destined by God "to bear a most effective part in the joint progress of civilization and Christianity." But especially it liked the idea of putting a good religious college on a railroad line where students could reach a pious education easily. "The genius of the age demands it. A College should occupy a wisely selected mean in local position — not in contact with the corrupting influences of the city—yet by means of facilities for travel, as near the homes of its pa-trons as the case admits."[16] Following such advice was precisely what Joseph and Mary undertook to do next in their saga of becoming an American success story. They would help build a college in suburbia, just beyond the zone of urban corruption, and they would resettle themselves in that same place—a shrewdly selected mean that had all the advantages of modern living, including railroad transporta-tion, and none of the dangerous urban influences.

A conference of Wesleyan Methodists meeting in Batavia, Illinois, in 1851, with Joseph likely in attendance, resolved to create a new comprehensive school and college under church auspices—an Oberlin for the prairie. Two brothers named Wheaton stepped forth to offer forty acres of land for a campus in the new town they were platting, a town bearing their name.[17] They conceived of a Christian community free of alcohol, with a Christian school at its core. The conferees readily accepted their offer, for the location was ideal. The new town of Wheaton lay on the outskirts of Chicago in DuPage County, twenty-five miles west of the city's Michigan Avenue, and the Galena and Chicago Union Railroad came directly through it. Within a couple of years five hundred inhabitants were living here, some of them commuting to work in the city, and they were a sober, diligent bunch. Soon a school, the Illinois Institute, was under construction in their midst.

The Powells, tired of their rustic life and now relatively affluent, did not hesitate. They determined to pull out of Boone County and move to this suburb of Chicago where they could be among like-minded neighbors who shared their Wesleyan principles. On 16 De-cember 1852 Joseph bought a forty-acre farm, including a small farmhouse, on the Geneva Road just outside the Wheaton brothers' estate—land that Joseph would rent out for income. Two more forty-acre parcels came into his possession, then three properties in the Illinois Institute Addition, residential lots adjoining the school. Then came more acquisitions, and still more. All of the wealth they had been accumulating since Jackson and South Grove days they now began reinvesting in this new home. And it would be their last home—offering the comfortable righteousness they had been seek-ing since they first came to America.

In the fall of 1853 Wes dutifully put aside his own affairs once again to help the family move.[18] He brought his mother and a younger sister into town, looked over their properties carefully, and decided to drag the farmhouse to their in-town lot on East Jefferson

Street, next to the school. Three strong men jacked the house up on rollers pulled by six oxen. In November the family unpacked in their new quarters. Uncle Walter and his family came from Ohio to establish residency in this new community too and bought part of a town lot for themselves. The rejoined families still had a large brood of children left to raise and educate, and now they could all go to school where they would be sure of a godly but scholarly atmosphere.

Illinois Institute opened its doors for instruction in December 1853, though it would not graduate its first college class for a while. The students themselves chose a motto: "For Christ and His Kingdom."[19] The school would be emphatically religious in purpose, rigorous in instruction, progressive and liberal on matters of race and gender, and highly conservative on issues of personal morality. Like Oberlin, the new school was not shy of politics: it was militantly abolitionist and moderately feminist. All qualified students, male or female, black or white, could attend so long as they observed strict rules of behavior. And those rules were spelled out for them in the school catalogue: they must attend church regularly; be in their rooms during study hours; use no obscenities, liquor, or tobacco; never play cards or billiards; never throw water or dirt from the windows; never invite members of the opposite sex to their rooms; never seek to marry a fellow student. A single three-story limestone building provided space for all the classes, the chapel, and fourteen dormitory rooms for advanced male students. Girls must live at home or as boarders in private residences. And most of the students in the first few years were indeed girls and boys; 111 enrolled as elementary students, 151 in the secondary department, and only 20 at the college level. An early picture shows a lone building topped by an immense cupola, standing forthrightly among newly planted trees in an open field of grass — a fortress for youth confronting the city.

Presidents of such religious schools were traditionally ministers whose main teaching responsibility was to put the seniors through a final course in theology. After the Reverend John Cross had proved inadequate to the task, the presidency of Illinois Institute passed to Lucius Matlack, a staunch antislavery agitator and founder of the Wesleyan Methodist church. But Matlack proved to be no better an administrator. Soon the school was teetering on the precipice of bankruptcy, and it remained there for several years. Finally, the Wesleyans asked assistance from the Congregationalists, who had acquired a great deal of experience in running church colleges, and offered to share control with them. In 1860 Illinois Institute (Wesleyan) became Wheaton College (Wesleyan-Congregational). Its newest president, the Reverend Jonathon Blanchard, was out of New England by way of Cincinnati, where he had been minister in a large church. He had been ordained by none other than Dr. Lyman Beecher, head of Lane Seminary, and Beecher's son-in-law Dr. Calvin Stowe offered his ordination prayer. Blanchard was thoroughly abolitionist and an ardent temperance man; the school continued to observe its founding principles. Blanchard had known the Powells in their Ohio days, so his move to Wheaton was a reunion after two decades of separation and a reminder of their troubled lives together in the antislavery fight.[20]

Within months of their move to Wheaton, Joseph Powell had become at least marginally involved in managing the Illinois Institute's affairs. He was elected to its board of trustees in spring 1855 and often opened the board's meetings with a prayer. He joined other supporters to provide funds for a student boarding house. But after only two years in office, Joseph resigned from the board in exhaustion. "Owing to general debility of health and prostration of the nervious [sic] system," he explained, "I find that business care of every kind increases it and my place will be much better filled by some other person. . . . I very reluctantly accepted the office and I feel that I have never performed the duties aright."[21] He was only fifty-two years old, but apparently the combined stresses of preaching several times a week, overseeing his large family, and coping with the school's early difficulties had aged him more than he realized.

The census of 1860 gave Joseph's worth as $7,000 in real estate and $1,500 in personal estate. That was not a grandiose fortune, but it certainly put him among the wealthier men in DuPage County. Three physicians recorded real estate values of $2–5,000, a lawyer claimed an estate of $10,000, and a hardware store owner one of $6,000. Most personal estates were under $1,000. Uncle Walter, identified as a watchmaker still, set his real estate worth at $1,000 and his personal worth at $500.[22]

For comparison, one could turn to another Illinois town, Jacksonville, and its distribution of wealth in the same period. In 1850 only 6 percent of the heads of Jacksonville's households owned $5,000 or more in real property; by 1860, that percentage had climbed to ten. At the other extreme, nearly two-thirds of the households owned no real estate at all in 1850, and by 1860 that number had climbed to 69 percent.[23] Owning real estate was not the common experience of town people in Illinois or other states of that period.

Clearly, Joseph had done well for himself. A mere artisan in England, he had risen to the middle class, perhaps even the upper-middle class, by the end of a decade in suburban Chicago.

The path to financial success in the antebellum North lay in two different lanes — staying put or moving on. The secret was knowing which lane to take and when. Every community had its small number of inhabitants who stayed put, who watched others come and go, while they added steadily to their rural or urban holdings. They made stability pay off in terms of both wealth and power. Mobility, on the other hand, was an engrained national habit that had self-betterment as its justification. The typical family moved and moved again, so that each ten years when the census taker came along to count a community's residents more than two-thirds of the names on average were new. Public leaders kept urging poor, landless, propertyless citizens to go west and find their opportunity instead of complaining about their condition or resenting those who owned most of Main Street. The message got through, and wagons rolled on and on.

The Powells had followed the official advice, and it had worked for them. They had shifted from one new community to another, gravitating toward the less crowded edges of settlement where land was cheap, and they had watched their economic worth increase over time. They had sold out and started over, doubling their net worth, and then done it again and again. But their last spurt of affluence had come not from moving farther west to new land but from moving to Chicago's environs, where real estate was booming through the 1850s. Once there, they stayed in place until death. They became pillars of the community. They could look back on their restless past as having led somewhere after all — toward security, affluence, and status.

Wheaton was a town filled with people like them — people who had risen from obscurity but always tried to give God credit for their good fortune. By the later 1850s the town had found a new political identity to go with its evangelical spirit and its upwardly mobile ethos. It had become a stalwart center of the new Republican Party that was emerging out of the disintegration of the American party system. The old Whigs had disappeared completely, the Democrats had cracked apart over slavery, the Liberty Party had faded quickly, the Free-Soil Party, which had taken the latter's place with a platform against the expansion of slavery into the western territories, had never won a national election. Suddenly, out of the chaos emerged a new party that met with enthusiastic reception all across the northern tier of states. It would capture and hold the majority vote of

Wheaton, and it would appeal to men like Joseph Powell and win their loyalty. With Joseph's support, the Republicans would win the Presidency in 1860, and their candidate would be Illinois's own Abraham Lincoln.

The Republican Party's ideology summed up much of what the elder Powell had come to believe in. America was the best society this world could offer. It was organized on the principles of free labor, free enterprise, and free men. As his own story documented, it was open to anyone with talent and determination. A good country was one that gave men a chance to rise out of poverty through their own efforts. Access to low-priced land and a good education could enhance that chance. The small-scale, independent entrepreneur, in town or country, who had used his chances wisely and made something of himself was the model American. The wealth that such a man achieved should be all his own, to use as he saw fit, but he should use it in godly ways. The good citizen should be an active, believing Protestant. A strong religious faith was needed to safeguard against false pride, selfishness, and greed. Protestantism, understood rightly, was the indispensable handmaiden of success. And capitalism under the steadying influence of Protestantism was God's plan for America.[24]

Such a society had many enemies, but by far the most menacing of them, in Joseph's view, was the great Slave Power sitting in the South. Slavery was a threat to the labor of free white men. It was relentless in trying to take over the West where deserving men wanted and needed to go to claim their opportunity. Slavery was bad for whites, and it was even worse for blacks. It denied a race of people their dignity as men and women, their independence, and their just rewards for hard work. The Slave Power, operating from its base in the plantation system, had gained control over the federal government, manipulating the law to its advantage, and it must be defeated. There could be no compromise. America must not be in its thrall any longer.

There were, to be sure, other enemies, including large industrial corporations that might subvert democracy, though this money power was a far less obvious or worrisome threat to the new party of Republicans. The great cities were filling up with followers of the Catholic Church—brewers of liquor, minions of the pope, a threat to Protestant control—and America must be vigilant against these too. But it was the Slave Power above all others that threw an evil shadow across the nation.

Joseph's sons would move with him into the Republican Party as their political home in an increasingly divided, discordant society.

They would remain loyal to its candidates through the Civil War and beyond, loyal at least nominally to the end of their lives. But the sons would not find a home in the Republican-dominated town of Wheaton, with its leafy streets, its fervent religious climate, and its good real-estate opportunities. This suburb was where their parents stopped, but it was one more place the boys would leave.

Nothing marks more clearly the break that Wes Powell made with his parents' world than the occupation he gave to the census taker in 1860. He identified himself as a "Naturalist." He was, that is, a man well versed in the natural history of plants and animals, could tell one species from another, knew the difference between Cretaceous and Carboniferous periods of geology, and had spent time collecting for a museum. One can almost hear Reverend Powell snort in sheer frustration with this willful child. What kind of career is that for the oldest son of a minister of God—wasting his life on muddy shells when his soul is in constant jeopardy, dabbling with the profane, mixing with people of suspect faith, speculating about what the earth was like thousands of years ago, doubting the literal truth of the Holy Word? Wes heard it all many times over, yet proudly he wore his new label with an air of independence if not defiance.

A frank appraisal would have to conclude that at this point Wes was about as much a naturalist as he had been a farmer ten years earlier. His training was minimal, his experience limited. He was puffing himself up to an identity that, at age twenty-six, he had not yet established. His source of income was now a small Illinois public school, yet he did not identify himself as a "schoolteacher" or even "principal," but as an expert in zoology, botany, the outdoor sciences. He was in fact still an amateur, but in democratic America anybody, no matter what their background, could aspire to be anything, and he aspired to stand within the admired circle of scientists. He was confident that he would make it there somehow and add something substantial to humanity's knowledge of the natural world.

Unquestionably this ambition involved a repudiation of his father and mother's long nurtured plans for him to become an evangelist of the gospel. He refused to ride a circuit as his father had done or go to Methodist conference regularly. The nation offered him another option, an alternative profession that had developed rapidly in recent years along with westward expansion. The founding heroes of that profession were Carolus Linnaeus of Sweden, Georges de Buffon of France, and James Hutton of Scotland. Among earlier Americans, the naturalist tradition included John and William Bartram, Thomas Jefferson, and Charles Willson Peale, followed in Wes's own day by John James Audubon, Thomas Say, Thomas Nuttall, and Henry David Thoreau.

Few of them had been orthodox Christians. They approached nature as eighteenth-century rationalists who believed in the capacity of the human mind to discover truth and order in the universe. Or they were nineteenth-century romantics, pantheists, and transcendentalists who felt a profoundly sympathetic bond with nature that was not exactly part of the Christian legacy. Whatever their philosophy, these naturalists consulted the texts of modern science more than the Bible. While evangelism was winning its converts, they too were quietly increasing in numbers, winning an audience for nature, and by the 1850s they were a force to be reckoned with in the intellectual landscape.

Natural history had its mother church in the American Philosophical Society, founded in Philadelphia in 1743 to promote the cataloguing of the country's wild bounty and the publishing of scientific work in many fields. A hundred years later its offspring assumed a variety of guises: natural history societies, agricultural societies, societies for the encouragement of meteorology, paleontology, ornithology, and Indian ethnology. The Smithsonian Institution, begun in 1846 with an endowment from a London philanthropist for the "increase and diffusion of knowledge among men," gathered those impulses together in Washington, launching a nation's museum with enormous ambitions to educate the populace about the natural world.

Those were all private initiatives, but government also supported the pursuit of natural history. The various states, beginning with Massachusetts in 1830, funded scientific surveys of their lands, usually with an emphasis on accumulating "useful" knowledge, and scientists such as Edward Hitchcock, James Hall, Henry and William Rogers, and David Dale Owen laid foundations for publicly supported geology.[25] The federal government also appropriated funds for comprehensive natural history surveys as part of its mission to occupy the trans-Mississippi West. Most famously, it sent Lewis and Clark over the Rockies to the Columbia River. They were followed by other soldier-explorers—Zebulon Pike, Stephen Long, and John Charles Frémont—all of whom kept an eye open for flora and fauna as well as American geopolitical interests. Frémont led no fewer than five expeditions across the Great Plains between 1842 and 1853, and in the popular mind he stood as the noblest explorer of the century, the great Pathfinder, riding his acclaim to the new Republican Party's presidential nomination in 1856.

Frémont's employer, the Army's Corps of Topographical Engineers (established in 1838), was perhaps the single most important federal expression of enthusiasm for science. The corps, though mainly military map makers, took along with them on their western expeditions many naturalists who depicted in illustration and text the astonishing native peoples, animals, forests, rivers, plains, and mountain ranges that graced the western country. The Pacific railroad surveys, carried out by the corps from 1853 to 1855 to determine the best route to the West Coast, added substantially to the continental catalog of species and their distribution. The surveys were disappointing in that no single route for a railroad emerged as ideal, but they produced seventeen volumes of official reports covering all aspects of the trans-Mississippi environment.[26]

Private and public, amateur and professional, this remarkable flowering of natural history occurred just as Wes was coming of age, and it overwhelmed the appeal of evangelical religion. Methodism, as far as Wes was concerned, had seen its day. It lacked vibrancy and excitement. After a remarkable success, Methodism was no longer the growing cultural force it had once been. The country was now intent on making progress in a more secular direction, and Wes wanted to be part of that shift.

He was in love with the land, the outdoors, the flow of rivers, and the nation's material life. To be sure, by the time he took the name naturalist much of the land had already been well explored. All those surveys and scientists had succeeded in giving citizens a broad outline of their country from New England to California. They had classified most of the native species. They had told the tale of rocks even in the remote desert wastes. Yet Wes was sure there was more to be done. He was certain that somewhere on the continent lay blank spaces where knowledge had not yet penetrated completely—empty spaces about which he could write his own reports.

Wes had to realize that he was entering not only an adventuresome but a controversial profession, and controversial not merely in his parents' household but in the broader culture. He left no indication of any inner turmoil over his decision; on the contrary, he seems to have chosen science with few misgivings. Others, however, expressed plenty of worries. Natural history, they warned, for all of its exuberant optimism might be leading toward dark, troubling conclusions—and those conclusions might be particularly dangerous to evangelical religion.

As science moved from cataloguing species to explaining why and how they existed, it entered sensitive territory. Religion thought it had answered those questions as well as they could be answered. The Reverend John Wesley had proclaimed, at the dawn of modern natural history, that "the design and will of the Creator is the only physical cause of the general economy of the world."[27] He echoed a view that repeatedly tried to assert control over natural history and subordinate it to faith and revelation. Its most widely read exponent was William Paley, author of *Natural Theology* (1802). Nature, from the bee pollinating a flower to the most devastating flood, Paley insisted, exemplifies the wisdom and benevolence of God. The study of natural history, rightly understand, should lead people to greater devotion.

Well into the mid-nineteenth century reputable scientists of England and the United States agreed with Wesley and Paley that their work had no claim to independent or superior explanation. Their studies of geology or botany, they agreed, must be subordinate to revealed religion. That humility, however, would not last for long. Increasingly, scientists began to challenge the church's right to determine the ultimate meaning of their work. They did so by ignoring the problem of finding a "final cause" behind the world's natural order, concentrating instead on immediate physical causes that could explain, in purely material terms, why things existed where and as they did. Such explanations became more and more comprehensive, until they threatened to squeeze God and the theologians right out of the picture. Scientists began restricting the frequency of divine intervention into the physical world. Nature, so far as they could see, followed its own laws without any need for immediate or direct supernatural interference. Scientists alone could explain those laws.

In the first half of the nineteenth century the Bible became for many intellectuals a work of poetry, fable, even myth. One of the first Bible stories to fall into disbelief was Noah's flood. Here were rocks that showed no evidence of a universal flood. Here were thousands of species, more than could be crowded into any man-made boat. And if Noah's story was fable, then what about other Bible stories that had been taken as factual? What about Adam and Eve or the Garden of Eden or Bishop Ussher's calendar that said the earth had been created in 4004 B.C.? What did all those fossils lying along the river banks or deeply embedded in the rocks reveal about time? What did they say about the Judeo-Christian theory of Creation? Perhaps humans were not even the special creation of God. The whole edifice of Western Christian thought, which put man at the center of nature, a fallen but redeemable child of God, was beginning to totter under the skepticism of natural history.

In the year Joseph and Mary had left England, a book was published that would rock Christian orthodoxy to its foundations: the *Principles of Geology* by Charles Lyell. Altogether, he produced three volumes under that title during the period 1830–33, and they provoked heated debate in both Europe and North America on fundamental questions about the history of the earth and of life itself. The earth has been undergoing constant, steady change for aeons, he argued; it has been rising, then eroding under the ceaseless power of water running across its surface — processes natural, observable, and going on this very minute. Lyell was not hostile to religion. He granted that the processes of geological change might well have been set in motion by God at some indeterminate point in the past. But after that point they operated all on their own. Scientists did not need God to explain the present land forms. Small, simple, everyday forces at work could account for the most stupendous scenes.[28]

Heretofore scientists, and the public generally, had supposed that miraculous powers, like enormous pent-up floods bursting through rock walls or volcanoes erupting from the core of the earth, had shaped nature, usually on instructions from God. That supposition might have satisfied the mind's craving for drama, but it did not fit the facts. The surface of the globe was the result of the continuing play of observable natural forces such as wind, rain, and sun on a pliable crust, a theory that Lyell's contemporaries called "uniformitarianism" to distinguish it from the "catastrophism" that had posited spectacular revolutions such as the Great Flood.

Geologists of the previous century had already started naming and marking off the periods of change the earth had passed through, but it was mainly British scientists of Lyell's day, and particularly Lyell himself, who organized most of the modern stratigraphic column — that great thick book of many chapters. The latest chapter, covering the most recent period of geological history, they called the Quaternary; it had two sections, the older of which Lyell gave the name Pleistocene, meaning the age of ice and glaciers. Before that came the Tertiary period, and it was Lyell again who defined several of its subordinate epochs — the Pliocene, Miocene, and Eocene. Other scientists identified the Mesozoic chapter, telling the story of extinct dinosaurs, and before that the Paleozoic. Finally, in 1862, Joseph Beete Jukes titled the immense first chapter in the book of nature the "Precambrian," the ancient era when primitive forms of life first appeared in the fossil record. The exact length of any of those chapters was still in dispute, but Lyell and other historically minded geologists were sure that all the chapters had been very long—much longer than humans had ever realized. Ussher's date of creation was a mere comma buried somewhere near the end of the volume.[29]

In 1841 and 1842, while the Powells were living in Jackson, geologist Lyell traveled through the eastern United States to study rocks. It was well known by that date that the stratigraphic column was the same on both sides of the ocean, suggesting a common global history for geology, and Lyell came to America to correlate the continents. He crossed New York state to take in the spectacle of Niagara Falls, journeyed south to the Carolinas, then crossed the mountains and came down the Ohio River. There he found the same Devonian and Silurian formations as in England and became particularly interested in the wealth of ancient marine mollusks preserved in the continent's sediments. He speculated that once this river valley had been a deep ocean filled with life, now extinct, while huge continents once stretched where both the Atlantic and Pacific oceans now lay.

What an astonishing past these Americans had to discover! Older than George Washington, older than the Indian civilizations commemorated in their burial mounds, that ancient world was a warning to the young, overconfident nation. "There is no other example in history, either in the old or new world," Lyell granted, "of so sudden a rise of a large country to opulence and power." Yet that success would be no more stable or permanent than the oceans that once lapped the shores of the interior, or the fossil shells that lay exposed at steamboat landings. On this trip Lyell spread his disturbing new theories of geological change among laymen as well as scientific leaders, unsettling them with his probing into the past.[30]

But the most severe shock to traditional Christian orthodoxy was yet to come—from Joseph Powell's former Shrewsbury townsman, Charles Darwin. While the Powells were arriving in Palmyra, Darwin was boarding the HMS *Beagle* as ship's naturalist. Returning home from Latin America and the South Pacific after nearly five years, he settled in the village of Down, not far from London, and began cogitating over his experiences, particularly the strange finches and tortoises of the islands named Galapagos. Twenty years of further reading and thinking led him finally to announce a revolutionary hypothesis. In July 1857 he put it in a letter to the Harvard botanist Asa Gray: "I *assume* that species arise like our domestic varieties with much extinction."[31] He did not believe, that is, that the flora and fauna of the earth, humans included, were the direct artifacts of God; they had evolved under the pressure of competition for resources. The next year he went public, presenting before the Linnaean Society, along with his codiscoverer Alfred Russel Wallace, a theory of evolution through natural selection. And the year after that event Darwin's *On the Origin of Species* appeared in print, arguably the most important book of the century. Religious leaders on both sides of the Atlantic immediately denounced it as promoting "atheism," but within a decade or two most scientists accepted the theory as true.

Step by step, natural science had been growing assertive about its ability to explain things. Wes Powell could not have been deaf to those claims or the tumult they raised. When in 1860—just months after Darwin's book was published—he announced that he had joined the ranks of naturalists, he had to know that he was, in some measure, defying not only his parents' wishes for his future but also their entire way of thinking. He risked being regarded as religiously unsound. Still, he had chosen his future, his mode of thinking, his deepest intellectual loyalties. From that point on Methodism, Christianity, or any other religion did not play an important role in defining his outlook on life.

On the death of Darwin in 1882, Wes delivered a memorial address that may help explain the abrupt shift in his youthful beliefs. "It remained for Darwin," he said, "to demonstrate the laws of biologic evolution, and the course of the progress of life upon the globe." Every generation in the long history of life, from the earliest era to the modern, shows "progress to a higher and fuller life; science has discovered *hope*." The new picture of the world that geology and evolutionary biology had drawn had appealed to a young man looking for a positive future, not in Heaven but in the here and now. "Darwin," he explained, "gave hope to philosophy."[32] Those words came more than two decades after his youthful announcement of a profession, but it was indeed in a spirit of hopefulness that he undertook to fit himself to a career.

The way to securing that bold label "Naturalist" was marked by much indecision and restlessness, and always by a lack of funds. Clearly, Wes had to finance his own intellectual gropings—Joseph was very firm about that. Had he grown up in an elite family of secular inclinations, Wes might have gone straight to Yale's newly established Sheffield Scientific School and joined there an affluent student body that included Clarence King and Samuel Franklin Emmons, both training for eminent careers in western geology. His teacher might have been James Dwight Dana, professor of natural history and author of the standard geological manuals and textbooks. Although Yale College itself was a notoriously conservative place where the classics and theology still dominated instruction, the quasi-separate Scientific School offered young men well-equipped laboratories to conduct sophisticated experiments with blowpipes and glass retorts. But Yale in any department was expensive at $200 a year. Wes, though he longed to go east to such a college, could not afford that sum, and his parents were not about to give it to him. He would have to find a less prestigious prairie education.

His first strategy was to leave home once again, this time bound for the midlands of Illinois where his sister Martha and her husband, John Davis, lived. They farmed in Long Creek township, just east of Decatur in Macon County. Wes, they promised, could find a teaching position there, paying $24 a month, nearly double what he had made in Wisconsin. In the fall of 1854 he went south to take the job. His brothers Bram and Walter and two of his sisters, Nell and Lida, followed the same trail south and into public-school teaching careers.

A mile along the section lines from the village center sat the Cherry Point schoolhouse, named for the wild cherry trees growing in the vicinity. The building was starkly plain and wooden, the furnishings primitive: log slabs for seats, pegs driven in for legs, desks made in similar fashion, all arrayed along the four walls.[33] Wes pulled out his notes and went to work. As in Wisconsin, he announced special evening lectures on geography. He drilled his audience on the states and their capitals with the aid of rhyming chants, then rounded off each evening with a group attack on the popular song, "Uncle Sam's Farm," filled with exuberant Yankee pride: "Come from every nation / Come from every way / Our lands are broad enough / Have no alarm / For Uncle Sam is rich enough to give us all a farm." Wes loved to sing; it was part of his Welsh heritage. He memorized many hymns, ditties, lullabies, poems, and parlor songs and sang them with a lusty voice. Whatever his students learned of geography, they rocked the rafters, with their teacher leading the chorus.

During that school year Wes decided to throw in with his brother-in-law on a commercial venture to improve his shaky financial situation. John Davis had been raising sheep and now wanted to expand into raising nursery trees for fruit orchards; another nurseryman, C.R. Overman of Fulton County, agreed to help them set up their own operation under the name "Davis & Powell." Wes had pointedly re-

signed from family farming, but now, under the promptings of an admired older relative and the pangs of necessity, he relented.

Martha Powell Davis had chosen well for a husband. John was her
match in intelligence and culture, and together they provided a core
for liberal, well-read, antislavery thinking in the community. John's
parents had immigrated from Kentucky to take up government land
still covered with native sod. They had created a profitable stock
farm, breeding horses, mules, cattle, and swine for sale, and raised
ten children, most of whom lived near them in Macon County. Like
the Powells, the Davises impressed on their children the importance
of an education. John, born in 1826 in a log cabin, left the farm at
age nineteen to attend a private academy in Springfield, while he
supported himself clerking in a drug store, then entered Illinois College in Jacksonville. His heart lay in agriculture, however, and he
came home to farm once more. Compared to the Powells, the
Davises were more rooted in place, and they were staunch agrarians
in their politics, none more so than John.[34]

John grew up as a farmer-philosopher, a scholar and writer, and a
lifelong promoter of the agricultural way of life. A local newspaper
published occasional articles he wrote, extolling rural culture and
seeking to improve the farmer's standing in society. One of those
pieces described for readers the strong community feeling among
the sheep growers of Long Creek township, where a "you-help-me-
and-I'll-help-you" ethos thrived, particularly during the June shear-
ing season. Whatever the size of his flock, each man came to the aid
of his neighbors to round up the sheep, wash their fleece, and clip
the wool from their backs. "Jokes fly as freely as in harvest time. Each
man marks the number of sheep he shears, and hence there is much
competition for the greatest number." [35] Like athletes competing in a
sport, they vied to see who could tally the most animals sheared, and
it was the market dealer among them who held the record of seventy-
five in a single day.

Another of his newspaper essays called on historians and biogra-
phers to write the life stories of farmers for a change. Farmers
needed to be inspired to stay in their calling, but the prevailing
canons of literature held up urban models of success that, in effect,
denigrated their work. Agriculture and the mechanical arts, John argued, "lie at the foundation of American prosperity"; therefore, it is
vital that men engaged in those occupations should be well read and
intelligent, and have a literature extolling their virtues. "Let us have
the lives of mechanics and farmers who have from small beginnings

succeeded to wealth and influence in their business, and through their own energy and industry."[36] The agrarianism represented in those two articles mixed, however inconsistently, a celebration of old-time rural communal values with the modernizing, individualistic ambitions of the self-made man. Some three or four decades later, after moving to Kansas, John was still pursuing that complicated agrarian ideal, but he abandoned his family's traditional affiliation with the Republicans to join the raucous new farmer's party of Populists.

If Wes wanted to experience another milieu than old-fashioned evangelical Methodism, he certainly found it among the Davises and their community, which extended into Decatur. He went into the shearers' barn, heard their salty jokes, and listened to his impassioned brother-in-law defend the agrarian life. Then there were dances at the county courthouse where the fiddler sat on the judge's bench tippling whiskey, a mildly scandalous scene for any strict-temperance Powell. Family rumor says that Wes met a lass in Decatur who won his affections, but no one remembers her name. It is clear that he was taken by this place in many ways. If he did not find a wife here, he did find a decent income, a big family who enjoyed themselves with parties and festivities, and stimulating conversation about the public issues of the day. What he did not find in this place, however, was a college to attend or the science courses he was beginning to crave. Hence the proposed venture with John to earn enough money to get to those things he wanted.

Wes had no capital to invest in the business, so he tried borrowing to come up with his share. When father Joseph heard the news, he exploded with anger. In a letter he insisted that Wes get out of the venture immediately, no matter how promising it was financially, because he was using other people's money. "The borrowing of money to make money," he wrote, "is not one whit better than highway robbery." Joseph had always paid cash in his land transactions; he was debt aversive to a high degree. Now he was bitter that his son had put at risk another man's capital, having little collateral or sufficient means to repay the debt if the business failed. Such behavior was immoral. Mary added a note of her own, backing up Joseph in gentler tones and warning that the venture might well divert Wes from ever going to college rather than get him there sooner. Reluctantly, their son withdrew from the partnership. Somehow he found means to pay off his loans, though he was left poorer than ever.[37]

Securing a college education was turning into a desperate obsession, now coming closer, nearly within his grasp, now receding into impossibility. His parents offered to pay his expenses to attend either the Illinois Institute in Wheaton or Oberlin College in Ohio, but he was not interested in either of them. He wanted science, not piety. John Davis fortuitously intervened again to suggest that Wes consider his own alma mater, Illinois College, where his younger brother Henry was heading. They could go as classmates and room together. Wes jumped at the suggestion, but painfully aware of his limited preparation (that one term in Janesville, those days up in the garret), he knew he must whip himself into shape before he could pass the admissions tests.

He went monkish. In Decatur he found a vacant shoemaker's shop and moved in as an anchorite going to his cell. For five weeks he lived there, subsisting on almost nothing except books. He had no cook stove, so his food must be bread, cheese, and milk, with occasional gifts of smoked sausage or boiled eggs from sister Martha. The air of his lodging reeked of old leather and grease. Ignoring it, he kept on reading. Fortunately, a learned man in the town, John Coleman, who ran a preparatory academy in the Methodist church basement, loaned him texts in Latin, Greek, mathematics, and science and gave him a little free advice on where to concentrate his frenzied energies. Somehow he worked up confidence; the fall saw him packing off with Henry to Jacksonville, hoping Illinois College would open its doors.

Another of John Davis's letters to the *Dewitt Courier,* dated April 1855, describes Jacksonville, which was then the premier college town in the state, as "the Athens of Illinois." It was an Athens whose largest educational institutions were an "asylum for the deaf and dumb" and another one for the insane. In his letter Davis described taking the train to the state capital of Springfield and transferring to the Jacksonville line which ran thirty-five miles west. At the end of the line he stepped down into a pleasant town of over three thousand people, with large, elegant houses and wide streets. Jacksonville boasted, in addition to all those schools, a county courthouse majestically sited in a town square. Illinois College lay on the western outskirts. Davis found the main building of his alma mater burned to the ground, but a red-brick gothic structure was rising from the ashes.[38]

The new building, bearing a striking resemblance to the Smithsonian's "Castle" on the Washington Mall, was named after the college's current president, the Reverend Julian Sturtevant, A.M., D.D., LL.D. The first president had been Lyman Beecher's son Edward, friend to the murdered abolitionist Elijah Lovejoy. The school had gained a radical reputation almost from the year of its founding,

1829, but Sturtevant had moderated its image considerably. The first faculty had come from Yale to transform the western frontier into a Christian civilization. Self-styled as the "Yale Band," they were bright young scholars rigorously trained in the classical curriculum. But in 1852, still following Yale's example, the college established a Scientific Department with a three-year curriculum, divided into freshman, junior, and senior years. Conspicuously missing from the premises by that point was former professor Jonathan Baldwin Turner, retired but still a resident in the town, one of the most remarkable men in Illinois history.[39]

John Davis should introduce his old professor, for he owed to him much of his thinking about the needs of an agrarian-based society. Two decades earlier, when Turner had been a young faculty recruit from Yale, he made "the discovery that Illinois would be the very first state in the Union, were it only fenced, and its industrial classes properly educated." Since wood is a scarce commodity on the prairie, Turner (as Davis explained) looked for alternatives to the split-rail fence and located an answer in the Osage orange tree, *Maclura pomifera*, a member of the breadfruit family, native to Texas and Arkansas. A natural hedge plant, it grew thick-set and loaded with thorns when cut repeatedly. Turner learned of this trait and promoted the tree for fencing.

Having "acted the part of a benefactor to the prairie farmers of Illinois," Davis went on, and having had the satisfaction of seeing hundreds of miles of Osage orange planted across the countryside, Turner then worked on his second brainstorm: getting the state to establish an "industrial" university where farmers and other practical-minded students could get a decidedly useful, nonclassical education. As a student, John Davis had been struck by this latter vision in particular, and he devoted much of his own energies to promoting it. So did other educational reformers, including Representative Justin Morrill of Vermont, who persuaded Congress in 1862 to establish the land-grant college system, a realization of Turner's dream. Despite these significant successes, Turner had been forced out of teaching at Illinois College for holding too radical views about religion and politics. He may have been the farmer's benefactor but he was "unreliable" in moderate Presbyterian eyes. Davis sought him out on his return visit and "spent every leisure moment in his company"; and he gave Wes a letter of introduction to the now self-employed gentleman, who had welcomed Davis to Jacksonville, walked him over his experimental farm, and talked enthusiastically of natural history.[40]

Such was the small-college environment that Wes had decided, on his brother-in-law's advice, must be the door to a career in science. With Henry Davis, he arrived in early October 1855 to begin classes. To enter the Scientific Department, he must first pass entrance examinations in English grammar, geography (a snap), arithmetic, and *Smyth's Elementary Algebra*. He passed. The curriculum for first-year science students included algebra, geometry, trigonometry, navigation, surveying, and elocution, a program that had to be a little disappointing to Wes; not until his senior year did he study natural history, and then it would be Paley's "natural theology" version.[41] On the positive side, by taking the science track he could avoid the normal heavy dose of theology, though President Sturtevant was making noises about adding the subject to the science program in the next year or so. Whatever his track or year, every college man must go daily to chapel and attend church on Sunday. So Wes was a college man at last and, with whatever misgivings, he fell to with relish. Right away he joined the literary Sigma Pi Society and, in November, found himself debating a burning topic of the day, "Is phrenology entitled to the rank of a true science?"[42]

Wes and Henry took rooms at Grove House with several other freshmen. A typical room's furnishings consisted of a plain table, two or three chairs, a pail, wash bowl, pitcher, andirons, shovel and tongs, bedstead and bedding. They had to board at a private residence for $2 a week; their stove wood, lights, and washing was all extra expense. Altogether, with tuition costing $30 a year, the experience was going to require $130 for each of the next three years, or about what Wes had been making as a schoolteacher annually. The school allowed students of limited means to sign a note for most or all of that amount in exchange for labor as needed, and John Davis obligingly signed a note for Wes. Although Wes did well academically in his first-term courses, with grades of 90 to 100, his financial resources soon ran low.[43]

By winter he was forced to drop out and take a teaching position in the town of Clinton, Dewitt County. The previous year the state of Illinois had passed a law requiring all counties to tax themselves to provide free public schools, opening up jobs and improving salaries dramatically; his salary was a munificent $60 a month. He saved his earnings carefully, and the next fall he was back at Illinois College, this time to study Latin and Greek along with chemistry.

Whether he actually finished the second year is hard to determine. What is clear is that he did not make it through the full three-year course. Money was undoubtedly the main reason, though the lack of sufficient natural history in the science department may have discouraged him too. More than once he had left his parents' house in a quest for independence, and more than once he had been frustrated. The way he wanted to go seemed clear enough, but when he put his foot on the path it turned treacherous. By the fall of 1857 he was dwelling under the parental roof in Wheaton once more and trying to get interested in the college across the street.

Had Wes remained a resident of Wisconsin, he could have gone up to Madison to enroll in a decently equipped, publicly funded university. Delay a few years, and he might even have been a classmate of John Muir, who enrolled in 1861 as a freshman in the chemistry and geology classes taught by Dr. Ezra Slocum Carr. Together, the two undergraduates might have rambled along the shores of Lake Mendota and talked snakes and rocks. Wes, however, did not consider Wisconsin, and Illinois offered him no good opportunity for a tax-supported university education.

It is true that, in October 1857, a new Illinois State Normal University set up temporary quarters in Bloomington with seven teachers and nineteen students. Money had been accumulating in a special fund from public land sales to support higher education. Although the denominational schools wanted it for themselves, Jonathan Turner had successfully promoted his dream of a public institution for training teachers, farmers, and mechanics in "useful knowledge," and the money went to establish a "normal" university. The new school was mainly for training teachers, whose credentials were often miserable; as one agricultural paper put it, "we believe that at least four-fifths of the teachers in the common schools of Illinois would not pass an examination in the rudiments of our English education, and most of them have taken to teaching because they hadn't anything in particular to do."[44] Mainly, the students who came to the State Normal University were from farm homes, and they wanted to be better prepared for the teaching posts opening up. Wes, however, was farther along than any of them, with teaching experience in two states and two years of college credit behind him. He needed a more rigorous challenge.

So it was either study with the Presbyterians in Jacksonville or with the Methodists in Wheaton. He had tried one of those options on his own coin and mettle, he was now ready to cave in, accept family support, and try the second. He was not the first Powell to enroll at the Illinois Institute. His younger siblings Nellie, Walter, Lida, and Juliet had all attended one level or the other during the previous year, along with cousins Morris, Ada, and Clement from uncle Walter's brood. Bram came back from Macon County to join them, so that Powells were soon as thick as termites on a log.

The Illinois Institute's school year, unlike Jacksonville's, was split into three terms. Science was represented in the offerings — at least pneumatics, optics, and electricity, though no botany or zoology. Wes enrolled as a sophomore, the most advanced class in the still organizing school. Whatever courses he took, extracurricular excitements of a very earnest nature soon overshadowed them. On 19 November he was "unanimously received" as a member of the college's Beltionian Literary Society.[45] Ellen and Lida were already active members. The society's program was to stage evening debates once a week on current topics, punctuated by singing from the choir, and to publish student literary efforts in a review. Wes's first debate was on the topic, "Have men of thought been of more benefit to the world than men of action?" His opponent, who took the negative side of the question, was a sophomore woman, and Wes won the audience vote. He followed that victory with another, taking the negative on the question, "Did William Penn deserve the laudation he had received?" then presented a talk on "The Defense of the Classical Greek and Latin." By January he was a member of the society's steering committee and busy proposing constitutional amendments and procuring a library. But by spring, after only two terms in attendance, Wes abruptly decided this was indeed the wrong place for him. Asking for a partial return of his society dues, he left the school.

Where he went, at long last and after much resistance, was Oberlin College, with a ticket paid for by father Joseph. In the popular mind the little school near Cleveland, Ohio, was still a breeding ground for self-righteous fanatics, radicals, and extremists. It was also a place where blacks felt uncommonly welcome; over four hundred of them had settled in the town, comprising one-fifth of the population, mostly living impoverished in the "Little Africa" part of town. Oberlin, in the words of the humorist Petroleum V. Nasby, was the school where "Ablishnism runs rampant—wher a nigger is 100 per cent. better nor a white man — wher a mullato is a objik uv pity on account uv hevin white blood!" Oberlin, he added, was the little school that started the Civil War.[46]

The Reverend Powell had admired Oberlin College's combination of antislavery views, puritanism, spirituality, and serious-minded learning ever since he had first met its students and faculty in Jackson. It was, in his mind, the place to go if one wanted to become a minister, and especially to become the right kind of minister. Wes did not object to the school's politics, but he still had little desire for the ministry. All the same, here he was. By 1858 there were more than one thousand two hundred students enrolled, most of them in the preparatory department. When he arrived that spring, many of the 180 college students (most of them males, though this was a coeducational institution) were returning from the traditional long winter vacation, having preached, taught, or agitated for reform somewhere in America, though many were poor and had to earn cash instead. Wes took a room in a house on South Professor Street, and then he enrolled in the nonelective freshman course of study.[47]

Even more so than in Wheaton, the curriculum here was almost wholly given over to the study of ancient classics. There was no scientific department and little science. Upperclassmen did take a smattering of botany, chemistry, and astronomy, and they read Edward Hitchcock's pious textbook on geology. But freshmen like Wes were expected to get their grounding in classical language and literature first. The registrar's records show that Wes took the required course on Livy, the Roman historian, and another on Homer's *Odyssey*; no record of his grades survives. Come summer term, he was still doing Livy and Homer, along with Latin prose composition, the *Acts of the Apostles*, with something called "Cryopaidia" thrown in. Classes began every morning at eight o'clock and went to noon, six days a week. The rules said he also must go to church twice on the Sabbath and attend a religious lecture at midweek, as well as be present for daily prayers every evening in the chapel and every morning in his lodgings. He did not survive the regimen. A few months of Oberlin and he was a dropout once again.[48]

In that short span of perhaps five months his main pleasure appears to have been botanizing in the woods and conversing with fellow student Carlos Kenaston in Kenaston's house. Together, they read Philip Bailey's book poem, *Festus*. Bailey, an English barrister, had produced a transatlantic sensation with this vapid imitation of Goethe's *Faust*. The main character in it, Festus, rolls out tediously long dialogues with Lucifer and flies over the earth with him to examine the state of humanity. They pass over America, "half-brother of the world! With something good and bad of every land." The poem's indifference to traditional religious dogma may have been the reason it was denounced as "irreverent," though its worst sin was to throb with hope for "a time when the world shall be / Much better visibly, and when, as far / As social life and its relations tend, / Men, morals, manners shall be lifted up / To a pure height we know not of nor dream."[49]

After their daily session with this unassigned, unapproved, and slightly risqué reading, Wes and Carlos liked to wander down the street to collect apples from a large orchard. Those were the main pleasures, but they were not enough. As Kenaston later recalled, one day "Powell disappeared, and only long afterward did I learn that the fatal sickness of his father occasion[ed] the change of plans which took him from this College."[50] In truth, Joseph had no fatal illness; he lived for more than another decade. The fact was that Wes had abruptly concluded what he had known all along: Oberlin was not the institution for him. Oberlin may have been the educated evangelical's lodestone, but something else — natural science — was pulling on his imagination and pulling him away.

Give the Illinois Institute one more try, his parents urged. In the fall he enrolled there again — late this time, paying his fees in mid-October for only three quarters of a term — and resumed studies with sister Nellie and all the kinfolk. But this too would not do. When the term was over, he dropped out again, and this time he dropped out of college altogether.

In three institutions he had accumulated about three years' worth of courses, though never making it beyond sophomore standing. He had hoped to earn enough money to go East for a final year or so and to finish his degree, but it was not to be. That patchwork of campuses and courses he had been through must be sufficient formal education for whatever career lay ahead. That, and whatever he had been picking up for himself on the margins.

During these years of searching for an education and wrestling with his parents, Wes discovered rivers. They flowed through the landscape of his mind like songs of freedom and escape. They sang of catfish, beaver, blue herons, grape vines festooning the trees, the smell of mud. He had known rivers since a boy — the Genesee, the Salt Lick and Scioto, the Rock of Illinois. Now he began to turn back to rivers to find what no college offered, an education out of doors where on his own he could learn to read the book of nature.

The summer before heading to Jacksonville's college, and right after being cooped up in that dreadful Decatur cobbler's shop, he struck out on a bold exploration in the spirit of Lewis and Clark. Purchasing a flat-bottomed skiff at a Mississippi River town, he set off upstream for St. Paul, Minnesota. A skiff will take a sail, so he may have had more than oars to work against the current. The river town of Hannibal, Missouri, lies directly west of Decatur and it is possible that he started there, in the native village of Mark Twain, another lover of rivers and his contemporary (they were born one year apart). Or Wes may have launched from Burlington or Rock Island or Dubuque. Whatever his port of debarkation, he toiled along day after day, dodging floating trees and steamboats, observing the water cutting its soft banks, camping at night on a sandy island beside a roaring fire.

He was, to borrow from Twain's experience, "a traveler! A word never had tasted so good in my mouth before. I had an exultant sense of being bound for mysterious lands and distant climes which I never have felt in so uplifting a degree since. I was in such a glorified condition that all ignoble feelings departed out of me, and I was able to look down and pity the untraveled with a compassion that had hardly a trace of contempt in it."[51]

Twain, who trained to be a steamboat pilot on the Mississippi, discovered an education that no university could have given him. The river was his Harvard and Yale College. With growing experience as a cub, he wrote, the face of the water

> became a wonderful book—a book that was a dead language to
> the uneducated passenger, but which told its mind to me without
> reserve, delivering its most cherished secrets as clearly as if it
> uttered them with a voice. And it was not a book to be read once
> and thrown aside, for it had a new story to tell every day.
> Throughout the long twelve hundred miles there was never a page
> that was void of interest, never one that you could leave unread
> without loss, never one that you would want to skip, thinking you
> could find higher enjoyment in some other things. There never
> was so wonderful a book written by man; never one whose interest
> was so absorbing, so unflagging, so sparklingly renewed with every
> perusal.

But the more Twain learned, the less poetry and romance the river held for him. He came to see the river as a pilot must—a series of dangers and warnings, a transportation utility devoid of all beauty.[52]

Wes, however, was not out on rivers for any economic purpose, and he never lost his fascination with their beauty and mystery. He came seeking adventure, and he came in the name of research. His design was to collect shells of mollusks, both the modern freshwater species and any ancient saltwater fossils he could find. Scientists were intensely interested in the *Mollusca*, which were good indicators of past geological eras; the minute variations in their huge phylum stimulated thoughts about the origins of species. Wes was only a collector, but his choice of species to collect suggests that he understood something of their importance in contemporary science. When he got to St. Paul, he sold his skiff and tramped across Wisconsin and upper Michigan to the Straits of Mackinac separating Lake Michigan from Lake Huron. All his collections he sent home to Wheaton, which served as his museum for a time.

Most of the details of that first river and land journey and the ones to come have vanished, but it is not difficult to see how such trips began to form a counterpoint to his existence as a college student and teacher. The next summer, following his employment in the Clinton school and before he went back to studying at Illinois College, he felt the pull of the Mississippi once more. This time he started at the Falls of St. Anthony (St. Paul) and floated downstream all the way to New Orleans — the entire navigable length of the river. No surviving journal tells what he ate or how much money he carried or what dangers he met from ruffians, cutthroats, slave traders, the whole miscellany of confidence men and shysters who throng the books of Mark Twain and Herman Melville. Wes was a small, slight man of twenty-two traveling alone on America's greatest highway at a tumultuous, seething time when sectional hostilities were mounting, few policemen existed, and nature was a constant threat. Despite several months of this life, he came home safely to Illinois, his imagination working hard to assimilate what he had seen.[53]

Back to the classrooms of formal education he went, but he grew restless as the seasons turned. In late spring 1857, after his second year at Illinois College, Wes took a train to Pittsburgh, where the Monongahela and Allegheny rivers flow together to form the Ohio, and prepared to descend to the Mississippi. In a letter to his mother, dated 14 May, he described the growing industrial metropolis from his room on the city's Mount Washington. He could see the confluence of the rivers, the barges and steamboats putting out from the docks, the chimneys belching out coal smoke, the twinkling lamps of a great metropolis below.[54] Leaving that vista of urban growth behind, he floated down the Ohio where Lyell had geologized, down to the Wabash and up the Wabash, trekking across to the Great Lakes and Michigan.

The immense landscape that Wes was learning slowly and intimately, mile by mile, from a seat in a small wooden boat or afoot overland, was the great interior basin of the country. *Harper's Magazine* called it "the body of the nation. . . . It would contain Austria four times, Germany or Spain five times, France six times, the British Isles or Italy ten times. . . . As a dwelling-place for civilized man it is by far the first upon our globe."[55] Americans saw it as a heartland of incomparable promise for agriculture, industry, and cities, and so it was becoming in these very years. Although railroads were quickly revolutionizing transportation, the rivers were still vital to the nation's development. They provided for Wes an education in economy, business, politics, the flow of population, and the diversity of cultures that made up the nation.

They instructed him as well about the geological history that had made the North American continent what it was. The Mississippi and its tributaries had begun as drainage channels for the glaciers that had once covered the land, and they had continued over thousands of years to carry away the melting winter snows, now and then slopping over their banks and flooding the flat surrounding plains. As they eroded the face of the earth, they exposed bones and shells, and those remnants of lost epochs and geological periods helped the naturalist piece together the history of the continent. Wes carefully labeled his shells and put them away in bags, but the lessons that he learned from his summer voyages were harder to identify or store. They formed fundaments of his thinking for the rest of his life, more important to him than reading Livy or the Greeks.

His fourth summer excursion occurred also in 1857, when he hiked from St. Louis south to Iron Mountain, an important mining area in Missouri. Now he was after minerals, and in his enthusiasm for picking them up he nearly ran out of money and had to pawn a watch to get back to Decatur and Wheaton. No wonder after such experiences that the Institute, and later the next spring Oberlin, seemed so boring. Sitting in classes with younger students, few if any of them experienced as he was in the arts of collecting, navigating, or exploring, not to mention the arts of self-reliance, forced to recite each morning the daily lesson, he grew restless fast. His heart and mind were both outside the window, where he could imagine the sound of a river flowing.

While Wes was toiling through those first terms at the Institute, taking on fellow Beltionians in debate, the state teachers' association met in Decatur and heard a proposal from Professor Cyrus Thomas, a botanist at the new State Normal University, to organize a Natural History Society of Illinois. The proposal stirred up some interest, and in June 1858 the new society came into being in Bloomington, home of the university, with Jonathan Turner chosen as its first president. Their aim was "to conduct a thorough scientific survey of Illinois, in order to afford new sources of knowledge to our citizens." They planned to collect specimens of every species of plant, bird, shell, fish, insect, and quadruped, along with fossils and minerals, and display them in a museum at the university. Thomas was an expert on plants and animals along the Ohio and Mississippi rivers. Another member, George Vasey, also a botanist, had a wide reputation as an authority on prairie grasses. They solicited assistance from the state geologist and the railroad engineers. And that same summer they added the membership, dynamic energy, field experience, and accumulated collections of one Wes Powell, hitherto unknown to science.[56] He had by now amassed a herbarium of several thousand plants, a large collection of shells, and a cabinet of reptiles, all stored somewhere in the Wheaton family residence, and he became one of the most active supporters of the Natural History Society.

Later in life Wes recalled for his first biographer, Martha De Lincoln, how the collecting he had done as a young man had given him a heroic reputation among the citizens of Wheaton. One day, as he passed a group of men, carrying a basket of glass fruit jars for his specimens, they asked where he was going. He told them he was headed out to the woods to get another rattlesnake for his collection. When he came through town that evening, they saw that he had a live snake in one of the jars. His prowess in the woods made a big impression. Soon rumor had it that he knew all the habits of the local fauna and could find any animal at any time he wished. Even the county paper told the story, which grew and grew until the whole upper floor of the Powell house was supposed to be a fabulous museum, filled with many crawling and pickled reptiles.[57] The truth was that he was mainly a mollusk man, he had trouble identifying many of the species he had collected—often labeling them according to the places where they were found rather than by their proper Latin names—and the elder Powells were not about to let their home be taken over by live serpents.

A young man like Wes, who liked to spend his summers rowing on a river and studying natural history, who had no financial means to go East to a more appealing college, seemed to have one choice left to him—teaching in the common schools. He had an impressive résumé for any school board and was highly marketable. In January 1859 Wes took a position in Hennepin, county of Putnam, midway

*Wes Powell as school principal and teacher
in Hennepin, Illinois, late 1850s.*
(Courtesy: Utah State Historical Society)

between Chicago and the Mississippi. There were two schools in town; he taught in the building with the higher-level classes, a solid two-story structure of classical proportions topped by a small belfry. For nearly two years he continued there, working his way up to principal at $100 a month. Of course, without question or hesitation, he introduced natural science into the curriculum.

The position suited him in many ways, and a portrait made at the time of employment, the first image we have of him, shows a prosperous-looking, self-confident professional. It is a ferrotype and it shows Wes with a long trimmed beard, no mustache, large, wide-apart eyes, a bulbous nose, a thick upswept pompadour. He wears a black velvet bow tie and coat, a starched white shirt, and a bright multicolored waistcoat — the dapper son of a tailor. When the school year was over, he changed into rougher garb and continued those summer expeditions for science.[58]

Hennepin sits high on the east bank of the Illinois River, an imposing tributary of the Mississippi. When Wes arrived, it counted seven hundred residents, including one hundred students. This neat little village of checkerboard streets was the county seat and a shipping point for agricultural produce. It had one flour mill and one distillery, which tells where some of the grain went. A colony of Pennsylvania Germans had settled here and planted extensive apple orchards for cider and pies, while a large population of Quakers made the town a strong abolitionist center.

Mainly, for Wes's enthusiasms, there was the river—broad, deep, and organic. If Wes wanted to be close to the water world of the Midwest, he could not have chosen a better position. During the winter and spring he spent his weekends examining the local soils for evidence of their glacial history. The school year was only eight months long, and when his first summer vacation rolled around, he took a boat down to the Mississippi, and then up the Des Moines River of Iowa as far as the mouth of the Raccoon, collecting all the way.

Through the Natural History Society he was now connected to other naturalists, professional and amateur, and science teachers of all levels, across the entire state. He aspired to greater recognition. When the State Agricultural Society met in Jacksonville in September 1860, he was there to show off his mollusks in the competition for "best collection illustrating the zoology of Illinois." The judges awarded him second prize of $25, behind a collection of stuffed birds. Thus, the small-town teacher was beginning to draw statewide attention as a naturalist and as a science educator. That same year he became a member of the society's committee on conchology and later its secretary. He was no longer in a state of agonizing uncertainty. He was now, as he told the census taker, a "Naturalist."

And at age twenty-six he was still a bachelor. None of the female college students he had met seemed to be very appealing, or perhaps it was the other way around; he was no college romeo even in the terms of strictly circumscribed, Protestant-college rectitude. The one woman who had caught his eye and held it was his half cousin Emma Dean, and she was no college student. She lived in Detroit, Michigan, with her parents, Joseph Dean and his wife Harriet—the Joseph Dean who was Wes's mother's brother, the one who had missed the sailing of the ship to America back in 1830. Now he suddenly showed up living in the United States, with a family of four children, Emma, Mary, Henrietta, and Charles, and a prosperous career in making and selling hats.

Sometime in 1855, when Wes was dwelling in Decatur or Jacksonville, a letter came to Mary from this long-forgotten brother, the son of her father and stepmother who had followed her to the New World some time later but knew no way to get in touch nor did he know where she had gone. Settling in New York City, he had pursued his craft as a hatmaker for several years. Daughter Emma was born in New York in 1835, a year and a half after Wes was born in Mount Morris. When she was fourteen the Deans migrated to Detroit, and a city directory for 1855 lists him as a "hatter" now living on that city's Michigan Avenue. Ten years later another directory has the family living in another house on the same middle-class residential street, and Joseph was now working as a clerk for Frederick Buhl's company, which specialized in the manufacture and wholesale and retail sales of an assortment of hats—silk, fur, wool, panama, leghorn, palm leaf, and straw. Buhl, one of the leading merchants in the city, had developed his hat business out of the old beaver fur trade and now bought and sold buffalo and deerskin robes for winter sleighing as well. Joseph got on well with the company, until by and by they made him a partner. After retirement he continued coming in to work; "the old business habit," his obituary reads, "was strong in him still."[59]

Joseph Dean's letter coming from out of the blue set the Powell household abuzz. Mary quickly took a train to Detroit to see this family connection that she had never realized was living in the Midwest. Then Wes, on the first of his long summer excursions, the one that took him across Wisconsin to Mackinac, went down to Detroit to meet the Deans for himself. The young woman of twenty years he met in the household was petite, almost a child in size, but she was no tender violet. She had a large-eyed, anxious gaze, a wide mouth with a slight smile, and thick brown hair bunched and curling around her temples. Wes would be back.

Over the next several years while he was trying to get an education, he found several excuses to go to Detroit. He said he needed mollusks from Lake St. Clair, which is near Detroit. Oberlin was only a boat trip across Lake Erie from that city, and part of his reason for enrolling there may have been a hope that he would see Emma more often. All in all, he managed several visits, and he and Emma carried on a correspondence, enough at least to make the Reverend Powell and his wife increasingly nervous: Would he marry his own cousin, even if she was only a half cousin? Wes did not heed their anxieties, however; soon he and Emma were engaged to be married.

Then the great catastrophe came that everybody had been dreading for decades: the nation abruptly broke apart over slavery. Everything that Wes had been doing for profit and pleasure came to a stop. Natural history had to be thrown into a storage chest. The books of science, with all their new theories and speculations about rocks, mollusks, speciation, evolution, deep time, their tense debates over

Emma Dean Powell.
(Courtesy: National Archives)

causality, their challenge to religious authority, had to be shut up. Even affairs of the heart had to be interrupted. During the spring of 1860 Wes arranged with a Janesville, Wisconsin, lyceum bureau to do a speaking tour through the backwoods of Kentucky, Tennessee, and Mississippi on geography and geology. While there, he felt a palpable tension in the air, a growing defensiveness toward any and all Yankee criticism. He heard Southerners defend slavery as a moral, godly institution—absolutely necessary for the advancement of civilization—and promise to seek its extension across the continent. Sensing that hardening of opinion and aware of what his own people in the North were feeling, he came home worried. In a letter to his father he concluded that only war could decide the slavery issue, and in that decision determine whether the Union could survive intact or not. The next few years proved him tragically right.

CHAPTER 3

The Hornets' Nest of War

Wes Powell was an eager warrior, ready to do battle for a righteous cause, and to his mind the cause of the Union was decisively righteous. Five days after President Abraham Lincoln called for volunteers to put down a rebellious South, the young school principal of Hennepin was at the head of a group of locals who went charging off to serve. They took a train to Granville where they enlisted, then went on to Joliet, a center for organizing volunteers into military units. Passing their medical examinations, they were mustered into Company H of the Twentieth Illinois Infantry Regiment of the United States Army. The men elected Wes to be their sergeant-major, but by mid-June the army had elevated him to a second lieutenant. Those college years were good for something after all. So were the days of teaching students often older and larger than he. And so were those months of exploring rivers, rowing a boat, developing survival skills, and gaining confidence in his ability to handle whatever came his way.

Wes may not have looked especially like a commander of men. Army records describe him at enlistment as twenty-seven years old, five feet six inches tall, of light complexion, with gray eyes and auburn (or sandy in one military record) hair. He was on the short and slight side, though exceptionally hardy. But in his mind, and apparently in the minds of other men, including the army, he showed promise of leading a company effectively into combat, though he had not an ounce of military experience.

All over the nation passions were running high that spring of 1861. Lincoln's election to the presidency had been the match lighting a fuse long in the laying. He was, in the eyes of many Southerners, a

"Black Republican" who would free the slaves, give them full citizenship with whites, and set loose an unholy terror of rapine, violence, and brutality. In fact, Lincoln had run on a platform of leaving slavery alone where it existed—condemning it as a moral outrage but not interfering with it except in the western territories where it could legally be prevented from spreading. He was no radical abolitionist, yet not a single southern state voted for him. Although the North gave him a landslide endorsement, he won office with only 40 percent of the nation's ballots.

The election split the rival sections like an ax cleaving a hickory log. Within weeks South Carolina voted to secede from the Union, and by 1 February, a month before Lincoln's inauguration, six more states had followed suit. The cotton-and-slave kingdom was frothing with anger over their threatened right to be different. Their freedom was in danger, they protested; their culture was despised; the blacks were to be set up as their masters. Lincoln and majority opinion in the North, on the other hand, was adamant that the South, which for so long had embarrassed the moral purity of the nation with its practice of slavery, was not going to destroy that nation now by secession. The split widened almost daily. In mid-April the commanding officer at Fort Sumter in South Carolina was forced to surrender to the newly proclaimed Confederate States of America, and Lincoln thereupon declared that an armed insurrection had commenced that must be answered by force.[1]

Wes Powell was one of tens of thousands who responded immediately to the President's call for volunteers. He signed up for a long spell—one that would stretch to nearly four years in all, lasting well beyond that first flush of furious excitement, years that would leave a tragic mark on his person. For the remainder of his life he would be reminded each and every day that he was a man who had heeded Lincoln's call and risked everything for the Union. That is not to say he was on his way to fame. His role in the conflict would be minor, his place in warrior annals marginal and often obscure. He left no letters or diary to help later generations understand what the war meant to him. In that way, though, he was representative of the vast multitude of men who fought in the Civil War, most of whom left no indication of why they fought or what it was like. Yet their lives, like his, were altered considerably by the experience of war.

While in Joliet waiting for orders, Wes asked leave to go into Chicago, ostensibly to purchase an officer's uniform but actually to buy a couple of books on military engineering and to travel to Detroit to see Emma. Always the autodidact, he wanted to read up on the role he was already envisioning for himself as an engineer designing and building defensive fortifications. He was not eager for hand-to-hand combat. What he hoped to learn by cramming with all of his practiced intensity was how to create the infrastructure on which armies must depend: forts, bridges, revetments, gabions, gun emplacements. The army seemed to sense his passion. Right away they sent him to a post where he could put text into practice.

On 6 July the Twentieth Illinois shipped over to Alton, then down to St. Louis, and on to the riverfront town of Cape Girardeau in southeastern Missouri, a strategic point for Mississippi River traffic. Dating back to the time of French empire in North America, Cape Girardeau sat on a high bluff overlooking the highway of brown, rolling water below. Whatever came up from the South had to pass under its scrutiny. Wes's regiment, along with three others, set up their tents among the nervous townsfolk and continued drilling with arms. No one was quite sure where or how they would be used in the insurrection, or when they would be ready to fight. Wes, meanwhile, perceived that this was an important site to protect, and he began mapping the terrain and drawing up a fortification plan just as West Point's engineering instructor Dennis Hart Mahan or France's Sebastien Vauban said it should be done.

The bright pupil drew attention and approval from the regular army men who had been put in command over these green troops. Wes's colonel encouraged him to keep doodling. Then in August no less a personage than Brigadier General John C. Frémont came into camp on an inspection tour, along with a large foreign advisory corps. Frémont was, as ever, vain, self-seeking, and given to the grand gesture, but for Powell he was also the awe-inspiring explorer of the West and former presidential candidate, now seated directly before him. The army had put Frémont in charge of the troops that were supposed to keep Missouri, a slave state, within the Union. With little credit to his generalship, the state was in fact lining up on the right side, though guerrilla attacks would burst out repeatedly for the duration of the war.

Frémont demanded that the troops put up grandiose fortifications immediately, and Wes's colonel stepped forward to say that one of his junior officers had already drawn up plans. They included four separate forts arranged in a great square surrounding the town, each triangular in shape, each supplied with cannon, two of them to be sited on the edge of the bluffs to control the river, two more on the interior corners to guard against hostile approaches from the rear. Wes presented his ideas to the general. Frémont approved but put one of his Prussian officers in charge of carrying them out, though because the man had little English, Wes remained in effect the consulting engineer. Later, Frémont sent down from St. Louis a Captain Fladd, who spoke the local tongue and had considerable engineering experience, to oversee construction, and Wes was happy to train under a true professional.

The summer passed, and the troops waited impatiently for a new set of orders. They were learning what it meant to be away from home for an extended time. They played cards, drank whiskey, visited prostitutes, used cannon balls for bowling nine pins, drilled repeatedly, arose at dawn to a bugle playing reveille, went to sleep with taps, ate hardtack and beans, fell homesick and wrote letters, sang sentimental songs, started fights, cursed the regular army and its officers, picked lice out of their hair. Some of them dug quarters into the soft bluffs, becoming, as one of them later said, "temporary troglodytes."[2] This war, if it ever got started, would be fought by a people's army composed mainly of amateurs and volunteers. Typically, they enlisted with great expectations; war was an opportunity for adventure and romance. In a popular phrase of the time, they were eager to "see the elephant"— that is, to experience some hugely dangerous excitement. But they were also filled with indignation toward their fellow countrymen in the South who were endangering much that these citizens cherished. It was their "duty," the Union soldiers heard repeatedly, to defend the ideals, indeed the very idea, of America.

On 1 September a new commanding general dressed in loose-fitting civilian clothes came to their encampment. He was Ulysses S. Grant, newly made a brigadier general and soon to take over the position of Frémont, who was proving ineffectual. Grant was a regular army man, a graduate of West Point and a veteran of the Mexican War, though a few months earlier he had been clerking in a leather shop in Galena, Illinois.[3] He had enlisted in the Twenty-first Illinois regiment and, like Wes, been sent to Missouri. Now Grant was elevated to general and was on his way to Cairo, sitting at the junction of the Ohio and Mississippi rivers, which would become his launching point for invading the South. He was of an offensive, not defensive, mind, intent on exerting force deep into enemy territory with no delay. Quickly, he began moving regiments south to Cairo, preparing them for a more aggressive thrust.

Grant reviewed Wes's plans and was not enthusiastic about building such elaborate military fortifications around a town that far north. He had a different assignment for this younger man. Instead of sending him to the front with his regiment, Grant decided he needed Wes to man the six twenty-four-pounder guns to be mounted in one of the corner forts. On 9 October he wrote the St. Louis command center that he had authorized "Captain Powell an efficient officer of the Twentieth Illinois volunteers who has been acting as engineer, to raise a company to manage the Siege Guns."[4] Suddenly, Wes was promoted to captain in charge of artillery, a rank he would hold for the next three years, though the downside was that temporarily he was stuck minding cannon that would never be used.

On a late November visit to Cape Girardeau, Grant spent several hours riding around the town with Wes, treated him with respect and cordiality, and invited him aboard his steamboat for supper. The opportunity was golden. Lonely after his Hennepin friends in the Twentieth had departed and anticipating a long winter coming on, undoubtedly bored with the job he had ended up with after such high prospects, Wes requested leave to get married to Emma and permission to bring her to Cape Girardeau. Grant consented—after all, his own wife was following him, as were the wives of other officers, into the theater of war. Wes made a dash for Detroit, arrived there at six P.M., 28 November, and married Emma at the residence of her father. By eight P.M. they were on a train headed back to Cape Girardeau.[5] Like Julia Grant, Emma would live with Wes in whatever accommodations the army provided for the duration of the war.

More relief from boredom was on the way. Grant was looking for officers to organize batteries of light artillery for use on the battlefield, and Wes was suitable and agreeable. On 11 December the former schoolteacher was mustered into service as captain of Battery F of the Second Light Artillery, Illinois Volunteers. The muster roll included 132 men whose duty would be to handle six six-pounder guns (Napoleons) mounted on two-wheeled carriages pulled by horses. Like Wes, these men had come from common civilian occupations of the day: bookkeeper, lawyer, druggist, painter, carpenter, saddler, merchant, chair maker, farmer, baker, clerk, butcher, physician, chandler, and one "segar maker." They were eighteen to forty-five years in age, though mostly in their twenties and thirties. (Wes was only slightly above their median in age.) His younger brother Walter, who had been teaching school in Macon County, signed up for service under

Wes's command and eventually advanced to first lieutenant.[6] For the next several months, until mid-March, Battery F drilled in the river town. Now and then they went on patrol into the Missouri countryside, hunting for rebels, but mainly they drilled and drilled. Wes was a demanding officer — a strict disciplinarian as his own father had been. As a kind of father or mature brother to his troops, he worked hard to get them ready for combat.[7]

War became a bloody reality in July 1861 when Confederate and Union troops clashed not far from Washington, D.C., in the battle of Bull Run (or Manassas). But it was Grant in the West who truly opened the war. He wanted to strike hard and fast, never mind the casualties. From his gathering point at Cairo, he moved up the Tennessee River with the aim of cutting straight through the South, severing the insurgent forces, disrupting their railroad lines, and crippling their supply system. In early February 1862 Grant's men took Fort Henry; ten days later they captured Fort Donelson and thirteen thousand enemy troops. The North was ecstatic. Lincoln made Grant a major general, subordinate in the western theater only to General Henry Halleck, and Grant pushed on. Now he called up more of his forces to drive deeper into the South.

Wes's battery, restlessly watching in Cape Girardeau, at last were summoned. On 14 March they marched off to fight, their red artillery stripes flashing on their blue-clad legs. They had added twenty-four men. In early April a steamboat brought them, their guns, and horses up the Tennessee River where Grant was gathering his forces. Emma stopped off at the general's headquarters at Savannah, Tennessee, while the boat went on to Pittsburgh Landing.

The next target Grant had in mind was Corinth, a railroad crossing just over the state line in Mississippi, a vital link between the east and west of the Confederacy. General Albert Sidney Johnston stood in the way, with forty-four thousand men ready to protect the railroad from Grant's incursion. The Union general had forty thousand of his own and was waiting to add another thirty-five thousand under Don Carlos Buell before moving south.

Wes's little group tugged their guns up the steep slope from the landing and found themselves on a broad tableland of oak woodland interspersed with farms and orchards and dissected by deep ravines. The noise and dust of a massed army lay heavy on the air. A few miles away was Grant's Army of the Tennessee, composed of six divisions under the command of John McClernand, William H.L. Wallace, Lew Wallace (later a famed novelist), Stephen Hurlbut, William

Tecumseh Sherman (Grant's most trusted underling), and Benjamin Prentiss. All but Lew Wallace's troops were ranged in a wide arc around a little log Methodist church called Shiloh, after a village in central Palestine.

Battery F were unassigned troops (shifting back and forth among the divisions). Their captain did not know where they belonged or how they would be used. For the next three weeks they faithfully drilled, exercised with the guns, and waited. Each of the six-pounders weighed nearly half a ton. The men practiced wheeling and backing these immense cast-iron tubes on wooden wheels, raising and lowering their muzzles, aiming them at some hypothetical target a half mile away. The swabbers learned how to clean out the gunpowder residue after each firing. Grant, meanwhile, still eight miles downriver, had given no instructions about putting up any fortifications. They were going into action soon, and he saw no point in building them. Nor did he believe they had anything to fear for the moment.[8]

The night of Saturday, 5 April, Wes had his men clumped together near the road leading up from the landing.[9] Before dawn the next morning, as they were still sleeping, a patrol ran into Confederate troops advancing rapidly toward the Union encampment. General Johnston nearly caught his opponent completely off guard. As the alarm sounded and men awakened, he threw six full divisions at them in rapid fire. The troops of Sherman, Prentiss, and McClernand were all at the front, and they ran to their weapons and began fighting back. Some were thrown into terror and raced for their lives back to the river. General Sherman, trying to rally his panicked troops, had three horses shot from under him. McClernand followed his men to the rear. Prentiss's brigades, in contrast, tried desperately to keep their ragged lines together and stop the onslaught. Soon they were in the thickest part of the battle, fighting all on their own. Outnumbered four to one, they formed a valiant knot of defense. The rebel bullets screamed about their heads, cutting the leaves from the trees in a steady green rain, cutting down the men with deadly missiles. They fell back to a sunken farm road where they had protection from the firing and held their ground.

That position a Confederate officer later called the "hornets' nest" for the vicious, incessant, lethal fire they created across an open field, repulsing each Confederate advance. Twelve times that afternoon Prentiss and his troops repelled fierce Confederate charges.

Meanwhile, Wes and his men at their camp near the river could hear muskets firing, bayonets clashing, rebels yelling their war cry, drums rolling, bugles calling. They could smell the smoke of guns and feel the thunder of cannons, but no orders came to join the fray. Finally at about ten A.M., making a decision on his own, Wes ordered his men to harness the horses, and they charged down the road toward the battle lines, looking for McClernand's position. They passed wounded soldiers on every hand, staggering along or lying by the road—Sherman and McClernand troops in retreat. As they galloped down the main road leading to Corinth, Wes suddenly realized they had passed beyond the Union lines and were nearing the enemy. Wheeling about, they upset one of the guns and had to leave it there. Back they came along the road until they ran directly into the Hornets' Nest. By now General Will Wallace had brought his Second Division forward to help Prentiss, and Wes reported to him near the left of his line. Wes arranged his battery alongside the other artillery already there, aimed the muzzles over his infantry's heads, and now the Second Illinois Light Artillery's firepower added to the din.[10] On the other side, the rebels brought up sixty-two field guns to bombard the Prentiss and Wallace troops.

For six hours the opposing forces blasted each other's lines, neither side able to stop the carnage or gain a victory. An Iowa infantryman, in a letter to his hometown newspaper, was struck by the contrast between the human violence unleashed on that battlefield and the springtime harmony of nature all around them: "While the battle was raging most terrifically, and when it seemed like a mighty hurricane sweeping everything before it; when the great storm of cannon balls made the forest in places fall before its sweep; when men and horses were dying, and a blaze of unearthly fire lit up the scene; at this moment of horror, when our Regiment was lying close to the ground to avoid the storm of balls, the *little birds* were singing in the green trees over our heads!"[11]

Grant, who had rushed to the battle scene from headquarters, commanded the forward troops to hold at all costs while he tried to reorganize a defensive position closer to the river. But by late afternoon Prentiss and Wallace realized that they could hold no longer. Their supporting flanks had all failed, and they were in imminent danger of being completely surrounded.

What happened next can best be told in Powell's own words, written down in a letter thirty-four years after the events but as sharply etched in his mind as though they had occurred only yesterday.

About four o'clock, as I have always remembered the time, Gen. Wallace asked me if I could not plant a section to his left in advance of the line where there were some trees near the corner of the Peach Orchard fields. This I did and the section was immediately engaged. Soon I discovered that there was a line of men concealing themselves in the fence and I dismounted and pointed one of the pieces along the fence loaded with solid shell. As I raised my hand for a signal to the gunners to stand clear of the recoil a musket ball struck my arm above the wrist which I scarcely noticed until I attempted to mount my horse. Looking about I found that infantry which had also moved with me into this position were running away as I thought from the line. I stood by a tree and tried to examine my arm, and looking about the field and at the running men, I was more angry than I remember ever to have been at any other time, but this was very quickly explained when I saw in the distance a confederate force coming down in double quick time, and that my supporters were engaged in repelling them. At about this juncture a medical officer rode up to me and commenced to cut my sleeve for the purpose of examining the wound; but immediately Gen. Wallace himself rode up and dismounting picked me up, for he was a tall athletic man, and put me on my horse and directed the sergeant to take me back to the landing.[12]

In shock, Wes clung to the saddle for nearly three miles, riding through a constant hail of gunfire before arriving at an Illinois boat tied up at the river.

The other men of the battery came along more slowly in his wake. Five of them had been wounded, three were missing, twenty-seven of the horses were dead, and two of the guns had been captured. Reaching their morning's encampment, they turned about to face the crushing enemy once again. For another hour that afternoon, until 6:30 P.M., they fired canister after canister, until at last the Confederate advance stopped and the Union line held. General Wallace was dead, shot within minutes of giving up his horse. Prentiss was captured, with two thousand of his men. And Grant had nearly lost it all — the battle, his men's lives, his reborn career, the Union cause.

Rain began falling over the carnage, leaving the dead and wounded lying in pools of muddy water. Twenty thousand had been killed or wounded that day, one of the deadliest battles in the annals of modern warfare. Among the casualties on the Confederate side was their commanding general, Albert Johnston. His troops, for a while so near to victory, were left as devastated as the Union forces.

The fight was completely gone out of them. For all the losses, neither gray nor blue had won the day.

Wes, nearly delirious from pain and loss of blood, was taken to Savannah by boat. Emma, his bride of only five months, was waiting at the landing and followed his litter to the town hall, turned into a makeshift hospital where a physician from Olney, Illinois, William Medcalfe, was on duty.[13] The doctor cleaned and examined Wes's wound and gave laudanum to help him sleep. Emma stayed through the night with a roomful of men all around her, feverish and groaning from their wounds. The next day Medcalfe decided to wait a little longer to see how bad the damage was to Wes's arm. For the moment he had no choice but to leave the bullet embedded in the limb. But by Tuesday he feared the wound would not heal; the bones were too smashed and gangrene would set in soon as the tissues died from lack of blood supply. He gave his patient a few whiffs of chloroform and amputated his arm about two inches below the elbow, stitching up the severed arteries, muscle, and skin to make a reddened stump.

So suddenly had the disaster happened, and so irrevocably. Wes had been a soldier for less than a year. Shiloh, his first true engagement since enlisting, his first real chance for glory, had left him maimed for life. He had Emma with him to be his nurse and support.[14] He had survived his brush with death. But all about him were men who, like himself, had been home with their families not so very long ago, planting crops or teaching classes or selling dry goods. Now mutilated or dying, they lay packed together in a forlorn little hospital in Tennessee, and the war for the Union had lost almost all its glamour.

For nearly three months Wes lay recuperating, his wife-nurse helping him feed and dress, while the Union forces, after burying their dead men and horses, followed the withdrawing Confederates south. Grant, now in disgrace for his inexcusable negligence at Shiloh, persisted in taking the Corinth rail center as planned. His troops then hunkered down while the general reassessed what the enemy was going to require from him, his men, and the United States government in order to be defeated. Surely it would take more than anyone had yet realized.

Emma and Wes came down to Corinth at the end of June to visit the troops. He had lost weight on his already spare form and was suffering intense pain. Others in the company had also been wounded, while still others were dead. The survivors, including Walter, were sleeping in their Sibley tents, cooking on outdoor campfires, gathering news from

Wes and Emma Powell, photographed in Detroit, 1862, several months after the Battle of Shiloh. (Courtesy: National Archives)

the eastern front, and waiting. Their captain came to bid them good-bye, as he now had orders from Grant to go home to Illinois on extended recruiting service. The army needed fresh, whole bodies to fill its depleted ranks, and Wes, whose crippled frame could hardly have been good advertising for the cause, went to Springfield to sign up more volunteers. He wanted and needed the break.

Why was he in this war? The question had to turn over in his mind after Shiloh as the process of buttoning his pants in the morning, mounting a horse, or writing a letter all became more daunting tasks. Millions of other eligible men had still not enlisted, and even after President Lincoln instituted a military draft in March 1863 many would either hire a substitute to go in their place or riot against conscription or evade the law somehow. John Muir, for example, escaped into Canada, declaring that he was a Scotsman by citizenship and a pacifist by principle. Mark Twain deserted from the Missouri rebels he had joined after he realized his life might be in danger. Clarence King, who graduated from Yale that summer when Wes was recovering from his wound, went salmon fishing on the Saguenay and geologizing in the Sierra Nevada.

Wes, in contrast to all of these contemporaries, had gone to war and without any coercion. By choice he would go back into the fighting. Later in life, in a letter to a friend, Wes provided some clues to his motives:

> It was a great thing to destroy slavery, but the integrity of the Union was of no less importance: and on and beyond it all, was to be counted the result of the war as an influence which should extend far into the history of the future, not only establishing in North America a great predominating nation, with a popular and powerful government; but also as securing the ascendancy of the Anglo-Saxon branch of the Aryan family, and the ultimate spread of Anglo-Saxon civilisation over the globe. Perhaps it is only a dreamer's vision wherein I see the English language become the language of the world; of the science, the institutions, and the arts of the world; and the nations integrated as a congeries of republican states.[15]

As an explanation of his thinking at age twenty-eight, this document requires some caution. Its language reflects the later nineteenth-century's fascination with "Anglo-Saxon" and "Aryan" ethnic mythologizing that was not so familiar to Wes in his youth. Yet the statement does indicate that his motivation as a warrior went beyond ending slavery.

Wes, like the rest of his family, hated the Slave Power intensely and wanted to see it defeated not merely because it was incompatible with a system of free white labor but because it was wrong to turn another human being into a commodity to be bought and sold. Despite the "Aryan" rhetoric in his letter, he was not a racist who believed in the innate biological inferiority of people of color, though he did maintain all along a confidence that English and Anglo-American culture was best and deserved to triumph over others.

More so than his parents, however, with their nearly single-minded devotion to Wesleyanism, Wes was an intense nationalist who accepted the idea of America's exceptional destiny completely. The growth and expansion of the United States was for him a more powerful moral cause than any church or creed. America was the great republican experiment seeking to demonstrate that people could be trusted to elect their own leaders rather than be ruled by a hereditary class. Like so many others fighting with him in the Union ranks, Wes saw his country as a benevolent force. The nation had succeeded in expanding to the Pacific, bringing the rule of law and the promise of liberty and opportunity where they had never been before. Now Southern planters and their deluded lackeys threatened to destroy that nation in order to protect their base economic interests. They were immoral, they were vicious, they must be destroyed even at the risk of Wes's own life and limb.

To be sure, Wes was moved by more than ideals. He clearly liked wearing a uniform, drilling his charges, exercising authority and discipline. A side of him was ever wanting to be the strong figure to whom less capable men looked for leadership. He was thrilled by the logistical challenge of moving large armies around on the map. Although so far he had played only a marginal role in Grant's campaigns, he had tried to gain a sense of the larger picture that the general and his advisory staff had in mind. Bloodshed in itself had little appeal. What he especially liked was the play of logic, strategy, mobilization, supply, and communication on a large theater of action.

But above all the principle of the Union was the reason why he fought. And it was Abraham Lincoln's articulation of that principle, and Lincoln's dogged determination to defend it through thick and thin, that kept Wes at the front. Lincoln was his commander, his hero, his avatar. One of his close friends in old age, the former Union general David J. Henderson, perceived the strong hold that Lincoln had over him. As Henderson recalled, "he was not an admirer of Napoleon, or Caesar, or any of the great slaughterers; but oh, how illuminated and beautiful became that rugged, bearded face when he talked of Abraham Lincoln!"[16]

While Wes was in Springfield with a safe, quiet assignment of signing up recruits, his admired president was on the job in Washington, tirelessly defending the republic against its enemies. Wes's comrades were still in the field, experiencing danger and privation. He could not stay out of action for long despite the fact that he was missing part of an arm. By mid-February 1863 he and Emma were on their way back into battle. His men in Battery F had finally received orders to travel west to the Mississippi and begin preparations for Grant's next target, the city of Vicksburg, well fortified on another high bluff above the river. Take the place, Grant realized, and the entire western half of the Confederacy would effectively be under his control. Wes and Emma arrived at Grant's new headquarters at Lake Providence, several bends and loops of the river north of Vicksburg. As officer and wife, they had waiting for them a comfortable room in an abandoned plantation mansion while the "boys" slept below on the lawn and drilled with new guns and horses. Acres of roses scented the air, and mockingbirds sang from the trees. The Powells were enchanted with their lodgings, but the next deadly campaign was about to begin.

The Confederates knew they were in the vicinity, for they could see them on the water or in the bayous around the city, and knew why they were there. Grant, however, could not find a secure way to approach his target. The Yazoo River came into the Mississippi just downstream from his command post, and the landscape was a tangled wetland of muddy sloughs and islands, oxbows, abandoned river channel, broad new river, jungle, snakes, raccoons, and mosquitoes. Finally, after much study and repeated failure, he decided to try going down the west side to a crossing point well below Vicksburg and coming around from the east. They went into vigorous action. Wes's company and two others that he had charge of had to throw down a corduroy of logs and construct bridges much of the way for their gun carriages to pass and for the foot troops to use as well. On 30 April the army, shedding all impedimenta, crossed the Mississippi and continued east, clearing away rebel resistance at Champion's Hill and Big Black River and wedging in between Joe Johnston's large, roaming land force and John Pemberton's defenders before Vicksburg.

In the aftermath of engagement at Champion's Hill, as he was bringing the guns up from the rear, Wes came upon an old acquaintance from Hennepin, a man named Morgrave, who was still with the Twentieth Illinois infantry. During the battle Morgrave had been taken prisoner by the enemy. His guard and he got down behind a log to await the outcome, and wresting the guard's gun away, the prisoner became captor. Wes found them hiding in that reversed position. Morgrave was eager to know which side had won, and Wes told him, to his delight, that the bluecoats had had a huge triumph. Morgrave and prisoner, Wes and Battery F, the whole union army now swept back west toward the ultimate goal.

On 19 May and again on the 22nd Grant threw his men against the fortifications on Vicksburg's eastern side, but both times they were severely repulsed. They would have to be more patient if they wanted this prize. Settling in for a long siege, they augmented their numbers to seventy thousand and waited for the city to get hungry. The one-armed captain of Battery F was now under the immediate command of Brigadier General Thomas E.G. Ransom, Sixth Division of the Seventeenth Army Corps, which was under Major General

"Our Works Before Vicksburg—Battery Powell." A sketch by Theodore R. Davis of the siege of Vicksburg, Mississippi, from Harper's Weekly, *4 July 1863. Among the figures is a man missing an arm, but it is the left arm that is missing, while Powell lost his right arm.*

James G. McPherson. The man behind them all, the master of their fortunes, General Grant, went on a drinking binge.

The Powell Battery took up a position on the Graveyard Road, running northeast from the city, to prevent the Confederates escaping in that direction. They began digging a tunnel, or sap, through the soft loess hills toward the enemy's fortifications, which would allow troops to move forward unseen and invulnerable to artillery. Night and day, Wes was out overseeing the tunneling, going without much rest or food. It was some of the hardest work of his life. Now and then he did pause to pull out of the tunnel walls and the open trenches a few fossilized mollusks, labeling them according to location and packing them away for his Wheaton "museum." But mostly he labored alongside the men digging. They cut cane from the nearby fields and wrapped it in telegraph wire, stripped from lines overhead; these bundles they set up as shields against enemy bullets.

From time to time their superior officers came by to inspect the battery's progress. Grant, sobering up for these occasions, met Wes repeatedly and asked pointed questions. Wes was impressed with his shrewd sense of what needed to be done. Still they kept digging. A full month of this sweaty toil, and at last they were ready to drag two of the twelve-pounder guns, weighing perhaps eight hundred pounds each, through the sap to a point within seventy yards of the Confederate works. Setting up the guns, they prepared to blast the city apart. On 3 July Wes reported to McPherson and Ransom that his battery was ready to begin action the next morning — a patriotic Fourth-of-July salute at daybreak. By dawn, however, the Confederates had run up a white flag, and Grant stood revived as a hero among his men and nation.

Simultaneously, a battle had been raging at Gettysburg, Pennsylvania, leaving twice the number of casualties that Shiloh left. It too was an electrifying victory for the North. But the rebels were not yet finished; they still had plenty of fight in them. Battery F ran down to Natchez to intercept a shipment of cattle, which they hauled to the occupying troops in New Orleans, then came back upriver to Natchez. Captain Wes Powell went along but then had to quit. For the next two months he was forced to take medical leave. Vicksburg had left him debilitated. He weighed only 110 pounds, his arm throbbed with constant pain, and he required professional medical attention. Emma and he journeyed to Detroit where a surgeon reoperated on his stump to deaden some of the raw nerve endings. After a period of recuperation at her parents' house, they headed back in September to their company, meeting them at what would become winter quarters, the village of Hebron near Vicksburg.

In mid-November Wes and company went out on a raiding party to Meridian, under the command of General Sherman, where they tore up railroad lines and bent them around the trees, a trial run for the blitzkrieg that Sherman would soon launch on the eastern redoubts of the Confederacy. The intent in that demolition was to leave Vicksburg permanently isolated, beyond all possibility of any rearmament, but the soldiers also burned farms along the way. Grant's Army of the Tennessee, meanwhile, had moved east to capture Chattanooga, and in the following spring he would himself go on to Washington to assume command of all the Union armies, leaving his trusted Sherman in charge of the western operations. Sherman would then set off for Atlanta, with Battery F lumbering along in the infantry's dust.

This time Wes stayed behind; he was asked to do so. During the spring and summer he had assumed responsibility for teaching a regiment of freed slaves how to use weapons and man the garrisons of Vicksburg. Not every northern officer wanted that work. Despite their opposition to slavery, many in the Union army, officers and privates, refused to serve alongside or in the company of blacks, whether free or ex-slave. Northern men of color had enthusiastically joined the bluecoats in substantial numbers to fight for freedom, but they were often given menial jobs around camp and paid half the pay of a white soldier. The Southern slaves who flocked to their liberators enjoyed even less regard from the military command, but they did furnish manpower needed to maintain the rear.[17] It was Wes's task to help them gain the skills and confidence to perform well this lowly but necessary work. By September, however, Wes was bored with his assignment, which threatened to leave him stranded in a dull garrison in Mississippi for the duration of the war. Turning down an offer of promotion to lieutenant colonel, he asked to be restored to his company, which was now tromping through the ashes of Atlanta.

Another worry may have been agitating Wes's mind. Battery F had suffered heavy losses in the battle of Atlanta on 22 July, and brother Walter had been captured and had disappeared into a Confederate prisoner-of-war camp somewhere. Situated so far away, Wes could hear nothing and was eager to go where he could get more news and be more engaged in the struggle. What he could not know, and would have been devastated to learn, was just how wretched Walter's situation was. Walter had been taken to a place called Camp Asylum, or Camp Sorghum, near Charleston, South Carolina, which was no better than the infamous prison at Andersonville. The prisoners were kept outside all day under a hot summer sun, given little food or water, and confined in the midst of their own excrement, until many died of dysentery or other illness. Walter had fallen seriously ill. Precisely what he caught — his medical records indicate either a case of sunstroke or some kind of fever — drove him out of his head. Another prisoner from the Illinois infantry, who had known him for a while, saw him on Thanksgiving Day wandering across a dangerous no-man's-land marked off between prison groups, "with arms aloft" and praying in a loud voice —"as mad as he could be."[18]

On 18 September Wes wrangled an order to return to his company and rushed eastward to the front. He had secured more than that long-awaited order — he had also won promotion to major. In contrast to his own dedicated mood, all across the North the critics of the war and of Lincoln had begun to raise the cry for peace. Though beaten severely and pushed back relentlessly, the Southern armies

showed surprising resilience. Some observers predicted that the president would lose his bid for reelection that fall, so unpopular had the
war become. But Major Powell was more determined than ever to see
the war through to an end. The new commander of the Army of the
Tennessee, General O.O. Howard, calling him "a straightforward
and attentive officer," named him chief of artillery "for the artillery
not in the field with me."[19]

In this enlarged role of looking after armaments behind the front
Wes now had the job of organizing a shipment of sixteen batteries of
guns to Savannah, Georgia, to support Sherman's march to the sea.
The only way to get them delivered was the long way around, via the
railroad to Nashville. Wes boarded the train with the guns and arrived in that city just as the rebels, under the recklessly aggressive
General John Bell Hood, were making a last-ditch effort to retake it
from the Yankees. Wes was put to work on a challenge that was the
exact opposite of Vicksburg: now he must help construct a defense
against a hard-charging enemy determined, in a last-ditch effort, to
break through that pacified border state toward the Ohio. Once
again he supervised the throwing up of earthworks. He unloaded
those sixteen batteries of guns, deploying them behind the foot soldiers shielding the city.[20] The attack came on 15–16 December, and
during those two days Wes was constantly in the saddle, riding back
and forth to check on more than a thousand artillery men and then
scaling the heights to stand with the commanding officer, General
George H. Thomas, monitoring the panorama with field glasses. For
the first time in his war career Wes was in a position to see the whole
of a battle as it pulsed and echoed before him.

Nashville would be his last battle. The rebels lost decisively there,
as they were now losing in Virginia — indeed, all energy in the Southern insurrection was fading. It was apparent that there was little more
that this tired, damaged man could do. He was ready to go home. On
4 January 1865 he was mustered out of service, and Emma and he returned to their homes in the North and to civilian life. The war
dragged on for another four months, until finally, at Appomattox
Courthouse on 9 April, Robert E. Lee in full-dress uniform surrendered to Grant.

For a brief moment the North knew indescribable joy and relief.
The demon that had stalked the region for so many decades, the
Slave Power of the old South, was dead and gone. Never had anyone,
even the most radical abolitionists, anticipated such a bloody war or

*Wes and his younger brother
Bramwell Powell, 1865.
Bram, who replaced Wes in
the Hennepin school, never
saw service in the Civil War.
Wes's empty right sleeve is
concealed from the camera.*
(Courtesy: Utah State
Historical Society)

such massive human losses, whether sacrificed to preserve the Union or to defeat the institution of African American bondage. Heaven did not make that war, the religious-minded noted, but heaven must have had a hand in the outcome.

The greatest evil that the nation had known was now wiped away. Prayers of thanksgiving went up all over the victorious states, but most certainly they were long and earnest in the household of Joseph and Mary Powell. Those two pious people would have been justified in seeing a divine power working in their lives and in that of their adopted country. Despite many dark days during the war, the North had come through to triumph over wickedness and had smashed the power that had held Congress in its unholy grip for so long, that had made Christian principles a mockery, and that had defied the will of God.

The cost of defeating the Slave Power, however, had been immense: over six hundred thousand lives lost, an unnumbered host of other casualties and heartaches. In their own parlor Joseph and Mary could look on two sons who had paid mightily for the victory. Wes had come home earlier, a man with a stump of an arm who was still learning to write and eat with an awkward left hand. Walter would not arrive until May, after his release from prison camp. This once robust man (he had been taller and heavier than Wes) who had been such an excellent student in college, so quick to pick things up, so promising a school teacher, was now shrunken, morose, uncommunicative, and given to fits of violence. But at least their chairs at dinner were vacant no longer. They had made it home.

The North had done well economically under the stimulus of wartime spending. Coal and iron production was up, traffic on the rails and canals was up, more land was in agricultural production than ever before. Not only had the Slave Power died, but Northern industrial power had an uncontested horizon before it. The West, with all of its vast soil, mineral, and forest resources, was beckoning both the settler and the capitalist. An army that had conquered the Southern insurgents stood ready to advance on the native peoples living there and force them to yield to America's claim.

Thus, the immigrants Joseph and Mary could look on the national scene with considerable satisfaction, despite the melancholy sight of two maimed sons. Thirty-five years earlier they had left their homes in Britain, a land that had been family ground for generation following generation, the country of their Welsh and English forebears, the evangelical domain of the Wesley brothers, the birthplace of industrialism, a nation green in the countryside, black and prosperous in the cities, to try their fortunes in America. The gamble had paid off. The young couple had now grown old in the New World. They had accumulated more wealth and status than ever would have been possible in Hull or Shrewsbury for people of their modest origins. Thanks to America, all eight of their children had gained some college education. Not least, they had raised their voice against evil, and at last that evil had been vanquished.

But then, tragically and inexplicably, their deity permitted the most wicked deed imaginable, and once more the Powells' faith in God and country was on trial. On the night of 14 April a rabid Southern fanatic shot President Lincoln in the back of the head as he sat in Ford's Theater watching *The American Cousin*. A second assassin stabbed the secretary of state, William Seward, in his own home. Seward was not mortally hurt, but the president, carried across the street to a private residence, was badly wounded, and he died the next day. The city of Washington was stunned. Telegraph lines carried the shock across the land. In the North prayers of thanksgiving for ending the war turned almost instantly to prayers for the soul of the dead leader and for some measure of comprehension. A governor's committee in Illinois declared that "the nation has been called by the mysterious decision of an over ruling Providence to mourn the loss of the first Magistrate of the Republic at a period when the best and brightest hopes of the people were centered upon him, and at the moment when his long faithful services had culminated in complete triumph."[21]

Much of the nation fell into deep grief, edged with despair, as preparations for Lincoln's funeral and burial were made. A cortege started by rail toward the President's home state of Illinois, and all along the tracks people stood with their heads bowed, silent and grim. Heavy rains added to the gloom. On Monday, 1 May, the cortege reached Chicago, and citizens came in from nearby towns to pay their respects to a man whom many had loved though others had criticized and doubted. Thirty-six thousand mourners marched four abreast behind the casket as it moved by carriage from the railroad station to the Court House, where the body would lie in state.

According to the *Chicago Tribune*, the funeral mourners came from all the diverse parties, classes, races, occupations, and cultures that had mingled to create the Northern states.

> Bronzed, war worn and grey bearded heroes of the army and navy; veteran soldiers incapacitated from active service by honorable wounds; Governors of States and grave, thoughtful faced counsellors of the nation; metropolitan officials irrespective of partisan differences; the children of the schools by thousands, unconsciously participating in a ceremony which in after years will be their most precious recollection; venerable Judges of Courts and the reverend clergy, all creeds merged in the one great sorrow, Protestant and Catholic and Hebrew, all moving side by side; Knights Templar and Masons, the mysterious symbols of their orders draped in mourning; Hollandish and Belgian, English and Scotch, Irish and Welsh, French and Norwegian, Danish and Spanish, Hebrew and Bohemian societies almost countless in members; the Arbeiter, Grueth Bildungs and Turnverein of stalwart, phlegmatic Germans, pledged to liberty and humanity; associations, unions of every description; and last but not least the men whom he has lifted from bondage and stamped with the dignity of manhood, the race which by a stroke of his pen he delivered from the task master, and made forever free.[22]

As they all walked along the muddy streets, according to reporters, the sun broke out and shone down on their resplendent banners and black arm bands.

Every sidewalk was full, every building showed faces peering from windows and rooftops, every doorway was packed with observers. Along Park Row the city's elite had draped their residences in crape festooned with flags of many designs, elaborate sprays of white roses, and banners inscribed with mottoes ("Our Country's Martyr," "The Union and the Constitution," "Bear Him Gently to His Rest"). They passed a congressman's house that was decorated with a bust of the president surmounted by cherubs and the "Anchor of Hope prettily arranged among the drapery." Merchants covered their storefronts with black and white cloth and put vases of evergreens in their display windows. Chicago did itself proud in this greatest of all funerals and in its grieving ironically celebrated its wealth, diversity, enterprise, and institutions.

The only sounds heard that solemn morning, besides the muffled tread of the marchers, was the distant tolling of a bell. By late afternoon people began to file through the Court House rotunda to see the President's corpse, dressed in black and lying in a casket mounted on an elaborate catafalque. They came at the rate of almost six thousand an hour, continuing until midnight.

Were the Powells—Joseph and Mary, Uncle Walter and his wife, Wes and Emma, many of the other children—in that line, glancing briefly at the great man's embalmed, discolored face before returning home? Surely they were. Lincoln had been their hero, the savior of their nation, their commander in chief, their symbol of high moral purpose, and now they bid him farewell before his body was taken south and buried in his home city of Springfield. With others across the state and country, Wes and the rest of the Powell family said good-bye to a long, troubled, dynamic, and painful era of America's history.

Part Two

Canyons of
the Colorado

CHAPTER 4

Westward the Naturalist

T he war fought over Southern independence was the young nation's most deadly hour, but exactly how it was deadly varied across the continent. In the states, territories, and unorganized lands lying beyond the Great Plains, where both slave owners and abolitionists were fewer and old political rivalries weaker, the war was a death knell to economic development. It stopped the westward movement. If that movement stopped forever, if the nation permanently broke apart, westerners would become pioneers for nothing. Their achievements would shrink back to a scattering of farms, mines, and dusty towns lying weakly on the fringes of a shattered ideal. They would have no glorious future ahead, no honored place in the vanguard of civilization.

That danger to the West loomed in the mind of William Gilpin and filled him with the rage of a day-dreamer smacking his face into an unanticipated wall. On the eve of war he warned that "the Union itself, incessantly assailed and perpetually menaced, has seemed to approach the twilight of its existence, and . . . has been in suspense between the infuriated passions of extreme sectional fanatics."[1] He knew plenty about those passions, for he was then living in Missouri, a state bitterly divided between pro-Northern and pro-Southern factions. For a time Missouri had been the pulpit of one of the greatest advocates of continental expansion, Senator Thomas Hart Benton: father-in-law of John Charles Frémont, ideological father of the concept of Manifest Destiny, and early promoter of the transcontinental railroad. Then the state fell into internecine fighting, and the vision of building the world's dominant nation on the North American continent, supremely prosperous and powerful and dedicated to the cause of liberty, was forgotten.

Gilpin, who had been a follower of Benton, had gone west with Frémont in 1843 and served in the war against Mexico to extend the national domain, then become a town promoter on the banks of the Missouri near present-day Kansas City. He had voted emphatically for Lincoln and the Union, even serving as one of Lincoln's personal bodyguards in the tense moments before his inauguration. But Gilpin could never forgive what both the North and the South alike had done to put at hazard the most important movement in world history—the one going past his door toward the Pacific shore.

The younger son of a wealthy Philadelphia businessman, Gilpin had taken a long time to identify his life's cause, but when found, he took it up with a zeal that was unmatched in his day. He could hold forth for hours on the beauty and virtue of this "republican empire" and on its progress toward encompassing the whole continent of North America, including Mexico and Canada, and then moving on to conquer the world. Abraham Lincoln, who shared some of that fervor, appointed Gilpin to be the first territorial governor of Colorado in 1861, and for the rest of his life Gilpin made Denver his messianic pulpit. He moved into a large, handsome brick house, with bay windows looking out on the boomtown construction of what must one day become (he was sure) the nation's capital city. His last few years were absorbed in private land speculation in southern Colorado, and he died rich in 1894.

Although Gilpin served in office only a year before being dismissed for imprudent government borrowing, he remained a popular prophet—especially on the Fourth of July, but always and whenever his fellow citizens wanted someone to tell them, at great length and in swelling, bombastic prose, what it was they were supposed to be achieving. In his own mind he was rational, factual, and scientific, offering irrefutable proof that the United States was destined for global dominance. Science, particularly the work of the German savant Alexander von Humboldt, had demonstrated that great civilizations can arise only in the northern temperate zone that girdles the earth. The United States, by acquiring the West, occupied more temperate-zone space than any nation in history. Happily, nature added an auspicious topography. While both Asia and Europe were large bowls turned upside down, with mountains at their center splitting people into warring ethnic fragments, the United States was a bowl turned right-side-up. The low-lying Mississippi basin formed its center, and people tumbled together, becoming one nation of unprecedented unity.

"Nature is the supreme engineer," Gilpin declared; "art is prosperous only whilst adhering to her teachings." He was speaking about finding the best railroad route across the continent, but the principle had a broader meaning. Americans must see, with the aid of science, that the great interior bowl, not the eastern seaboard, must become the political and demographic heart of the nation. The bowl must be filled with immigrants, until there were over a billion people living in the continental interior, raising a cornucopia of food from its dark fertile soils.

Malicious rumors in the older states suggested that much of the western country was a grim desert that could never support so many people. It was a lie, said Gilpin. Nowhere in the West was any real desert. "This dogmatic mirage" had first been spotted hovering over the Great Plains, but when settlers actually arrived there, the desert disappeared. It drifted farther west—until, again, knowledge blew it away. Now it was "about to be expelled from its last resting-place, the basin of the Colorado." Explorers soon penetrated that last stretch of hidden country, and when they did they discovered that even there Americans possessed a land of unlimited opportunity.

The Colorado River, Gilpin explained, flows across a high plateau with enormous agricultural potential. With rose-tinted maps, he described several such plateaus lying in a chain from Mexico to Canada, all of them remarkably suited for farming and grazing. They enjoyed a year-round spring. All that was required to grow crops was to draw off the rivers for irrigation—and then even plows were not necessary in the soft, moistened ground. The Colorado Plateau, like other parts of the West, had been "prepared and equipped by nature in all departments at every point, and throughout its whole length, for the immediate entrance and occupation of organized society, and the densest population."[2]

A skeptic might have asked why, if nature was so good to westerners, a mountain chain as high as fourteen thousand feet above sea level had been raised across the path of the republic. Gilpin, unfazed by any apparent anomalies in nature's great plan, was quick to insist that here too all was providential. The mountains held inexhaustible amounts of gold and other mineral wealth—gold so abundant that someday every American would possess it with the same ease as a cotton shirt.

If the West had a common ideology after the Civil War, it was this vision of Gilpin's. Politicians, businessmen, and engineers tirelessly extolled the region's potential for settlement and growth. Many easterners shared their enthusiasm, none more passionately than Samuel

Bowles, a Massachusetts newspaper editor, loving admirer of the poet Emily Dickinson, staunch Republican, and personal friend of powerful men in Washington, including Schuyler Colfax, Speaker of the House of Representatives and eventually Vice President of the United States. In 1865 and 1868 Bowles traveled through Colorado, which he called the nation's "Switzerland" (so much for North America being radically unlike Europe in topography). Like Gilpin, he was struck by the dazzling promise of the West. "If we stand together in the future," Americans will achieve "such a triumph of Man in race, in government, in social development, in intellectual advancement, and in commercial supremacy, as the world never saw,—as the world never yet fairly dreamed of."[3]

The only threat to a renewed American empire, rising from the ashes of the Civil War and led by western boosters, came from Indians. They posed more of an obstacle than any mountain chain. Neither Gilpin nor Bowles had any doubt that the Indians must go down to defeat, though each man prophesied different fates for them. Gilpin, who had opposed the prewar policy of removing eastern Indians beyond the Mississippi and resettling them on reservations, wanted to abolish those reservations and refuse any of the western tribes exclusive territories too. The proper role for the Indians, he advised, was to work as herders on the white man's ranches where domesticated livestock replaced the bison.

Bowles, on the other hand, saw Indian reservations as temporary necessities—at least until the native peoples died off from alcohol or disease. His frank words are worth presenting at length, for they reflect dominant attitudes of the whites immediately after the Civil War.

> We know [the Indians] are not our equals; we know that our right to the soil, as a race capable of its superior improvement is above theirs; and let us act openly and directly our faith. "The earth is the Lord's; it is given by Him to the Saints for its improvement and development; and we are the Saints." This old Puritan premise and conclusion are the faith and practice of our people; let us hesitate no longer to avow and act it to the Indian. Let us say to him, you are our ward, our child, the victim of our destiny, ours to displace, ours also to protect. We want your hunting-grounds to dig gold from, to raise grain on, and you must "move on." Here is a home for you, more limited than you have had: hither you must go, here you must stay; in place of your game, we will give you horses, cattle and sheep and grain; do what you can to multiply

them and support yourselves; for the rest it is our business to keep you from starving. You must not leave this home we have assigned you; the white man must not come hither; we will keep you in and him out; when the march of our empire demands this reservation of yours, we will assign you another; but so long as we choose, this is your home, your prison, your playground.

The Indian was doomed, Bowles believed, by his inability to adapt to the changing order. "All we can do is to smooth and make decent the pathway to his grave."[4]

What Major John Powell thought, at the conclusion of the war, about the West or the Indians' fate or the white man's destiny went unrecorded. He had ventured only a little beyond the Mississippi and had little firsthand knowledge of the territory stretching from the prairies to the Pacific Coast. He had, however, grown up with influences that in the years to come predisposed him as he formed ideas and assessed visions.

Powell, as we have seen, came from immigrant people whose otherworldly piety persisted in uneasy contrast with their worldly success. While his family was not inclined to doubt that America was part of God's plan, they had a strong sense of human fallibility in carrying out that plan. Like his parents, Powell wanted to see farms and towns spread westward from Illinois, but he knew firsthand what hard work farming was even under favorable soil and climate conditions. Success was possible, but it was never sure or effortless. From boyhood on he was fascinated by the native peoples, their history on the land and their radically different ways of life. He had settled on natural science as his professional calling, rejecting the authority of revealed religion, but for him science meant the slow, careful accumulation of facts and their application to limited hypotheses, not Gilpin's spread-eagle prophesies. And then Powell had seen something more to the Civil War than hot-eyed fanatics quarreling over trivialities. All the dying and maiming had been necessary to defeat an evil power that could no longer be tolerated. Taken together, such predispositions produced a way of coming into the West that was different from Gilpin's or Bowles's.

In the decades following the war Powell became one of the country's leading experts on the West — its topography, geology, and climate as well as indigenous peoples. He joined the cause of continental conquest, and joined excitedly, but he never breathed out the same overheated zeal as Gilpin or was driven by a desire to augment his private wealth. He believed in the American mission, but he showed more sympathy for the plight of the natives, more hope for their amalgamation into American society, even while convinced that there was no future for them in continuing their traditional way of life. In contrast to Gilpin, he found the facts of science supporting pragmatic planning in the region. He acknowledged real deserts staring Americans in the face, setting terms for settlement and requiring careful arrangements to safeguard democracy. He did not find such conditions discouraging but, rather, a challenge to accept and work with. In short, he did not dissent from the project of western expansion nor question the grand idea of progress, but he did argue that progress must always keep its feet firmly on the ground.

The Civil War ended just a few days after Powell's thirty-first birthday. Nearly half of his allotted three-score-and-ten had gone by, and so far he had done little except acquire a character. He also now had a wife and a war record to go with his scattered college education and high-school teaching experience. He had no job, however; brother Bram occupied his old principal position in Hennepin. And he had no income except a war pension.

On the last day of January 1865 Powell was in Detroit staying with the Deans and applying for a disability pension from the federal government. His statement of application explained that the loss of his right arm "totally disabled him from manual labor." It was witnessed and signed by father-in-law Joseph Dean and his friend and fellow employee Joseph Sparks, with supporting letters from Joseph Mitchell, who had been Powell's second-in-command at Shiloh, and by William Medcalfe, the physician who did the amputation. The application was successful, and he began receiving $20 a month, a sum that was increased to $24 in 1883 and $30 in 1886. So modest a sum could hardly support a family. The Republicans in DuPage County offered to run him for the office of county clerk, which he was sure to win on party affiliation alone, a position Powell later claimed was worth $5–6,000 per annum. His father, on the other hand, advised him to go back to teaching, one of the few professions open to a maimed man, and that was what he decided to do.

Undoubtedly through his father's church connections, an offer fortuitously came of a teaching position at Illinois Wesleyan University in Bloomington. A professorship, and a professorship of science at that! The school was only fifteen years old. As Illinois Institute shifted over to Congregational management, the state's Wesleyans pinned their educational hopes on this downstate institution. So far it was prospering, well enough at least to pay a salary of $1,500 the first year. While Powell was stationed at Vicksburg, the Wesleyans had awarded him an honorary master's degree, a shrewd move as it turned out for both parties. With no earned degree of any kind, he looked very unqualified to offer advanced instruction, but now Wesleyan could see no obstacle to making him a faculty member. By fall he was ready, and ever so eager, to show what elevated place science should occupy in a modern institution of higher education.

Powell joined a small faculty of men, learned and pious, including the president, the Reverend Oliver Munsell (who taught ethics and metaphysics); Henry DeMotte (mathematics); Jabez Jacques (ancient languages); the Reverend W.H. Daniels (belles lettres); the Reverend W.R. Goodwin (principal of the preparatory department), and the Reverend M.A. Lapham (ancient languages). Among the nearly two hundred students, also all males, nearly three-fourths of whom were enrolled at the preparatory or precollegiate level, there were a number of war veterans, two of whom would figure later in Powell's western adventures—Lewis Keplinger, who had marched with Sherman through Georgia, and Francis Bishop, who had taken a bullet in the chest at Fredericksburg.[5]

That first year Powell, the erstwhile college dropout, charged across the campus like a whirlwind, overwhelming both the faculty and students. He quickly set up a tiny museum, with himself the curator. Professor DeMotte and he set about reorganizing the curriculum and faculty duties, while alone he drew up plans for a new central building; when carried out, they gave the college its "Old Main." Professor Powell then took on the task of designing a college seal, which likewise was accepted: the sign of an open book with the words "Scientia et Sapientia" written across the pages. He filled his students' heads with plenty of "scientia" of a distinctly nonclassical variety. To the freshman in the scientific department he taught chemistry, botany, and physical geography; to the sophomores systematic zoology, comparative anatomy, and physiology (with added lectures on cellular histology, the vertebrate skeleton, and insects injurious to vegetation); to the juniors, natural philosophy and organic chemistry (with lectures on agricultural chemistry); and to the seniors his specialty of mineralogy and geology (with lectures on the history of geology). His syllabi consisted of going through the standard texts by Dana, Gray, Agassiz, and Gould, but the new professor had no intention of being conventional.

Powell wanted to get his students outdoors and inspire them with reading the book of nature in the field. As one student wrote several decades later, "We all recall how text-books went to the winds with Major Powell. Third floor, . . . southwest room, materializes, and we see the artillerist, true to his artillery instincts, firing his batteries all the while at the entrenched enemies. Ordinary views of physics and geology seemed insignificant under his broad generalizations. . . . He made us feel that we had conquered the commonplace, broken our way through the accepted, and come into the heritage of free thinkers."[6]

The town of Bloomington heard a few volleys from him too, as he was invited to participate in the annual lyceum series, along with the temperance advocate John B. Gough, the humorist Petroleum V. Nasby, and a lecturer on African gorillas. Powell's own topic was, appropriately, "Perpetual Motion." At the school year's end the college board of trustees commended Professor Powell for setting a fine example of perpetual motion among the faculty and hired him back for a second year.[7]

But, as a professor Powell proved no more steadfast than as a student. Midway through his second year he was angling for another position at Illinois State Normal University, a campus located only a short way from Illinois Wesleyan, and a campus where Powell's mollusks were already on deposit. During the war, in idle moments, he had kept up his natural history interests by reading scientific reports and making notes on the southern regions he was seeing and by filling up boxes of invertebrate shells, sending them to Normal. The Normal faculty also knew him well through his work as secretary of the Illinois Natural History Society, which kept its collections on their campus. As secretary he had delivered lectures on natural history to their students.

At the society's annual meeting, which was dominated by professors from Normal, Powell proposed that they lobby for a legislative appropriation for their museum as an educational benefit to the whole state, and naturally, since it was his idea, he was given the task. Early in 1867 he charged into Springfield to get money out of the legislature, and he came home waving an appropriation that included a salary of $1,500 for a museum curator along with $1,000 for "the necessary expenses of improving and enhancing the value of the museum."[8] Without much subtlety, Powell had created an opportunity for himself. The society, duly appreciative, immediately recommended him for the position and salary, while the university made him a professor of geology, with the expectation that he teach in the winter term, leaving the rest of the year free for museum work.

So, good-bye Wesleyan. At a mock graduation ceremony, one of the students gave him a ritual caning, which, according to the newspaper, he took "in a most excellent manner." Nobody seemed much offended by his self-seeking moves. Officially, he was going on leave for the next two years to get the Normal museum in better shape, but he did not come back. Ambition was burning in his brain. He had always been restless, but now he was restless with a purpose — academic advancement and scientific recognition.

Nor did he continue as a classroom teacher for much longer. During the next academic year, 1867–68, Powell offered his first and only course at Normal, and then gave up college teaching altogether. He was now performing the role of "curator," with boxes to unpack, labels to affix, glass cases to fill. Within three years the number of specimens in the Normal collections rose to over 130,000. The greater portion were plants pressed between covers, but there were some fifteen thousand shells on hand, many of them Powell's own.

Even that curatorial job quickly lost its appeal. His commitment to Normal, and to the campus museum lasted no longer than his commitment to Wesleyan. In fact he was beginning to lose interest in Illinois — its rivers, rocks, and institutions. Already he had his eyes trained on the golden West, where opportunities lay like nuggets on the ground.

At the same March 1867 meeting where he was officially appointed curator of the natural history society's museum, Powell asked the board of education's permission to use part of his support funds to lead a collecting expedition into the Rocky Mountains. They allowed him $500, which he matched with $500 from the brand-new Illinois Industrial University in Urbana (later the University of Illinois) and $100 from the Chicago Academy of Science. That was enough to get him started. In April he took a train to Washington, D.C., to see what financial support he could get there. His old commander General Grant, now head of the Armies of the United States, authorized a military escort and rations from military commissaries at low government rates. "A party of Naturalists, under the auspices of the State Normal University of Illinois," Grant's letter read, "will visit the Mauvaises Terres of Southwestern Dakotah for the purpose of making a more thorough geological survey of that region. From thence the party will proceed to explore the 'Parks' in the Rocky Mountains." That was a more ambitious itinerary than the Board of

Education had agreed to — indeed, it was impossible for a single summer's jaunt. But then Powell had been used to going on long trips, and he was eager to engorge as much of the western landscape as he could.

He did not go alone this time. His party consisted of friends, relatives, and college students from Wesleyan and Normal, twelve of them in all. The list included Emma, who became assistant ornithologist, the only woman in the party. Powell's brother-in-law Almon Thompson ("Harry" or "Prof" to the family), a native of New England, husband of sister Nellie, graduate of the Illinois Institute, and superintendent of public schools in Bloomington, went along as head entomologist, with a minister from Rock Island, William Spencer, as his assistant. Joseph Hartzell, the senior at Wesleyan who had mock-caned Powell, traveled as zoologist, along with three other students (W.H. Bishop as Hartzell's assistant, Martin Titterington as herpetologist, and L.H. Kerrick as mineralogist). Everyone soon learned how their leader expected to supplement the scanty expedition funds he had raised; they were expected to contribute $300 each in the cause of science and the museum collections. When Bishop couldn't come up with the sum, Powell allowed him to work his way as cook, while Titterington borrowed his share. And why not? This was a far more stimulating course of study than any classroom could provide. It was one of the first, if not the very first, extended field trips in American higher education.

Professor Powell gave orders that they must all get themselves to Council Bluff, Iowa, the point of debarkation, where they assembled and organized their excursion. He arranged free railroad passes for them to that point, the end of the line. Emma and he arrived in late May and began purchasing teams, wagons, and camping equipment. Two years after the war, and still the way west was by dusty wagon trail, the well-rutted route of the Oregon- and California-bound pioneers and gold-seekers of the past two decades.

Powell found another of his old commanders, General William T. Sherman, in residence at the Council Bluff military post; and from Sherman he learned that the Mauvaises Terres (today called Badlands National Park, just east of the Black Hills) were a dangerous destination. The Sioux (Lakotah) were angry over white incursions into their hunting grounds and were threatening violence. Powell abruptly cut that part of the expedition out of the plan, along with the military escort. They went, without any protection, straight to

Colorado and its high mountain parks (South, Middle, and North) to do their summer collecting. Each expeditioner carried a repeating rifle and a heavy revolver. As Titterington remembered, the professor said that "he didn't expect any trouble with the Indians, but thought the moral effect of the guns would be good. We had no trouble, but the wrecked wagons, new-made graves and deserted sod houses told what might happen any time."[9]

Their route took them across the Missouri and along the meandering Platte River. Samuel Bowles had followed the same route two years earlier and described it as heavily populated by long trains of wagons and carts laden with food, clothing, machinery, and luxuries for the frontier, or coming back empty. The typical wagon on this highway was hitched to four pairs of mules or oxen, and the trains might stretch one-third of a mile long. Twilight found them circling around blazing campfires, their stock let loose on the prairie to feed. Every ten or fifteen miles appeared a stagecoach station, some of them serving meals, and every fifty to a hundred miles a grocery, a blacksmith shop, and a military post. This was by no means a lonely, self-reliant road, but it had become more menacing. The natives of the central plains were no more happy than the Lakotah about the hordes of whites coming through, and that summer their angry young men went on a campaign of retaliation, striking at whomever they could. They attacked farms, stage stations, and the more vulnerable wagon trains. Powell's group of greenhorns was understandably nervous, especially after they came upon a vandalized wagon with blood and hair smeared on the wheels and a crude grave where a victim lay buried.

On 17 June they reached Fort McPherson, near present North Platte on the semiarid High Plains. Here they met General Sherman again, with General George A. Custer and six companies of soldiers, in pursuit of the Indians. The next fall a federal peace commission came out to parley with the southern plains tribes—Arapaho, Cheyenne, Comanche, and Kiowa—at Medicine Lodge Creek in Kansas. They signed a treaty that the Indians probably neither fully understood nor accepted, requiring them to move to reservations in present-day Oklahoma, giving up their traditional territories and becoming farmers. That treaty marked the beginning of a new government policy of confining the western Indians within specified boundaries and trying to domesticate them to white standards. Powell's little company thus found themselves in the midst of a conflict that they had hoped to avoid.

The plains were hot as well as perilous, feed and water were scarce, and they hurried along as fast as the mules could go. As expeditioner L.H. Kerrick reported, it was a "tedious" journey "over long stretches of rolling prairie, alternating with bleak sand hills and cactus fields, besieged by mosquitoes and buffalo gnats, reconnoitered by cowardly, thieving Indians, scorched by a June sun, and tossed and torn by such storms as visit only the Plains."[10]

On 6 July, forty days out from Council Bluff, they arrived safely in Denver, a site that passed for civilization. The only thing impressive about the place was its superb view of the Front Range of the Rockies. Earlier in the year the town had been designated the permanent seat of Colorado's territorial government, though it was a long way from being any kind of capital at all. It counted fewer than five thousand inhabitants clustered near the confluence of Cherry Creek and the South Platte. The streets were dirt, and there were only a few boardwalks to elevate the pedestrian out of the dust, mud, and animal filth. A new set of irrigation ditches ran along the streets, bringing water to a few young shade trees that had been planted, but otherwise Denver was still a windblown spot in the road with more saloons than churches.

Eight years earlier the place had popped up on the map when miners found gold while panning in the South Platte—and the '59 gold rush was on. Within a few months the city had attracted forty thousand people. Their real interest, however, was not Denver but Clear Creek, which came tumbling fast and cold out of the mountains, bearing a few gold flakes to the flatlands. The miners moved up its canyons in search of the mother lode. They threw up shacks in the little ratholes they called Central City, Idaho Springs, Silver Plume, Georgetown, and Empire. The murder rate soared. Gilpin County, named after the visionary governor, became for a period the world's most fevered mining community. Then the easy pickings failed and the hordes began to leave as fast as they had come. The value of gold taken out of the pocked hillsides was cut in half from 1864 to 1867. Denver nearly collapsed as a consequence, and in the mountains the picks fell quiet, many shafts stood empty, the machinery for crushing ore began to rust. When the Powell scientific party arrived, the city was still coming out of a depression, and conditions were only beginning to revive. They could not have been much impressed.[11]

Powell and Thompson called on ex-governor William Gilpin, interrupting his daily preoccupation of getting capital together to buy up Mexican land grants in the San Luis Valley. What Gilpin said to

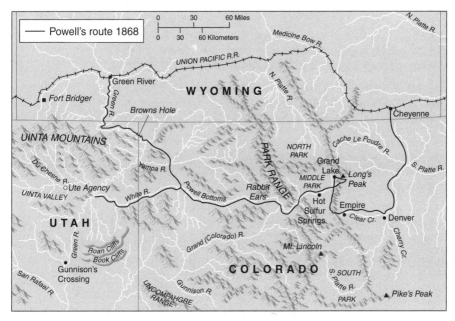

The Rocky Mountains at the time of Powell's 1867 and 1868 summer excursions.

them is speculation, but it is safe to suppose that he waved his arms grandly over the dreariness before them, foretold a brighter future for Denver—much brighter than Chicago, boys!—and urged them to get in on the coming bonanza while prices were low. He may have been the first person to suggest to Powell that the Colorado River needed a bold man to explore and describe it over its entire length.[12] If he did, the notion had to wait and germinate for a couple of months. Right now, what Powell could see was that he and his party had a collecting mission to perform in the mountains. And whatever the bargain prices of Denver land, the price of food in the city was extremely high; they had hungry animals to feed and no cash to spare. Without further delay, they left town, heading south toward Pike's Peak, the towering sentinel that juts out into the High Plains.

The original plan had been to cross westward into Middle Park, but lingering snows blocked the way. So they decided on a more roundabout itinerary. They would begin making their contribution to science by climbing that legendary mountain, acting more like tourists than naturalists, and only later when the snows had melted would they enter Middle Park via South Park to begin collecting the flora, fauna, and minerals.

The route they followed from Denver south, suggested by a local who said it would save time, diverted them from the foothills and directly into the mountains via Bergen's Park, a route that might have been suitable for a packhorse caravan but was hell on wagons and mules. At one point they had to dismantle the wagons and carry them in pieces over a torturous patch of rocks. The party's amateur newspaper correspondent, Joseph Hartzell, sent a letter to the *Bloomington Pantagraph*, describing that ordeal: "To our prairie-accustomed eyes ascent and descent in safety seemed wholly impossible. Often, had not our baggage been securely fastened with ropes, it would have slid endwise from the wagon, and sometimes it seemed that nails instead of hoofs could only accomplish the journey." Over one section of the trail it took them four hours to gain a mile. Nonetheless, they were camping nights among aromatic pines and firs, not out on the shortgrass plains, the water was pure and abundant, the pasture was free, and they were safe from Indians. On their right hand they could see the snowy divide. "With these advantages," Hartzell wrote, "the Rocky Mountains must yet become a source of national wealth far greater than the golden sands have yielded or ever can. . . . Tomorrow, we start for the ascent of Pike's Peak."[13]

That day of climbing was 27 July. Eight of the twelve in the expedition party, including Emma, who (Hartzell speaking again) "has uniformly borne the hardships of the trip with a courage and fortitude far beyond that usually attributed to her sex." She rode side-saddle on a Mexican pony, getting off and proceeding on foot where necessary, clambering over fallen timber charred by forest fires, panting like the others in the high-altitude atmosphere. They spent the night high on the mountain, wrapped in blankets and ponchos, and the next morning after breakfast they successfully finished their climb. Many others had been there before them, including one or two white women, but Hartzell, destined for the ministry, broke into spiritual rapture for the readers back home: "With a picturesque landscape of hundreds of miles in extent spread out beneath us, the clear, blue arch of heaven above, no wonder that it seemed to our rapt vision something like enchantment. Surely the Creator intended the grandeur and beauty of the world as a foretaste of the hereafter. What a prediction of the unknown! Eternity itself may easily seem short!"[14]

Unlike heaven, however, mountains have to be descended, and the work coming down can be more difficult than going up. Emma trekked along gamely with the young men, and Powell, for all his disability, was a coiled spring of energy and strength. Exhilarated by their triumph, they headed west—in a late July snowstorm—across the wide flowery meadows of South Park toward Mount Lincoln on the continental divide, slightly higher than Pike's Peak at 14,235 feet. They climbed it too, and now their wagons were brimming with dead insects, birds, snakes, prairie dogs, marmots, jack rabbits, and all manner of western flora, so radically different from the species of the Mississippi Valley. Returning through Central City, they added minerals and ore samples to the load. Kerrick reported to his Chicago newspaper that they had amassed "over 2000 pounds of choice minerals, 6000 plants, and a large 'assortment' of beasts, birds, and reptiles, and Indian curiosities. It is gratifying to add that they brought back a human scalp apiece, and as this is the endowment each set out in life with, it cannot be deemed cruelty to the redskins to bring them away."[15]

By early September they were down in Denver again. Winter was rushing into the high country, and it was time for students and faculty to get back to school. Fortunately, the two Powells were free of that necessity; as curator and wifely assistant, they could linger for another two months.

Powell was invited to speak on "the Peaks, the Parks, and the Plains" in the Presbyterian church of Denver. The newspaper report gives a good idea of what he had learned from that summer's adventures and how he was trying to fit it into what he already knew about geology.

> He illustrated the lapse of countless ages upon the globe, their influence and effects, from its early formation down to the present existence. He described the time when our mountains were encompassed by a torrid sea, laving a shore that grew tropical plants, and on which strange animals roamed. He described the growth of forests and their decay—occurring again and again—and the formation of our coal beds thereby. As the mountains became fixed, they dried and shrank into less space, and many crevices were formed, which eventually became mineral lodes. . . . The pouring rains and the frosts crumbled down the mountains, and decomposed the iron cubes of the lodes, carrying some of the gold to lower places and forming the placer diggings. He described many things in geology interesting to our people who live in the midst of this great field for study, and evinced himself thoroughly at home with his subject.[16]

After one summer he was speaking authoritatively to a western audience about their own landscape, helping them fit their new territory into the perspective of science.

The Powells went on alone to Middle Park and Grand Lake, where the Colorado River has one of its headwaters, and there they met and interviewed several trappers familiar with the topography. By this point, if not earlier, Powell had decided on his next goal. He had glimpsed a country beyond the Rockies, down their western slope toward Utah, a mysterious canyon land where no miners had yet penetrated, a country that the map makers still left blank. By September 1867 Powell had determined to go there and unlock its secrets.

Among the men Powell met in Middle Park that fall was Jack Sumner, who was trapping, hunting, and running an Indian trading post at the Hot Sulphur Springs, a property belonging to his brother-in-law William Byers, founding editor of the *Rocky Mountain News.* Jack Sumner would figure importantly in Powell's projects over the next two years and in controversies that would plague Powell for the rest of his life.

There is only Sumner's account of their first meeting, and what it most reliably reveals is the man's highly inflated sense of himself. He had come into Colorado only a year and a few months before Powell, but already in his own mind he was one of the last of the legendary "mountain men," much as Powell hoped to be one of the last of the "pathfinders." The two men had other characteristics in common: Sumner had been born in Illinois in 1840, had been raised on an Iowa farm, and had spent many days exploring midwestern rivers. He had served as a private in the war and a year after mustering out had come west, probably at his sister's invitation, to help with some of the Byers enterprises. When Powell showed up in Middle Park with a letter of introduction, Sumner was pleased to share his briefly accumulated fund of knowledge with the "dude." Powell, he recalled, had all his learning from books and even believed the old folklore about beavers using their tails as trowels in plastering their dams. Powell was the college-educated innocent; Sumner was the wise old man educated by the hills.

According to Sumner, Powell offered him a job on a geological trip to the Bad Lands of Dakota, but he countered with the idea of going down the Colorado from the junction of the Grand and Green to the Gulf of California. "After several windy fights around the campfire," Sumner recalled, "I finally outwinded him, and it was agreed that he should come out the following spring and we would make the attempt. . . . The idea was certainly not his own."[17] Thus Sumner remembered their conversation forty years earlier. More likely, Powell was debating with himself over which direction he should go next, and the appeal of adding another river to his life list was stronger than heading into agitated Lakotah territory which he had been repeatedly warned by the Army to avoid.

When the Illinois State Board of Education met on the Normal campus on 18 December, Powell stood before them to give his report on how he had spent the funds allocated for the western expedition. He thanked various railroads and express companies for offering free transportation. By that fall the Union Pacific had reached Cheyenne, Wyoming, making a return wagon ride across the plains unnecessary. Much of his report, however, dealt not with travel, finances, or even specimens collected for the museum. Instead, Powell talked about the edenic places they had visited and he listed the names they had given them: the Park of the Peaks, Lincoln Park, Platte Lake, Cascade Lake. The intention behind the naming was to echo Frémont's laying claim to a continent: in these places, the professor was saying, we were the first (forgetting the Indians) to come and see, and we gave them an identity for the sake of science, American expansion, and our own egos. Compared to Frémont's Wind River Range or Great Basin, those names were neither inspired nor significant, but Wes Powell was lining up himself alongside his explorer heroes. Then, ever so casually at the end of his report, he announced that, having seen its headwaters, he hoped to "complete the exploration" of the Colorado River during the next year.

Clearly, in his own mind he had already begun mapping the greatest and most mysterious river of the West. All that remained was to "complete" the task. But when, how, and with what funds? What kind of party did he need? How long was that river, anyway, and how could he make it through a country that had for so long defied exploration? The expedition he had just led cost in the neighborhood of $10,000 when cut-rate military rations, railroad favors, and his party's time and food were all figured in. He had even sunk over $1,000 of his personal funds into the venture, nearly as much as all the funds advanced by his institutional sponsors. How could he now finance a "complete exploration" of the Colorado with such means as he had? Details to follow. The board did not ask any questions but commended their curator with enthusiasm: "In the exploration of the country and the collections he was successful beyond expectations. In the prosecution of this enterprise Professor Powell had exhibited indomitable energy and rare skill. The money appropriated by the legislature for this object has been most judiciously expended. It has been efficiently used in the cause of science and education."[18]

A few weeks later the Illinois Natural History Society arranged for Powell to give his Colorado geology lecture in Chicago, Urbana, and Bloomington. The weather for the latter was cold and icy, the audience small, so he came back to try again in February, this time with a better response. The hometown newspaper described the lecture as offering "very interesting descriptions of the grand scenery he visited and details concerning the vast wealth there deposited." Powell, who just a short while ago had been an unemployed, uncertain war veteran was now a state celebrity, filled with self-confidence and authority. Everything he did seemed to meet with public approval.

The local Bloomington editor came to look at Powell's museum that winter and found its curator "emphatically 'master of the situation' and everything seems to be going on like clockwork. . . . Too much credit can not be given to Professor Powell. He works sixteen hours a day and pays his assistants out of his own meager salary."[19] But Powell was not working only to catalogue the summer's plunder (in fact much of it never got properly identified) nor was he resting on the acclaim he had received. Unknown to the editor, he was considering a job offer to join the faculty at what would become the premier public university in the state — a chair in natural history at Illinois Industrial University, to begin whenever he was ready. He accepted but never occupied that chair. The West was calling him back. Another year was fast unrolling, and already he was planning ahead for the return of warm weather when he could be in the field once more, among the peaks and parks if not the plains.

Powell needed every coin he could pick up if he was going to make a full scientific exploration of the Colorado River, from its sources in the Rocky Mountains down to its warm, navigable lower basin. He must invest some of his own funds besides raising money from private citizens, museums, and educational institutions in his home state. And even that would not be enough. Such a project must also attract support from that wealthy patron of science and exploration in Washington, the Congress of the United States.

On his previous trip west, Powell had been permitted to buy food at low commissary rates from the western military forts. This time, for a project of much larger scope and covering more than a single summer, he needed to draw rations free of charge. Only if he did not have to pay high frontier prices for his flour, bacon, apples, and coffee, prices often five or six times higher than in Illinois, could he afford to go. To secure that privilege, however, he had to play every card he could with Congress: wounded Civil War veteran, experienced hand in the outdoors, rising star of science, frugal Republican from the Midwest, a man of courage and intelligence at his country's service. Before he could navigate a river, he had to navigate the lobbies of the nation's capital.

In a letter to General Grant of the War Department, dated 2 April 1868, Powell explained that he intended to lead a party of no more than twenty-five naturalists, including two "civil engineers," to make a scientific and topographic survey of the Colorado River. "It is believed," he continued, "that the grand cañon of the Colorado will give the best geological section of the continent." A better understanding of the country would be valuable, inhabited as it is "by powerful tribes of Indians, that will doubtless become hostile as the prospector and the pioneer encroach upon their hunting ground." He promised to do this vital work far cheaper than military expeditions had cost. General Grant quickly endorsed the request, calling it "of national interest," and Joseph Henry, head of the Smithsonian Institution, pointed out that the project had practical as well as scientific value. "The professor intends to give special attention to the hydrology of the mountain system in its relation to agriculture," noted Henry. From the expedition would come knowledge "on which a judious system of irrigation" could be founded for that rainfall-deficient region.[20]

On 15 April Shelby Cullom of Illinois introduced a joint resolution in the House of Representatives to authorize the Powell expedition to draw free rations from western military forts. The reception was not altogether positive. Many congressmen were in a budget-cutting mood, and expenditures to support a private, unofficial adventure such as this one seemed a good place to start being thrifty. Many could not see much return in it for states located in the East. They complained that they had funded expensive government surveys before the war, costing millions of dollars, none of which in the end had produced the route selected for the transcontinental railroad. They pointed out that the nation was already financing military men on the frontier, including many who were skilled in making maps. The resolution, with a load of questions to answer, went to committee and stayed there for the next month.

Powell's main hope for support lay in a single word written across all the available maps of the West—"unexplored." It was a word that no right-thinking, patriotic politician could look on with patience. Still the most authoritative map of the region was the one first published in

1855, in Volume 11 of the *Pacific Railway Reports* (subsequently revised), by Lieutenant Gouverneur Warren of the Army Corps of Topographical Engineers. Much of it was admittedly sketchy and uncertain, but blazoned in the middle of its four-foot expanse was that word "unexplored" stretching across southern Utah and down into Arizona. The word covered a territory some three hundred miles east to west and two hundred miles north to south. A dotted line, indicating high uncertainty, traced the course of the Colorado River across that empty space. Warren was more sure about the lower reaches of the river and about the route of the Green River as it runs down from the Wind River Range and loops around the Uinta Mountains. But the other main branch of the Colorado, the Grand, he had flowing from the west side of Pike's Peak, while the River Blue was supposed to drain the area around Long's Peak. Where the Grand and the Green came together was likewise unfamiliar; few white men had seen the junction and no one had fixed its location for the map maker. Those were precisely the gaps in knowledge, the errors in fact, that Powell was promising to remedy.[21]

The Colorado River had been a part of the European and American imagination for three hundred years, but little had been done in that span of time to gather systematic knowledge about its course and watershed.[22] First called El Rio de Buena Guia (the river of good guidance) by Hernando de Alarcón in 1540, it later became the Rio del Tizon (the river of half-burnt wood) and then Rio Colorado (the red or colored river). Alarcón had recruited local natives to tow his ship a hundred miles upstream from the Gulf of California to the junction with the Gila, and perhaps beyond. Seeing a desolate landscape all the way, he saw no reason to continue. That same year his fellow commander, Francisco Vasquez de Coronado, traveling across the desert in search of gold, heard about a great river to the north and sent his subordinate officer, García López de Cárdenas, to discover it. Cárdenas glimpsed it distantly, from the rim of the Grand Canyon — a chasm so large that he could not find his way down — and he too returned with discouraging news.

Nearly two and a half centuries later, in 1776, the Spanish priests Francisco Tomas Garcés and Silvestre Vélez de Escalante picked up the broken thread of exploration. Garcés poked along the south rim of the Grand Canyon (he named it "Puerto de Bucarreli") and found his way into the hidden sanctuary of the Havasupai Indians. Escalante, with his fellow padre Atanasio Dominguez, circled northwest from Santa Fe to the Grand and Green rivers before turning back across southern Utah, fording the Colorado at the point known thereafter as the Crossing of the Fathers.[23]

After them, in the 1820s and 1830s, came a motley gang of American fur trappers: William Ashley, Jedidiah Smith, Jim Bridger, James Beckwourth, James Pattie, and Denis Julien, most of whom focused on the tributary Green where the beaver lived. Pattie and his companion trappers, however, followed the Colorado up from the Gila and may have reached the lower end of the Grand Canyon. A decade later, in 1836, Julien scratched his name on rocks as far south as Cataract Canyon, below the junction of the Grand and Green. Brave, colorful adventurers, they did not leave much information for the record nor did they help the nation understand precisely what it had to deal with in the heart of the West.[24]

By far the best data a congressman could find on the Colorado River had been gathered by a military officer, Lieutenant Joseph C. Ives, just a few years before the Civil War. A member of the Topographical Engineers, Ives had first come into the country in 1853 to assist Lieutenant Amiel Whipple's survey of the 35th parallel from Albuquerque to California. They followed the Bill Williams Fork until it joined the Colorado River, then turned north to cross at the Needles, a cluster of slender, sharp spires rising from the west bank of the river. Four years later Ives was back on the scene, in command of his own expedition to discover how far upriver a steamboat could travel. He had purchased his boat in Philadelphia, a small, iron-clad, paddle-wheel steamer named *Explorer*, assembled it on the mud flats of the Colorado delta, filled its boiler with driftwood, and chugged upstream against the silty current. Constantly grounding on sand bars, his party afforded considerable amusement to the Indian spectators along shore. The Army, nonetheless, was seriously taking hold of the river at last—and taking hold at its business end, where it entered the waters of commerce and geopolitics. Ives set out to discover what the river could offer in the way of military control over a still contested desert interior.[25]

Ives was temporarily eclipsed by a disgruntled competitor, a private entrepreneur named Alonzo Johnson, who wanted to be the first to push his own steamboat to the head of navigation on the Colorado. Congress refused to fund his enterprise, so in retaliation he got the jump on Ives, and in January 1858, reached a point 320 miles above the mouth of the Gila and some 30 miles above the Needles.[26] Ives, completely disregarding his rival, steamed on past that point into Black Canyon, before hitting a rock and giving up his water entrada.

He was now within a short haul to the Mormon outposts, which even more than the Indians along the river the Army was determined to intimidate and keep under the federal government's authority. Ives had proved that guns and supplies could be carried by water deep into the interior deserts, should the Mohaves or Mormons forge an alliance against the United States; farther upriver, however, he discovered that there were imposing rapids and gloomy canyons that defied modern military transport.[27]

Sending the repaired boat back to Yuma, Lieutenant Ives, accompanied by two German artists, Baron von Egloffstein and Balduin Möllhausen, his civilian geologist, John S. Newberry, and their Indian guides, struck out overland, following a trail east along the southern border of the Colorado's canyon lands. They came upon and named Diamond Creek. Following it down a steep declivity to its mouth on the main river, they stood where no white explorers had stood before — at the bottom of the Grand Canyon with dark-brown walls rising on both sides and a roaring dynamo at their feet. Unfortunately, Ives was no man of imagination; he called the place (after the practice of trappers) "the Big Cañon." Nonetheless, he was awed by the spectacle and wanted to see more. Leading his troop down another creek, Cataract, into the Havasupai homeland, making a dizzying and treacherous descent into those "infernal regions," he stopped short of touching the river again and climbed back out to the high, flat plateau and headed east toward home.

In his published report Ives mixed a trembling wonder with a practical-minded judgment on the stupendous worthlessness of this country.

> Ours has been the first, and will doubtless be the last, party of
> whites to visit this profitless locality. It seems intended by nature
> that the Colorado river, along the greater portion of its lonely
> and majestic way, shall be forever unvisited and undisturbed. The
> handful of Indians that inhabit the sequestered retreats where we
> discovered them have probably remained in the same condition,
> and of the same number, for centuries. The country could not
> support a large population, and by some provision of nature they
> have ceased to multiply. The deer, antelope, the birds, even the
> smaller reptiles, all of which frequent the adjacent territory, have
> deserted this uninhabitable district. Excepting when the melting
> snows send their annual torrents through the avenues to the
> Colorado, conveying with them sound and motion, these

dismal abysses, and the arid table-lands that enclose them, are left, as they have been for ages, in unbroken solitude and silence.[28]

Although this was not a country made for military or economic uses, it was made for scientists and artists. Professor Newberry of the party celebrated the canyon as "the most splendid exposure of stratified rocks that there is in the world."[29] The painter Egloffstein produced a number of wildly exaggerated images of the canyons — lonely birds flying through gothic shafts of gloom — to titillate the public; while Balduin Möllhausen's majestic panoramas of the desert and portraits of brightly attired native peoples were the expedition's most striking achievements. But budget-conscious congressmen who knew the Ives report must henceforth wonder why they should put more dollars into studying so "profitless" a place.

One other official government exploration preceded Powell's request for support, this one led in 1859 by another Army engineer, Captain J.N. Macomb, and including geologist Newberry again. They angled northwest from Santa Fe, following the Old Spanish Trail into Utah, searching for the junction of the Grand and Green Rivers. Though they did manage to see that point of confluence, from a distance, they did not attempt to penetrate the impassable terrain before them or follow the Colorado on its way south from there. Instead, they retraced their route over the sagebrush plains, Macomb complaining, "I cannot conceive of a more worthless and impracticable region than the one we now found ourselves in."[30] Newberry was happy once more to make field sketches and take notes on the massive red and brown Triassic sandstones, the first geological analysis attempted of this country, but his studies had to be brief.

Now, nearly a decade later, Congress had simply to decide whether they would furnish a little free food for the one-armed man from Illinois who proposed to navigate the unknown Colorado from its upper waters down to the point where published knowledge began. On a slow day in May, lacking larger matters on the agenda, the senators debated what John Sherman of Ohio, the main opponent of the resolution, referred to as "a foray on the subsistence department." Lyman Trumbull of Illinois took up Powell's cause, though he was neither quite sure where the Colorado River actually was nor what academic position Powell held in his state. A more effective advocate was John Conness of California, who acknowledged how difficult it was "for gentlemen who live in the East to understand or sufficiently estimate the extent of the West, and the extent of that West belonging to their own country which is not yet understood." Powell, like other explorers before him, promised to "bring that great country forward," to open its blank spaces for settlement, and ultimately to bring "the populous regions of the West and the capital with the West in connection with the great unknown West and make them one." Convinced by the argument, the Senate amended the resolution to put limits on the amount of rations that Powell could draw and then on 11 June passed it twenty-five to seven, most of the nays coming from the northeastern part of the country. The House had already approved. Powell had his meal ticket to study the whole river, and thus to study the last (nearly) unexplored space in the West.

A small discordant claim to priority slipped into the Senate deliberations. Senator Sherman, denying that no "civilized man" had ever seen the six or seven hundred miles above Ives's encampment at the mouth of Diamond Creek, declared that the river "was run recently, during the last fall, I believe, by three men to escape the Indians, and one of them got through alive." Is that claim authenticated, asked Senator Trumbull, who was surprised by the news. "The man lives," answered Sherman; he went in one end of the Grand Canyon and "came through at the other." The debate shifted away before giving that man a name, but he was James White, a tenderfoot prospector then living in Callville, Nevada, claiming to be the first man ever to run the Canyon.

On 8 September 1867, the Mormon residents of Callville spied a wreck of a human being floating offshore in the Colorado on a raft of logs roped together. He was nearly naked, and sun, water, and lack of food had left him bruised, burned, and emaciated. His reason was so nearly gone that it took weeks to bring him around to tell his story. In a personal letter to a brother in Wisconsin, oddly given a title, "Navigation of the Big Canon A Terrible Voyage," White claimed that he had been prospecting for gold with a Captain Baker and a George Strole (or Stroll) in the San Juan Mountains of southwestern Colorado and into Utah. A band of fifteen to twenty Ute Indians attacked them, killing Baker. White and Strole fled a short distance to the San Juan River, where they made a two-foot-wide raft of cottonwood logs and launched into the current, eventually floating into the Colorado. The fourth day Strole washed overboard and drowned. White continued on alone, encountering Indians who took his pistols in exchange for a piece of dog meat, his only food during the voyage besides a few mesquite beans. Two weeks on the river, and he arrived at Callville.

"[I] see the hardes time that eny man ever did in the World," he wrote home, "but thank god that i got thrught saft."[31]

Was any of it true? The locals believed him, and so did a California newspaper that quickly published his story. So too did Dr. C.C. Parry, a botanist in the survey party organized by General William J. Palmer to find a route extending the Kansas Pacific railroad to the Pacific Ocean. Parry interviewed a recovered White in Callville and calculated that he must have floated on his raft for 550 miles, a journey, Parry concluded, that might safely be made by anyone in a good boat with waterproof supplies. Parry added that "there is not the least reason to doubt that he actually accomplished the journey in the manner and in the time mentioned by him."[32] So also believed Parry's boss, General Palmer, though he did not interview White himself, and so also a British traveler, Dr. William A. Bell, who published a version of the story in his *New Tracks in North America* (1869). All agreed that White, who did not appear to be a self-promoter but was a quiet, modest fellow, somewhat embarrassed by the attention he was getting, had no motive to lie.

For decades almost everyone who came to know the river first-hand doubted White's story. They could not see how anyone could successfully ride a makeshift raft through so many canyons, many of them filled with pounding rapids, cataracts, and falls, nor did they find the descriptions White gave of the geography at all convincing. He placed the Little Colorado on his right rather than left hand, as he was coming down, and he was astonishingly wrong about the height of canyon walls, the color of rock, and the absence of rough water. His most determined critic, Robert Stanton, who came to know the river as well as anyone after Powell, pursued White to his last place of residence, Trinidad, Colorado, and after interviewing him in 1907, decided that the old man had actually floated only sixty miles, from Grand Wash to Callville, points well downstream from the Grand Canyon itself.[33] His rescuers and supporters had led White to assume, through their leading questions, that he had achieved the miraculous. Someone may even have helped write his letter home, suspected Stanton; the spelling seems an incongruous mix of good and bad.

There are alternative explanations. White's prospecting party was a tough, violent bunch that had commenced their quest by stealing horses from Indians in western Kansas. White and another man had fallen into a quarrel over whose horse should carry their bread supply, and according to the interview with Stanton they traded five shots over the dispute, which left White's opponent wounded and unable to travel.[34] White blamed a band of Indians for attacking them, but the number was reduced over the years to one — a single murderous savage who shot Baker through the heart for unexplained reasons. Might it have been that White lost his temper over a trivial matter, as he had done before, and killed one or both of his partners, then made up a harrowing story to divert attention?

Whatever happened to his companions, it seems plausible that White indeed came down the Colorado — more plausible at least than that he made his way overland from the San Juan River to Grand Wash Cliffs. The most direct route by land was well over two hundred miles long, across Indian lands and wide, waterless expanses of rabbit brush and sage, thick low jungles of pinyon and juniper, across the deep canyon of the Little Colorado, not to mention many smaller ravines — and all without maps or knowledge of the country. Surely he would have remembered such an ordeal; it would have been seared on his brain as hotly as any perilous canyon voyage. But he did not remember that route because he did not go that way. He went by water, clinging to his so-called "raft," which was nothing more than a few logs tied together — clinging like a bug to the wood, half in and half out of the chocolate-colored river, again and again pushing himself out of back eddies into the current, getting knocked about to the point where he could stand erect no longer, arriving nearly dead. If it seems improbable, all other explanations are more improbable still.

Many of White's sympathetic believers, including the good senator from Ohio, wanted to think that the Colorado River was an easier force to conquer than it really was — that it was more like eastern rivers. Any good oarsmen could run it. Yet for thousands of years the Indians had not really learned to navigate the long river, except for making crossings here and there in bullboats, nor for hundreds of years had the Europeans succeeded in penetrating its long, central stretch. There was nothing easy about it.

Undeniably, Powell wanted to be the first man to claim victory over a river that others had called unconquerable. He wanted to be the "discoverer" of this place, and he could not accept that somebody else, by accident, had achieved what he was setting out to do by careful planning. James White denied him that pristine achievement. But Powell need not have been so defensive. White had not brought out any reliable knowledge of where he had been or what the country looked like. He was no explorer. In particular the middle stretch of the Colorado, some five hundred miles long by water, remained virtually unknown and unmapped in 1868. To change that condition would be Powell's achievement—not to be the first to make it through the Canyon alive but the first to make it through with intention and understanding. Now that he had secured congressional patronage, he was ready to attempt the heroic: to take full, systematic possession of this last, hidden West.

Major Powell's second western expedition left the Chicago railroad station on 29 June 1868, just three weeks after Congress granted him a supply of rations. There was some ambiguity about the company's proper name; the newspapers called it the "Rocky Mountain Exploring Expedition," while a banner draped on the side of their car read "Colorado River Exploring Expedition." Powell himself was clear about their larger purpose but not about how far they would get that summer.

His party was larger in number this time but as green as before. He and Emma were the only carryovers from the first expedition; everybody else was a new recruit, filled with anxious excitement and plenty of questions. Among them was Walter Powell, still recovering from his prisoner-of-war ordeal—moody, often melancholic, given to violent outbursts. The list of college students going this time included Lewis Keplinger, a war veteran at Illinois Wesleyan who would become a Kansas City judge; Rhodes Allen, Edmund Poston, and Lyle Durley, all also enrolled at Wesleyan; and Samuel Garman, a Quaker undergraduate at Normal who one day would join the science faculty at Harvard. Henry Wing, a physician who sat on the State Board of Education, was included in the party, along with Dr. George Vasey of Bloomington, who in a few years would be appointed botanist to the Department of Agriculture. Then there were a trio of Protestant ministers: the Reverends W.H. Daniels, J.W. Healy, and W.C. Wood, of various denominational affiliations. Twenty-one expeditioners in all, nearly twice as many as went on the first trip, none of them "civil engineers," as promised, some of them familiar with science, some not.[35]

Powell recruited so many hands because he had to. He needed an army of laborers to collect all those museum specimens he had promised to no fewer than sixty-seven schools and colleges in the state. Everybody, it seemed, wanted to get their stuffed magpie or rattlesnake, and some expected nothing less than their own grizzly pelt. Acquiring museum specimens was the popular notion of science. Illinoisians were less interested in opening a passage to the Colorado River than in getting exhibit material for their hometown edification.

Powell, already the shrewd, accommodating politician, understood the needs of his supporters well and knew he had to satisfy them first in order to achieve his larger dream. But he suffered many headaches from his expedition's large size, its general inexperience, and in some cases its whininess.

Chief among the whiners was the good Reverend Wood, a Presbyterian from Joliet with a Yale degree. How he joined the party illuminates Powell's often hasty, haphazard style of management under the pressures of time and circumstance. Wood had been suffering from a chronic sore throat; one doctor advised him to take up smoking, which was against his moral principles, but another recommended a trip to Colorado, which was not. He brought along his thirteen-year-old son Henry for an interview at Prof. Powell's office in Bloomington. Emma met them first and took a liking to the son, so much so that she intervened with the boss to get him added to the party. She was "a charming active little woman," Henry remembered, and they got on famously ever after. Powell accepted the father and son, but let the minister know that it would cost him $325 for equipment, freight, mess kit, and two pack mules. In other words, he would be expected to work hard and help pay for the collecting of all those specimens. Wood agreed, but really what he wanted was a holiday in the mountains. Over the coming summer he parted company with the expedition, as did a few others whose notion of exploration did not mesh well with the Major's.

Exhilarated, they rode the new iron rails across the interminable plains, passing the now defunct stagecoach stations and eating houses that only a year ago had catered to the covered-wagon traffic. Whenever a large wild animal came into view, every man was at the window firing madly through the smoke and cinders streaming back from the locomotive. The sport was encouraged by the crew; if passengers killed a pronghorn or bison, the engineer offered to stop the train. He did not have to do so. Young Henry, packing a large Colt and a muzzle-loading shotgun, was sent to the baggage car for the safety of the other passengers. Now the prairies offered only a little sport and amusement where they had once threatened danger from roving Indian parties.

They arrived at Cheyenne on 2 July and descended from the train among the dregs of humanity, the leftovers from the very recent past when the town had been "Hell on Wheels," a violent, tumultuous staging site for constructing the railroad. The bars were still there, and so were the squalid little whorehouses where the out-of-tune pianos played and the lights burned all night. Wood wrote in his diary that vice was reportedly worse farther down the line toward Laramie, but "here its bad enough." Dr. Vasey promptly went back home to Illinois, deciding that he had better work to do as interim curator of the museum. The rest billeted down near the station until they were ready to move a few miles out of town to a quieter, less profane setting. A party of Christian desperadoes, they wanted to look tough in their big hats, neckerchiefs, and fringed leggings but still keep their language clean and their bodies pure.

The problem of getting some horses that could take them to Denver, a hundred miles south of the railway, forced a delay of several days. Fortuitously, several drovers arrived from California with a herd of Mexican ponies to sell, and the Illinois naturalists went to look them over. "From this tramping, seething, wild mass of horseflesh," noted Wood, "we were to select our animals for the Expedition, to be broken on the spot and ridden back to camp, each man on his own."[36] The expeditioner was supposed to point at a horse that looked potentially docile, and the drovers threw a lasso over its head, jerked it off its feet, thrashed it all over with the rope, stomped on its mouth until it calmed down enough to take a bridle and saddle—and then invited the new owner to climb aboard. All day on the Fourth of July the party tried breaking their purchases to ride. Most of them were bucked off a few times, but the worst part was that the stock kept running away and had to be chased.

After subduing the animals, they started at last for Denver, passing through what the Reverend Daniels called "the Great American Desert," an area "comparatively uninhabited and uninhabitable." Yet, he admitted, "the country is not worthless. It is destined to be the great pasture of the nation." (At least that part of the Gilpin vision was getting through.) They had expected big game to shoot along their route, but "with the exception of a few antelopes, a single prairie wolf [coyote?], and an elk, no wild animals have been seen."[37] Though the plains were alive with wildflowers and birds, which they dutifully collected, like most travelers before and after them they had eyes mainly for the romantic peaks to the west, beckoning them to green forests and high mountain lakes.

The newly acquired ponies stampeded along the way, and Powell had to stay behind to round up the missing stock while the rest of the party continued on at a slow, plodding pace. Toward evening a stock detective came into their camp and seized one of the horses, which was bearing a United States government brand (rustled, he charged), and took it back to Cheyenne. When Powell pulled in, he found that he had to go back along the trail after the detective and try to get the animal returned; they had none to spare. He succeeded by showing a bill of sale, but by that point his weary expeditioners were getting cranky and impatient. When Powell rejoined the group, Emma insisted that the two of them catch a stagecoach to Denver, ostensibly to advance their preparations there, but it was beginning to look to the rest like their leader was more concerned about himself, wife, and grand design than about his men.

Those left behind on the trail felt abandoned; they groused and dragged along. Divided into four army-style "messes," they rotated the chores of night guarding, cooking, and dish washing. Their inexperienced preparation of rations over a fire of buffalo chips left much to be desired. One of the boys stopped at a little adobe store and bought canned peaches and crackers, which he passed around like manna from home. The water they found was usually alkaline; one after another they fell sick. Or they nursed a bruised leg from falling off the horses or pulled cactus thorns out of tender flesh. Then it rained, then it hailed. Their commander had turned down the suggestion that they carry along tents, so they were sleeping out with all the elements. Wood began to complain that this was not what he had expected: "I find there are quite a number in the Expedition who are here for the same purpose as myself, health. . . . On the whole [we are] somewhat scattered and demoralized . . . [by] this filthy ill arranged way of traveling. . . . My voice seems affected by the least dampness. The cooking I abominate mostly because of our limited knowledge and facilities. Its greasy, filthy work so that we live more like pigs than human beings."[38]

A particular bone of contention with the Major was keeping the Sabbath day holy. Powell believed in always pressing on, treating Sundays like any another, but the religious men in the party were scandalized by such behavior. They insisted on stopping over on Sundays, doing no work of any kind (well, they argued over what was permissible and what was not), and holding ecumenical services, under the open sky if need be. Reverend Daniels assumed much of the preaching, and his congregation sang psalms to lift their spirits and reviewed their moral responsibilities to the expedition.

But by 14 July hopes were brightening. They had finally reached Denver and were supposed to move quickly up Clear Creek Canyon and into Middle Park, where the trout were biting and the air was piney. The *Denver News* greeted their arrival and explained Powell's program: what was left of the summer would be spent on figuring out the topography and hydrography of the Grand River, and possibly the Green. Then next spring or summer, "the railroad meanwhile having reached Green river, new supplies and boats will be obtained thence and the great canon of the Colorado will be descended and explored. The professor contemplates thorough work, even if it takes two or three years."[39] That was what Powell had in focus, not Sabbath rituals or creature comforts or the medical ailments of his party. He listened to their complaints, he was always cheerful and optimistic, but he was distracted from their woes by the grander picture he had formed in his imagination.

Denver had a distinguished visitor when the expeditioners arrived. The country's next president, General Ulysses Grant, was staying at the American Hotel, hoping to win the territorial vote in November, small though it might be, for his Republican ticket. Puffing on the ever-present cigar, Grant took a coach to Central City to meet with miners, and the expeditioners came along in his wake, heading for the summit of Berthoud Pass. Filling his journal with gauzy effusions, Reverend Daniels described the shadowed ravines through which they climbed, the plains below them stretching away like a cloud, the dark purplish polish of the cliff faces. "We all tonight," he wrote, "feel inspired by what we have seen, and more, perhaps, but by what we expect to see — a free, let-loose, grand, indefinite sort of feeling. The scenes today have passed before me like a panorama and left more of an impression than a picture. I feel as if I had had a sublime dream and kept the sublime feeling though I couldn't for the life of me recall what I had seen."[40]

The expeditioners spent a week and a half at Berthoud Pass, elevation over eleven thousand feet, slaughtering the wildlife wholesale. They picked bunches of wildflowers — alpine forget-me-not, purple fringe, saxifrage, moss campion, blue columbine, shootingstar, parry primrose, western fringed gentian — for their sponsors. Keplinger improved the time by taking hourly barometric observations, going without sleep most of the period; on his birthday, he sat through a furious six-hour snowstorm to get his readings. The newspaper editor Byers showed up, after seeing Grant off to Denver, and brought his wife and two children into their now happy camp, who amused the expeditioners with summer snowball fights. They all had to marvel over the fact that they were standing on the continent's divide where melting snow flowed either into the Gulf of Mexico or the Gulf of California.

The demands of high-altitude science fulfilled, they followed the water running west, plunging down into the broad vale of Middle Park, the Byers family with them. Keplinger described the scene where they camped for several weeks:

> The park is an elevated depression surrounded by mts 25 [miles] long & from 6 to ten wide we are now camped on the Grand river at the Hot Springs The Grand River is the most beautiful river I ever saw just barely small enough to be fordable & just as clear as it is possible for water to be & full of the finest trout we have more than we know what to do with Raspberries & Gooseberries & Utah Indians in proportion the[y] are friendly, entirely to friendly begging & Stealing. The Hot Springs are something new to me the water is actually hot & a large enough stream for a good sized creek. Just as I rode up to day Maj. met me said he was just waiting for me to come up, that we were to start (four of us) to go to Longs Peak 50 miles distant to attempt to ascend it. I at once washed my clothes in that Hot Springs (The last they are likely to get soon & wrote two letters & it is now dark Tomorrow morning we start for the Peak & nothing pleases me better I never felt abler to climb mts in my life The party are all in the highest spirits & best of health extraordinary appetite an[d] an abundance to eat.[41]

All their trials and discomforts, their perfidious treatment in getting to this paradise, were forgotten. Even Reverend Wood, now camping with son Henry apart from the rest of the expedition, was delighted with everything he saw and was pulling in fifty trout a day.

The Grand River comes out of Grand Lake, which lies on the western side of Long's Peak, a mountain that had not yet been climbed for the record. A first climb would add little to scientific knowledge, but it was an irresistible challenge and the symbolic point of origin for the Colorado River. On 20 August a small group of expeditioners — the Powell brothers, Keplinger, and Samuel Garman — along with Byers and two local residents, Jack Sumner and Ned Farrell, set out for the summit, each mounted and each leading a pack mule laden with ten days' rations. They had bedding tied behind their saddles, pistols strapped around their waists, rifles and scientific instruments secured on the mules. Sumner, the grizzled twenty-eight-year-old trader whom Powell had met the previous fall, had accompanied them over Berthoud Pass; Farrell was also reputed to be experienced in mountain survival. The group blazed a rough, torturous, and lengthy path up the mountain, one that has seldom been used since. Two days out, they stopped overnight at the base of Mount McHenry (near present-day Powell Peak), making a corral for the horses, and the next morning they proceeded afoot, leaving guns and blankets behind, carrying only a little bacon and biscuit in their pockets.

Swinging around to the south, they could see Long's jutting above them but could not find the way up. Sumner led them along a narrow ridge. Then he sat down, refusing to go any further and declaring, "By God, I haven't lost any mountain." Keplinger passed him, estimating the ridge to be no more than eighteen inches wide at that point. "After seeing me pass [Sumner] said he could he go anywhere I could, and he did, but he got down and 'cooned' it."[42] Unfortunately the ridge did not connect with Long's, so they retreated and overnighted at timberline near Sandbeach Lake. Keplinger, his competitive juices now flowing, went out to find another route, made it to within eight hundred feet of the summit, but lost his nerve to go on. Trembling all over, he could see Estes Park far below but none of his party. Worried about losing him, the rest kindled beacon fires and hallooed, until about ten o'clock they heard him coming into camp. "The night," Byers wrote for his paper, "was a most cheerless one, with gusts of wind and sprinkles of rain; our only shelter under the sides of an immense boulder, where we shivered the long hours through."[43] When dawn came, they followed Keplinger back the way he had found, and at mid-morning they reached the summit.

To the south they could see Pike's Peak and the Denver area, to the north the Medicine Bow mountains, and to the west the Gore range and the Grand flowing toward the main-stem Colorado. To mark their triumph, they put their names with the date, 23 August, in a baking powder can. One of them pulled out a biscuit that their commander had made—hard as a rock, "the kind which when cut with a sharp knife would show a fine-grained, smooth, dark-colored surface"—and stuck it in "as an everlasting memento of Major Powell's skill in bread making." The Major was not amused by their antics and told them to take it out. Then he bared his head and made a solemn speech: "We had now accomplished [he intoned] an undertaking in the material or physical field which had hitherto been deemed impossible, but . . . there were mountains more formidable in other fields of effort which were before us."[44] They finished the ceremony by raising a flag and throwing wine on their little monument. Garman, a Quaker, noted that "the little that remained in the bottle was drank by 5 of the party. 2 of us withstanding all entreaties did not drink on Longs Peak, whatever the papers may say to the contrary."[45]

Keplinger and Garman stayed on nearby Mount McHenry for over a week, taking barometric readings and botanizing, while the rest headed back to Middle Park. Garman wrote to his female friend about the mosses and lichens he found: "We exulted just a little in the thought that here if any where on the footstool were things just as God had made them."[46] Down below, however, things were turning decidedly less idyllic. Once more, the vaunted Eden seemed threatened by dangerous Indian uprisings.

Over a hundred white people had suddenly materialized around Hot Sulphur Springs, gathering for protection against what they feared was an imminent attack from raiding Plains tribes. The Utes, whose tipis had greeted the expedition's eyes when they first arrived, had abruptly departed for South Park where they ran against a party of Arapahos and Cheyennes, their enemies, and lost to them in battle. The raiders had killed a few whites too, burned ranches, and driven off livestock that spring and summer. Several days after the Long's Peak ascent, word came that the mutilated bodies of a white woman and her son had been brought into Denver, stirring up cries of vengeance and exaggerated rumors about the numbers of Americans that had been killed. The whole region seemed in flame.

Among the white folks huddled near the thermal springs was fourteen-year-old Emma Shepard, daughter of a judge, along with her mother and siblings. In her diary she wrote that Major Powell came down from the mountain to take charge of them in the crisis. He barricaded the females, including his wife, Emma, in Sumner's trading post and put his men to work until nearly midnight digging rifle pits on the hillside behind the cabin. Very early the next morning, as they were waiting tensely for a barrage of arrows, a dog began to bark, and Powell sent a man down to the river to see if enemy Indians had arrived — but none were there. A few hours later, while it was still dark, the girl's father and a friend came riding up to the cabin, telling them that there were no Indians anywhere, that the scare was over.[47]

Elsewhere, General Philip Sheridan was chasing the Indian recalcitrants all over the plains, and in late November General Custer attacked and defeated the Cheyennes on the Washita River in Oklahoma, a victory that the Sioux avenged less than eight years later on the Little Big Horn. But in Middle Park there was really nothing violent to see or fear.

Although the Utes had remained friendly toward the whites, seeking them as allies in their tribal wars, they met mostly with amused contempt. The Powell party was no exception. Generally, except for Powell himself, they treated the native people of the park as unwanted nuisances. Durley, who had been left to tend camp while others went climbing, found them "most awful sassy" and knocked one of them down for his poor manners. "Us fellows," he wrote, "felt considerable easier [when] Ed Douglass and Anteroe [two Ute leaders], with bands moved camp today."[48] Rhodes Allen, also left behind to collect birds, described the Utes as "the most decent & intelligent looking Indians I have seen although they are not by any means beautiful or neat. Their dress is various, no two being dress alike either in style or material, & none have a complete sute. . . . They live nearly entirely on meat, only getting what little bread they can beg of the few whites that travel through this country."[49]

Powell had put some of the expeditioners to work assembling a Ute vocabulary, but, as Garman wrote, "'tis most stupid work these children of the mountains have little or no idea of the eternal fitness of things and 'Heap lie' and 'Heap steal' as if being the laziest creatures of God's make wasn't enough to fit them for the influence of the missionary or the civilizing hand of the white. While they have enough to eat & can keep moderately warm they are perfectly happy & 'want but little here below'. Some of the boys are disgusted with them almost beyond endurance."[50]

When Byers took control over the hot springs in 1861, he had ignored the Utes's long-standing use of them for bathing and for healing their sick horses. He simply took possession under federal land laws with the idea of turning the springs into a profitable spa, located on the 160-acre homestead he was also claiming and developing. The setting for his estate was auspiciously lovely. The springs erupted out of the hillside north of the Grand River, ran into a large pool and then streamed down to the river, edged with willows and cottonwoods, where the water was icy cold. Byers had a shed constructed over the thermal pool for his customers. In doing so he was only extending an appropriation that earlier had been made by a succession of white trappers, including Bill Williams, Jim Bridger, and Kit Carson. Tourists began to show up that same summer the Powell expedition did, appropriating the Indian resources for their purposes too.[51]

Soon after the Arapaho scare, Powell met at the springs no less a dignitary than General Grant's running mate, Schuyler Colfax, traveling with the governors of Illinois and Colorado and the Massachusetts journalist Samuel Bowles. They were there to talk with the local Indians, gather beautiful agates, and do a little fishing and bathing. Bowles, in his book *The Switzerland of America*, recounted meeting with "the Professor" and his "enthusiastic young men." "He is every way the soul, as he is the purse of the expedition," Bowles wrote. "He leads the way in all danger and difficulty, and his wife, a true help-meet, and the only woman with the party, is the first to follow." Powell made a strong impression with his plans to stay the winter on the Green River and then to explore "the grand canyon of the world, and one of its most wonderful marvels."[52]

Bowles marveled at how little was known of the land that lay beyond Colorado's mountains, despite decades of travel and exploration, and how well prepared Powell seemed to be to reveal that country.

> Is any other nation so ignorant of itself? All that we do know goes
> to show that, beginning with the union of the Grand and the
> Green Rivers, the Colorado is confined for three hundred miles
> within perpendicular walls of rock averaging three thousand feet
> high, up which no one can climb, down which no one can safely
> go, and between which in the river, rapids and falls and furious
> eddies render passage frightful, certainly dangerous, possibly
> impossible. . . . The general conviction of the border population is
> that whoever dares venture into this canyon will never come out
> alive. . . . The whole field of observation and inquiry which
> Professor Powell has undertaken is more interesting and
> important than any which lies before our men of science. The
> wonder is they have neglected it so long. Here are seen the central
> forces that formed the Continent; here more striking studies in
> physical geography, geology, and natural history, than are
> proferred anywhere else. New knowledge and wide honors await
> those who catalogue and define them. I can but think the inquiry,
> vast and important as it is, is fortunate in its inquirer.[53]

Bowles was about as good a publicity agent as a man could want, and Powell had forcibly impressed on him and his companions the great work of exploration he was preparing to do. He struck them as a man without fear or misgiving. He seemed filled with a sense of mission whose significance he fully grasped. And now as Bowles, Colfax, and the others left for the East and the national election campaign, now as the Colorado highlands were turning frosty and golden, it was time for the Powell expedition to be moving on to establish a more long-term encampment, closer to the edge of the unknown.

The trail out of Middle Park ran down Cedar Canyon, then climbed out of the valley of the Grand and over Gore Pass, named after an eccentric big-game hunter from Ireland. Countless Indians had taken it, but the frontier scout Jim Bridger was the first white man to follow that route into western Colorado. In the summer of 1861 he had led a Swiss-born engineer, Edward Berthoud, over the trail in search of a wagon road to carry mail between Denver and Salt Lake City. Powell had a copy of the map produced by that search, and he had hopes that the fading traces of wagons that had passed over Berthoud's trail would be legible enough to follow. His guidepost was Painted Rock, 125 miles west, beyond which he would find a winter-ing-over site on the White River, perhaps where it joined the Green in Utah. Little did he realize how rough the road would get.

On 7 September Powell directed brother Walter to start their pack train down the trail. The advance guard were to be the "ornitholo-gists"—all Wesleyan students, either skipping the fall semester or as recent graduates free to go on with the adventure. With them went two young trappers, Gus Lankin and Bill Rhodes (a.k.a. Billy Hawkins or "Missouri"), both of them looking mighty tough, the latter ru-mored to be a fugitive from the law, though he would later figure in Powell's Colorado River trip. Wes and Emma stayed behind to finish up the work in Middle Park, promising to follow with the "botanists" in a few weeks. The ministers returned to Illinois filled with fish and renewed benevolence.

For the lads forging ahead on the Berthoud trail, the summer idyll quickly turned into a dispiriting ordeal of bone-chilling mornings, constant rain showers, and pummeling hailstorms. Worse, they had trouble finding and staying on the trail. On the other side of Gore Pass it turned north toward the junction of the Upper Bear and Yampa Rivers, followed the Yampa (then called the Bear) as it flowed north and straightened west, cut over a divide into the headwaters of the White River and came down the long slope of the White to the Green. Easy to mark on paper, hard to follow on the ground. The most thorough account of their gropings is the diary of Rhodes Allen, one of the youngest of the students, who complained that they were traveling "over the worst country I ever saw," a bewildering maze of thick sagebrush, willows, quaking aspens, pines, and scrub oaks. The impressive Keplinger, skilled in scientific instruments, helped get them back on trail by taking a fix on the star Scorpio, but they were soon lost again.[54]

On the 12th, when they were camped somewhere in the upper reaches of the Yampa, they awoke to find that Lankin had cleared out, taking two of the animals and a large share of the food. His sidekick, Hawkins, remembered that Lankin had a cache of steel traps not far away, and the lads went out to track the thief down. Lankin was watching for them and opened fire when they came into sight, nearly hitting one of them. The lads flew pell-mell back into camp for reinforcements. A well-armed posse went out to capture Lankin, but they too failed and returned to camp. Rain started falling in the night, the water running into their tent and soaking their bedding. A wolf dragged off some of their bacon and chewed one of the saddles. Running low on food, Walter decided to send Woodward, Durley, Bishop, and Hawkins with the mules back to Middle Park for more supplies. The rest of the party hunkered down to wait, weary of fighting their way forward. For the next two weeks they waited, doing a little bird shooting for food and specimens but mainly enduring the cold and the boredom. "I did nothing today," wrote Allen, "& the other boys helped me." Discouraged, he was "ready to go home at any time."[55]

Meanwhile, Powell was not through mountain climbing. By this point he had climbed nine of the higher peaks in the Rockies, and his tenth was the highest one in the Eagle range south of the Grand — a peak over thirteen thousand feet high that he would name Mount Powell. On the morning of 22 September he set out, along with an editor and printer for the *Rocky Mountain News* named Oramel Howland and a veteran of the Long's Peak climb, Ned Farrell. After dining on elk and mountain grouse, they fell asleep on fresh-cut boughs stuffed under their blankets. On the fourth day they reached a dangerous zone of ice and snow, and Farrell tried to convince the Major that it was useless to proceed, particularly in view of his disability. But Powell did not give up. By three P.M. they had gained the top — and gained a view far surpassing any they had seen so far, with the dappled green and gold valley of the Grand far below, a bird's-eye view of how the western rivers were produced.

Farrell, in reporting the climb for the *Chicago Tribune*, could not restrain his admiration for Powell's tenacity and courage. In the spectacle of Mount Powell and Mount Lincoln facing each other like twin sentinels on the continental divide, he found "worthy monuments of men who have devoted their lives to the service of their country."

Powell had given his arm, Lincoln his life "in the same glorious contest for freedom, and while the one has been called away and the other spared, the record he has left is a sufficient guarantee that he will never dishonor the name given to the companion mountain of that which will remain for all time our national monument to our martyred Lincoln."[56] Contorted syntax it may have been, but the honor Farrell intended was clear enough; Powell, in his gutsy assault on the peak, had made a powerful impression as a man destined for heroic achievement.

The lads, meanwhile, still waited patiently for their leader on another mountainside farther west. At last on 6 October the Major, Emma, Farrell, and Hawkins came riding into their camp, with the pack train laboring along somewhere behind them, bringing a double load of food and other supplies. Powell also brought them a revised plan. He had given up on the idea of spending the winter on the Green and instead had chosen a more salubrious spot on the White River, where there was little snow in the winter, where the game was abundant. Other humans would be there too — several bands of the familiar Ute Indians, the Yampa and the Grand River bands. Earlier in the year the government had granted them the western half of Colorado for a reservation, and a federal agency dispensing annuities would soon be set up in the grassy bottom lands of the White River. Here the Powell expedition decided to establish a base until they were ready to confront the Colorado River in the spring.

The reunited party, well fed on pronghorn steak, bread, and coffee and in high spirits once more, now went looking for the White River. They had left one of their number behind, however, and he was going through his own private hell. Young Bishop, a student from an Illinois farm who had become their pack train specialist, had been sent by Powell back to Empire to mail home an updated report. By the time Bishop returned to Middle Park, the place was deserted. He followed the now well-trodden trail over Gore Pass but then was seriously confused. On a tree at the full party's last encampment he found pinned a paper note by Keplinger: "We have moved camp to a point on White River, 50 miles distant. General directions South of West. You will find provisions cached in the rocks 20 steps North. Come along as fast you can." The White River? Bishop assumed it must be the one before him, and he rode his mule briskly along an Indian path on its banks. Unfortunately, he was on the Bear (Yampa), not the White, and he was heading in the wrong direction.[57]

A two-foot fall of snow blocked his way, and he snuggled down by a fire to think his way through his predicament. It dawned on him that something was wrong with his calculations. Going back to the paper note, he struck off in a new direction, looking for traces of his friends' passage among the high sagebrush — a trail of broken twigs, for the ground was covered with snow. His situation was desperate, but he kept on moving, clinging to his tired mule for companionship. He was nearly out of grub, for ravens had pillaged the cached provisions, and had to live on what he could shoot — sage hens, jack rabbits, and a single pronghorn brought down by a lucky shot of over a hundred yards. He shot a mother grizzly too, her cubs scattering into the brush, and skinned it in hopes of winning a pair of five-dollar top boots promised by the Major to the first one to kill a bear. Jack the mule, however, refused to carry the hide, bucking and kicking and tearing it off with his teeth, and it had to be left behind.

Thirty-three days out from the Springs, a month alone in the wilderness, Bishop at last found his party on the White River. During his long trek he "had not seen a living soul, white man or red." The country belonged to the Utes, but he did not meet any of those owners. Interviewed at his home in San Diego in 1917, he remembered that the worst of the experience had been "the uncertainty and the lonesomeness. . . . You can imagine that the camp boys looked pretty good to me." But what chagrin when he found Walter Powell walking about the camp in that pair of prize boots, a fresh bearskin hanging in his tent.

The spot they chose for winter quarters lies where the White enters into a broad valley, now called Powell Bottoms or Powell Park, a few miles west of the modern town of Meeker, Colorado.[58] Clumps of cottonwood, a wide stream purling through, mountains rising to the north and south, white teepees and Indian ponies nearby all formed an Albert Bierstadt painting that said unspoiled country. To get ready for winter, they cut oak limbs for hay forks and shocked the bottom land grasses for their stock. They built log cabins with stone fireplaces. Emma, the lone woman in the party, made a home with Wes in one of them, the rest of the men and boys bedded down in the others, all forming her winter-long community. Here in this remote valley, Farrell explained in another newspaper dispatch, they intended to live in the coming months "away from politics, from wine and women, from miserly landlords and dingy boarding houses; away from neighborhood gossips, Christmas parties, elopements and divorce courts; away from all these, but worse than all, away from home and friends."[59] Thus isolated, they concentrated on assuring their physical survival and on adding still more to the fund of human knowledge.

Now that the cabins were built it was time for several in the party to take their leave. On 2 November Powell set off for Green River Station, due north of their winter quarters, with the idea of seeing them back to Illinois via the Union Pacific Railroad. The doctors Wing and Vasey, who had been in and out of the expedition were among those leaving, along with the students Akin, Poston, Durley, Taylor, and Allen. Keplinger and Woodward preferred to retrace their path to Denver through Hot Sulphur Springs. Their departure left Emma and Walter, Sam Garman, and the mountaineers Jack Sumner and Bill Dunn behind in the cabins, waiting the return of Powell, Howland, and Farrell.

The trek north to the railroad took nine days on horseback, averaging fifteen miles or so a day.[60] As the sky turned cold and cloudy, they crossed the rough divide between the White and Yampa rivers and dry, sandy gulches where any pool of water was likely to be unfit to drink. A few days out and they began to suffer from thirst. Allen spread the rubber blankets from his bed to catch a rain that seemed to be brewing, but he got only a teacup full, which he shared with two of the others. They fared better on finding meat: a herd of wild cattle, strays meant for the railroad camps, came along, and they killed one of them for roasting.

Then at last, striking a wagon road that led them past log cabins occupied by wood cutters, they approached Green River Station. Allen could hear the locomotive whistling from his last night's campsite in the bush. Arriving in the town, the lads sold their mules for $100 apiece (all except Allen, who had to take the $25 offered by the Major for his used-up animal) and then went off to visit the dance hall. At twelve noon on 15 November they took seats in the railroad cars, bound for Cheyenne and Illinois. Their summer and fall in the Rockies would be one of the lasting memories of their lives: an initiation into a West of men who shot to kill, of terrain that was often unmarked by any roads, often not even a trail, of Indian parties and rumors of massacres all around, of bull elks bugling in the early autumn mornings, of the sound of mountain brooks in a high meadow.

What was left of the Powell exploring expedition turned around to go back to White River, and as they rode the Major thought long and hard about the challenge of the coming spring, when they would revisit the railroad town. All along he had been collecting every scrap of information he could about the territory ahead. He had studied the work of army engineers, their maps and descriptions, and had gathered data from Mormons, Indians, and frontiersmen of all sorts.

In late January the still-present Bishop, turning down an offer from Powell to join his river crew (being lost once, he was not eager for more), left for Fort Bridger and his own railroad trip home. Powell was not discouraged by the dwindling size of his party; he penned an upbeat letter to President Richard Edwards of Illinois Normal, describing their layover months as an elysian interlude. "We have found the winter so very mild," he wrote, the most delightful he had ever experienced.[61] Little precipitation had fallen in the valley, but the distant mountains glistened with snow, and the game reliably came down to the river to drink. The stock had fared well on the hay they had cut. The party was in good health. Sumner and the other hunters had brought in plenty of food, and piled up many wolf, fox, mountain sheep, deer, and antelope skins to dress. Emma had practiced her taxidermy skills on 175 birds, and Powell had busied himself collecting rocks and fossils along the valleys, mesas, and hillsides nearby.

Mainly, though, Powell had spent days and nights in the adjacent camp of the Utes, making a vocabulary of their language at "the request of the Smithsonian." He bought their clothing, ornaments, and cooking utensils for the Normal museum, packing them with the stuffed birds and pressed plants. It was his first extended, undistracted opportunity to study native Americans at close range, people whom he was beginning to find among the most fascinating residents of the western territories and a subject that would one day become his chief intellectual interest. "In all," he claimed, "we have had fair success" in understanding these people, a claim which by the standards of his day, when Indians were commonly regarded as vermin, was probably true.

The overriding need, however, was to prepare for next season's survey of the Colorado and its downriver canyons, which must be done with the same thoroughness he had given its headwaters. "I have explored the canyon of the Green," he told Edwards, "where it cuts through the foot of the Uintah mountains, and find that boats can be taken down. So that the prospects for making the passage of the 'Grand Canyon' of the Colorado is still brighter. The Canyon of the Green was said to be impassable." It would seem that he was, in addition to collecting specimens and vocabularies, building up confidence in his project during that short moderate winter.

In mid-March the last of the Illinois students, Sam Garman, the teetotalling Quaker naturalist, took his departure. How he had endured those close quarters with the rough, whiskey-drinking Jack Sumner and Co., all of them smelling of blood and animal skins, is beyond telling. The complaints he put in his letters to Friend Gertrude back home all were directed at the Powells, and they were more expressions of pique than anger, of the small resentments that accumulate after months of forced intimacy. The Major, he wrote, commanded too much of his time: "He found I could do almost any work he had to do and that appeared to be excuse enough for setting me at it, no matter what became of the work I came to do." Emma, too, came in for reproof; though most of the lads had found her warm and sympathetic, a woman of unusual spunk, Garman resented her self-importance. She thought him too independent and tried to impress on him "that *herself* and the major *commanded* the expedition and *members* until I announced my intention of leaving when matters changed suddenly and took a much pleasanter aspect, but too late."[62]

Spring temperatures brought the White River to flood level, the water rising into their cabins. They relocated one of them to higher ground for the commander and his wife, while the rest had to sleep outdoors. Lengthening days told them it was getting time to break camp. Powell had to see a man in Chicago about building a few boats, and he had to report in person to his institutional sponsors. One morning the Powells left the others to their guns and traps and went off to find their own train home.

As they rode north, Powell reconnoitered the land one more time, passing from the White to the Yampa, through Browns Hole to the Flaming Gorge where they camped for several days, studying the Green River and the surrounding geology, then west up Henrys Fork and north to Fort Bridger, near the railroad line. All three of the Powells, man, wife, and brother, were getting used to this vertiginous landscape, dangling their feet over the edge of cliffs and calmly looking down several hundred, even a thousand, feet to the water below. They descended the cliff walls to examine the rapids closely and to wonder whether they could be safely navigated or not. Powell would come back to float down a Green that, at least in parts, he had pretty thoroughly canvassed in advance.

Two years had gone by since Powell had first proposed a scientific excursion into the Rocky Mountains, and in that time he had shifted from being a teacher of undergraduates to a bona fide explorer of the West. He had demonstrated the personal qualities that would carry him into the great work ahead, and indeed throughout the rest of his career. Clearly, he was a man who liked taking charge of others in pursuit of a goal. He pushed, he rallied, he gave orders, and he expected them to be obeyed. He loved being Major. The people in his summer expeditions who had served in the late war may have been used to such military style, but those who had not often found him insensitive to their needs, demanding of their time, and intolerant toward any assertions of their individuality. He set them hard at their task while absenting himself from his post for long stretches of time in order to satisfy his own curiosities and enthusiasms.

Whatever his digressions, Powell went into the field with system and purpose. He carried a large scheme in his head. Compared to Lieutenant Ives, who had confined his work on the lower Colorado within the narrow lines set by military strategists, Powell had conceived of the river's exploration in the broadest possible scientific terms. He had framed a comprehensive plan of research and, for all his restless energy, had carried it out with deliberation: start with the great mountain range that tapped the clouds for snow and rain, decipher the rocks and their history, follow the drainage to lower elevations, note the variations in flora and fauna along the way, pay attention to the native people who have devised their own fashion of living in the country, move into the unknown spots on the map only when you have carefully and scientifically located them in the adjacent known.

Powell had marked himself as a man of emphatic, extraordinary ambition — everyone said so who met him. Whatever his deficiencies of education or social standing, he was not bothered by any sense of inferiority. He felt his own manifest destiny. If it was not the western vision of Gilpin — impersonal, global, economic — it too was without apparent limits. He wanted nothing less than to possess the vast interior space of the Colorado River as his own intellectual property, to measure it off and stake it out in seven-league boots.

Yet for all his imperiousness Powell came into the West as a man of commonplace origins, a democrat in his approach to knowledge, a homespun leader of the people. He had brought a cross-section of Illinois, that quintessential midwestern society, into the Rockies: an indiscriminate assortment of farm boys, ministers, students, and teachers, the products of small towns and public schools, and mingled them with frontier editors, printers, trappers, bartenders, and miners — and yes, with Indians still living in traditional ways and wrapped in blankets — and he had called that enterprise scientific exploration. This contrast with the party organized by Lieutenant Ives, or by any other western explorer, is striking. Powell, to be sure, did it that way because he had to and because he knew no other.

Underlying all his other qualities was a hunger to know and experience the land itself. Since those days of rowing on the Mississippi and other inland waterways, those solitary treks across forests and prairies, Powell had been insatiable in his love of topography. Colorado, a new revelation, had sent him climbing. And it had sent him riding. Day after bone-wearing day, uphill and down, he had clopped along on a horse, disregarding his aching stump of an arm, taking in the smells and sights before him, sleeping in a muddy draw or under ponderosa pines.

More than anything else that winter spent on the White River demonstrated his passion for the outdoors. Explorers before him had commonly, when their summer ended, gone back to the city where they planned their next outing in the comfort of a parlor or hotel room. Powell, in contrast, put himself and his wife through months of primitive discomfort in a makeshift cabin in the bush. Science did not demand that he do so, nor did ambition. He simply hungered for the experience of being in the natural world.

CHAPTER 5

Down the Great Unknown

The Green River begins among the high, persistent glaciers and ice-cold tarns of the Wind River Range in Wyoming. At first a mere trickle from the rooftop of the continent, it swells to muddy grandeur along its 730 miles through alpine meadows, sagebrush flats, spectacular sandstone canyons, and alkaline wastes. Entering Utah, it bends around the east-west trending Uinta Mountains, forming Browns Park and the deep chasms of what is now called Dinosaur National Monument. Resuming its course south, the river flows through the Uinta Basin and the dry Gunnison Valley to a confluence with the Grand. Altogether the Green falls nine thousand feet, many of them foaming white-water rapids. The river's name may derive from the brush growing along its banks, offering a brilliant contrast to the often blasted country on either side, or from the name of a St. Louis businessman who dealt in furs. The legendary heart of the fur trade and the scene of its annual rendezvous, the Green was known to trappers by an Indian name, the Seedskadee.[1]

Powell had assumed throughout his 1867–68 explorations that the Grand was the true source of the Colorado River and the logical starting point for penetrating the western country. In 1875, however, he acknowledged that it was the Green, not the Grand, that is "the proper continuation of the Colorado," and he was right.[2] The Green is four hundred miles longer than the Grand, drains an area nearly twice as large, and therefore by the rules of geographical nomenclature ought properly to be considered the upper mainstem. In 1921 the state of Colorado, with support from the U.S. Congress, perversely declared the Grand to be that mainstem, as though chauvinism could repeal the facts of nature. Powell, whatever his earlier

*The first transcontinental railroad under construction at the crossing of the Green
River in Wyoming Territory, 1869. Taken by Andrew J. Russell.*
(Courtesy: Oakland Museum of California)

confusion, wisely chose to launch his exploring boats into the waters
of the Green, though he had not tracked its point of origin among
the Wind River glaciers.

Powell had another, more compelling reason for starting out on
the Green in his journey down the Colorado River. Early in 1869 the
transcontinental railroad had crossed the Green, making it possible
to unload boats directly from a flatbed car into water flowing to the
Gulf of California. While Lieutenant Ives and others had tried to
push heavy steamboats upstream from the Gulf, until the Grand
Canyon blocked their passage, Powell had decided that a better strategy was to put small wooden boats into the upper basin and descend
on the power of the current. He later explained to the English writer
William Bell that he had talked with Indians and white hunters, consulted the Mormons in Utah, read reports of the government surveys, and with his own eye examined the upper reaches from its

banks and canyon walls, until he was convinced that he could successfully go down the entire river in small boats.[3] But first he needed to find money to buy those boats.

When he and Emma left their winter quarters on the White River to go back east, via Green River City (or Station), Emma went to Detroit to stay with her parents while Wes stopped in Chicago. There he took his boat sketches to a master boatmaker, Thomas Bagley, whose workshop was located where Clark Avenue meets the Chicago River. Powell ordered four boats made to his carefully considered specifications. Three of them were to be twenty-one feet long, four feet wide, and two feet deep, each made of oak, double-ribbed with wineglass transoms (they strongly resembled ferry tenders used on Lake Michigan), and each divided into three compartments, the fore and aft compartments decked and watertight in anticipation of rough waves. The fourth boat was to be a shorter, lighter craft of pine, sixteen feet long and similarly divided into compartments. The first three needed to be heavy and rugged in order to carry food supplies through dangerous, rock-filled rapids, while the smaller boat should be fast and maneuverable to pilot the expedition through treacherous places.[4]

While the boats were under construction, Powell went after a renewal of funding from his benefactors. The 1868 resolution of Congress, allowing him to draw free rations from western army posts for twenty-five men, was still in effect; he could take part of his meat rations in the form of cash, which allowed him to hire four hunters to supply his party with fresh meat along the way so they did not have to subsist on bacon only. Other support came from the Smithsonian Institution and the Chicago Academy of Science in the form of scientific instruments, but money for the boats must come from the Illinois Natural History Society (of which he was still secretary), the Illinois Industrial University, and various private sources, including $2,000 of his own salary. In other words, this first expedition down the Colorado was not to be a federal project.[5]

On 7 May, after giving an interview to the *Chicago Tribune* and promising them a few reports from the field, Powell left to rejoin the Colorado River Exploring Expedition, now gathered at Green River City. The boats proceeded him, gratis, on an earlier train. Waiting to receive and outfit them were the core of his brigade encamped a half mile from the Union Pacific Railroad bridge. Most of them had arrived weeks ago and had long exhausted the scarce entertainments of the town. They had taken some of their meals at the Fields' boarding house and others at Ah Chug's dining room at the train depot. They

Jack Sumner. (Courtesy: Utah State
Historical Society)

had drunk Jake Fields's home brew and staggered back to camp
through the dusty streets, past adobe and wood frame buildings,
many of which were uninhabited since the railroad construction
crews had moved on. They had cleaned their guns a few times,
thought about the fabled country that lay downriver, and waited with
increasing impatience.

Most of the exploring party were the same men who had been with
the Powells through the previous winter. Brother Walter was in the
party, moody as ever and isolated from the rest. Jack Sumner was the
acknowledged leader of the group in the Major's absence, and he was
still working at the role of a frontier tough, a deflater of dudes, a self-
described descendant of trappers and scouts. W.W. "Billy" Hawkins
(or Rhodes), the lad from Missouri with the shady reputation, was
also in the party; like Sumner, he was in his late twenties but acted the
ancient one. William Dunn, about the same age, notoriously dirty
and unshorn—Powell described him as dressed in "buckskin with a
dark oleaginous luster"—was another holdover from the summer of
'68. So were the Howland brothers, Oramel and Seneca, hailing

from Pomfret, Vermont, age thirty-six and twenty-seven respectively—two handsome men of long bearded faces and deep-set gray eyes. Oramel, who had been a printer and editor in Denver, had promised letters from the field to the *Rocky Mountain News*. Whatever their differences in literacy, all these men were close friends, except Walter, and most were Union veterans from the late war, used to taking commands but feeling very independent by now.

Besides these holdovers several newcomers were recruited to fill the boats. Andy Hall, though only eighteen years old and the "kid" of the party, had already spent several years roaming the West, working as scout, bullwhacker, mule driver, and boatman. He was a son of Scottish immigrants, though he had cut his family ties to join the rough-and-tumble company of western men, playing the clown and jokester among his elder companions. Another new face was Frank Goodman, a young florid Englishman who was a less skilled and experienced variation on the frontier runaway type that Hall represented; he was so eager he offered Powell money to take him along. Powell had particularly sought the addition of Sergeant George Bradley, who would turn out to be one of the stalwarts of the expedition and the author of its most important journal. Bradley was two years younger than Powell; like him, he was the son of British immigrants and had been wounded in the war. During the previous fall, Powell, while he was reconnoitering the country, had met Bradley at Fort Bridger, located on Black's Fork of the Green, and induced him to leave the boredom of post life to go down the Colorado. On 14 May Bradley received his discharge papers from the Secretary of War and rushed over to Green River, eager for adventure. He would prove to be fearless in a crisis but a petulant man and an inveterate worrier. A lifelong bachelor, he carried his family's pictures wherever he went, homesick with memories but refusing to go home.[6]

One day while they were waiting for the Major to arrive, a stranger approached their campsite and declared that he had been authorized by the former secretary of war, Edwin Stanton, to take command of the Powell expedition. This audacious fellow called himself Samuel Adams, and he showed around several official-looking letters to prove his appointment. The men let him stay to eat at their mess and loaned him funds.[7] When Powell finally pulled in on 11 May, he was immediately confronted by Adams, but one look at the so-called authorizing letters showed them to be nothing more than polite wishes for success in all of Adams's endeavors, and Powell quickly showed him the exit.[8] Adams went away rebuffed but determined to match and surpass whatever Powell and company would achieve. They would hear more about him later. In fact, he would turn out to be one of the oddest ducks the river would ever see: a charlatan, a dreamer, a hopeless incompetent, a half-demented and self-deluded entrepreneur who thought the Colorado belonged to him.

What Powell promised each of his recruits verbally is impossible to determine, though some of the men in later years complained that they had been promised more than they got. The only evidence that survives is an agreement dated 25 February 1869 between "J.W. Powell, party of the first part, and J.C. Sumner, W.H. Dunn and O.G. Howland, party of the second part." In it Sumner agreed to take charge of the sextant, Dunn to make barometrical and other observations, and Howland to make a topographical drawing of the course of the rivers all the way down to Callville, or Call's Landing, the Mormon settlement at the head of sea-going navigation. They were in effect designated the scientific staff, though all of them were more used to handling a rifle or a skinning knife than a scientific instrument. They were also expected to collect animal skins for which Powell would pay them according to an attached schedule: $1.25 for a deer skin, $10.00 for a "grown grizzly" bear, 35 cents for a squirrel, rabbit, woodchuck, or weasel. Powell would allow the men five-day stopovers for gold and silver prospecting, "if not too often," another thirty days between 1 September and 1 December for hunting and trapping, and an additional sixty days between 1 January and 1 June 1870 for the same. They had been thinking about exploiting the river's resources for a while, and it was their chief motive for going along. Each was to receive for services rendered, including the boat work, the sum of $25 a month, and Powell was to furnish all boats, supplies, and ammunition. The contract covered a full year, which indicates the time the expedition was expected to take.[9]

Powell kept his party encamped for two more weeks below the bridge, painting and caulking the boats and packing away the supplies. The large boats could carry 4,500 pounds each, though they were not loaded that heavily—perhaps the three carried 7,000 pounds in all. Food rations sufficient for ten months, consisting of flour, sugar, bacon, beans, dried apples, and coffee, were divided among the cargo vessels, along with a large store of ammunition, several dozen animal traps, axes, hammers, saws, augers, nails and screws, and scientific instruments—two sextants, four chronometers, several barometers, thermometers, and compasses.

The ten men likewise had to be divided among the boats. In the smaller lead boat, which they named the *Emma Dean*, sat Major Powell as commander, with Sumner and Dunn at the steering and bow oars.[10] Behind them came *Kitty Clyde's Sister* (named after somebody's heartthrob), manned by Walter Powell and Lieutenant Bradley; then the *No Name* (here imagination failed them), with the Howland brothers and Goodman aboard; and finally, bringing up the rear, the *Maid of the Canyon*, in charge of Hall and Hawkins. "We are quite proud of our little fleet," wrote Powell, "as it lies in the river waiting for us to embark: the stars and stripes, spread by a stiff breeze, over the Emma Dean; the waves rocking the little vessels, and the current of the Green, swollen, mad and seeming eager to bear us down through its mysterious canyons. And we are just as eager to start."[11]

On 24 May the Colorado River Exploring Expedition pushed off from an island in the wide, shallow Green, as the town folks stood on the bank cheering and waving. Or, as Sumner put it, "after much blowing off of gas and the fumes of bad whiskey, we are all ready by two o'clock and pulled out into the swift stream." Almost immediately, the *Kitty Clyde's Sister*, riding low in the water with its heavy load, grounded on a sand bar. The crew jumped into the cold current and pulled her off. Another boat broke an oar within a short time after departure. Despite those initial mishaps, the whole fleet managed to proceed seven or eight miles that afternoon before reaching their first encampment under an overhanging cliff among cottonwoods. Sumner confessed that they pilfered somebody's stacked cordwood to keep warm that night, which was raw and cold and threatening rain. "We turned in early, as most of the men had been up for several proceeding nights, taking leave of their many friends, 'a la Muscovite.' The natural consequence were fog[g]y ideas and snarly hair."[12]

Major Powell gave a somewhat different account of their first evening out, featuring himself climbing up the cliff and admiring the desolate beauty of the Green River badlands and, in the far distance, the jagged line of the Uinta Mountains. On all sides stretched the multicolored sandstones and shales, carved by rain into fantastic sculptures never seen in eastern lands covered by vegetation. "Standing on a high point, I can look off in every direction over a vast landscape, with salient rocks and cliffs glittering in the evening sun. . . . heights and clouds and mountains and snow fields and forest and rocklands are blended into one grand view. Now the sun goes down, and I return to camp." [13]

Little of that description was written on site; it first appeared in a series of articles entitled "The Cañons of the Colorado," published by *Scribner's Monthly* in 1875. That same year Powell expanded his magazine articles to form a government report that, two decades later, was expanded into a commercially published book, *The Canyons of the Colorado*. For the latter he once again revised the account of his voyage, adding several chapters describing the broad landscape features of the Colorado Plateau.[14] Any reconstruction of the original expedition must, therefore, consider not only the differing newspaper articles and journals of Sumner, Powell, and Bradley, along with a few letters to newspapers sent in by Walter Powell and O.G. Howland, but also Major Powell's various accounts published over his lifetime.

Each embellishment of Powell's narrative strengthened the impression that here was a vast unknown part of America that was at last being revealed as unified and coherent. Order was replacing blankness, beauty emerging from the most hostile-seeming environment. A place that had repelled everyone before him was in fact proved to be a place of exquisite color, diversity, light, and form, of natural harmony. Every motion of the river had a rational explanation. All the strangely contorted physical features, the boulder-choked passages, the pine-covered slopes overhead were part of a single, coordinated design based on the laws of nature and natural processes. As they rounded each bend, as they climbed from the river to the surrounding highlands, the expeditioners, he emphasized, gained new verification of that complexly integrated whole that he called "the valley of the Colorado."

Likewise for Powell, the little group of men whom he had assembled in so haphazard a fashion — men gathered from the wayside and by chance meetings, men who were all misfits by the standards of domestic middle-class life (none but himself was married or living with women or family) — now supposedly moved together down the Green River with a singleness of purpose. They did not quarrel or show resentment. They performed their assigned roles conscientiously. Everyone was cheerful, even Walter, and no mishap was serious enough to disturb their collective sense of purpose. Like their commander, they were a band of optimists, confident of their eventual success. From the beginning Powell portrayed his expedition, like the landscape through which they moved, as an expression of harmony, one that he had organized and nurtured, but also one reflecting the deeper harmony of nature.

Others in the party did not altogether share Powell's sunny optimism. They concentrated on the day-to-day events more than on the broad view of the landscape and the cosmic harmonies of nature: hard rocks in the river, mosquitoes swarming around their faces, a lack of sleep. When they looked around the evening campfire, they saw a few tensions simmering among them, tensions that grew more and more serious. Powell inevitably became the focus of their darker emotions. Though they regarded him with respect (Sumner called him "the Professor"), they mixed respect with sardonic humor, sometimes criticism, other times anger, much of which he did not see, or seeing, he ignored.

From the first day the Major often sat apart from the men to eat his meals, and Billy Hawkins, who served as one of the cooks, brought him his food plate and cup of coffee. He also sat apart from their grumblings and resentments. In his eyes the mission was self-evidently important, and the natural world was an endless source of intellectual and aesthetic delight. His motley crew must see what he saw and behave accordingly, with selfless cooperation and constant good humor. They must work together as one. So he felt, but the other men, as reflected in journals and later memories, were inclined to feel things differently.

The second day out, everyone agreed, it rained. They were in the boats by six A.M. and by mid-morning two of the men were already thoroughly wet from jumping in and out of the river to push the boats free of rocks and gravel bars. Then around noon the skies opened up, and they were all soaked. During a brief stop Hawkins found a young mountain sheep asleep on a cliff and threw it down by the heels to the men below, which furnished a mid-afternoon dinner. Powell and Bradley, the two geological experts, climbed another cliff "to see how it was made" (as Sumner put it). So the pattern of the trip was established as a daily struggle between being wet or dry, in-water or out-of-water, between satisfying the demands of science or sustenance. It continued raining for several more days, and the geologists continued to tramp "around most of the day in the mud and rain to get a few fossils" (Sumner again) while the hunters went in pursuit of sheep, beaver, geese, whatever they could find to roast over the campfire. Darkness found them bedded down in pairs on a pile of cut willow branches. Bradley recorded: "Got pretty wet but expect to be wetter before we reach our destination."[15]

The Green flowed along easily for several days, down to Henry's Fork, where they dug up provisions and instruments Powell had earlier cached. As they approached the mountains, the walls began to magnify and the water to tumble over rocky deposits in the stream bed. Their first canyon they named Flaming Gorge for the brilliant red color of its sandstone, which the evening sun seemed to set afire.[16] Another canyon appeared, and another, and then a rounded bluff which they called Beehive Point. The first day of June found them in the spectacular Red Canyon, whose walls rise half a mile high. Here the water began to rumble more loudly, contesting with the sound of their shouts and oaths. They were moving along at "railroad speed," Bradley reported, and some thought they must at times be running at the rate of a mile a minute.

In fact the ride was getting a little too exhilarating, as the boats leaped and rolled like wild animals running through a forest—like "blacktails jumping the logs," as Powell remembered. He was forced to begin reining in their enthusiasm for the sport with an insistence on caution. A bad rapid must not be chanced. They must get out and unload all the boats, line them downstream carefully or portage them, and carry all the baggage over shores strewn with large boulders and tangled driftwood. They had no smooth, easy path by land. Portaging was not nearly as fun as plunging along in the boats, "singing, yelling, like drunken sailors," Sumner wrote, or "like sparking a black-eyed girl—just dangerous enough to be exciting."[17] Not fun at all: more like hauling elephants on their sweating backs. Each boat took four men to carry it over a portage.

Lining the boats was somewhat easier than portaging, though not all that easy when they had to drag the baggage out of the compartments first to let the boats down empty. They attached a strong rope to the bow and another to the stern. One rope was made fast downstream, the other let out slowly by five or six men, easing the boat past sharp rocks and holding it against the powerful current. They let down over falls that way, the rope burning their hands and pulling them off their feet, until at the last minute they let go and the boat plunged over the edge. The Green grew deeper and stronger as they went, and their combined strength felt puny against it.

A few traces of white-man's civilization had punctuated their river journey so far, some antedating the railroad. But they were startled to find, as they were hauling their cargo around a rapid, an English name painted in large black letters on a rock wall: "Ashley, 1825." Or was it "1855"? Sumner thought it was some obscure trapper's graffiti, but no one, including Powell, knew much about who Ashley was or what his fate had been, though Powell had heard rumors of a drowning here and wrote that the name "is a warning to us and we resolve on great caution."[18]

The correct date was 1825, and the autograph was William H. Ashley's, the man who had organized the American fur trade in the Rocky Mountains. It was he who had hired the intrepid Jedidiah Smith and sent him pathfinding all the way to California, and it was Smith who had first discovered the beaver-rich Green River. Ashley had followed up that discovery by coming down the river himself in bullboats — bowl-like vessels made of buffalo skin — proceeding past this point and past the mouth of the Uinta River before turning around and coming back to Henry's Fork. His was the first navigation of the Green, and he understood that he was on the headwaters of the Rio Colorado of the West. Powell's sources had told him little about this important anticipation of his own exploration, and indeed he had missed a few other accounts of earlier river travel. Much of the upper Green was by his time fairly well known not only to Indians but also to whites who had been poking along its banks for several decades.[19]

At Browns Hole (or Browns Park, as Powell changed its name to give it more dignity) the walls pulled back, and they glided into a wide, lush oasis of meadows, scattered trees, and wetlands, more than twenty miles long and five wide. It was named after an employee of the Hudson's Bay Company who had come here with his Indian wife forty years earlier. The river now became a broad mirror, running smoothly over sandy bottoms and reflecting back the dark-red mountains that form a border.

Gathered here were a large bunch of cattle and their herders, and no one dared ask any questions in this remote valley about whether the men were rustlers or not. Bradley evaluated the prospects of growing vegetables as well as livestock —"think it would pay well," he mused. Sumner was thinking like a farmer too, as schemes of irrigation, rye, barley, and potatoes danced before his eyes; "there is money for whoever goes in there and settles and raises stock." Prospectors, along with the cattlemen, had discovered the valley; a Colonel Jackson, formerly a railroad inspector and now head of a silver prospecting company, had earlier proceeded them overland from Green River City. Likely, they headed up the Vermilion valley to the east, through which Frémont had found his way into Colorado and where three years later, in 1872, the great Diamond Hoax was exposed by Clarence King.[20]

Powell, on the other hand, had birds, not cattle or minerals, on his mind. Waterfowl flocked here in multitudes, and swallows dipped and skimmed over the river's surface. (Today much of Browns Park is preserved as a national wildlife refuge.) He was awakened at daybreak by a chorus of warblers, meadowlarks, woodpeckers, and flickers overhead in a cottonwood. Reclining on his elbow, he listened to their sweet voices — the romantic lover of nature, the devotee of wild beauty. Sumner was half-awake and listening too, soothed by the birds and the "low, sweet rippling of the ever murmuring river at sunrise in the wilderness, . . . as lovely as a poet's dream." He began to dream of an Oriental harem in which he "could see the dim shadow of the dark-eyed houris." But then Andy broke into their reverie with a bullwhacker's call to breakfast: "Roll out! roll out! bulls in the corral! chain up the gap! roll out! roll out!"[21] Once more they must rise from their bedrolls and get on their way, leaving the glorious paradise behind. They prepared to enter what turned out to be one of the most disastrous places of the entire expedition.

At the end of Browns Park stood a dark vermilion portal controlling the entrance to an even darker canyon more than twenty miles long. The cliffs on either side, rising two thousand feet, were an extension of the Uintas through which the river had cut a course. Examining the formidable scene before them, Andy Hall recalled a popular poem from his schoolboy days, Robert Southey's "The Cataract of Lodore," and so Powell, who knew the poem by heart, named the canyon Lodore. Sumner protested, but to no avail; "the idea of diving into musty trash to find names for new discoveries on a new continent is un-American, to say the least." Soon there was little leisure to argue about the nationality of names, for they plunged into one of the more hazardous stretches of white water they encountered on the upper river.

The Major later explained that at this point he ordered the little pilot boat pulled to shore and went ahead on foot to reconnoiter the scene. He had worked out with the men a set of flag signals to use when he was sitting amidship — dip the flag left or right for landing in the event of danger ahead. Now he had left Dunn in the boat with the flag, signaling the others to stop. Looking back, Powell saw two of the crews pull in behind the pilot boat as they were supposed to do, but the third, the *No Name* with the Howlands and Goodman aboard, failed to see the signal and went plunging on down the boiling current. They dropped two or three feet over a fall, then careened down a second fall of twenty to thirty feet, crashing into a rock, rebounding and filling with water, then smacking broadside against another rock. Their boat cracked in two, and the men were thrown into the foaming avalanche, passing from sight. Powell and the others raced down the shore, frantic that the men were lost. But there was Goodman clinging to a rock with a deathlike grip, his head bobbing up and down, and there was the elder Howland stranded on an island, trying to reach Goodman with a pole. The younger Howland had been the last to leave the boat, but he had managed to follow his brother to the island. Sumner leaped into the pilot boat and rowed hard to pick up the trio and bring them back to shore, alive, bruised, and badly shaken.

Their boat, however, did not survive. It drifted downstream into a maelstrom, was smashed again and again, finally sinking from view. All provisions aboard were lost from sight, all the clothes of the men (save the shirts and drawers they were wearing) were gone, along with rifles, a revolver, all the maps Oramel had made, many of the notes taken so far, and all of the barometers. Powell's self-confidence was shattered almost as badly as the boat. That night he could not sleep, worrying about the disaster's implications for the rest of the expedition. Three months' supply of food was gone. And why had they put all the barometers in one boat?

Next morning, however, the situation looked a little brighter. Overnight the wrecked vessel had washed up on an island, and the men hastened to see what they could salvage from it. They found the barometers and a package of thermometers intact. Powell heard a happy shout and was pleased to hear the men value the scientific instruments so highly. But what they were shouting over was a keg of whiskey that had been packed away without his permission and now was found safe in the wreckage. Powell was pleased to let them have it—two gallons of well-deserved comfort, he said, after their cold, hard trial in the water. Sumner, who measured the keg at ten gallons, passed it around for all to swig. "The Professor," he noted, "was so much pleased about the recovery of the barometers, that he looked as happy as a young girl with her first beau; tried to say something to raise a laugh, but couldn't." Everyone was relieved, but no one was in a joking mood.

The disaster in the Canyon of Lodore left its shadow over the rest of the voyage. From that point on Powell could never quite believe that the Howlands were trustworthy or competent or that any of the men were as careful and cautious as he wanted them to be. Howland excused himself by claiming that the accident was due to their misunderstanding, not missing, the signal and also to their having so much water aboard their low-riding boat "as to make her nearly or quite unmanageable; otherwise, the mistake was seen by us in time to save her."[22] Whoever or whatever was to blame, it was clear to all that they were a mere two weeks into their project—the date was 9 June—and already they had lost one-third of the clothing and food needed for the remainder of the trip. Ruefully, Powell named the site Disaster Falls and concluded that they must be more prudent than ever to avoid a fatal replay.

For the next few days Bradley's spirits took a turn toward the somber and negative. On the one hand the mishap brought out his religious impulses; he was always the most pious member of the group. In Lodore's dark depths and turbulent river he felt that he had faced the awesome power of God: "O how great is He who holds it in the hollow of His hand, and what pygmies we who strive against it." Two days later he had come back to earth, griping about his secular commander: "Where we are tonight it roars and foams like a wild beast. The Major as usual has chosen the worst camping-ground possible. If I had a dog that would lie where my bed is made tonight I would kill him and burn his collar and swear I never owned him." Earlier that day he had stumbled while portaging the boat and blackened his eye; "it can't disfigure my ugly mug and it may improve it, who knows?" After another two days of toiling through the canyon, he was complaining that their remaining rations were being ruined by too much wetting and drying. "I imagine we shall be sorry before the trip is up that we took no better care of them. It is none of my business, yet if we fail it will be want of judgment that will defeat it and if we succeed it will be *dumb luck*, not good judgment that will do it."[23]

He had no good words for the hunters either, for they had consistently failed to bring in much game for the table.

> We frequently see mountain sheep as we pass along, and if we kept *still* we might kill them but as soon as we land the men begin to shoot and make a great noise and the game for miles around is allarmed [sic] and takes back from the river. This makes one think that these are not *hunters* and I believe that if left to maintain themselves with their rifles they would fare worse than Job's turkey. They seem more like school-boys on a holiday than like men accustomed to live by the chase, but as I am no hunter myself I must not criticize others. Still as usual I have my opinion.[24]

He spoke a certain truth; often it was the one-armed Powell who succeeded as well as Sumner and company at bringing in meat. But it would have taken more than a fat piece of mutton to put Bradley right.

Bradley's increasingly critical mood toward his fellow travelers could not have been improved by their next disaster in the bowels of Lodore. After a day of lining and portaging past several whirlpools, they set up camp on a bar covered with dry willows and pines. Hawkins started a cooking fire that a sudden wind scattered into the trees, until the whole camp was "one sheet of flames. We seized whatever we could and rushed for the boats and amid the rush of wind and flames we pushed out and dropped down the river a few rods." Bradley, whose neckerchief caught afire, had his ears and face badly scorched and his eyebrows and mustache singed. Hawkins had gathered up the mess kit and was heading for a boat, his clothes aflame, when he stumbled into the water and lost it all—bread pan, baking oven, frying pan, kettle, spoons, tin plates, cups, pick-ax, shovel. Once aboard the boats, they watched the fire spread toward them and had to push off and run a rapid or lose everything. Powell, who had been following their frantic movements from a high rock without seeing the fire, was astonished and came scurrying down to see what was going on. He led the men back to the burned campsite where they salvaged a few utensils and recovered some bedding. An-

"Fire in Camp." (Illustration from "The Cañons of the Colorado," *Scribner's Monthly,* Jan. 1875)

other misadventure, but this time the Major took it more philosophically. "We do just as well as ever," he wrote. Later he remembered more enthusiastically that Lodore's "walls and cliffs, its peaks and crags, its amphitheaters and alcoves, tell a story of beauty and grandeur that I hear yet—and shall hear."

The Canyon of Lodore leads into an even grander and more beautiful "story," the most beautiful anywhere on the river, a pocket-sized park where the Yampa enters the Green on the left. Weber sandstone, beige with tints of gray, green, and black streaked with manganese and iron oxides (the famous desert varnish), forms nearly vertical walls here. Box elder, cottonwood, and willow grow in the silty soil that makes a shifting floor at the junction, providing enough land for a farm. The combined flow of the two rivers becomes a surging, broad current the color of the rock. On the right it runs along the bottom of an immense block seven hundred feet high and a mile long, then turns around and runs up the west side in a horseshoe loop. Later generations would call this Steamboat Rock, but Powell referred to it as Echo Rock. A shout reverberated off its walls again and again—ten or twelve times he counted. They spent three days here, pushing up the Yampa a short way, climbing with the barometers to the highest elevations.[25]

In the later telling of his experience Powell now and then embellished his memories to the point of fictive invention. For example, he tells how Bradley and he set out to climb Echo Rock, not an easy task for a skilled rock climber with two good arms let alone a one-armed man. They ascend nearly to the top, when Powell finds he can go no farther. He is stranded on the face of the precipice, unable to go forward or back. Bradley, who is above him, takes off his drawers and reaches them down to Powell, who releases his tight grip on the rock and grabs the drawers. Bradley pulls him to safety. They take atmospheric measurements on the top and descend by an easier route. As an anecdote, it emphasizes at once Powell's disability, which one tends to forget, and his cool courage in the face of danger. Both aspects of the man were true. And such a rescue did indeed happen— not at Echo Rock, however, but three weeks later when Powell and Bradley were climbing a one-thousand-foot mountain farther south.

Leaving Echo Park, the river turns west through Whirlpool Canyon, Island Park, and Split Mountain Canyon, then south again through the Wonsits Valley. Rough water alternated with smooth, but the scenery was consistently splendid. Bradley mooned over his family tintypes, which were getting spoiled by moisture, but the food was

"The Rescue." (Illustration from "The Cañons of the Colorado,'" *Scribner's Monthly,* Jan 1875)

getting distinctly better as the men were catching trout. Overall their spirits were recovering. Oramel, despite his near brush with death, had come to live for the excitement of rapids. "Danger is our life," he wrote. "As soon as the surface of the river looks smooth all is listlessness or grumbling current, unless some unlucky goose comes within range of our rifles. But just let a white foam show itself ahead and everything is as jolly and full of life as an Irish 'wake' or merry-making, or anything of that sort." On 28 June they reached the mouth of the Uinta River, where they stopped until 6 July. Looking back on the voyage so far, the disaster receding from immediacy, Powell declared, "never before did I live in such ecstasy for an entire month."[26]

They were now stopped at a major crossroads. The wagon road from Denver to Salt Lake City that E.L. Berthoud had surveyed, the one that gave the Powell party so much trouble finding the previous fall, crossed the Green River where the Uinta debouches into it. Less than two miles farther down, the White River, which had flowed past the Powells' winter camp, came in on the left. The Uinta River drains the south-facing slopes of the Uinta Mountains, and its valley had been designated the site of an Indian agency, located forty miles upstream. Sumner noted that according to the 1868 treaty with the Utes this whole valley was now a reservation, but whether the Indians "will be permitted to keep it or not remains to be seen."[27] Powell sent Walter and Andy to the agency, then two days later went himself with Billy and Frank Goodman. They carried letters, fossils, plant specimens, and newspaper articles to be posted home, and a hope for provisions to replace those that had been lost.

Unfortunately, the agent, Pardon Dodds, was away in Salt Lake City, and there was little food to be traded for — three hundred pounds of flour was all. Goodman, who had been in the wreck at Disaster Falls and was unreassured about their supplies, used this opportunity to follow in Dodds's departing tracks. He abruptly resigned from the exploring expedition and headed back to civilization. While earlier he had wanted to pay for the experience, so eager was he for adventure, now he was eager to escape with his life still intact.[28] Powell wished him well and turned away to interview the Indians who had settled at the agency and were learning to farm. He examined their crops, noted that they still preferred to live in traditional lodges rather than white men's houses, and traded for an old man's pipe.

Powell spent the Fourth of July at the agency, while the men back at the boats were trying to get up some appropriate patriotic sentiment on their own. "The musical little mosquitoes bite so badly,"

Bradley complained, "that I can write no longer." So instead he counted up all the Fourths he had spent in the wilderness and thought of home, its comforts contrasting with the privations he now suffered, asking himself why he was here. "But those green flowery graves on a hillside far away seem to answer for me," he concluded, and with moistened eyes he repaired to his tent and privately indulged in a day of nostalgia and remembrance.[29]

What the good folks at home, and indeed across the nation, were thinking about the Powell expedition was a good deal less than sentimental. No word had come from any of the party since leaving Green River City. Their articles from the field were not be published in the Chicago, St. Louis, and Denver papers (or reprinted in the *New York Times*) until 17 July at the earliest, and in the absence of any direct news, rumors began to fly and fears to mount. While they were taking a respite from travel, a sensational story of their demise got out, became wildly embroidered, and, unknown to them, was agitating many friends and family members with doubt and controversy.

On 28 June the *Omaha Herald* announced, and newspapers in Denver, St. Louis, and Bloomington picked up the story, that the entire Powell expedition had been drowned while trying to run a dangerous rapid—"save one, who is now reported to be at Fort Bridger." Or, another report had it, the survivor was now at Green River City, after having walked five hundred miles out of the wilderness—details were confused. A note of skepticism accompanied some of those stories. The *Bloomington Pantagraph*, where Powell was well-known, was doubtful, noting that the Major combined unusual prudence with daring. It also carried a letter from former expedition member Lewis Keplinger, who cautioned that "Major Powell himself taught me not to put much faith in 'sole survivors' especially when they witness the loss of their comrades at a safe distance. . . . this report is just such as we might expect from some deserter from the party who lacked the nerve to face the dangers of the trip."[30]

On 2 and 3 July, while Powell was at the Uintah agency, another Omaha newspaper flashed news it had received from William Riley, a self-described trapper and Indian fighter, who had met the sole survivor of the wreck, Jack Sumner, at Fort Bridger and received the full details from him. The expedition had passed "Hell's Gate" (the Gate of Lodore?) below Browns Hole, and soon after all the boats and the men aboard were destroyed while Sumner watched helplessly from the shore. In this account Sumner traipsed a mere seventy-five miles overland to Fort Bridger. "These rapids," the paper went on, "are extensively known throughout the Western country as the spot where several different parties who have attempted a descent through the destructive chasms have perished in the foolhardy undertaking." Disregarding the fact that Lodore was hardly known at all, the account had taken on somewhat more credibility and precision in the space of a few days.

As this Sumner-centered story was gaining circulation, another supposed survivor popped up with a tale that was as tall as the Uintas and as bald-faced as any riverboat swindle. John A. Risdon, now in Springfield, Illinois, told a *Chicago Tribune* reporter that he alone had escaped from the Powell wreck and had struggled home with the bad news. He had joined on, so he said, back in July 1865 as a "chainman" for land surveying, after serving under Powell in the war, and had been with the party every day since it had left Illinois. He furnished a list of names in the party, including Durley, Knoxon, Sherman, Duncan, and a "half-breed named *Chick-a-wa-nee.*" On 7 or 8 May the party had reached the Colorado River near a small Indian settlement named Williamsburg, where they stayed for a week scouting and observing. Then they moved downstream to explore two tributaries, the Big Black and the Deleban, where the whole group of twenty-five men climbed into a large bark canoe (except for Risdon) to cross the river, and, losing control, they plunged down a fall of 160 feet in a mile and a quarter. Powell had stood in the stern, steering, as the canoe was sucked bow first into a whirlpool and disappeared from sight. "Good bye, Jack," the men aboard shouted, "you will never see us again." "For two hours I lay on the bank of the river crying like a baby," Risdon went on. Tearfully, he trudged up and down the river, looking for remains (apparently expecting the whirlpool to throw a few bodies upstream), but all he could find was a single carpet bag belonging to Powell, containing his sketchbooks and memorandum. On 1 June Risdon, driving two wagon teams, made it to the small military post of Le Roy on the Red River, where a Colonel Smith arranged transportation for him back to St. Louis. Risdon was now visiting the governor of Illinois, hoping for a ticket home to Lasalle, and the carpetbag was on its way to Mrs. Powell. The reporter concluded that "the fate of Major Powell's expedition is left without a doubt, and another name is added to the long roll of martyrs to science."[31]

The next day, however, the *Detroit Press* carried a letter from Mrs. J.W. Powell, dismissing "the whole story as a fabrication." She had never met any John Risdon, knew for certain that he was not connected in any way with the expedition, and herself had a letter from her husband datelined Green River City several days after the supposed drowning had occurred. The party's goal was to reach the Grand Canyon in September, after doing preliminary scientific work during the summer months; they could not have made it that far downriver so quickly. The notion of having wagons and horses along was absurd; there were no roads out there; they had sold all their stock, and were relying solely on the boats. While she was at it, Emma sent another letter to the *Tribune*, questioning the Sumner story as well. The Sumner she knew would, in the event of a mishap, have come directly and immediately to Chicago or Detroit to give details first-hand, not lolled around a military fort.[32]

Powell's brother Bram blasted Risdon too, pointing out that all of the names he had given were wrong and the number was double the true size of the party. "Besides all these falsehoods, Risd[o]n has invented a geography which upsets all the maps. He makes rivers run the wrong way; transfers others hundreds of miles from their former location; establishes unknown military posts; builds a canoe which the Indians call a yawl and makes it hold 20 men. His whole story is a tissue of falsehoods from beginning to end; but what was the motive for their invention?" Bram speculated that Risdon might have committed theft or murder and was trying to cover it up. "Our own opinion of the whole matter is that Risd[o]n found himself out West without money, and invented this story to excite sympathy and raise the wind to get home."[33]

The *Chicago Tribune*, which had been taken in so readily by Risdon's yarn, pointed out three days later all the improbabilities in it. The paper recalled that Powell had taken sturdy Chicago-made boats with him and was unlikely to have abandoned them before reaching the Grand Canyon itself, for according to its information the Colorado River before the Canyon was "a placid, almost sluggish stream." Why, it asked, did Risdon drive the wagons all the way to the Red River rather than to the Pacific railroad or to Denver? Such questions, though evidencing a sudden skepticism, revealed once more that the paper was as ignorant as Risdon of western geography. The entire hoax in fact reflected a widespread lack of information about the West, a journalistic passion for disasters, and a credulity that outran common sense. Few observers believed that the Colorado and Green could be mastered by any boating expedition. But now they decided to wait for more news. The Illinois governor, sensing public opinion shifting against the importuning Risdon, refused to furnish him a free ticket home. The last anyone heard of the man who had

cried like a baby as he witnessed Powell sinking below the waves was
that he was in the Springfield jail, accused of stealing a horse.[34]

Beneath all the dark rumors lay a sad kernel of truth. Three weeks
after Powell's party had left Green River City, a man named Theodore
Hook, the mayor of Cheyenne, had embarked on his own expedition
down river. Not long after starting he was drowned, and searchers
could find no trace of him, nor for that matter of the Colorado River
Exploring Expedition, not even a campfire. Meanwhile, oblivious to
all the rumors flying about, Powell and company dispatched their
mail and climbed back into the boats to resume their odyssey.

B elow the mouth of the Uinta they entered more truly unknown
county, at least unknown to American civilization (except for
Monsieur Julien), country from which they were be unable to send
out any word until they were through the Grand Canyon. Nor could
they expect any replenishment of rations. The flour they had added
at the agency would do little to remedy the fact that, due to the boat
wreck and the constant wetting, nearly half of their rations had been
lost. The lack of food was on everybody's mind. "We are quite careful
now of our provisions," noted Bradley, "as the hot blasts that sweep
through these rocky gorges admonish us that a walk out to civilization is almost certain death, so better go a little slow and safe." Yet in
fact they were going at a very fast clip in order to reach the junction
of the Green and the Grand in time to make observations of the 7
August solar eclipse; indeed, they were making such haste that they
would reach that point in only ten days' time, on 16 July.

A few upsets slowed them down. When only five days away from the
Uinta's mouth, Powell's pilot boat swamped, rolling over and over,
dumping rifles and blankets out, losing the oars, and forcing the
Major to swim awkwardly to shore. Luckily, the boat was saved. They
made only a half mile that day. Much to Bradley's pious satisfaction,
the Major had no choice but to observe this particular Sabbath, as he
sat drying out by the fire and Sumner cut new oars from driftwood.
But then they made up for lost time with subsequent daily runs of 15,
18, and 33 1/2 miles, passing quickly through a shaly, unvegetated
country, which Powell named Desolation Canyon, then through a
darker section named Coal Canyon (later revised to Gray Canyon).

Starkly beautiful, austere, and eerily quiet, these shores did not invite them to linger. Powell, who had commenced a daily journal written shakily in pencil with his left hand, skipped over these uneventful
days. Sumner, however, did note in his journal their arrival at the old

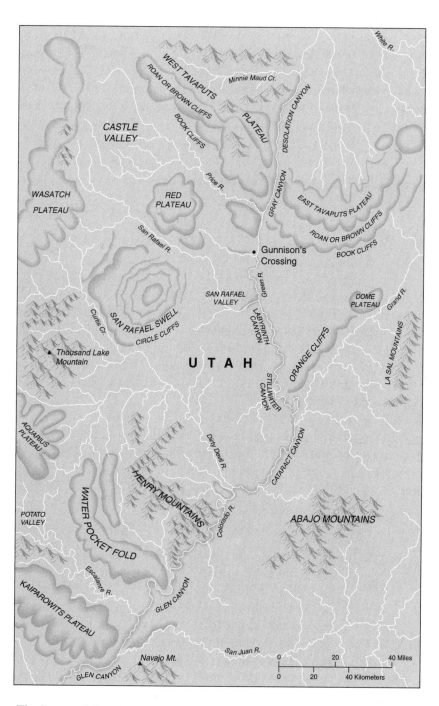

The Green and Grand rivers of Utah, converging to become the Colorado River.

Spanish Crossing, a wide, shallow ford where Green River, Utah, now sits. The Utes had long used this ford, but it took its English name from traders pushing cattle from Santa Fe to California; though requiring a long detour north, this was the easiest point for them to get across. In 1853 Captain John W. Gunnison of the Topographical Engineers came through following the 38th parallel on a railroad survey. He was killed a few months later by the Paiutes, but the prominent feature of Gunnison's Butte, which marked the crossing, commemorated his brief transit.[35]

Continuing through the San Rafael valley, the river sinks into Labyrinth and Stillwater canyons (the latter now bisects Canyonlands National Park). Then, with little warning, the Grand comes in from the left, wider than the Green—125 yards compared to 70 or 80 in width—somewhat colder and clearer but about the same depth at ten feet. Bradley was surprised to find that this junction, which creates the Colorado River, was so calm, wide, and quiet. He had expected raging waterfalls or foaming rapids, something frightful to behold. "We float in upon a scene never before beheld by white men and by all regarded as dangerous of approach," he marveled, "and the last 75 miles of our journey through a dark calm cañon which a child might sail in perfect safety. Surely men do get frightened wonderfully at chained lyons."[36]

Because of the deteriorating condition of their flour, which they sifted through mosquito netting to get rid of the spoiled lumps, they had to give up staying around for the eclipse. But they did remain here five days, camping a short way up the Grand, to get the latitude and longitude of the junction securely fixed. For a change of diet, they killed a beaver and tried beavertail soup, but it was too heavy a food for this hot summer climate. Temperatures were in the high nineties, and their bare feet sizzled on the rocks.

Despite the heat and their troubled stomachs, they managed to climb the adjacent cliffs and to look out on a sterile but awesome moonscape. Powell penned this description a few later years later:

> The landscape everywhere, away from the river, is of rock—cliffs of rock, tables of rock, plateaus of rock, terraces of rock, crags of rock—ten thousand strangely carved forms; rocks everywhere, and no vegetation, no soil, no sand. . . . When thinking of these rocks one must not conceive of piles of boulders or heaps of fragments, but of a whole land of naked rock, with giant forms carved on it: cathedral-shaped buttes, towering hundreds or

thousands of feet, cliffs that cannot be scaled, and canyon walls that shrink the river into insignificance, with vast, hollow domes and tall pinnacles and shafts set on the verge overhead; and all highly colored — buff, gray, red, brown, and chocolate — never lichened, never moss covered, but bare, and often polished.[37]

So at last, two months out and with barely two months' supply of food left, they had arrived at the promised land of their dreams — the hard, naked desert country of the Southwest.

From this point on Bradley's chained lion began to roar once again. Past the junction, they entered what they called Cataract Canyon, forty-one miles of sheer hell. Rapid followed on rapid, one every half mile or so, pounding the boats mercilessly. The portages that the weary men stumbled along added damage to the boat bottoms. The resulting leaks they tried to repair with pitch. Powell brought down a load of it, tied up in the sleeve of his shirt, from the scattered pine trees growing overhead. It did not last for long, and they had to caulk and recaulk in such makeshift ways many times before the trip was over. Fortunately, they suffered no bad accidents in this perilous channel, for by now they were learning to respect the river's power and to handle themselves with more skill.

They had not, however, learned to get along with each other through all the vicissitudes. Days of backbreaking toil under harsh conditions frayed their tempers. When they arrived at the mouth of a vile little stream coming in on the right below Cataract Canyon, the expedition reached a crisis in their relations. The stream was muddy and smelly. Sumner described its water as "about as filthy as the washing from the sewers of some large, dirty city, but stinks more than cologne ever did."[38] According to Powell, it was Dunn who muttered "dirty devil" when he saw it, and the stream thus acquired a name. Bradley, however, understood that the name had come from Powell, not Dunn, and was a commentary on the despicable condition of the entire party; he added that such name-calling was "in keeping with [Powell's] whole character which needs only a short study to be read like a book." On the other hand, according to Billy Hawkins, Powell had earlier taken to calling Dunn in particular a "dirty devil" and now named the squalid little stream after the man. "It was here," Hawkins continued, "we had the first trouble in the party."[39]

Billy Hawkins did not keep a diary during the trip, but in 1919, a half century after their ordeal, he recalled that at some point — his memory was vague — the men reached a state of "mutiny." They became so unhappy with Powell's leadership that they refused to recognize his authority any longer. Sumner and Bradley, who did keep journals, gave no indication in them that relationships had sunk so low, but in later years Sumner agreed that a serious revolt against Powell had occurred somewhere near the end of Cataract Canyon.

According to both Sumner and Hawkins, it was Dunn who provided the spark, or the tinder, for rebellion. Disaster-prone in Lodore Canyon, he now confirmed his carelessness by dropping the Major's gold watch into the water, ruining it, and its owner demanded $30 compensation or Dunn's departure. Powell was adamant that Dunn must either pay or leave. Walter added to the clash by sneering that if Dunn were drowned it would be no loss, a remark that outraged the others. Sumner warned Powell that "he couldn't come any damned military there"—that is, behave in an autocratic, abusive way as though the men were enlisted under him.[40] Hawkins and Hall likewise jumped to their feet to protest but were told (the story goes) to shut up and stay out of the controversy, to which Hawkins responded by refusing to bring Powell's dinner to him any longer. "I told him that he had just said that he was going to make a change in the outfit and I told him that I had made that change to start the ball rolling, and that he would have to come and get his grub, like the rest of the boys. His brother then handed his dinner to him."

Walter's popularity, never high to begin with, had reached nadir with some of the men. "He had a bulldozing way that was not then practiced in the west," Hawkins said. Walter was immensely proud of his baritone singing voice, and when Hawkins tried to imitate him, he threatened to slap his face. More than once, Walter questioned the expertise of Dunn. When the Major called Dunn "a bad name," Dunn replied that "if the Major was not a cripple he would not be called such names." Walter then charged into Dunn with an oath— "swearing and his eyes looked like fire"—and the two began to scuffle in the water, until it looked like Walter's greater strength would drown Dunn on the spot. Hawkins leaped in and seized Walter by the hair. "He cursed me to everything," Hawkins remembered, even to being a 'Missoury Puke,'" and threatened to kill him. Andy now joined the fray, drawing a gun on Walter and forcing him to surrender his hold on Dunn. The Major came hustling up and reproved Hawkins for "going back on him," but Hawkins had had enough of the Powell brothers, their self-important airs and their insults. Like Sumner, he tried to avoid all-out mutiny for the sake of the expedition, but he no longer honored the expedition leader.[41]

How much truth and how much exaggeration post facto these stories contain is impossible to determine. What seems probable is that a hot blaze flared up but then died down to a smoulder as the main river turned a more kindly face toward them. The river affected all with its shifting moods. The next long segment went down on the map as Mound Canyon, and then on reflection, as Glen Canyon, a better name to suggest the stretch of peacemaking and tranquility they now entered.[42]

No more charming place existed along the Colorado than this 150-mile stretch of quiet, purling water. Their boats glided without danger of upset through a series of softer rocks, the Glen Canyon group of Navajo, Kayenta, and Wingate sandstones. All are easily eroded, the Wingate most of all, so that the river bed was free of the hard, resistant boulders that make treacherous rapids. Along the walls the scanty rainfall had carved a wonderland of domes, coves, nooks, intricate folds, arches, alcoves, curving walls, and chambers. One of the largest of these hollowed-out caverns, large enough to seat several thousand people, they called Music Temple. Walter, recovered from his murderous anger of a few days back, gave them a concert, singing his favorite melody, the antislavery song "Old Shady," or some other popular piece. They ventured into other grottoes and into side canyons where they found secluded enclaves of Eden — maidenhair fern, mosses, and flowers growing beneath groves of oaks, willows, and cottonwoods, patches of shimmering green against the variegated walls of white, orange, red, purple, chocolate, and yellow rock. The sunlight penetrating these alcoves gave them a soft, ethereal glow.[43]

Native people had discovered Glen Canyon long before Powell did, a fact he began to realize more fully after coming upon the ruin of a building high up on the left wall, built as it seemed for the magnificent view. It had once been a three-story structure, though now only the bottom floor was intact, and it had been laid up carefully by a skilled mason with mortar. Not far away he found a series of steps cut into the stone and a rickety old wooden ladder leaning against what looked like a watchtower. Powell read these structures as defensive redoubts against dreaded enemies who long ago had driven this people into the canyons for safety. He found traces of their pottery, etchings on the cliff faces, and a deep excavation that he identified as a kiva, a chamber for religious ceremonies similar to those of the modern-day pueblos of the Southwest. The Navajos called such kiva-making people the Moqui, or Hopi, and Powell applied the same name to the culture that had constructed these ancient dwellings. They were, he realized, the ancestors of those now living in Arizona (today they are known as the Anasazi).

In Chicago a few weeks earlier Powell had told a reporter that he was heading toward a country "where we expect to see no human being." Three years' study, he said, had made him doubt whether "these canons have ever been seen by man. The Indians never go into them, and there is little game on the cliffs to tempt them." But now he began to find traces of humanity where he had not expected them, and such traces continued as he moved into the Grand Canyon itself. They were, to be sure, mere pinpoints of settlement, hardly domesticating this vast rocky wilderness; but they suggested that men and women had certainly seen these canyons before and in fact had managed to scratch out a living here, though exactly when he could not say. "I stood where a lost people had lived centuries ago," Powell marveled, "and looked over the same strange country."[44]

While gliding through the ornate stillness of Glen Canyon, they passed the San Juan, which enters through a wide gap in the left-hand wall, pouring into the main stream the sediment-heavy water from the New Mexico and southwestern Colorado mountains. That junction was more than a hundred miles farther downriver than either government or Mormon maps had had it, another argument for why the Powell expedition was necessary. Looming on the near horizon was the massively rounded peak of Navajo Mountain, which the Major named for the Howland boys. That bestowal did not survive, but all the expeditioners, Dunn included, could take pride in seeing their names added to the new map that was in the making. On the right hand they drifted past the place that Fathers Dominguez and Escalante had discovered a hundred years earlier on their return to Santa Fe: the Crossing of the Fathers, El Vado de los Padres. Farther on the river cut directly through the divide that had once closed this watershed off and sent the Colorado due south; on the left side the divide could still be seen as the dark-hued Echo Cliffs and on the right, curving back toward the west, as the Vermilion Cliffs. This once continuous wall through which the river had breached a course marked a major transition from a zone of younger, softer rock into a zone of harder, older, uplifted rock, a transition from the upper to the lower basin of the Colorado.

On the yonder side of the wall, after making a day's run of thirty-eight miles, they pulled out at a low, wide delta where the Paria River joins—another small, dirty stream in Sumner's estimation. He confused it with Escalante's ford, though in fact the padres had passed this spot without crossing the Colorado. More recently, the Mormons, represented by their roving scout Jacob Hamblin, had discovered the site, named it the Paria (pronounced Pah-ree-ah), and constructed a provisional fort here. Navajos also knew this valley and delta well, for here they butchered cattle stolen from the Mormons and packed the meat over the river to their hogans. The place would figure importantly in Powell's future explorations, but on this occasion he hardly commented on it, merely noting that he found green sandstone in this place.

Science was now absorbing the Major's attention to the point of distraction. Each day he wanted to stop the boats and go climbing to where he could see more of this intriguing country. Downriver from the Paria the canyon walls became chiefly limestone (inspiring the name Marble Canyon); because the layer of rock was stained by overlying, dark-red sandstone, Powell called it the Redwall limestone and traced it farther down into the Grand Canyon itself. No geologist had ever closely studied this formation, or any of the other formations exposed by erosion, and to make that study was a large reason why he had come: to examine rocks and to make collections of natural history, antiquities, and ethnology for the institutions sponsoring him. He was as keen as ever to add facts to the store of knowledge. On 7 August, the day of the eclipse, they lay over so that he might make observations, but clouds interfered and he had to be content with bagging a couple of fossil brachiopods. It was pitch-dark when he finished, so he and Walter had to sleep overnight on the chilly heights.

The rest of the party, meanwhile, was turning impatient. They had their minds fixed on getting the exploring over and done with as quickly as possible. Bradley had nearly forgotten his own amateur fascination with geology. "We are interested now only in how we shall get through the cañon and once more to civilization," though he added that "we are more than ever sanguine of success." When they passed the mouth of the Little Colorado (they called it Rio Chiquito or the Flax River) on 10 August, the point that conventionally marks the beginning of the Grand Canyon, Bradley dismissed it as "a lo[a]thesome little stream, so filthy and muddy that it fairly stinks." Only in contrast with his life at Fort Bridger did the expedition still look like a positive experience. "Thank God the trip is nearly over," he wrote, "for it is no place for a man in my circumstances but it will let me out of the Army, and for that I would almost agree to explore the river Styx."[45]

While waiting for Powell to satisfy his scientific urges, Bradley scribbled furiously in his journal.

> The men are uneasy and discontented and anxious to move on.
> If Major does not do something soon I fear the consequences,
> but he is contented and seems to think that biscuit made of sour
> and musty flour and a few dried apples is ample to sustain a
> laboring man. If he can only study geology he will be happy
> without food or shelter but the rest of us are not afflicted with
> it to an alarming extent.[46]

As for the bacon, it was nearly gone, threatening them with no meat for the last, most arduous part of the journey.

Now the scheme of trading their salted army rations for cash to pay the hunters was looking like poor policy. None of the four hunters had at any point proved reliable in bringing in a daily supply of fresh venison or mutton, largely because the game was far more scarce than they had imagined — and it was getting more scarce all the time. Sumner managed to shoot a bighorn sheep before they left Glen Canyon, but the meat quickly spoiled and they had to throw most of it away. Fish might have been a substitute, and the Colorado had, at this time before any major dams were built, an abundance of native species — several kinds of chub and suckers, along with squawfish, also known as the Colorado or white salmon. The latter were big, often exceeding thirty pounds, and might have fed the men sumptuously. They had no luck in snaring them, however. "Fish were very plenty as we passed along today," Bradley noted, "but they will not bite as they get plenty to eat all along; where the water is still we could see them catching small flies that that river seems covered with."[47]

So they entered upon the final stage of their journey in a spirit of anticipation mixed with lingering resentment, frustration, and impatience. Their leader seemed persistently insensitive to their privations, cavalier about the risk they were running with such low food supplies. And once more the river began to make a frightful roar — a roar they could feel in their bones.

Powell may not have been paying much attention to his men's needs at the time, but describing this moment retrospectively he conveyed fully the tangled emotions they all felt.

> *August 13.*   We are now ready to start on our way down the Great
> Unknown. Our boats, tied to a common stake, chafe each other as

they are tossed by the fretful river. They ride high and buoyant, for their loads are lighter than we could desire. . . . We are three quarters of a mile in the depths of the earth, and the great river shrinks into insignificance as it dashes its angry waves against the walls and cliffs that rise to the world above; the waves are but puny ripples, and we but pigmies, running up and down the sands or lost among the boulders. We have an unknown distance yet to run, an unknown river to explore. What falls there are, we know not; what rocks beset the channel, we know not; what walls rise over the river, we know not. Ah, well! we may conjecture many things. The men talk as cheerfully as ever; jests are bandied about freely this morning; but to me the cheer is somber and the jests are ghastly.[48]

The Holy Grail of western exploration lay almost in their hands, the secrets of the greatest canyon on earth, but they understood fully the dangers it posed.

Powell's "unknown distance yet to run" was painfully true; it was not clear exactly how far they had come nor how much river was left to run. Like any sailor at sea, they had been using a sextant to determine their position by measuring the altitudes of celestial bodies. The barometers, when they were working, told them their elevation, so they knew how many feet they had descended and how many more were left to descend to sea level. Each day the men also compared personal estimates on how far they had come, averaging their estimates to establish their log—a crude way to measure but the best they had. By their reckoning they had traveled more than six hundred miles from the railroad, most of that at the leisurely rate of four or five miles per hour.[49] They knew the location of Callville, the Mormon settlement that marked the beginning of the "known," and they could figure out where it was in straight-line distance and in change of elevation. What they could not know was how many more turns the river made before reaching that point, or how many rapids it went through, or how many days of portaging and lining they had ahead of them, or whether their victuals would see them through.

The Colorado was now a river running due west. All the existing maps had that general direction right. But if the Grand Canyon's head lay in the east and its tail in the west, its body coiled and looped sinuously like a great snake through all the compass points. The first great loop brought them southward into a formation that so far they had not encountered, one lying deeper in the earth than all the sedimentary

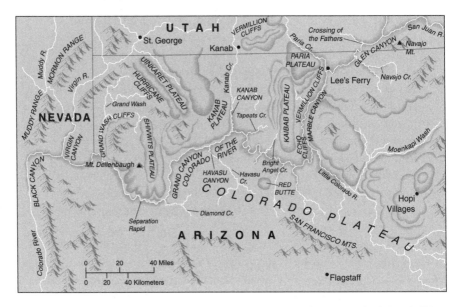

The Grand Canyon of the Colorado River.

formations they had seen. Powell called it "the granite," and even today the Canyon is known as a series of Granite Gorges—Upper, Middle, and Lower. More accurately, the deep basement rocks they ran into are called Vishnu Schist, formed of ancient sand and mud that had metamorphosed into an immense mountain chain, streaked with pink-colored bands of granite and then worn down by over three billion years of erosion. It was hard stuff, harder than any rock they had encountered. The way was west, but the way was also down, down, down into the depths of time.

Shortly after leaving the Little Colorado, as they came into hard rock and more rapids, Bradley exclaimed, "this is emphatically the wildest day of the trip so far."[50] They estimated their daily progress at no more than six miles. Again and again they nearly capsized, as the waves broke over the gunwales, filling the boats like buckets. Miraculously they came through, often working their way along the side channels by clinging to the canyon walls with tense, bruised fingers. Shores and sandbars disappeared; often the current ran from wall to wall so that they could not get out to investigate but must run any rapids that appeared. When night came, only the Major and Sumner had room to sleep in their customary two-man bedroll, while the rest must lie scattered among the cracks and on the lip of a narrow ledge above the current.

Rapids are not continuous in the Grand Canyon; they mark no more than one in ten miles throughout its length. But they came along with such force that the expedition was rendered, in Powell's words, "entirely unmanageable; no order in their running can be preserved; now one, now another, is ahead, each crew laboring for its own preservation."[51] Further adding to the disorder was rain. Although they were passing through one of the driest parts of the nation, they encountered rain that did not stop—hours and hours of it pounding down, making their nights a complete misery and their daylight hours gloomy and wet whether they were splashing through rapids or not. Making things even worse, when the sun came out the temperature could soar to 115 degrees.

What the torrents of rain did for them was to illustrate exactly how the canyons and rapids had been formed. Water cascaded over the rims, adding to the deafening noise of the river, water carrying mud and silt of various hues. It came plunging down the side canyons with locomotive force, flowing not as clear rainwater but as an avalanche of moving earth, boulders, and trees. Hundreds of tons of loose rock and soil could rumble down in such a debris flow, tearing loose boulders the size of houses and dropping them into the main channel. Nothing so terrifying occurred to the Powell expedition, but they could clearly see what had created the rapids that gave them so much trouble. The suddenness with which the river could rise, or the side canyons become a Niagara, or the rocks be covered by a flash flood, or huge boulders loom suddenly in their way made them realize that this was not a place that could be easily learned and mastered once and for all. A single storm could diminish all the expertise they had acquired.

The sun was out, shining bright and hot, when they arrived at a crystal-clear creek coming down from the north rim; Powell named it Silver Creek and later in a lecture revised it to Bright Angel Creek. It became, in his telling and retelling, the symbolic counterpart to the Dirty Devil River—the beautiful, benign face of nature contrasting with the evil, repellent face. By this point their food was wet through and through, despite the watertight compartments. They had broken or lost a few of their oars, and Oramel had lost the map he had been drawing since the Little Colorado. It was time to make an extended stop. They spread the food and bedding out to dry on the gravel and then stretched out themselves under a willow to sleep. Next day the whole party headed upcreek, looking for a suitable piece of wood to cut into oars. Gigantic old cottonwoods rustled overhead as they walked through the grass and bushes, the sound of canyon wrens and ravens more audible away from the river. They found a great pine log and skidded it back to cut down for oars. Their food, however, needed more than drying out; the last of the bacon was so rancid that it had to be thrown away. The can of baking soda, or what they called "saleratus," got knocked over into the river and washed away, a minor calamity that meant their bread henceforth was flat and unleavened. Soon they were reduced to half-rations of bread and stewed apples, though there was plenty of coffee to wash that mix down. Clearly, they must not relax too long here but push on.

Powell found another "Moqui" (Anasazi) ruin near their Bright Angel campsite, including the foundations of several houses and an old grinding stone for making corn meal. Why, he wondered again, had people ever sought such inaccessible places to live and farm? He decided that it must have been because the Spanish conquerors, who had come into the country with "a monstrous greed for gold and a wonderful lust for saving souls," had driven the native people to hide in these canyons. The Indians either had to give in and accept the invaders' religion or feel a rope around their necks. "Doubtless," he concluded, "some of these people preferred another alternative, and rather than be baptized or hanged they chose to imprison themselves within these canyon walls."[52]

Prison was exactly how the expeditioners were beginning to regard their own experience in the Grand Canyon. They were feeling incarcerated in an endless and worsening privation. The rain resumed, and now they had no protection from the cold, drenching nights — no canvas or ponchos left, few hats or blankets, not enough clothing to cover their bodies. Getting a fire started in the downpour was hopeless. The gloom of the canyon, whose walls towered to unprecedented heights, was getting oppressive.

While the men did the portaging, Powell seized the opportunity to climb the walls as high as he could. Men and boats diminished to mere dots, the river itself shrank to a mere brook, "and still there is more canyon above than below."[53] As he climbed, the inner gorge of dark schist gave way to shale and sandstone, but then came a sloping terrace (later generations would call it the Tonto Platform), and beyond that terrace he could see looming still more cliffs. He guessed that the distant rims were a mile high, and he was right — a mile high and requiring many hours of strenuous climbing to get out. Downstream all he could see was more of the brown-black granite gorge.

Mid-morning on the 25th, after an easy twelve miles of floating, they entered a stretch of river that had once seen tumultous volcanic activity. A great fissure slashed across the canyon, a geological fault, and out of it in the distant past had erupted a vast flood of lava. Magma had filled the entire inner gorge to a height of twelve to fifteen hundred

waters, gathering rapidly on the bare rocks back of the cañon into a small channel, have carved a deep side cañon, through which they run until they fall into the farther end of this chamber. The rock at the

"Running a Rapid." Illustration from "The Cañons of the Colorado," Scribner's Monthly, *Feb. 1875.*

feet, forming a dam against the river. "What a conflict of water and fire there must have been here," Powell marveled. "Just imagine a river of molten rock running down into a river of melted snow. What a seething and boiling of the waters; what clouds of steam rolled into the heavens!"[54] Looking up, they could see the cinder cone of a crater (and there are more in the adjoining country, out of view). Eventually, the Colorado had eroded the lava away, restoring its channel, but lava still lined the walls and chunks of lava still sat in the river bed, creating one of the worst rapids they had encountered. Despite three hours of portaging around Lava Falls Rapid, they made thirty-five miles that day.

They were in the Lower Gorge, passing Parashont Wash, 205 Mile Rapid, and Granite Spring (to use modern names), where they came upon a garden growing on the delta of a tributary stream. Indians, it seemed, still had a living presence in the canyon. Whoever they were (Hualapai? Paiutes?), they had planted corn, melons, and squashes, Bradley noted, "with considerable care." Assuming that the owners were up in the mountains hunting and that their own hunger justified a raid, the Powell party sneaked through the garden, took a few ripe squashes, and moved quickly downstream, where they cooked and ate their plunder. Powell wrote, "never was fruit so sweet as these stolen squashes." The fresh food gave them new strength, and they made another thirty-five miles that day. "A few days like this," he promised, "and we are out of prison."[55]

But there was more darkness before there was light. On 27 August, a little before noon, they came upon a patch of river that seemed worse than any they had met with since Green River City. Rapids marked a fall in the river of eighteen to twenty feet, then rough water extended for another two to three hundred yards, leading to another fall whose scale they could only guess. Even if they made it past those hazards, there was still an immense rock projecting halfway across the downstream current that they might have trouble avoiding. All afternoon they scanned the situation, looking for answers. No portage seemed possible; they would have had to haul the boats straight up the cliff, requiring many hours, even days, and an extravagance of energy. Lining would have required a longer rope than they possessed. In reconnoitering, Powell at one point got himself caught once again in a dangerously narrow place on the cliff face, looking four hundred feet down and unable to move forward or back. The others passed him a line, but he could not let go to grab it. They then brought oars which they used to brace him from falling and to give him a plank on which he stepped back to safety. Descending to camp, he was undaunted, announcing that they would run the rapids in the morning.

After dinner the elder Howland asked Powell to walk up a little side creek with him to discuss their predicament. The trip must end here, Oramel insisted when they were alone; they must climb out onto the rim and head for the Mormon frontier outpost of St. George, which was somewhere to the north. Dunn was ready to leave, and his brother Seneca would go along, though reluctantly. The two men came back to camp and said nothing, but Powell was now agitated and worried by these men's reluctance to go farther.

That evening he reviewed the notes of their route and tried to calculate how much of the canyon was left to run. He checked his figures against the sextant's readings. As nearly as he could calculate, they were forty-five miles away from the mouth of the Virgin River coming out of southwestern Utah, a figure that he knew must be doubled on account of the river's meanderings. Many of those miles must be through open country, beyond the canyon's terminus. His authority in that prediction was the manscript journal of a trio of Mormon explorers, led by Jacob Hamblin, which described exploring the main river from the Virgin eastward to the Grand Wash. Once they reached that tributary, they could easily follow it upstream some twenty miles to St. George. So the party was that close, if they could hold together and get past their last deadly obstacle.

Howland fell asleep by the river's edge, but in the night he was awakened to hear Powell lay out his calculations. There was no sleep at all for the latter, who paced up and down the sand the whole night. If they decided to abandon the boats and climb out, then what would they face? A desert that was perhaps seventy-five miles wide before they reached St. George. It could be crossed, if the recent rains had left standing a few puddles of water. For a few moments Powell leaned toward accepting Howland's proposal, but then he stiffened his resolve: "For years I have been contemplating this trip. To leave the exploration unfinished, to say that there is a part of the canyon which I cannot explore, having already nearly accomplished it, is more than I am willing to acknowledge, and I determine to go on."[56] He roused Walter, who agreed to stay with him on the river, as did Hawkins, Sumner, Bradley, and Hall.

That evening Bradley wrote in his journal, "There is discontent in camp tonight and I fear some of the party will take to the mountains but hope not. This is decidely the darkest day of the trip but I don't despair yet." Hawkins, remembering back years later, was sure that Powell had decided to abandon the expedition, at least temporarily in order to get food supplies replenished—that is, until Andy Hall and he, the youngest two in the party, announced that they at least meant to continue on, whether anyone else accompanied them or not. Dunn tried to dissuade them; he was upset about leaving these young friends and was sure they would die in the rapids. "While we were talking," Hawkins recalled, "the Major came up to me and laid his left arm across my neck, tears running down his cheeks . . . and the Major said to me, Bill, do you really mean what you say? I told him that I did, and he said that if he had one man that would stay with him that he would not abandon the river." So, with that show of his men's resolve, Hawkins claimed, the expedition leader decided not to abandon the cause.[57]

Aside from the Powells, the men had gotten along well with one another, and now they were upset by the prospect of parting, tears rolling down their faces like children. In the morning, as they sat solemnly around the campfire, they could not come to an agreement. Each side of the dispute felt that the other was risking suicide. The Howlands and Dunn still insisted on walking out, the others still insisted on staying with the boats. And so they must separate.

Those continuing on the river were now too few to man all three of the boats. The *Emma Dean*, which had taken a heavy beating, must be left behind, and the remaining six men must crowd into the two oak-planked vessels, *Kitty Clyde's Sister* and *Maid of the Canyon*. All the barometers, fossils, minerals, and part of the ammunition must be left on the rocks to lighten the vessels. The cook baked the remaining flour into a supply of biscuits, which they divided into two piles, and Howland picked up two rifles and a shotgun. He also took along a duplicate set of the expedition records (or he thought he did; in fact he took the only set of records from the last part of the trip), a letter from Wes to Emma, and a watch from Sumner to give to his sister in Denver in the event they were drowned. "They left us with good feelings," Bradley wrote, "though we deeply regret their loss for they are as fine fellows as I ever had the good fortune to meet."[58]

Once more the boats pushed off from shore, the crews mustering all the courage they could. Sumner told the outcome with characteristic terseness: after lifting the boats over a line of rocks they "ran the rest of the damned rapid with a ringing cheer, though at great risk, as the boats shipped nearly half full in a perfect hell of foam." Somehow they even managed to swing free of the big dangerous monolith blocking the channel and come quietly into an eddy around a curve. Behind them, the three left behind stood watching them succeed in running the rapid. It had not been so serious a threat after all, no worse than many other places the party had run without harm. For a couple of hours Powell and the others waited, firing their guns and hoping that the three had changed their minds and would follow in the abandoned boat. They did not do so, however, and the expedition went on without them, worrying and wondering what they were doing.[59]

That afternoon the river-runners had another near disaster, as they tried to line one of the boats through a hazardous stretch of white water. Luckily Bradley, ever cool in a crisis, was sitting in the boat when it broke free, and he rode it through to safety, with only the loss of a sternpost. That was their last scare. At noon on the very next day, just as Powell had calculated, they came drifting out into the Grand Wash, its low hills and broad skies lifting their spirits, and when night came, having made 42 1/2 miles, they camped for the last night in a mesquite thicket, sitting up until after midnight talking of home, talking of the three who had left them, talking of the ordeal of the canyon.

Powell was filled with relief and joy that evening, but his joy had little to do with having experienced the great declivity out of which they had just come. Quite the contrary, when he thought of the Grand Canyon, he flashed back to those grim days after the battle at Shiloh, when he lay delirious from his wounded arm, wondering whether he would survive or die.

> When he who has been chained by wounds to a hospital cot until his canvas tent seems like a dungeon cell, until the groans of those who lie about tortured with probe and knife are piled up, a weight of horror on his ears that he cannot throw off, cannot forget, and until the stench of festering wounds and anaesthetic drugs has filled the air with its loathsome burthen — when he at last goes out into the open field, what a world he sees! How beautiful the sky, how bright the sunshine, what "floods of delirious music" pour from the throats of birds, how sweet the fragrance of earth and trees and blossoms! The first hour of convalescent freedom seems rich recompense for all pain and gloom and terror.[60]

The Grand Wash was his coming out of the horror. For all the spectacle of wild, archaic nature he had witnessed, for all the beauty and the intellectual challenge presented by the canyon, he now associated it with a fetid hospital tent, as earlier he had associated it with a prison. Such had not been his feeling back at the Uinta, after spending more than a month on the Green. There he had been at a high pitch of ecstasy. Two weeks in the canyon, however, had been a brush with death, comparable only to the war, and now his first impulse was to forget the ordeal and revel in his release.

Continuing on their way, they passed a band of Paiutes, the first people they had seen in a couple of months. Most of them fled at the sight of these strange bearded men emerging out of the walled river, except a man and woman who seemed reassured by the half-familiar Ute words that Powell spoke to them. How far to the Virgin River was the question he tried to ask, but he could get no answer. Sumner, though himself nearly naked, reddened by so much sun, and poorly fed, sneered at the impoverished couple: "Her ladyship's costume was nice and light and cool. It consisted of half a yard of dirty buckskin and a brass ring. She was as disgusting a hag as ever rode a broomstick." [61] Lacking any tobacco, he gave her a piece of soap, and they went on.

At midafternoon on that day, 30 August, they encountered three white men and an Indian hauling in a seine at the junction with another river—and, yes, it was indeed the Virgin. The white men were Mormons, Joseph Asey and his sons, engaged in building a new town where the Virgin and Colorado meet to replace the less well sited Callville farther west. They had instructions from Salt Lake City to watch for any fragments of the Colorado River Exploring Expedition that might have drifted downstream. After so long a silence the Powell party were all assumed dead, drowned, and destroyed, though in fact they had once more come through alive and well, and with ten pounds of flour to spare.

The Mormons treated them with a ready hospitality that Powell would remember gratefully for years to come. As soon as the bishop of St. Thomas, James Leithead, got word of their arrival, he rushed to meet them, bringing mail from home and a wagon filled with fresh melons. Starved for fresh food, the men "ate melons till the morning star could be seen."[62] They were offered a free ride back to civilization if they were interested, an offer that the Powell brothers quickly accepted. As soon as they were fed and rested, they left for St. George and tarried there for only a few days before catching another ride with a driver and mule team headed for Salt Lake City.

The four others in the party decided to follow the river on south to look over the country and its prospects. They had come to improve their means, but so far wealth had eluded them. Powell gave them part of the cash he had left in his pockets, along with the two remaining boats.[63] They had never had a chance to do any prospecting or hide-collecting, as called for in the original contract, but then after the wreck at Lodore and other mishaps, and after so severe a loss of rations, no one could realistically insist on the old financial terms or schedule. Altogether, they had been on the river for sixtynine days, including stopovers, not the ten months or year they had projected. Powell calculated that they had come a little over nine hundred miles.

So on 1 September came a second day of separation, this one with fewer tears and less anxiety. Before leaving, Bradley penned a letter to his sister, "but I was so intoxicated with joy at getting through so soon and so well that I don't know what I wrote to her."[64] He went on to Fort Yuma and then over to San Diego, where he set himself up in the orchard business, never going home to Massachusetts until a few weeks before his death in 1885. Andy Hall made it all the way down to tidewater, after which he went back to a career of mule driving in Arizona Territory. In 1882 he was working as a stagecoach guard when he was killed near Globe by a band of robbers. Hawkins traveled along as Hall's companion to the Gulf, and he too settled in Arizona, farming until his death in 1919. This former renegade from the law ended up a justice of the peace.

Sumner, who made it down to Yuma, later headed back to Denver; he lived out his life in Colorado and Utah, enjoying a certain local renown as one of the last of the old frontiersmen. Most of his later years were spent in prospecting for silver and other minerals, ever chasing after a rainbow. In 1907 he died in Vernal, Utah, as poor, crusty, and prideful as ever. Resentment toward Powell grew on him in later years, for he had had little success of his own and insisted that he, not Powell, was the true "discoverer" of the Grand Canyon. If that were so, he had never been very enthusiastic about what he discovered. At the end of the 1869 expedition he summed up his view of where they had been: "I never want to see it again anywhere. Near the Grand Cañon it will probably remain unvisited for many years again, as it has nothing to recommend it, but its general desolation as a study for the geologist."[65]

And the fate of the men who had determined to walk out of the canyon? Tellingly, Powell did not organize a search party to go look for them. It would be another year, in fact, before he made any effort to track them down, and then it would be done as part of a more general survey of Indians and geography north of the canyon. The men had left of their own will, rejecting his entreaties and his leadership. They had used the rapids as an excuse more than as a reason to leave, or they would have followed after when they saw the party go through unscathed. Bad feelings, not bad water, was the real cause of their separation, a fact that Powell understood all too well. Although publicly he would say nothing harsh against them, he was manifestly not torn with anguish about their fate.

By this time modern communications in the form of the telegraph had reached the remote village of St. George, and on 7 September a telegrapher's dispatch to Salt Lake City reported that, five days earlier, a friendly Indian had reported to the local whites that the "Shebits" (or Shivwits, a band of Paiutes) had found three men north of the Canyon in an exhausted state and fed them, before sending them on their way, but then had followed and killed the men. Later reports suggested that the men, still unidentified by name, had come upon an Indian woman peacefully gathering seed, and had raped and killed her.

Whether the news came while Powell was still in St. George is impossible to say, but he certainly had received it by the time he arrived in Salt Lake City, and he did not go back to verify it or to determine whether those were his men who had been killed or to recover their bodies. A later telegram from Mormon elders in southern Utah claimed that corpses had been discovered, but Powell's only response was to question whether those were really his men. When it seemed possible that the dead were indeed the Howlands and Dunn, Powell defended their honor with no hesitation, Oramel Howland's in particular, whom he stated was incapable of rape or murder. "I have known O.G. Howland personally for many years and I have no hesitation in pronouncing this part of the story a libel. It was not in the man's faithful, genial nature to do such a thing." Nonetheless, for Powell the expedition was over, and so was his responsibility for the men.[66]

The capital city of Utah treated the Major like a conquering hero come home from the front, draping him with garlands of praise and glory. On 15 September an article appeared in the *Deseret Evening News*, complimenting Powell on his achievement: "He appears to have endured the fatigues and anxieties of the trip remarkably well. There are but few men who have the opportunity in this life of learning what the world thinks of them after they are supposed to be dead." On the next night Powell gave what the paper termed a "gratuitous lecture" on his Colorado River expedition to an audience that packed the Thirteenth Ward Assembly Rooms; the level of popular interest was intense. The lecture described the sequence of canyons along the Green and Colorado that he had named, the main features of their geology, the changing color of the river reflecting the formations through which it flowed, the absence of timber along the banks, the "tribe of diminutive men[,] kindred to the Aztecs" who had once lived in those inaccessible places, the tense last moments when they almost lost Bradley. If the report is a reliable summary of the lecture, it seems that Powell had not yet had time to organize his thoughts more systematically, but the audience did not care; they were hearing directly from the man who only two weeks before had come floating out of a hidden, fabled land.[67]

When the applause died down, the Powell brothers took a night stage north to Corinne, where they caught the Union Pacific cars and headed home to Chicago, arriving on 20 September and putting up at the Tremont Hotel. The following day Wes gave an interview to the *Chicago Republican*, "direct from scenes of his great exploits and discoveries."[68] A few weeks later he was again lecturing on the river expedition to the Chicago Academy of Science and from there went on to lecture at Pike's Hall in Cincinnati, Ohio, at Wheaton College in Wheaton, Illinois, at the Parker Institute in Brooklyn, New York, and again in Chicago at Plymouth Church. He had been a Utah hero, now he was an American hero. The entire nation wanted to hear about the extraordinary country in the West that had been opened at last and to see or hear from the extraordinary man who had opened it.

On the first day of November a report was finished and submitted to the War Department that read like a parody of the Powell expedition. Its author liked to style himself "Captain Samuel Adams," though he had never been in command of any vessel larger than a raft. Adams, who had tried to take over the Colorado exploring party back in Green River City, had dreamed up his own project to run alongside Powell's and try to steal a little attention from the media and Congress. He too was setting out to unlock the mysterious country and the river running through it.

Green River having been claimed, Adams hied himself down to Breckenridge, Colorado, located near the headwaters of the Blue River, and made that his embarkation point. The Blue, after all, had appeared on a fewer older maps as the upper continuation of the Grand. The only boats available were those he had to make himself, which he proceeded to do, hammering them together out of local pine: four of them in all, each of them one foot longer than Powell's cargo vessels. With promises of finding gold, he recruited one man more than his rival to make up an expedition of eleven, and they launched on 12 July, while Powell's boats were racing through Desolation Canyon. Adams's course was north toward the Grand, with Mount Powell and the other peaks of the Gore Range on his left. The second day out their boats crashed into rocks, and he lost all of his papers, instruments, and maps, including those precious "authorizing letters" from high government officials. By the time they reached the Grand, half the party had gone back home, leaving him with Messrs. Twible, Waddle, Lovell, Lillis, Day, and himself riding in two of the boats. On 7 August the last boat wrecked, and he was down to a crew of Twible and Lillis, the others leaving in a huff, threatening retaliation for gross mismanagement and breach of contract. The shrunken crew now threw a raft together — then after an accident another raft, and another, and still another, until finally their leader decided he had made a thorough job of it. They had "gone over the most difficult portion of our route," he abruptly proclaimed. How far they got down the Grand is hard to say, perhaps as far as Glenwood Canyon.[69]

Three years earlier, Adams reported, he had gone up the Colorado some eleven miles beyond Callville until he could see a broad, open valley ahead, obviously navigable (and obviously the junction of the Virgin with the main river). Now, standing on a high point above the wreckage of his fourth raft and looking downstream, he thought he could see that same valley on the horizon. Ergo, commerce could easily come up this river system all the way from the Gulf to the Rockies. Wild, extravagant rumors about immensely deep canyons that were hundreds of miles long, filled with terrific rapids and dangerous falls blocking the path of economic progress, were nonsense. Here, in truth, was the easy water-route west that Americans had been seeking for generations.

So much for his "report" on exploration. Adams went on for another ten pages, laying out the incredible potential of the Southwest, once its principal river was properly utilized. The Colorado would be to the Pacific Coast what the Mississippi was to the East. Down its current barges would move mountains of grain, coal, and lumber. Railroads would connect the river across the plains to markets and factories, and one day Arizona would stand with Illinois and New York as a national center of industry. All that prevented such a dream from coming true was bad publicity about the river itself — a negative image created by those who had had no direct experience with it — and despotic concentrations of capital that sought, through whatever means possible, legal or illegal, to keep down men of enterprise such as himself.

For his labors in behalf of the nation, Adams sought compensation from Congress in the amount of $20,000, but it was over a year later before such a bill was introduced in the House. To bolster his case he persuaded the *San Francisco Chronicle* to reprint his journal of exploration in nine installments during March 1872. His last article ended with the promise that "in his next communication" he would tell of the remarkable Indian tribes that lived along the Colorado "and the ruins of cities, canals, missions, and fortifications of a people whose history is forgotten, and which today stand as the silent monuments of the long, unbroken Sabbath which has rested over this once populous territory."[70] He would inspire readers with hope that such monuments could be built again.

But there would be no next article, nor indeed any compensation coming from Congress. The territorial delegate from Arizona, Robert McCormick, who had long considered Adams "a lunatic," asked Major Powell for a critique of his rival's explorations. Powell pointed out that between Adams's eleven-mile voyage upriver from Callville and the endpoint of his aborted mission down the Blue and Grand lay more than eight hundred miles of country. That Adams could have looked over all those miles with the naked eye was patently ridiculous. That he missed seeing the nearly impassable canyons that Powell had gone down was incredible. "The absurdity of designating [the Colorado] as a central route between the Atlantic & Pacific Oceans is made very glaring by a moment's consultation of the map of the United States." The case dragged on, however, until 1875, when the House committee on claims, relying on Powell's critique and calling Adams's report "a complex tissue of errors and exaggerations," refused his claim.[71]

Politicians have not always been so skeptical toward visionaries of western economic development; as often as not, they have given away the store. But in the instance of the Colorado River they had at hand a man whose 1869 expedition had made him a genuine authority and an authentic hero. Powell did not need a lunatic, a buffoon, a pathetic imitator like Sam Adams to make him look commanding, though the contrast between the two explorers underlined how remarkable Powell's trip had been, how hard-won his expertise was, and how easily things might have turned out differently.

Powell, to be sure, heightened his own adventures with a dash of romance, embellished a few anecdotes to dramatize his personal

Powell with burnsides, taken in Wheaton, Illinois, Dec. 1869, a few months after his first Colorado River expedition. (Courtesy: Utah State Historical Society)

heroism, and, disregarding his own notes, exaggerated the dangers of some of the falls he went over. He also created a picture of harmony where there was often hostility and resentment. But he did go down the river — a real river — every single mile from Green River City to the Virgin. He slept on hard rocks and sand with his men for over three months and suffered with them through all the dangers and hardships. He did so with only a stump of an arm that gave him more pain than he talked about — a disability that would have kept other men at home. When he looked back over where he had been, he had no illusions about easy wealth lying out there, waiting to be exploited. In fact, he had only limited interest in any wealth that the Colorado River could offer anyone.

Powell's journey down the legendary river of the West was one of the greatest events in the history of American exploration. Only the travels of Meriwether Lewis and William Clark some six decades earlier compare in significance or drama. Those two intrepid men set the standard and no one ever surpassed them, though their achievement rested mainly on the extraordinary journal they kept over a span of two years, a journal filled with wonderfully vivid descriptions of landscape, encounters with Indians, and details of natural history that intrigued readers for a long time to come. They each had two good hands with which to write that journal. They had as audience a highly literate president who first imagined their exploration and gave them everything they needed, and they had each other to share the writing as they did the command. Powell, in contrast, raised his own funds and recruited his own party, with no one else to depend on. He had a brother for companion who was as maimed in mind as he himself was in body. Instead of feasting off a land and sea of wild abundance, his party went through one of the harshest territories on the continent, forced to hurry because of the uncertainty of food. His men were not soldiers to the bone, and they left behind more commentary on their leader than Lewis and Clark's rank-and-file did, much of it unflattering. For all of those differences, if Lewis and Clark opened a century of exploration, Powell closed it with comparable success. He removed the phrase "unknown" from the last large area of the coterminous United States.

No one else of his own generation was prepared to do what he did and did so well. Sumner and the other boys may have justly felt that more credit was due them, but they did not organize the expedition nor push it through; without Powell it is hard to imagine them getting to Green River City with a set of boats, let alone making it as far as the Grand Canyon. As for other scientists of the day, they had avoided the challenge or failed to see it. Perhaps the brightest geologist around, Clarence King knew what it was to traipse across rough country, but always he needed his lavender gloves, his comfortable bed, and his supply of good wine. He did not risk his life in a wooden boat going down a river filled with big, hard rocks, nor did he sleep on the ground doubled up for warmth with the likes of Jack Sumner. Nor did John Strong Newberry of Columbia University take on the Colorado as Powell did, though Newbury had been with Lieutenant Joseph Ives and Captain J.N. Macomb in traversing the southwestern desert. The army engineers whose careers immediately preceded Powell's had done great service to the nation, but they were more limited men than he. Usually they required a whole troop bearing guns wherever they went, yet for all their entourage they were circumscribed in purpose, and perhaps in imagination, reconnoitering the country mainly for military or transportation purposes. Powell, in contrast to all of these, brought to the Colorado a simplicity of means and a richness of ends. He had ambition, scope, determination, and a willingness to risk all for the sake of science. Thereafter, the Colorado and its tributaries would rightfully be identified with him.

Had Powell been content with making a single, heroic voyage, putting a few names on the map, that identification might not have held. Having run the river, however, he went back east to lay the foundations for a longer, more detailed exploration, one that would bring together science, art, ethnology, and public policy. He would be back, for there was a lot more he wanted to know about this place.

CHAPTER 6

Surveying the
High Plateaus

Exploration is a linear path blazed across the blank spaces of a society's knowledge. In the half-decade following the Civil War the exploration of the American West, including most dramatically the Colorado River and its borderlands, reached an end. By that point Americans had followed every river, crossed every mountain range, and traipsed through every desert and plain. They had made rough, approximate maps to guide others. Now the nation shifted toward a more systematic survey of that huge, austere interior, and Powell the explorer became Powell the surveyor.

A survey is more comprehensive than an exploration, involving as it does the careful mapping of every square mile, the inventorying of natural resources, the explaining of how things came to be where they are, the assessing of future economic possibilities. The survey demands scientific expertise; it is a project characteristic of a modern nation-state steeped in the perspective of science. The survey is a more thoroughgoing way of taking possession, of establishing empire. The land must now be divided into geometrical shapes, measured with exquisite precision, and given exact boundaries. Names must go down in the record book. Plants, animals, and minerals must be extracted from their tangled web in nature and put into ordered cases within museums. The citizen seeking land or wealth must be able to find its coordinates accurately on a map.

Powell, the last of the great western explorers, was aware that a new generation of expert surveyors were already in the field, some more than a decade or two ahead of him. They had carried out the Pacific railroad surveys of 1853–55. Although they did not manage to define the best transcontinental route, they did introduce the survey as a concept. Even earlier scientific surveyors had appeared in the East; the first state-funded survey was established in Massachusetts in 1830, and it diffused from there into the Old Northwest and the South. Thus, by the time Powell went down the Colorado, the idea of a systematic survey of the West's resources had appeared, and its practitioners were capturing public attention and government support.[1] If he wanted to enjoy more than a brief moment of fame, he would have to join their ranks and become a surveyor himself. Indeed, that was what he had been hoping to do when his food supply ran out.

The best known of the western surveyors was Ferdinand Vandiveer Hayden, an unprepossessing man of no outstanding qualifications. He was five years older than Powell, had been a student at Oberlin before him, and a graduate of the Albany Medical College. But medicine was not his calling; he had gone west to collect natural history specimens for his mentor, James Hall, and then, breaking with Hall, had become a field collector for a long list of distinguished men of science. Starting first in the Dakota Badlands in 1853, he had swept a wide arc from the upper Missouri toward the Rockies. Whole wagon loads of bones and fossils, rocks and ore samples had come out of the ground, bearing his name. In 1867 he won appointment as the director of the Geological Survey of Nebraska, and two years later he parlayed that into the new directorship of the Geological Survey of the Territories of the United States, under the Department of Interior, with $10,000 per annum to spend. Soon thereafter, a complaisant Congress allowed him to upgrade his title to director of the U.S. Geological and Geographical Survey of the Territories and raised his budget to $75,000.[2]

As a scientist, Hayden was no great figure; his mind was a jumble of facts, his powers of reasoning limited. As a human being he was even less impressive: vindictive, insecure, manipulative, self-promoting, a plagiarist. But in the eyes of Congress he spoke with scientific authority, and that authority always confirmed what Congress wanted to hear: that the West is a glorious land of opportunity. The grass is greener there than anywhere else on earth, the mines richer, the waters more abundant, the soil a fount of fertility, the scenery incomparably magnificent. At least the last part of that litany was true.

While pleasing the politicians, Hayden managed to supplement his munificent salary by arranging a few private deals on the side, including one that involved William Gilpin's real-estate investments in southern Colorado. No one saw any great conflict of interest in that.

In 1869 Ulysses S. Grant had been inaugurated as president and had plunged Washington into an unprecedentedly loose era of political spoils and corrupt administration.[3] Conflict of interest had become the national pastime. Grant's own Vice President, Schuyler Colfax (who with Samuel Bowles had visited Powell in Middle Park that campaign year of 1868), stood accused of taking free stock from the Credit Mobilier, the railroad construction company that had bilked the transcontinental line. By comparison with the Grant administration and the Congress, Hayden seemed an honest man who earned every penny in his pocket.

The Hayden Survey had plenty of money to hire good scientists and topographers, and their publications were a lasting achievement. Fielding Bradford Meek, Elliott Coues, James Gardner, James Stevenson, Cyrus Thomas, C. Hart Merriam, Henry Gannett, and William H. Holmes were all on his payroll for a time, along with the famed landscape photographer William Henry Jackson. Undoubtedly, the Hayden Survey's greatest contribution was the highly professional *Atlas of Colorado*, published in 1877. Thanks to Hayden's entrepreneurial success, the federal government began to underwrite the accumulation of knowledge about the western lands on a scale never before seen.

While Hayden was enlarging his survey into a new kind of Rocky Mountain imperialism, another surveyor, Clarence King, was building a rival survey extending from California eastward. King was eight years younger than Powell and already enjoyed an impressive reputation and wide acclaim. After graduating from Yale's Sheffield Scientific School, he had joined the California Survey, which was designed and directed by Josiah Dwight Whitney, himself the product of an elite eastern education with postgraduate training in Germany and France.[4] But King, always restless and supremely self-confident, had left Whitney's employ to organize his own show. Though a civilian and only twenty-five years old, he went directly to Washington and convinced the secretary of war to fund a federal survey of the entire country lying along the fortieth parallel, from the northern Sierra through Pyramid Lake, Nevada, across Utah all the way to the Front Range of Colorado near Boulder. His chief selling point was that the country's prosperity would be enhanced by knowing the exact location and potential scale of wealth lying along the route of the transcontinental railroad. The King Survey was established in 1867, with a staff of thirty-five geologists, topographers, and military personnel — the last to protect the survey against marauding Indians — and a budget of $100,000 over the first three years.[5]

King was an altogether different scientific entrepreneur than Hayden. He had a reputation as a quick study and a versatile genius. Everyone loved him—loved his amusing stories, loved his generosity of spirit. He hired the finest young brains coming out of Harvard and Yale, especially if they also had a little European polish, men like James and Arnold Hague and Samuel F. Emmons. Like King, they were bon vivants who came slumming to the rough camps of the West. It entertained them to put on boots and guns or to sleep in a canvas tent while maintaining their discriminating tastes, their impeccable standards of connoisseurship. They were the best and brightest of their generation when it came to reading the rocks, and King was the best and brightest among them. They set a standard for surveying the western landscape that Hayden could never hope to match.

By summer 1869 King and his men had advanced into the Uinta Mountains and, at season's end, passed through Salt Lake City just a few weeks before the river-weary Powell. Nervous that the obscure major from Illinois was stealing a march on his domain, King considered making his own expedition down the Green River in the fall of 1871.[6] By that date, however, it was a little late to beat Powell in the river game; and in any case, King was already bored with the hard, rambling life of the field and longing for a New York gentleman's club where he could write with better concentration and more comfort about the geology of the Great Basin.

King's survey had been sold as a practical investigation into mineral resources, from gold and silver in California to coal in Utah, resources that if properly mined and smelted, could make the nation a lot of money. King himself was bewitched by the prospect of acquiring great personal wealth in the mining business. But all the same he was devoted to geological science for its own sake, and he insisted that a survey must not be distracted from producing first-rate theoretical studies—not by the call of adventure, nor by the temptation of making a private fortune, nor by the trivial demands of museums. The two leading publications of his survey exemplified those antithetical goals: the utilitarian *Mining Industry* (1870), coauthored by King and James Hague; and the more theoretical *Systematic Geology* (1878), King's solo work.

In addition to publishing reports, King believed that the new generation of western surveyors should produce more detailed, reliable maps of their assigned terrain. This he learned not only from observing the U.S. Coast and Geodetic Survey but more directly from sitting at the feet of Josiah Whitney and his German-born topographer C.T.

Hoffman, who introduced to the United States the most advanced techniques of topographical mapping developed in Europe. Using ancient Euclidean principles, European map makers had learned to cast the whole landscape into a series of enormous triangles. They fixed a base line, and from its end points they projected lines to prominent mountain peaks or other highly visible features. If one knew the length of the base line and the size of the two angles formed by the projections, one could compute the distance to the peak — that is, complete the triangle. One such projection led to another, and then to another, until the whole West could be plotted and measured. Within that web of abstract lines the topographer could fill in the slopes and contours that wrinkled the earth's surface. King's Fortieth Parallel Survey promoted the techniques of triangulation as a more precise of system of large-scale mapping.

Neither Hayden nor King was a military officer, trained at West Point, and that was a significant departure from tradition. Before the war the Army Corps of Topographical Engineers had nearly monopolized the work of investigating the country. But now Hayden, a civilian scientist, scorned and contested the military's role in the West. Although King was in the employ of the War Department, he too was independent of their control and hired only civilians to do his scientific work. The army was a much diminished force, reduced to the work of subduing the native peoples. But one young officer, Lieutenant George M. Wheeler, who was King's age and a high-ranking graduate of the Point, refused to accept this decline of intellectual status; he reasserted a more scientific role for the military by establishing and directing the Geographical Surveys West of the Hundredth Meridian. That meridian ran through Dodge City, Kansas, so that Wheeler was claiming as broad a terrain as Hayden — in fact, was competing for the same terrain.

The Wheeler Survey did not get organized until 1871. When Powell was going down the Colorado, Lieutenant Wheeler was stationed in Nevada, stuck and bored, looking for some outlet for his mathematical and engineering talent. First he mapped the territory of Nevada, and then, inspired by his success, announced that he was ready to take on the rest of the West. He moved into the California deserts and in the furnace-heat of July and August traversed Death Valley. Then he looked eastward into Arizona and Utah. He recruited a civilian photographer, Timothy O'Sullivan; a civilian journalist, Frederick Loring; and a civilian geologist, Grove Karl Gilbert to bolster his public image; mainly, however, he put military men to work at gathering the data. The most significant of his reports did not appear until 1889, long after his survey was officially ended. It was an extraordinary compendium of useful information: altitudes of every high place, distances from point to point, population figures of each town and territory, whole tables of facts on industry, communication, irrigation, and Indians.

All of those federal surveyors ignored, by and large, the native peoples whose land this once had been. Hayden found them an annoyance and an obstacle. King was more sympathetic, but his interest in natives rarely rose above the libidinous; he was irresistibly attracted to women of darker skin. Wheeler, though a reliable source on native demography, counted Indians with the hope that they soon would become extinct, and soon would not be soon enough. "While the fate of the Indian is sealed," he wrote in his final report, "the interval during which their extermination as a race is consummated will doubtless be marked . . . with still more murderous ambuscades and massacres."[7] A brutal man, Wheeler understood his survey to be another instrument, along with cannons and cavalry, of military conquest.

As Powell rode home to Illinois following his journey deep into the canyon country, he realized that he had this well-heeled, well-staffed, highly ambitious competition pressing on all sides. Much that he wanted to accomplish had not been possible in that first pass at the river. His collections were woefully incomplete, his maps were primitive, his scientific understanding of the surrounding landscape was sketchy. More than that, he had not had the opportunity to study closely the native peoples, and in contrast to Hayden, King, and Wheeler, such a survey was what he wanted to attempt. He did not want to take the West away from the other men, but only to return to the blank spaces of Utah and northern Arizona, lay claim to that as his personal territory, and produce a full, careful investigation of its land and people.

Over the winter of 1869–70 Powell stayed in the college town of Normal, at home with Emma once more and tending to his museum curatorial duties. On 12 March his mother died in Wheaton. Friends eulogized her spotless life, her sound judgment, her warm and earnest heart. Then Mary Dean Powell was laid to rest in the local cemetery, far from the place of her birth. Her eldest son was among the most stricken mourners. For the rest of his life he kept on his library wall a small painting done by her hand of a faraway England, which he described in verse: "A cottage with thatch, and a tree standing near, / A mother and child in the foreground appear. . . . Oh its charm for me now is not found in its art; / I rejoice / in the voice / That appeals to the heart."[8]

In contrast to Mary's Bible-centered life, however, Wes was focused on creating a secular career in science, with scientific surveying his new ambition. Instead of sermons in church he gave lectures on geological uplift and erosion, on secular wonders in nature. His audiences received him enthusiastically, though reporters sometimes commented on his low, indistinct voice and his casual manner of address; for all his sometimes florid rhetoric, he was no platform orator by the standards of the day.[9] In addition to his public lecturing, he began to lay siege to Congress, looking for friendly politicians and other supporters in the capital who would fund his researches.

By May he was seeking an appropriation of $12,000 to "prosecute to completion the geographical and topographical exploration of the Colorado River and its tributaries, and to establish, by astronomical observations, four of the most important points, viz: the junction of the Grand and Green Rivers, the mouth of the San Juan, the mouth of the Little Colorado, and the mouth of the Virgin River." The appropriation allowed him to hire a small scientific staff and a pack train of horses and mules, and it supplemented the free rations that he had been permitted to requisition from army posts at Fort Bridger and Camp Douglas.

Once more Joseph Henry, secretary of the Smithsonian, offered a letter of support for this man who had shown "remarkable perseverance, sagacity, and intrepidity." A more detailed study of the Colorado River region, Henry argued, would advance understanding of that unusual environment and, in particular, might show how its surface water might be usefully captured to irrigate crops. Another powerful figure, Secretary J.D. Cox of the Department of the Interior, added his own justification. Although his department was championing Hayden in the survey competition, "a long time must necessarily elapse before said river will have been reached by public surveys, and it is important that its geographical locality should be accurately determined." Congress apparently agreed with those powerful endorsements, for on 12 July 1870 it appropriated the full requested sum "for completing the survey of the Colorado of the West and its tributaries."[10]

In making that appropriation, granting Powell his first federal dollars, Congress in effect created still another survey in the West — a fourth that within a few years would officially be designated the "Geographical and Geological Survey of the Rocky Mountain Region, J.W. Powell in charge." The Rockies would figure hardly at all in Powell's program; a better title would have been "the survey of the high plateau country of Utah and Arizona through which the Colorado River flows." Year after year he had to come back to get his appropriation renewed and increased. He never enjoyed the largesse that Hayden, King, or Wheeler did. But within a year of his first trip down the Colorado River Powell, the self-made explorer, had won a niche for himself in western surveying. He had entered a new career and was learning how to use his elbows to push forward through the competition.

By late August Powell was in Utah once again, backtracking along the road he had taken a year earlier, heading south from Salt Lake City toward the frontier settlements. He had received letters, now nearly a year old, from the mother and the brother of the Howland boys, asking for more information than they had gotten from the newspapers about the dead men's fate; but he had nothing personally to give them. More on his mind at this moment was the problem of locating accessible points along the river where he could supply another flotilla of boats. Making a more thorough survey meant staying longer in the river canyons, and that in turn necessitated a system for bringing in food—establishing a depot, say, every one to two hundred miles, which a pack train could reach. Below Gunnison's Crossing there was the Crossing of the Fathers and there was the mouth of the Paria, but below those access points Powell knew no way to get down to the river before the taking-out point at the mouth of the Virgin—a stretch of nearly three hundred miles.

At the town of Parowan on 5 September Powell joined President Brigham Young, the heavy-set, domineering patriarch of the Mormon Church, and traveled with him toward the headwaters of the Sevier River. The Sevier originates in the highlands of southern Utah, over ten thousand feet in elevation, not far from the sources of the Paria, the Kanab, and the Virgin Rivers. Young was heading toward that divide on his way to consecrate the fledging village of Kanab, and he left Powell in the hands of his most respected explorer-scout, Jacob Hamblin.[11]

Hamblin, now fifty-one years old and twenty years a resident of the territory, had family roots in the same part of the country that Powell did. Born in Ohio, then moving to southern Wisconsin as a teenager, he had converted to Mormonism against his parents' wishes; eventually he emigrated along the trail that led from Nauvoo, Illinois, to Salt Lake City. In 1854 Young sent him on a mission to the Indians of southern Utah. An unquestioning follower, Hamblin had done his best to obey Young's instructions; he learned the native dialects, took two wives from among the Paiutes (along with two white wives), taught the Book of Mormon to the tribes, and served as a diplomat in time of conflict. He was widely known as the "buckskin apostle." Frederick Dellenbaugh, who would serve with Powell and come to know Hamblin well, gave a non-Mormon's testimonial to the latter's abilities:

> He was an extraordinary character and had a great influence over the Indians. He was always fair with them and his slow, quiet way of talking suited their ideas. He never exhibited any fear or excitement, whatever might have been his inner feelings. I never saw anyone so quiet, calm and self-contained as "Old Jacob" as everyone in Kanab called him.[12]

Dellenbaugh might have added that, in 1870, no white man knew the lands adjacent to the Colorado River as well as Hamblin.

The others in the Powell party included Hamblin's brother Fred, several other Mormons in charge of the pack train and wagon team, and two young men from Illinois, whom Powell had hired a few weeks earlier as the first members of his new survey team: Francis Bishop, topographer, and Walter Graves, assistant. Bishop (who should not be confused with the lad of the same name who got lost on the Bear River in the fall of 1868) was a twenty-seven-year-old war veteran, a former captain in the Union Army who had taken a bullet in the left lung at Fredericksburg and, later, had become Powell's star pupil at Illinois Wesleyan, graduating with distinction the preceding spring. Unlike his teacher, he had remained a reverent Christian; his address at commencement had been on "The Bible, the Keystone of Civilization." Bishop had just married, and his bride died while he was away on this expedition.

Joining the group at the headwaters was Chuarumpeak, one of the leaders of the Kaibabs, the band of Paiutes who inhabited the Kaibab Plateau to the south in Arizona, and some of his fellow tribesmen. Chuar, as Powell familiarly called him, or "Frank," as the Mormons called him, became a longtime friend and instructor on Paiute mythology. Sharing the lead with Hamblin, he took the survey party on a strenuous, meandering route toward the Grand Canyon and the site of a possible supply depot. As they went along, Powell was impressed by the intimate knowledge of landscape possessed by his Indian companions. "I have prided myself on being able to grasp and retain in my mind the topography of a country; but these Indians put me to shame." His own talent, as he appraised it, was to grasp the whole of the place, engraving a broad map of spatial relations on his mind, while Chuar and the others had a very detailed, unerring knowledge of every rock, ledge, gulch, and canyon. "They cannot describe a country to you," Powell wrote, "but they can tell you all the particulars of a route."[13]

According to Powell, writing in *Canyons of the Colorado* more than twenty years later, he first descended into the east fork of the Virgin River — literally into the water, for they were forced to wade up to their armpits where this swift, cold stream runs through narrow canyons — during this overland expedition of 1870. The Paiutes called the fork Parunuweap, or Roaring Water Canyon, and the north fork of the Virgin, which they soon came to, they called Mukuntuweap, or Straight Canyon. Turning up this second gorge, Powell wrote, the party found themselves in one of the Southwest's most stunningly beautiful places (now protected within Zion National Park). The colossal Towers of the Virgin, monoliths of Navajo Sandstone rising nearly four thousand feet from the river bed, loomed overhead, and columbines, red monkeyflowers, and maidenhair ferns sprouted in the hanging gardens along the cliffs.

Actually, this trip into the upper reaches of the Virgin River did not occur in 1870, but in late September 1872, in the company of Stephen Jones. But it was on the earlier overland reconnoiter that Powell first topped the prominent escarpment his boat party had seen a year earlier, when they were at the mouth of the Paria — the long, conspicuous line that he named the Vermilion Cliffs for their warm, reddish glow in early morning or late afternoon.[14] At the base of the cliffs lay Pipe Spring, one of the Kaibab tribe's most important water sources until the Mormons seized it; here President Young encountered the Powell party again for he had come to lay out an enlarged fort and ranch headquarters called Winsor Castle.[15] Then across the dusty bunch grass of the Arizona Strip the surveyors rode, heading toward a high volcanic peak that Powell named in honor of his ever helpful Illinois senator, Lyman Trumbull. Likely they came down the Toroweap Valley, passing Mount Trumbull on the right, to the canyon rim, and then down a steep, narrow path, which the horses had trouble negotiating, down to the great river once more. This spot they agreed, though difficult of access, could be one of their supply depots; it was near the Lava Falls Rapid and about sixty miles upstream from where the Howlands and Dunn had separated and left the river.

Returning to Mount Trumbull, Powell found a number of Shivwits waiting for him, summoned by Chuar to talk peace. These were the very people who had been accused of killing the three Powell men. They lived on the next plateau to the west and were a potential threat to the survey's operations; Powell did not want any further troubles with them. Like the Kaibabs, the Shivwits band lived as poorly as any natives on the continent. Most of the year they slept in the open and went about scantily clothed. In winter they sought shelter in their wickiups, rude dwellings of branches covered with cedar bark. Their diet was mostly seeds, pinyon nuts, and cactus fruits, with an occasional rabbit and, in the autumn, roasted grasshoppers. Powell sat down with them to parley.

Loading his pipe with tobacco, he passed it around the circle, but when the Shivwits' pipe reached him, he saw it had been broken and tied up with a piece of buckskin, well soaked with saliva, and he quietly passed it on. It was hard to explain to the Indians why he was there, since he did not wish to trade nor did he want their lands, but he tried to suggest that "all the great and good white men are anxious to know very many things, that they spend much time in learning, and that the greatest man is he who knows the most." However the Shivwits looked on his motive in being here, they likewise sought friendship and readily gave it, naming him "Kapurats," meaning "arm off."

The Shivwits confessed their poverty and ignorance, and then without hesitation confessed that they had killed the three white men a year earlier. "Bad men said they were our enemies. They told great lies. We thought them true. We were mad; it made us fools. We are very sorry." Later, after the session broke up, Hamblin collected more particulars about the murders, and they confirmed what had been reported earlier: the Paiutes had ambushed and shot Powell's men full of arrows after first feeding them and then hearing that they were miners from the other side of the river who had killed a Hualapai woman in a drunken brawl. Despite their confession of murder, Powell rested easily that night, marveling that he could sleep in peace among them. He neither resented nor distrusted them, nor after their explanation and apology for the killings did he pursue the matter any farther.[16]

One reconstruction of what may have happened back in August 1869 has the Howlands and Dunn watching their compatriots successfully run the rapids and then hiking up Separation Canyon on nearly empty stomachs. They followed a Paiute trail, topping out in the vicinity of Kelly Spring on the second day and continuing across the pine-forested Shivwits Plateau toward what is now called Mount Dellenbaugh. That mountain, which is some two thousand feet in elevation, afforded a good vista from which they could get their bearings to the Mormon settlements. On its summit has been found an inscription reading "Dunn 1869" and "Water," with an arrow pointing north across Lake Flat and toward Parashant Wash. If in fact Powell's men followed the arrow, they may have reached the copiously flowing Log Spring as early as four or five days after leaving the river. A short time later the Shivwits found them, fed them generously as related above, and shot them on 2 or 3 September, somewhere in the vicinity of Parashant Wash, perhaps among the junipers at MacDonald Flat.[17]

Did it actually happen that way? If the Shivwits killed Powell's men, what happened to their bones, clothing, guns, or the letter to Emma, or the records they were carrying? Was it possible, or even more likely, that someone else was guilty of the crime? Jack Sumner eventually recovered the watch he had sent out to his sister, and he was convinced that it had been Mormons, not Indians, who had done the killing. His theory was that the Danites, a secretive, militant group of defenders of the faith against "gentile" enemy forces, had taken the Powell men for spies and shot them, burying their remains. More recently, a letter written by Mormon dissident William Leany has surfaced, which, in the course of recalling the old days of repression against him, cryptically mentions three men being killed in a church house in Toquerville, a village nestled in the shadow of the Hurricane Cliffs. Were those murdered men the Powell men? Did their guilty assassins then make a covenant of silence, and did the church connive in hushing up the bloody deed?[18]

Whether this alternative theory is true depends on whether Powell understood enough of the Southern Paiute tongue to have actually understood them make a confession. If not, then he must depend on Jacob Hamblin to translate. If Hamblin, who certainly knew the Indian's language better than the Major, was translating for him, he had to fabricate a confession without Powell suspecting, and that fabrication had to have been part of a well-orchestrated conspiracy directed from above. None of these hypotheses seems plausible. The Paiute and Ute languages were closely related, part of the Numic group, and Powell had spent much of a winter among the Ute, writing down vocabulary lists. On this reconnaissance to the North Rim, he encouraged Chuar and the others to perform their tales of ancient times, when the animals were gods and talked with people, and he followed those elaborate stories in detail. He surely could not have missed a confession of murder.

Powell, from his first moment among the Mormons, stood in sharp contrast to those non-Mormons who looked on the church and its polygamous followers as a cesspool of lies, treason, and sexual license. He liked and trusted Mormons. He came to trust Hamblin completely and never doubted that the scout spoke the truth about the three men's fate. And the Mormons, from the top of their hierarchy down, reciprocated Powell's good will; they supported his survey with enthusiasm and aided him in many ways over many years.

On 30 September Hamblin, reporting to his commander-in-chief Brigham Young, described the meeting with the Shivwits and Powell's plans to go on to the Paria and, after crossing the Colorado, to the Hopis and Navajos. The tone of this private letter is not at all conspiratorial.

I have been to the Colorado with Maj. Powel, found a place where we can get supplies down to the River for his exploring Party another season, yet it will be with concidrable difficulty. This point is sixty miles south of Pipe Springs, at Windsor Castle, two watering places, abundance of grass, & dwarf sage the most of the way. we visited the small band that killed two or three of Maj. Powels men, last season. I gathered them together & explained to them Maj. Powels business, sent one of them over the River to visite the remainder of the band, and left our Hourses, & most of our lugage with them while we climed down to the River. The Maj. expressed some anxiety about his goods & Horses, found on our return, that every thing was right, being absent nearly two days, the Maj. & 3 of his men will go the Navyos with me. There is a small flat boat being built at the river, at the mouth of the Pahreah. This will be don mostly at the expence of Maj. Powell. I will communicate to you on my return.[19]

Hamblin could not spell, but neither could he have lied or engaged in an elaborate cover-up to protect a fanatical assassination of innocent men.

The party, including Chuar's contingent, returned to the Vermilion Cliffs and followed them east toward the gap through which Kanab Creek runs. A new white settlement was taking form in that gap, laid out on the high sandy banks of the creek under the supervision of

Young and the local bishop, Levi Stewart. President Young owned several lots in the center of the village, as he owned property all over the territory, enhancing his worldly estate as he enhanced the Mormon cause. Powell was so impressed by the optimistic spirit of the new community and by its surrounding red-rock canyons that he sought to buy one of Young's lots. He promised to improve it, wrote Young, "and seems much interested in developing the country." That may have been more cooperation with a "gentile" than the Mormon leader wanted to encourage, as no sale of land took place. But Young was apparently influenced by his conversations with Powell the science teacher and educational reformer: not long after their meetings, Young began promoting academic instruction in mineralogy, geology, and chemistry. "I want my children girls & boys," he wrote, "to go thoroughly into these Sciences. . . . There are branches of knowledge which we ought thoroughly to understand and are particularly adapted to these mountain regions."[20]

From 24 to 30 September Powell's entourage roamed over the Kaibab Plateau, a high tableland averaging over seven thousand feet in elevation and supporting a dense evergreen forest. Kaibab is a Paiute name meaning "mountain lying down," a more telling topographical description than Buckskin Mountain, the name the whites gave this place because here they could get deer hides in abundance. The southern edge of the Kaibab forms the North Rim of the Grand Canyon, and they followed along that edge, with the river in sight below, starting from a promontory around which the river bends sharply—later called Powell Plateau—all the way east, before descending to the Paria. Meanwhile, Bishop and Graves had brought a load of lumber to the Paria's mouth for making a boat. While they finished their task, Powell rambled up the broad flood plain of the silty tributary. The little craft, when ready, carried men and freight, while the animals swam along behind the boat to the opposite shore of the Colorado.

From this point on they traveled mostly by night to protect their animals from thieves. Their course took them along the Echo Cliffs (paralleling what is now Highway 89) toward the Hopi towns collectively known as Tusayan. Powell had been eager to see this pueblo-dwelling people. He found them the most interesting of all the western natives, and in future years he would write about this visit and about Hopi folkways and religion. The party stayed two weeks, visiting the mesa-top towns of Oraibi, Shupaulovi, and Walpi. Hamblin was intent on assuring the Hopis that the Mormons supported their cause against the neighboring, aggressive Navajos, who had nearly destroyed a whole Hopi town not many years earlier. On 28 October the party came at last to the notorious Navajos, widely regarded by everyone else, native or white, as a dangerous threat to peace.

A meeting between the Navajos and Hamblin's delegation took place under the supervision of the Indian agent at Fort Defiance. Six thousand tribal members had gathered there to receive rations and annuities from the government. "It is a wild spectacle," Powell wrote, "groups of Indians are gambling, there are several horse races, and everywhere there is feasting. At night the revelry is increased; great fires are lighted, and groups of Indians are seen scattered about the plains." Before Hamblin took over the negotiations, Powell made a little introductory speech on behalf of the Mormons, praising them as industrious and peaceful. All Americans are one people, he told the Navajo leaders, and they all—Mormons included—pay taxes to one common government, which allows the government in turn to give gifts to the Indian. Any further depredations on Mormon livestock, any show of hostility toward Mormons or others, would be an attack on all Americans and would be punished by the American troops.

Four years earlier the Navajos had surrendered to the U.S. Army, following a period of raids and clashes, and over eight thousand of them had been imprisoned at Bosque Redondo in eastern New Mexico. A treaty in 1868 had allowed them to return to a government-established reservation of over three million acres in Arizona, and now the issue was whether they would live there harmoniously with the neighboring Hopis, Utes, Paiutes, and Mormons, as they had agreed to do in the treaty, staying within their assigned borders and leaving the property and territory of the others alone. They promised Hamblin to do so to the immense relief of the Mormon emissaries.[21]

That was nearly the end of the fall reconnaissance for Powell and his men. They paid a visit to the Zuni pueblo, near Fort Wingate, and then went home via Santa Fe and Denver. William Byers, Powell's former companion on Long's Peak and brother-in-law to Jack Sumner, was "surprised and gratified" to have him call at the *Rocky Mountain News* office: "Major Powell," the paper noted, "whose name has become familiar to every western man, woman, and child . . . , has formed elaborate plans for next year's work." He had also managed to identify, in his just-completed travels, a possible railroad crossing over the Colorado River, requiring a suspension bridge—location unspecified but probably the mouth of the Paria, where they had built their boat. A railroad could cross from there through the

Navajo reservation to the Rio Grande, the Major noted. From this newspaper interview it seems that Powell was indeed interested in developing the country, as he had told Brigham Young — was interested in more than simply pursuing his scientific work.[22]

In December a letter came to Powell from Jacob Hamblin, reporting on a safe return from the Navajo parley. Powell's pack train had come through all right, though the Major's horse had gone lame and might need a year to recover. The Hopi artifacts for the museum had come through in good shape too, except for a few pieces of pottery. He mailed "one Cochena suit, 6 fancy legging strings, 2 Cwawa's or womans belts, one fancy belt, one stone mortar, one stone axe, 1 pr moccasins, one fancy Blanket, one large blanket, 2 images." Through a gift of scarlet cloth, he arranged for the Hopi leader, Tuba, and his wife to come to Kanab and make a set of bridal clothes there. And he tried to get a few goods from the Superintendent of Indian Affairs in Salt Lake City for the faithful Kaibabs, to be "used in a way to favor your business and season."[23]

If 1869 had been the season of exploring the Colorado River, this succeeding year had been a season of discovering the lay of the surrounding land, making a traverse from the Utah plateaus down to the river and then from that river southeastward into New Mexico. Powell spent long days in the saddle, days when every muscle was sore, days when he might well have wished he were back in a boat again. Along the way he engaged with all the native peoples whom he wanted to incorporate into his investigations. He was now established as "Kapurats" among those peoples, a maimed but amiable friend who honored them by wanting to know their culture. In Jacob Hamblin he recruited the most knowledgeable foreman he could have found and put him in charge of local staging and provisioning. Finally, capping his success, in March 1871 Congress renewed his $12,000 appropriation for a second year. With funding extended, the Powell Survey could return to the high plateaus in full force and with systematic method begin truly to open this country to the American mind.

Science said that Powell must run the Colorado River once more, devoting the better part of a year to doing a proper survey. None of the first crew was to be rehired for that work except Jack Sumner, who agreed to join a second crew at the old embarkation point of Green River City. This time Powell mainly recruited in his home state, among the farms and towns of Illinois. He looked for neither hunters nor outdoorsmen. He did not secure many skilled hands in managing a boat. Nor, on the other hand, did he acquire highly trained scientists comparable to those in the survey parties organized by Hayden and King. After all, Powell himself still enjoyed little recognition in the intellectual world, despite that letter from Joseph Henry, and had developed few connections for professional recruiting. Among the many individuals who volunteered, he chose those who had a modicum of knowledge and culture, a useful talent or two, but none had a degree from an elite college or had done any postgraduate study in Europe.

Including Powell, they numbered eleven. The Major was the oldest at thirty-seven. Five years younger, and second in command, was the husband of sister Ellen (or Nellie), the superintendent of schools in Bloomington, Illinois, Almon Harris Thompson, who was nicknamed "Prof" or "Harry." Practical, levelheaded, a master of details, he went down in the roster as chief geographer, astronomer, or topographer, subjects that he had been studying since August. The expedition, as a day-to-day operation, was his as much as Powell's.

Stephen V. Jones and John F. Steward were a year or two younger than Thompson. The former was principal of schools in Washburn, Illinois, and a friend of Thompson, whom he served as assistant topographer. Melancholic in temperament and inclined to dyspepsia, Jones had dark hair, a long face, long nose, long ears. Steward came from a farm near Plano, Illinois, and had met Powell at the siege of Vicksburg, where they collected fossil shells together. His assignment was assistant geologist. A forceful, independent, and worldly fellow, he had strong opinions and expressed them with volleys of profanity.

Francis Bishop, the first to be recruited back in August, stayed on for the coming river trip as a second topographer. Still highly pious, still mourning his dead wife, he was scandalized by Steward's rough language and Powell's indifference to religion. The most taciturn of the new crew was Andrew Hattan, or Andy, another farmer and war veteran; he signed on as cook and boatman, neither of which jobs he had done before. There was once again a family member in the party: Walter Clement Powell (or Clem), the Major's first cousin and son of uncle Walter. He was twenty-one years old and lived with brother Morris in Naperville, Illinois. Uncle Walter had died in the summer of 1869, while Powell was away on the first expedition, and Powell wanted to give his immature cousin a change of scene and a dash of experience beyond the family's combination drugstore and bookstore. He was hired to work as a photographer's assistant with no previous experience. Probably about the same age as Clem was Frank

Richardson, called Little Breeches by the rest, though little is known about him except that he was from Chicago.

The Hayden Survey, and before it the railroad route surveys, had made a splash by taking along distinguished artists to record the unspoiled West, and Joseph Henry from the Smithsonian (from 1871 on Powell answered directly to the Smithsonian rather than to the Department of Interior) insisted that Powell do the same. Where to find someone willing to go, however, someone who knew how to mix a proper collodion and spread it evenly on a glass plate, who knew how to expose and develop that plate properly under difficult field conditions? After a couple of good prospects changed their mind, Powell had a professional man, E.O. Beaman, recommended to him by the E. and M.T. Anthony Photographic Supply Company of New York. A second artist came from Buffalo in the same state: Frederick Dellenbaugh, well-to-do son of a physician, handsome with a shock of dark red hair, adept at pencil and brush. Eighteen years old, he was the youngest in the party. Fortunately, both artists came experienced in handling boats. In temperament, however, they came with large differences, particularly when dealing with the trip commander: Beaman tended toward insubordination, Dellenbaugh toward hero worship.

On 21 April Powell ushered Emma, Clem, Dellenbaugh, and Richardson aboard the train leaving from Chicago for Omaha and Wyoming. The other recruits, including Harry and Nellie, chose a newer rail line that ran from St. Louis across Kansas to Denver. Traveling with them was the Reverend Joseph Powell, now a widower. Several members of the Powell clan had become interested in Kansas as a future home, as the old family restlessness began to work on them. Soon two of the siblings moved to the prairie state: Martha Powell Davis and her husband, John, to Junction City and Lida Powell Garlick and her husband, Charles, to Cedar Point.[24]

After visiting Denver, father Joseph returned to live with the Garlicks, and on 28 December he died at their home among the tall bluestem grasses of the Flint Hills — dying, as Mary had done, a long way from his childhood home of England. His body was buried next to hers in the Wheaton cemetery, and next to his brother Walter's. In those final few months of life, he came west to see the pronghorn, the prairie dog, the thousands of bison carcasses left by hunters along the track; he saw the western plains and mountains that his son had crossed many times and shared his thrill of western adventure. But he would never see those canyon lands or that stonewalled river that his son was intent on understanding.

Powell's second Colorado River exploring expedition at Green River City, Wyoming, May 1871. Taken by E.O. Beaman, whose dark box is on the extreme left. The men, dressed formally in honor of the moment, are, from left to right: Beaman, Hattan, W.C. Powell, Jones, Hillers, J.W. Powell, Dellenbaugh, Thompson, Steward, Bishop, and Richardson. (Courtesy: U.S. Geological Survey)

The Powell Survey expeditioners converged at Green River City where they went into camp for three weeks to prepare and pack the boats. Powell had ordered only three craft from the Bagley boat works, dispensing with the smaller pilot boat for this second voyage. The men named the boats the *Emma Dean,* the *Nellie Powell,* and the *Canonita* and fixed to their stern posts American flags sewed by Nellie. Built to the same dimensions as the first set of cargo boats, with the same low, curving sides and deep keels, they had a third covered compartment installed amidships, leaving less room for the crew. Powell purchased a captain's chair from the Fieldses, who were still running a boardinghouse in town, and affixed it to the cover of the middle compartment in the *Emma Dean.* He went downriver on this little throne, a rubber life preserver at his side. Jones was assigned the steering oar, Dellenbaugh the bow oars. After the lead boat came the *Nellie Powell,* with Thompson steering at the rear, Steward and Bishop at the oars, Richardson sitting flat on the middle deck. The third boat was reserved for the photographers and their equipment, with Beaman, Clem, and Hattan aboard.

First campsite of the second Colorado River exploring expedition, 4 May 1871, near Green River City, Wyoming. Taken by E.O. Beaman. Left to right: Thompson, Hattan, Jones, Steward, W.C. Powell, Richardson, Dellenbaugh, and Bishop.
(Courtesy: U.S. Geological Survey)

Jack Sumner was supposed to be among Powell's crew, but he sent word that he was snowed in, trapping furs in the mountains, and could not join them. They had a copy of his journal aboard, as they did Howland's maps, but no Sumner. With a stroke of luck, Powell and Thompson found a replacement in a young man born in Germany and now working as a teamster in Salt Lake City, where they went visiting. He looked big, strong, and agreeable. His name was John K. Hillers, or Jack—and inevitably he became "Bismarck." Before following a brother west, he had grown up on the immigrant-packed streets of New York City. Hillers liked a ribald joke as much as he liked his whiskey. Unenthusiastic about the Mormon capital, he readily agreed to sign on as general assistant. On cold nights Powell had him for bedroll mate, "spooning" up together, instead of the cantankerous Sumner.

Emma was five months pregnant, and undoubtedly she was anxious about whether her husband would come back from another river trip. She and Nellie settled in Salt Lake City rooms for the summer to await the outcome. Three men from the first party having been killed, she had some reason for concern. If not Indians, then the river and its dangers might take any one of them. It was exactly as long as it had been before, with the same number of ferocious rapids, the same chances of falling from the rocks, the same risk of an accident or drowning.

Second expeditions never seem as thrilling as the first, pioneer expedition. The nation is less interested. The newspapers tend to ignore repeat performances. Powell himself found it hard to stay enthused about going down the Colorado again. His interest in the sport of river running was limited. Having made that overland trip the previous fall he was more eager to learn about the landscape through which the river moved and about its native peoples and their ways than he was to improve his skills of white-water navigation. He was more worried about provisioning his food depots, more intent on creating a complete map, more worried about negotiating another round of appropriations, more concerned to get pictures for distribution in Washington. Not least he was thinking about becoming a father. He would stay with the boats for only a part of the voyage.

His crew, on the other hand, was aglow with excitement. Nearly a thousand miles of unseen wild country lay before these greenhorns of the second Colorado River Exploring Expedition. With a high sense of adventure they launched on the morning of 22 May 1871. Many townspeople, including all the whites but not the local Chinese, came down to wave them off.

Compared to the first river trip, this expedition was as well documented in personal accounts as it was in topographical data. Thompson, Jones, Steward, Bishop, and Clem Powell all kept nearly daily records, some of them starting in Chicago; and the Major wrote a few sentences each day in his own journal.[25] In 1874 Beaman published a seven-part narrative, "The Cañon of the Colorado," in *Appleton's Journal*.[26] Young Dellenbaugh proved to be the most articulate, comprehensive scribe. On the basis of his own notes and the others' journals, he brought out a detailed, if belated, account of the expedition in his book *A Canyon Voyage*, published in 1908, with a revised edition appearing in 1926. The last account to appear in print was Jack Hillers's diary, long held in family hands but finally published in 1972.[27]

As they floated down the Green River, places of incomparable beauty met them around every bend, places that now had names and memories attached: Flaming Gorge, Kingfisher Canyon, Ashley Falls, Browns Park. Once more Powell felt himself in paradise as the river threaded its way around and through the Uinta Mountains. His journal, at this point and later, had little to say about the men and their

happenings; all the longer entries were descriptions of scenic landscape, with words such as "beautiful," "fine," "grand" frequently
recording his mood. He became a painter of rocks and crags, of
graceful curves in the stream, of fossils dug from the soil. Science he
let slide, as he did the mundane chores of camp life.

Most of the others shared his nature enthusiasm, though Thompson did not like to "gush" over how lovely the country was and Hillers
seemed wholly indifferent to the landscape, concentrating on his
rowing and mending. Schoolmaster Jones was in full ecstasy, but he
gave nature's West a religious interpretation that Powell did not. Seeing it inspired feelings in Jones of an unseen power who defied
human comprehension, an awareness of God—"He who set in motion the wonderful machinery of the universe." Geology must reconcile itself to the Mosaic account of creation, Jones believed, by
acknowledging that "there is, there must be a power higher than nature, that controls her works and I try to look through nature up to
nature's God."[28]

In contrast to the first expedition, religion became a recurring
motif among this second party gathered so largely from pious middle-class circles of Illinois, circles that Powell understood well from
his youth, though once again he refused to give in to demands that
they keep the Sabbath holy on their travels. They could stop for photograph making or data collecting but not to idle away an entire day
in meditation. For several of these travelers, on the other hand, Sabbath observance was more than an expression of piety; it was also a
precious link to cultural refinement and domestic ties. Clem grew
misty-eyed on Sundays remembering how his family at home was sitting around the parlor, enjoying one another's company and improving their minds. The Green River campfire, he felt, needed a day "in
the parlor" to be complete. Some of the men, who daily grew more
shaggy and ragged, felt they needed time off when they could bring
out their better garments and think about higher things. They
needed to keep in touch with respectability.

Powell was not indifferent to the spiritual needs of his crew as they
left civilization farther behind. In contrast to the first expedition, he
packed a load of books, mostly poetry, and as they were going along
in the boats, sometimes lashed together, or as they gathered around
the fire in the evening, the stars shining brightly overhead, he read
from those books or had Thompson do so. The first volume out of
the box was Walter Scott's *The Lay of the Last Minstrelsy*, in six cantos,
followed by *The Lady of the Lake* and *Marmion*, until the river canyons

Frederick Dellenbaugh sitting on a sand bar at the Gate of Lodore, Utah, 1871. Taken by E.O. Beaman. (Courtesy: National Archives)

rang with scenes of the Border Country, of heath and forest and tumbling burns, of castles filled with friars, huntsmen, and bards. "He died a gallant knight," read Powell loudly to his boatmen, "With sword in hand, for England's right." Longfellow's "Hiawatha" was also in the box, along with Emerson's essays and Whittier's poems. Powell, the preacher's son, packed no Bible (Bishop, of course, had his Holy Scriptures along), but he did reflect his mother's love of the best that British and American literature of the day had to offer.[29]

While riding in the boat the teenager Dellenbaugh sat at Powell's feet, with his back to the bow and his hands on the oars, looking up to the Major on his elevated chair. They talked at length about the previous voyage and the men who had been on it. But mainly Fred was impressed by this magnetic leader, with "his magnificent will, his cheerful self-reliance, and his unconquerable determination to dominate any situation." [30]

When Powell got anxious about the river ahead, noted Dellenbaugh, he broke into exuberant song. If the current was more tranquil, he sang quietly but still with passion. His favorites were some of the old hymns ("The Home of the Soul"), popular operas ("Figaro"), and sentimental tunes ("The Laugh of a Child," "Shells of Ocean," "What Are the Wild Waves Saying?," "Annie Laurie," "Way Down upon the Suwanee River"). Some of the other men joined in, Hillers particularly who had his own extensive repertoire, while Steward played the mouth organ, Richardson the flute. But it was the leader in charge, J.W. Powell, who led their singing and who rallied their spirits through each day's labors.

Darker stretches, however, lay ahead. They were approaching the dreaded Canyon of Lodore, site of the first trip's most disastrous boat accident, and Powell was anxious about coming through intact. When they stopped at Browns Park, still filled with thousands of head of cattle, he dismissed Frank Richardson from the party and sent him out with the drovers. Richardson was not up to the level of work that was required of all hands. "It seems rather sad to part with him after all," wrote Bishop, "His heart is kind and although he is not of much value, yet he is one of us."[31]

Lodore, however, turned out to be less rugged than before. They made it past Disaster Falls without mishap, although downstream they came up on the two-year-old wreckage of the *No Name*—a few wooden fragments, an issue of *Putnam's Magazine*, a bag of flour lying perfectly preserved on a rock, all reminding them of what tragedies were possible. Powell was now careful to an extreme, running ahead along the shore to study the rapids, insisting that they portage or line wherever there was any risk of upset. With such strenuous management, they managed to glide safely into Echo Park, where they took a couple of days to investigate the tributary Yampa. July the Fourth found them a short way downstream from Steamboat Rock at Brush Creek, feasting on ham, canned peaches, and a bag of candy smuggled aboard. Then, abruptly, Powell decided he must go ahead with one of the boats to the Uintah Indian agency in order to collect mail and supplies. Thompson figured he was really going to Salt Lake City to see Emma, and he was right. She was having a difficult pregnancy, and Wes beelined across the mountains to be at her side.

When the other two boats arrived at the mouth of the Uinta River, they found an old oyster can containing a note from the Major, instructing them to wait. They had to wait a long while—from 15 to 24 July, when at last Powell rode into camp with a change of plans. During his time in Salt Lake he had word from Jacob Hamblin that the scheme of packing provisions to the mouth of the Dirty Devil River was inadvisable; the packers could not bring horses down its narrow, twisted canyon, and any detour around it would take one into a wasteland, made more intense by this summer of drought. The Dirty Devil was to have been a critical food depot, midway between Gunnison's Crossing and the Paria. Here Powell had experienced a bad patch before, when the first expeditioners had commenced to quarrel. So concerned was he about getting through more successfully this time that, after a few days of discussion, he concluded that he must personally go in search of a depot. He hired the former Uintah agent Pardon Dodds, now raising cattle on the reservation, to help him search for the Dirty Devil's headwaters and to see for himself the difficulties of provisioning.

In Powell's absence the party occupied themselves by criticizing the Utes and inspecting the conduct of their reservation, which was a forty-mile hike from their camp. Coming down the Wonsits Valley, entering into Ute territory without Powell to calm them down, some of the men had begun to get nervous about a possible Indian attack. Then at breakfast one morning two natives had materialized out of the bushes — a young couple who were running away from their tribe, eloping to avoid an arranged marriage; the man turned out to be the son of Chief Douglass, the wife a girl of only fifteen years. They were probably the first Indians most men in the party had seen up close, and they turned out to be harmless and a little romantic.

Indian life at the agency was, by contrast, unromantic in the extreme. The expeditioners were repelled by what they saw — not at all like the poetic world of Hiawatha or Whittier's Mogg Megone. The "bucks" drove in cattle and horses stolen from the Mormons while the federal agent, the Rev. J.J. Critchlow, was away buying a sawmill; the Ute men indulged in horse raising or loafing while their "squaws" did all the hard physical work. The agency was trying to teach the Utes how to farm by plowing the ground for them, providing seed, tools, and irrigation water, even cutting grain, but the effort was not succeeding. "Washington (who they believe is yet alive) has sent them all things," wrote Jones. "Poor simple people. Someone has been deluding them." Thompson agreed: "The Agency as at present conducted is a cheat, a swindle. The Indians do not make good agriculturists." Hillers, who found the reservation inhabitants repugnantly dirty, complained that "these Indians will steal and when caught only laugh."[32] The party was eager to leave the Utes behind, and they proceeded down river without the Major, hoping to meet him at Gunnison's Crossing.

Once launched, however, they began to find fault with each other. The next stretch of the Green River passed through Desolation and Gray canyons, and the party moved through that land (so bleak beyond the riparian edge of cottonwoods) at a slow, monotonous rate. Thompson was now in charge of the work, enforcing a daily ritual of taking barometric readings of their elevation, recording changes in the compass direction, and drawing a map of the river's course. Bishop was their draftsman, and he put into his map a few features of the surrounding landscape and their campsites, numbered and dated, along the river course.[33] That was not enough work, however, to keep nine men happily employed and at peace with one another.

Other than rowing the boats in a slow current, the hardest physical work was taking the all-important landscape photographs along the way. Beaman had the necessary skill to do this work well, but it took brawn and sweat as much as finesse and technique to carry it out. Wet-plate photography made use of large, fragile pieces of glass, which had to be coated with chemicals carefully mixed and applied on site. They must be wet when exposed in the large camera, and then they must be immediately developed in a portable dark tent. All of the elaborate equipment—plates, chemicals, camera, tent—had to be hauled up and down the cliffs in a large, heavy box to reach the best vantages for panoramic shots. That was the work of the photographer's assistant, cousin Clem, who began to despise the work—"that infernal box on my back," he wrote, that "infernal howitzer." It soured his relations with Beaman, and they spatted and sparred. Beaman was careless, Clem complained; he was uncultured and coarse; he disobeyed Prof's orders; he was "disliked by all."[34]

Jones was becoming another of the unpopulars because he gave himself too many airs and turned out to be, so Clem said, incompetent at his job. Jones and Steward disagreed over the quality of Andy's cooking, and the others complained about Steward's bad manners. The homesick, distraught, ever fastidious Bishop was particularly hypercritical; he felt himself thrown "among so many who, if not infidels full-grown are embryotic, and I fear are germs of vigorous growth." Only Powell and Thompson seemed suitably cultured to him; the rest were too unrefined, though Fred and Clem were passable, "and so would be Steward only for his unhappy style of talking, for profanity and vulgarity are of all things with me the most inexcusable." That left Jones, Andy, and Jack in the class of barbarians, though in truth Jones was one of the most well-read and articulate in the party. Bishop and Clem, nursing their feelings of superiority, formed a little clique of

*Almon ("Harry" or "Prof")
Thompson, Powell's brother-
in-law and second-in-
command on the second
Colorado River expedition,
photographed late in life.*
(Courtesy: U.S.
Geological Survey)

the discontented, sitting apart and playing chess together. Fred got tired of all the petty bickering and, at one point, moved his bedroll away from the rest. And Thompson, left in charge, wondered where Powell was and when he would show up again.

The Major met them, as promised, at Gunnison's Crossing on 29 August, bringing with him Fred Hamblin and three hundred pounds of flour, a little meat, and twenty pounds of sugar. Those were all the supplies he could lay his hands on quickly. He had spent most of his time crossing the West Tavuts Plateau south of the Uinta valley, examining its geological structure before going over into the Sevier River drainage. Much of the time he had traveled with Indians to learn more about their culture, and they had confirmed Hamblin's judgment that the Dirty Devil was not a practical route for a pack train. He had not actually gone to look for himself. The alternative he decided on was to bring supplies to the Crossing of the Fathers, or what Powell called the mouth of the "Escalantis."[35]

The situation disgusted Thompson, and he unloaded a ton of resentment in his diary: "I cannot learn that the Major made any serious effort to get in [to the mouth of the Dirty Devil] and do not believe he did. . . . I do not care a cuss whether he comes with us or not on the river, but it makes one mad to wait and then have him come in and report a failure. . . . I knew how things would be before starting, so ought not to grumble." Thus, a new tension had developed within the party, this one between the first and second men in command; the latter was now on the prod, looking for further examples of mismanagement from Powell, rather wishing he would go away and leave Thompson in charge of getting the job done promptly and right.

With Powell back in his captain's chair, the boats plunged into Labyrinth Canyon, wound their way to the junction with the Grand, and then entered the long ordeal of Cataract, which Powell dreaded most of all the river's turbulent stretches. The surrounding country changed from desolate to utterly sterile, with little vegetation in sight. Powell turned more moody as they went, singing to himself with a look of abstraction, "Flow gently, sweet Afton, among thy green braes." The boats were getting hammered by the rocks, in and out of the water, running the rapids or bumping along the portages. The food supply was diminishing fast, with no assurance that Dodds would meet them ahead with replenishment.

On the last day of September the party arrived at the mouth of the Dirty Devil. Clem noted, "Tis a small dirty stream and that is all." Powell decided to leave the *Canonita* here, storing it in a cave and half filling it with sand, and burying some of Beaman's photographic chemicals to be retrieved in the following spring, when they might find their way down the fetid stream and resume their scientific investigation. Now they must move on quickly. After taking the tributary's picture, Beaman had one glass negative left. There was less than a week's supply of flour.

While the men were repacking their stuff into the remaining boats, Powell and Jones climbed two thousand feet up the sandstone bluffs to peer into the vast wilderness beyond. Powell named this unusual landscape the "Plateau Province," for its distinctive feature is not the peaked mountain but the flat terrace or plateau, high and endless to the eye, its edges fretted and sculpted into long meandering cliffs that flash with every color of the rainbow. Earlier Thompson had described it as "weird and wild, barren and ghost-like, it seemed like an unknown world. The river is sunk. No appearance of gorge or canon a mile away. All is level to the eye, so abruptly has the river cut its channel."[36] Actually, the many plateaus (part of the broad Colorado Plateau) are not level but tilt northeast toward the clouds, and their higher elevations are green with forests; in the winter they are deep with snow and in the spring they are filled with the sound of running water. The Colorado River receives the flow from those plateaus, streaming down a thousand smaller canyons and gorges. The Dirty Devil, corkscrewing from the north, passing malodorous sulfur springs along the way and picking up its disgusting smell, was part of that flow; but elsewhere the water was crystalline and sweet.

On the first trip Powell had noticed, without comment, a range of impressive mountains immediately to the west of the river, sharply contrasting to the prevailing horizontality. No American had ever given them a name nor explored them, hence he referred to them as the "Unknown Mountains." Along with the distant plateaus, they had defied even Jacob Hamblin's navigational skills. They intrigued; they awaited the surveyor's persistence and penetration. Far to the west somewhere was the valley of the Sevier and the Towers of the Virgin, the village of Kanab and the Pipe Springs ranch. But what lay between those places he had been and the place where he now stood? Still a large blank spot remained on the American map.

Overloaded now with ten men and all their gear, the two remaining boats raced through Glen Canyon and past the San Juan's mouth. Spirits were high again, though rations were low. Powell was disappointed not to be able to climb the mountain he had named after the elder Howland (now Navajo Mountain), but they stopped briefly at the Music Temple where they discovered the names Howland and Dunn carved eerily on the wall and added their own names. They spotted long-deserted Anasazi ruins, picked up arrowheads, examined the barrel cactus. Then they came upon a fire-blackened shore, fresh tracks of shod horses, the sound of a gun. They had arrived at the Crossing of the Fathers, and there was Dodds with a load of food, mail, magazines, heavy shoes, and overalls. Dodds had been here for two weeks, in the company of a couple of miners, George Riley and John Bonnemort, who had come looking for gold in the river; Hamblin had been with them before heading down to Fort Defiance. The Major, it turned out, had managed the logistics well, and the expedition was safe, though Thompson continued to grumble.

The date was 6 October — and autumn was in the air. Time to prepare for winter quarters, which Powell had decided to establish in the new settlement of Kanab. Taking Hillers along as assistant, he rode out with the pack train, heading for Salt Lake City to see Emma and the new baby, Mary Dean (named for Wes's mother), born on 8 September. He carried fossils collected by Steward, a copy of Bishop's map, some sketches by Fred and prints by Beaman, Clem's diary to date, and letters home to loved ones from all the crew. For Powell the river expedition was over for that year. Next summer, he told the men, they would run the Grand Canyon. Now they should get themselves down to the Paria, wait there for further word, then come overland to Kanab where he would meet them once again and they would set up winter lodgings.

A good scheme, one that had been broadly planned as far back as Illinois. But the men who climbed once more into the boats were as weary of the river as the Major. Poor Clem had received only two letters from friends and family, and he was thinking anxiously of home: "Ah me! I wish the trip was over with. Am feeling rather blue." Jones had injured his ankle; then his rheumatism flared up; soon he was hobbling around on a pair of makeshift crutches. Steward was sure he was the worst off of all. A letter informed him that his wife was seriously ill, and then he himself took sick, unable to stand or eat, the causes of his ailment unclear.

A group of Navajos came into their camp, and the men rallied to inspect this unfamiliar, good-looking people. Clem got off a few jokes at the Indians' expense, though he was impressed enough to proclaim them "*the* Indians of the West [who] can more than hold their own against the rest." Jones, trying to keep his dignity intact, rubbed cheeks with one of the older natives. But the expeditioners could not be diverted for long; they wanted to finish the season's work as quickly as possible. Finally, the boats were ready to push off from the Crossing, and on 23 October they arrived at the Paria's mouth, camp 86.

The change of scene was not a great improvement, if civilization was what they wanted. The Paria presented them with high walls on all sides, seemingly cutting them off from the outside world. They had food enough; their pack animals came in, though a little late, driven by Riley who was guided, or misguided, by an incompetent old man who lost the way. But for drink they had to choose between the dirty-white tributary or the reddish-brown main river. Nights were getting cold, days were still hot and glaring. After getting instructions to move camp over to House Rock Valley, west along the Vermilion Cliffs, they readily cached the remaining boats, along with oars and instruments, and changed location. Now they hoped, they were in a spot from which they could at least go adventuring on the Kaibab.

Thompson took the two sick men, Jones and Steward, out to Kanab, while Steward announced that he was resigning from the survey. "I have had splendid opportunities to pursue my favorite study, that of paleontology," he wrote, "but could have spent the time much better in some other parts of the globe, though a better opportunity to study the effects of the forces of nature can hardly be found elsewhere—wonderful and beautiful scenes without end."[37]

The others, Jones included, decided to stay on the payroll. But those left in the House Rock camp soon were as unhappy as ever, having nothing to do but shoot wolves and read and reread their magazines. Clem read Ferdinand Hayden's descriptions of the Yellowstone, an excerpt from Clarence King's *Mountaineering in the Sierra Nevada*, and the plays of Shakespeare, but he was unbearably bored. "The whole party is disgusted with the way the expedition is run," he put in his journal; "even Prof. said if things did not go differently he would leave. . . .We are wasting valuable time by staying out here. . . .I am getting heartily sick of this infernal fooling and the haphazard manner in which the expedition is run."

When word of mouth came that Chicago had burned down a month earlier, they remembered how far they were from Illinois and urban civilization. They were hearing so little, doing even less. Not until the end of November did Powell make it back to Kanab and summon the crew from their lonely, isolated, do-nothing camp life. By that time they had been almost eight months out of doors, away from all comforts, living each day on a diet of fatty bacon and Andy's efforts at bread. They had to live thus in order to gather information about the river. Now, at last, they were heading for the nearest human settlement—a community where people lived along streets and slept in beds, where women and children dwelled, where vegetables grew in backyard gardens. The second river expedition of the Powell Survey, though not quite finished, was going into recess.

K anab may have offered a certain urbanity to men who had been away from civilization for so long, but in truth it was a tiny, struggling village out on the far edge of American settlement. Its population was fewer than fifty families, all Mormons, with a few Paiutes coming through now and then, begging for food or seeking to trade. Although an old fort dated back earlier, the effective founding of the town had occurred only the previous year, 1870, when Brigham Young had ordered Levi Stewart to lead a migration down here to create a community.[38] They came by wagons through Toquerville and along the Vermilion Cliffs to this gap out of which a shallow river flowed, a river fringed with willows that the Paiutes called "kanab." Young's visit in September of that year had been to consecrate Stewart as bishop and to see that the town was laid out in the approved design.

The town was one mile on a side, divided into large residential blocks around a public square, and the streets followed good Mormon practice: First Street North, First Street West, Second Street North, Second Street West. Dellenbaugh later remembered fences of willow wattling and ditches filled with irrigation water lining the wide, regular streets.

> Fruit trees, shade trees, and vines had been planted and were
> already beginning to promise near results, while corn, potatoes,
> etc., gave fine crops. . . . The houses that had been built outside
> the fort were quite substantially constructed, some of adobe or
> sun-dried brick. The entire settlement had a thrifty air, as is the
> case with the Mormons. Not a grog-shop, or gambling saloon,
> or dance-hall was to be seen; quite in contrast with the usual
> disgraceful accompaniments of the ordinary frontier towns.

In contrast to the western norm of hodge-podge shacks in a sea of tin cans, Kanab, like other Utah settlements, was well-ordered from the beginning. "As pioneers the Mormons were superior to any class I have ever come into contact with," Dellenbaugh declared, "their idea being home-making and not skimming the cream off the country with a six-shooter and a whiskey-bottle."[39]

The presence of "gentile" surveyors from the East was bound to be intrusive, but the Kanab townspeople tried to be generous and hospitable, some of them forming lifelong friendships with the Powell party. (Dellenbaugh was still corresponding with a descendant of the Hamblins in 1934.) Economic self-interest helped reinforce their wary goodwill, for the survey crew had cash to buy vegetables, bread, and milk, to hire the men folk to pack provisions, repair wagons, and take care of their riding stock — though at least once when their cash ran low, the surveyors paid the locals in coffee beans. Another time they took up a collection to help a local family rebuild their burned-down house. Nellie in particular got on well with some of the women, and for a spell when Harry was away she lived in a tent set up in Jacob Hamblin's garden.[40]

The surveyors, however, immediately gravitated to the community's edges, first setting up camp at Eight Mile Spring, which lies east of town along the base of the cliffs. When the lads came in from exile, they found Jack Hillers there at the campfire, his big voice booming out a welcome. Emma was there too, and Nellie, and the new baby, and a young Mormon nursemaid, who was, said Clem, "rather pretty." The Major had persuaded Emma to join them for the winter, though it may have taken a while to convince her. Emma had followed her husband through the Civil War, climbed Pike's Peak with him, and endured a log-cabin winter on the White River, but now she had a child to care for and was distinctly less enthusiastic about going into primitive quarters. The nursemaid may have helped decide her. So did the companionship of Nellie and her dog, Fuzz. In any case, here the womenfolk were, and suddenly for the men, all was domesticity and warm-hearted cheer.

Following Clarence King's model, the first desideratum for the winter phase of the survey was to establish a baseline for topographical mapping. Any flat place was as good as any other flat place for putting such a line, so Powell and Thompson decided to establish their baseline on a desolate plain south of Kanab. It was level out there but also windy and dry, with the sandy soil blowing much of the time. Here they set up the work camp where the boys slept and ate, just over what turned out to be the Utah-Arizona boundary.

The base line was forty-eight thousand feet, or nine miles, long. Its course along the meridian had to be fixed with transit and theodolite, its length measured off with as much precision as they could manage. Bishop had the job of preparing three wooden rods, each sixteen feet long, oiled and varnished, setting them on trestles, and aligning them with small steel pins. They served as the rulers. If the wind was blowing, the rods trembled so badly they could not make exact contact. It took considerable patience to get the line right. Let Powell explain how they proceeded when the line was finished:

A system of triangles was expanded from the extremities of this line, so as to embrace all the country from the Markagunt and Paunsagunt Plateaus on the north to salient points a few miles south of the Grand Cañon, and from the Beaver Dam and Pine Valley Mountains on the west to the Navajo Mountain beyond the Colorado on the east, and still farther to the northeast, so as to embrace the country from the Sevier River on the west to salient points immediately beyond the Colorado on the east, and as far north as the southern tributaries of the Dirty Devil River. The angles of these triangles were measured with a seven-inch theodolite. At the geodetic points mounds were built and flagstaffs erected, and in that clear atmosphere it was found that

it was practicable to make the sides of the triangles from twenty-
five to thirty miles long, and occasionally, when the artificial
points were on very salient natural points, the sides of the triangle
could be made much longer.[41]

Patience was required, and exactitude, and a survey crew with iron
lungs, brass butts, and legs of steel. Somebody had to climb each and
every one of those geodetic points, build those mounds, erect those
flagstaffs, walk or ride those long sides of the triangles.

A few days after arriving in Kanab, Powell invited brother-in-law
Harry to go out riding with him to discuss the coming year. He was
improvising as usual, looking ahead and shifting his plans around, a
habit that Harry often found irritating. Now Powell ventured that he
should go to Washington during the winter to try for another appropriation; they could use the money to survey the valleys of the Sevier and Virgin or to publish reports of their results. Harry,
confident as ever that he could manage the topographical fieldwork,
agreed to stay behind. "If I fail," Powell asked, "will you work without
salary next year to complete this work?" Harry was still agreeable, as
long as he could get enough money to live on. Count on being supported, Powell promised. He and Emma, therefore, would stay in
Kanab until February, then leave; and he would not return until
next summer.

While the baseline was being staked out, Christmas came and winter came with it. It rained and snowed and rained again. Jack bought
a jug of Mormon wine, and Nellie prepared a huge plum pudding to
go along with Andy's ham, bread, sorghum molasses, and sardines.
After dinner everyone's thoughts turned to home. But then they sad-
dled up to ride through the sagebrush into Kanab, with the moon
shining through the gap in the cliffs, to join the community celebra-
tions. That night the Mormons put on a big dance at the schoolhouse, with fiddles playing, candles burning, feet stomping. The
dance opened with a prayer by the bishop — a strange custom to the
"gentiles"—after which the dancing partners took their positions.
"One can but be amused at the queer style of the Latter-day Saints, as
they style themselves," wrote Bishop; "so uncouth in all their movements; so void of grace of look or action. The boys are somewhat incensed at the treatment they have received, being somewhat
unceremoniously snubbed by the Kanab belles." The Powell group
was welcome to watch, but none of the girls danced with them, so
eventually the surveyors drifted back to camp in the dark.[42]

Before the Major could depart, he had one more task to finish. Congressmen, he knew, wanted to see the spectacular plateau province; more than reading about it, they wanted pictures. His lecture audiences loved pictures too — transparencies on glass projected from a magic lantern. The public was in a rage for stereoscopic views of the western landscape. Beaman had collected plenty of negatives, so he was instructed to get them printed on paper and to make transparencies for the Major to use as needed. Beaman began to do so, but he was not pleased to see his artistic work become the property of Powell and the Powell Survey. He had other, private ambitions for his pictures, though he had obligated himself to serve the Major's mission. Soon they were feuding, and the day before Powell left, Beaman resigned from the survey, selling out his interest in the photographs and negatives, and collecting $800 for his eight months' work. He proceeded to Salt Lake City before returning with pack stock to traipse down to the Hopi towns, now free to take pictures on his own.[43]

Seeing the breach coming, Powell had set Clem, the long-suffering photographer's assistant, the task of filling Beaman's place. Whatever he knew about mixing cough syrup in the drugstore, Clem proved to be a failure in the art of wet-plate photography. All his pictures came out poorly exposed or spotted or streaked or fogged, and he blamed Beaman for ruining the chemical bath before leaving. He had Thompson convinced that his equipment had been sabotaged, but the problem was not in the chemicals. Clem had no gift; he was clumsy as well as careless. Failure made him incensed and, once more, he vowed to quit. "The Maj. thinks he can do anything with us because he has us out here," he complained, and he threatened to join the train of miners who were heading down Kanab creek to pan for gold in the Colorado. The threat was empty, but finally he was excused from camera work; and Powell, as soon as he got to Salt Lake City, recruited James Fennemore, a rather frail young man fresh out of England, and sent him down to do the work.

Bishop chose this moment to announce that he also was leaving the survey, after suffering through many abuses and insults at the hands of his fellow employees and putting up with their uncouthness and irreligion. He resented the Major's command of the amenities: "They have a very soft thing up at the 8 mile spring with their fine large tents and stoves, while we 'poor scallawags' can take what we can get to help our lot, if we can." Worse yet, the Mormons, though emphatically religious, had a theology that was too "queer" for his orthodox religious views, and a moral standard that was appalling. They

were all "vile, miserable sinners with but few exceptions," was his
judgment; and when one of the local girls seemed to be falling in
love with him, he was determined to resist that entrapment. "I must
not let the fire [go] too long," he decided, "before throwing water on
it." Powell was undoubtedly happy to let him go, agreeing to pay
$400 in back wages and to furnish a railroad pass to Illinois. As it
turned out, Bishop did not leave immediately but stayed around all
spring. And a few months later this sad, lonely man, looking for more
pious companionship than anyone seemed ready to give, abruptly
changed his mind about the Mormons, settled in Salt Lake City, and
became a Mormon himself—indeed, a bishop and a science professor in the University of Deseret.

The survey had dwindled some, but there was a sufficient work-
force left to start measuring angles and plotting distances; beside the
Thompsons, there was Jones, recovered from rheumatism but still
acting the "baby," Clem, Dellenbaugh, Hattan, and Hillers, as well as
the Mormon packers (various Hamblins, George Adair, Will Johnson, the Nebeckers, John Stewart, and one of Brigham Young's sons).
Reassured by the strength and willingness of the remaining party, the
Powells put their baby between them on a wagon and on 2 February
began their long journey north and east to the nation's capital,
where committees were already making up next year's budget. Emma
and Mary would not come back to the West, and Wes would not do so
until August. Most of the subsequent work of the survey was directly
supervised by Thompson, who doggedly worked away at the mapping
while paying the bills and keeping the boys occupied. Nellie stayed
with him, the only woman in the party, until the following fall.

Thompson was now in charge, but Thompson peppered the Major
in his absence with letters detailing their problems, and sent him
plenty of telegrams as well. A telegraph line had reached Kanab via
Pipe Springs and St. George, connecting the frontier with the metropolis, so Powell could be kept instantly informed of what was happening. After the Beaman affair, the chief problem was assuring
sufficient funds in a bank account to cover the party's expenses. They
consumed a hundred pounds of flour a week. "Think you can see,"
Thompson wrote, "that if payment is refused my checks it will put us
in a devil of a fix and probably cause trouble to the expedition." A
week later he wrote again: "Do not fail to attend to the matter immediately. Only flour to last four weeks longer—and hell to pay if our
credit is not kept good." Apparently Powell, now in Washington, responded with a deposit to the Salt Lake City bank, though Thompson

The Grand Canyon at Lava Falls, looking eastward. Taken by James Fennemore or J.K. Hillers, April 1872. (Courtesy: U.S. Geological Survey)

had no direct reply from him about any of his requests or queries until well into May. One bitter line tells Thompson's mood completely: "In fulfillment of your agreement last winter with me I do not think you have acted squarely or honorably."[44]

A little more money in the till, however, could not end all the problems of the field staff. The weather foiled them repeatedly whenever they went out to the higher elevations to plot their lines. One day's snowfall on the Kaibab left two feet on the ground, and the accumulated drifts were ten to fifteen feet deep. As spring approached, the party decided to risk a lengthy excursion across the Uinkaret Plateau to Mount Trumbull, the first of three trips that kept them occupied until July. The new photographer Fennemore came along, and his assistant was now the strapping young Hillers, who was beginning to try his own hand at the camera business and discovering he had a knack that Clem did not.

Nellie went along on this spring excursion, dressed in men's clothing and riding her pony astride like a man. She had been studying botany, probably since college days at Wheaton, and was using her stay in Utah to make collections of the flora, pressing them between

The Grand Canyon at Lava Falls, looking westward. Taken by James Fennemore or J.K. Hillers, April 1872. (Courtesy: U.S. Geological Survey)

drying blotters and classifying them with the aid of a botany text. Some of the two hundred species she collected went to the country's most eminent botanist, Asa Gray at Harvard, and ended up in the famous Gray Herbarium. But on this excursion her botanizing was thwarted by sickness. After climbing Mount Trumbull, where she found a new figwort, she could not get out of her bedroll one morning. Harry fell sick too, likely because of bad food or water, and then it snowed heavily on them for several days.[45]

The party angled north across the Hurricane Cliffs to reach the warm valley the Mormons called Dixie. Stopping at a farmhouse to eat, Ellen began to recover some of her strength — enough to comment on how abusive the Mormon men could be to their women, and how used up the women often looked. The party stayed over at Berry's Springs for two weeks, gathering topographic data, but Ellen did not recover fully. On 4 May she wrote, "Sick all day. Could not even change driers on plants. Laid under trees all day. The water yesterday made me much worse and in fact has made all sick and the horses too."[46] The trip lasted more than five weeks. She gamely endured it, but the experience illustrated how hard the survey work could be for anyone who was not accustomed to the rough field conditions.

The foiled trip did establish in Thompson's mind that they had a talented photographer developing in their ranks. "Jack is really a better artist" than either Fennemore or Clem, he wrote to Powell, "that is[,] has better ideas as to what comprises a real representative view or salable one even."[47] He warned that Fennemore, who was not able or willing to climb heights, could never make it through to the Grand Canyon. The other discovery was how fast and furiously the gold miners were flooding into the area, pushing up and down the Colorado in both directions despite the weather, and already said to be prowling around the mouth of the Dirty Devil. The boats left there and at the Paria were in danger from those miners; according to one report the miners had broken into the party's cache at the Paria, stolen the oars and other property, and might next steal the boats. It was time to go to their rescue. Thompson began preparing to search for that elusive path along the Dirty Devil. They must come down that stream if they meant to reclaim the *Canonita* and get ready for the final river excursion ahead. Thompson took Hillers and Fennemore as photographers, and all the other men went along to map and pack.

Before leaving, Thompson wrote Powell about the plan they had discussed to make the country yield a little personal wealth as well as science. Powell had tentatively agreed with Captain Dodds to throw in on his cattle-raising enterprise on the Uintah reservation, this despite evidence that Dodds was a violent fellow who nearly killed one man in a fight; threatened to shoot another; and took an axe to Old Mormon, one of the mules belonging to the survey, putting that poor creature out of commission until it died of its wounds. Whatever the reason, whether because of Dodd's character or Powell's priorities, that partnership did not get off the ground. But Thompson had another scheme of his own — trading cattle with the "half-breeds around Ft. Defiance." "Now if we can get a permit to trade with the Navajos etc. that is to trade guns am[m]unition etc. we can make a big thing of it, and make a big museum of Navajos implements etc. *including cattle*. Wish you would look into the matter a little."[48] Since Powell was not in a corresponding mood, it is not clear what he thought about the proposition, though like the Dodds partnership it never came to fruition.

On 29 May Thompson led the survey party on a second major excursion, this one northeastward to find the way down the Dirty Devil. The trip was his triumphant moment, amply repaying all the frustrations of the winter and the false spring. They packed six weeks of rations on a dozen animals and headed up Johnson Canyon, which lies a few miles east of Kanab. Their route took them toward and along the Pink Cliffs that mark the edge of the Paunsaugunt Plateau (just below what is today Bryce Canyon National Park), then over into the upper Paria valley. The fifth day out brought them across a high ridge and down into a place the Mormons called Potato Valley.[49] A small, clear creek flowed out of this grassy basin, but for two days it rained and they were too sick to do much. When it cleared and they could move on, the possibility began to excite them: Was this valley the headwaters of the Dirty Devil, and was this little stream the Dirty Devil itself?

Thompson and Dodds climbed to a point where they could see all the country around: on the southwest stretched a line of cliffs (the Kaiparowits Plateau), on the north a still higher set of cliffs, and forty miles to the east they could see those "Unknown Mountains" that had intrigued Powell from a riverside view. But it also dawned on Thompson that the little creek below was not the Dirty Devil, which must come down the other side of those mountains. What then was the stream that ran this side of the mountains and southeastward to the Colorado? Was it the Escalante (or what Powell had called the "Escalantis" in honor of the Spanish padre who a hundred years earlier had traversed this region)? If so, it did not flow toward the Crossing of the Fathers, as Powell had thought, but took an unfamiliar course and was in fact an undiscovered, uncharted river.

The party turned north toward the sources of the enchanting little river, up the "mountain" as Thompson called it; in fact, it was not a mountain at all but another of the plateaus, flattish like a table on top. The barometer registered 10,910 feet, so it might well have been a mountain. Looking around him, Thompson could not resist making a little "gush":

> The landscape from the divide which we came over is beautiful.
> The mountain slopes a little west of south from the mountain up
> to the sand rock, a distance of 20 miles, and is 20 miles wide.
> Slope quite easy. Creeks every mile or two. Often groves of aspen
> and pine and clear meadows. Is a perfect paradise for the ranch-
> ers. Indians have been in, but not for years. Have camped here for
> the winter. Cold enough to freeze last night. Boys report four
> lakes. Jack got two views.[50]

J.K. Hillers in camp on the Aquarius Plateau. Taken by James Fennemore, spring 1872. (Courtesy: U.S. Geological Survey)

There were actually at least a hundred lakes on top, not four, and Thompson the would-be cattle trader could not help but appraise the grass and water in terms of economic potential as well as aesthetic charm. He was standing on the highest of the high plateaus that comprise southern Utah and northern Arizona, and from it they could look over one of the most spectacular landscapes that nature has created in the West. Because of its abundance of lakes and streams, so rare in the arid country, he named the plateau after the eleventh sign of the zodiac, Aquarius the water-bearer.

They had still to locate the damned Dirty Devil. Descending from the Aquarius Plateau they surprised eight Utes of all ages, who scattered into the brush, leaving one old man to meet the whites. Thompson speculated that these were the guilty Indians who had killed a Mormon boy over in the Sevier settlements and were fleeing because they feared their avengers had come. But gradually the Utes came out to parley and pointed the surveyors toward a trail that ran east toward the unnamed range of mountains. The trail led through what is now Capitol Reef National Park, past its ancient Triassic sediments and Waterpocket Fold, until it emerged on a broad sagebrush flat leading up to the mysterious peaks.

As they walked around and climbed those peaks, Thompson could not explain their geological origin, so like a volcano but without any visible eruption through the earth's surface; later, geologists would label them laccoliths, meaning intrusions of magma from below along a crustal fault. But if Thompson could not explain the geology, he could name the highest of them (at 11,522 feet) after his wife, Ellen, and another after Jack Hillers, his budding photographer. The mountains were unknown no more. Eventually, they were recorded collectively as the Henrys, after Joseph Henry of the Smithsonian.

On their far side, between the mountains and the Colorado, ran the Dirty Devil at last, but Thompson no more than Hamblin or Powell tried to follow it through its torturous canyon. Instead, they came down a broader wash to the edge of the Colorado. But if he had not managed what he had criticized others for not doing, Thompson justifiably felt that he had succeeded wonderfully. It was his dogged determination to map this country to its innermost parts, and his experienced understanding of topographic logic, that had brought him across the last great blank. Thompson had, in effect, made the survey his own. In Powell's absence he had effectively taken command, met a hundred demands from staff and suppliers, suffered through bitterly cold nights camping in the snow, pounded leather over steep trails, and solved one of the biggest remaining puzzles of the Colorado Plateau's geography. If there was any justice in assigning names, the Unknown Mountains should have become the Thompson Mountains, and at least one of them should have been called Harry.

Repairing the Canonita, *June 1872. The boat had been left behind at the mouth of the Dirty Devil River the previous fall. Left to right: Will Johnson, Frederick Dellenbaugh, and J.K. Hillers. Taken by James Fennemore.*
(Courtesy: U.S. Geological Survey)

On 22 June the party came up to the point where the Dirty Devil flows into the Colorado River, a spot they had left last October. The water was higher, running faster. Thompson instructed Dellenbaugh, Hillers, Fennemore, and Johnson to retrieve the *Canonita* out of its cave, work her back into shape, and bring her down to the Paria. He then turned around and went back along the newly blazed path to Kanab, where he awaited the return of Major Powell.

One forgets just how slow and tedious travel could be even in the advanced year of 1872, how much time it still took to cover the vast expanses of the American nation. The telegraph had revolutionized communications, the railroad had integrated the country into a single, centralized whole that reached across more than three thousand miles. But it was a long, long way from the village of Kanab to the territorial capital of Salt Lake City—a journey of ten or twelve days by horseback or wagon, moving at a rate of thirty to forty miles a day. Connecting from there to the Union Pacific line, crossing the mountains and prairies to Chicago, and riding the cars on to Washington, D.C., was no instantaneous process: the cars moved at thirty to forty miles an hour; they stopped or broke down repeatedly; and they could leave a traveler stranded at a station for hours on end, sleepless and fatigued, waiting for a connection. Such was Powell's new life as the director of a western survey, shuttling back and forth between the field and the base, which was necessarily in the national capital.

How much time Powell actually spent in Washington that spring and summer is hard to determine. Coming and going, he had friends, family, and institutions in Illinois and Michigan to stop over and see, though he was cutting free of his former institutional responsibilities. In late June the Illinois State Board of Education accepted his resignation from the office of curator of the museum on the Normal campus, though they went on wrangling with him and the Smithsonian over which of Powell's collections belonged in their museum.

His rapid moves from position to position, his frequent western travels since 1867, his tangled sponsorship for those expeditions, and his own inattention to detail had left the museum bewildered about what really belonged to them and where the missing pieces were. He had entered into the museum work with furious energy, but when the Colorado River started running through his imagination that energy had found a new, more enticing goal. Which box of shells belonged to which period of his life, and who owned them, were questions that seemed trivial distractions from the great work that was afoot, and Illinois had to compete for his attention with scientists and politicians in the East. The home folks who had supported him before he became famous were not satisfied with basking in his reflected light; they wanted what was rightfully theirs, properly labeled and identified.[51]

Powell stopped to discuss the missing specimens with them, but mainly he stopped only to leave permanently. He contracted with a real estate agent to sell their house in Normal, for which they received close to $2,500, and arranged to leave his books there until they could be moved to Washington. Even before that sale the Powell's new address, effective 1 June, had become 910 M Street, Washington, D.C., where the Major lived the rest of his life.

Once in Washington, he had a busy round of people to see, correspondents to answer. While Thompson and the boys were freezing on the Uinkaret and struggling to find the Dirty Devil, Powell was succeeding in getting a substantially increased appropriation of $20,000 out of Congress, made official on 10 June. He was also getting letters from and responding to people who were eager to join his project, however temporarily, including Clarence King's right-hand man S.F. Emmons, who wanted to arrange a trip down the Green River with the Major (a trip that never occurred). He was getting to know the leaders of the other surveys, including Lieutenant Wheeler, and guardedly sharing information with them as competing scientific investigators do. Then there was the matter of claims being made by the cracked visionary Samuel Adams, the self-proclaimed explorer of the Colorado, claims that Powell was called to assess for the congressmen.

And through it all he was courting one of the greatest landscape painters of the day, Thomas Moran, who had accompanied Hayden into the Yellowstone country and whose massive painting, the "Grand Canyon of the Yellowstone," fourteen by seven feet, was hanging in the halls of Congress and was heavily credited with the creation of Yellowstone National Park, the nation's first, earlier that year. On 24 June Moran wrote Powell: "I shall not be able to accompany you this season in your exploration of the Colorado Cañons, as accumulated work will prevent my going westward at all this year. I feel that I miss a glorious opportunity in not being able to take advantage of your very generous offer."[52]

On 17 July the Major arrived back in Salt Lake City, as Thompson learned from the *Deseret News,* and with him was a former colleague and professor of mathematics at Illinois Wesleyan, Henry DeMotte, who had come to spend his summer vacation with the Powell surveyors. DeMotte left the city on the 22nd in a wagon drawn by four unbroken mules ("wild broncos") that Powell had purchased and reached Kanab on 2 August. Powell, who stayed over to synchronize watches and arrange a telegraph signal to Kanab so that they could determine, with DeMotte's help, the village's precise longitude, came along behind, arriving in late afternoon on the same day. Naturally, the esteemed former colleague had to be taken down through the Kaibab pine forest to see the abyss. His visit was honored by a new name on the map, Demotte Park, a few miles from the Canyon. On the north rim they "sat in silent awe, spellbound, not speaking lest the magic power which held our spirits in mute ecstasy might vanish." And then, expressing a reluctance to leave that tourists ever after expressed, the visiting professor wrote, "we left the scene and turned our steps toward camp. Our view of the Grand Canyon was ended and we were now to make due haste to reach the Pahria [sic] river at which place the boats lay anchored and the boys awaited our arrival."[53]

The boys had been awaiting that arrival for a long while, so long that they had learned much about patience and the fine art of killing time. While Thompson had returned to the work of triangulation, those left with the *Canonita* had run down through Glen Canyon, passing what they now recognized as the true mouth of the Escalante River, so small and narrow and so easily overlooked on the previous two trips, and arrived at the Paria on 13 July. They were out of all supplies except coffee and flour.

Fortunately, the Paria's junction with the Colorado was not the same uninhabited desolation that it had been. People were now living here, or at least trying to scratch a living out of the hot, baked sands. A half mile up the tributary stood a freshly made log cabin, and near it a man was plowing a field. His name was John Doyle Lee, one of the most notorious figures in Mormondom, and he had settled here to be safe from the law. One of his eighteen wives, a sturdy woman named Emma, stood watching them arrive, and another, Rachel, ducked into the house out of sight and stole away after dark to hide out at their other farm at Jacob's Pool.

John Lee had been a member — some said the instigator — of the party of Mormons and Paiutes who in August 1857 attacked a "gentile" wagon train at Mountain Meadows in the Bull Valley range of southwestern Utah. The Mormons were being invaded by U.S. troops, their independence and hegemony threatened by an American president determined to put non-Mormons in control. The wagon train, carrying immigrants from Missouri and Arkansas to California at this tense moment, threw out a few taunts and sneers as it went along. Spurred to anger, Lee and other prominent Mormon leaders of the frontier formed a militia, with Indian recruits, and in the night slaughtered 120 men, women, and older children — virtually the entire wagon train. Although the territory soon made peace with the federal government, President Young and others in the hierarchy were shocked and embarrassed by the brutal killing. They chose a strategy of concealment. Publicly, Lee was excommunicated, but privately he was told by Young to take some of his family to the

Paria and there serve the kingdom in exile. His wife Emma called their new home "Lonely Dell," but the maps henceforth called it Lees Ferry.[54]

Twenty years later, in 1877, Lee was captured and executed for the massacre; the only individual to be brought to justice, he was clearly a scapegoat for a wider guilt. Thus, on that day when the Powell boys came up to his new farm, they were walking into a potentially dangerous encounter with a man who was constantly on the lookout for the law and fearing a warrant for his arrest. Not two weeks earlier a Cincinnati journalist, J.H. Beadle (passing under another name), had penetrated Lee's isolation; in his book *Life in Utah* (1870) Beadle had called Lee a butcher, and in another book, *The Developed West* (1873), he published an interview with him. Lee was understandably on his guard for spies of that sort, or thrill-seekers or government agents, as well as for Powell expeditioners. But the boys handled the situation well. They offered to trade their flour and coffee for cooked meals until more supplies could be brought in. They were not there to arrest or make a report, merely to await Powell and then go down the Colorado to the Grand Wash Cliffs. While waiting, they volunteered to work on Lee's garden, repair his irrigation ditch, and share the table of the renegade and his family. In all ways they found him to be "genial, courteous, and generous."[55]

While idling at the Paria, the boys pulled out a new novel, *Overland*, published the previous year by John W. De Forest; it was the first work of fiction ever to feature the Colorado River. Inspired by a lecture Powell had given in New York City, De Forest told a wildly improbable story, filled with invidious racial stereotypes, about a young woman who must get from Santa Fe to San Francisco to see her dying uncle. She is escorted across dangerous Indian territory by two suitors, one an upstanding American military man and the other an unscrupulous Mexican. After treachery and sabotage by his rival the military man and his comrades find themselves adrift in the Colorado River in a collapsible boat made of canvas and sticks. When the canvas gets ripped on a rock, they cover the bottom with a hide from a grizzly, killed as it stands on the riverbank. For days they ride their patched craft through stupendous canyon rapids until eventually they reach Diamond Creek where at last they can get out of the imprisoning river. The story ends when the two lovers meet again in a shipwreck on the California coast, escaping another watery grave, and go off to live happily on their inherited funds. Clem read and liked the book, which was more than he could say about waiting for the Major in this place. The reality of their situation — hot, monotonous, and lacking any grizzly bears — could not compete with the romantic imagination of a far-off novelist.

Their own boats were not such flimsy craft as De Forest concocted. They were the same heavy, oak-framed vessels that they had unloaded at Green River City more than a year ago. Now they must be dug out, rehabilitated, and made ready to go through the canyon. The *Nellie Powell* and the *Emma Dean* had been left stowed high in the rocks at the Paria where they had weathered and aged. Dellenbaugh explained, "as they had dried out for eight or nine months we had to soak them a long time to bring the planks together and that made them lack buoyancy in the water and made them terribly heavy on land in portages."[56] Their oars were gone, taken by the miners, the caches broken into and stores stolen, but the boats were still fairly intact. Beadle had used the *Emma Dean* to get over the river to interview Lee. The *Nellie Powell* was in the worst shape of the three, and they decided to leave her behind for Lee's use. Now that Beaman, Bishop, and Steward had resigned, there was not enough crew left to man three boats.

Suddenly, after so much lying about, the pace quickened. A sense of urgency was in the air, as Powell arrived in a hurry to get the river trip finished. On 13 August he came riding into Lee's hideaway with the Thompsons, Jones, and DeMotte. Nellie and DeMotte climbed into a boat for a short test run, while the Major helped Lee pick a few watermelons and vegetables for a valedictory feast. The very next day the second Colorado River expedition resumed, with the familiar captain's chair mounted once again on the middle deck of the lead boat, with Dellenbaugh and Hillers in their accustomed positions at the *Emma Dean*'s oars, and with the others —Thompson, Jones, Clem, and Hattan — following behind in the *Canonita*. As predicted, the photographer Fennemore had fallen ill and could not go along for the final, dramatic ride, leaving Jack Hillers the honor of recording for the first time by camera the view of the Grand Canyon from the river. By nine A.M. they were off into the tumultuous Marble Canyon, and their next stop, Camp 88 as counted from Green River City, was dead ahead.

Roaring past Marble and the Little Colorado, they entered the great stone portals of the Grand Canyon, which Powell told them was "the sockdologer of the world"[57] (sockdologer, meaning a one-two punch, became the name of a fierce rapid at mile 78.5 from Lees Ferry). Already they had descended 480 feet since the Paria, with al-

Marble Canyon, Aug. 1872. Taken by J.K. Hillers.
(Courtesy: U.S. Geological Survey)

most two thousand feet more to fall. Clem was unimpressed by the canyon; the place was not up to his expectations (or up to the gothic descriptions of De Forest). But when the waves got higher and higher, leaping twenty to thirty feet in the air, with the spray rising twice as high, they realized they were in for as wild a ride as any of them had ever experienced. The boats quickly proved unable to handle this heavy pounding and began to leak, so the men bailed as fast as they could while pulling hard on the oars to keep off the rocks. It was the hardest work they had done, harder than climbing up cliffs to set up a survey flag, and at night they fell asleep as soon as dinner was over, despite the thundering current only a few feet away from their ears.

The river was not only higher than it had been on the first expedition — eight to ten feet higher — but it was also rising fast. Rain had commenced falling, pouring down on them and on the country all around, flooding into the canyon. Their rations, blankets, guns, and clothes all got thoroughly soaked. During a single afternoon, while they had the boats out of the water for repairs, they calculated the river rose three feet. Camp that night had to be moved high up on a ledge. The boats had to be lifted high too to prevent their washing away — hauled up and hung on the walls by ropes. "We felt like rats in a trap," Dellenbaugh recalled, and when they put the boats back in the water the *Emma Dean* was soon leaking again through a hole big enough to stick two fingers. Powell, throwing caution to the winds, decided they needed to get downstream quickly and find safer ground. "By God, we'll start!" he yelled. "Load up!" He was not a man to swear or use an oath like that, so the crew knew just how seriously worried he was.[58]

In hauling and portaging the boats Jack had sprained his back badly and had sprawled, agonized with pain, on the shore. The strongest oarsman among them, he needed a few days to recover and get back his powerful stroke. But now he was ready again for action. Dellenbaugh and he pulled hard on the oars, and the *Emma Dean* shot downstream, with the gunwales barely an inch out of the water. Later that day they pulled in at Bright Angel Creek, all of them in need of a long, dry night of rest.

Three days later, and an estimated twenty-four miles downstream from Bright Angel (possibly at Waltenberg Canyon), came an accident that nearly cost the life of the director of the survey. It was the closest Powell ever came to drowning in the river that had made him famous. As Clem was beginning to realize, "high water is a great labor-saving institution as long as one is right side up with care, but if one met with an accident then look out."[59] The *Emma Dean* encountered a rapid that quickly swamped her, spilling out the crew, camp kettles, axes, and cups. As Jones, steering in the rear, put it, "a wave struck the port side, a whirlpool caught the stern and in an instant the boat was keel up and we in the water."[60] Dellenbaugh, with his hat jammed down over his eyes, clung to the boat, and Jones grabbed a ring at the stern. But both Powell and Hillers had been sucked down into the whirlpool, disappearing from sight. Hillers recorded the sensations he felt as he sank:

> Wind by this time began to tell. I done some of the tallest kicking I ever done in my life. I thought it an age — all at once I felt myself brought up suddenly, and the next instant I had hold of the gunwale of the boat. Major and myself came up together in a boile. Must have been in the same whirlpool with me, as he spoke of being taken down by one, but he fortunately had his life preserver on or else he might have been drowned, having only one arm.[61]

Powell caught hold of the bowline, and together the crew righted the boat and maneuvered her into an eddy, where they could bail with their hats, still miraculously on their heads, in lieu of the kettles. The Major's expensive chronometer had stopped running at 8:26:30 in the morning. Dellenbaugh joked about Powell's zeal in examining the geology at the bottom of the river, "but as a matter of fact he came near departing by that way to another world."[62]

That was 3 September, and four days later they reached the mouth of Kanab Creek, or Kanab Wash, where George Adair, Nate Adams, and Joe Hamblin were waiting with rations packed in from the town of Kanab fifty miles upstream. This had proved to be an easier access point than the depot Powell had located a year earlier downriver, especially after the miners had beaten a path down to the water. The food in the boats was spoiled by too much wetting, and now the careful advance planning to replenish supplies at a number of critical places paid off. Nellie had sent down potatoes, cheese, butter, and canned fruit, for which Hillers called her "the most thoughtful little woman I have ever known."[63]

The packers brought news that the whole Shivwits band was in turmoil over several killings of their people near Mount Trumbull and in St. George; they had gone back into their mountains, threatening revenge on the whites. White ranchers north of the canyon had retreated to safety, and Jacob Hamblin sent word that it was unsafe for the boat expedition to go farther: "It would not be for you to send men into their country until we lurn more about it."[64] He was worried that the Powell party might be ambushed, repeating the tragedy of two years earlier. Nellie had also sent a letter urging them to leave

Powell's empty boat with his chair and life preserver stashed under the seat, Marble Canyon, Aug. 1872. Taken by J.K. Hillers. (Courtesy: U.S. Geological Survey)

the river at Kanab Creek because of the Indian threats. The men sat up late into the night discussing their situation. They had come over 164 miles by Thompson's estimate, with 114 miles more to go before they were out of the Grand Canyon.

The next morning Powell announced that the trip was finished; they would go no farther. "All very pleased," wrote Thompson. The fate of the Howlands and Dunn must have been weighing on everyone's mind that night. And the river, so much higher than before, was a second threat that no one underestimated, certainly not Powell after his near-death experience. They were, after all, in the business of making maps and collecting data, which so far they had managed to do much better than on the first trip. The course and topography of the lower part of the canyon could be examined from the rims when the Indian troubles were over.

With some reluctance, nonetheless, the boys unpacked the boats and prepared to abandon them on the bottom of the canyon, among the detritus left behind by the miners, none of whom had ever found any significant amount of gold. The photographers scrambled to take a few last pictures. Dellenbaugh took home the flag of the *Emma Dean*; the departed Steward was awarded the flag of the *Nellie Powell*, the boat they had left at the Paria; and Clem, who had at last decided he could go back to brother Morris with his head held high, claimed the flag of the *Canonita* as his parting reward. Dellenbaugh wanted to pack the lead boat out in sections, and later Powell regretted not taking the suggestion and saving some memento from this historic voyage. They even left behind the chair that Powell had occupied amidships. Years later Dellenbaugh came back and found the chair still lying in the sand; he carried it to Salt Lake City and presented it as a souvenir to his old comrade Bishop.

If there was disappointment at not being able to finish the voyage as planned, there was also in the end a renewed spirit of harmony and goodwill among all the crew, present and absent. They had suffered and succeeded together, in spite of many moments of dislike and irritation, and they had survived one and all. No one had died, no one had been permanently injured. And no one was truly sorry that they had undertaken so long and perilous a journey. For all that success they had to be grateful to the man who had planned and fretted about and financed the trip, and who in the end had brought them through to safety.

In 1874 Powell was called before the appropriations committee of the House of Representatives to explain estimates he had made for future expenses. After raising his funds to $20,000, Congress had slashed them to $10,000 for the current fiscal year so he was more than a little eager to be accommodating. The chairman of the committee, James Garfield of Ohio, a longtime supporter of the western surveys, asked why "no history of the original exploration of the canyons had been published." Powell's answer was that he did not look on his field work as "an adventure," that he was only interested in the scientific results and their publication. Garfield, in a friendly manner, advised him to work up that history in a government report or risk losing all of his appropriations. He promised to do so, and the next appropriation was raised to $15,000—a lesson in power politics. By 16 June of that year he had Garfield's history ready for publication.[65]

Obviously, the congressman meant him to tell the story of the famous expedition of 1869, the one covered in newspapers and shrouded in rumors of death and disaster. Powell wrote that he had kept a daily journal of that trip on long, narrow strips of brown paper, which he bound in small leather volumes, and it was this journal he now decided to publish. So he later remembered. A sketchy journal on long brown strips of paper survives, but not one bound in leather volumes, and not a journal in any form comparable to the report Powell published. Contrary to his memory late in life, he did a great deal of embellishing and expanding in order to prepare a history of an event that had been completed almost five years earlier. He added details of incident and landscape from subsequent trips, correctly entitling the report, *Exploration of the Colorado River of the West and Its Tributaries, Explored in 1869, 1870, 1871, and 1872.*

When he came to do the report as instructed by Garfield, he could not resist giving it a more scientific aura. Thus, only half of the pages were Powell's "history of the original exploration of the canyons." He included a chapter by Harry Thompson on the search for the mouth of the Dirty Devil, he added two chapters of his own on the broader physical characteristics of the Colorado River valley, and he added a third section on fauna by scientists who were never part of his survey team. The report was in fact quite a miscellany. Apparently, Garfield was satisfied with this compromise between adventure and science. But some of the men from the second journey down the river were not satisfied, Dellenbaugh in particular. They saw the names of Sumner, Bradley, and the rest in print but not their own, and they read about the wreck in Lodore and the separation of the Howlands and Dunn but nothing about the long months they had rowed and portaged to collect a better set of data. Their adventure somehow had slipped by unrecorded and unappreciated.

Fred Dellenbaugh, a lifelong admirer of Powell, never accused the Major of deliberately ignoring the men of '71–'72; on the contrary, he continued to defend Powell's character and generosity for decades to come. But Almon Thompson did accuse and went on accusing for years. In his mind he had never been given proper credit for the work he had done. The Major was not "a fair and generous man — to put it mildly." Decades after their river trips, Thompson wrote to Dellenbaugh:

> The phase of the Major's character which led him to ignore the second expedition is no mystery to me. He had no fine sense of justice, no exacted loyalty to a high ideal and honor and so far as his subordinates were concerned did not know the meaning of noblesse oblige. He was generous, sympathetic, and possesed all the estimable qualities you and I assign him but you will notice neither you nor I speak of his justice or loyalty. He was sadly deficient in these.[66]

This has the familiar, grudging tone of a brother-in-law who always resented the relative who had outshone him in every way. As for loyalty, Powell rescued Thompson from a small-town school superintendent's job, gave him a priceless opportunity to spend years in the West's most stunning and unspoiled region, and then maneuvered him into a well-paid, high-level career in the scientific establishment of Washington.[67]

Deserved or not, and largely it was undeserved, the image grew of Powell as an ungrateful man who deliberately overlooked the achievements of the second party. He seemed unaware of the wounded feelings among some of his old crew, though he was certainly aware of the hard attitudes taken by the first party of hunters and miners. When, in 1895, he came to dedicate his book *Canyons of the Colorado*, Powell singled out the men of '69 and spoke of them in the most positive terms—"my noble and generous companions, dead and alive"—when they had been neither especially noble or generous toward him. But once more he failed to mention the men of the "second expedition," as Dellenbaugh termed it.

Of course, there was, in Powell's mind, no "second expedition," and in a sense, he was right. What occurred in 1871–72 was a fragmented but scientifically thorough survey of the Green and Colorado rivers, one that included Powell on site for only a portion of the time. Could an "expedition" mean those long times when he was on his way to and from Washington, lobbying Congressmen, arranging for supplies? In his annual reports to Congress he acknowledged Dellenbaugh, Thompson, and the rest by name, gave their exact itinerary, and honored them as "scientists" engaged in a proper survey.[68] He put their names on the landscape just as he did the names of the first party. But he did not look on their contributions as a mere "adventure" to be gotten up for popular consumption nor did he have any reason to think that Garfield's request for a history of the "original exploration" included them, any more than it included the dozens of other men who were hired for a season or more to carry on the survey.

When at Kanab Wash on 9 September 1872 Powell called the second trip through the Grand Canyon finished, the survey as a whole was by no means finished. Jack Hillers and Clem were immediately sent with old Jacob to take pictures of the Hopis and their ancient towns.[69] Thompson went off to complete the topographical survey of the Grand Canyon, while Powell and Jones headed for the headwaters of the Virgin River and studied the geology around Kanab. Near the end of October they joined together for a month-long survey of the Uinkaret Plateau and its sixty-some volcanic cones, of which Mount Trumbull was the highest. Here Powell once more met with the local Paiute bands—Kaibabs, Uinkarets, and the strongly anti-Mormon Shivwits—talked peace with them, recorded their vocabularies, traded for their artifacts and for the seeds and fruits on which they subsisted, and made notes on their mythology. Altogether he filled twenty cases of material for the Smithsonian. Then, on the last day of November he left Kanab for Salt Lake City and was back home in Washington—yes, it was home now—on 5 January 1873.[70]

The Thompsons and Dellenbaugh stayed on for the winter, renting a lot in Kanab where they set up several tents for dwelling and working. In one of the tents they placed a large drafting table next to an iron stove, and in that narrow space they began to transfer all their topographical data to paper, drawing a full, comprehensive map of the Colorado Plateau. It took weeks to finish, but in mid-February they were done. The original drawing was transferred to a large sheet of tracing cloth, which was rolled up and inserted into a long tin tube. Dellenbaugh then rode through a snowstorm to Salt Lake with the tube on his back. Taking a room in the best hotel in town, he slept for the first time in nearly two years in a real bed; the next day he turned the map over to Wells, Fargo for delivery to the Major and went off to San Francisco for a holiday before returning east.

Nor was the Powell Survey completed then; it went on for six more summer-fall seasons, with changing personnel on the payroll and changing terrain to study. In 1879 Congress consolidated the Hayden, King, Wheeler, and Powell surveys into a single institution, the U.S. Geological Survey. Thompson continued through the '70s to work as Powell's main field lieutenant and later, after the consolidation, worked as a geographer in the new Geological Survey. Hillers also stayed with Major Powell for more than two decades, achieving acclaim as one of the nation's greatest photographers—an extraordinary outcome for a poor young immigrant who had been recruited at the last moment off the Salt Lake City streets. Dellenbaugh came back regularly to the Southwest, though as an independent traveling artist and historian. In 1878 he went to Paris to study painting, though he never became the artist he hoped to be. Instead, he turned to writing and illustrating books about American exploration and became one of the founders of the Explorers Club. In 1899 he served as an artist on the Harriman Alaska Expedition. With Hillers, he outlived all the other members of his Colorado River crew; Hillers died in 1925, Dellenbaugh in 1935.

The others in the crew had no more reason to feel shortchanged by Powell, by history, or by fortune. John Steward went back to Illinois to work for the Marsh Harvester Company (later the International Harvester Company) and became a successful, well-paid businessman. Captain Bishop, as related earlier, moved to Salt Lake City and taught college science there for years. Beaman failed to leave much of a trace after his magazine articles appeared. Fennemore, whose role in the survey was so short, continued to work as a photographer in Utah and became famous for his picture of John D. Lee sitting on his coffin just before he was executed by a firing squad. Andy Hattan returned to the family farm and lived out his life in Illinois, unmarried and obscure. And Stephen Jones went back briefly to his career as public-school teacher before taking up the practice of the law; in 1883 he moved to South Dakota, became an influential lawyer there, and had a hand in drafting the state's constitution.

Few of them looked on Powell as their personal hero. They had lived too close for that kind of adulation and had seen his foibles and deficiencies. His science, some of them realized, could be superficial and casual, and he did not set the same high standards for himself or his men that Clarence King did. Repeatedly, he left his employees with insufficient explanation about what they were trying to achieve and how they should be spending their time. He did not communicate with them fully; often he seemed more intent on communicating with the newspapers, lecture audiences, and Congress than he did with the men who were working under him, or else he was lost in his own thoughts. Too often when he was with them his mind seemed in another place. For all his geniality, cheerful optimism, and high spirits, he stood aloof and apart. In their eyes he was a flawed leader as he was a maimed man.

On the other hand, Powell's second group of recruits were not themselves free of flaws. They did not come well prepared or well trained to do advanced science, at least compared to members of the other surveys. They were a party of amateurs, self-taught like their leader; a group of rather ordinary Americans who wanted to see the fabulous river of stone for themselves and then sometimes found it too much for them. They brought along a few petty weaknesses — intolerance, vanity, suspicion, and ego. A culture demanding unblemished heroes would not find any of them particularly heroic. They were not paragons of courage or military discipline or scientific brilliance or entrepreneurial genius.

But for all their weaknesses, together they did great work. The Powell Survey, like the original exploration that it built on, represented a triumph of ordinary people confronting an extraordinary landscape. The Major and his men, with few exceptions, successfully answered the old challenge made by the West: Could people of no particular status or breeding or elite education, through diligence and ambition, achieve something special in this place? They could and they did.

Like the men he recruited, Powell came west as a rather ordinary, undistinguished man and found himself challenged to rise to a new, higher plateau than he had known. The Colorado and its highlands inspired and compelled him; they transformed him from a floundering preacher's son who could not find himself into a charismatic figure, into a hero for his time. The land called out his great gifts of intelligence, prudence, understanding, and resourcefulness. A half dozen years after his first, improvised field trip into the West he had succeeded in navigating, not once but twice, the most formidable river on the continent. With his staff he had produced a map filled with information about a place that had defied knowledge, and in doing so he had made himself one the country's most informed experts on the realities of this awesome land.

CHAPTER 7

Kapurats

A photograph taken by John Hillers in October 1873 shows the Kaibab Paiutes sitting in a circle under a pinyon, holding an earnest tribal council. The center figure is Chuarumpeak, his long black hair falling forward on his shoulders. Many of the other figures are a blur of black mop that moved before the exposure was complete. Then there is Wes Powell, whom the Paiutes called Kapurats ("He is who is missing an arm"), solemnly sitting on the side of the circle next to Jacob Hamblin and made conspicuous not by his height but by his pale face. It was a characteristic place for Powell to be during his field seasons, for he constantly sought the companionship of Indians and sat long hours in their midst, flat on the ground.

He would be collecting, of course — a trader in words, stories, artifacts who believed that in the jumble he collected lay a mode of thinking that was different from his own, a mode he could penetrate and understand as a scientist. But unavoidably he would also be hearing about the plight of the Indian peoples undergoing an invasion of monumental proportions. They told him about the hillsides where they had once gathered seeds that were now a cattleman's pasture, the riverbanks where they had grown corn and squash that were now a white man's village, the game they once had hunted that could no longer be found. He could see other forms of invasion that were undermining a once self-sufficient way of life: a white man's gun replacing the bow and arrow, machine-made cloth that seemed superior to the old rabbit-skin robe, a sulphur match that was more convenient than a palm drill for starting a fire. Even more profoundly than the loss of land, those commodities purchased from the industrial economy turned autonomy into dependence.

Powell and the Mormon scout Jacob Hamblin meeting with a band of Paiutes. Taken by J.K. Hillers on the Kaibab Plateau, 1873. (Courtesy: National Archives)

Whatever he may have thought about their chances of cultural survival, Powell never doubted that the dark people with whom he sat were as human as himself. They were not a contemptible species of vermin to be exterminated. Occasionally he found them comical or ludicrous, repellent or disgusting, but never subhuman. This acceptance of the Indians as fundamentally human, not a commonplace attitude among Americans of the period, was undoubtedly the legacy from Powell's parents and their intense Methodist belief in the equality of all people before God — a belief that had made them abolitionists and for which they had suffered serious threats of harm. Powell himself had been a pupil and a teacher in racially integrated colleges.

He had come west with little of the prejudice against people of color typical of his day.

The complaints the Indians made to him were, by and large, against the Mormon kingdom that was expanding into their territory. "Gentile" miners and ranchers were crowding in too, but they were fewer in number and they came a little later; the most immediate threat, at least in Utah, was from the people who called themselves Latter-day Saints. Their vision was nothing less than imperial. Soon after arriving at the Great Salt Lake in 1847, they began dreaming of a godly state that would stretch in all directions of the compass, but particularly southwestward along an axis that ended in Los Angeles, their intended seaport. The Colorado River was to be their Mississippi River, bringing converts in from the ports of England, Denmark, and Sweden; bringing in sugar cane from their plantation in the Sandwich Islands; bringing in whatever they needed to defend their independence against a competing American empire. Brigham Young, one of the great imperialists of the century, kept pushing his people farther and farther into Indian lands, instructing them to saw up forests for houses and fences, to quarry rock for religious temples, to seize every available source of fresh water, and to transform the desert into cotton, wheat, and cattle farms.[1]

Mormon expansion meant Indian starvation. Seeds of grass could feed the white man's cattle or they could feed the native people's children; they could not do both.[2] Naturally, the natives fought back, trying to hold the land that they had lived on for centuries. In 1865 a small group of Utes, Paiutes, and Navajos, numbering no more than a hundred, answered the call of Autenquer, or Black Hawk, to retaliate by raiding the Mormon settlements. They stole thousands of head of cattle and killed some ninety settlers before the Mormons raised a twenty-five-hundred-man militia to fight what they called the Black Hawk "war." The Indians did not have a chance against such numbers. They surrendered and even apologized. Black Hawk trudged from congregation to congregation explaining that they had turned to violence because they were hungry. When Powell arrived to study their languages and culture, they were still hungry.[3]

Ironically, Brigham Young himself had proclaimed an official policy of feeding the Indians instead of fighting them, however hard it was to enforce in frontier settlements.[4] More than that, their holy word taught Mormons that the Indians were brothers and sisters who must be redeemed from their fallen state and brought back into fellowship, not slaughtered or starved. According to the *Book of Mormon,* whites and Indians had a common set of parents in ancient Palestine, Lehi and his wife Sariah; their eldest son, Laman, was the father of all Indians, their youngest son, Nephi, the father of Mormons. The sons sailed together to the Land of Promise (the west coast of America) about the year 590 B.C. But they subsequently divided into two conflicting groups, the Lamanites and the Nephites, until in A.D. 421 the Lamanites wiped out their rivals completely and Moroni, the last prophet of the Nephites, stashed their records in the Hill Cumorah near Palmyra, New York, where they lay hidden for fourteen hundred years until Joseph Smith dug them up and tried to revive the Nephite lineage. The Lamanites, or American Indians, thus were blood relatives, though they were also bloody enemies.

By the light of this story the Mormon empire builders had to acknowledge that they were invading the homeland of people like themselves, however benighted those people had become. The Saints, of course, had by the authority of scripture a moral right to do so, since they, or their spiritual ancestors, had once been invaded and destroyed by those same people. But as the better half of the family, they could not do to the Indians what the Indians had done to them. They must bring the Indians over to righteousness. So when Mormons gave away food to the Indians it came with a packet of theology and, on a number of occasions, it had to be paid for by mass baptisms.

Powell did not in the least believe that *Book of Mormon* history. It was no more factual to him than the stories told by Indians about how Coyote brought fire to mankind or how Tavwoats rolled a magic ball before him, crushing a great canyon through the earth and filling it with water. Powell collected all such "mythologies" but put them under the heading of primitive "superstition." The Mormons and Indians were nowhere more alike than in their capacity to invent stories of origin and to tell them endlessly around the fire. Telling such stories, however, did not give either people a divine right to territory or natural resources. The land was not promised to anybody in particular.

The ruins Powell had seen along the Colorado River told him that other peoples—neither Paiute, Ute, nor Mormon—had once claimed ownership but had disappeared. What he did not know, but would have instantly accepted, was the story that modern science in the form of archaeology tells about the deep human history of the region. The masonry ruins he and his party came upon and puzzled over can now be radiocarbon dated back to A.D. 800–1000, their abandonment to about A.D. 1150. They were constructed by the people

Powell called the archaic Moquis or the Shinumos, and his men called the Aztecs, but that we now call the Anasazis, the ancient ones. They may first have appeared in the canyon country, expanding westward from the Four Corners or from the south, as far back as the beginning of the Christian era, though their roots lie in the Clovis and Folsom hunting and gathering cultures. A long, slow evolution (through cultural stages identified as Basketmaker I, II, and III and Pueblo I, II, and III) brought them to a pinnacle of material achievement before they abruptly slipped away. Their descendants, as Powell rightly guessed, are the Hopis, the Zunis, and the various Pueblo communities along the Rio Grande.[5]

Why they left the stone houses and kivas they had constructed in a number of places below the canyon rims is still an open question. The most common explanation is that long-term drought set in, drying up their irrigation possibilities, forcing them to move down to more well-watered sites.[6] But it is also the case that as they moved out of the canyonlands, they were succeeded by another culture — and not only were they succeeded but they may have been pushed. The invaders came from the southwest, the Mohave Desert, spreading in a fan across the Great Basin. They were people of the desert who knew how to forage in the driest of environments. Along the south rim of the Grand Canyon they became the Havasupai and the Walapai. Along the north rim, high up on the plateaus, and into western Colorado they became the Paiutes and Utes. Agriculture provided a small, scattered part of their diet, but most of their food came from hunting and gathering: a low-intensity, seminomadic relationship to the land.

Between the Utes and Paiutes there was no more stable harmony than between the Lamanites and Nephites. The Utes, who came into contact with the Plains tribes and adopted their horse culture, including the tipi and bison hunt, regularly ran roughshod over their horseless Paiute brethern, stealing their children for slaves and selling them in Santa Fe. Some Paiute bands were severely depopulated by this practice, and they often hid in the most inaccessible places to evade the Ute raiders. The role of the Athapascan-speaking Navajos in this shifting mosaic (they arrived in the Southwest not long before the Spanish) added even more tension and competition. Thus, the Mormons, and the whites generally, were by no means the first group to invade the region nor to try to push aside others and command their resources. They were only the latest in a series of people in motion, though they moved in faster and more disruptively than any people before had done.[7]

As a student of the Indian Powell understood the main lines of that science-based story well enough, and through the study of their languages, affinities, and geographical distribution he hoped to uncover the origins of the various tribes. But it was not possible for him merely to study them in an academically detached way; the complaints he heard constantly, the favors he was asked by Indians, the hunger and bloodshed he witnessed all drew him into political involvement. He could not remain completely neutral. Even the maps his survey parties produced had a potential use in the struggle going on between the competing cultures. That was well understood by the Mormon hierarchy, and that was why they were willing to offer him assistance.

On the whole Powell supported the new white invaders, for apart from their theology they were creating an advanced society in this part of the West. They were writing a progressive new chapter in the old story of human occupation and use. On the other hand, he found the people they were invading interesting and sympathetic. Their lives stimulated his curiosity, while their suffering touched his heart.

In January 1872, a few weeks before Emma and he left the Kanab survey camp for Washington and while he was wrestling with the uncooperative photographer, Beaman, Powell gave Jacob Hamblin a letter of introduction to the U.S. Indian agent for southern Utah and Nevada. He wanted to draw the agent's attention to the destitute condition of the Paiutes. As the letter described, grasshoppers had eaten so much of the vegetation that the humans could gather no seeds or pine nuts; "and now the Indians are begging from the whites who are themselves poor by reason of the grasshoppers." The Kaibabs were camped only a few miles away, and Powell had visited them regularly, exchanging food for their "ornaments." Can you do something for them, he asked? "It will be an act of humanity to them[,] prevent difficulties that must arise from their begging excursions and tend to give greater security to my parties who are surveying this region."[8]

The agent addressed was another man called Major Powell — Charles F. Powell — who had been appointed to his post in the summer of 1871. He was stationed in the mining town of Pioche, Nevada, a hundred miles north of the Colorado River near the Nevada-Utah territorial line. Remote and penurious, the post was part of a new federal system set up to address Indian problems. Letters and reports went from places like Pioche up to Washington, D.C.; letters and instructions came back down. Accordingly, agent

Powell sent surveyor Powell's plea to his superior, Francis Walker, Commissioner of Indian Affairs, with a plea of his own: "I can do nothing until funds are sent me for their relief." No such funds came during that winter. Money was the one thing that did not circulate well in the new system. But it was clearly becoming the federal government's responsibility to find a solution, immediate and long-term, to the worsening plight of the invaded natives of the West. Peace, security, and humanity all argued that.

Each of the western states and territories had a superintendent appointed to find solutions and prevent violence. The Nevada superintendent lived in Carson City, with a subordinate agent in Pioche to handle local matters: two men, with a small staff, to cover a territory larger than a hundred thousand square miles. They were poorly paid, and the temptation to squeeze out an extra income by selling annuities designed for Indians or by arranging kickbacks from overgenerous contracts was strong. Understandably, the turnover in office was rapid, from the superintendent down to the local agent far out in the sagebrush. Before Charles Powell there had been Henry Stewart, a staunchly religious man recommended by the Baptists' national association; his health was so bad he was prevented from ever taking hold. And before Stewart was Captain Reuben Fenton, another military man, who bilked the government and his own charges and was locked in jail by the sheriff.[9] After Charles Powell came still another agent, George W. Ingalls of Springfield, Illinois, who lasted only from July 1872 to September 1874.

If anything held those loose, mobile bones of a system together, it was the "peace policy" announced by Ulysses Grant soon after moving into the White House. Although he came from the military, Grant surprised many by not unleashing such violently anti-Indian commanders as Philip Sheridan, George A. Custer, or William Tecumseh Sherman to pacify the West. He listened to a group of reform-minded Protestant ministers who asked that, henceforth, agents be appointed from their ranks to bring the kindly moral power of Christianity to bear on the Indian problem. If the natives could be made into Methodists or Quakers, it would take the fight out of them. Grant went along with the request, and the Methodists assumed jurisdiction over California, Oregon, Washington, and Idaho; Baptists were put in charge of all agencies and reservations in Nevada; while the Presbyterians had responsibility for the Indians of Utah and Arizona. Conspicuously absent from the list of religious supervisors were the Mormons, whom Grant did not like and the major Protestant denominations regarded as renegades from decency.[10]

With the shift from military confrontation to religious pacification went a shift from forcibly removing Indians thousands of miles away from the white man's settlements to amalgamating them into the dominant society. They must become regular Americans. The government must stop making treaties with them or otherwise treating them as independent, sovereign nations. Indians in turn must come to the government not as members of tribes but as free-standing individuals, each responsible for securing his or her own welfare within the commonwealth. They must acquire a piece of private property, learn how to raise food for their own families and a surplus to sell in the marketplace, and practice thrift and self-discipline. They must go to school and learn to read and write English and do sums. The country must see that the only good Indian is a good American citizen.

That Indians were not yet ready for such an amalgamation was clear to everyone advocating the new reforms. They needed time to adjust, to learn new ways, and they needed space where they could be secure from the white invasion. Reservations of land for Indians were an essential part of the peace policy. Setting up agencies to distribute foodstuff or medicine or Bibles was not enough; native people also needed a guaranteed base of natural resources where they could learn to follow the white man's mode of livelihood. The prevailing federal land laws did not allow for such a base. In fact, Indians as such did not even exist in terms of the laws governing the distribution of land. Any American citizen, or any alien who had declared the intention of becoming a citizen, could go onto the public domain and stake a claim to 160 acres. If those acres had not yet been officially surveyed for homesteading, the citizen could claim a right of preemption—a right to settle and at some later date to buy, free from competing bids, at the minimum government price. Mormons and non-Mormons commonly used the right of preemption to plunk themselves squarely down on the Indians' food and water supply, and the Indians had no legal means whatever to drive them away. A reservation of land exclusively for Indians was a vital necessity so long as such land laws were in force.

Besides the huge Navajo reservation, the government marked off reservations on the Walker River and at Pyramid Lake in Nevada (1859), in eastern Utah (1861), and in western Colorado (1863). Tribes that refused to move to those places, or that had no reservation to go to, could be mercilessly harried by the army, miners, farmers—by anyone who came through—for they were people without title. To be sure, those who now lived on reservations had limited protection. Whites could squat and defy anyone to evict them. More serious yet, any title that Indians obtained was constantly under threat. As Major Henry Douglas, superintendent of Indian affairs in Nevada, warned Commissioner Ely Parker in 1870: "There is a constant hankering after the land on these Reservations, and white men are determined to have them if they can by any reasons obtain them;—they will not scruple to hire and make use of the power weilded [sic] by 'wickedness in high places' to secure the desired object, and such a conspiracy is now actually in progress."[11]

The turnover at the top of the government's system, in the office of Commissioner, was as rapid as that at the agency level. Ely Parker, Grant's first appointee to the office, a Seneca Indian, resigned after only two years under a cloud of accusations that he had failed to enforce government rules requiring open bidding on contracts. He was replaced by H.R. Clum, then by Francis A. Walker (who was really interested in perfecting a national census and soon resigned to become president of the Massachusetts Institute of Technology), then by a Congregational minister, Edward P. Smith, who served from 1873 to 1876.

After Parker, the so-called peace policy regularly betrayed its original purpose of Christian benevolence. Walker, for example, looked on the reservations as confinement centers for wild, bestial tribes: "If they stand up against the progress of civilization and industry," he warned, "they must be relentlessly crushed. The westward course of population is neither to be denied nor delayed for the sake of all the Indians that ever called this country their home. They must yield or perish." His successor, Smith, insisted that any Indian living on a reservation should not expect a handout. "The call to labor must come to him, not through memorials or treaties, councils or presents, but through his necessities. He must be driven to toil by cold and the pangs of hunger. Then, when he has taken this first step toward self-support, his wants, which at the beginning were registered only in his stomach, take on multiplied forms, and urge to increased industry."[12]

By the late 1870s Smith and others within the government's Indian bureaucracy were beginning to advocate breaking up reservations into discrete pieces of private property. They spoke of "allotting" the land in "severalty," or individualized titles, destroying the traditional Indian practice of community ownership. "The starting point of individualism for an Indian," according to still another commissioner, E.A. Hayt, "is the personal possession of his portion of reservation. Give him a house within a tract of land, whose corner-stakes are plainly recognized by himself and his neighbors, and let whatever can be produced out of this landed estate be considered property in his own name, and the first principle of industry and thrift is recognized."[13] The passage in 1887 of the Dawes Severalty Act, also called the General Allotment Act, drawn up mainly by Senator Henry Dawes from Massachusetts, came only a decade after Hayt's words and defined federal policy toward Indians well into the twentieth century.

From his encounters with native peoples Powell did not come up with any profoundly original ideas about how to reconcile white and Indian culture. He cared about Chuar and the other Paiutes, but he did not see how they could go on sweeping seeds into their conical baskets or congregating around the Mormon settlements to beg for food and clothing. He understood that they were terrified by what was happening around them, far more so than the whites with all their talk about "massacres" and "scalpings." The Indians were afraid, worried, uncertain, despairing, and demoralized. They needed friends to help them make a transition. Powell saw himself as such a friend but one whose job it was to bring bad news where necessary and insist that the Indians accept and adapt.

Their way of life could not longer be sustained. It had to pass away, with the scientific naiveté of the savage. Detaching them from their ancestral homelands was the first step, Powell argued.

> All of our our Indian troubles have arisen primarily and chiefly
> from two conditions inherent in savage society. The first is that the
> land belonging to an Indian clan or tribe is dear to it not only as a
> region from which it obtains subsistence but chiefly because it is
> the locus of its religion. The Indian religion is localized. Every
> spring, creek and river, every valley, hill and mountain as well as
> the trees that grow upon the soil are made sacred by the inherited
> traditions of their religion. These are all homes of their gods.
> When an Indian clan or tribe gives up its land it not only
> surrenders its home as understood by civilized people but its gods
> are abandoned and all its religion connected therewith, and
> connected with the worship of ancestors buried in the soil; that is,
> everything most sacred to Indian society is yielded up.
>
>   Such a removal of the Indians is the first step to be taken in
> their civilization. . . . The great body of Indians of North America

has been removed from their original homes. Only a few now remain to worship at the graves of their ancestors. This portion of the problem is almost solved, but the wisdom and patience of the American people must be exercised for a few years longer — demanding as they should on the one hand, that the progress of civilization and the establishment of homes for millions of civilized people should not be retarded because of the interests and superstitions of a small number of savages, but demanding on the other hand that strict justice and the widest charity be extended to the Indians.

The second great step in the civilization of the Indians consists in inducing them to take lands and property in severalty. . . . The greatest crime is the claim of an individual to land and it is also a heinous sin against their religion.

Breaking the emotional bond between Indians and their land, Powell was saying, could open their minds to a more advanced interpretation of nature. They must cease worshipping the earth and begin exploiting it. Private property ownership hastened that shift in attitude. Such changes, however, "should not be abruptly enforced upon" the Indians, for they needed patient tutoring to bridge the gulf that separated them from their white conquerors.[14]

Replacing a military with a peace policy was one that Powell heartily welcomed. After his trip to the Dakota Badlands under military escort failed, Powell never again requested any soldiers to accompany him in the field. His men carried guns, but they never had to use them against Indians. "If I should go into that country with a body of troops," he explained, "I would thus take a hostile attitude, and would be compelled to fight my way among them, but in all that country I can go alone or with one or two men, or I can send out one or two men and they can travel anywhere without trouble."[15] If a mere fraction of the money spent on supporting troops in the West were allocated to help civilize the Indians, the conflict would be over. Indians dreaded the soldiers. They could not understand why Americans set apart a professional military whose sole purpose was killing and "who care nothing for social life, and do not desire to have wives and children as other men." Soldiers, in their eyes, were always "a source of trouble and loathsome disease."[16]

Although he was in favor of the peace policy, Powell was opposed to putting religious indoctrination ahead of practical economic solutions. He defended that view carefully in a time where so many humane reformers saw the saving of Indian souls as a first priority. "I should be sorry to offend the hosts of earnest, humane, religious men in the United States," he wrote, "but I am constrained to affirm that bibles, and religious songs, and missionary teachings are powerless with the Indian in his present condition."[17] He did not deny that good might come from preaching the gospel to the heathen. He did not insist that all religions were equal or that Christianity was no better than paganism, though in his own private thoughts the Protestant evangelical worldview was as dead as primitive animism. He simply maintained that a practical solution must begin with satisfying material wants.

A final contrast between Powell's notion of a peace policy and that of the Grant administration, or indeed that of the Dawes Act some years later, lies in the fact that he did not see the reservation as a short-term expedient to be abolished as quickly as possible. He was less vociferous than others in pushing a social ideal based on private property, economic individualism, rigid self-reliance, and competition. In fact, he had a few doubts about that social idea stirring in the back of his head, doubts that later grew into a critique of American ideology. For now he tended to agree that the Indians needed to acquire and cherish private property as a first step toward civilization, but he also continued to emphasize that they needed the security of a carefully run reservation to do so. He was to have the opportunity to help Indians achieve that security, for he was about to take a temporary leave from the Powell Survey and go to work gathering Indians on reservations.

A troop of Army regulars barged into the camp of Keintpoos (a.k.a. Captain Jack) and his Modocs on a November morning in 1872, to disarm and send them back to a reservation. The reservation, located in southeastern Oregon, was inhabited mainly by the Klamaths, who resented having the Modocs thrust upon them. None of the Keintpoos runaways wanted to go back to face that Klamath resentment, so they gave the soldiers the slip and hid in the Lava Beds of northern California. Through the following winter they defied all demands that they surrender and all efforts to negotiate their return. When they killed a U.S. general in self-defense, the government sent more troops to defeat them. Suddenly, President Grant's peace policy was in shambles. The white frontier community was in uproar everywhere, as newspaper editorialists raged against the audacious Captain Jack and darkly warned that a "Modoc war" was on. There was no war, and there would be no war. Keintpoos was captured on 1 June, hanged a few months later, and the Modocs offered no further resistance.[18]

Despite this pathetic outcome, Secretary of the Interior Columbus Delano worried that the neighboring tribes of the Colorado Plateau and Great Basin might next catch fire, and then the Apaches, Comanches, Sioux, and Blackfeet would be smoking hot too. Better send somebody into the desert interior to cool things off and define a strategy to prevent any more Modoc-like outrages.[19] Delano called in Major Powell, who was preparing to take the field with his survey crew. Powell reassured Secretary Delano that there was no need to be alarmed. Indians had never succeeded for long in overcoming their deep-seated differences and animosities to form an offensive alliance against the whites. Nonetheless, the secretary continued to worry. Powell was en route to Salt Lake City when a telegram caught up, appointing him, as of 21 April 1873, to the office of special Indian commissioner to undertake a full study and make recommendations. A snowstorm delayed his train in the Rockies, but on 6 May he arrived in the Utah capital with a huge task and only the vaguest of instructions.

Powell's co-commissioner was George Ingalls, the agent at Pioche, Nevada.[20] They were well acquainted with one another, for after Powell's second run through the canyon he had joined Ingalls at St. George and St. Thomas to powwow with the Paiutes. It may have been Ingalls who brought Powell to the commissioner's attention when he reported that Powell acted as his interpreter and "delivered quite an address, setting forth the advantages derived by the Indians if they would generally adopt the propositions I had submitted to them." Those propositions amounted to giving up "their savage, wandering life, and [diverting] their attention to agricultural and mechanical pursuits, and adopting a civilized mode of living, and securing the benefits of an education."[21] The Paiutes told him that was exactly what they wanted to do. They seemed, he believed, well-disposed toward the whites and all their propositions.

Ingalls, in reporting the powwow, shrewdly noted that Brigham Young was preparing to build a railroad south from Salt Lake City to join the new Atlantic and Pacific line following the 35th parallel, intensifying pressure on the Indians. Washington, it was hinted, must protect them from the ambitions of Mormon imperialists. The Indians must get their own reservation, and get it soon. A few weeks before the two special commissioners arrived in Salt Lake, Congress authorized a Paiute reservation in Lincoln County, Nevada, covering

Powell and Taugu, one of his informants among the St. George band of Paiutes,
taken by J.K. Hillers in 1873. (Courtesy: National Archives)

almost two million acres, including the valley of the Muddy River (or the Moapa), a tributary of the Virgin. The commissioners agreed they must make a visit to the new reservation a high priority.

Simply to locate all the Indians in their assigned territory was a formidable job. Powell's instructions, which he had to go back to Washington to clarify, were to design a large-scale program for the Utes of Utah; the Paiutes of Utah, northern Arizona, southern Nevada, and southeastern California; the Shoshones of Idaho and Utah; and the Western Shoshones of Nevada. Somehow they were to induce all those peoples to accept life on a reservation, a goal that the army had failed for months to achieve in the case of a mere handful of Modocs. The removal program must be legal, practical, and humane. It must follow the strict letter of treaty obligations; no Indian should be moved beyond geographic limits they had formally specified in writing. And certainly the commissioner did not want to provoke another "Modoc war" by mixing incompatible peoples on the same reservation.

Designing such a program was a big job for a couple of commissioners, no matter how well they knew the country or the Indians. They hired a young Ute named Richard Komas, a student at Lincoln University in Pennsylvania, to help them with interpreting, and together they went off to find the tribes and talk to them. If the whites were in a high state of fear that they were about to be slaughtered, the Indians were even more terrified and many had fled into the mountains for refuge. From spring to the first of December the commissioners were hard at their task of locating and persuading them to accept the government's conditions. By sending out word that they had annuities, or government supplies, to distribute, they hoped to induce Indians to come together and listen to what the commissioners proposed. The message was consistent: You cannot survive any longer on your own, the land is almost all taken up by whites, your only hope is get to a reservation and stay there. In other words, you have been whipped and have no choices left.

In early May the commissioners met with Utes, Gosiutes, and Shoshones near Salt Lake City. After that they faced long days of bumping down rough dirt roads in their ambulance wagon, carrying flour, beef, bacon, and other provisions to the Indians, sleeping in tents many nights far from hotel comforts, sitting in council for days on end. "It was often necessary," Powell explained, "to go where there were neither railroad nor stage lines," even at times to rely on shank's mare as the only mode of transportation.[22] During June they were in Utah's Cache, San Pete, and Sevier valleys, then in Kanab and St. George. The month of September found them on the Muddy River reservation, while later that month Powell traveled to Las Vegas and Ingalls headed northward in Nevada.

Altogether they identified more than one hundred tribes, or bands, in the region, each with its own name and government. Their combined population came to 10,437—only a third of what the Indian bureau had assumed. Half of them were already on a reservation, but that still left a large number of people to uproot and resettle.

The Powell-Ingalls report, delivered 18 December 1873, and reviewed in testimony before the House Committee on Indian Affairs in early 1874, proposed dividing the native peoples into four groups and concentrating them on four large reservations. The Western Shoshones, who numbered 1,945 in Nevada and another 400 in Idaho, should go to Fort Hall on the Snake River of eastern Idaho, where there is "abundance of timber, plenty of water for irrigating purposes, extensive and valuable grasslands, abundance of agricultural

Taugu and Powell, taken by J.K. Hillers, 1873. (Courtesy: National Archives)

lands, and altogether the valley is very beautiful and valuable."[23] Already over one thousand Indians were living there at least part of the year. Some of the nonreservation tribes sent delegations to take a look, and they were pleased with the prospect and ready to join those already there.

All the Northern Paiutes, whom Powell preferred to call the "Paviotsoes" to distinguish them from the Southern Paiutes, were to pack up and go to an existing reservation on the Malheur River in Oregon's Harney County.[24] Their Nevada lands were too small for their population, lacked much agricultural potential, and were likely to be claimed as part of the Central Pacific's railroad land grant. The total number on that reservation was to rise to twenty-three hundred.

The remaining two reservations were far more familiar to Powell and Ingalls than Malheur or Fort Hall, and they occupied most of their attention: the Uintah Reservation in eastern Utah and the Muddy in southeastern Nevada. Both were prompted by Mormon expansion in particular. Both typified the headaches that any reservation program anywhere must face.

The biggest headache was that many Indians did not want to move to them, and for reasons that mixed the rational and the irrational. Paiutes, Gosiutes, Pahvants, and Utes wanted to stay where they were, dispersed on smaller reservations. Powell rejected that notion as against their self-interest. "Where the Indians are now scattered about the country," he told congressmen, "there seems to be no way by which justice can be secured to the Indians." Lacking any understanding of the American court system or legal proceedings, they required military forces stationed in every neighborhood to guard against white depredations. Congress was not likely to be more generous with future funding than it had been with past funding. The protective troops would not be forthcoming, and the Indians would not want them around if they were. The cause of justice, therefore, could only be served if the Indians could be concentrated in a few places under the protection of civilians who "have a care for their rights."[25]

A better reason for resistance was that Indians realized the larger reservations were not yet able to offer them a secure, safe, appealing home. The Uintah was a case in point. It covered the whole drainage system south of the Uinta mountains, including the Strawberry, Duchesne, and Uinta rivers, an expanse of nearly 2.5 million acres. Here Powell had walked and ridden during stopovers on both his Green River explorations. He realized that for much of the year heavy snow closed the reservation completely from the outside world, and even in summer a hellish road was its only connection to Salt Lake. Yet the land was, according to Powell, blessed with good soil, plenty of water, and convenient timber. "The climate is good for the growth of smaller grains and vegetables, but not favorable to the raising of corn. Good range for cattle is practically unlimited — in fact, there is room enough for all the Indians of Utah. Perhaps there is no finer valley than the Uintah [Uinta] in the territory of the United States west of the hundredth meridian."[26]

By executive order Abraham Lincoln had set the valley aside as a reservation during the Civil War, but the Senate had never ratified a treaty with the Indians to give it a stable status. Compared to the reservation established for the Utes in western Colorado, this one had always been underfunded, a stepchild easily forgotten. Powell's packer, Pardon Dodds of Ohio, had been appointed its first agent, and he felt compelled to raise and sell cattle to the Indians he was supervising in order to survive. His successor was an Army officer who spent his days at Fort Bridger, playing cards and drinking whiskey.

When the Reverend John Critchlow arrived from New York, it looked as if the Grant peace policy might have recruited a more caring administrator. He was sincere, hardworking, and very determined to succeed. His first impulse, to be sure, was to turn around and go back. The small agency staff appeared depraved and worthless, the Indians completely discouraged. No more than seventy-five acres were under cultivation for a population that averaged five hundred Utes. Most of them were from seven tribes organized into a confederacy under Chief Tavwi, or Tabby. They stayed around for spring planting but then left during the summer growing season to go hunting. On reflection, however, Critchlow decided to accept his agency assignment: "This is a beautiful valley. . . . I would make it a Home, then compel all the others to come here to receive their presents, let them see its beauty and desirableness, then it will not be difficult to induce them to make this their home."[27]

When the special commission arrived, Reverend Critchlow was enthusiastic. He wanted, for starters, to convince them that his agency needed more money — perhaps five times more in order to do an adequate job. His most expensive project involved setting up a steam-powered sawmill to make logs and boards for building permanent houses. If they had houses, the Utes might throw away their tipis and stay put the year round. If they had fenced lots surrounding those houses, all with individual family names on them, they might acquire a more conservative character and put down roots.

So Critchlow hoped, and perhaps it would have worked. But the commissioners heard that the Utes did not leave simply to go hunting. They left also because they despised their new agent. Critchlow, they said, was harsh, demanding, rigid, and unfriendly. What Powell and Ingalls soon realized was that getting Indians to stay on reservations depended on more than treaties and paper agreements or successful councils; it required the recruiting of white agents whom the Indians liked and respected, and such were not common.

Those agents should not be Mormons, said the government, a prejudice that created a special problem for the reservation program in Utah. By opposing the hiring of Mormons, indeed by trying to remove Indians altogether from Mormon influence, the federal government touched off a cold war of religion. Powell was himself caught in sniper's fire. Friendly to the Mormons but also friendly to the Grant administration, he could not take sides openly. From Brigham Young he received a warm promise of cooperation if "we would assure him the Indians when on the reservation would be well cared for."[28] Young and his supporters, however, did not really believe that Indians would be well cared for by the government—not as well cared for as by the Mormons. The Saints were not happy to see the Indians disappear from their pool of laborers, or to have all government rations distributed by non-Mormons, or to lose all means of bringing these children of Laman back to the light of Moroni's word. Some persisted in encouraging the Utes to set up small farms and learn sheepherding in and near the Mormon communities rather than accept federal lands and "gentile" influence.

A year before Powell and Ingalls accepted their commission, another federal agent, George W. Dodge, had uncovered what he believed was a conspiracy on the part of the Mormons to sabotage the reservation program. "The entire Mormon influence is working dead against the Government policy for the Indians," he wrote, and was trying to impress them with the idea that the U.S. was their enemy who would send soldiers to "kill every Mormon & Indian who has more than one wife."

> They were dissatisfied with the agents appointed by the U.S. because they were Americans & not Mormons & not acquainted with the Indians. . . . It means that these Indians have been tampered with by Mormon agents. They have been taught that they were the descendents of Joseph & therefore properly the wards of Mormons. . . . Found great trouble with the interpreters they would not translate correctly & honestly & he (Dodge) understanding something of the language had to correct them & make them do their duty. The Mormons had secret signs & signals which they had taught to the Indians & used them in interpreting

so that it was very difficult to detect deception . . . it is injurious in high degree to the interests of the U.S. & the Indians to allow any Mormons to aid in any capacity among the Indians.

Critchlow, according to Dodge, was from the beginning of his tenure an agent against whom the Mormons whispered. If Dodge was right, the Uintah Reservation faced a deeper problem than simply finding a likeable agent or putting the Indians in wooden houses.[29]

Whatever was making them restless and unhappy, the Utes did not stay where they were assigned nor stick to farming. In May 1872, for example, several hundred came off the Uintah and White River reservations into San Pete Valley and refused to go back. Telling Dodge they were under no obligation to comply with any government requests and recognized no authority over them, they lingered through the summer months until the military was called out to enforce obedience.

Meanwhile, Critchlow and his staff went on trying to raise crops and build rail fences for the missing Indians, reducing themselves as Dodge put it to "little less than slaves to their wards." Critchlow kept hoping for a breakthrough to self-reliance. "I sometimes feel discouraged at the little progress made in view of the means and efforts expended," he reported, "but I apprehend I am not the only one in the service who has been compelled to modify his views with regard to what can be accomplished in a given time."[30]

The Muddy River Reservation presented somewhat different problems. There the land set aside was big enough to feed all the Paiutes who lived within the Colorado River basin, though not to support a hunting and gathering mode of life. Its 1.9 million acres were mostly barren mountain and sandy desert, but along the Muddy lay ten or twelve thousand acres that, with irrigation, could raise an abundance of food. "Altogether the situation is good and sufficient," declared the commissioners, for in this low-lying place with warm climate the people could grow grain and subtropical fruits successfully.[31] The Paiutes were generally more experienced at farming than the Utes, who had adopted the horse culture, and with infrastructure and guidance this place might allow a flourishing agricultural life for the southern tribes. During the month of September the commissioners brought in between four and five hundred Paiutes, out of a potential two thousand Paiutes, and three hundred Chemahuevis from California. However, the white man had already entered this land and blocked further reservation development by insisting on a set of claims that the government had to acknowledge.

Kit Carson had named the river "Muddy" when he camped on it in 1847, a name the Mormons accepted when they arrived in the winter of 1865. Once more, Brigham Young was the guiding power behind frontier expansion. He sent a small party to strengthen the Southern Mission with a cluster of settlements growing cotton and improving transportation. St. Thomas was one of the new villages, along with others aggregating some five hundred families in all. From these settlements came the men who had pulled Powell's first Colorado River expedition out of the water and fed them on melons.

But a boundary survey showed the Mormon outposts to be located on the wrong side of the Nevada-Utah line, which meant they must pay taxes in gold and silver coin to a "foreign" capital. The settlers chose not to live under such oppressive conditions, and in February 1871 virtually all of them left their farms (four thousand cultivated acres in all), along with irrigation canals, hundred of thousands of newly planted cottonwood trees, and adobe homes covered with tules, to resettle in the Long Valley of Utah. It was an ominous retreat for the Saints' empire.[32]

Only one family stayed behind, Daniel Bonelli's — and then another set of whites arrived, a trickle of non-Mormons looking for agricultural possibilities. When by executive order the president created an Indian reservation here on 12 March 1873, there were some ten white claims to the land, most of them unpatented. The claimants were mainly poor people, often living in pitiable conditions, and they made a loud wail of protest against being dispossessed without full compensation, a wail heard all the way to Carson City and Washington. As Bonelli wrote to Powell, "This seems to be a big field to withdraw from the use of civilization in so desert a country but seeing I cannot hinder it I will cease to grumble if the Government will only come as near doing me justice as it comes being extravagantly generous to the savages."[33]

Powell's first response was to hope that the Paiutes could be persuaded to change course and settle on the Uintah Reservation hundreds of miles to the northwest, avoiding the displacement of the angry whites. But he soon saw that the Paiutes remembered bitterly their longtime feuds with the Utes and refused to settle next to them. So a reservation on the Muddy was the only realistic possibility, and that meant facing up to the white squatters. As Powell explained to the Commissioner in Washington:

Not a word has been said to any of the white people that there has been any thought of abandoning the Muddy as a reservation. We have apparently kept up a bold front, and a number of the people who came into the valley last winter have left and the difficulties which the Commission anticipated with the settlers will not be as great as expected; some of them have been to see me, others have written us. It would be a great advantage to the management of the affairs of the reservation if they all could be induced to leave the valley this summer or coming fall. In the main, they are a class of people whose presence and influence would be bad.[34]

The squatters made huge claims, covering far more than the standard 160 acres allowed them under the preemption acts and including all the irrigation improvements made by the Mormons before they left, improvements worth hundreds of thousands of dollars, improvements that the new settlers had had no hand in making.

In the end Powell and Ingalls affixed the sum of $32,050 as just compensation for all claims in the valley, but to the white settlers it was not nearly enough. Bonelli wanted at least twice as much as recommended ($5,700 in his case) and felt ill-used by the Major. He had forsaken "that fossilized religion" of Mormonism to "move in and with the progressive, homey age" and was not being well rewarded for his wise decision. "It is simply enigmatical to me," he complained, "that the only man of all these settlers who has toiled here since first the white man redeemed the valley from the desert, should be singled out to perpetrate such injustice upon."[35] But then he gave away his motive when he called for eliminating from the reservation all the "metalliferous territory." Like others, he was sure that great wealth lay buried in the barren mountains.

The government physician appointed to the reservation, Henry Geib, interpreted the white settlers' unhappiness to be over the mining potential there and warned the government that there was widespread discontent over establishing any reservation in this place. The reservation included mountains, and mountains meant minerals, and minerals were the region's leading industry. The two million acres locked up in the reservation included much potential mineral land — land that the Indians, whose only interest was in raising food for themselves, could do without. Geib proposed, and Bonelli agreed, that the reservation could be reduced to the valley lands along the Muddy, leaving the rest of the land open to miners. "Such a concession to a dominant sentiment might conciliate much opposition and would appear to involve no sacrifice of essential points that would be the best interests of the Reservation."[36]

This was not, however, the way Ingalls and Powells saw the situation. Mines (most of them were only salt mines at this date) offered a source of revenue for the Paiutes to supplement their farming economy, while an influx of white miners would be unwholesome for reservation morals. Rather than cutting large chunks out of the Indian domain, the commissioners proposed to expand it to take in several thousand more acres of timber and arable land while maintaining the rest for Indian cattle grazing.[37]

Each of the four designated reservations had complex problems to solve, for both Indians and whites. Yet Powell was characteristically optimistic about making a success of this program, and doing so in a short span of time. The first year's cost to develop the reservations would be $400,000, or $100,000 for each of the reservations, the Muddy River appropriation to include buying out the whites at Powell's appraised value. That $400,000 was twice as much as the government was currently spending on Indians in the region. On the other hand, it was less than the single Modoc episode had cost the government for military action, not counting the loss of lives. The commissioners estimated that it would take three such large annual appropriations before the Indians could become mostly self-sufficient, after which the appropriation could be reduced. With such an investment in reservation development, carefully spent and sustained, the nation could buy peace.

No more presents or gratuities, however, no more free tents, no more machine-made garments. Instead, the Indians ought to be paid government wages to work on their farms, houses, and roads — not wages in the form of cash, which they would gamble away, but wages in the form of foodstuffs and fabric for making clothes. They should get a free cow, house, irrigation ditch, blacksmith, carpenter, saddle and harness maker, medical department, and school.

The commission does not consider that a reservation should be looked upon in the light of a pen where a horde of savages are to be fed with flour and beef, to be supplied with blankets from the Government bounty, and to be furnished with paint and gew-gaws by the greed of traders, but that a reservation should be a school of industry and a home for these unfortunate people. In council with the Indians great care was taken not to implant in their minds the idea that the Government was willing to pay them for yielding lands which white men needed, and that as a recompense for such lands they would be furnished with clothing and food, and thus enabled to live in idleness. The question was presented to the Indian in this light: The white men take these lands and use [them], and from the earth secure to themselves food, clothing, and many other desireable things. Why should not the Indians do the same?

Under this policy, the Indians must surrender hope of future hand-outs and give up claims on another 420,000 square miles of land, including the greater part of Utah, Nevada, Idaho, and Oregon. In exchange they would get firm legal title to 10,000 square miles of reservations. In the end, so the promise went, they would live more securely and comfortably than before. They would no longer have to "fight the battle of life for themselves."[38]

As commissioner, Powell saw himself in the position of realist and harmonizer trying to find a solution that hurt neither Indians nor whites. He did not believe that blame or guilt stood wholly on one side of the racial line or the other. Both sides offered virtue and vice. Indians stole, murdered, and invaded; so did whites. In his 1875 article "An Overland Trip to the Grand Cañon," Powell summed up his basic philosophy for resolving what had become one of the country's most troubled racial encounters:

> He who sees only their crimes, and studies the history of their bar-
> barities as it has been recorded for the past three or four cen-
> turies, can see in the Indian race only hordes of demons who
> stand in the way of the progress of civilization, and who must, and
> ought to be destroyed. He who has a more intimate knowledge of
> Indian character and life sometimes forgets their baser traits,
> and sees only their virtues, their truth, their fidelity to a trust,
> their simple and innocent sports, and wonders that a morally
> degenerate, but powerful civilization, should destroy that primi-
> tive life. Social problems are so complex that few are willing or
> able to comprehend all the factors, and so the people are divided
> into two great parties, one crying for blood, and demanding the
> destruction of the Indians, the other begging that he may be left
> in his aboriginal condition, and that the progress may be stayed.
> Vain is the clamor of either party; the march of humanity cannot
> be stayed; fields must be made and gardens planted in the little
> valleys among the mountains of that Western land, as they have
> been in the broader valleys and plains of the East, and the
> mountains must yield their treasure of ore to the miner, and,

whether we desire it or not, the ancient inhabitants of the country must be lost; and we may comfort ourselves with the reflection that they are not destroyed, but are gradually absorbed, and become a part of more civilized communities.[39]

It was a philosophy of racial integration, one that depended on the federal government for enforcement and intervention. But it was also a philosophy of integration that affirmed the superiority of the white man's civilization, without affirming the innate superiority of the white man.

The antebellum abolitionists had preached more or less the same gospel of integration, though usually infused with a perfectionist's hope for the moral regeneration of the species. Powell was no perfectionist. He worked with the imperfect, secular tools of government policy—agents and commissions, data-collecting, appropriations, and agricultural training—to effect change in human behavior. Behind his report lay a conviction that all people, regardless of their color of skin, were alike in wanting the same things. Whites and Indians both wanted security of livelihood, peace, stability, and the opportunity to improve themselves. They could manage to find all of those things in a more or less satisfactory way only if government helped—in this case, by maintaining the reservations with diligence and good faith.

Reason, it was soon clear, did not prevail to the extent that Powell hoped. Neither the whites nor the Indians followed the commission's recommendations in the next few years. Bonelli and the other settlers at Muddy River refused to leave, and with the intervention of their legislative representatives the reservation was cut down drastically in area until there was not enough land for Indian subsistence. By 1878 Powell was pointing out to still another commissioner of Indian Affairs that the Paiutes were reduced once again to begging: "The promises made by Mr. Ingalls and myself have not been fulfilled. . . . I am constrained to protest against their neglect and against a course which must sooner or later result in serious trouble."[40] The other reservations lost considerable portions of their land too, and Malheur eventually vanished.

As the large reservations diminished, smaller, more scattered reservations appeared throughout Nevada and Utah, so that even the Shivwits and Kaibabs managed to hold onto their scraps of identity. They did not, however, secure a substantial enough land base for self-maintenance. On the positive side no more wars broke out between the region's Indians and whites, but neither did integration or true harmony appear.

Powell even found it hard to be reimbursed for the expenses he incurred as a special commissioner. He submitted a bill of $3,319 (somewhat more than his annual salary), figured at a rate of $8 per diem and ten cents a mile. The bill was "irregular," the government auditor insisted; it did not have proper approval from the government's advisory Board of Indian Commissioners. After a flurry of explanations and receipts, he was finally paid off in full. That was the relatively easy part of putting an end to the work he had done. What was not so easy was persuading whites and Indians to accept the idea of a common West and to make progress together.

While Powell was parleying with the Great Basin tribes and bands, the Powell Survey had to be managed, once again, by Harry Thompson, who put men in the field all summer and fall mapping the country. Yet Powell's service as special commissioner advanced the overall objectives of the survey. Powell used his time, and the Indian Bureau's money, to enhance his knowledge of native cultures, a goal as significant for him as topographical mapping.

In September Jack Hillers of the survey staff met him in St. George, and wherever they went to see Indians that fall Jack had his camera ready to record not only the meetings themselves but the traditional lifeways that were in imminent danger of disappearing. The photographs he took—a native woman with empty cradle, another arrayed in calico dress and jacket, three bare-breasted girls in traditional fringed buckskin skirts and straw beanies, a circle of naked old men gambling, children on their haunches playing the game of wolf and deer—are among the most valuable records compiled by the survey during its existence. More than that, those pictures speak eloquently of an almost forgotten people who make a timeless appeal for understanding.[41]

Anthropologists have pointed out that some of Hillers's pictures were stage-managed to create an idealized (or eroticized) Indian for white consumption. The bare maidens titillated Victorian mores. Other figures sometimes do look coached and awkward; in a few pictures they are even wearing somebody else's clothes. Powell brought along fancily beaded garments and feathered headdressess from the Colorado Utes, either to give as gifts or to deposit in museums, and on a few occasions he had Chuar, his wife, and others put them on for the photographer—gussying up the poor, drab Paiutes in Plains

"The mirror case." Powell, dressed in native garb, is examining the case with the Ute woman Tuaruv. Taken in the Uinta Valley by J.K. Hillers, 1873.
(Courtesy: National Archives)

Indian glamor. Nonetheless, the pictorial record became invaluable documentation of native life before and as it underwent assimilation. So also did the boxes of artifacts that Powell shipped to the Smithsonian, including seed fans, winnowing trays, chipped arrowheads, hafted stone knives, bullroarer "whirrers," parfleches, war clubs, and stone pipes.[42]

The extensive vocabulary lists that Powell compiled were also a remarkable gift to scholars who came along much later to study the Indians, after their informants may have forgotten some of the old words. Powell lumped all those hundred tribes he identified into one people, the Numa, because all their dialectics derived from common Numic roots, though isolation had produced significant barriers to communication. The Kaibabs said "pian" for "mother," as did the Utes that Powell had wintered among on the White River; but the Gosiutes said "piats" and the Paviotsoes said "ivwia." The varying terms of family relationships, animals, utensils, place names, common verbs, and sayings he copied down awkwardly with his left hand, as he did stories long and short and lines from songs and chants translated into English. A man who loved poetry as he did was not unmoved by the beauty, humor, and feeling in such Paiute recitatives as "The crest of the mountain forever remains, forever remains, though rocks continually fall" or "In the blue water the trout wags its tail" or "Over the land over the land I walked at morn singing and trembling with cold."[43]

Powell met several new informants during his commission work, among them Tapeats (a Shivwits man), Kanosh (Pahvant Ute), Naches (Northern Paiute), and, most important, the college-educated Richard Komas, who came to work briefly for him in 1874–75 before dying an early death. None of them became Chuar's equal as a friend, but they expanded considerably Powell's insight into how Indians understood the world around them and related to one another. After the commission's work was over, the pile of manuscripts relating to Numic culture and linguistics continued to grow, with significant additions from a field trip to western Nevada in 1880. Powell also delivered scholarly lectures in Washington, D.C., and popular lectures in Milwaukee and other cities on his Indian researches during this period. On the basis of his informants, his further researches, and his public talks he projected a volume, a "Report on Indians of the Numa Stock," to be published by the federal government. Unfortunately, that project never came to completion. There is only the fragmentary manuscript which he left behind. Covering a broad stretch of country and a wide spectrum of cultural beliefs and practices, it reveals not only his considerable skill as an ethnographer but also his ambivalence about the people he was studying.

Their medical practices came in for the most graphic descriptions. Powell was shocked by the cruel torture that Ute medicine men performed on their sick patients. Medicine seemed to be unimportant, unless one called the sweat bath a form of medication; generally, treatment focused on exorcising evil beings that had invaded the body. The methods were barbaric. Live coals were placed on the sick person's flesh, fanned by the breath of the medicine man until they raised terrible blisters. That was Indian treatment at its worst. They jumped up and down on the patient's body, beat him or her with clubs, made crude incisions with stone knives in order to drive the spirits away. Powell describes one elaborate treatment he witnessed in the tent of Chief Douglass in which the healer howled, chanted, blew smoke, sucked at the patient's heels, and appeared to extract the guilty spirit through the navel, carrying it outside and burying it in the ground. Later, Powell, when no one was looking, dug up the offending spirit and found it was nothing more than a little fossil shell.[44] This side of Indian life — harsh, uninformed, draconian, gullible — he described without editorializing but could not have wanted to preserve. The people were better served by American physicians treating them on reservations.

Powell believed that schools that taught the Numic peoples to speak English were another liberating influence. Even as he was preserving vocabularies, he looked on the native languages as a trap for those who could speak nothing else. "Into their own language," the Powell-Ingalls report declared, "there is woven so much mythology and sorcery that a new one is needed in order to aid them in advancing beyond their baneful superstititions; and the ideas and thoughts of civilized life cannot be communicated to them in their own tongues."[45] A belief that illness came from evil spirits infiltrating the body was such baneful thinking. The treatment following that diagnosis was the rankest sorcery. People suffered grievously as a consequence, becoming victims of their own stumbling, inadequate knowledge.

A far less dangerous expression of Indian mythmaking came in the form of tales and stories of the ancient days when animals spoke to humans and were part of a race of beings endowed with extraordinary powers. Powell was captivated by those stories and recorded dozens of them: Tavwoats Has a Fight with the Sun, The Abandoned Boys, Corn Is Brought to the Earth, Huna Is Chosen Gravedigger, How Pasowavits Won His Wife, The Disposal of the Widow. But they did not add up, in his mind, to a consistent or coherent, let alone scientific, account of the world.

The Paiutes, for example, explained their origin by a tale in which the Old Woman of the Sea comes ashore and leaves a heavy, squirming, tightly bound sack on the ground, with instructions that it be delivered to the middle of the world. The Shinauav (Wolf) brothers carry it away, until one of them decides to open it. Immediately, hosts of people jump out and run off into the desert, where there is no food to support them. As the old woman worried, they scatter in many directions. Luckily, a few people remain in the sack, the knot is retied, and they are carried to that destination of beauty and abundance where they have all that is needed to make a good life: the land of the southern Paiutes. When Powell tried to suggest that this story contradicted other stories of origin he was given, his informants grew angry. They neither had any knowledge of other, more richly endowed places to live nor any concern about whether their beliefs and explanations were consistent with one another. For the scientifically minded Powell the charm and creativity of the stories was not enough.

On the other hand, Powell's research notes for the Numa book also pointed to many praiseworthy aspects of native culture. He emphatically denied that Indians were "savages" in the conventional American sense of people roaming through the forest like wild beasts, with no purpose, social organization, moral discipline, or knowledge of their environment. Though they did not hold Americanlike attachments to private property, Indians did lay claim to definable territories and defend them against other tribes. Those territorial attachments were powerful. "An Indian," he wrote, "will never ask to what nation or tribe or body of people another Indian belongs but to 'what land do you belong and how are you land named.'" A kind of nationalist pride or patriotism, as well as a sense of home and family livelihood, animated the native. "Every thing that is dear to him" is associated with his place on earth. Powell offered that sense of territorial belonging as evidence that these people were not wild beasts, even as he was recommending that their traditional attachments be severed.[46]

Indians knew the meaning of government, though their governments were in some ways unlike that of the United States. Tribes (or bands) came together to form nations, and nations formed confederacies. Among the Paiutes in Utah and Arizona were fifteen or twenty bands that recognized Taugu, or Coal Creek John, as their principal chief. At all levels chiefs sat with councils to make policy. They did not pass laws in the Euro-American fashion, nor set up police departments or courts of justice that resembled those in more civilized nations, "but a profound sense of the duty of obedience to leaders and superiors exists."[47] Children learned to obey their elders early on, and when they grew up they looked on obedience to chief and council as a supreme virtue. Consequently, Powell explained, crime, violence, and resentment against authority were all rare among them. They lived together with little of the social conflict that affected white society, and (he may have had in mind) much less of the inner turmoil or disharmony infecting the white communities that were springing up in the West.

Powell's reading of the strengths and weaknesses of the Numa resembled almost exactly his reading of the Mormons, the children of Nephi. Like the Indians, the Mormons offered impressive social organization and spirit of community. But also like the Indians, the Mormons were held in the grip of mythology and sorcery that was closed to the challenges of modern science and indifferent to its standards of evidence and truth. Mormons may have been receptive to the newest inventions — the railroad or telegraph — but their philosophy was, like the Indians, based on primitive superstitions. America was right to reject that "revelation"— to dismiss the fantastical stories about Lehi and his sons sailing in a wooden boat to a new world, or how the great civilizations of ancient Mexico were built, or how the truth had been revealed to an uneducated farm boy in New York State. Nonetheless, the Mormons, like the Indians, had many virtues when it came to organizing their social life or getting a living together on the land.

Most Americans of the time looked on Mormons and Indians alike as outlandish people, practicing immoral acts, inclined to be violent toward outsiders, guilty of massacring the innocent pioneer who fell into their clutches. Powell, in contrast, defended these widely misunderstood peoples. His attitude toward them, however, was ambivalent, and often it is hard to know what separates an ambivalence from a contradiction.

On the hundredth anniversary of the Declaration of Independence, 4 July 1876, the nation celebrated by opening a grand Centennial Exhibition on the grounds of Philadelphia's Fairmount Park. Ten million people, equivalent to a fifth of the American population, attended the fair before it closed a few months later. Among the dozens of buildings in the park the largest by far, indeed the largest in the world, was the Main Building, looming over the popcorn stands, balloon pedlars, and beer gardens like a gargantuan factory surmounted by gothic cathedral towers. The building's exhibits were carefully arranged to compare the varied nations of the world — and of course the United States stood preeminent among them, flanked by the other great white powers of England, Germany, and France. Now that the war between the states was fading into a memory, and the most recent economic depression, the worst ever experienced, was losing its grip, the country was in a mood to celebrate its ascension to glory. The past century of world history, the fair proclaimed, had featured the rise of the United States to global stature, and the next would see its dominion over all.[48]

Down the Main Building's long central hall, well down from the high civilization of the United States and the European powers, was the exhibit organized by the Smithsonian Institution on the American Indian. For it, Major Powell, with a grant of $5,000, had collected a large number of the artifacts, showing the material culture of the Utes, Paiutes, Hopis, and other southwestern peoples. Those artifacts were crowded into glass cases set alongside a totem pole, a canoe, and a dog sled from the Pacific Northwest and Alaska and an Indian tipi from the Great Plains. Powell had not only been an active contributor himself but had also recruited one of the other major collectors, Stephen Powers, a farmer from Marietta, Ohio, who had been put in charge of bringing in the California exhibit.[49] When the fair ended, the assistant secretary of the Smithsonian, Spencer Fullerton Baird, a man of keen acquisitive appetite, happily filled dozens of freight cars with artifacts and shipped them down to Washington where they became a permanent part of the National Museum.[50]

The beauty and craftsmanship evident in the Indian objects were far overshadowed by the material culture of industrial America on display at the fair. The massive Corliss steam engine installed in the Machinery Building spoke powerfully of the impressive technological sophistication of the national mind and hand, as did such new inventions as the telephone, sewing machine, refrigerated storage, and patent medicines. Indians by comparison seemed primitive. They were still clothing themselves in hairy animal skins and pounding corn with a piece of stone. In the material terms set by the fair, a vast gulf existed between the races. Nowhere could the Indian life, at least as represented in the glass cases, compete successfully for admiration or inspire hopes of easy assimilation.

For the organizers of the Centennial Exhibition, and for the largely white fair-goers, the superiority of American technology indicated moral superiority as well. The underlying theme of the fair in fact was that technology and economic growth were the foundations of moral progress. Indians were backward when it came to manufacturing; therefore, they must be "savages" in all ways, demonic and cruel. The wiping out of General Custer and his regiment at the Little Big Horn only a few days before the fair opened confirmed that view.

Powell wanted to bring real Indian people to Philadelphia to promote a more sympathetic understanding between the races. The Navajos should show how they wove their blankets, the Utes how they dressed a buffalo hide. They should come from the most authentically traditional tribes — true native cultures as unaffected by white influence as possible — and yet they should speak English, be clean and pleasant, never unruly or violent. The idea was to put the best possible face on the least Americanized peoples for the edification of middle-class whites. Baird agreed with the plan, but it had to be scratched when Congress refused to provide the funds.

Although Powell shared the common assumption that superior technology must always triumph over inferior, he did not simply equate the material and the moral. Possessing railroads did not make Americans better in every way than people who traveled on bare feet. If he had to draw up a scale of civilization, he would, like the fair organizers, put the United States high on one end and the Paiutes and Shoshones low on the other end. He did not challenge the prevailing hierarchy of his day. But the cultural judgments made in the Centennial Exhibition halls did not speak the full truth, as he had seen and experienced it, and that is why he wanted to bring living Indians to meet and talk with the well-dressed crowds.

While the Philadelphia exposition was in preparation, Powell published an essay on his first trip to the Hopis that reveals, as his Numic manuscript does, a more complicated picture of native people than one could find at the Centennial Exhibition. That trip occurred in fall 1870, but his account, "The Ancient Province of Tusayan," waited until late 1875 to appear in print. For some reason he claimed that he had spent two months in Tusayan, the name commonly given to the seven Hopi (or Moqui) towns in Arizona. In fact, he was there only two weeks before going on to Fort Defiance with Jacob Hamblin. Still, those weeks left a profound impression on him. The Hopis, more than any other Indian nation, attracted his sympathetic interest, perhaps because they had built so impressive a civilization in the past — those imposing ruins along the Colorado River — or because they lived so appealingly in the present.

Each of the towns he described as having its own architectural form, well adapted to its site, but in all of them the Hopis lived closely together in terraced multifamily houses. The outside of the houses was not attractive, with their irregular walls and filthy streets, but inside he found an appealing domestic environment. Climbing up and down the ladders and stairs that connected one floor to another, he noted a "great cleanliness" within and a warm hospitality toward the guest. The Hopis practiced the most careful economy in the consumption of resources, for their food and fuel was hard to come by, located outside the towns and often at great distances. Corn of several different colors was grown, each painstakingly stored in a different room. The women prepared from those stores a platter of thin, neatly folded patties that suggested a strongly developed aesthetic sensibility. They also made an abundance of pottery, showing "great skill in ceramic art," and wove bright clothing from their wool, which they wore with style and grace. Powell admired the women's habit of washing their hair each morning on the roof tops, using a yucca shampoo, and the young maiden's technique of coiling their black glossy hair on each side of their heads like a ram's horn. All the men, women, and children were attractive, healthy, vigorous, well-organized in their daily duties, and amicable in their relations with one another.[51]

Repeatedly Powell asked permission to descend into the kiva to witness one of the Hopi ceremonies, and always he was refused. But then one day he was allowed to join an important thanksgiving to Muingwa, the god of rain, for the harvest just completed and for the growing season to come. Disrobing with the other men and wrapping himself in a blanket, he sat through a twenty-four-hour ritual of singing and dancing, the women and men taking different parts, after which they all came out onto the rooftop for games and races. Because he did not understand the language, Powell could only observe actions, the arrangement of seating, and the roles played by the elderly priests and the young women with their pitchers of water and their trays of corn meal and sand. The conclusion he drew for readers was that the Hopis were "remarkable for their piety," no matter that they worshipped a large number of unfamiliar gods or told strange — to the ears of the white man — stories of creation.

The Hopis that Powell described were, like the Numa, neither noble nor villanous. They were a people to be liked, respected, and in some ways admired: agriculturists whose moral standards were not essentially different from the American ideal. Powell did not deny that there were significant differences, particularly in religion and belief, but his point seemed to be that the Indians presented, despite those differences, no threat to virtue or decency. Some of their food, to be sure, was a little bizarre; what he called their "virgin hash" was produced by young women chewing up meat and bread into soft little lumps which then were boiled like dumplings and distributed to the men. But bizarre differences did not indicate degeneracy. The Indian race, like the white race, could offer something beside gore and violence.

Powell's brief presentation of the Hopis, popular and superficial as it was, contrasted sharply with the views of some of the Indian agents appointed to superintend their welfare. Although they had no reservation until 1882, the Hopis had had agents among them for a dozen years, agents who had to contend with all the familiar problems of Mormon and non-Mormon, as well as Navajo, incursions into traditional Hopi land.

Sympathetic though they may have been toward their charges, the agents were often repelled by signs of immoral behavior. Agent William McAteer, for example, complained about the Hopi mode of living, "huddled in villages, each house communicating with the other induces promiscuous intercourse (adultery) to such an extent that many at present are afflicted with venereal and kindred diseases and on account of jealousy, the married men hesitate to leave their homes to perform their labor, without taking their wives with them." Another agent, J.H. Fleming, though he had never attended the Hopi dances, knew from reliable authorities that they were an evil influence. "The dark superstition and unhallowed rites of a heathenism as gross as that of India and central Africa still infect them with its insidious poison; which, unless replaced by Christian Civilization, must sap their very life blood." The difference in tone from Powell's essay on the Hopis is striking, and it suggests how other Americans judged the Hopis, and judged them harshly as moral beings.[52]

During the pivotal decade of the Centennial Exhibition, the years of the Grant peace policy and of the creation of Indian reservations out of the western public domain, the nation's white majority was challenged to rethink its traditional approach to native peoples. The Indians, some began to realize, might not fully disappear from the continent. They might be around forever, and it might be necessary to find some accommodation with them as part of American society. Utter extermination may have been what some still wanted, but it was not the only, or even the dominant, attitude. Assimilation in some form was where American thinking was heading. Assimilation, to be sure, could be ruthless in its own way, and the underlying racial fear and hostility that had characterized white attitudes for centuries had by no means vanished. But a policy of assimilation did involve, at the very least, a guarantee of physical survival.

Powell's idea of American nationhood included whites and Indians living together as fellow citizens. Indians frightened him far less than they did most Americans, especially most western Americans, both because he saw their vulnerability before the advancing white man's technology and institutions and because he saw their essential humanity. In those seasons spent in the field, he had learned to see Indians as complicated people and enjoyed being with them. For him they were not, as dominant stereotypes had them, unredeemably cruel savages or incompetent children. They were, nonetheless, a people whose world was coming to an end.

CHAPTER 8

The Sublimest Thing on Earth

Following a tumultuous river into the unknown, Major Powell discovered a cause and a mission. He wanted to lead his countrymen toward a deeper understanding of the natural world and of the human cultures it supported. He hoped to uncover new facts and better ways to settle and inhabit the land. A strong conviction told him that the public needed that understanding, that it came into the country ignorant and unprepared. The survey was his instrument of education. Through it he wanted to explain and interpret a West that Americans did not know, one that lay well outside their expectation and experience.

The particular landscape he chose for deep mapping he called the Plateau Province, stretching from the Uinta Mountains and the Great Salt Lake down to Arizona's San Francisco Mountains, from the western slope of the Rockies to the Great Basin. (Today this area is usually designated the Colorado Plateau.) In the last quarter of the nineteenth century, it was still the least known part of the country. The other surveys were likewise trying to bring unknown places into public consciousness, but their boundaries were less clearly set by nature; King's survey, for example, was defined by the transcontinental railroad and the fortieth parallel, purely man-made determinants. Powell's, in contrast, was a single watershed defined by the Colorado and its tributaries.

The dominant natural feature of the Plateau Province, after the river, was the Grand Canyon, but there were other canyons, plateaus, and even mountain ranges. A thorough survey must also include the flora and fauna that had evolved across the province, from chuckwallas and junipers to bighorn sheep; and it must reveal the origins of land forms and their intricate history. Also, it should include the native peoples who had been inhabiting parts of the province for millennia. All of that was no small challenge. Unlike some of his fellow survey directors, whose scope was more superficial, Powell realized he had more than enough to do and he had no designs on any other territory.

Science must furnish the method for understanding this colossal coherence. Already science was fragmenting into many specialties, but Powell believed that all the specialists might work together in order to achieve a more scientific understanding of this single, unified place. No other approach to nature promised as much practical insight for a nation contemplating its patrimony. Certainly religion, though it continued to influence American thinking about the natural world, could not offer so much. Nor did either antebellum romanticism or transcendentalism, which elevated feeling over reason, subjectivity over observation, a search for the ideal behind the veil of the material over the steady accumulation of facts and hypotheses.

The leading mode of expression for romanticism had been art, especially the visual arts. Powell was no by means hostile to the artist; on the contrary, he incorporated the arts into his mission to awaken the nation's interest in its land. But in the future art must follow, not lead. Poets or painters must pay attention to what the scientists discovered about the natural world and keep their passions disciplined by practical knowledge.

Art in the nineteenth century had meant the making of beautiful pictures, and beautiful pictures had meant pictures celebrating the beauty of the land. Painters of landscape were the best paid, most revered artists in a young country that wanted to know all that it possessed. They showed off its assets and promised excitement, adventure, even a sense of national identity. They encouraged piety. Following their lead, Americans went outdoors to find God. Painters as much as ministers served as keepers of the national soul. The canonical artists of the landscape—Thomas Cole, Asher Durand, Frederick Church, Albert Bierstadt—all enjoyed substantial fame, and the unveiling of their latest canvases became sacred events both for what they revealed of the nation's nature and for what they could do to lift the nation toward moral greatness.

In early July 1873 a rising star in the landscape painters' firmament, Thomas Moran, stepped off the train in Salt Lake City to meet an awaiting Powell. Moran was tall and gaunt, with long hair and the start of a beard; his eyes were pale and hollow, giving him a vacant, dreamy look. The two men planned an excursion to the most spectacular expression of raw, unmediated nature on the continent, the Grand Canyon.

The name as well as growing reputation of that place were largely Powell's achievement. Though the name "Grand Canyon" had appeared in a few early writings, including William Palmer's report on a railroad route across Arizona, others, such as Joseph Ives, had persisted in calling it "Big Canyon"—that is, until Powell decisively stepped forward and instructed Fred Dellenbaugh to write "Grand" on the topographical maps they were making. No one henceforth disputed that declaration. Powell used the name "Grand Canyon" in all the lectures he gave in eastern and midwestern cities, and he threw the phrase at Moran for more than a year to entice him to come, see, and paint. Although the pressure of work had forced Moran to turn down an invitation to join the previous summer's river voyage, he hankered to see the canyon for himself, to paint it for the public, and now he was here to do so.

Moran, like Powell, was the son of a working-class artisan who had fled Britain's industrial trap for better opportunity in America. The family had arrived in Philadelphia in 1841, when Thomas was seven years old, and a decade later he was apprenticed to a wood engraver and was teaching himself to draw and paint. While Powell was fighting on the battlefield, the young artist went to England and marveled at the intense colors, the brilliant light and atmospheric effects, and the contemptuous disregard of mere representation of the painter J.M.W. Turner. Returning home, Moran turned out a number of picturesque scenes of eastern autumnal woodlands, but was still no Turner or Bierstadt in achievement or reputation. His golden moment came when Richard Watson Gilder, editor of *Scribner's Monthly*, hired him to rework some amateur drawings submitted to illustrate a couple of articles about an 1870 expedition into the upper Yellowstone River valley. General H.D. Washburn, the surveyor-general of Montana, commanded the expedition, and in his party rode the author of the articles, Nathaniel Langford. It was this expedition that later claimed to have first proposed preserving the Yellowstone area from exploiters.[1]

Ever alert to any incursions on his turf, Ferdinand Hayden immediately pushed his Geological Survey of the Territories into the Yellowstone area, ostensibly to determine what was fact and what was fantasy. He had shrewdly guessed that this place of lodgepole pines, deeply incised canyons, boiling mudpots, and hot geysers trailing clouds of steam was capturing the imagination of a landscape-hungry populace, and he wanted to capture its charisma for his survey. On his staff he employed one of the country's most talented landscape photographers, William Henry Jackson, and the artist Henry Wood Elliott, for he realized the usefulness of the visual arts in bringing attention to his operation.

Galvanized by the Yellowstone pictures on which he worked without ever actually seeing the place, Moran determined to join the Hayden group. With backing from Jay Cooke, the financial power behind the Northern Pacific Railroad, and from Gilder, he wrangled an invitation to join the exploring party. The outcome was a third article on Yellowstone, published in the *Scribner's Monthly* of February 1872, written by Hayden and exquisitely illustrated by Moran, who was at last seeing the fabulous place with his own eyes. He was also glimpsing a more brilliant career for himself in painting the western scene; the article's lead black-and-white engraving, *The Great Canyon and Lower Falls of the Yellowstone*, furnished the basis for the magnificent oil painting of the same title that Moran finished and Congress purchased in spring 1874, two years after Yellowstone became the first national park.[2]

After years of relative obscurity , Moran rose to national celebrity, a high priest of America's cult of the outdoors. He earned bundles of money, he had a mountain in the Teton range named after him by Hayden, and he acquired a new moniker, "Yellowstone Moran," which gave him credit for shifting the mind of Congress toward preservation. Grateful toward the employer who had made his success possible, he decided to stay with Hayden as honorary member of the survey.

In the summer of 1873 they planned to make an expedition down the Colorado River to the Grand Canyon, a brash invasion of the Powell Survey's assigned territory. In anticipation Moran contracted with several editors to buy his drawings of the canyon. But then, after some reflection, Hayden changed his mind and decided he must confine his field work that year to the Rockies. The painter was left caught in his contracts. "I felt it obligatory on me," he apologized to Hayden, "to accept the offer made by Maj. Powell as the only chance of getting there within the limits of the time that I could give to it & I agreed to accompany him. . . . [M]y business relations with others & and my intense desire to see the Grand Canyon force me to change my original plan of accompanying you this summer."[3]

When he arrived in Salt Lake City, Moran brought a traveling companion, Justin Colburn, a journalist with the *New York Times* who came along to do a series of stories. Powell arranged an interview with Brigham Young and other Mormon leaders, after which the travelers headed south along the Wasatch to camp, climb mountains, and find Indians. Moran had showed up just as the Powell-Ingalls commission was getting into its work, and the Major was forced to juggle his schedule between competing demands. The travelers scaled Mount Nebo, then thought to be Utah's highest peak, and Moran, who had by now seen not only Yellowstone but Yosemite Valley in California and other western wonders, reported to his wife that he had just encountered "the most magnificent sight of my life. . . . [A]lthough I do not think I would undergo the labor of another ascent, I would not have missed this for ten times the fatigue. I stood it first rate but Powell, Colburn, and Pilling [Powell's assistant] were sick and vomited when we got down."[4]

Because the Pahvant Ute chief Kanosh was waiting to see him in Fillmore, Powell sent Moran and Colburn ahead. Moran sketched all the way. At Powell's base camp in Kanab, the travelers met Thompson and Hillers, who showed them the trail into the canyons of the Virgin, which in Moran's judgment topped Yosemite for scenic grandeur.

On 5 August, again in the company of Hillers and with ten days of rations packed on mules, they set out for Mount Trumbull and the flanking Toroweap Valley, riding to the very brink of the Grand Canyon. Cameras, pencils, and brushes all were busy. Colburn contrasted the chasm to the better known Niagara Falls for impact on the senses and feelings:

> At the Grand Cañon, the feeling of grandeur is not produced
> by power in activity, for the river is too far away, and forms too
> insignificant a part of the scene. Nor is it produced by the vastness
> of the chasm alone, for every one has seen other things giving a
> more distinct impression of great extent or size. I think the feeling
> is one of awe and wonder at the evidence of some mighty,
> inconceivable, unknown power, at some time terribly, majestically,
> and mysteriously energetic, but now ceased.[5]

Moran was moved by the rainbow of colors before him, as rich as any palette he had held. Bright violet was the dominant tone, he jotted on one of his drawings, but also there was gray intermixed with red and yellow and cream and — well, the autumnal woods of Pennsylvania could not compare in chromatic splendor.

Back in Kanab they rejoined Powell, who was still negotiating with Indians but willing to steal time to show the travelers his own favorite spot along the Canyon rim. On 14 August they broke camp and rode their animals across the hot, dry desert up into the cool green Kaibab forest, to Big Spring, Parissawampitts Spring, the Muav Saddle, and then the Powell Plateau, an immense rampart around which the Colorado River bends, running so far below it looks like a tiny creek. Standing on the plateau's edge, they could see for twenty to thirty miles up and down the declivity and beyond the south rim to the San Francisco Mountains more than sixty miles away. A rare summer storm blew through the canyon at that moment, pelting down rain and generating dozens of waterfalls that dwarfed Niagara in height. Moran sketched furiously, finding at this breathtaking spot the inspiration for a second sweeping canvas to pair with *The Great Canyon and Lower Falls of the Yellowstone*.

Finishing that project must wait until he was back home in Newark, New Jersey. For now, he had plenty of less grandiose pictures to plan for his clients, including William Cullen Bryant, editor of the elegant two-volume picture book, *Picturesque America*, published in 1874 by D. Appleton and Company. This was the most comprehensive collection of American landscape views ever put together so far, and Moran contributed forty pictures, including several of Utah and the Grand Canyon. Another client was the art magazine *The Aldine*, which was setting new standards in printing wood engravings for a discriminating audience. Also among his clients was Major Powell, who agreed to buy a number of Moran pictures for use in magazine articles, a book, and government reports he had in mind to write. Many commissions — more than an artist could possibly fill on the spot, involving more places than he could personally visit. Moran relied on Hillers to send him photographs of the Powell Survey's other scenic discoveries from which he could work up drawings. *The Aldine* touted those drawings for "their wonderful clearness" of atmosphere, "untainted by the smoke of great cities," though many were actually copied in an urban studio from a Hillers photograph tacked onto an easel.[6]

All four of those traveling companions — Powell, Moran, Hillers, and Colburn — were eager to use their skills to capture the growing market for western scenes. None was intent only on making money, but none showed any reluctance in turning the canyon into cash. Colburn had his newspaper to satisfy, which he did through a series of three dispatches from the field.[7] Moran had rather different links to the market. Passionate though he was about the extraordinary

Overland expedition to the Grand Canyon, 1873. Powell is seated at the base of the tree. The man with a hand to his face is the artist Thomas Moran, and the balding man standing behind him is his travelling companion, J.E. Colburn, a writer for the New York Times. *Taken by J.K. Hillers.* (Courtesy: U.S. Geological Survey)

beauty of the places he had seen, he was a shrewd businessman when it came to selling his experiences. He developed an entrepreneur's keen sense of what would sell, and over the succeeding years he did not scruple to turn out cheap, popular illustrations for railroad companies and tourist promoters as well as creating highbrow works of art. Until his death in 1924 (he was then living in Santa Barbara, California) he came back to the canyon regularly to paint its elusive tints in oil. Yellowstone Moran thus became Grand Canyon Moran, and his substantial financial success was in no small part due to his standing as the greatest painter of America's greatest landscape.

By the time they met Moran, Powell and Hillers had also become artistic entrepreneurs and readily turned the landscape into profitable commodity. Neither Congress nor the Smithsonian objected to their doing so; after all, others such as photographer William Henry Jackson were doing the same. Powell bought out Beaman's negatives of the Green and Colorado rivers for promotional use.[8] He also acquired the smaller Fennemore portfolio. Then he sent the self-taught Hillers into the field to gather photographs that Powell could show on the lecture circuit or in the halls of Congress, promoting his career as he did so, just as he was promoting the unknown country.

Hillers perfected a technique for transferring pictures onto glass transparencies that could be projected before lecture audiences, and for a while he went along as Powell's projectionist. But far and away their most lucrative joint enterprise was the making and selling of stereographs. These pictures were taken by a camera with dual lenses and mounted in pairs on a card; when looked at through a binocular device the images dissolved into one, creating a three-dimensional effect. They were easily produced and reasonably priced, so that Americans of even modest means could sit in their parlor and experience the thrilling vistas of Arizona or Wyoming. Every stereograph produced by Hillers was only in part his property; he received 40 percent of the sale price, while Powell and Harry Thompson divided the rest. Altogether Powell prepared some 650 different stereographs for commercial distribution, usually in thematic sets, and the business became a considerable sideline to his survey work.[9]

It is impossible to say how much Powell or Hillers pocketed from this enterprise, since no account books were kept, many pictures were distributed free to politicians, scientists, and friends, and some of the profits may have been plowed back into a painting contract with Moran or the purchase of equipment. Rumor said that Powell made enough money from selling pictures to pay off a substantial mortgage on his new house in Washington, but that seems an exag-geration.[10] Undoubtedly, he did add something to his bank account, and with little sense of charity. One of the most popular subjects among stereograph buyers was the Indians of the Southwest, and Hillers's best pictures were of those people. None of the Indians saw any return from the sale of their images, though in many cases they were desperately hungry and begging for food. Neither Powell nor Hillers, who knew first-hand the plight of the Indians, seemed sensi-tive to the fact that they were exploiting these people for gain, either to enhance their own incomes or to win support for the survey.

The survey, it should be added, was going through a financial squeeze, due largely to the Panic of 1873. Powell's budget for the fis-cal year that began in July of that year was slashed in half, down to $10,000, by far the smallest appropriation of all the western surveys. After paying his own and Thompson's salaries (they each got $3,000), he was strapped to pay his other staff. Hillers had to take un-paid leave, which he spent in San Francisco with his brother, using the opportunity to get professional advice from the West Coast pho-tographer Carleton Watkins. When in the next year the appropria-tion was restored (but only to $15,000), the survey was still in a state of hardship. Hillers may then have moved in with the Powell family in Washington to save money, and he and the Major may have had little choice but to sell pictures in order to keep a roof over their heads. Publicizing their work by delivering public lectures, giving free sets of stereographs to key Congressional committeemen, writing popular articles, and forging liaisons with artists such as Moran were all part of a strategy of survival more than of accumulating wealth.

Powell's driving sense of mission overrode any idea of gain. He managed, to be sure, to work out a few private deals along the way that may have had a modest profit in them. They helped secure a comfortable urban life for Emma and little Mary, but it was not one Powell shared for much of the year as his work kept him in the field, on dirt road and iron rails, sleeping in farmers' door yards or under a canvas tent. When Moran showed up wanting to revel in the beau-ties of the canyon lands, Powell ran to accommodate him. He had lured Moran away from Hayden to advance his own cause, and now he watched him leave with the hope that the artist would give back more than he took away.

On Thanksgiving Day 1873, Powell stopped in Newark to consult Moran in his studio before going on to Washington to turn in his special Indian commission report. He wanted to inquire about the seventy drawings he had commissioned. He found the artist just finishing the charcoal design for a painting entitled *The Chasm of the Colorado*. It was going to be big—seven feet high, twelve wide, exactly as large as the Yellowstone painting—and Powell was thrilled with the prospect. Moran's backlog of work was staggering, and the artist was staying up until 1 or 2 A.M. to get it all finished. On 16 December he wrote Powell: "I have been working pretty constantly on the Big Picture for the last two weeks & it progresses wonderfully for the time & promises all that I could desire of it. I have got our storm in good."[11] In late January he sent a photograph of the painting to his congressman, and on 30 April he exhibited the finished painting in Newark, after which it traveled to New York City and then to the Corcoran Gallery of Art in Washington. On 14 July Congress appropriated $10,000 to purchase the painting and hang it alongside its companion portrait of the Yellowstone canyon on the second floor of the Capitol. The purchase price was the same as Powell's total budget for that fiscal year, yet he was as excited as everyone else to see what Moran had wrought.

Most remarkable about the painting is how little sense of the chasm's vastness it gives. Moran positions the viewer safely back from the rim of a side canyon, peering across a rounded basin in the foreground that is too dark and gloomy to convey its full depth. The lower half of the picture forms a protective barrier walling the viewer off from the Canyon proper; richly colored in somber browns and reds, it shades into blackness, not inviting any passage, saying in effect that man's place is here on the edge, not there in the depths. For living companions, however, the viewer has only a few clumps of brown grass, a small twisted tree, and a tiny snake in this harsh world dominated by rock and sky. Beyond the barrier a terrible storm is passing to the east, raining down like fire, the canyons filling up with smokelike vapor. This is not a gentle, beneficent shower that brings life but a thunderous power that even the rocks cannot withstand. Beyond the storm's fury a patch of sunlight appears, blue sky and glowing rock, the only brightness in this somber majesty. The viewer stands before the scene like Noah, witnessing the purification of the world by a force greater than humankind, greater even than nature. Something transcendent and divine has been at work here, demonstrating a primordial capacity for creation and destruction that no soft, green river valley in the East could ever reveal.

Moran's editor at *Scribner's*, Richard Watson Gilder, confessed to a feeling of dismay when he viewed the painting. Its subject was "Ti-

Thomas Moran, "The Chasm of the Colorado," 1873–74. Oil painting on canvas (84 x 145 in.). The original hangs in the National Gallery of American Art, Washington, D.C.

tanic," he wrote, a godlike strength that left the mere human confused and disturbed. The picture lacked order, coherence, or repose. It seemed to be a glimpse of another planet where "all is terrible, fantastic and weird." He struggled to praise the work but finally had to admit that "its subject is less fortunate, because less pleasing," than Moran's picture of the Yellowstone river canyon. The reviewer for the *New York Times* complained that the picture did not give a "true" impression of distance, depth, and color and thus failed as a work of art. Moran's hometown newspaper, the *Newark Daily Advertiser*, was more affirmative, but noted that "for native savageness these volcanic [sic] tracts of the great West are as different from the Alps of Europe as are the wild Comanches or Sioux from the 'merry Swiss boy' who blows his Alpine horn among the reverberating rocks of his mountain home."[12] No one, it seemed, found Moran's Grand Canyon an inviting place for recreation or pleasant thoughts. It said nothing about a land of hope and promise, nothing about the bright prospects of America.

The Grand Canyon painting reached back to an older notion of the sublime that did not suit American, middle-class, or Christian needs. The Irish-born politician Edmund Burke's influential essay distinguishing between the beautiful and the sublime (1757) had identified the latter with ideas of pain, danger, even death; the sublime was a feeling of terror evoked by the landscape, not a feeling of pleasure or relaxation, though it could bring a peculiar kind of delight. The experience of the sublime lay beyond reason; it defied human understanding, control, or activity. To feel the sublime was to be swept by incomprehensible powers.[13] That was exactly what Moran felt standing on the edge of the Grand Canyon, but that was not what most Americans wanted to feel about themselves confronting the natural world. They wanted to feel a surge of wonder, but the wonder should leave them in control, or at least leave them reassured that nature was under the control of a God who looked kindly on the American people and had their welfare in mind.

Moran's reputation was not harmed by this disturbing picture, but never again did he paint so "Titanic" a landscape. His future canyons were all lighter, happier places, where green and ochre replaced the dark browns and black, diminishing the terror. They also happened to be pictures painted, in his later period, from the comfortable terrace of a South Rim hotel. He also found more reassuring subjects for his bourgeois audience. A year after finishing the *Chasm of the Colorado*, he turned out a popular canvas, the *Mountain of the Holy Cross*, inspired by a fourteen-thousand-foot peak near Leadville, Colorado. Ice had carved a perfect cross on its face — two intersecting crevices filled with snow that Spanish explorers had reverently named and that Hayden and his crew had rediscovered. Moran composed the painting after a photograph by William Henry Jackson. Newspaper reviewers pronounced it decidedly superior to everything else that Moran had produced. It was sublimely Christian. It sent a frisson of pious emotion down the spine but did not threaten man's exalted place on earth. The painting, like the mountain, declared that God was out there in the West, supervising the nation's future.

Far more than Edmund Burke's terrifying notion of the sublime, Americans were drawn to the aesthetics of John Ruskin, the English author of *Modern Painters* (1846). Ruskin preached that art must be true to nature; the artist must study carefully the geological formations, the botany of plants, the dynamics of clouds, and be faithful to that material reality. But the artist should not pursue the facts of nature for their own sake. The purpose of art was to lead the viewer upward from the material to the ideal, which is to say, to God. Every painting, every sketch or drawing, should speak without ambiguity about the divine order in the universe. The natural world is not chaotic or titanic but planned and designed. Ruskin drew his aesthetic theories in large part from the Reverend William Paley, whose *Natural Theology* (1802) argued that by studying the natural world, discerning the rational design that underlies it, we come to know the will of God. Nature daily furnishes proof that a transcendental power exists. Every mountain, canyon, or herd of deer, if understood rightly, is a proof of divinity.[14]

Continental ideas about the close, harmonious relations of science, art, and God concurred with those of Ruskin. Nature, whether approached through science or art, was supposed to teach lessons about transcendental benevolence. The world out-of-doors was a mirror of the mind of God. No conflict, therefore, should exist between the scientist and the artist, for both served the same pious end. In the words of Louis Agassiz, the Swiss-born biologist and disciple of the German scientist Alexander von Humboldt, who joined the Harvard faculty and dominated American science before the Civil War: "In our study of natural objects we are approaching the thought of the Creator, reading his conceptions, interpreting a system that is his not ours."[15] That system was expected to stir up feelings of the sublime, but not feelings of terror that left one passive or prostrate. Nor should one be left confused about the power behind the natural world, as Moran's painting of the Grand Canyon apparently left viewers. The message written in nature was supposed to be unambiguously reassuring.

So it was believed in the decades leading up to the postwar western surveys. Science had served as an agreeable companion to art. But by the mid-1870s that old confidence in harmony was beginning to break down. The Ruskinian landscape tradition represented most lately by Thomas Moran was at its zenith of popularity but already showing signs of decline. Fewer after Moran claimed spiritual authority in portraying the outdoors. Art continued to play a role in interpreting the West, but increasingly it was a role subordinate to that of science.

Among all the survey directors Powell was in the forefront of a new materialism.[16] The canyons of the Colorado were not for him places to go searching for God or moral instruction, and he was less intent than others on reading that primordial place according to conventional pieties. He felt elevated by the landscape, but his emotions were completely secular and always checked by scientific reason. Powell wanted art on his side, and he even went so far as to place a personal order with Moran for another oil painting of the Grand Canyon. But in truth he was not seeking moral guidance from any artist's canvas.

In spring 1875 Moran wrote repeatedly to Powell, complaining that he was not getting any response (forgetting his friend's physical handicap in the letter-writing department). Had the Major taken "A Journey to the Center of the Earth"? The artist, eager to savor more of the Plateau Province, wanted to know where the survey crew were going during the coming season and how he could join it. While waiting for an answer, Moran reported with satisfaction that "The Mountain of the Holy Cross has been on exhibition for some time & has received the highest praise from the Artists & the public with a fair share of newspaper laudation. I know you have no interest in the subject for a picture & I have therefore made no reports during its progress. Shall send you a photo as soon as I get some printed."[17]

There are a couple of explanations for why Powell was indifferent to this particular painting. The mountain with the spectacular crucifix lay outside his survey boundaries, in Hayden's domain. But also mountains interested him more for their scientific problems of glaciation, volcanism, block faulting, and erosion than for their superstitious omens. He was interested in geophysical rather than moral uplift.

Somehow, despite the press of his ethnological studies and Indian commission duties, Powell managed to stake a small claim for himself in the field of geology. It was an age when amateurs could make good. Although Powell had little formal academic training in the subject, neither had others winning names in science. Even the great Clarence King had only a couple of years of undergraduate study at Yale — a general science education with no advanced training except what he got in the California field from more experienced hands. In contrast to King, Powell relished topography, geomorphology, and physiography. He was, and had been since his adolescent years in Illinois, a passionate student of the lay of the land. Where did rivers come from and where did they go, was always his beginning point. Rivers changed their course over time, and that history made him curious. Rivers washed away dirt and uncovered a past when strange forms of life swam the waters and walked the earth. The land was constantly in motion, presenting a different face to its inhabitants from year to year, a restlessness that matched his own.

Powell's first scientific publication was an article on the geological structure of the country lying north of the Grand Canyon, which appeared in 1873 in the *American Journal of Science and Arts*, edited by Benjamin Silliman and James Dwight Dana of Yale. It was the first attempt by anyone (not excepting John Strong Newberry's cursory notes on the region) to describe systematically the stratigraphy in both the main and tributary chasms and the escarpments that rose like "a great geographical stairway" toward the north. Powell adopted the local Indian names or their English equivalent for each step in that stairway: first, the *Shinarump Mukwanikunt* (the Shinarump Cliffs), a series of hummocky, light-colored outcroppings running two hundred miles eastward from the Virgin River; behind them, the *Unkar* or Vermilion Cliffs, made of dark-red sandstone; then the *Atsigar* or Gray Cliffs, capped by fossil-bearing limestone of the Jurassic; and the *Untsawar* or Pink Cliffs, composed of limestones and sandstones. That staircase was split apart by north-south fractures, out of which floods of lava had oozed over the country, forming in places hard, protective caps over older sedimentary rocks that stood out as buttes or table mountains on the horizon.

The amount of erosion that had occurred in this place, Powell observed, "is so great as almost to stagger belief." One hundred replicas of New Hampshire's Mount Washington could be dropped into the Grand Canyon without filling it.

> A vast labyrinth of deep gorges has been excavated, extending to every part of this region, and should we compute the amount of rock necessary to fill these to the general level of the country, we should still have but a meagre term of comparison for the sum of the material which has been carried away by rains and rivers.

The result of that long process of differential erosion was "an *ensemble* of topographical features embossed on the face of the country, wild, grand, and desolate."[18]

Professor Dana asked for a follow-up paper setting forth "the special geological evidence in stratigraphical facts sustaining your conclusion that the so-called faults are faults."[19] But another four years passed before Powell got around to submitting to Dana a second article, and then it was another broad overview of "orographic structure." Meanwhile, his next scientific effort appeared in 1875, a series of three articles on the "Physical Features of the Colorado Valley," published in the *Popular Science Monthly*. In them Powell tried to convey complicated scientific concepts to a nonspecialist audience, varying the technical details with a few flights of rhetoric. "Among the buttes on the lower terraces rattlesnakes crawl," he wrote, "lizards glide over the rocks, tarantulas stagger about, and red ants build their play-house mountains. Sometimes rabbits are seen, and wolves prowl in their quest; but the desert has no bird of sweet song, and no beast of noble mien."[20]

Take away that flourish and Powell had a few unadorned scientific concepts to propose and explain, concepts that earned him a respectable footnote in the history of geological thought. They were mainly worked out in the Uinta Mountains of Utah and formally stated in his *Report on the Geology of the Eastern Portion of the Uinta Mountains*, issued in 1876. In the two preceding years Powell had explored that range with Henry DeMotte, a former colleague at Illinois Wesleyan, and Charles White, a paleontologist.

The most puzzling feature for him was not the folding that had occurred, shoving up mountains once thirty thousand feet high, or the erosion that had ensued, cutting those mountains down to less than half their original height. Rather, it was the fact that the Green River had cut right through the rising wall of rock. Why did the river not go around this great obstruction? The question had relevance throughout the Plateau Province. Powell's answer was that the surface folding had happened so gradually that the river kept its course, "as the saw revolves on a fixed pivot, while the log through which it cuts is moved along. The river was the saw which cut the mountains in two." He called the result an "antecedent valley," where the waterway had established itself before any faulting or folding took place and persisted in holding its course. In other parts of the West valleys were "consequent" to (that is, came after) a more rapid process of surface upheaval or corrugation, while in still other cases a valley was "superimposed" on an older, underlying rock formation as its original, younger bed was washed away. Although later geologists might dispute whether the Green actually represented an antecedent or a superimposed valley, or where and how much of the whole Colorado River system was antecedent or superimposed, the broad concepts stuck.[21]

Another of Powell's enduring geological theories posited a "base level" in fluvial erosion. The base level was "an imaginary surface," an abstraction that helped geologists understand the varying rates of corrasion that occured along a river or creek. The ocean was the ultimate base level, below which land could no longer erode. But other base levels, local and temporary, existed too, and no running stream could cut below them. A tributary, for example, could not cut lower than the main stream into which it flowed. Flowing water sought equilibrium; it distributed energy from head to mouth, cutting faster here and more slowly there depending on how closely it approached its base level. An obstruction in the river, a hard ledge of lava or a pile of rocks falling from the cliffs, created a natural dam that changed the base level all the way upriver. "The more elevated any district of country is, above its base level of denudation," Powell noted, "the more rapidly it is degraded by rains and rivers."[22]

What those scientific concepts revealed was a mind that was quick and intuitive but not particularly interested in following up a hypothesis with disciplined investigation. Powell sought a broad overview, a place where he could stand and grasp the logic of the landscape. He was a generalizer rather than an experimentalist. The weaknesses of that temperament are many, but it is also the case that such a mind is likely to be creative, radical, quick to challenge established theories.[23] Science needs more than one sort of temperament. It requires more narrowly focused geologists on the ground who will work on a problem for months or years until they solve it. But it also needs the bold thinker who can ride up to an overlook, handle a few rocks, fearlessly speculate and hypothesize about the big picture, and ride on.

The boldest theories of the period came from England's evolutionary biologist Charles Darwin and historical geologist Charles Lyell, and Powell did not hesitate to make those theories his own. He took from them the view that the natural world is the product of observable forces operating in the here and now, and that those forces have been operating all the way back, as far as the mind can travel. Nineteenth-century scientists called this perspective "uniformitarianism," for it looked on nature as the outcome of slow, steady, unvarying processes. Given enough time, a small stream could move a mountain or carve a canyon; a mere five or six inches of erosion per thousand years could eventually produce a Grand Canyon. Similarly, minute variations among organisms could accumulate until they produced the full diversity of species on the earth.

The uniformitarian perspective, though no longer new by the mid-1870s, was still hard for many people, including many scientists, to swallow. They could not believe that little actions could have big consequences. Surely, they countered, the world began with some dramatic moment of creation, and surely such events continued to erupt from time to time. The Grand Canyon, for example, must have been caused by a deep cracking of the earth's surface, a cataclysmic collapse of rock into a yawning gulf.

This older view saw the past as a series of catastrophic events — hence the name "catastrophism." The biblical flood was one such catastrophe, a single abrupt event that remade the world. Like the flood, other catastrophes had a divine origin. God was actively engaged in making and remaking the earth. Uniformitarianism, on the other hand, led to a denial of the superintending power and agency, perhaps even the existence, of God.

Nowhere on the Colorado Plateau did Powell find evidence of a catastrophic past. He was a uniformitarian through and through. "The agencies of Nature," he wrote, "produce great results — results no less than the carving of a mountain range out of a much larger block lifted from beneath the sea; not by an extravagant and violent use of power, but by the slow agencies which may be observed generally throughout the world still acting in the same slow, patient manner." Seas advanced and receded, thick sediments formed on the bottom of those seas, the sediments rose slowly into mountains, rivers cut canyons through them. "No great convulsion of Nature, but steady progress." There will come a time, he predicted, when

> this desolate land of Titanic rocks shall become a valley of many valleys, and yet again the sea will invade the land, and the coral animals build their reefs in the infinitesimal laboratories of life, and lowly beings shall weave nacre-lined shrouds for themselves, and the shrouds shall remain entombed in the bottom of the sea, when the people shall be changed, by the chemistry of life, into new forms; monsters of the deep shall live and die, and their bones be buried in the coral sands. Then other mountains and other hills shall be washed into the Colorado Sea, and coral reefs, and shales, and bones, and disintegrated mountains, shall be made into beds of rock, for a new land, where new rivers shall flow. Thus ever the land and sea are changing; old lands are buried, and new lands are born, and with advancing periods new complexities of rock are found; new complexities of life evolved.[24]

The cadence of his language was biblical; he had, after all, been raised on pulpit oratory and the King James edition of the Scriptures. But the view that Powell expressed was decidedly not a biblical one.

Ironically, some of his superiors in geological science, men whose claims to scientific expertise exceeded his, had a great deal more trouble accepting that modern perspective on nature. They remained catastrophists for reasons that were essentially religious. The outstanding case in point was Clarence King. For all his sybaritic ways and risqué sense of humor, King was a religious man who packed a Bible along with elegant waistcoats in the field. In biology he was a disciple of Louis Agassiz, who opposed the Darwinian hypothesis of evolution through natural selection. In aesthetics he was a disciple of John Ruskin and saw in the beauties of the natural world the hand of divine intelligence. In geology he was a catastrophist, convinced that the earth's story had been written by stupendous volcanoes and glaciers whose power he could only imagine from fragmentary remains.

King's survey of the Fortieth Parallel produced outstanding geological work—more and better scientific publications than the other surveys. His own report, *Systematic Geology*, published in 1878, was eight hundred pages long, beautifully illustrated and exquisitely written, and it traced the succession of rocks from the Archaean (Precambrian) to the Cenozoic in the mountains and basins of the West. Though historical in approach, it incorporated chemical and physical analysis into the study of geology. But King felt besieged by the new wave of uniformitarian thinking, and in an address delivered in 1877 at Yale's Sheffield Scientific School he lashed out at "the army of scientific fashion followers who would gladly die rather than be caught wearing an obsolete mode or believing in any penultimate thing." Entitled "Catastrophism and Evolution," the address demonstrated that, however fashionable his personal wardrobe, he still wore an old hat when it came to scientific theory.[25]

Cleverly, King attacked the uniformitarians as being prosaic and unimaginative. "They are bounded—I might almost say imprisoned—by the evident facts and ideas of their own today and their own environment." He had a livelier imagination.

> Uniformitarians are fond of saying that give our present rivers
> time, plenty of time, and they can perform the feats of the past. It
> is mere nonsense in the case of the cañons of the Cordilleras.
> They could never have been carved by the pigmy rivers of this
> climate to the end of infinite time. . . . [T]here is not water
> enough to quench the thirst even of a uniformitarian.

King granted that there had been long periods of "geological serenity," the present period being one of them. "But then all at once a part of the earth suffered short, sharp, destructive revolution, as unheralded as an earthquake or volcanic eruption." Later on he maintained that there simply had not been enough time to work the slow, gradual changes that the uniformitarians favored. The earth was only about twenty-four million years old, he calculated, while the new school needed billions of years to achieve their results.[26]

King's sense of time proved to be ludicrously shortsighted. The earth is indeed billions of years old, and his brief span of twenty-four million years would get us back only into the mid-Tertiary period. But the most significant issue in this confrontation was not who had facts on his side and who do not. Nor was it about who had imagination and who did not. The real issue was theology versus science. A strong catastrophist position like King's retained the notion of divine intervention — sublimely powerful, terrifyingly dramatic — as the dominant force in nature. The Darwinists in biology and geology, on the other hand, did away with any need for God. Species evolved without supervision or plan, just as the surface of the earth changed without any purpose in mind. King denounced this view of nature as "valueless." He denied that "a mere Malthusian struggle" was the "author and finisher of evolution" rather than "He who brought to bear that mysterious energy we call life." "Moments of great catastrophe," he concluded, "thus translated into the language of life, become moments of creation, when out of plastic organisms something newer and nobler is called into being."[27]

Powell, in contrast, turned away from creationism and its companion catastrophism and, in doing so, proved to be more in tune with progressive scientific reasoning. King's beliefs could not explain the development of the Grand Canyon or the Plateau Province. They were, in fact, no more helpful than a Thomas Moran painting, with which they had much in common: pious in feeling, beautiful to look at, grandly imaginative, but not to be taken seriously as science.

Astonishingly, the man who had ridden the wild Colorado in 1869 with the likes of Jack Sumner and Billy Hawkins had become, a mere six years later, director of the best scientific team in the West. It helped that the King survey had, after 1874, deserted the field and was comfortably quartered on New York's Fifth Avenue while they wrote up their reports. But King had seen some of his best men leave earlier: his close friend James Gardiner had gone over to the Hayden party, the photographer Timothy O'Sullivan had left to explore with Wheeler, and Samuel Emmons had tried to join Powell.[28] Underfunded though he was, Powell had a visionary zeal, a wide-ranging intellect, and a prodigious energy that drew men like a warm campfire on a winter range.

Thompson, grumbling but faithful, kept up the wood supply for that fire. Other stalwarts included Hillers, the photographer; John Renshaw, a topographic assistant; and James Pilling, a native of Washington, D.C., an expert in the new art of stenography, and now Powell's personal secretary and disbursing agent. Then in 1874–75 dozens of young men began seeking a place in the Powell camp. They enlisted powerful figures in Washington and elsewhere to help them. The Chicago architect William Le Baron Jenney, inventor of the steel skeleton and curtain wall that made the modern skyscraper possible, recommended his brother to Powell. James Angell, president of the University of Michigan, and Frank Marvin, chancellor of the University of Kansas, lobbied for their students. Secretary of Interior Columbus Delano had a candidate, and so did Spencer Baird, who supported an old boyhood friend—"I would be exceedingly glad if you could find something for him to do to tide over a tough passage in his life." Clarence King pushed forward a young civil engineer whose "heart turns westward as ours did and I commend him to you." Graduates of Yale, Columbia, and Harvard offered themselves for staff positions.[29] Few, however, could be hired because Major Powell lacked funds.

Jobs depended on Congressional appropriations, and in 1874, as the national hard times dragged on, those seemed in doubt. Congress began to ask whether there were too many surveys and whether they might be consolidated into one. It took five more years to achieve that consolidation, during which time Powell survived and, indeed, gained in reputation at the expense of his competitors. John J. Stevenson, on the staff of the Pennsylvania Geological Survey, wrote to thank Powell for a "very large number of stereos" and confessed to being an admirer: "Were it not that I owe a certain degree of fealty to Lt. Wheeler I would throw up my hat for you as the best chief in Washington. There can be no harm under the circumstances in my saying that you are a good second anyway." Later that year, after Powell managed to secure another appropriation, Stevenson wrote, "I hope the day is not far distant when you will be in charge of the Civilian explorations, with that infernal humbug, Hayden, hopelessly out of the way. Your chapter on Physical Geography is worth more than all he has given to science by personal labor in twenty years."[30] Hayden, to be sure, had his resolute defenders, but the talent clearly was beating a path to Powell, and the Major had his pick of the best.

It helped recruiting that no other landscape surpassed the canyon country for geological or artistic interest. Lieutenant George Wheeler, the most scientifically inept of the four survey directors, rankled by Powell's meteoric success, determined to steal the Colorado River for his own and the Army's glory. In the late summer of

1871, after marching his men through 120-degree heat in Death Valley, he loaded them into three barges at Fort Mohave and announced that he intended to finish the exploration of the Colorado begun by his predecessor, Lieutenant Joseph Ives. He pushed upstream against the current, with the aid of sails, oars, ropes, and a hard-used team of Mohaves and Paiutes. On 4 October Wheeler's party reached the Grand Wash Cliffs where Powell and company had come out of the canyon two years earlier. On they went, struggling up rapid after rapid, grunting and pulling their way over the rocks, breaking ropes, losing rations. Two weeks of these demented heroics, and they reached the mouth of Diamond Creek, which Ives had followed down to the Colorado's banks. Wheeler grandly reported that with this laborious traverse "the exploration of the Colorado River may now be considered complete."[31] Little credit to Powell, who had run the canyon segment already. The army man simply declared victory. Luckily there was not a war on, or Wheeler in command might have lost a whole battalion.

Among Wheeler's boat crew were O'Sullivan, who soon drifted off, and a budding young civilian scientist, Grove Karl Gilbert. Eventually the latter deserted too. A tall, lanky young man (born in 1843), he had little more training in science than Powell did when Powell first came west. Gilbert had studied the ancient classics at the University of Rochester, though one of his favorite teachers, H.A. Ward, was a naturalist who had hired Gilbert to work in his business of preparing and arranging museum collections. For a brief time he worked as a volunteer on the Ohio Geological Survey under Newberry, and it was through Newberry's influence that he joined Wheeler's field party. [32]

In 1872 Wheeler sent this young geologist straight into Powell's face, on a reconnaissance of Utah's natural resources. Gilbert traipsed over well-trodden terrain from Salt Lake City south to Pipe Spring, Lees Ferry, and Kanab, encountering the Powell entourage in Kanab.[33] Winters he spent in Washington, trying to pull his hasty field notes together into a report or two, often showing up at the Philosophical Society's meetings. Here also he mixed with the Powell men, including the Major himself. Over brandy and cigars, they talked about the western rocks and the big geological questions. No one Gilbert had met thought in such expansive terms, going far beyond the collecting of specimens, the cataloguing of resources, or even the making of maps.

In September 1874 Gilbert signed a contract to work for Powell, and in the following season he was back in Utah as a Powell man,

Grove Karl Gilbert.
(Courtesy: U.S. Geological Survey)

doing real, probing science for the first time in his life. Meeting Powell proved to be the career-making event of his life, and for nearly three decades the two were inseparable, Gilbert serving Powell as his right arm — a quiet, self-effacing, generous, and uncomplaining assistant. He was good at geology; in fact, Gilbert turned out to be the most important scientific talent recruited to the Powell Survey, and indeed ranked one day as the leading geologist in government service.

In his first season under the new boss Gilbert traipsed over territory that Powell had discovered and Thompson had explored, the Henry Mountains. An anomaly in the Plateau Province, the mountains posed unusual questions to the geologist. Even from a distance it was obvious that their slopes were light sandstone, their domes a dark rock that must be lava. The dark rock proved to be an igneous intrusion that had shoved overlying sediments upward into mountains without breaking the surface. Gilbert called those bulges laccolites (which others refined to laccoliths) and dated them to the middle Tertiary. Beyond naming and explaining, he meticulously analyzed the processes of erosion that had carved canyons in the sandstone and laid bare the black, underlying domes. The resulting report, published in 1877, was one of the Powell Survey's most valuable contributions to geological science.[34]

Gilbert was clearly a more impressive geologist than Powell; the science was, after all, his true and only calling, one he pursued with little distraction. He scrutinized the minutest details and formed careful hypotheses which, in the eyes of other scientists, were models of scrupulous research. That was not Powell's way to fame. Although he was a good observer, classifier of facts, and coupler of cause and effect, he did not put in enough time on the ground. His contributions, Gilbert noted, were not "elaborately or adequately illustrated." Powell believed that "a scientific fact needed no argument, but only statement." [35]

Powell was a man of large thoughts that he liberally threw out as seeds for others to plant and nourish. "Phenomenally fertile in ideas," he was, according to Gilbert, "absolutely free" in communicating those ideas to others, which they often appropriated without giving full credit. "Gathering about him the ablest men he could secure," Gilbert wrote, "he was yet always the intellectual leader, and few of his colleagues could withstand the influence of his master mind." Gilbert claimed that the careers of a half-dozen scientists were based on extending and applying Powell's insights. Together those protégés formed a school known as the "new geology." It amalgamated geology and geography, earth and water, past and present. "Whereas geologic history was formerly read in the rocks alone," wrote Gilbert, "it is now read not only in the rocks but in the forms of the land and the arrangement of the streams."[36]

Within six years of the first river expedition and three years of the second, the Powell Survey had shed its amateur status and become nationally respected for scientific professionalism. What could such a pool of talent offer in the interpretation of nature's West? If Thomas Moran's romantic, vaguely religious approach to the landscape through painting was a late expression of the fading transcendental line, what alternative vision could the geologists suggest?

During the second half of the nineteenth century the American perception of nature shifted from the authority of the artist toward that of the scientist. The Grand Canyon and its environs stood at the very center of that shift. Masters of the brush and pen went on trying, as Moran did, to incorporate its hard beauty, its mind-bending scale, into their vocabulary and technique, but citizens increasingly reached out to scientists for guidance. Powell and his staff stood ready to serve. Although they had lively aesthetic sensibilities, they insisted that art must not violate their view of the natural world as secular, profane, rationally ordered, and utterly material.

Among Powell's recruits the most eloquent exponent of that scientific view of the landscape was not the abstruse Gilbert but a remarkable Army captain named Clarence Dutton, who joined the survey in that fertile year of 1875. Seven years junior to the Major, he had set himself up in a professional military career when they met through the Philosophical Society of Washington and began having spirited conversations. Dutton was soon won over; though he did not ask for a transfer of duty himself, he was willing to have Powell approach the War Department. For fifteen years he remained on seasonal leave from his military duties, during which time he produced a number of significant geological writings on the West. What he brought to the Powell organization was a rare blending of aesthetic passion and scientific erudition.[37]

Dutton was from a rural home near Wallingford, Connecticut. As a child he set up a "laboratory" to study minerals and, as he recalled in an autobiographical sketch, took to running away from school and violating the Sabbath "in the pursuit of knowledge not supplied in the current text books & Sunday school books." His parents sent him to a boarding school that had "Holiness of the Lord" written all over it, and soon it was written all over him too — he memorized large portions of the Scriptures and even tilted toward a career in the ministry. At age fifteen he entered Yale College but within two weeks dropped out of the theological program run by neo-Calvinists Noah Porter and Timothy Dwight and turned to mathematics and physics instead. An indifferent, bored student, he graduated well down in his class, though he won the Yale Literary Prize with an essay on the English novelist Charles Kingsley. Rather than academic honors, he pursued Kingsley's ideal of manly sports for the young gentleman by excelling in gymnastics and rowing. After graduating in 1860, he accepted the position of adjutant to his older brother in the Union army and saw "pretty rough service." Midway through the war he took a competitive examination that won him a place in the Ordnance Corps, where he could stand on the developing instead of receiving end of military explosives.[38]

After Appomattox the U.S. Army did not really need this officer of insatiable curiosity. He put in his time at the Watervliet Arsenal in Troy, New York, then at the Frankford Arsenal in Philadelphia, still later in Washington. Duty satisfied, he was free to learn about the Bessemer steel process, the chemistry of gunpowder, the microscopic structure of rocks, the fossil record. In Washington he cultivated the Powell men, and Powell, seeing a great talent going to waste, gave him the geology of Utah to study. Like Gilbert, Dutton was drifting until he found a leader.

Dutton might have been a twin of Clarence King, except that he lacked any enthusiasm for the limelight. For a brief year they were classmates at Yale. Both represented a liberated New England mind that sought the good life: fine booze, smokes, flirtatious women, ribald tales, a clubby life among other males. Both men read widely— Dutton called himself "omnibiblical"—and both aspired to scientific authority while seeing themselves as artists and poets as well. Both were great talkers. Dutton could lecture impressively on any number of topics. When they looked at rocks, both men thought of sex. King was amused to get a geological letter from Dutton one day "full of erotic similes." It "does me good," he replied. "There must be something in the atmosphere of the place, which makes you speak of catching faults *in flagrante delictu*," or else it is "the anchorite abstinence of your life" driving "secretions to the brain."[39] Where they differed most was on religious matters; King was still a believer, Dutton had become an agnostic. Thus Dutton chose to join the nonreligious gang out surveying the Plateau Province.

Powell not only pointed Dutton to a new career but also instructed him about what to look for when he got to Utah. The great book that Powell had projected for himself, a description of the region adjacent to the Grand Canyon and its geological history, had to be handed over to someone else who had more time to do it justice. Dutton was that person, grateful for the assignment. He traversed the plateaus with Hillers, collecting ideas and pictures of "the great lesson which this country teaches—erosion." To Powell he wrote, "your great conclusions regarding the erosion of the Colorado plateau I concur in to the utmost & I think I can now add a chapter to them derived from the study of the side canons & you have yourself indicated the scope of it by your suggestions about consequent[,] inconsequent & antecedent drainage."[40]

Dutton's first major production on that subject was a *Report on the Geology of the High Plateaus, Utah* (1880), but it was his second work, *The Tertiary History of the Grand Cañon District* (1882), which carried out the Major's assignment with surpassing skill. This report's 260 pages matched anything that King wrote for literary grace and, though a scientific document, was worthy of comparison with Moran's paintings for artistic expression. It was published in only three thousand copies, with more than forty plates, including heliotropes made from Hillers's photographs, wood engravings and wa-

Captain Clarence E. Dutton.
(Courtesy: U.S. Geological Survey)

tercolors by Moran, and pen and ink panoramas by William Henry Holmes, and was accompanied by an elephant folio atlas of more than twenty sheets, all printed with exquisite craftsmanship by Julius Bien and Company of New York, which had become the favorite engraver for all the surveys. It may well be the most elegant book ever to come out of a government office.

The Grand Canyon District, as Dutton defines it, covers thirteen to sixteen thousand square miles in all. Besides the Colorado River and its tributary canyons, it includes five plateaus on the north side — moving from west to east, Sheavwits (Shivwits), Uinkaret, Kanab, Kaibab, and Paria, all edged by those multicolored terraces ascending into Utah — and one on the south side, the less thoroughly studied Colorado Plateau (which today gives its name to the entire region).

Dutton takes a Powell-like position up on the Markagunt Plateau and peers over the whole district. Where he stands the rock is all Tertiary, equal in age to the Uinta Mountains far away. He gives no dates of deposition, and on the last page of the report he tells why: "Unfortunately there is no mystery more inscrutable than the durations of geological time. On this point geologists have obtained no satisfactory results in any part of the world. . . . [H]ere, as elsewhere, whenever we interrogate [Nature] about time other than relative, her lips are sternly closed, and her face becomes as the face of the Sphinx."[41] Later geologists made the Sphinx speak and traced the Tertiary back from about two million to some sixty million years ago, the period during which modern flora and mammals emerged.

The Grand Canyon District is an immense cavity that is missing the entire Tertiary period, and indeed missing much of the rock from the Cretaceous, Jurassic, Triassic, and Permian periods as well. The dominant rock in the district is Carboniferous, over three hundred million years old. Where did all the later strata go? Downstream to the Gulf of California. That in simplest terms is the story the district has to tell—what Dutton calls "the Great Denudation." No sudden catastrophes, just the daily wearing away of rock ten thousand feet thick, rock worn away by the simple flow of water and the weathering effects of sun and wind and frost.

Dutton's strategy is to lead the reader on a series of excursions across this denuded surface, reconstructing the missing eras as he goes. One must first realize that the Colorado River, old as it may appear, is really only a recent feature of the landscape. Before it began running, before even the Rocky Mountains arose, a series of inland freshwater lakes and saltwater arms of the ocean flooded the land; alternating with them were a series of hot, sterile deserts filled with moving dunes. All those early regimes might have lain invisible to the human eye had not the whole district begun to rise slowly in elevation, heaving twelve to eighteen thousand feet upward during the Tertiary period. The elements cut and sawed that upheaval, eventually leaving only traces of the former worlds when pelagic fish swam across Utah or palm trees rustled in the warm, moist nights or the only sound was grains of sand rolling along the ground.

"I have in many places departed from the severe ascetic style which has been conventional in scientific monographs," Dutton warns in his preface.[42] Imagination can be safely let free in this place, for it cannot easily exaggerate the astonishing facts. Indeed, the scientist must stimulate the popular imagination sufficiently so that it can fully comprehend what has occurred here.

One of Dutton's excursions leads across the Kaibab Plateau ("the most enchanting region it has ever been our privilege to visit") to the canyon rim, just as Moran and Colburn had advanced in the company of Powell and Hillers. But Dutton ends up at another spot that he names Point Sublime, and there he finds a more enticing view of the canyon and a more secular notion of the sublime than Moran.

He calls on the reader to drop all inherited ideas of what constitutes the beautiful in nature.

> The lover of nature, whose perceptions have been trained in the Alps, in Italy, Germany, or New England, in the Appalachians or Cordilleras, in Scotland or Colorado, would enter this strange region with a shock, and dwell there for a time with a sense of oppression, and perhaps with horror. Whatsoever things he had learned to regard as beautiful and noble he would seldom or never see, and whatsoever he might see would appear to him as anything but beautiful and noble. Whatsoever might be bold and striking would at first seem only grotesque. The colors would be the very ones he had learned to shun as tawdry and bizarre. The tones and shades, modest and tender, subdued yet rich, in which his fancy had always taken special delight, would be the ones which are conspicuously absent. But time would bring a gradual change. Some day he would suddenly become conscious that outlines which at first seemed harsh and trivial have grace and meaning; that forms which seemed grotesque are full of dignity; that magnitudes which had added enormity to coarseness have become replete with strength and even majesty; that colors which had been esteemed unrefined, immodest, and glaring, are as expressive, tender, changeful, and capacious of effects as any others. Great innovations, whether in art or literature, in science or in nature, seldom take the world by storm. They must be understood before they can be estimated, and must be cultivated before they can be understood.

The newcomer does not arrive fully prepared to appreciate the canyon. But with long, careful study it begins to appear what it truly is: "by far the most sublime of all earthly spectacles. . . . the sublimest thing on earth."[43]

Those were unwonted words to come across in a science report. They assumed a wider audience and a more unconventional role for the western surveyor than anyone, except Powell, had done. Dutton was acting as the nation's aesthetic guide. But he was not speaking as a member of an educated elite trying to instruct the benighted American masses how to find grandeur in the Grand Canyon. Few people of any class or race or nationality have ever missed the grandeur. The native Americans walked in awe of the place; the Spaniards, along with Anglo miners and hunters, were staggered by it even when they did not tarry. It was the bourgeoisie, their heads filled with aesthetic theory—Ruskinians who defined the beautiful and the sublime in terms of Swiss mountains, Niagara Falls, the Tuscan countryside, the Hudson River valley—who most needed to be reeducated.[44]

Now the sublime took on new meaning. It continued to refer to those peak emotions that bring a shiver, a thrill, a sense of extraordinary power beyond the human. But now the sublime experience came from grasping the full story of a geological landscape developing over hundreds of millions of years—building up land forms and tearing them down, creating with quotidian forces the most incredible effects. "It is hard to realize that this is the work of the blind forces of nature," Dutton writes. "We feel like mere insects crawling along the street of a city flanked with immense temples, or as Lemuel Gulliver might have felt in revisiting the capital of Brobdingnag, and finding it deserted." Deserted by God, mind, spirit, the ideal, the good, even by the monstrously evil.[45]

That sense of walking through some vanished giant race's capital recurs throughout Dutton's report. The agnostic's sublime is not chaotic; it is architectural. This is most true in the canyon itself, whose name does not convey a full sense of what is here. More than simply two walls rising from the river, the canyon is a complex architectural wonderland some ten to twelve miles in breadth at its widest point. "The contrast between Saint Marc's and the rude dwelling of the frontiersman," Dutton continues, "is not greater than that between the chasm of the Colorado and the trenches in the rocks which answer to the ordinary conception of a cañon." But Dutton denies that he is offering a mere analogy. What nature has done here is precisely the work of an architect: chiseling, sculpting, cutting out large amphitheaters, naves, arches, and columns, leaving walls, spandrels, lintels. "Hundreds of these mighty structures, miles in length, and thousands of feet in height, rear their majestic heads out of the abyss, displaying their richly-molded plinths and friezes, thrusting out their gables, wing-walls, buttresses, and pilasters, and recessed with alcoves and panels." Overall, no plan has arranged these buildings into a unity; each structure obeys the same laws of form and function. Properly understood, the analogy does not run from the human to the natural, but from the natural to the human. The art of civilization takes its inspiration from the art fashioned by the blind energies of nature.[46]

Yet even Dutton could not resist trying to pull the canyon into some more familiar, cultural frame of reference. The natural buildings needed names. Pointedly, he does not draw them from the Christian religion—a Saint Peter's or a Church of the Redeemer. Instead, he turns to the ancient pagan religions, which make no belief claims on Americans but suggest a poetry of power. Asia furnishes the Hindu Amphitheater, Vishnu's Temple, and Shiva's Temple. In that borrowing Dutton initiated a trend that produced temples named for Confucius, Mencius, Isis, and Zoroaster, along with the Tower of Ra, Cheops Pyramid, and the Buddha Cloister. On the south side eventually appeared a contrasting section named in honor of leading scientists: Darwin Plateau, Wallace Butte, Lyell Butte, Newton Butte, Tyndall Dome, Geikie Peak, and the row houses of New World geologists and paleontologists (Newberry, Marsh, Cope, Dana, Le Conte, Shaler). The eye can move from the old city of superstition to the new one of enlightenment.

Dutton was reluctant to use the native American names that some of those features already wore, for they did not convey an appropriate sense of grandeur. The native tongues were hard to pronounce, and their names attached to places were apt to be too long, often telling a story. So the canyon became a strangely foreign city divided between ancient pagan gods and modern scientists, with the local Christians, Mormons, and Indians all studiously ignored.

Dutton's names are meant to reduce the incomprehensible to the manageable. Yet he acknowledges that names cannot really capture the overwhelming power of nature in this place—a nature whose antiquity far exceeds the most ancient human civilizations and whose power can make even industrial America catch its breath. When late afternoon comes to the canyon, all names and stories dissolve into a haze of color. As the sun reddens toward sunset, the walls turn bright yellow, orange, crimson. "The blaze of sunlight poured over an illimitable surface of glowing red is flung back into the gulf, and, commingling with the blue haze, turns it into a sea of purple of most imperial hue—so rich, so strong, so pure that it makes the heart ache and the throat tighten."[47] Nature still has the power to summon up all the feelings of the sublime—feelings instructed and not suppressed by the discoveries of geology, physics, and paleontology.

Among the artists contributing to the report, none was more completely in tune with Dutton's aesthetic science than William Henry Holmes, whose three-plate panorama composed from Point Sublime forms the book's centerpiece, shoving Moran aside. Those panoramic drawings are all done in black ink on white paper (larger color versions appeared in the *Atlas* issued with the *Tertiary History*), in part

William Henry Holmes.
(Courtesy: U.S. Geological Survey)

because printing technology was not yet ready for Dutton's throat-constricting purple haze but also because Holmes was intent on show-ing, with the aid of numbers and alphabetic letters, the chief geological features of the place. All color is gone, and all haze; what remains are the fracture lines, the stratigraphic layering, the bold es-carpments carved by the elements. No one has ever drawn the canyon lineaments better. From the rim down to the Great Unconformity, the line separating the basement rocks of schist and granite—the foun-dation of this natural metropolis—from the sedimentary strata in which the buildings had been carved, Holmes leads the viewer into the intricate but insistently material forms of nature.

Holmes was not trained as an artist in any of the prevalent tradi-tions of the century. He was not the product of the Hudson River or Rocky Mountain school, nor of Barbizon or Dusseldorf, though in 1879 he traveled to Europe briefly to study art. A native of Ohio, he found work sketching natural history specimens at the Smithsonian, until in 1872 he was recruited by Hayden as artist for his survey. Hay-den set him to drawing mountains, designating him an "assistant ge-ologist," and Holmes learned to observe rocks with uncommon skill. In July and August 1880 he met Dutton at the Grand Canyon to pre-pare illustrations for the latter's report. His notebook from that ex-cursion is filled with geological references: "The rocks at the spring

William H. Holmes, "Panorama from Point Sublime: Part I: Looking East." Shaded and tinted drawing for the atlas accompanying Clarence Dutton's report, The Tertiary History of the Grand Canyon District *(1882).*

are triassic, but the plain across which we marched is underlain by the permian." He saw the color and reveled in it, as his frontispiece, "Smithsonian Butte—Valley of the Virgen," and his watercolors in the Dutton atlas demonstrate. But his principal assignment was to reveal the structure of geological panoramas and that he did with gusto. "Sketched with greatest pleasure from sunrise until half past three marvelous buttes and most interesting geology."[48]

The first plate of Holmes's Point Sublime panorama shows a seated man, a pad resting on his knees, sketching a distant Red Wall limestone and the Lower Carboniferous sandstones. Behind the figure stands another man bending over him, his hand on the artist's shoulder. Is it Dutton supervising Holmes? Geology instructing art? Science redefining the sublime? The vignette suggests all of these possibilities. The Grand Canyon challenges both the artist and scientist to redefine their relationship to one another and, together, to reeducate their perception of the earth.

If the test of a good manager is whether she or he can recruit first-rate talent and then allow that talent the freedom to do its best, then Powell met the test. He ought to have, for he had learned management the hard way by patching exploring parties out of anarchic fur trappers and frontier runaways, college students, pious, valetudinarian ministers, disgruntled military men, assorted family members, complainers, dabblers, dreamers—the standard American lot. By comparison Dutton and Gilbert were easy to handle. They simply asked to be pointed in a direction, furnished adequate means, and supported until the project was complete. The foibles and frequent inattention of their leader they quickly forgave, staying with him as they rose out of obscurity into national prominence—the best testimony an administrator could want.

But Powell aspired to be more than an organizer of other people's talents. Everyone he recruited from 1873 on was, to some degree, an alter ego who shared his sense of mission. He allowed them independence to pursue questions that he wanted answered. They, in turn, acknowledged his role in shaping their ideas about physical geography, geological change over time, upheaval, volcanism, and erosion. Dutton, in his report on the Mount Taylor and Zuni Plateau district of New Mexico, confessed that he could not say where his own ideas left off and those of Powell and the others began; "all observations and experiences were common stock."[49]

Throughout his life Powell was never much of a book writer. Compared to Gilbert and Dutton, he tended to write short articles, a chapter or two, a lecture or paper. A shining exception was the *Exploration of the Colorado River of the West*, the book-length report that Congressman Garfield had pressured him to complete; it was submitted on 18 June 1874 and published in 1875. When it appeared, it was more of a compendium of individual pieces than a tightly integrated monograph. Nonetheless, it provided an introduction to the Powell Survey's work, an indication of the broad outlines of the region's distinguishing features, and a guide to future work. It was the basement rock on which Gilbert and Dutton, as well as Powell himself, laid down sediments and carved them into ornate forms.

Several of Powell's shorter pieces were amalgamated into the *Exploration*, including a series he did for *Scribner's* on the 1869 expedition, "The Cañons of the Colorado," and the same magazine's "An Overland Trip to the Grand Cañon," both published almost simultaneously with the government report. Also incorporated were Powell's pieces for *Popular Science Monthly* on the "Physical Features of the Colorado Valley" (1875), along with the chapters by Harry Thompson, Elliott Coues, and G. Brown Goode. Eighty-one illustrations, some of them by Thomas Moran, were interspersed among the chapters, most of them depicting scenes along the Colorado River, such geological phenomena as faults in cross-section and monoclinal folds, and sensational events such as the wreck at Disaster Falls. The whole was purposely gotten up for popular consumption, rather than for a scientific audience, but it succeeded in transforming the adventure of going down the river into more than an adventure story.

It took a couple of years for Powell to get it all into print. New York editors had been after him to tell his exploits to the public, and he wanted to do so, if for no other reason than to beat out the photographer Beaman who was going the rounds with his own manuscript. In early 1873 Powell first approached the commercial publishers. A response came from H.O. Houghton of the Riverside Press in Cambridge, Massachusetts, saying that the fragmentary record of the first expedition needed amplification and polish before it could be a market success. "We find the manner of the book admirable: it is fresh and attractive in style and marked by good taste throughout: the explanation of geologic facts is free from technicality and the narrative of the exploration of the canon is clear and intelligible." Nine days later Houghton returned the manuscript but kept the photographs Powell had sent. On 12 April a letter from Henry Alden of Harper Brothers gave him a similar response: they wanted to see more manuscript before they could make a decision to accept or reject. A few days later Ticknor & Fields wrote from Boston that were eager to look at the manuscript, but by then Powell was gearing up for his Indian commission assignment and had to put aside his publishing ambitions.

Not until more than a year later, in July 1874, was he back in negotiation with publishers, and now it was with Richard Watson Gilder of *Scribner's Monthly*. Gilder, however, wanted to buy only a few articles, and he wanted plenty of raw, throbbing excitement in them: "Please send one or two more incidents of the expedition of a bloodcurdling nature." Powell sent in the requested articles, and they were printed, but they were less than bloodcurdling. Although he had a dramatic streak, he was not up to mass-market standards. Thus, the full story of the first expedition down the Colorado did not appear from a commercial house.[50]

Thomas Moran may have explained best why Major Powell did not quite measure up as a popular writer of western adventure. After reading one of the *Scribner's* articles, Moran professed to like it very much but complained about its lack of emotion.

> You do not once (if I recollect aright) give your sensations even
> in the most dangerous passages, nor even hint at the terrible &
> sublime feelings that are stirred within one, as he feels himself in

the strong jaws of the monstrous chasms. It seems to me, that the expression of these impressions & thoughts tend to realize the descriptions to the reader & are almost as necessary as the descriptions themselves. I know that you will forgive this plain criticism, because you know I wish your articles to have the greatest success.[51]

Moran echoed the lecture reviews that Powell sometimes received: he was a clear, effective speaker, they said, but lacked sufficient flourish and pounding emotion. He was too cool and scientific for an American public that preferred lurid dime novels. Henceforth, he confined his publishing efforts to scientific journals, philosophical reviews, and government reports.

Powell, nonetheless, knew how to tell a compelling story and proved he could reach a large public. When the *Exploration* came out as a Congressional report, requests for copies poured in from railway executives, grocers, and scientists, and they came from Brazil, Canada, Scotland, England, France, Germany, Italy, and Australia as well as all parts of the United States. Soon the supply was exhausted. For years it remained a difficult book to obtain, and well-thumbed copies passed from hand to hand.

Twenty years after its government publication, the *Exploration* experienced a rebirth as a commercial work. In 1895 the publishers Flood & Vincent of Meadville, Pennsylvania, brought out a new edition, reentitled *Canyons of the Colorado*. In that form the report endured; it was reprinted again and again in the twentieth century, until it became the most popular literary product of all the western surveys. Over the next century no one among his contemporary explorers and surveyors, not Dutton, King, Hayden, or Frémont, was as widely read as Powell.

Gone for the 1895 edition were the miscellaneous chapters by Thompson, Coues, and Goode; this was now all Powell's book, his final statement on the country he had set out to understand and interpret more than two decades earlier. He doubled the number of pages to nearly four hundred and included three times the number of illustrations in the original edition. The day-by-day description of the first expedition remained largely unchanged—a few words altered here and there. Now, however, the grand topography of the Plateau Province moved front and center and dominated the first four chapters, which he entitled "The Valley of the Colorado," "Mesas and Buttes," "Mountains and Plateaus," "Cliffs and Terraces." Powell

directed the reader's gaze from the Mogollon Rim of Arizona northward to the Wind River Mountains and the Grand Lake of Colorado,
headwaters of the Colorado, then circled back south, and ended the
grand tour with the Kanab River flowing down to join the Colorado
in the heart of the Grand Canyon, the heart of the province. A final
chapter on the canyon takes readers to the water's edge, a place
where even as late as the final years of the nineteenth century few
American travelers managed to reach. Perched high on the canyon
rim, Dutton had seen a vast deserted city of temples and towers,
awash in color. Down on the river, Powell gave a very different sense
of the place — less architectural and more musical. What he most remembered was the sound of water running through this land — "the
land of music . . . a land of song."[52]

Then to the 1895 text Powell added illustrations galore. Some of
them were relevant, some were not: a picture of gambling Paiutes appears on the page discussing the geology of the Henry Mountains,
for example, and a Hopi hairdresser is on the page facing an account
of the passage through the Middle Granite Gorge. He kept the original edition's drawings by Moran and added a few more, including the
"Mountain of the Holy Cross." He gave equal space to the line drawings that William Henry Holmes had done for Dutton's report: "Towers of the Vermilion Cliffs," "Temples and Towers of the Rio Virgen,"
the full "Panorama from Point Sublime," and Holmes's masterpiece,
"Grand Canyon at the Foot of the Toroweap, Looking East."

But the most striking change Powell made in his text had nothing to
do with either the geologists' or artists' depiction of the natural landscape. He now filled the book with Indians — Apaches, Navajos, Utes,
Paiutes — people who had effectively been erased from Moran's, Dutton's, and Gilbert's pictures and accounts. Harry Thompson's report
on searching for the Dirty Devil's headwaters was replaced by a chapter
on Powell's travels in fall 1870 to the Shivwits, inquiring about his lost
men, and to the Hopi and Zuni villages. Two-thirds of the illustrations
and a larger part of the revised text had Indians for their subject, several of them derived from John Hillers's photographs. Instead of Dutton's land of Oriental temples and palaces, Powell gives us a Zuni
court, a passageway in Mashonognavi, the kivas of Shumopavi, an Indian tipi in the Uinta Valley, a sweat house, a Tusayan interior. He is
nearly obsessed by stone-worked pueblos, inhabited or lying in ruins.
Ovens, mealing stones, fetishes, ladders, basketry, effigy pottery are all
on view, along with Indians riding on horseback, hunting, gambling,
spinning, making belts, praying for rain.

Powell inserts Indians into the story even where they were not really there. Where the text tells the story of white men alone on a wild river, the accompanying pictures tell a different story: Hopi women dressing their hair or Indians making smoke signals. In each of those first four chapters, describing the region's land forms, he introduces the native cultures that dwell among the rocks and plateaus. The impression he leaves is of a land densely peopled by Indians, not a wilderness but a fully settled and inhabited place. In fact, most of the Plateau Province was not so thickly settled; even before the white man it had been, over much of its extent, relatively wild and unpopulated, compared, say, to the Mississippi or San Joaquin or Columbia river valleys. But Powell had an important point to make: this land, he was suggesting, is not so unpeopled as Dutton or others have portrayed it. And the peoples living in this environment must be studied and appreciated along with the facts of geology or the sublime color and spaciousness of nature.

Even the white man is included in Powell's revised work, though he shows up merely as a cartoon figure desecrating the scene. One of the book's illustrations shows a tiny male figure descending a ladder propped against an immense balanced rock. He has a paint pot in his hand, and the newly painted face of the rock is an outdoor advertisement reading: "Vandals & Shameless/ Secondhand Store/ Colorado Springs."

By including so many human figures and activities Powell was not repudiating the search for the sublime that had animated men like Moran, Dutton, or himself in the 1870s. After all, he had deliberately brought them into this place to admire its natural wonders and convey some sense of the land. The canyon, in his estimation, surpassed all other experiences in emotional impact. "It is a region more difficult to traverse than the Alps or the Himalayas," he writes, "but if strength and courage are sufficient for the task, by a year's toil a concept of sublimity can be obtained never again to be equaled on the hither side of Paradise."[53]

What Powell seemed to be arguing, however, was that it was not enough for Americans to understand or appreciate nature or be inspired by its order. People belong in our pictures and places. The Indians are also a source of beauty in the landscape, as are their crops, adobe cities, brushy huts, and household artifacts. They must not be erased or dismissed. A science that leaves the native people out is partial and inadequate. So too is an art that does not integrate them into its sense of beauty. The American mind must stretch back into the distant past to see what the land had been like before any humans existed, but it also must come forward into the more recent past, the non-European past, tracing the sequence of cultures and their stratigraphy on the land. Powell's mind leaped nimbly back and forth between those unpeopled panoramas of Holmes and Dutton, on the one hand, and, on the other, a Hillers photograph of three Paiute girls sitting on the ground or an Indian family preparing their meal.

Thus, Powell's mission was to promote a more secularized, but still sublime history of the land while also promoting a more inclusive, deeper understanding of human settlement and inhabitation. No one else on his staff fully shared that integrative ambition, nor for that matter was it the way in which most Americans coming into the country looked about them and tried to understand. It was Powell's special vision. Such a vision of land and people, old inhabitants and newcomers, of people trying to inhabit a place successfully, would inevitably embroil him in politics and economics as well as in art and science.

CHAPTER 9

Democracy Encounters the Desert

A smell of graft and corruption rose through the floorboards of the Grant administration, one dead rat joining another, until the public nostrils could stand it no longer. The president himself seemed indifferent to bad odor. If his house was full of rats, dead or alive, he saw no reason to do any cleaning. But disgust with this state of affairs, and with Grant's Republican Party, which once had proclaimed itself the party of virtue, was mounting across the country. In the election of 1876 both parties ran reform candidates for the presidency: Samuel Tilden, a Democrat, opposed Rutherford Hayes, a Republican. When Hayes, after losing the popular vote, won in the electoral college by an infamous compromise with white supremacists in the South, the stink got worse than ever. A new spirit of reform, however, was rising, and Hayes, a conservative Republican at heart, had to heed and try to join.

That irresistible wind blowing through Washington caught up Major Powell and changed his life. From his parents he had inherited a certain readiness to challenge power and authority in the name of principle. He could not have liked the degrading spectacle of the Grant presidency, though for a while he kept his principles to himself, sticking to his work until he could find support for reform. The evil he wanted to attack was the disposal of public lands in the West to private individuals, a subject filled with powerful implications for American society. Who got land and how much of it, how it was divided it up, were among the most critical matters to decide in the postwar years. Powell thrust himself into the very center of that discussion. Eventually the issue of public land reform made him one of the most influential — and one of the most hated — men in Washington.

The public lands were the responsibility of the Department of the Interior, Powell's own employer, among the smelliest agencies in the federal establishment. Under Grant's indifference that department had become scandalously mismanaged and corrupt, and it is worth remembering a few of the sordid details.

The Office of Indian Affairs vied with the General Land Office (GLO) for bad appointments, larceny, bribery, and dereliction of duty. Indian Affairs repeatedly appointed local agents who were unscrupulous or incompetent. They often failed to keep the government's promise to deliver decent annuities of food and clothing to their charges in exchange for territorial cessions the Indians had made. It took an outsider, Professor Othniel C. Marsh, a distinguished paleontologist at Yale, to blow the lid off that failure. In 1874 he met the Ogalala Sioux leader Red Cloud near the Black Hills to get his permission to make a fossil-collecting expedition into Indian territory. Red Cloud was more interested in showing him the scrawny cattle and the putrid pork, flour, and beans they had been given by their federal agent, who was lining his pockets with the funds with which he was entrusted. Shocked by what he saw, Marsh raised a protest in Washington not only against the guilty agent but also against the whole national "ring" that worked to steal funds meant for the Indians and against Commissioner E.P. Smith and Secretary of Interior Columbus Delano, both of whom knew about such theft but did nothing to stop it. Despite a torrent of denial and vilification, Marsh persisted until Smith and Delano were forced out of office.[1] The greatest moral claim of the Grant administration, establishing a more benevolent treatment of Indians, was revealed to be a cover for further graft and exploitation.

Meanwhile, the General Land Office, which was in charge of conveying title to federal lands to private citizens, was doing an outrageously bad job. It had neither the staff nor the principles to handle its responsibilities in an efficient, honest way. Simply keeping the books on all the land transfers going on was a daunting task. The federal domain originally stretched from Florida and Michigan to California and Washington (not to mention Alaska), nearly 1.5 billion acres in all. By 1875 that domain had dwindled by more than a third, though any statistics were estimates rather than certain knowledge. Among the largest recipients had been the railroad corporations, receiving directly over ninety million acres of free land. The railroad grants were finished by 1871, taking less than two decades to dispose of an area larger than California. The states then took possession of hundreds of millions of acres through swamp land grants, internal improvement grants, and land grants for education. Then a bewildering array of laws and special acts had given the public domain away to individuals through direct sales, military bounties and warrants, and preemption (or purchase by squatters). The best organized and best staffed civil service in the world would have had difficulty keeping up with that blizzard of titles, papers, acreage, and owners. The General Land Office, one of the poorest bureaucracies ever created, was hopeless.[2]

All of this had happened very quickly, and when the dust cleared it was apparent that the tillers of the soil had not done very well compared to the corporations or other large interests. During fifteen years of Republican rule, the class of common farmers had received less than a hundred million out of the six hundred million acres sold or given away. The Homestead Act, which had been designed to prevent this outcome, had barely kicked into action by the end of the Grant presidency. Passed in 1862, that act entitled any person who was the head of a family or twenty-one years old, whether a citizen or not, to acquire title to 160 acres of land free after five years of occupancy. In its first decade only about twenty thousand individuals met those requirements, though eventually 1.6 million did so. But over half a century, the legendary homesteaders received only a fraction of the federal largesse.

Two supplements to the Homestead Act were touted as enhancing opportunities for poor, struggling farmers looking to improve their estates. Neither made a big difference, though they opened new possibilities for fraud and abuse. The Timber Culture Act, passed in 1873, promised an additional 160 acres to any settler who planted 40 acres (later reduced to 10 acres) of it to timber. Over two million acres in each of three states, Kansas, Nebraska, and South Dakota, passed into private hands under this act, but years later it was hard to find any substantial forest growing in those prairie states. The Desert Land Act, which became law in the month that Hayes became president, March 1877, offered to sell 640 acres at a cost of $1.25 per acre to any individual who irrigated some portion of that land — exactly what portion and how much water must be used and how the water could be obtained all left unspecified. What is unspecified is open to interpretation. The Desert Land Act was a challenge thrown down to the cunning imagination, which tried to interpret the ambiguous law to its advantage. The largest portion of land disposed of under its authority went to Montana, Wyoming, and Colorado livestock grazers, many of them syndicates looking for a home base from which to exploit the unfenced public domain.

The GLO administered a body of public land laws that were poorly drawn, easily subverted, and hopelessly incongruous with one another. Making a bad situation worse, the agency contracted out its land surveying to local entrepreneurs, many of whom barely knew their work or performed it as quickly as they could. Surveyors went out into the field with rods and chains to section off the land, going over hill and dale with little oversight or accountability. Frequently their section or township lines did not meet—they could be many miles off—and then a jag or two would be drawn on the ground, with the hope that some landowner would straighten out the mess at his own expense later on. The surveyors marked sections by cutting a blaze on a tree, raking up a mound of dust, or driving a wooden stake into the earth. Finding a given piece of land after the surveyors had been through was no easy matter. Indians regularly pulled up the stakes for fuel, the blazed tree fell down, or wind blew the dust piles away.

Adding to this incompetence was plenty of venality among the citizenry trying to get their piece of land. They knew the best methods for making fraudulent claims—a boat could be pulled on wheels across a dry piece of ground, for example, with the claim that it was all swamp land, worth only a few cents an acre. All one needed to make a claim good were the right kind of witnesses, the right amount of bribe proffered to a land-office recorder, the right friends in high places. Examples of the latter went straight to the White House. President Grant's own brother won a surveying contract for which he did no work, not even bothering to go to the territory. Secretary Delano's son was able to win surveying contracts over better qualified rivals. The administration of the public land law was rife with lies, confusion, and cheating from bottom to top.

Cleaning up the Department of the Interior, therefore, became one of the key projects of reformers rebelling against the Grant legacy. They wanted more virtue in government, and they wanted more efficiency. Under pressure to achieve those goals, President Hayes appointed one of the most dynamic idealists of the day, Carl Schurz, as Secretary of the Interior. Schurz had been an outspoken student radical in his native Germany. Coming to the United States, he joined the Republican party, supported Lincoln with eloquent speeches in newly learned English, rose to become minister to Spain, Civil War general, newspaper editor, and U.S. Senator, before breaking with the Grant administration over corruption. When he took of-

*J.W. Powell in 1874, the year
when he became forty years old.*
(Courtesy: Grand Canyon
National Park Museum)

fice as Secretary of the Interior, he set out to bring enlightened treatment to the Indians, merit-based appointments and promotions to
his department, a more efficient system of surveying land to the
West, and the conservation of natural resources to the nation.

As director of the Department of the Interior's Geographical and
Geological Survey of the Rocky Mountain Region (Second Division),
Powell was bound to come under intense scrutiny for his steward-
ship. How he spent his funds, how he sought to influence legislators,
whom he hired, what he produced were all subject to the new questioning. On the matter of virtue Powell could rest easy; he was far
above the Grant standard—a model of rectitude, one in spirit with
the reformers of public ethics. When it came to efficiency, however,
he stood in danger of losing his position, not because he was himself
inefficient but because there were clearly too many surveys and surveyors on the federal payrolls. Beside his own office and that of Hayden in the Department of the Interior, there were Wheeler's and
King's organizations in the War Department and the Coast and Geodetic Survey in Treasury. None of them had any connection with the
GLO's sixteen surveyor-generals distributed through the states and

territories, nor with all the private contract surveyors who were marking off sections and quarter-sections. Could money be saved and the
opportunities for abuse curtailed? The answer was yes, but who on
the list must close up shop? Powell looked like a good possibility for
unemployment.

Back in 1874 an investigation of the overlapping and competing
surveys by the House Committee on Public Lands had concluded that
things should be left as they were for the moment. "Each of the surveying parties," the committee said, "has been doing very excellent
work for the benefit of the people and appropriate for the particular
end it had in view." Competition was desirable for bringing out the
best in each group. "The time is approaching, however, when it may
be proper so to consolidate them" into one organization under one
department to produce a grand map of the western territories. When
that time came, the committee strongly hinted, the War Department
would not be the best home nor military men the best directors; civilians ought to be put in charge of all surveying. Wheeler's work had
not been cheap nor scientifically advanced enough to continue indefinitely. He and Hayden repeatedly clashed on the field, making a
spectacle of themselves. The most sensational moment in the committee's hearings came when an army surgeon related how Hayden had
once threatened, "You can tell Wheeler that if he stirs a finger, or at-
tempts to interfere with me or my survey in any way, I will utterly crush
him — as I have enough congressional influence to do so, and will
bring all to bear."[3] Such strutting and fist-shaking was already exceeding any healthy competition, but Congress allowed it to continue.

Three years later, when the issue of overlap and waste resurfaced
in the Hayes administration, Powell's, not Wheeler's or Hayden's,
seemed the most vulnerable among the western scientific surveys. He
had the smallest staff and, in early 1877, he still had an unimpressive
publication record of three short reports and two volumes, the *Exploration of the Colorado River of the West* and the report on Uinta Mountains geology. He had published very few maps, despite all the
topographical work that had been done, because Congress had failed
to pay for them. Gilbert and Dutton had only work in progress, nothing in print. To be sure, Powell had begun preparing what he hoped
would be a long series of scholarly monographs, *Contributions to North
American Ethnology*, but to some cost-minded reformers that kind of
scholarship was a waste of tax dollars.[4]

To bolster his case Powell agreed to publish a controversial report
on the potential mineral wealth of the Black Hills — a place that was

a long way from the Colorado canyons he had been assigned. The report originated in an expedition in 1875 by two geologists, W.P. Jenney and Henry Newton. Gold had been discovered in the hills, setting off a mining rush into what was Sioux land. The federal government followed the rush by authorizing a scientific investigation of the mineral prospects; but when the report was done, Ferdinand Hayden, who had staked out his own claims to this part of the West, refused to publish it as part of his survey. Some said he was jealous. The report showed his own previous work in the area to be inadequate. Newton's former teacher was J.S. Newberry, now on the faculty of Columbia's School of Mines, and he approached both Secretary Schurz and Major Powell to rescue the report "from the selfish and unworthy opposition of another geologist also in the service of the Department of the Interior."[5]

Powell was in no position to turn down a request from Newberry, so he agreed to take charge of it. He more than agreed; he rushed to get the report prepared for publication before he had secured money from Congress to pay for it. When the report finally appeared in 1880, Newton had died of typhoid fever, cutting short the career of a young scientist who might have become another of Powell's protégés. The publication, moreover, came too late to do Powell any good in the search for Congressional approval. What it did do was all harmful; it opened a breach between Hayden and himself that never fully healed. Hayden now saw that he had more than Wheeler to crush if he was going to dominate western surveying.

As a new president and Congress prepared to take office, making noises about a thorough housecleaning, Powell's anxiety intensified. His survey had been cut the previous year, and he might be cut again, or even abolished. On 23 January 1877 he wrote to the friendly Clarence King, who was winding down his own work: "I beg of you to come and help me pull through this year. . . . I have some warm friends who are helping me and some pretty strong opposition and believe your influence here in certain quarters would be sufficient to carry me through. Let me state further that there is no time to lose." Two days later he wrote to Newberry: "I fear that it will be a tight squeeze for us this year, but hope to get through all right." He was confident that the Republican-controlled Senate was "unanimously in favor of increasing my appropriations" but feared what might happen in the Democratic-controlled and more reform-minded House, though there he had recruited both Republicans and Democrats to his support, including James Garfield of Ohio, Samuel Randall of

Pennsylvania (the Speaker of the House), and Abram Hewitt of New York, all prominent in reform circles.

Newberry responded by lobbying vigorously for Powell. In an unsigned letter to Garfield that was probably written by Newberry the author argues that "if it becomes necessary to retrench in the matter of Western explorations, there may be some discrimination made between the good and the bad and the retrenchment may fall where it will do the least harm and the most good." Powell should get the nod, for "he is honest and energetic, and has been doing excellent work, part of which has been paid for from his private means." In contrast, Hayden "is now given to the *political* management of his surveys. . . . [W]hile one organization is purely egotistical and selfish in its object and the scientific work which is accomplished by it costs the country more than it is worth, the other is inspired with the true scientific spirit," and is accomplishing impressive results. Newberry also sent a letter to Congressman Hewitt contrasting the two surveys to Powell's advantage and criticizing Hayden as a fraud who "has lost the sympathy and respect of the scientific men of the country."[6]

On 3 March Congress awarded $50,000 to the Powell Survey for the coming fiscal year, almost twice the sum he had received for the current year and, indeed, the highest sum he had enjoyed since his survey began. Temporarily, his anxieties eased. Despite the political shift that had occurred, he was not only safe but more highly regarded than ever. When a year later the House asked him and Hayden to account for their management over the preceding decade, he had reason to be confident that he had used his monies wisely. Nothing in his financial record had a Grantish smell to it. His men had mapped nearly sixty million acres of the Plateau Province and had completed a rough reconnaissance of another twenty million acres.

Powell's appropriations from 1871 to 1878 totalled $209,000, ranging from a low of $10,000 in fiscal year 1874 to the latest figure of $50,000. (Over that same period Hayden had spent $615,000; Wheeler, $499,000; King, $387,000.) Yet he had managed to recruit outstanding talent, often without paying them a dime. Captain Dutton was paid by the Army as was Colonel Garrick Mallery, a new assistant who took leave from his post to help with the ethnographic work. The government had also paid nothing for the survey's transportation expenses; its members had enjoyed free railroad passes much of the time, or if they were charged half-fares, they often paid their own way. For years Powell had run his organization out of his own house, and when he took over a floor in the Wright Building, at the corner of Eighth and G Streets in Washington, he did not use his direct appropriation to pay any of the rent. As for his publications, he claimed to save money by publishing only final monographs rather than "elaborate annual reports composed of hastily prepared materials, crude and undigested."[7]

The problem of overlap with Hayden was a more difficult embarrassment, though except for the Black Hills report, Powell had been careful to avoid any territorial infringement. Secretary Delano had drawn up separate districts in the mountain West for Hayden and Powell. Within those districts, they were to make topographical and geological maps, on a scale of four miles to the inch, which when joined together would provide a common, standardized atlas. But in making museum collections, they still risked duplication. Powell had recommended that all natural history collecting—vertebrate and invertebrate paleontology, mammalogy, fossil plants, entomology—be turned over to Hayden, while Powell concentrated on ethnography. "The other parties engaged in Western exploration were doing comparatively little in this field," he explained to congressmen, "and hence I determined to push these investigations the harder as I greatly desired to avoid unseemly rivalry and to waste [sic] energy and money in duplicating the work of others."[8] But so far his superiors had not formalized any such division of responsibility.

More sweeping changes than those, however, were going through Powell's mind. The whole survey morass needed cleaning up. Science needed to have a hand in the settlement of the West. The very nature of the West, particularly its arid climate, needed to be understood more clearly. The indiscriminate giveaway of the public lands needed to stop. Small farmers deserved a larger share of the nation's territorial conquests. Time had come for fundamental reform, and Powell was ready to lead it—indeed, to take charge of the nation's westward movement.

By joining the wave of reformers Powell joined a move to elevate an ideal of public service among all who held government jobs, elected or appointed. The Democratic congressman from New York City, Abram Hewitt, an iron manufacturer who had jumped into politics to clean up Tammany Hall, expressed that ideal in a speech before the House of Representatives in May 1876. "The spirit abroad is the spirit of reformation. . . . The people are determined to bring back that better era of the Republic in which when men consecrated themselves to the public service they utterly abnegated all selfish purposes."[9] It remained to be seen just how far that consecration could go in reforming America and how long it could keep itself unspotted in the world.

That "better era of the Republic," the age of Jefferson and Franklin, had given the nation a method of disposing of public lands that had been revolutionary when it was first devised. Its greatest virtue was its seeming simplicity. It was made for newcomers like the Powell family on the recently settled prairie of southern Wisconsin, unfamiliar with the plants and animals, soils, creeks, and climate. They could identify their property lines quickly. Everything else they must learn slowly, by experience.

After nearly a decade of traipsing over the western landscape, Powell was convinced that Jefferson's scheme needed to be reinvented. In a statement to the House Committee on Public Lands on 23 March 1878, he summed up his case:

> The present system of parceling the public lands into townships and sections, arranged systematically in reference to certain meridians and parallels of latitude, and the method of measuring these parcels and determining their position so that they can be readily identified and described, were devised more than eighty years ago for the great valley of the Mississippi. The country in which they were originally adopted was comparatively low, level, and wooded; and the methods of survey were adapted to these conditions. The lands themselves were, as a great body, continuously valuable for agricultural purposes. There were no mountain or desert wastes, and the system of parceling and the method for surveying, then employed, were well suited to the peculiar conditions of that region; but the lands for which the system of parceling and method of surveying were originally intended have mostly been surveyed. In the great mountain region, which is more than four-tenths of the whole United States, exclusive of Alaska, new conditions obtain, which seem to demand some modification of the system of parceling and surveying.[10]

The basic insight he had gained was that the West was not "continuously valuable" for agriculture. Its lands were too heterogeneous, a quality that made them interesting to the scientist but difficult for the settler. How to devise for that huge region a more adaptive land system — and keep it simple and easy to understand — was the challenge.

Compared to Thomas Jefferson, Powell witnessed first-hand the western land's capabilities and the trials of trying to live there. But like all observers his data had to be fitted into his values. Jefferson had sought an America that was secular, rational, friendly to farmers, and individualistic. Powell agreed with all of that except the last term. In place of "individualistic" he put "cooperative."

From the beginning Powell was attentive to the practical implications of his survey work, though he was never much interested in practical military problems, as Wheeler was, or the contributions the West could make to mining corporations and the industrial economy, as King was. Powell studied the land with the eyes of a farmer. Any farmer wanted to know which acres were good for cropping or pasturing livestock or providing fuel and fencing. Such practicalities suggested the need for land classification. The GLO surveyors had often noted on their field maps where woodlands or wetlands lay, but they mainly had in mind the plotting of sections and townships rather than classification. Powell's survey, once the topographic outlines had been established, began to distinguish what the capabilities of the land might be.

Pressure from the Secretary of the Interior's office to make the scientific surveys more useful to the public confirmed Powell in this inclination. From 1874 on it became boiler-plate instruction that Hayden and Powell indicate on their maps "the areas of grass, timber, and mineral lands, and such other portions of the country surveyed as may be susceptible of cultivation by means of irrigation."[11] In effect, land classification had become an objective of government science. Hayden claimed that his *Atlas of Colorado*, covering an area of over one hundred thousand square miles, "shows with remarkable clearness, by means of colors, the agricultural and pastoral lands, the pine and other forests, the barren lands, and those above timberline — all the valuable mineral deposits, as coal, silver, and gold."[12] But how that broad-gauged information helped a settler know where to locate a farm or mine was not so clear. Powell wanted to go beyond the instructions to coordinate the laws of land disposal and settlement with a scheme of classification.

He began to study rainfall over the entire West, relying on the Smithsonian Institution for help. When Joseph Henry became director of the Smithsonian in 1846, his first major project was to obtain regular weather reports from a nationwide group of voluntary observers, many of them surgeons or their assistants at western military forts. In 1873 the Smithsonian published all of its available rainfall records as a contribution to the study of climatology.

The author of that monograph was the cadaverous-looking Charles Schott, a scientist in the U.S. Coast Survey and member of the National Academy of Sciences. Schott was another of the talented refugees from the aborted 1848 revolution in Germany—trained as a civil engineer at the Technische Hochschule in Karlsruhe before his career was cut short by political upheaval. In America he gained international recognition for his studies in terrestrial magnetism. Along the way he took up the investigation of climate. With Cleveland Abbe, a mapmaker, he put together a national map of isohyets, or lines connecting points receiving equal rainfall, for a volume in the Census of 1870, the *Statistical Atlas of the United States.* They color-coded the map, using shades of blue to designate areas getting more than twenty inches per annum and white to show those getting less. Most of the West was as white as a sheet of muslin. Their twenty-inch isohyet ran up the Rio Grande and Pecos River and, with a broken line to indicate incomplete data, wobbled northward over the plains toward Minnesota.[13]

The significance of the twenty-inch isohyet was that agricultural crops generally required that amount, or more, of rainfall per year to mature. Imported European crops such as wheat and oats needed that amount, and so did indigenous crops such as beans and corn. If it did not fall as natural precipitation, then the water must be added artificially, as the Indians of the southwestern deserts had been doing for centuries.

Powell's first effort to get financial support from Congress, in 1868, had been endorsed by Secretary Henry for the light his explorations might throw on how to get sufficient water in a dry land. "The professor intends to give special attention to the hydrology of the mountain system in its relation to agriculture." High mountains, Henry explained, trap the vapor floating inland from the Pacific Ocean, depriving the soil of "an essential ingredient of productiveness." But this vapor could be "reclaimed for the uses of the husbandman by a judicious system of irrigation, founded on a critical knowledge of the hydrology and topography of the country."[14]

In an April 1874 letter to the House Committee on Public Lands, Powell pointed up the social and economic issues he saw posed by the rainfall data and western topography. The letter called for a new scientific survey under the Department of the Interior "for the purpose of determining the several areas which can . . . be redeemed by

*Charles A. Schott, "Rain Chart of the United States." (From J.W. Powell, Report
on the Arid Lands of the United States [1878].)*

irrigation." He warned that two-fifths of the country "has a climate so
arid that agriculture cannot be pursued without irrigation." The crux
of the problem was not simply that the westerner needed to irrigate
but that there was not enough moisture running down from the high
mountains to irrigate the entire region. Perhaps a mere 1 to 3 percent of the enormous white space on the map could be "redeemed"
through irrigation. Already the smaller streams had been put to use.
"The larger streams, which will irrigate somewhat greater areas, can
only be managed by cooperative organizations, great capitalists, or by
the General or State governments."[15] In other words, the country was
facing a different frontier than it had ever faced before, with momentous institutional and technological implications.

Powell tried to interest the scientific community in the aridity
problem when he addressed the spring 1877 meeting of the National
Academy of Sciences in Washington. His address on "The Public Domain," as reported in the *New York Tribune*, was illustrated with colored charts showing the nation divided into two parts—humid and
arid. Agricultural settlement had nearly reached its limit in the

humid part. Florida, Alabama, Louisiana, and Mississippi still had their unsettled spaces, but those were mainly swamps and salt marshes—not land that any farmer could use. Only a small part of Minnesota offered any new agricultural potential. Almost all the good land in the eastern states had been sold or given away.

That left for future agricultural expansion only that vast arid country to the west, extending over some 1.5 million square miles, yet only a tiny portion there was irrigable. The present land system, Powell warned, with its promise of a self-sufficient homestead for the landless family, was no longer workable. It must be scrapped and something new put in its place. After he finished his remarks, Joseph Henry commented that he too had long been convinced of the "unfitness of our public land distribution." His meterological studies had led him, as they had led Powell, to see that the country was not uniform in its characteristics. And if it was not uniform, then it could no longer be cut up into exactly rectangular sections all promising exactly the same potential.[16]

Nothing less than the Smithsonian Institution, then, stood behind Powell's dawning awareness that the Jeffersonian grid was out of date and out of place. But it was Powell who went beyond the scientific data to see a danger looming for democracy. For if the land system was outmoded, then the people hurt most were the common folk— seeking land as his own parents had done and bound to be defeated.

The West was a land of paradox—strikingly heterogeneous in its terrain, starkly homogeneous in its scarcity of water resources. Although many chose to see the land through a haze of extravagant optimism, as William Gilpin did, others were more realistic. The journalist Justin Colburn, who accompanied Moran on his first trip to the Grand Canyon, did not miss the shift from wet to dry. One day out of Omaha, his train entered "the rainless realm, where drouth and aridity hold indisputable sway. This is the great fact, the fact gigantic in proportions when considered in its economical aspects and its importance to the American nation." Colburn wrote those words after talking with Powell in Salt Lake City, but he was ready to listen after days of looking out the train window. "The one fact that impresses itself constantly, till it fixes an indelible impression overlying all others," he wrote, "is the utter desolation, the barrenness, the worthlessness of all the country passed through west of a point—say 150 miles from Omaha."[17]

What struck a traveling journalist so forcibly became a daily fact of life for the people who made their homes in this country. Prominent among them were the Mormons, who had migrated by foot across that barrenness Colburn described, pulling heavily laden handcarts behind them. When they tried to plant a patch of potatoes in their new Zion, they first had to soften the baked earth with water. By the time Powell first encountered them, the Mormons had two decades of experience with aridity, and their experience profoundly influenced his thinking and the message he took to Washington.

A federal land office did not open in Salt Lake City until 1869, giving the Mormons plenty of time to devise their own approach to settling the country. Without hesitation, they ignored the section and township grid and devised a more flexible, adaptive plan. Wherever there was water, they planted a community: Logan, Provo, Parowan, St. George, Kanab, each as square and geometrical as they could make it, with wide streets, deep house lots, and irrigation ditches flowing to backyard gardens. Moving outward from this core, they established farms in the valleys, allotting the land in ten-acre increments according to the needs and abilities of different families, some of them large, with a dozen or more wives, some small and poor. An average farm was ten to fifty acres—a minuscule estate by the standard of the 160-acre American homestead ideal. But each of those farms was irrigated, and the work of irrigating twenty or thirty acres was more than enough to keep a family busy. When the water was adequate, those acres were also enough to provide a sufficiency of production.[18]

In the beginning they permitted no free market in land. Without federal surveyors and the homesteading system in place, there was no one to buy land from, no one to pay, so they squatted without permission or clear legal status. The Saints looked to the Church, its bishops, and its president, Brigham Young, for guidance on where to live and how to divide up the land. They were orderly and obedient. The outcome was hardly egalitarian, for the best lands and water rights usually went to those well up in the church hierarchy. But the most humble farmer was guaranteed at least a minimum of ten acres and a share of the water. After they had taken care of themselves, the church officials divided the land "by ballot, or casting lots, as Israel did in the days of old."[19]

Water as well as land had to be divided, and this necessity led the Mormons to create a set of water rights that had no precedent in the East. In a water-rich country the law of riparian rights dominated. Land owners had the right to use water flowing over or adjacent to their property so long as they did not diminish its quantity and infringe on downstream users. Irrigation, however, required taking the water out of its course and consuming it, leaving little return flow. The farmer whose land lay well away from a stream or river must either take the water across someone else's land or perish. So, facing those new realities, the Mormons abandoned the riparian law and devised a set of rights that apportioned the supply of water among all those who owned farm land, giving to each cultivator what was needed and no more. Water rights inhered in land ownership.

Before abandoning their earlier home in Nauvoo, Illinois, the Saints went on trade missions to Santa Fe where they observed the irrigation practices of the Hispanic communities in the Rio Grande Valley. The basic principle in those towns was that water must be shared for the common good, not made the exclusive property or right of any individual. Beyond picking up that cooperative principle, Mormons borrowed the time-tested methods of building community ditches, or *acequias*, brought from Spain to the New World and merged with native American techniques.[20] Then the Saints set about diverting Utah's streams by constructing brush, earth, and rock dams, forcing the flow into ditches that ran to every farmer's rows of crops. Such an infrastructure required the careful organization of all the settlers to keep the dams repaired — they washed out frequently in spring floods — to keep the ditches free of obstructions, and to assure that the agreed-upon amount of water went to every user.[21]

Beyond their narrow circle of irrigated farms lay the dry lands that no system of irrigation could ever reach or turn green with crops. That persistently brown horizon was extensive. Utah counted only 119,000 improved farm acres in 1870, virtually all of them irrigated, out of a territorial area of over fifty million acres. The only possible agriculture across most of the countryside was the grazing of sheep and cattle. This the Mormons did too, managing the land as a commons. They did not establish isolated, independent ranches as other Americans were doing at the time. Instead, they created a village herd, to which each owner provided only a few head, and drove them onto the nearby bench lands or mountain slopes to graze under joint supervision. By the late 1870s this system prevailed throughout the territory and was expanding southeastward toward Moab and Bluff and westward into the Great Basin, though already "gentile" cattlemen were beginning to crowd in and contest the range.[22]

Before he died in 1877, Brigham Young kept his people on a cooperative path in their use of land and water. While the rest of the nation was in full cry for laissez-faire freedom, the Mormons struggled toward prosperity within a communitarian ethos. That was so from their first arrival in Zion, but it became especially pronounced in Young's last years. As mainstream American society bore down on them, he called for a renewal of the cooperative spirit. Those most willing to try were the towns lying on the remote southern edge, where survival against the Indians and the natural elements was most difficult. Colonists there began organizing themselves into a new institution, the United Order of Zion, based on community property and the redistribution of wealth. The colony on the Muddy River that had been abandoned, where Ingalls and Powell worked to create a Paiute reservation, had been such an Order, and when they retreated into Utah those colonists determined to try again. In 1875 they formed Orderville in the Long Valley north of Kanab and organized their economic life into a series of departments, all owned and worked in common: Boarding House, Store, Grist Mill, Farm, Canal.

Powell and his men were carrying out their investigations precisely during this time of communitarian renewal among the Mormons, and their base camp at Kanab sat squarely in the middle of that ferment. In 1871 the people of Kanab created a Farmer's Association with power to "dictate the putting in and cultivating of the land, to put a price upon all labor, grain, and produce of all kinds." The next year a cooperative farming area was planned just below the town, near where the Powell men were setting up their base line for triangulation. Two years later those communitarian gropings led to a fullfledged United Order, presided over by Brigham Young's nephew, though it was soon riven by a party spirit and the United Order fell apart.[23] But if the utopian dream of a propertyless society did not fully materialize, the idealism from which it sprang was more long-lived, as was the view that living successfully in this water-scarce environment required more cooperation than Americans usually practiced.

Such idealism did not mean that the Mormons always took better care of their natural resources than anyone else. They drained streams dry, destroyed riparian habitat, and assaulted the native flora and fauna even more violently than they assaulted the Indians. As their herds increased, they overgrazed the scattered grasses until erosion became a serious problem. The many rules they made for themselves did not prevent them from overstocking and depleting. Clarence Dutton, describing the Kanab-Pipe Spring region in 1881, noted that

> ten years ago the desert spaces outspreading to the southward were covered with abundant grasses, affording rich pasturage to horses and cattle. Today hardly a blade of grass is to be found

within ten miles of the spring, unless upon the crags and mesas of the Vermilion Cliffs behind it. The horses and cattle have disappeared, and the bones of many of the latter are bleached upon the plains in front of it.

The cause was in part a natural shift toward an even drier climate. But "even if there had been no drought the feeding of cattle would have impoverished and perhaps wholly destroyed the grass by cropping it clean before the seeds were mature," a practice, Dutton noted, that was generally the case throughout Utah and Nevada.[24]

A cooperative spirit avails nothing if a people do not understand or acknowledge the limits of the land. Mormons often did not. They were like other Americans moving west in their desire to force the natural world to yield a substantial livelihood for them and all their numerous progeny. They sometimes talked expansively of their Zion as though it were an earthly paradise created for them by a benevolent God, who would favor them with abundant rain, a gentle climate, a bountiful harvest if they worked hard enough. But the people whom Powell met were also, on the whole, like him in their capacity for realism. They were not so trapped in tradition that they could not innovate to meet the environmental challenges before them, even to the point of scrapping a well-established eastern system of dividing the land and water.

Powell, as he was puzzling over the implications of Shott's rainfall map, found among the Mormons an inspiring model of adaptation and innovation. They provided a fund of tested folk experience that had been hard-wrestled from this exacting place. Other Americans, including congressional legislators, paid little attention to that experience because Mormon society looked so bizarre, so threatening in its marriage customs, its theocratic politics, its anticapitalist tendencies. All those peculiarities must disappear, "gentiles" insisted, and the Saints must conform to the American way. To a very large extent that capitulation in fact occurred soon after Young's demise. But for Powell the model of a cooperative commonwealth growing up in the desert could and should be salvaged from the Mormon experiment. The essential lessons that democracy must learn in the West were: Be prepared to work together and be prepared to change.

On 1 April 1878 Powell transmitted to the Commissioner of the General Land Office, J.A. Williamson, a report on the lands of the arid region of the United States. It speedily made its way to Congress, which ordered it printed as the latest publication of the Powell Survey.[25] At first glance the report looked like any other scientific document, for it was loaded with statistical tables, charts and maps, and scholarly prose. It included Charles Schott's rain chart along with a map of Utah Territory folded into a back pocket. The latter was more than two feet wide, three feet long, drawn on a scale of five miles to the inch, with the rugged topography shown in hachures, the rail roads, wagon roads, and telegraph lines in inked lines, and the irrigable and forested lands in splotches of color. This was where Harry Thompson's and Fred Dellenbaugh's sketches in a canvas tent had finally led. Thompson was represented also by a chapter on the irrigable lands drained by the Colorado River, Dutton on the irrigable lands of the Sevier valley, and Gilbert on the Great Salt Lake and its rising water level. A chapter by Willis Drummond Jr. on land grants in aid of internal improvements followed a national map showing the broad swaths that had been given to the railroad corporations. But finally this was J.W. Powell's book. His two opening chapters set forth in sweeping terms the physical characteristics of the arid region and the new land system needed there.

Once more Powell began with an apology. He had intended to write a full-blown work on the public domain, but, as in the case of his big book on the Plateau Province, he had been distracted. What he did not say was that everything he wrote — every letter, memo, chapter — had to be dictated to a secretary and transcribed in longhand before revision and printing. Added to his physical handicap was his restlessness of mind, his constant flitting from subject to subject, all of them connected in his own mind but none covered in great depth. What he lacked in discipline or focus, however, he made up for in creative synthesis. His brief chapters, sober and authoritative, did as much as any larger book could have done to lay out the fundamental choices facing the westward-moving democracy.

Although Utah provided the archetype, Powell addressed the entire arid region whose eastern border he identified as the one hundredth meridian, a line roughly equivalent to the twenty-inch isohyet. Geographers would later use the ninety-eighth meridian (Hutchinson instead of Dodge City in Kansas) as a closer approximation, but the point was that climate divided the country into almost equal halves. The western boundary was the Pacific Ocean, except for the rainy belt of northwestern California, western Oregon, and western Washington that Powell called the anomalous Lower Columbia Region.

Other complications broke down an oversimplified picture of "two Americas," one wet, the other dry. Most important, a transition zone, the Subhumid Region, ran straight across the path of settlement, covering, for example, much of Kansas. And within the predominantly arid states and territories the heterogeneity of relief provided a diversity of vertical zones: irrigable lands at the lower elevations, forests growing on the moisture-abundant mountains, and "pasturage" lying between.

The timber lands did not, for Powell, require any new legislation to protect them from misuse. In Utah only a minuscule part of the territory supported any forest suitable for lumber. Most of the trees were too small to be valuable for more than fencing or fuel, and their inaccessibility made them safe from excessive cutting. But they did need protection from fires that every summer raged across the high country. His boat parties had smelled smoke as they floated down the Green and Colorado rivers; at other times the haze had interfered with his survey crew's triangulations. "In the main," he wrote, "these fires are set by Indians."[26] As they were pushed out of the lowlands by white settlers, the natives turned to collecting upland furs and selling them. They set the fires to drive wild animals to their guns, turning forests into charcoal. Encourage the Indians to move onto reservations and take up farming, and the burning would stop, the forests survive. Lumbermen could then be allowed to harvest whatever they could sell in a sparsely populated market.

The other two categories of land, however, required new legislation, and Powell offered two bills for Congress to consider. The first would allow any nine or more people to organize themselves into irrigation districts. They should take up only land that had been certified by surveyors as irrigable. Within such a district no individual should own more than eighty acres. Every individual property within that district should have a guaranteed share of the water. Together, the settlers should build their own water system. "The redemption of all these lands," he explained, "will require extensive and comprehensive plans, for the execution of which aggregated capital or cooperative labor will be necessary. Here, individual farmers, being poor men, cannot undertake the task."[27]

Apparently, since his proposed bill is silent on the point, Powell would leave each district to decide how to carry out its plans. He was emphatic on only one particular: local farmers must own the water. It must not fall into the hands of private companies who might, if they controlled it, achieve a monopoly.

If in the eagerness for present development a land and water
system shall grow up in which the practical control of agriculture
shall fall into the hands of water companies, evils will result
therefrom that generations may not be able to correct, and the
very men who are now lauded as benefactors to the country
will, in the ungovernable reaction which is sure to come, be
denounced as oppressors of the people.[28]

That unambiguous principle of ownership left, nonetheless, a few
questions unanswered.

"All the waters of all the arid lands will eventually be taken from
their natural channels," Powell predicted, and be totally consumed.[29] Even the mighty Colorado, running through its stupendous canyons, a river that had afforded Powell the most thrilling
moments of his life, must some day become a dried-up channel as irrigators diverted its entire current to their fields. But how were irrigation districts of nine or more persons supposed to achieve such a
feat? Requiring vast sums of money and expertise, the capture of all
the water in the West inevitably threatened to remove power from
the hands of poor farmers.

Powell, to be sure, offered no grandiose vision of plenty. If every
drop of water in Utah was captured for agricultural use, only 2.8 percent of the entire territory could be irrigated—or 1.4 million acres.
Gilbert and he derived that estimate from the fact that irrigators
needed a flow of one cubic foot of water per second for every eighty
to one hundred acres. Measure the total stream flow across Utah and
they could determine the irrigable potential. That tiny fraction of the
land allowed plenty of room for agricultural growth—in fact an increase of ten times over current development—though 97 percent
of Utah could never become another Illinois or Ohio.[30]

The unredeemed part of the country had only one conceivable
use for the rural settler: a pasture for livestock. Powell's second proposed bill would authorize pasturage homesteads (or ranches) organized into districts on the public lands. Given the scantiness of
vegetation—the fact that ten or more acres of grass were needed to
raise a single cow—those homesteaders would need at least 2,560
acres each, along with a water right sufficient for twenty irrigated
acres for raising winter feed.[31] Again, a group of nine or more persons would have to come together to set up such a grazing district.
Once organized, they would pasture their cattle or sheep in a common, unfenced herd, much as the Mormons had been doing.

As many copies of the report as Powell could lay his hands on went out to newspaper editors and other influential persons. Recipients included the *Rocky Mountain News*, the *Chicago Tribune*, the *San Francisco Chronicle*, various scientists, clergymen, and professors. Some of them responded quickly. The *New York Tribune*, for example, devoted two long columns to reviewing the report the day after it reached Congress.[32]

In that legislative body Powell lobbied his old friend and supporter, Garfield of Ohio, throwing in a little flattery ("knowing that your interest in public affairs extends far beyond the local and transient contests of the hour"). Powell warned that, since about 1870, the great tide of western migration had been forced to halt because it is "impossible for poor men to obtain homes and become agriculturists" in the arid region. "Thus agricultural industries have not kept pace with mining industries." Read the first two chapters, he urged. "I do not wish to claim too much for the plan proposed, but I do wish to urge the importance of some change in the present system."[33]

At least one western congressman took up the challenge. On 1 May the *Deseret News* reported that Peter Wigginton, the Democratic congressman who represented California south of Sacramento and was a member of the House Committee on Public Lands, had introduced two "very novel and important land bills, which are likely to give rise to considerable discussion."[34] Wigginton was confident that they would pass. But on 21 June the same newspaper reported that the bills had not been taken up and had to be carried over into the next session. When that session began, Powell had a second edition ready for distribution, but still there was no action. In fact, the bills would never get out of the Public Lands committee, which was dominated by men who were far less sympathetic to Powell's ideas than Wigginton.[35]

The large economic interests did not line up in support, understandably, since Powell's motive was to save the West for the people, not the corporations. Among the conspicuously silent voices was that of Collis P. Huntington, vice president of the Central Pacific Railroad, an aggressive monopolist and the driving force behind the company that Frank Norris portrayed in his novel *The Octopus* (1901). When Powell's talk before the National Academy of Sciences made the New York papers, Huntington wrote enthusiastically: "My own mind has been revolving something of the kind for some years." The country needed "a radical change" in the manner of surveying the West.[36] But the only change he wanted would allow railroad corporations to consolidate their checkerboard land grants into larger blocks that could be developed and sold as irrigated farms. Otherwise, the lands were useless. Huntington had misunderstood what Powell had in mind, and when the truth came out the mogul said no more.

Powell's bills failed, according to his critics, because he did not understand the economic forces that were revolutionizing the West and the nation, transforming the country into a modern industrial state. He was too old-fashioned, agrarian, backward-looking, and nostalgic for a vanishing village America, which he wanted to see recreated in the arid region. Naively, he expected individualistic Americans to follow a communitarian ethos that belonged to a precapitalist, preindustrial era. The celebrated explorer of the Colorado River turned out to be an impractical dreamer.

Such were the reasons commonly given for the deadly silence that fell around the Powell report of 1878. But the author's naiveté was not the main difficulty. Most of the failure to face reality lay with those congressmen who refused to give the proposed bills careful thought or to confront the scientific evidence behind them or to take the Mormon experience seriously. Among them were politicians from eastern, southern, and western states who stubbornly resisted change. The land system that had been good enough for America over the past eighty years was good enough still. They expected, indeed they insisted, that the West not be different from what they had known.

Powell's land reforms failed to get a hearing mainly because many politicians were in the grip of a dream of their own. It promised that the West would become another Eden of easy, abundant wealth and happy, innocent, people. They ignored the warnings of journalists such as Colburn and the sobering hardships of real, on-the-ground settlers. No matter how arid the climate or how limited the water, they insisted, the West was sure to become another promised land. God would make it so. His chosen people would never suffer denial.[37]

The world of science included a few believers in that Edenic dream. Ferdinand Hayden, for example succumbed — eager, as he admitted he was, "to report that which will be most pleasing to the people of the West, providing there is any foundation for it in nature." More than a decade before Powell's reform proposals, Hayden thought he had evidence that the planting of trees on Nebraska homesteads was ameliorating the climate. Rainfall had increased with agricultural settlement and was becoming more equally distributed through the year. Plant enough trees across the Great Plains and aridity would give way to well-watered fertility. A member of Hayden's survey team who became a professor at the University of Nebraska, Samuel Aughey, also bought the dream of unlimited bounty and paired up with a town promoter, Charles Dana Wilber, to sell the idea that "rain follows the plow."[38]

Whether tree planting or plowing could work such magic across the entire arid region was never addressed by Hayden or his disciples, but the Powell survey did give it serious consideration. Gilbert, in his chapter on the Great Salt Lake, allowed that the lake might be rising due to human agency. He went on, however, to criticize the Hayden circle for leaping to conclusions about plow agriculture, nor did he take seriously another popular argument, that telegraph wires were affecting precipitation. What he concluded, and Powell followed him, was that stream flow was being enhanced by deforestation in the highlands. They did not expect that the desert would vanish any time soon.[39]

The West, according to Wallace Stegner, "has not been so much settled as raided—first for its furs, then for its minerals, then for its grass, then in some places for its scenery," and with every raid the raiders have ignored consequences.[40] Powell warned about those consequences, ecological and political, that persistence in old land policies must bring, and the raiders and boosters fought him as they fought reality.

But it must be added that the failure of the arid lands report was more complicated than a losing confrontation between popular myth and scientific reality. Powell was himself responsible for some of the resistance he met, for he made a strategic mistake in trying to sell his reforms. He tied them to a scientific establishment in the East that was beginning to demand that the West be brought under their intelligent control. They called for more centralized authority that could bring greater efficiency in the use and development of the region's resources. Powell wanted their support and approval. Where they led him, however, was not exactly where he wanted to go.

In mid-October 1878 Powell was in the field with his survey crew when a letter reached him from a committee of the National Academy of Sciences, soliciting his views on what plan should be adopted for surveying and mapping the territories. He had been expecting the letter—indeed had earlier sent copies of his arid lands report to the committee. Immediately he hustled back to Washington. On 1 November he had his statement ready—a long, brilliant, combative treatise that threw into the shadows much briefer communications from the Corps of Engineers, the Land Office, and Dr. Hayden.

More than that, he instantly assumed the generalship of a battle to re-organize science in the federal government — a battle he would deci-sively win, though it would cost him a war.

In the previous spring Congress had ordered the academy to look into the survey jumble. The idea came from Abram Hewitt, though he probably borrowed it from his friend Clarence King, a member of the academy since 1876.[41] The academy had been chartered by Con-gress during the Civil War to provide expert advice on demand, and its membership was the self-selected elite of American science. Hay-den was a member, Powell was elected in 1880, Gilbert in 1883, and Dutton the year after that. Its president was Joseph Henry, but his death in May left the vice-president, Othniel Marsh of Yale, as acting president. Marsh moved quickly to establish a committee of eight to carry out Congress's order, including James Dana, William Rodgers, John Newberry, W.P. Trowbridge, Simon Newcomb, Alexander Agas-siz, and himself as chair.

Powell's statement was a blast that reduced the entire jerry-built sys-tem of western surveying to a pile of kindling. "The present multipli-cation of organizations," he charged, "is unscientific, excessively expensive, and altogether vicious, preventing comprehensive, thor-ough, and honest research, stimulating unhealthy rivalry, and leading to the production of sensational and briefly popular rather than solid and enduring results."[42] The private contract method of land-office surveys came in for his heaviest fire. He reminded the academy how hard it is to run a straight line on a round earth and how little training the typical contractor had to do that. But the contractor did have an interest in making a profit; and since he was paid by the number of townships he marked off, he had good reason to turn them in fast and full of errors. In the arid West, where settlements tended to be widely scattered oases, there was no need to lay out ephemeral townships across the wide intervening desert where no one would ever live — yet that is what the contractors did repeatedly and got paid for doing. The system required them to do so because it had to be continuous; each new section line had to be one mile from the last.

Altogether the government had spent $23 million on contracted work, and "it was absolutely valueless for scientific purposes." Other than the coordinates of a claim, Americans could get little useful in-formation out of it.

> Forests, prairies, plains, and mountains have been traversed in
> many directions; millions of miles have been run with compasses

and chain; chart after chart has been constructed with great labor; folio on folio has been placed among the national archives, containing facts incoherent and worthless; and the record has been made that here are trees, there swamps, and yonder glades; that the lands surveyed are level, hilly, or rolling; that sandstones are found here, limestones there, or granite elsewhere; and so the records of useless facts have been piled up from year to year until they are buried in their own mass. That all of this labor and expense has been lost to science may well challenge the attention of the learned men of America, and when properly understood, they will not be slow in demanding a reform.[43]

The solution he offered was to put all of this work into the hands of scientific experts employed on a fixed federal salary. In the end it would be cheaper, more reliable, and more informative to do it that way, because the scientists could identify which lands had coal or lead deposits and which did not, which lands had water and which did not.

Behind Powell's withering critique was his desire to enlarge the leadership role that science played in a modern democracy. Science, he argued, had become essential to American life and deserved government support. But the government should fund scientists only where they had a practical bearing on the wealth and welfare of the greatest number of people. A single comprehensive "geographical and geological survey" qualified because it would produce a better understanding of the country's natural resources — minerals and the products of the soil. Botany and zoology were not proper subjects for federal subsidy since they were more philosophical than useful inquiries. The government should stay out of such fields and leave them to private initiative. On the other hand, the study of ethnology deserved funding because it held answers to the pressing question of what to do with the Indians.

The Major expected enormous social benefits to flow from government science. It could help settlers find a secure home and solve the country's "great engineering problems." A single centralized bureau of experts could figure out how to drain swamps, stop disastrous flooding, and control rivers as large as the Mississippi. Millions of acres in Florida could be "redeemed" by draining Lake Okeechobee and growing cotton or sugarcane on the bottom. "The time must come soon when all the waters of the Missouri will be spread over the great plains, and the bed of the river will be dry."[44]

Then there was the West, "a region of vast and inexhaustible wealth," waiting for expert scientific investigation to locate that wealth and show how to develop it. Just a few months earlier Powell had idealized small Mormon villages of self-organizing common folk, but now he spun out a Faustian dream of scientific experts managing the earth and all its resources. Nature put limits on humankind, but they could be eased by the power of organized science.

The National Academy's recommendation took a more restrained approach, though its main outlines followed Powell closely. On 6 November the full academy voted to accept the committee report (the sole dissenter was Marsh's bitter personal rival in paleontology, Edward Cope of the University of Pennsylvania), which called for dismantling the Wheeler, Hayden, and Powell surveys, along with the GLO's district surveyor-generals, and putting the entire public domain under two agencies to be set up within the Department of the Interior. All mensuration of land should be done by a Coast and Interior Survey, successor to the Coast and Geodetic office. All investigation of "geological structure, natural resources, and products," including land classification, should be the work of a new "Geological Survey." Civilians should run both agencies, nothing being left with the military, and those civilians should be properly credentialed scientists. Finally, the academy called for a high-level commission to codify the morass of public land laws and devise a new method of parceling land in the arid region where the homestead and preemption system was "both impractical and undesirable." Nothing was said about draining Lake Okeechobee or about the utility of studying Indians.[45]

Powell's hand in the outcome was obvious. His stenographer and assistant on Indian work, James Pilling, wrote, "I see the Academy has made its report and it sounds wonderfully like something I have read — and possibly written — before. What will become of we poor ethnologists?"[46]

If Powell was disappointed by the omission of ethnology, he did not show it as he wheeled his energies into full battle position. Congress had to implement the recommendations, and powerful agencies, particularly the War Department, were ready to fight. All the GLO surveyor-generals and their contractors, many of them political friends of congressmen, were not prepared to fade away into the sunset. Nor was Hayden ready to retire. He was not unhappy to see his nemesis Wheeler recommended for retirement, but if there was to be a new superagency established, Hayden wanted to be its director. Such an outcome was inconceivable to Powell, and he took charge of lobbying the academy plan through Congress — and of stopping Hayden from vaulting into power.

Powell made it known that he was not himself a candidate for director of a consolidated survey. His future, he had decided, lay in ethnological research, not the natural sciences. Some urged him to be more ambitious. A geologist at the University of Cincinnati insisted that "no other man in the continent [is] so well qualified to take charge of this work. . . . What is wanted is a man who has the proper appreciation of the *comprehensive character of such a work*." Certainly, no one else had spoken as authoritatively as Powell about what a new system must achieve. But as Dutton explained, "he renounces all claim or desire or effort to be the head of a united survey and would merely ask for a subordinate position under it secured to him by executive appointment. The administrative duties of such a position would render it impossible for him to acquire the only thing he really covets and that is a standing among men of science resting upon his own personal contribution to it."[47]

Powell's nominee for director of a consolidated survey was his friend Clarence King. No substantial help in the battle, however, came from King, who was living the good life in New York City, though always as an attentive spectator and a willing candidate. Hayden, in contrast, began pulling in all favors due, soliciting any testimonial he could get from abroad, working old political connections. All through the previous months he had failed to take the lead on or show any grasp of the large issues being debated. His statement to the academy committee was a pathetic bit of self-advertising, but then he had gone along with the nearly unanimous vote in utter silence. Secretly, he was suffering from syphilis contracted from a prostitute, a disease that would kill him in another nine years.[48] His ailment left him lethargic and ineffectual at critical moments. But if he was confused about what was going on, he was certainly clearheaded about grabbing the proposed directorship. On 20 February 1879 Powell wrote to Marsh that "the most vigorous efforts are being made by Dr. Hayden to get the appointment under the bill, which is almost sure to pass." Powell requested letters from scientists around the country to counter those Hayden was collecting.

The danger was that if Hayden grasped control of the government's chief science department, he (the optimist about rain-making plows and man-made forests) might fail or refuse to push through any substantial reform in the land survey system. For Powell, Hayden was a symbol of the Grant era's incompetence and corruption that must be swept out of office. In response to a request from Congressman Garfield he sent a devastating assessment of Hayden's fitness to do science: "He is a charlatan who has bought his way to fame" by taking credit for the research and ideas of others, contributing nothing himself. For all his ambition, his work had been fragmentary, disjointed, unsystematic, incoherent — the harsh adjectives piled up and up. In contrast to King, who has "an orderly, sagacious, logical mind which places him among the truly great men of science," Hayden is incapable of drawing up any plan or method. For twenty years "he rambled aimlessly over a region big enough for an empire," frittering away large appropriations while trying to impress "the wonder-loving populace." He is "a wretched geologist," his mind "utterly untrained to severe scientific logic and analysis."[49]

Severe but true, an assessment that leading scientists like Newberry had uttered before. It went, however, beyond what was called for and bordered on invective and animosity. Having been treated with condescension and contempt by him for years, Powell despised Hayden in every way and was worried that the wily, mean-spirited conniver might once again fool Congress and gain command over a creation that Powell had worked hard — much harder than anyone else — to achieve. Nonetheless, he might have been more restrained, considering that his own work often had something of the fragmentary and disjointed about it too. Like Hayden, he had curried favor by furnishing photographs to the wonder-loving committees that controlled his funding. Though his own expertise in geology was greater than Hayden's, he too borrowed extensively from King and others.

Before any man could get the new position in his pocket, it first had to be authorized. Congress took the entire winter to make up its mind. Fearing that the Public Lands Committee would simply sit on the academy report (as they had done on the arid lands report), the House leadership sent it to the Appropriations Committee, chaired by the reform-minded John Atkins, a Democrat from Tennessee. Naturally, that left a few politicians sputtering threats when it came to the floor in February, most of them westerners who dominated the Public Lands Committee.

Slyly, the essentials of the academy plan were embedded in the Sundry Civil Appropriations bill, one of the last and largest pieces of legislation that had to be passed before the 45th Congress could adjourn. Even Garfield, though he supported the academy plan, was not happy that so important a reform was slipped into a bill to tie up loose fiscal ends. Confident of success, Atkins and Wigginton ignored him and argued the bill on the floor, following a script crafted by Powell.

Those who spoke against the academy plan, it turned out, were not all members of the Public Lands Committee. They included Horace Page, who had been a mail contractor representing the mining community of Placerville, California; Dudley Haskell, a shoe merchant from Lawrence, Kansas; Martin Maginnis, a Helena, Montana, newspaper publisher; Mark Dunnell, a lawyer from Owatonna, Minnesota; and most prominently, Thomas Patterson, a trial lawyer from Denver, Colorado (who was a member of the Public Lands Committee).

None of them could match Powell's familiarity with land and water issues in the arid West. For example, Patterson had only arrived in the region in 1872. Five years Powell's junior, he had been born in Ireland and raised on Long Island, New York, and in Crawfordsville, Indiana, where his father ran a jewelry store. After being admitted to the bar, he moved to Colorado and two years later was elected territorial delegate to Congress. He served one term, was defeated for re-election (by one vote out of thirty-eight thousand cast), contested the count successfully, and came roaring victoriously back to the House just in time to get Powell's arid lands report on his desk, a report he instantly rejected. Patterson was no tool of the special interests. Eventually he left the Democratic party for the Populists, and after acquiring an interest in the *Rocky Mountain News*, used his paper to champion the cause of labor and denounce corporate power. Had he read Powell's words more carefully, he might have found a potential comrade in arms. Instead, he rushed to judgment and denunciation. But why he and the others did so is worth a closer examination.

To a man, the opposition pooh-poohed the notion that the sweeping reforms proposed by Powell and the academy were needed because the West was a desolate wasteland. Maginnis defended the region's potential for settlement: "It contains in its rich valleys, in its endless rolling pastures, in its rugged mineral-seamed mountains, traversed by thousands of streams clear as crystal and cold as melting snow, all the elements of comfort, happiness, and prosperity to millions of men." Denying that only 1 or 2 percent of the region was "good land," he promised that someday the West would be "one of the richest and greatest parts of the vast domain of the United States."[50]

So far the opponents sounded like Governor William Gilpin, inexperienced men fitted with rosy spectacles. But it is hard to find a sharp distinction between them and the reformers when it comes to realism and expectations of growth. Patterson admitted that "our agricultural lands . . . are limited, and the number of our population following agricultural pursuits must also be limited. But to have that number as great as possible, to swell it to its maximum," the 160-acre homestead must not be exceeded. The land must not be given away as ranches — vast holdings that would become "baronial estates" for "an aristocratic and wealthy few." The proposed survey reforms, he feared, if they led toward Powell's pasturage farms, must greatly diminish the number of poor people who could settle in the West.[51]

What separated the two sides in the debate over survey reform was the question of who should decide what nature's limits are. Who should be in control of surveying, shaping, and distributing the land — the common people or an elite group of scientists? Who should determine what the capacity of the land was? Who should the land system serve? Patterson and his allies believed it should be the little people, who needed a land system that they could easily understand and control. And Powell's ideas about bringing science to the West seemed to threaten them.

Congressman Page protested that the National Academy plan represented "a radical and abrupt method of wiping out the entire system of public land surveys — the repeal, in effect, of all laws which are simple and easily understood." Dunnell added that, although the present land system was not perfect, he supported it because it was "well understood by all of the people," not only those who had previously secured a homestead on the public domain but also "those who are on their way to this country at this hour to become settlers." That foreigners should be the main beneficiaries of the public lands was not, to be sure, the original intention of the homesteading act, which had been aimed at relieving American citizens trapped in cities, landless and impoverished. But by this time a growing proportion of the West's population growth was coming from new European arrivals. They spoke little or no English, but they could grasp what the northwest quarter of section 12 in township 30 meant. Now it was proposed to "introduce a system whose animus and methods shall be scientific and theoretical rather than practical."[52]

The opponents to reform also conjured up a plot by elite scientists to get work for themselves and funding for their quixotic pleasures. Haskell raised a few laughs at the prospect of scientists spending thousands of federal dollars collecting "bugs and fossils," measuring "the rotundity of the earth," and making "bright and beautiful topographical maps that are to be used in the libraries of the rich." Turning the public lands over to such fellows to measure and study would cost the taxpayer huge amounts of money. And it would throw out of work, Maginnis complained, "the hardworking, faithful, competent surveyors upon the border [who] by education, by constant practice, by superiority of attainment, [are] better fitted to make these surveys than any body of men to be employed by bureau officers here in Washington."[53]

The scientist who came in for the most vicious attack, however, was the college dropout from Illinois, the former professor of natural history, J.W. Powell, who was fingered as the mastermind behind an elitist conspiracy to rob the people. Patterson saw in the academy plan, as he had seen in Powell's arid lands report, a disastrous scheme that "will throw almost insurmountable obstacles in the way of the settlement of the public domain." Homesteaders or miners would no longer be able to walk into a local land office, with friendly witnesses, and claim that they had met the law's requirements and deserved a piece of free land. Instead, they would have to petition scientists far off in the nation's capital and wait for them to decide which land was suitable for occupancy and whether the settler had made a proper use of it or not. Patterson bitterly denounced the architect of this power grab:

> Sir, this is principally the work of one man. Four and two years ago he appeared before the Committee on Public Lands and sought to influence it in its [sic] favor. After hearing an exhaustive argument by this revolutionist, and other arguments from Lieutenant Wheeler, Dr. Hayden and members of the Coast Survey, the committee closed its door upon the proposition and its author. He then set out for pastures new and found them within the limits of the room of the Committee on Appropriations. I regret beyond measure, sir, that the great committee of this body should have listened to the chimeras of this charlatan in science and intermeddler in affairs of which he has no proper conception.[54]

Unfair though it was, the attack revealed just how much anger Powell had stirred up—anger that he had never really appreciated or tried to defuse. Of course he knew more about the country than this braying lawyer, and the criticisms he had made of the land system were carefully reasoned. Patterson was a fool to think otherwise. But if Powell truly wanted to save the West from monopoly power, then that was also what the congressman wanted, and they missed an opportunity to come together to devise a way to make that happen.

The most powerful speaker for land and survey reform in the House debate was the New York capitalist Abram Hewitt. At first he had opposed the academy plan, thinking that the military was the department best equipped for western surveying. But with further study he came around with eloquence and enthusiasm. "There are millions of acres where a church mouse would starve on a homestead tract," he warned. The lesson to be learned from that condition was not to lower American expectations but to apply scientific knowledge. Hewitt was no pessimist about the economic potential of the West. More than any of the westerners, in fact, he spoke in the purplest prose about vast coal beds, silver bonanzas, magnificent ranches, affluent cities and states springing up "in a day from a golden soil." He extolled the incomparable riches "with which the Maker of the universe has loaded this continent on which happily our lot is cast." The time has come, he urged, to exploit that wealth in a far more systematic and comprehensive way—"if we desire to develop in our day the measureless possibilities of the industrial destiny which awaits us."

Science held the key to the fullest exploitation of the West. By establishing a single, consolidated U.S. Geological Survey, putting scientists in charge of overseeing western lands, the nation could avoid making foolish investments. Sound development depended on expertise—"the very brightest and strongest scientific intellects of the age; men powerful to investigate and free to press their honorable professional ambitions to the full limit of their strength." Business depended on expertise in order to subjugate nature fully to the uses of humankind. "Thus the science of geology and the science of wealth are indissolubly linked together." Hewitt the iron manufacturer was a man bent on environmental conquest, seeking power over nature and over the resources of the world. Science, he urged, must become an indispensable tool of empire.[55]

Hewitt sat down to "great applause," and his colleagues in the House quickly passed the academy plan. It went to the Senate, where it was defeated. But Atkins and Hewitt wasted no time in getting appointed to the conference committee to reconcile the differences. On 3 March, the very last day of the legislative session, that committee presented their solution. It was exactly what Hewitt and the reformers had wanted all along. The competing surveys would be unified under a Geological Survey, set up to examine geological structure, mineral resources, and all "products of the national domain," as well as classify the public lands. Also, a public lands commission would codify existing laws, set up a scheme for land classification—irrigable, timber-bearing, pasturage, swamp, coal lands, etc.—and decide how those classes should be distributed to the public. Little time remained for debate. The House and Senate both approved the conference committee's version by comfortable margins, and a more science-based era for the West began.

Powell, through his allies in the National Academy and Congress, had won a substantial victory, but it came at a cost. He was now ironically identified in many people's eyes as one of the scientific and economic imperialists who were threatening western democracy. He had portrayed the lands beyond the hundredth meridian as a desert or near desert, a view that some did not want to hear. More seriously, he had joined those who insisted that only the nation's best minds could understand that problem and deal effectively with it. His vision of an alternative West—based on decentralized irrigation and pasturage districts copied from Mormon villages—had been obscured.

Powell's enthusiasm for science betrayed him. Somehow he ended up standing with moguls of industry and intellectual elites who threatened to impose a system on the West that it feared, did not understand, and did not want. Economic and scientific rationality, Powell's opponents worried, would bury justice and equality. If that was a misapprehension or a misstatement of Powell's views, he had not managed to make himself clear.

When the smoke of battle cleared, the accused "revolutionist" and self-interested job seeker found himself out of his old job. Since that first summer over a decade earlier when he had brought Emma and the Illinois Wesleyan students to climb Pike's Peak, he had spent a large part of every year on western expeditions. How many mountains he had climbed, how many rapids run! How many nights he had slept under western stars, or in a stranger's cabin or a hotel room or a leaking tent, waking in the morning to begin another arduous day. Now the Powell Survey was over, its director was (temporarily) no longer in charge of any organization or agency. His protégés, Gilbert and Dutton, had positions in the new science bureau that Clarence King consented to lead, though they were working to finish books begun under Powell's direction. Thompson was raising sheep in Greenwood County, Kansas. The Major, forty-five years old, put *finis* to his career as western naturalist, geologist, surveyor, explorer.

"Now that the battle is won," Marsh wrote, "we can go back to pure Science again."[56] Unlike the Yale man, who had his Peabody Museum of Natural History and his fossil bones demanding attention, Powell had no elaborate scientific facility where he could retreat. To be sure, he was not out of all government-supported work. An appropriation of $20,000—tucked into the Sundry Appropriations bill—allowed him to finish up his projects on Indian ethnology. On 20 February he had made a formal request to Chairman Atkins for that extension.

> There is in my office a large amount of material relating to the
> Indians of North America, consisting of vocabularies, grammars,
> notes and materials on their habits, customs, governmental
> organization, mythology and religion, arts and industries, etc. etc.
> This material has been collected very largely by myself or under
> my assistants. A large part of my time during the past ten years has
> been directed to this branch of research, and I have endeavored
> to push it with the utmost vigor.

Three volumes on ethnology had either appeared in print or were in process of publication, but "the greater part of this material . . . yet remains in an inchoate condition," and he wanted funds to assemble and edit. The new Geological Survey excluded such research, so Powell requested that he be assigned to work out of the Smithsonian, now headed by his good friend Spencer Baird.

Beyond those editorial chores, Powell had in mind going back to visit the native people who fascinated him above all others, the Hopis, and to produce a substantial monograph on them. Since that first visit when he sat in the darkened kiva wearing only a blanket, listening to the women chant for rain, he had thought about them often. The secrets they held, their strange beliefs and philosophy, could only be opened by learning their language. Indeed, it was vital to learn all the languages of all the tribes before those tongues became extinct and English became the common language. Pilling and he wanted to make that salvage mission their first priority, while a full investigation of the Hopis was to be his own contribution to science.

While he was lobbying Congress through the winter and then preparing for the transition in the spring, letters came in from many directions, reminding him of all the friendships he had neglected during the campaign for reform, of old days in the field, of all the problems agitating the West. Nathan Meeker, the Ute agent on Colorado's White River, wrote him about the changes that had come to the valley where Powell had camped through the winter of 1868–69. Meeker had acceded to Indian desires and renamed the valley

"Major Powell" (it is now called Powell Bottoms). Where the old cabins stood in ruins, a canal brought water to the crops the Utes had been taught to raise. "If you ever come again in this neighborhood, you must stop with us." Nearly a year after writing that letter, however, Meeker and six of his assistants were killed by his charges, who were angry over his efforts to force them away from buffalo hunting and into farming and cattle ranching.[57]

Midway in the battle over the land surveys a letter came from Billy Hawkins, a member of the first Colorado River party, who seemed much more friendly toward Powell now than he would be later on. He had spent part of the '78 season with the Powell Survey, having a good time rambling over the mountains. He was eager to be on the payroll again the coming summer, if it paid well. "I have been with you longer than any of the other Boys," he wrote, and the income would allow him to pay a visit to Washington to see old friends. Unfortunately for Hawkins, the survey was at an end and so was his chance to see the nation's capital.[58]

The painter Moran was still filling canvases with plateaus and canyons. He wrote Powell to send $150 "on account" for a Green River picture. It was a second try, after the first request received no reply, leaving the artist "on the mourners bench until I hear from you." Still no answer from the Major. Another letter went off: "It is quite incomprehensible to me why I have no reply to the two letters that I have written you." Bills mounting, he was desperate. "If you cannot let me have the amt I asked for let me have what you can." Two weeks after the legislative session ended with victory, Powell finally managed to send a postal order with an apology for his tardiness. "I have been in an absorbing contest," he explained, "and have neglected every thing else." Moran was grateful for the money but was flustered over a request for a picture of the Virgin River—one he had painted for Powell, then sold under the impression that Powell did not want it, and now must trade it back so that Powell could get it after all. No hard feelings over the confusion. His wife sent greetings to Emma and an invitation to stay with them if she came to New York that spring.[59]

The amateur archeologist Philetus Norris, who became the second superintendent of Yellowstone National Park after Nathaniel Langford, serving from 1877 to 1882, wrote Powell about the future of the park. He was gratified that King had been offered the Geological Survey directorship—"coveted, but not deserved by Prof. Hayden, and trust that the latter will be kept away from the Park and from making eronious maps and models and affixing or suppressing names of lakes, mountains etc with far less regard to merits of others than to gratify his notions of favouritism or his vengeance." If Norris should lose his superintendency, he wanted Powell to become his successor. But in no event did he want to see Hayden or any of his cronies take over the park, "as I have no cause to doubt he mostly [sic] gladly would." Norris need not have worried. Hayden was kept on by King and given an appropriation of twenty thousand dollars to finish up his work, though increasingly he was a sick shell of a man. And Norris remained in office until Patrick Conger, an obscure Indian agent, was appointed to oversee the park, who proved to be a weak protector of its natural beauty.[60]

Then there was a letter from a still older acquaintance, requesting a copy of the arid lands report but seeking support on a far more revolutionary project—nothing less than the defeat of Christianity. A fellow student from Wheaton College days, W.S. Bell, now resident in New Bedford, Massachusetts, wrote to remind Powell of a debate they had twenty-one years ago on "the utility of creeds, I affirming and you denying." Ever since that occasion the author had moved toward Powell's position. "I have got so far away from creeds as to apply my efforts daily to the work of overthrowing them."[61] No record survives of any reply Powell made. Apparently, in theology at least, he had learned to keep his views to himself.

Abruptly, the lull in Powell's life came to an end. President Hayes appointed members to the Public Lands Commission authorized in the same bill establishing the U.S. Geological Survey (USGS). By law, Clarence King must be a member, along with James Williamson, commissioner of the General Land Office. Three civilians had to be added, and Powell was asked to be one of them. In early June he sent King a telegram of acceptance. "I am more delighted than I can express," King replied. "Hamlet with Hamlet less is not to my taste. I am sure you will never regret your decision and for my part it will be one of my greatest pleasures to forward your scientific work and to advance your personal interest." King went on to confess his anxieties about taking on the USGS. "I feel like a condemned culprit ascending the gallows but I suppose you are right in predicting that when my blood gets up I shall enjoy being hung."[62]

The other two civilians appointed were Thomas Donaldson of Philadelphia and Alexander Britton of Washington, D.C. Donaldson was a lawyer who once had ties to Thaddeus Stevens and other Radical Republicans pushing for strong civil rights enforcement in the South. He had been appointed by Grant to be land register in the Boise,

Idaho, land office, and the exile may have softened his views, for on his return to the East he became a close ally of the conservative Hayes. Britton was originally a New Yorker, also a friend of Hayes—a lawyer who had developed a lucrative career representing the railroads and other large corporations with interests in western lands.

The two may have been picked by the portly, bearded Williamson, who was still another lawyer by training. He been recruited by Schurz to disinfect the GLO, serving as commissioner from 1876 to 1881. After leaving office, he became general solicitor and then president of the Atlantic & Pacific Railroad, which merged with the Atchison, Topeka & Santa Fe. A few weeks before joining King, Powell, and the others, Commissioner Williamson had reversed a previous Interior Department decision and granted patent for nearly two million acres to the Maxwell Land Grant Company of New Mexico. All of these lawyers brought an undeniable expertise to the Public Lands Commission, but not one of them had shown any sympathy for the small family farmer looking for a homestead. On the contrary, they represented the Republican Party's post–Civil War elite of rich capitalists and corporate entrepreneurs.[63]

King had an ambivalent relationship to that elite. He was critical of its vulgar materialism but eager to make a great deal of money to support his expensive tastes. He had not scrupled to exploit the public domain over the preceding years, even while serving as director of his own survey. In 1871 he had invested, with former field assistant N.R. Davis and others, in a large herd of cattle. Huge amounts of capital were then flowing into the West from eastern U.S. cities, London, and Edinburgh to stock the unfenced, unsettled grasslands—whether they were Indian lands or federal domain did not much matter—with longhorns. While he served on the Public Lands Commission, King remained part-owner of the twenty-five thousand head that he and his friends put out to graze on the public lands of Wyoming, Nebraska, and Dakota. For a few years he made an annual return of 25 percent. Yet he and his partners professed to deplore the greedy race for wealth going in the country. As King's friend James Gardiner put it: "However rich we may become we will by simple living, and use of our money for others, do our part to stem the tide of selfish extravagance."[64] Still, for all their repugnance toward the buck chasers, there was no reason to believe that King or his associates cared anything about improving the opportunities of the lower classes.

Powell had seen his warnings about land and water monopoly, his defense of small homesteader opportunity, his ideal of a cooperative commonwealth, trampled in the debate over land surveys and land reform. The Public Lands Commission was his last chance to see those warnings made into law. Realistically, however, he could not expect much from a commission composed of so many stalwart conservatives, friendly to corporations and vested interests.

For support he might have turned to the likes of George Julian, former congressman from Indiana with roots in the antebellum free-soil movement. Julian warned: "If our institutions are to be preserved, we must insist upon the policy of small farms, thrifty tillage, compact settlements, free schools, and equality of political rights, instead of large estates, slovenly agriculture, widely-scattered settlements, popular ignorance, and a pampered aristocracy lording it over the people. This is the overshadowing question of American politics." Powell was inclined to agree with that kind of thinking and with Julian's argument that "the unrestricted monopoly of the soil is as repugnant to republican government as slavery is to liberty."[65] But how to get the Commission to share such concern and ensure that the West was saved for the common people?

On 18 August the commission, with Clarence Dutton as its secretary, opened its inquiry with a public hearing in Denver. They distributed a questionnaire and collected oral testimony. Powell was not yet with the commission, nor subsequently in Leadville, Pueblo, Santa Fe, or Las Vegas, New Mexico. According to the *Salt Lake Tribune*, he had gotten lost. He stopped at Denver "to discover himself, and then telegraphed here to find out where the Commission was."[66] When he caught up with them, it was mid-September, and they were starting north across Idaho to Helena and Butte, Montana. From there they traveled west to the Nevada and Sierra mining districts and to San Francisco, where they held hearings from 6 to 16 October. In early November they came back east to Evanston, Wyoming, then went on to Yankton, Dakota Territory, before returning to Washington. On 24 February 1880 the commissioners submitted their recommendations to Secretary Schurz, appending nearly six hundred pages of testimony.

Over half of the testimony came from California, Nevada, and the Pacific Northwest. Among those best represented were men who had worked as contract surveyors or in a GLO land office, including several district surveyors-general. Judges, engineers, lawyers, stockmen and ranchers, merchants, and publishers also appeared before the commissioners. In Utah only one of the testifiers identified himself as a Mormon farmer, and he was disgruntled over interference by the church bishop. Thus, the commission encountered a different western society from the one that Powell had known most intimately—small farmers learning to irrigate. Aside from a follower of the reformer Henry George, who opposed the sale of any federal land, the commissioners met mostly with nonfarmers, economically successful men for whom the land system had worked well.

None of the testifiers shared Powell's criticism that the rectangular grid survey was outmoded or ill-adapted to the arid environment. But they did echo his view that water was scarce in the region, and they deplored the chaotic state of water rights. Two statements from Montana must suffice as illustration, one from the governor, Benjamin Potts, the other from a prominent rancher, Granville Stuart. Potts described his territory as agricultural only "*to a limited extent.* There is no land here that I can point to as really agricultural land without irrigation." The potential area of Montana that could be irrigated did not exceed one-twentieth of the whole. The rest had to become a cowman's country. Potts wanted to see the public domain (and most of the Indian reservations) sold to grazers. "I think the real wealth of the Territory is stock-raising, and the bunch-grass is worth more than all the mineral of the country."[67]

Stuart agreed with that assessment. He too wanted land made available to the stockgrower. As for farming, he saw no hope without the aid of large capital investment.

> I think irrigation will never amount to much here except by
> companies, and I think the government ought to aid them by
> giving them grants of land. It is a system that must be
> incorporated. It is too great an undertaking for individuals. The
> land will not be worth the money it takes to put the water on it.
> These great rivers can be taken out by companies and made
> valuable, thus rendering the land capable of sustaining a
> large population.

In other words, the agricultural West must develop by giving the public land away to capitalists—following the railroad example—or by selling it at ten cents an acre to ranchers.[68]

The commission's recommendations for new legislation followed, in its own phrase, "the conservative view," denying that any sweeping changes were needed but offering several modest ones. As the commissioners saw it, the great evil in the current laws was that it was both too easy to get land and too hard to get enough. Taken together, the various homestead and preemption acts allowed an individual to obtain as many as 1,120 free acres (not 160 acres, as the public assumed). Those acres might be highly valuable mineral or timber properties. Such a giveaway was foolish and unrepublican. On the other hand, most western land, covered as it was with sparse vegetation, was economically worthless even in such quantities. The first need, therefore, was to combine the traditional rectangular survey with a land classification program under the supervision of a new set of salaried civil servants.

Classifying lands for settlement was part of Powell's own program. But then the commission veered off in another direction that ran counter to his own views. First, they argued that irrigable lands should be sold "in unlimited quantities, subject only to the condition that the purchasers do actually redeem the lands by constructing the hydraulic works necessary thereto." The government should not enter into that work on behalf of small farmers, for it was too expensive and "not in consonance with the traditions of the American people." Irrigation must be turned over to well-heeled private developers. The commission dismissed fears that their approach might lead to land and water monopoly by arguing that it would not be in the self-interest of capitalists to hold on to irrigated lands. In the long term such lands would be more profitable if subdivided and sold. No mention was made of Powell's 1878 proposals for self-organizing irrigation districts, or of an eighty-acre limitation on irrigated farm ownership, or of "cooperative labor" as a more democratic method of development.[69]

The commission did adopt Powell's "pasturage farms," which they allowed might be settled by a "colony homestead plan." The grazers, that is, might be allowed to cluster in villages and irrigate their tracts together. But instead of placing a limit of 2,560 acres (or four square miles) on each pasturage farm, as Powell had recommended, the commission called for selling rangelands in very large blocks with no ceiling put on the purchaser. They shoved the Jeffersonian small homesteader aside for the cattle baron.[70]

In effect, the recommendations would have ended the free homestead ideal over most of the West even while professing satisfaction with the values it represented. If irrigable land could be sold in unlimited quantities—and the commission said it must be to get the land watered—and if all rangelands could be sold in unlimited quantities, and if anyone wanting either a small irrigated farm or a small homestead ranch had to buy that property from capitalists or the government, then traditional homesteading was finished. The commissioners, to be sure, did not emphasize that implication. They praised the "tillers of the soil" and claimed to want to reserve all arable land for them only, but then they would allow the selling of the West to the highest bidders and the biggest pockets.

Their approach to the timberlands confirmed that policy, though in a novel way. No settler, they said, should be allowed to file on redwoods, white pine, or other valuable timber. The government should retain all such lands in perpetuity. But it should sell the standing timber to private interests and allow them to harvest it. That would put an end to all theft and fraud while making the wood available for use. By selling the trees only on alternate sections, the western forest could regenerate itself by natural processes and become a permanently useful asset, offering fuel, lumber, and watershed protection for future generations. The recommendation was an important anticipation of the national forest idea that materialized a decade later. Like the other recommendations, it would effectively place the region's natural resources in the hands of men with capital.[71]

Whoever wrote the Public Lands Commission's report, it could not have been Powell—at least not the Powell who authored the 1878 arid lands report. The outcome was "Hamlet with Hamlet less" after all. The commissioners readily accepted that the environmental conditions of the West were unlike those of the East, but they used that difference to return to a policy of disposing of land directly to the well-to-do. They would put the development of the region more securely under elite control.

Yet Powell made only the faintest protest. To be sure, he gave a "qualified" approval. He would limit the amount of water any individual could appropriate to water actually used and he would explicitly tie that property in water to property in land. He also would give the miner the right to go on to the ranches to locate a mineral claim, particularly coal, so that that valuable fossil fuel would not all pass into the hands of the baronial estates. That said, he went along with the commission, signing off in his usual way, "your obedient servant."[72]

The boyhood farmer from Wisconsin and Illinois proved in this case not to be a revolutionist at all. If he had more radical thoughts, he did not insist on them when confronted by these men of wealth and power. King he depended on for career advancement, while the others also wielded considerable influence in Washington. In his silence, he followed the engrained ambivalence of Methodism toward those in power. Powell's parents had been driven by their religious and social principles to protest against slavery in the South, but they never challenged the rule of the moneyed classes in the North. Their son, despite strong principles of his own, chose not to raise his voice loudly against those who stood over him in learning, wealth, or authority.

As it turned out, the commission's recommendations went nowhere. Congressmen looked them over and filed them away. No bills incorporating the recommendations were reported out of the Public Lands Committee nor debated in either chamber. The home-steading law remained in place, with all of its misfittedness, fraud, and susceptibility to failure. Donaldson prepared a fat volume on the history of the public domain, but the other commissioners went back to whatever they had been doing before being summoned to serve. In February 1889 Powell returned, at least temporarily, to finishing his ethnological projects.

With the end of his Public Lands Commission work, a significant phase of his life came to a close. For more than a dozen years he had spent large amounts of time in surveying the faraway country. His name had become synonymous with the fabled West. He was hon-ored as the fearless explorer of the country's most sublime river, the Grand Canyon, and the enigmatic Plateau Province. He was re-garded, especially by easterners, as knowing more about the arid lands, as well as the native peoples, than anyone else. The United States in the post–Civil War years needed such an authority to advise on public policy. More than ever, it was a nation flowing west, into rugged mountain valleys and onto dusty sagebrush plains. It was flow-ing toward the lands of the Navajos, the Sioux, the Paiutes, threaten-ing to flood them out completely. Powell, responding to that call for advice, would seek to forge a new career for himself—Washington's resident expert on the West.

For all his deep affection and concern for the western country, for all his hard-won understanding of it, however, he was even more de-voted to the larger entity of America. The nation was his true home — the nation restored and triumphant after its dark days of war, the nation with a grand destiny yet unfilled. Powell was still the patriot he had been nearly two decades earlier when, as Abraham Lincoln's eager follower, he vibrated to those "mystic chords of memory" that bound the United States into one great organism and must not be dis-solved. Like the poet Walt Whitman ("Thou Union holding all, fusing, absorbing, tolerating all, / Thee, ever thee, I sing"), he had shining expectations for his country: America was the best hope of hu-mankind. Over its broad continent, on one coast as well as another, on every river and every hillside, in cities as well as in the country, it was the promised land. Settled in its capital on the historic banks of the Potomac, he wanted above all to serve that nearly sacred cause.

What his beloved America needed was exactly what the West needed: knowledge of itself. Knowledge of its diverse parts. Knowledge derived from science. Knowledge that was secular and free of outworn creeds. But also knowledge delivered into the hands of the people. Knowledge that could help secure the foundations of democracy. Knowledge that was hopeful and progressive. To promote that self-understanding, Powell sought to remain in Washington as long as he could. He continued to go west, but his trips were fewer and shorter. He was ready to survey the nation.

Part Three

Washington, D.C.

CHAPTER 10

Myths and Maps

The nation's capital was badly bitten by a small novel in the year 1880. Published by an anonymous author under the mocking title *Democracy,* it featured a rich widow from New York who moved into Lafayette Square, across from the White House, wishing to study more intimately "the clash of interests, the interests of forty millions of people and a whole continent, centering at Washington; guided, restrained, controlled, or unrestrained and uncontrollable, by men of ordinary mould; the tremendous forces of government, and the machinery of society, at work. What she wanted was POWER."[1]

Mrs. Lightfoot Lee found herself drawn, to the verge of marriage, by a powerful senator from Illinois, Silas P. Ratcliffe, a two-hundred-pound ego in a white waistcoat who wanted very much to be president. He was a great statesman, everyone said, but his only principle turned out to be "the want of principles." Almost too late the widow discovered that he was "a moral lunatic" who talked about virtue and vice "as a man who is color-blind talks about red and green."[2] Democracy was no better than any other form of government in its capacity for corruption, she discovered, and much worse in its tendency toward hypocrisy. The natural grace of the Potomac River, the soft, languid air of the southern spring, the thickly wooded hills nearby could not redeem the raw streets and ugly cynicism of this city.

Major Powell was on speaking terms with the novel's author, Henry Adams — four years Powell's junior, son of New England and descendant of two presidents, formerly historian at Harvard University, admiring friend of the geologist Clarence King, and now himself resident in Lafayette Square. They met in the same clubs, but they saw a different Washington. For Powell the capital abounded with splendid possibilities. It offered him the prospect of an important career in building the nation, now that his western survey was finished. It offered the potentiality of virtue as well as vice, and it offered plenty of stimulating associations with men and women of intellect and noble purpose. Unlike Adams or the fictional Mrs. Lee, he put down roots in this city and lived here nearly thirty years, all of them in government service.

The fame of the Powell Survey segued into directorates of two fledging scientific agencies: the Bureau of Ethnology and the U.S. Geological Survey. Powell established the former in the Smithsonian Institution in 1879, the year his old survey ended. And he assumed command of the latter in 1881. The two agencies kept him tied down in Washington, though the far western states and territories continued to dominate the attention of both. But his imagination was no longer limited to one region only; it expanded to encompass the broad American landscape, and indeed the whole meaning of humanity's place in nature.

In 1880 Powell was elected to the National Academy of Sciences, an acknowledgment that he now stood in the foremost ranks of American scientific research. That honor was followed eight years later by his election as president of the American Association for the Advancement of Science. It would not be his own research, however, that would occupy his future in Washington; he would specialize in the organizing of other people's research. He would continue what he had begun in Colorado, Wyoming, and Utah—surveying the territory, marking off work to be done and questions to be asked, setting others to the task of nailing down answers. To borrow from William Morris Davis, he was ever the scientific frontiersman, leaving others to plow and plant.[3]

Unflagging optimism was the quality of mind most needed in a frontiersman. Powell was every inch that man of hope, one who believed in the unlimited promise of America and, also, in the unlimited promise of human intelligence. That trait alone set him apart from the world-weary Henry Adams, who even in his youth could see in Washington, and indeed in America, only a spoiled dream and a bleak future.

Son of the Midwest's prairie farms and small rural villages, intrepid explorer of the Colorado River and its plateaus, Powell in his later years became a thorough metropolitan. His formidable drive and energy did not change, nor his capacity for hope, but to keep both alive was not easy in the city that drove Mrs. Lee away.

The Powells purchased in 1872 a brick townhouse at 910 M Street, N.W. (though they do not appear in the city directory as permanent residents until 1876), securing a mortgage for a little over half of the $14,000 purchase price. The house stood three stories high, was surmounted by an imposing cornice, and counted three tall windows across each story. A granite stoop, a deep-set front door, a basement entrance for tradesmen and servants, and a low wrought-iron fence confronted pedestrians passing on the sidewalk. No front lawn or trees — the street was decidedly urban, paved with asphalt, the entire block elbow-to-elbow houses. But in the back were small gardens, a patch of shade, a dirt alleyway, and small wooden outbuildings.

The typical Washington townhouse of the era was a Victorian advertisement for conspicuous consumption. A front parlor with floral carpet and a heavy oak fireplace mantel, surmounted by a mirror and porcelain vases, was commonly set off for company. Gas lights flared overhead, and the water vapor in the gas condensed on the heavy curtains, upholstered chairs, and embossed wallpaper. An upright piano was de rigueur, over which hung family portraits in gilt frames. On another floor were the bedrooms, with bulbous bedsteads and overstuffed wardrobes. The Powells likely followed the conventional taste, with the addition of a home office, out of which in the early years Wes ran his western survey — an office well filled with books of science and philosophy. Likely too the family employed one or more servants — black women with drawling southern accents — and they had their rooms off the basement kitchen.

How the Powells managed domestic life is hard to determine in detail. Emma, it is clear, ran the place as a stay-at-home housewife, though her maternal responsibilities remained small. They had only one child, Mary, who grew to adulthood in this house. Why there were no more offspring must be left to mere guesswork — was it due to infertility or incompatibility? How Emma passed her days, year following year, is also a mystery. She had charge of the budget for clothes and furnishings. She had friends who regularly came for tea and conversation, but it is beyond knowing what they talked about or whether the Major joined them in a laughing circle or retreated to his office.

The block on which the Powells lived was solidly middle-class. It was also racially integrated. Their neighbors included a black physician, a white hardware store owner, a widow, an architect, and two politicians — James Jones across the street, a Democratic senator from Arkansas who became one of Powell's staunch defenders on

Capitol Hill; and Blanche Bruce, also just across the street, a Republican senator from Mississippi, born a slave and elected in the Reconstruction era to become the first African American to serve a full term in the Senate.

In 1880 the population of Washington reached 178,000, making it the eleventh largest city in the country. Another hundred thousand settled here by century's end. Few of the European ethnic groups beginning to arrive in the United States in record numbers found their way to this city. Heavy industry was nearly nonexistent here, and jobs for them were less plentiful than in New York, Pittsburgh, or Chicago. Washington's growth depended on an influx of older-stock whites and blacks looking for government positions. A consistent one-third of the residents were African American in the latter decades of the nineteenth century, forming the largest concentration of the minority in the country and sustaining a middle class that was, depending on one's point of view, either a shining example of the race's potential or a showy, selfish elite who had little to do with the vast majority of blacks living in back-alley tenements.

The wife of a real senator from Illinois, Mrs. John A. Logan, characterized the city's population as a mix of "darkies," ever at hand in government offices or on the streets to do indispensable, if often desultory, service; a white Southern majority who ran the small stores and boarding houses, though with little hustle or energy; and the "predominating type" of the "Westerner," who was "quite apt to have a sharp eye and a long beard or heavy moustache." The latter, in her opinion, were beginning to control the city, as they were beginning to control the nation. Because most incomes came, directly or indirectly, from secure government paychecks, Logan noted, all Washingtonians, regardless of race or region of origin, seemed relatively prosperous.[4] They dressed to a common standard. Outwardly the city appeared more democratic than most, though in fact a wide divide separated blacks, even those in government employ, from whites, and the sectional hostilities of the Civil War lingered on.

Powell came to know the social life and topography of this city and its environs intimately, better than he knew any other place in America. He frequented the neoclassical Capitol building, with its large, resounding chambers and ceaseless flow of lobbyists. And occasionally he visited the other end of Pennsylvania Avenue, the president's inner office as well as his glittering reception hall. But the most agreeable of Powell's personal landmarks in this often treacherous terrain was the dark-red stone edifice of the Smithsonian Institution,

"Our National Capital," Harper's Weekly, 20 May 1882. Drawn by Theo. L. Davis.
Standing in the foreground are the Castle (the Smithsonian Institution)
and the National Museum. Other prominent features include, reading from the left,
the unfinished Washington Monument, the Department of Agriculture building,
the Mall, the Federal Market, the Baltimore & Ohio Railroad station, and the Capitol.
Prominent in the background is the Patent Office Building, and beyond lies M Street,
where the Powells lived from 1872 to 1902.

nicknamed the "Castle," thrusting into the Mall with a kingly air. It is unclear whether Powell ever occupied an office in the building, but as one of the Smithsonian's staff members he was frequently in its rooms and halls. More than any church or cathedral, it was for him the true temple of the city, where science occupied the pulpit.

The route from his home to the Smithsonian was one that Powell came to know well, on foot and by buggy. Walking south on Ninth Street he passed Mount Vernon Square and the gigantic Patent Office, where the Department of the Interior and the new Geological Survey were accommodated. Then he passed Ford's Theater, where Lincoln had been shot and where now was sited the highly popular Army Medical Museum, with its macabre display of amputated legs of army generals, the neck bones of the assassin Booth, various diseased organs pickled in jars, and a diverting sample of artificial limbs.

The one-armed pedestrian then skirted the massive Central Market, sprawling over two full blocks along Pennsylvania Avenue, the hub of the city's economic life where all the streetcar lines converged. When it opened in 1872 it was acclaimed as the largest and most modern food market in the nation, with stalls for a thousand vendors. Early in the morning gaunt-faced farmers from the Virginia countryside pulled up at the rear to sell corn, cabbages, apples, or green beans from their wagons; within, other sellers hawked fresh crabs from the Chesapeake, dressed muskrat or beef, roasted peanuts, or freshly baked breads and pies.

Immediately behind the market stretched the Mall. Fifty acres had been marked off for the Smithsonian grounds and landscaped by Andrew Jackson Downing into curvilinear carriage ways and picturesque urban forest. Directly ahead and adjacent to the Castle stood the new National Museum, completed in 1881, and here Powell kept an office for several years. He worked among growing collections that included a stuffed plains bison, a Rocky Mountain sheep, an extinct great auk, a giant fossil egg from Madagascar, a gorilla's head (all exhibited in the two-hundred-foot-long Main Hall); assorted Indian and Eskimo artifacts, locks of presidential hair, a sample of Chinese paper money, historic treaties made with other nations (displayed in the Gothic Hall); hundreds of mineral and ore specimens, many of them brought back by government exploring expeditions, including his own (West Hall); a marble sarcophagus from Syria, a few Central American stone idols, and bark from a California redwood tree (the Vestibule).[5]

Crossing the grounds to the Museum, Powell could glance left toward the imposing white dome of the Capitol, though it was often obscured by the smoke of a locomotive pulling out of the Baltimore and Potomac Railroad Station. That Victorian Gothic excrescence was plopped down on the Mall in 1873—a multi-hued and multibanded pile of brick inspired by the writings of the English author John Ruskin. Looking to the right, Powell could see the Agriculture Department building, with its flat-sided Second Empire mansard roof and extensive formal gardens. Further to the west were the still unfinished and bankrupt Washington Monument (it would not be completed until 1885) and the noisome Potomac Flats, rank at low tide with the stench of untreated sewage and mud. Somewhere in all that melange of architectural styles, that miasma of odors and aromas, was buried the simple, spacious design of the city's original planner, Pierre L'Enfant.

Charles Dickens, in an earlier decade, had dismissed Washington as the "City of Magnificent Intentions." It was then, as it was in Powell's day, a place of unfulfilled promises — a few grand gestures incoherently mixed among the mundane, the vulgar, the choleraic, and the ramshackle. A writer for *Harper's Magazine*, in 1881, described it more pleasantly as a "a city without a commerce and without suburbs — drive a mile or two in any direction and you find yourself in the midst of woods set but sparsely with houses and cabins, and with only the great pillard dome, like a shining cloud in the air, to remind you of the human mass so near."[6]

After shuttling between the Castle, the National Museum, and the Patent Office for several years, Powell took up rented offices in the Hooe building at 1324–1334 F Street, N.W. When first erected, it was the largest privately owned office building and the largest cast-iron-fronted building in the city. On the ground floor were small shopkeepers, but most of the remaining five floors eventually became Powell's own territory as his administrative responsibilities enlarged. It became the home of the Geological Survey and the Bureau of Ethnology. Geological specimens were stored on the top floor where it was too hot to work much of the year. The staff had to trudge up and down the staircases, summer and winter alike, carrying rocks and memoranda. In the long muggy seasons that Washington suffered through they opened the windows wide for cooling ventilation, putting up with the dust and noise of the city below.

Around the corner on Fourteenth Street was Newspaper Row, including the offices of the Associated Press, the *Washington Star* and the *Washington Post*, and the Willard Hotel, where the city's most distinguished visitors stayed. The Hooe quarters were a mere block and a half from the Treasury Building, immediately behind which stood the Executive Mansion. A short walk in any direction put Powell in the presence of any or all of the movers and shakers of public policy. He had a newfangled machine called a telephone installed in his office by the Chesapeake and Potomac Telephone Company, so that he was well and truly in communication with the whole nucleus of power that lay around him.

Thus, the restless western explorer had become a settled bureaucrat, a man bound to a desk much of the time, one of the army of federal employees. In 1880, nearly eight thousand people were in that army, a number that would nearly quadruple in another decade. Powell rose fast in the bureaucracy, as he had risen fast under Grant in the late war, and for many he became the very ideal of a civil servant.

As Powell rose in administrative power and significance, he and Emma did not rise much in social rank. Their income remained constant over a period of twenty years, and they stayed put at 910 M Street, unable or unwilling to move to a more fashionable address. Meanwhile, the city rapidly expanded northwestward, leaving behind the old downtown commercial center and creating new centers of wealth and consumption. Congressmen and senators were tired of staying in the traditional boarding houses around the Capitol. They wanted fine private residences in this city where they were spending more and more of their time, and they wanted bigger and better shops. They could afford to create them. A newspaper estimated in 1882 that the combined personal fortunes of seventeen senators was over $600 million.[7] Such affluence began to lay out another Washington to which the Powells did not belong.

A syndicate of rich westerners, led by Senator William Stewart of Nevada, invested hundreds of thousands of dollars in land near the city's northwest limits in the early 1870s. They were the first of a series of real-estate speculators seeking to profit from the increasing appeal of Washington as a place of residence. While Powell was signing the mortgage papers on his own house, they were preparing to refurbish the capital's domesticity in a grander style.

William Stewart had made his first fortune in the California gold fields, after dropping out of Yale College, but he added substantially to it by going into mining law and defending the original claimants to the Comstock lode. He enhanced it further by marrying an affluent young heiress from San Francisco. When he contrived to get Nevada legislators to send him to the United States Senate in 1864, he was proclaimed the wealthiest man in that body—the "Silver Senator." Even his whiskers were silver. He stood over six feet tall and always sported a wide-brimmed white hat—the very picture of Mrs. Logan's brash and self-assured westerner. After organizing his real-estate syndicate, he hired Arnold Cluss, the architect of the Center Market and the Agriculture Building, to build him a house in the wilderness of Pacific Circle, later renamed Dupont Circle. A massive Second Empire mansion, it boasted a turreted entrance tower, five floors of teak furniture and Aubusson tapestries, and a ballroom seventy-five feet long. The public ridiculed it as "Stewart's Folly" and "The Honest Miners Camp"; nonetheless, they flocked to see it, acknowledging that it surpassed the boring old White House in conspicuous display. Stewart left the Senate in 1874, though not before being offered a seat on the Supreme Court. For another decade the

"Folly" stood empty, except for a brief period when it was rented to the Chinese for their legation. But in 1887 Stewart returned to the Senate, restoring the house and his claim to dominate the city.[8]

Such aspirants to grandeur sought a new urbanism, though one that paid little heed to the poor underclass packed into back-alley shanties. In 1882 they convinced Congress to begin filling in the Potomac tidal marsh, sending the sewage that had been accumulating there downriver. They designed a magnificent park along Rock Creek, another dangerously polluted waterway, planted thousands of trees along the main thoroughfares, improved water supplies, and discouraged industry from coming to the city. Their Washington was a clean, livable, residential place, especially appealing to the well-to-do.

Throughout these developments the Powells stayed put in their original neighborhood and rarely crossed the social threshold into the northwest suburbs. Early on they achieved a respectable plateau, and there they lived contentedly, if not quite simply. A nearby livery stable sheltered their brown mare, Josie, and her successors, Snowfleet and Prince. They bought their groceries at R.C. Yewell's a few steps down the street. Former staff from the western survey days—Hillers, Thompson, Gilbert, Dutton, Stevenson—clustered nearby.[9] The Powells did not need to travel far for the necessities of life or for social intercourse, and evidently they were satisfied with what they had in material terms.

Now and then, some of the more powerful men in the city deigned to call at the M Street townhouse. E.W. Gallaudet, founder of a college for the deaf, was invited for a meal one March evening in 1881 and found at the Powells' table the secretary of war, Robert Lincoln (the late president's son); the secretary of the interior, Samuel Kirkwood (formerly senator from Iowa); Senators David Davis and John Logan from Illinois; and Senator J. Donald Cameron from Pennsylvania.[10] Their host was not reticent to court political support in his projects and budgets, nor slow to pass the cigars, if he thought there was any advantage to be gained. He learned to lobby and cajole and stroke important personages when necessary.

With almost everyone else in this city, Powell and his fellow scientists in politics craved power. The power they craved, however, was power independent of wealth—power that came from ideas and intelligence. They wanted to run this place, but run it in a way they saw as more disinterested. In contrast to the sticky-fingered Grant administration and the aggressive bonanza kings from the western mines, they anticipated a Washington that distributed power to those free of any expectation of personal profit—scientists in the main.

Above all, they dreamed of a new America arising from the ashes of war, disunion, and corruption. It was to be a nation standing in the vanguard of the world's cultural and scientific progress, master of the sciences of earth and man. It was to represent enlightenment and reason, much as Franklin and Jefferson had hoped in the early days of the Republic. A truly advanced America would extend benevolence and justice to oppressed and conquered peoples. It would protect its natural resources from destruction and distribute them fairly. Powell and his friends looked for a country that was as great in spirit and intelligence and principle as it was in physical assets.

Which way of thinking would dominate the capital city and the nation — that of Powell or Stewart, the scientists or the politicians, the middle-class bureaucrats or the self-made aristocrats? Which group contesting for power in the city had the interests of the American people most at heart? Those were questions to which Powell thought he knew the answer.

On 3 November 1880 a letter came to Powell from Lewis Henry Morgan, the dean of American anthropologists, now in his last months of life:

> I congratulate you and myself on our great Republican victory. It will give four years of steady encouragement to your work, and enable you to get it upon a solid foundation. This is something apart from the general good of the country which is now assured. Hurra for Garfield and the Ethnological Bureau.

The "Ethnological Bureau" was the office that Powell directed within the Smithsonian Institution. "Garfield" was James A. Garfield, formerly senator from Ohio, now president-elect of the United States. Chosen on the thirty-sixth ballot at the Republican convention, he had squeaked to victory over Winfield Scott Hancock in one of the closest presidential contests in history.

Born in a log cabin near Cleveland, formerly a minister in the Disciples of Christ church, Garfield was something of a self-made scholar. He respected science almost as much as religion, serving on the Smithsonian's board of regents, and he respected Powell in particular. For nearly a decade he had supported the western explorer at annual funding time (as chairman of the Appropriations Committee) and, early on, had spent a Sunday afternoon in his company looking at maps and photographs of the Colorado River country. On another occasion he attended a Powell lecture on Indian mythology and, at the conclusion, delivered his own erudite commentary. And of course he too had been drawn to dinner at 910 M Street for high-minded conversation. Conversely, Garfield appealed strongly to Powell after the contagion of cynicism spread by U.S. Grant, Rutherford Hayes, and so many other politicians in the capital—at last a political leader of moral principle, substantial intelligence, racial tolerance, and high-minded idealism.[11]

The friendship tightened when Powell briefly loaned a young personal aide, Joseph Brown, to help with correspondence while Senator Garfield worked to pass the bill establishing the Geological Survey. The aide, adept at shorthand and an efficient worker, stayed on for permanent duty when Garfield began his race for the presidency. After the election Brown moved into the White House as private secretary and had charge of the hungry mob of office seekers who wanted their part of the spoils.[12] Powell had given the new president one of his brightest recruits and in return had secured the gratitude of the most powerful man in the country. In cultivating Garfield he had cultivated access to power that no money could buy.

The director of the Geological Survey, Clarence King, in contrast, had no such fellowship with the new president and no enthusiasm for staying on in his administration. He wanted out of government duties altogether. Within only a year of taking the directorship, he had grown sour and discouraged. Congress had given him $100,000 to spend, a fraction of what the old western surveys had spent in toto, and was reluctant to expand his authority. In a few senators King stirred up hostility and distrust—too irresponsible and selfish, they complained, too vain and condescending, too friendly with the satirizing author Henry Adams, too easy in his associations with private investors.[13] Frustrated by failure, King sent word to Garfield that he would resign from the survey soon after the inauguration.

"It was for my health, more than for any other reason," King wrote his close friend Samuel Emmons, "that I resigned the Survey. I felt that I could not longer sustain the terrible pressure of the Washington office, with my health slowly giving way under me. My illnesses of the last four summers leave me each year a little weaker; and I have been frankly warned by both my doctors that if I am to be saved at all, it is by the most complete rest. Th[u]s I look forward to having another year; and am striving to tie up the ends of my affairs, so that I can either recover, or go out like a candle in peace."[14]

King need not have gone into his other motives for leaving his post. He still longed to be wealthy and had an eye to making a pile of money by salvaging flooded mines in Mexico and getting them back into production. While on the government payroll, he had visited gold and silver fields in the Sierra Madre. Moreover, Emmons knew about still other lusts that were pulling King south: "I can imagine H.R.H. after a bout among the dusky fair ones of Mexico," he wrote to George Becker; "he has a peculiar weakness for color, and especially when it is on a fair cheek."[15] Miraculously, they noted, His Royal Highness always seemed restored to health when he came back from flirting with dark-eyed beauties of Spanish tongue.

The inaugural ball took place in the newly finished National Museum, appropriately for a president avid for science. King immediately sent in his resignation, as promised, and Garfield had his secretary invite Powell in for discussion, which the secretary did with "great pleasure." A meeting of minds took little time. On that same day, 11 March, Garfield noted in his diary, "Appointed Maj. Powell Geologist *vice* Clarence King."[16] Within half an hour of their discussion, in fact, a nomination sped to Capitol Hill, and it was approved without dissent. Within a few more days Powell took the oath of office to become the second director of the Geological Survey—fittingly, for it was he who had done more than any other individual to get the survey established in the first place.

King backed his successor enthusiastically, even thinking that Powell was his own idea. He telegraphed Becker in Virginia City, Nevada, that "I will be behind the throne and your position and interests will be taken care of." Henry Adams's wife, Marion, wrote that King had brought them unwelcome news of his resignation: "a great blow to us—but he can do more valuable work as geologist out of harness and his successor will carry out his wishes." Another of King's confidantes, Arnold Hague, consoled himself by admitting that "Powell is, I suppose, the best man if not the only man who can raise money." He too assumed that the money Powell raised would carry on what King had started. With such reassurances and a few hasty farewells, King fled south to the border, little realizing he was starting down a spiral toward a disappointing end. Nor did he imagine that Powell would turn out to be nobody's stooge.[17]

That Powell was taking on the directorship of the Geological Survey when he already had a full-time job in the Bureau of Ethnology did not come up for discussion. Apparently, he himself did not for a moment consider resigning the latter. Self-confident as a rooster, he was certain that he could manage both offices without difficulty. He wanted to see the survey grow—grow far beyond anything King or anyone else had contemplated. At the same time he had lost none of his interest in ethnology and could see enormous potential in its development too. This man of humble origins and limited academic achievement intended once more, as he had on the Colorado, to seize his opportunities and make a name for himself by going where no one had gone before.

Fortuitously, he had a newly elected president firmly on his side, one who for all his solidly Republican fiscal conservatism was generous toward science. So at least it appeared in the springtime of March. Three and a half months later, however, Powell's world turned upside down. On Saturday morning, 2 July, the president climbed down from his carriage and entered the Baltimore and Potomac Railroad station on Sixth and B Streets. He was hurrying with his two sons to catch the 9:30 train and journey to meet his wife for a holiday at the New Jersey shore. As he crossed the ladies' waiting room, a man named Charles Guiteau stepped out of the shadows and shot him with a British Bulldog pistol. Garfield fell to the floor, severely wounded. The stunned attendants managed to transport him by ambulance back to the White House, where the physicians gathered to see how bad the wound was.

Guiteau, who was quickly apprehended, called himself a theologian and a lawyer, but in truth he was a longtime religious fanatic who had nurtured fantastical hopes of being appointed minister to the Austro-Hungarian Empire. For weeks he had besieged Secretary Brown and was repeatedly rebuffed. In frustration, he purchased a gun, honed his marksmanship down on the Potomac Flats, stalked Garfield for weeks, and finally found his moment of crazed revenge.

Brown later called the shooting a deed "which plunged a nation into gloom, brought the deepest anguish to a loving and devoted family and condemned the gallant gentleman to eighty days of suffering and ultimate death. No experience of mine in after life offered such a shock. The temple had fallen, and the idols lay shattered."[18]

Powell was just as shaken by the assassination as the younger man. Immediately he sent a handwritten note over to Brown: "The surprise this morning is overpowering. Tell me what you think."[19] While the president lingered on at the edge of consciousness, showing no sign of recovery, and as the summer heat and humidity intensified, Powell thought hard about what he could do to relieve his friend's suffering. A week after the shooting, he met Simon Newcomb, head of the

Naval Observatory, and reported that the physicians were trying out all kinds of devices to cool the air in the president's bedchamber. He urged Newcomb to go over to the White House to make recommendations.[20] But no experiments in air-conditioning could stave off death, and on 19 September Garfield died, leaving Vice President Chester Arthur to take his place.

It was Powell's second experience with presidential assassination. Lincoln's death had robbed him of the leader he admired above all others, but Garfield's took away a comrade who had stood beside him on the front lines, a peer and a colleague he had touched and talked with for nearly a decade. Never again would he enjoy such support from any politician. Still, there was work to be done. Wipe away the shock and grief and get on with one's plans. The future of American science was waiting to made, and Powell, through the unpredictable workings of politics, had now been given a powerful role in that making.

By the time the Powells settled permanently in Washington, the American project to construct a continental empire was complete—3.6 million square miles rolling westward from the Atlantic Coast to the Arctic Sea. Alaska was the last piece to be added, in 1867. Only there were the native peoples still in effective possession of the land. Everywhere else, they were removed from their homelands, decimated by disease and alcohol, or concentrated on reservations. Even the Comanches, the Sioux, and the Navajos, who once drove terror into the hearts of their enemies, had been subdued. They lived only on the sufferance and charity of their white conquerors. Their choices seemed few—fester in anger or accept a subordinate place in the American empire.

Powell believed that the government should substitute the science of ethnology for the arts of military conquest. It should support scholarly investigation of the social, economic, and cultural systems of the vanquished Indian peoples. Needless to say, not everyone agreed with that peculiar way of treating one's vanquished enemies. As one southern congressman retorted, Americans preferred to spend their tax revenues on studying the diseases of the horse rather than the superstitions of the Indian.[21] He spoke, however, after more than two decades of federal appropriations for ethnologists—not munificent but steady—and for that support Powell deserves most of the credit.

Indians, though losers in the struggle to possess the continent, had long appealed to a sympathetic, if often sentimental, white audience. In Thomas Jefferson's instructions to Lewis and Clark and

James Fenimore Cooper's novels of the frontier, the Indian was a charismatic figure to be understood and, within limits, admired. The founder of American ethnology was Jefferson's secretary of the treasury, Albert Gallatin, who gave up the study of monetary policy to collect lists of Indian words and, in 1843, publish the most comprehensive collection of native vocabularies to date. Gallatin became the first president of the American Ethnological Society of New York, a private venture that served vaguely as a model for Powell's Bureau of Ethnology. Learn their languages, Gallatin insisted, and you will gain access to the minds and hearts of these remarkable people.[22]

The decision to concentrate his scientific researches on Indians rather than on geology was a critical step for Powell, but what it revealed about him is complicated. Some part of the decision must be put down to shrewd opportunism. Indians sold books and articles, rocks did not. Indians had few serious students, rocks had many. Indians were rarely part of any university curriculum, rocks had their distinguished chairs. Yet, an even shrewder appraisal might have warned, go where the money and prestige are going, and that was not toward Indian research. Powell went where his curiosity and moral passion took him, and he became for a crucial period of time the country's most important student of the vanishing Indian world.

In pursuing research Powell was above all an organizer. If he walked into a messy room, his first instinct was to put everything into the proper cupboards. The study of the Indian was a truly big mess, as generations of amateurs and antiquarians had unsystematically collected everything from arrowheads and medicine bundles to half-finished word lists and scattered folk tales. Gallatin, Lewis Cass, Henry Rowe Schoolcraft, Constantine Samuel Rafinesque, along with Army doctors, warriors, engineers, missionaries, explorers, and commercial travelers had all added to the pile and the confusion. It was time that the study of Indians be put on a systematic basis, with a comprehensive view of parts and wholes. That could only be done in Washington, with Smithsonian guidance and federal investment. Powell persuaded the first secretary of the Smithsonian, Joseph Henry, to turn over the hundreds of questionnaires that Henry had sent out to solicit information regarding Indian numbers, vocabularies, and lifeways. Once these were in hand, he set himself the challenge of turning them into science.[23]

At no point did Congress explicitly authorize a federally funded Bureau of Ethnology. In the 1879 legislation abolishing the western surveys and establishing the Geological Survey, Powell had modestly asked for and received $20,000 to complete "the reports of the Geographical and Geological Survey of the Rocky Mountain Region with the necessary maps and illustrations."[24] But a year later he was back, asking for $50,000 to fund his new "bureau" in the Smithsonian. Such was his modus operandi. He understood what Congress meant to do — or at least should have done — and he held them to it. The second appropriation was no larger than the first, but for the fiscal year 1882–83 he secured $40,000, a funding level he maintained for another decade. Congress thus put a de facto stamp of approval on the bureau, persuaded by its director that it was the proper role of government to study systematically the tribal peoples it had defeated.[25]

The Indians were no longer enemies — they were wards. Back in 1873, when he had served as Indian commissioner with Ingalls, Powell had operated under a practical rationale: setting up reservations where diverse tribes could live together in peace and stability required knowledge of who was compatible with whom. Assimilation required intensive language teaching, agricultural self-reliance, and proper medical care, all of which meant that whites had to know as much as possible about the minds of those being assimilated. Now Powell justified his bureau with more pragmatism. Indians had signed a welter of treaties and land cessions, which someone in government needed to sort out. The bureau would do so, thus becoming the intelligence arm of the U.S. Army and the Indian Commissioner, as they tried to manage their wards.

Congress needed such rationalization for spending its money, but it had plenty of opportunity to understand that Powell's bureau had far more than immediate problem-solving in view. He was forthright about his larger intentions. The first annual report of the bureau announced that it would "prosecute work in the various branches of North American anthropology on a systematic plan, so that every important field should be cultivated, limited only by the amount appropriated by Congress." His scheme was long-term and basic. All "customs, laws, governments, institutions, mythologies, religions, and even arts" would be investigated. Since language was the only possible door into Indian ideas and thoughts, it must have priority. Exhaustive grammars and dictionaries must be published, along with "a large series of chrestomathies"—texts of literary passages for the study of literature and language. These would be the keys to unlock the mythic imagination of the native American.[26]

To guide field workers Powell published in 1877 an *Introduction to the Study of Indian Languages*, which three years later he updated in a second edition. He suggested making lists of words and phrases used for parts of the body, dwellings, food, colors, animals and plants, kinship, religion, amusements — the gamut of human activities. All Indian words should be rendered in the roman alphabet, each sound represented by a separate character. Aligning those lists into a "synonymy" would follow — parallel lists to enable the scientist to compare the different Indian languages, locating clusters of similar words for similar things, the similarities indicating genetic relationships. Eventually all Indian languages would be grouped into "families," which like biological species had points of origin and paths of diffusion. They could be plotted on a map showing their track across the landscape.

The ambition of the bureau must be nothing less than founding a "Science of Man," a phrase that first appeared in the annual report for 1892–93 but was the dream of its director from the beginning. Powell saw no one else in America organizing such a science, so he set out to do so. In the second annual report he marked off four great "departments" in this science: the study of arts, institutions, languages, and opinions.[27] They formed a seamless whole, each depending on the other for understanding. Scholars working in isolation from one another could not see the full picture, or how their specialized research fitted into it. But a center for ethnology could bring people together in a common effort. Set up in perpetuity, it could keep them moving toward a single end, generation following generation, slowly closing in on the ideal of complete knowledge.

The Indians were a vital natural resource to be mined and transformed into knowledge. Among them the scientists worked to record and interpret, deriving insights into the broader human condition. Powell did not ask the Indians whether this was a role they wanted to play. On the contrary, he took their cooperation for granted. While struggling to adjust to the vast changes visited upon them, they had to put up with his field anthropologists scrutinizing their daily habits, writing down their every word, and asking to be let into their innermost secrets. Defeated, they had no choice in the matter, though Powell was sure that, in the long term, they would see their best interest well served by more scientific insight into their cultures.

The problem was finding not subjects but skilled investigators. In 1879, and indeed for another dozen years, no one in the United States could boast any advanced academic training in anthropology or ethnology from any American university. Although William D. Whitney at Yale might be consulted on linguistic questions and Frederick W. Putnam, curator of Harvard's Peabody Museum of Archaeology and Ethnology (established in 1879), might give advice on artifacts, there was nary a Ph.D. program in the land until the immigrant Franz Boas set one up at Columbia. Even the great Lewis Henry Morgan had no professional training; he was a lawyer who had taken up the study of Indians as an avocation. The Bureau of Ethnology had to be staffed with self-taught amateurs.

The western surveys had left behind an outfit of experienced but unemployed field men, some of whom had traveled much among Indians or, at any rate, would not mind doing so. From his own crew Powell recruited John Hillers, boatman and photographer of the Utes and Paiutes, and James Pilling, stenographer and general factotum. From Hayden's entourage he chose James Stevenson, a surveyor of Yellowstone and the Grand Teton range; William Henry Holmes, geological artist extraordinaire; and Cyrus Thomas, an entomologist originally from Illinois. From Wheeler's survey he hired Albert Gatschet, a Swiss immigrant with exceptional linguistic skills, and Henry Henshaw, an ornithologist of weak constitution who was ready to substitute words for birds. Others came from the Army—Colonel Garrick Mallery, a stalwart gentleman with pince-nez and dragoon's moustache—and from the Christian missions—the Reverend J. Owen Dorsey, a slight-bodied Episcopalian who loved languages. Then there were the miscellaneous walk-ins: F.W. Hodge, Jesse Walter Fewkes, Cosmos and Victor Mindeleff, James Mooney.[28]

Males had taken exclusive possession of western surveying, but Powell opened the bureau's funds and publishing opportunities to a few female enthusiasts as well. The irrepressible Erminnie Smith of Jersey City, New Jersey, was given a small sum to pursue her interests in the Iroquois and Onondaga.[29] Alice Fletcher, though never on the payroll, was a regular around the offices when in Washington and a knowledgeable authority on the Sioux and Omaha whom the staff consulted.[30] The formidable Mathilda (Tilly) Stevenson, wife of the mild-mannered James, became a full-time staff member. For years she accompanied her husband into the Southwest, wrote several books on the Zunis, and on James's death in 1888 moved into a bureau office. She gave Powell more distress than anyone else in this generally happy family by heatedly insisting on her prerogatives, spending money without approval, and threatening him with powerful friends if he dared to take away her position.[31]

Others came and went through the bureau's doorway, but those were the persistents who intended, with Powell, to redefine the Indian, not as an obstacle in the path of empire—hated, feared, scorned—

but as an intricate text for scientific analysis. Stevenson became, until his death, Powell's chief executive officer, after which Henshaw assumed the managerial post. Pilling took charge of the treasury—paying bills, collecting receipts.[32] All worked against the ticking clock of cultural loss, fearing that the Indians might soon forget traditional ways and even forget their native language under the pressure of invading whites.

Agreeable as his recruits generally were, they confronted Powell constantly with a difficult question of how much control to exercise. As director, he was intent on marching his troops toward a common destination on which he had personally fixed. The bureau was his creature, the budget his achievement, the science of man his dream, the staff his collective instrument. However, he was operating in a culture where individual genius and personal freedom were the celebrated norm; somehow he must instill a counterethos of teamwork. Yet how to do that without driving off his more idiosyncratic, creative scholars? Too much direction from the top, and the troops might rebel. Too little, and he might stand accused of indulging private whims at public expense, not to mention failing to bring scientific order out of chaos.

Some of the foot soldiers in this ethnological army immediately started marching to a beat that was not consonant with Powell's orders to classify and map languages. Holmes, for example, went his own way from the beginning. Art and architecture were all that engaged him. He rambled from pottery to textiles to stone implements, while Powell looked on indulgently. Likewise, the Stevensons had their own ideas, archaeological as well as ethnographic, and they too enjoyed considerable freedom. Mathilda recalled these liberal instructions from Powell: "Go and do the best you can, you know best how to pursue your work and I know that you will accomplish all that is possible."[33] What he may actually have said was, go away and leave me in peace, but she was right that dictatorialness was not the director's style.

Putting aside those who had little interest in language study, Powell still had a few willing researchers awaiting orders. He set them the challenge of collecting all the vocabularies still extant in North America. With that data they could build a system of classification, which was the first step toward a science of culture. Different language groups reflected different cultural evolution, and that evolution in turn must be explained. Powell, it must be said, never got a firm grasp on the project. The Indians were more prolific in languages than the Europeans, defying his small band of collectors. Explaining human differences was an even more daunting task. He marched his men ragged, looking for a way over the mountain.

Pilling, who had the docile and agreeable temperament of a pack horse, was loaded down with the task of assembling a bibliography of everything that had ever been written about Indian languages. Off he went to the major libraries in the land, consulting their holdings and filling in stacks and stacks of note cards. The Reverend Dorsey set about writing what turned out to be an 812-page treatise on the Omaha language, while editing the Reverend S.R. Riggs's massive Dakota-English dictionary. Colonel Mallery delved into sign languages and picture-writing, those first stages of communication before humans had assembled verbal sounds into words or invented alphabets. Gatschet was put to work collecting a hundred different languages, but whenever Powell stopped pressing him hither and yon, he returned to puzzling out the single, complex grammar of the Klamaths of Oregon.

That left Henry Henshaw, last of the inner circle and as devoted as any individual to the ethnographic cause. In the early days Powell could afford to hire him only by putting him out on contract to the Census Bureau, which needed assistance in gathering population figures. As the frail little man went about enumerating the Indians of the Great Basin and West Coast, he tried to fill in the data gaps for Powell's map of linguistic families. After the census money dried up, Henshaw came home to work on the synonymy project, lining up columns of the various ways to say "dog" and "rat," "moon" and "stars." He could never complete that Augean task alone and, worn out at last, sailed off to Hawaii for an extended rest cure, leaving the project unfinished.

No day was long enough to achieve what Powell had in mind with his "Science of Man." Remarkably, the staff he recruited drove themselves as much as he drove them. Though often frustrated by his shifting about for a way up the mountain, they nonetheless did not desert him. Powell was loyal to them — he seldom let anyone go — and they were intensely loyal to him.

The greatest impediment to this enterprise was not Powell's own assistants but Spencer Fullerton Baird, second secretary of the Smithsonian. Somber-faced and self-assured, Baird had taken over the institution upon Henry's death in 1878. He was an insatiable collector. It was he who planned and built the National Museum and filled it with rows and rows of glass cases — a mausoleum of taxonomies and curiosities. In place of Henry's enthusiasm for exploring scientific hypotheses, Baird was more happy fixing labels and making inventories. The death of living creatures did not move him, nor the extinction of species, nor questions of social justice. A dull black coat was his usual dress.

Yet so determined was Powell to find a home in the Smithsonian for his Indian work, a home away from the politicized Department of the Interior, that he did not hesitate to put his Bureau of Ethnology under Baird's control. Moreover, he came to like and even admire this stolid administrator, for they had a few things in common. When Baird died in 1888, Powell eulogized him for his abilities as "an organizer of the agencies of research," including the U.S. Fish Commission, which Baird set up and headed without compensation to promote the artificial propagation of fish for American consumption. Powell praised his "sagacity," his "modesty," his "minute and comprehensive knowledge," his skill in setting a whole body of men to work on "a continuous line of research."[34] Yet this same "wise and venerable patriarch" who evoked such affectionate respect gave no end of trouble.

From the outset of their relationship, Baird asserted tight control over Powell's expenditures and exercised a heavy hand on the direction of ethnological research. There was to be no "divided sovereignty" within the Smithsonian. It was the secretary's prerogative to force all salaries into conformity, scrutinize all deliveries of goods into his building, and keep a close watch on all railroad passes that bureau employees secured. He proved to be a fuss-budget who could not let the smallest trifle go unnoticed, scratching out queries and imperatives at an unrelenting pace. "Of course I want it distinctly understood," Baird explained, "that we are not attempting a system of espionage, but simply keeping our records so that there will be no confusion."[35]

More galling still was Baird's practice of withholding part of the bureau's appropriation as a "reserve fund" for his own projects. By 1882 this sum amounted to $5,000 a year, enough to pay two or three of Powell's top staff members. No appeal to Baird for a restoration of the money availed. His frustration mounting, Powell raised his voice in protest:

> I beg permission to state that I think it unwise that the fund
> should be diverted from the purpose for which the appropriation
> was made, namely, for research, and devoted so largely to the
> building up of the Museum. I also wish to express a regret that the
> Secretary of the Smithsonian should take a part of the fund from

under my control, and should further employ assistants in the
Museum who are not under my direction; . . . I beg leave to suggest that the Bureau of Ethnology is an institution created by
myself, that it[s] plans are my own, and that whatever success it
has achieved has been through my labor; that to this work I have
devoted the larger share of my time for the last 13 years, and that
I cannot see it gradually taken from me without some feeling of
disappointment.

"With profound respect for your superior judgment," the letter concluded, "and confiding in your love of justice."[36] Baird, however, remained unmoved in his exercise of sovereignty.

Levying a tax on Powell's funds was only a small part of the pressure brought to bear on the ethnographic priorities. The secretary
was clearly out of sympathy with the emphasis given to studying languages and, through them, trying to understand the mental world of
the American Indian. He disrupted that program repeatedly by forcing Powell to become an artifact collector for his glass cases. In that
same letter of protest, the bureau's director wailed that more than
half of his congressional appropriation was being turned away from
philology and philosophy to artifact collecting. In an earlier letter
Powell insisted that "it is a narrow view of the subject which would
confine investigations among the North American Indians chiefly to
the collection of works of art."[37] Complain though he did, he was
forced to modify his plans in order to meet the secretary's views.

Baird did not yield, but he did try to justify his personal prefer-
ences as a matter of political expediency, an expediency that he deliberately promoted. In appealing to Congress to renew Powell's
funding, Baird warned "that exhaustive researches are now being
prosecuted within our own territory by foreign nations." The French
had hired an agent to acquire "an immense collection from the
coasts of California, Oregon, and Alaska"—whole shiploads of America's relics going abroad—and soon another French expedition
would be sent to "the most virgin archaeological fields of Arizona and
New Mexico." The United States was losing "its own historical monuments" to the rapacious Europeans.[38] Never mind that white Americans had no more right to those Indian relics than the French or
Germans; Baird stoutly claimed them as national property, hinting
not so subtly that such property belonged in the nation's museum in
Washington. Powell was worth funding, in other words, not because
he might help Americans understand the origins of the Indian or the

development of humanity but because he was defending valuable national antiquities.

If the subordinate missed the point, Baird drove it home in a personal letter to Powell, which could only be taken as a warning to conform or else. "I have always found members of Congress very impatient in considering the question of pure philological work," the Secretary wrote. "Of my arguments before the appropriation committee, I have found the most potent to be the urgency of securing, at the earliest possible time, the archaeological and ethnological aboriginal matter which could be carried off to Europe, either by travelers sent out for the purpose, or by dealers in the U.S. collecting material for export."[39]

High on the list of sites to be defended from foreign fingers were the ancient burial mounds scattered throughout the eastern half of the country, but particularly in the Ohio and Mississippi river valleys. Powell was only mildly interested in excavating them, regarding their rotting contents as a vulgar curiosity offering little scientific information. But Baird and Congress were interested in the mounds, so Powell put Cyrus Thomas in charge of the work and gave him sufficient money to hire assistants. They contracted with rural landowners to dig into those large piles of earth and cart off whatever artifacts and bones they contained. The stray crania went to the Army Medical Museum for keeping, but the Smithsonian acquired a good number of human skeletons for its own vaults. Some whites could not believe that Indians had ever been able to construct such imposing structures and speculated that a superior race, now extinct, must have been responsible. But Powell took the view (which turned out to be true) that the architects were indeed the Indians, and that their complex social organization and funerary rites were not to be underestimated.[40]

Still another way in which Baird imposed his will and priorities on the bureau's program was by sending over personnel he wanted hired. Usually these were men who thought like museum curators and were unsuited for the study of Indian languages or work on the synonymy. But in one outstanding case Baird's protégé turned out to be someone whom Powell agreed was one of most promising ethnologists of the age, Frank Hamilton Cushing.

An emaciated fellow of dreamy eyes and oily skin, Cushing had a keen intelligence and knew how to express himself well. Baird hired him at the age of eighteen to work on arranging Indian artifacts, but plodding museum work was not thrilling to the youth. On a bureau-sponsored trip to New Mexico in 1879 Cushing visited the Zuni tribe and quickly resolved to move in with them — indeed, to try to become one of them and penetrate their mysterious ways. For five years he stayed among the Zuni, dwelling with the tribal governor, dressing and speaking as an Indian, and eventually becoming a member of the priesthood and a head war chief. He also secured his transfer to the bureau's expense account and began sending in extravagant bills. Powell was at once captivated by this intrepid investigator, who Indianized himself more fully than he had ever dared do, and chagrined at what he was costing the office.[41]

"The expense of my work at Zuni may, at times, seem large," Cushing soothed, "but the *results also* are large." Powell might have agreed, but he had to account for every penny expended and he had no control over this Baird-appointed man. "I have from time to time assisted Mr. Cushing, in various ways," he wrote to Baird, "but have not considered him to be under my instructions and have in no way given him orders or controlled his work." Cushing's excesses were cutting into other branches of the bureau's mission. He should be put under Powell's direct control. Baird complied, but then he let Cushing know that he might "continue to communicate with me as freely as ever."[42]

This awkward arrangement might have continued indefinitely, but a powerful U.S. senator intervened and sent all the parties scattering for cover. John Logan of Illinois (the same potentate whom Powell had carefully cultivated) had a pampered son-in-law who wanted to set up a private ranch near the Zuni reservation, and a copious spring claimed by the Zuni as their own would be very useful for watering the ranch's cattle. The Logans worked the back corridors of federal offices to get title to the spring. The Zuni protested, and their case was taken up by the *Boston Herald*, in December 1882, embarrassing the senator who, in turn, accused Frank Cushing of being the source of the newspaper story. Baird demanded that Cushing issue a categorical denial of any involvement in order to save the Smithsonian from retaliation. Senator Logan, he trembled, "is indomitable and relentless; and while is he a most valuable friend, he is a very dangerous enemy."[43] Cushing, who knew the arts of the courtier as well as any man, quickly penned a "not guilty" letter to Baird, and the flap quieted down. The rumor, nonetheless, was probably true. Cushing had been outraged by the high-level conniving against his adopted people and had come to their defense. But pressed to the wall he was fearful of upsetting his generous patron at the Smithsonian, a patron who looked on any sign of political controversy as the rumble of approaching doom.[44]

Powell was thus dragged into battles he did not want to fight. Out west he had been known as a cautious man when human life was at risk, but he could be outspoken and aggressive when he chose to take a stand. He had fought a fierce fight against the old fraud Ferdinand Hayden, though he had been distinctly more muted as a critical voice on the Public Lands Commission. Under Baird's authority he had tried to avoid fights and stick to science, even if that meant retreating from his promise that the Bureau of Ethnology would serve as a guide to Indian land and treaty issues.

Aside from hiring Charles Royce to look into the history of land cessions (published as part of the bureau's eighteenth annual report, which did not appear in print until 1899), Powell carefully distanced himself from the still smoldering territorial conflict between Indians and whites. He was compelled by those over him to keep out of trouble, to avoid giving offense to powerful men. But it was also his own decision to emphasize basic, noncontroversial research on language and mythology rather than disputes over land and rights. Caution became the bureau's middle name.

When Baird died in 1887, the astronomer Samuel Langley succeeded to the secretaryship. Langley, who was a man of Powell's exact own age, large, red-faced, and painfully shy, proved no more willing than Baird to give the bureau much autonomy. He too withheld a portion of each appropriation for the Smithsonian's own uses, over Powell's protests, and he too wanted no controversy over Indians to endanger his institution's always meager funding. Controversy, nonetheless, would come, and once more it would catch Powell in the cross hairs.

In 1891 the Bureau sent James Mooney to investigate a new messianic religion that was spreading from Nevada toward the Dakotas. The Paiute Wovoka had a revelation from a Christian-like God who promised that a new world was coming, where whites would disappear into the ground and the slain Indians and bison would arise to live once more as in the old times. The tribes must not take up arms but trust God and Wovoka for their deliverance. Called the Ghost Dance because of its emphasis on the return of the dead, the movement reached the Sioux just as they were mourning the killing of their legendary leader, Sitting Bull. For several years thereafter their reservations echoed the chants and dances of Wovoka's vision. Mooney left his studies of the sacred myths of the Cherokees to talk to Wovoka and then observe how his prophecies were affecting the people who had not so long ago rubbed out George Armstrong Custer but were now roiling in despair and rage.[45]

Mooney had been a journalist until Powell, appreciating a self-trained intelligence like his own, hired him at the bureau. Unlike Powell, he was from an Irish-Catholic family and carried resentments toward the Protestant hegemony. He embraced the Indians with fellow feeling for the ethnically marginalized. As he moved about the Dakota reservation, he was struck by similarities between the swaying, singing cultists of the Ghost Dance, so oblivious to the white man's guns, and the impassioned Methodist followers of John Wesley, whose "assemblies were characterized by all the hysteric and convulsive extravagance which they brought with them to this country, and which is not even yet extinct in the south."[46] The Methodist Church was scandalized by Mooney's analogy. Secretary Langley was scandalized too, and so perhaps was Powell, son of two of those fervent disciples of Wesley.

Earlier, the similarity between the Indian sachem telling stories around the campfire and the Methodist preacher exhorting his outdoor audience had crossed Powell's own mind. Moreover, he had long lumped all expressions of religion together as "mythology."[47] But now he denied any analogy between Wesley and Wovoka. "This curious evanescent cult" of the Ghost Dance, he explained, "seems rather a travesty on religion than an expression of the most exalted concepts within human grasp." With Langley looking over his shoulder, he urged caution "in comparing or contrasting religious movements among civilized peoples with such fantasies" as that described in Mooney's memoir. "While interesting and suggestive analogies may be found, the essential features of the movements are not homologous. . . . Red men and white are separated by the broadest known chasm in the development of belief, a chasm so broad that few representatives of either race are able definitely to bridge it in thought."[48]

On the other hand, Powell argued sensibly that the Ghost Dance was no threat to the whites. "The misconception of Indian religious philosophy," he wrote, "which in fact presents rather apparent than actual antagonism to civilization as it is in the stage commonly traversed toward higher culture, has occasioned needless loss of life and treasure."[49]

Ethnological science, so susceptible to the winds of politics and racial conflict, was turning out to be harder to pull off than Powell could have imagined. But for all his distractions and embarrassments he was succeeding to an impressive degree. By the mid-1880s, it was clear that the Bureau of Ethnology was the most important institution in anthropology America had ever seen, and indeed it would remain among the most important such institutions America ever would see. The bureau's annual reports were magnificently produced on heavy paper, lavish with illustrations. They opened the public's eyes to the exquisite arts, the settlement history and ceremonies, the intricate calendar systems, and the bewildering variety of languages of the native peoples. If Powell did not manage to achieve a full science of man, as he had hoped, he achieved more than any other individual of his generation toward that end.

The cost of this success was high, however, in several ways. First, Powell's health began to sag and fail. After years of hard labor in the field, which he had seemed to relish, he found, as Clarence King had found, that Washington was hard on his constitution. His wounded arm still bothered him, though that was a pain he was used to ignoring. Other ailments came along, however, that he could not ignore. In late fall 1881, Pilling wrote Erminnie Smith that "the Major is down again. You remember he went into a dark room early in October and staid there until the latter part of November. He then came out for a week and probably caught cold. At any rate, he has a second attack and just how long it will last we cannot tell."[50]

Powell's physician diagnosed the problem as iritis, an inflammation of the iris of the eye which brings severe pain and danger of permanent injury. Powell must cease all work, or risk losing his eyesight altogether. The darkroom cure worked, but a little over a year later, he was back home again, unable to read. The inflammation again eased, but then in early December, 1884, he was once more back in his bedroom with the curtains drawn.

For a man who had so much animal vitality, this enforced idleness had to be galling. In compensation he began taking to the western field for a month or two in late summer and early fall, less for scientific purposes than for toning up his constitution. Many of those trips were made in the company of James Stevenson, with whom he liked to poke about in the ruins of the Southwest: 1882, northern New Mexico; 1885, the San Francisco Mountains, the Little Colorado district, and Oak Creek in Arizona; 1887, the Tewan Mountains of New Mexico. Secretary Langley went along on the last of those outings to see what the Bureau was doing in the field. But after Stevenson died, Powell's archaeological trips west ceased.

Valetudinarian excursions from Washington did not put the bureau's director in much contact with native Americans. That was a second serious cost of institutional success. Fewer and fewer Indians came into Powell's life. Once on close terms with the likes of Chuarumpeak and Tapeats, he no longer was immersed in their lives or engaged in their problems. Increasingly they became memories and abstractions.

Shrewdly, Powell realized that ethnological research needed a strong institutional base and that the federal government was best equipped to give it. He must be in Washington as a consequence. Yet the nation's capital was a long way from its wards. How easy it was to ignore them now that they posed no real danger to white citizens. Even the bureau, devoted to knowing more about them, could lose them among the pages filled with census numbers and vocabularies, the linguistic maps, the monographs for publication, and the boxes and boxes of stuff for the museum. Powell's field workers, of course, spent much of each year living with their subjects; but the director was perforce preoccupied with many bureaucratic details. Not surprisingly he felt a greater gulf than ever between the races —"a chasm so broad that few representatives of either race are able definitely to bridge it in thought." He lost touch with the daily struggle for cultural survival still taking place among the Indians. He lost interest in what his ethnology might offer policy makers, all the while he was drawing nearer to the ideal of science.

When Powell acceded to President Garfield's request and added the Geological Survey to his responsibilities, he was instantly set upon the pinnacles of American science. Geology was the most advanced and respected of fields; it had come of age fully a half-century earlier. Geologists in the United States had long-established ties with their European counterparts, cooperating with them to correlate strata on both sides of the Atlantic. Their field was vast, their knowledge sophisticated. The names of James Dwight Dana, James Hall, and the brothers Henry and William Rogers rang from rock to rock.

As the nation moved west, geology advanced too, now in the vanguard of settlement, now in the rear studying the ground that pioneers had passed over. State legislatures supported that research, nowhere more impressively than in New York, where the idea of a state geological survey had its finest realization. The irresistible effect of that public support was to put the stamp of utility on science. Legislators tended to prefer applied over basic research. Dreaming of a great empire rising out of the land, they wanted geologists to tell them what kind of wealth lay underfoot and how that wealth might be developed as quickly as possible.

"Eighteen hundred and sixty-seven . . . marks, in the history of national geological work, a turning point when the science ceased to be dragged in the dust of rapid exploration and took a commanding position in the professional work of the country."[51] So declared Clarence King in the first annual report of the U.S. Geological Survey. The date he referred to was the year when his own survey of the Fortieth Parallel was launched. Not altogether unfairly, he was claiming credit for transforming geology from a secondary to a primary agent in economic development. Its bias toward the applied would continue but, following King's example, scientists themselves would define what was useful and what was not.

The American empire, King predicted, must in the future shift from an agrarian to an industrial economic base, and in that shift geology must assume greater power and importance. Already he sensed that, as the population spread over the land, it was approaching a state of equilibrium with local resources. Farmers using traditional tools to produce for their own consumption faced a built-in limit, one they would soon reach when all the arable soil was occupied. Industrialism would then appeal as a postagrarian system in which science and technology would show how to expand production on a fixed base. "Every intelligent student of the country knows that we are yet at the very threshold of the industrial life of the Republic," King told Congress, and the coming challenge is "to utilize with the highest technical skill and with the utmost scientific economy, all elements of national wealth."[52]

The Geological Survey promised to help shape that industrial future. It could show the mineral industries, now worth one billion dollars a year and sure to grow, where to find a deeper wealth and how to transform it into unlimited prosperity. But stability was as necessary as growth. The European mining industry, which, in contrast to the American, acknowledged its dependence on geological science, had learned how to extract a stable community as well as ore from the earth, much as European forestry had learned how to manage trees for sustained yield. There lay the route to permanence. Americans, through the aid of the survey, some of whose experts were German- or French-trained, could likewise learn how to create an industrialism that was conservative and steadfast.[53]

Left to themselves, on the other hand, the private mining companies would never rise above their careless, wasteful past. They would continue to speculate wildly on rumors of mother lodes and bonanzas. Lacking reliable knowledge, they would overinvest in some veins of ore while underinvesting in others. They would see gold where there was only pyrite. The prospect of a quick profit would always pull them away from slow, steady work in place. Greed would forever corrupt honesty.

The dominant trend after the Civil War was not only toward an industrial economy but also toward an economy controlled by the large private corporation, which alone could amass the colossal amounts of capital required for new technologies of production and transportation. Railroads were the most stunning achievement of that new corporate economy. At the end of every railroad line stood a mine or a factory or a mail-order house that increasingly depended on corporate capital too. No single entrepreneur or small-scale producer could resist that power for long. Even farmers were losing much of their traditional independence to become the vassals of incorporated railroads, grain merchants, and banks.

The Geological Survey, as a state-supported agency, was embroiled in the most burning questions of the day in political economy: What should the role of government be in a corporate regime, and what should the role of science be? Director King gave unequivocal answers. The state should liberally fund science, particularly a science oriented toward practical research. And both the state and its scientists should act as partners with the private capitalists.

None of this program was exactly authorized in the legislation establishing the survey, though it may have been foremost in the mind of some of its backers, Abram Hewitt among them. The law spoke only vaguely of "the classification of the public lands and examination of the Geological Structure, mineral resources and products of the national domain."[54] "Classification" meant specifying whether lands had agricultural, timber, or mineral value. "Structure" meant scientifically describing the land forms and strata in their relation to one another. "Mineral resources" might include the precious or base metals, the inorganic (gold, iron) or the organic derivative (coal, oil), the miscellanies of granite, gravel, phosphates, or phosphorous. And "national domain"—where exactly was that? Was it the same as the "public domain," those lands still held by the federal government, or was it a more inclusive space, perhaps as inclusive as the entire nation?

Several months into his job, King asked the legal authorities in the Department of the Interior what "national domain" meant and was told to take a constricted view and confine his operations to the states and territories in which there were public lands. His appetite was larger than that, however, and he appealed to Congress for authority to enlarge the survey into a national institution—to make it "one of the most powerful elements in the development of the National mineral resources." He would narrow its focus, on the other hand, to empha-size "practical or economical geology," setting aside more academic subjects such as the origin of rocks or the laws of continent making. Above all, he would have the survey serve the nation's mining indus-try, which "has been more than overlooked, it has been pointedly cold-shouldered."[55] Neither the enlargement nor the restriction he sought was granted, and King lost interest and resigned.

Enter his friend and successor, Powell. Eager to help Congress make up its mind, Powell assumed from the start that the survey should serve the whole nation. The day after his appointment he received a letter from a geologist in New York, urging federal attention to the Atlantic seaboard states because most of the state surveys there were so poorly funded and crudely done. "Only a few capitalists" understand the min-eral potential, while "the vast majority of the people have been and still are totally ignorant, very often, of the very resources under their feet." The writer further urged expansion into the war-devastated South, which desperately wanted economic development but lacked the en-abling scientific knowledge. Here too the people, without adequate in-formation, might part with their mineral wealth "for a mere song."[56] Similar pleas from state survey employees fed Powell's resolve to make the Washington agency the nerve center of American geological intel-ligence, in service to all regions and all people. He proceeded to do just that, in a way that earned him, in some circles at least, a reputation for deviousness that followed him for years to come.

Powell's budget request in his second year carried a small sug-gested amendment, permitting the agency "to continue the prepara-tion of a geological map of the United States." In the House it was introduced by Atkins of Tennessee, one of the chief advocates for es-tablishing the survey in '79. A lively debate ensued in which limited-government, states-rights legislators charged that the phrase "to continue" was a deliberate trick. They had never agreed that govern-ment should make any such map. Further, they steamed, the expan-sion eastward was a scheme to fatten the pockets of private landowners, most of them located in the Appalachian mountains, by finding minerals for them that they could then sell to the railroads. Powell's friends answered that, since it was taxpayers in eastern states who were paying for the survey, they deserved to know as much about their states' potential as westerners did about the West. "We want the benefit of scientific exploration," one of them admitted, to enable us to get at our "vast, hidden wealth." The survey would "transform mountain wildernesses to bee-hives of industry."[57]

The glitter of neglected wealth was a powerful motivator, one that convinced both houses to give Powell his mandate to "continue." By summer 1882 he was rushing to extend operations into the older states, from Massachusetts and New Jersey to Texas, until the East rivaled the West in field activity. Where the vaunted King had failed, Powell had triumphed. He would go on triumphing, winning larger and larger appropriations from a Congress that panted for development.

Nor did his friends let Powell's star dip below King's in terms of salary. When his professed friend Senator Logan proposed to cut the director's compensation from $6,000 to $5,000 per year (bringing it down to the level of distinguished legislators like himself), Conger of Michigan protested that it was unfair and insulting to a great hero.

> The enterprise of that one-armed soldier, as he has passed down the rapids of the Colorado, as he has climbed the mountains of the continent, as he has explored the whole range of the formerly unexplored regions of the United States, is a perfect romance; it is a wonder; it is a marvel. . . . [A]nd he did all that on a pitiful compensation, less than a teller in a bank gets.

Senator Dawes of Massachusetts interrupted, "That was in the past." But Call of Florida rose with equal vigor to defend Major Powell, whom he described "as modest as he is intelligent and learned and indefatigable and laborious. . . . The question is whether we are to degrade American genius and learning and the highest scientific attainments." In his fields, Powell stands "chief and head above others, at least in our own country."[58] The salary was not cut.

The nation's geology thus became another jumbled space for Powell to put in order, though King had already started the process. Four highly autonomous divisions of research were operating in the West, beyond the 101st meridian, with old, experienced hands at their head. The Sierra mining district was under the gaze of King's personal friends Arnold Hague and George Becker. He assigned to another friend, Samuel Emmons, the Leadville region in western Colorado, lying over ten thousand feet above sea level. A boom had begun there in 1877 with the discovery of silver-bearing ore, and within three years the population was fifteen thousand. Cultural enrichment followed when Oscar Wilde lectured, with a white lily in his hand, on the stage of the town's Tabor Opera House. Enormous fortunes were projected in lead, zinc, and copper as well as silver. It was Emmons's duty to show the mining capitalists how to explore and develop the underground wealth over the long term, a duty that, through no fault of his own, he failed to fulfill. Within a decade the town was sliding into decline.[59]

King had absorbed other employees of the defunct western surveys. Grove Karl Gilbert had charge of the Great Basin district, where he ignored economic geology completely to focus on the geomorphology of ancient Lake Bonneville. The Colorado River and Plateau Province went to Clarence Dutton, who hunkered down to write his *Tertiary History*, another study that had nothing to do with King's industrial priorities. Closer to King's heart was the study of iron and coal extraction techniques (assigned to the Harvard mining engineer Raphael Pumpelly) and the collection of national mining statistics for the Tenth Census. Congress's mandate to classify the public lands was simply ignored.

Powell scrupulously continued all the appointments King had made, including a position for the ailing Ferdinand Hayden, living at home in Philadelphia and supposedly finishing up the research from his years in the West. Like the other heads of divisions, Hayden collected $4,000 a year, though it was more of a pension than payment for a job well done. Old animosities forgotten, Hayden congratulated Powell on his appointment and offered "my loyal services." As his syphilis advanced, he fell deeper into depression, unable to meet his obligations or even to leave his house where he hobbled around on crutches. To John Newberry he wrote that Powell had "been far more than just and magnanimous toward me, and I wish it were in my power to make some adequate return." That magnanimity raised a few awkward questions for Powell at budget time, but at last Hayden took himself forever off the accounts by dying at age 59.[60]

Those divisions represented order as decreed by King, and Powell did not dismantle them. But he did undertake to increase survey chambers dramatically in size and number and to rearrange them so they looked radically different from King's original floor plan. The chemistry laboratory remained intact, quietly responding to hopeful queries. Becker and Emmons went on running their mining offices as before. Gilbert stayed in his sublime deserts, though Hague, ready for a change, went off to the Yellowstone National Park — no mining allowed there — to observe erupting geysers and other curiosities. Dutton, finishing his book, shifted toward volcanic landscapes and traveled to the Sandwich Islands. Now the East had its own divisions, including the glaciated region around the Great Lakes and upper Mississippi (where Powell put Thomas Chamberlain and Roland Irving in charge) and New England and Appalachia (Raphael Pumpelly and Nathaniel Shaler). Powell also signed cooperative arrangements with various state surveys.

By fiscal year 1885, he had raised the agency's budget to $500,000 and his employees and their field staff to 283. "General geology" had become one of the biggest rooms in the house, bigger than economic geology.[61]

A striking example of the shift toward a less utilitarian science was the room designated "paleontology," filled with fossil bones of Cretaceous, Jurassic, or even older age. Powell recruited Yale professor Othniel C. Marsh to head that division. King had anticipated such support by arranging to publish Marsh's first comprehensive treatises, *Odontornithes* (1880), on the extinct toothed birds of North America, and *Dinocerata* (1884), on the order of extinct giant mammals that Marsh had excavated in an Eocene lake basin in Wyoming. Visions of fossil serpents and flying reptiles, of horned beasts lumbering across the plains of Nebraska and Kansas or the Green River basin, of lost tropical lakes in the West, excited the public imagination almost beyond anything else the study of the earth could offer. King, acceding to public interest, had not hesitated to include Marsh in his enterprise, even if it meant making another exception to industrial geology. Powell did more than follow along. He put Professor Marsh on the federal payroll (the professor had a position but no salary from Yale, though he had an independent income) and gave him enough funds to hire additional staff at the Peabody Museum of Natural History over which he presided. Powell went even farther, setting up laboratories for invertebrate paleontology under William Dall, Charles White, and Charles Walcott, and one for paleobotany (the fossil plants) under a brilliant young recruit, Lester Ward.

Marsh was an important figure to cultivate, an eminent and powerful ally in the academic establishment. This large, robust man, scowling and imperious, had an international reputation in his field. The leading biologists in England had lauded his finds in the boneyards of the West. Thomas Huxley, who stayed a week with him in New Haven in 1876, had declared his collection of fossil horses "the most wonderful thing I ever saw." And the great Darwin had written that "your work on these old birds and on the many fossil animals of N. America has afforded the best support to the theory of evolution, which has appeared within the last 20 years."[62] Marsh's research had elevated him to the presidency of the National Academy, first as a stand-in for the ailing Joseph Henry—and that at a crucial time when the academy was pondering Powell's western-survey consolidation scheme—and then on formal election in 1883. He remained president until 1895, longer than anyone else in academy history. Marsh looked like a gilded asset. His name on the payroll would do more than any number of mining experts to raise the scientific stature of the survey.

More than political advantage lay behind such an appointment. Powell was sincerely devoted to the ideal of basic research as a government responsibility. That had been true in his western journeys; it was true now in his Washington moves. Geology was foremost an intellectual adventure, dedicated to the pursuit of knowledge, and only secondarily should it be a servant of industry or public utility. All that adventure King had dismissed as secondary, even irrelevant. Powell wanted to put it back. He had never demonstrated much enthusiasm for solving mining problems, though he might praise the industry as one of the most important in the civilized world.[63] Mining was about producing wealth, and wealth was not an obsession with Powell as it was with King. Wealth, he was sure, would come along, in due course; it would naturally follow from the accumulated achievements of science. But the increase of wealth should not be the immediate or controlling purpose of the scientist, nor of the survey.

In throwing so much support to basic research, Powell took a calculated risk, given the traditional bias toward the utilitarian and profitable in American attitudes toward science. Basic research had no clear, immediate payoff. Like poetry or painting, it appealed to nonmaterial pleasures—curiosity, mental gratification, a love of order. Surprisingly, Congress went along with Powell's shift of emphasis, at least in the early years. Either the people's representatives assumed that science, no matter what problems it worked on, would yield an economic return, or they were beginning to be persuaded by Powell that basic science offered more important rewards than money alone.

By no means did Powell ignore the utilitarian aspect, though he found ways to promote it that King had never imagined. "Without a good topographic map," Powell explained, "geology cannot . . . be thoroughly studied."[64] The biggest new room in Powell's reorganization was a division for making a topographic map of the entire United States, similar to the one that had been completed for parts of Utah and Arizona. It would show every large rise and swell of the land surface, the contours of every valley, the course of every river, the height of every mountain and coastal plain. Americans could walk west with their eyes. For the first time they could gain a sense of the land that no Land Office grid could impart. They could see the

structure of the continent, unroll it across a table, and begin to understand the geological forces that had made it. They could know
more fully where they were.

"A Government cannot do any scientific work of more value to the
people at large," Powell declared to Congress on 5 December 1884,
"than by causing the construction of proper topographic maps of the
country." Engineers could use the maps for plotting highways and railway lines, sanitarians for solving urban water supply problems, and
farmers for selecting the best agricultural sites. This was unabashedly
"useful" science, but it was science that served not a small number of
mining corporations, or even the interests of industrialists particularly, but the most basic environmental needs of a whole society.[65]

The plan was to send teams into all the nation's regions to triangulate the landscape and plot its contours on a plane-table. Where the
terrain was simple, as on the prairies, the scale of the map would be
four miles to the inch (1:250,000). Where there were important mining districts, the scale would be larger, two miles to the inch
(1:125,000). Where people lived densely clustered, the scale would be
even larger, one mile to the inch (1:62,500). Leaving Alaska aside for
the present, the survey would prepare some 2,600 sheets. These could
be gathered into a great atlas, whose pages would improve in accuracy
as time went on and new surveys were done. Powell's estimated date
for completion, at least in preliminary form, was the year 1900.

Nothing in the survey's founding legislation specifically called for
such a national mapping project, but Congress had the power,
through appropriations, to approve or disapprove. Powell put
$170,000 into his 1885 budget for "geography," one third of his total
request, and Congress approved. The maps that resulted were uneven
in quality, some of them hastily or inexpertly prepared. But they became Powell's most significant legacy in earth science. As William
Morris Davis observed in 1913, "no publications of the Survey have
had . . . a greater general usefulness. . . . The change from geographic
barbarism of that earlier day to the relative civilization of the present
time is due more to Powell than to any other one man."[66] Generations
would run their fingers over brown lines of contour, blue lines of waterways, green patches of vegetation, black lines of cultural features —
the cartographic conventions that Powell adopted for this, his most
cherished project.

To supervise the large new division of topographical mapping,
Powell appointed as chief geographer Henry Gannett, a native of
Maine, graduate of Harvard's Lawrence Scientific School, and for-

mer field man for Hayden. Gannett joined the survey in 1879 and remained there until his death in 1914. Like his boss, he was an organizer of science and a lover of maps. Quietly diligent, highly exacting in his standards, he became one of the great figures in the history of American map making. For Gannett's lieutenants Powell tapped, among others, his own brother-in-law and Colorado river companion, Harry Thompson, who abruptly gave up sheep ranching in Kansas to get back into the topographic business. Another family member came at the receipt of a telegram: "Send Arthur to Washington to join my scientific corps. have a good place where he can learn and grow: start at salary $60 per mo. and expenses in field."[67] Son of sister Martha and her husband John Davis, formerly of Macon County, Illinois, now of Junction City, Kansas, Arthur Davis entered the survey as a topographer before switching at the turn of the century to the new federal Bureau of Reclamation, whose commissioner he eventually became.

Powell's criteria for making appointments were as eclectic as his scientific interests. In some cases he hired men who were the best in the nation at what they did—Gilbert, Marsh, Gannett. Other times he was swayed by ties of family or personal friendship. Or by the life story of an individual who, like himself, had risen from obscure origins through a mix of genius and perspiration. Lester Ward was one of those, as was a young farm boy from Iowa, William John McGee, who after teaching himself geology had applied for a position with the survey in 1883. Powell liked the brash palaver of McGee and put him to work at whatever came to hand. Others joined the survey through the intervention of a powerful politician or scientist whom Powell wanted to please. Requests to hire came in regularly, and where possible he accommodated, though the job given out was usually a lowly one of carrying a transit or packing a mule.

More questionable than any of those hiring practices, though in fact it was not questioned at all by Congress, was the shifting of several Bureau of Ethnology employees over to the Geological Survey payroll. Like the Green and the Grand mixing their waters, the two agencies flowed as one under Powell. To be sure, he kept separate accounts, reported to different superiors, and launched distinctive research programs for each, but he also made many joint appointments that blurred the bureaucratic boundaries. Besides himself, there were James Stevenson, who served as chief executive officer for both agencies, William McChesney, James Pilling, William Henry Holmes, and Jack Hillers. All of them had their salary paid by the survey while continuing on at the bureau, though it must be added that often they worked two jobs now instead of one, as Powell did, and without a pay increase. The survey, whose budget was ten times larger than the bureau's, subsidized ethnology and helped free it from the constraints under which it labored.

When the staff of the two agencies became too large for their old, separate quarters, Powell lobbied for a new building in which all could work together. After some delay, in 1884 they were authorized to rent space in the Hooe building. Here Powell positioned himself in a corner office on the second floor, consulting with ethnologists or geologists in quick succession, shifting from myths to maps, word lists to ore samples, rug weavers to swamp drainage, and back again. Undoubtedly, no other scientist in America had his eye on so diverse a set of inquiries. And undoubtedly, only Powell himself, wandering through his many chambers, could have said how they were all connected or what they had in common.

Certainly King's surviving appointees could not discern any coherence in this Powellian labyrinth. They remained far off in their mountain fastnesses, doing what King had wanted them to do, rarely visiting the Washington office. But from a distance they sensed that in the rapid expansion and amalgamation going on, they were no longer in control of government geology. "The latest Survey news," joked Albert Williams, "is that next year we are to absorb the Land Office and Indian Bureau, having already swallowed the Northern Pacific and Coast Surveys; in 1886 we take in the Dept. of Agriculture, Interior, War, State, Navy and Post Office Depts.; and in 1887 the White House, Treasury and anything that may be left."[68]

Emmons in the Rockies was the most querulous about the changes. Tall, slender, with carefully trimmed beard and moustache hiding a weak chin, he was a dandy among the tailings, albeit much respected by those he advised. King's departure had left him devastated, morbid, on the edge of resignation, a mood that did not brighten when he realized that Powell and not himself would be appointed successor.[69] Salary he did not need. He enjoyed as much as $17,000 a year from private investments, more than four times his USGS salary, and kept a summer house in the fashionable seaside resort of Newport, Rhode Island. Mining, however, was his profession, and he longed to have the old agency back where mining was king.

Watching the skirmishes with Congressional cost-cutters, Emmons was not impressed with Powell's leadership, though in the end it won through. "He always has a word of his own for anything," Emmons

The Hooe Iron Building, 1324–1334 F Street, Washington, D.C. Here the U.S. Geological Survey and Bureau of Ethnology had their offices during the 1880s and 1890s. The building was constructed in 1873, demolished in 1926.
(Courtesy: U.S. Geological Survey)

complained, "but as it generally conveys no idea to any mind but his own, it is difficult to remember." Indecisiveness added to the linguistic confusion. Faced with a problem, Emmons learned from Gilbert, the director "will think it over for some days, come to half a dozen minds about it, and then decide suddenly without any reference to what we have said about it." Becker stoked Emmons's indignation with a cynical comment on the recurrent bouts of iritis: "Altho' he may be unfitted to attend to Survey matters, the Major seems to be able to play his regular game [of cards]. I wish he would attend to our financial matters."[70]

If Powell dithered, he dithered mainly over how much autonomy he should allow the mining experts. Becker, perennially aloof in California, tried the director's patience most of all. He seemed unable to focus his research or make any progress toward publication, though

Powell had little doubt about his abilities. Similarly, Emmons was slow in getting his Leadville mining tome to the printer (it took eight years). Allocations went out to these two; nothing but receipts came back. To Powell it seemed that they answered only to God — or to King. But from their point of view, King was lamentably nowhere in sight, despite his promise to stand behind the throne. Powell was threatening to centralize everything in Washington, and no one was stopping him. He was constantly interfering with decisions that they had made, closing, for example, the independent office in Denver that Emmons had set up.

The disagreement touched deeper issues than decision making within the agency. King's men had a contrary notion of what the survey's role in society should be. Becker admonished that they must "furnish the country with information of direct industrial utility. For my part I believe that it is only on condition of doing something of the kind that the Survey will be permitted to become a permanent institution." "My object," Emmons wrote to Powell, "has been primarily to arrive at results which should be of immediate and practical value in the development of the mineral resources of the country, leaving to those of more purely scientific interest, which were by no means neglected, a second place." At the very outset of Powell's administration, Emmons had reminded him indirectly, in a speech given before mining engineers in Washington, what the survey's true mission was supposed to be: "Prominence should be given to economical geology."[71] Government should serve mining engineers in the private sector, just as those engineers served their employers, by placing before them "in an intelligible manner the character, mode of occurrence, and probable quantity and value of the mineral deposits" which their property may contain, "and the best method of utilizing them." Put another way, the USGS should give place of honor to its mining geologists, who should serve the industrial economy by helping the capitalists and their hired experts.

Powell had failed to get that relationship right. While he did not reduce the money going to mineral resources, he did not increase it much either. "I have appreciated from time to time," Emmons told him, "that you are reluctant to devote the amount of money to our work, which its general plan made at the commencement of the Survey involves."[72] Instead, money was lavished on paleontology, topographical mapping, Ice Age studies, and the geology of Martha's Vineyard.

In reply, Powell tried to justify to the dissidents his strategy, which was to broaden the program's activities in both basic and applied research. He was responding to what he conceived as opportunities and pressures. The politics of governmental science forced him to take on work that he might not want to do. For him too it was a matter of survival.

> I wish to make the Survey of such magnitude that the whole area of the United States can be properly occupied with a corps of topographers and geographers doing efficient work which will be available during the present generation. In order to grow from year to year, it is necessary to interest a large body of legislators and to obtain the friendly cooperation of the public press. In order to do this, I am compelled to vary somewhat my plans from what I would otherwise do, and yet such change is no injury to the work in the sequel. Having been committed to an extension of the work in the eastern portion of the United States, it became necessary to show that we were actually doing work in a number of Eastern states. In order to allay certain antagonisms which have arisen, I have found in necessary this spring to commence work in certain regions not contemplated last summer. . . . I fully appreciate your willingness to sacrifice your special branch of the work to the general good of the Survey. Please accept my thanks.[73]

A disingenuous defense it was, for in truth Powell was guided as much by his own convictions and enthusiasms as he was by political pragmatism.

The dissidents Emmons and Becker (and the more temperate Hague) came to Washington only now and then, passing through on their way to Newport boat races and summer lawn parties. They were not on hand enough to insist on their views. Meanwhile, Powell drew around him many loyal supporters in the capital, who formed a happy dining group that they called, in memory of old field days, "the Great Basin Mess." Gilbert was at the center of that group, along with Dutton, Gannett, Holmes, Pilling, Walcott, and McGee. Gathered around the linen-covered table, they were a convivial gang, aware of their leader's foibles but sure that he was on the right track.

Who was right in this rift within the agency? It was not to be decided by an appeal to the ghost of Clarence King. His was only one interpretation of what the country needed and wanted. Powell's vision was more open-ended, egalitarian, and diversified. It would be up to those who controlled the purse to choose which science they wanted.

National science was proving to be a fast-growing bush with strong, well-fertilized roots. Congress might severely lop and prune, but in a few years the bush would again be bursting with vigorous new growth. The year 1879 had seen a heavy pruning, with the consolidation of the western surveys into the Geological Survey. Five years later the bush was more rank and overgrown than ever. Not only had Powell nurtured the survey itself into a half-million-dollar enterprise and grown a whole new branch in Ethnology, but other science programs not in his hands had flourished as well. The Coast and Geodetic Survey, once in charge of making charts of harbors and headlands, had now expanded across the continent and had a half million of its own to spend. Then there were the military's Signal Service Corps and Hydrographic Office, not to mention the National Museum, the Fish Commission, and the National Observatory. It was time to get out the shears once more.

A special House-Senate commission, known as the Allison commission, was authorized in July 1884 to determine how to nip away the waste and overlap. Its chair, William Allison, was also chair of the Senate Appropriations Committee (a position he would occupy for 27 years). A lawyer from the Mississippi River town of Dubuque, Iowa, a moderate Republican, he was the sort of man whom Powell knew well and with whom he had much in common. Republicans dominated the commission, including the naval enthusiast from Maine, Eugene Hale, and the author of the act establishing the civil service system, George Pendleton. The Democrats had a strong voice in Hilary Herbert, former secretary of the navy in the Confederacy and now congressman from Alabama.

Immediately, the commission appealed to the National Academy of Sciences for suggestions on how the federal government could support scientific inquiry more efficiently. President Marsh appointed a special committee, which promptly recommended that a Department of Science be established in the President's Cabinet, which would draw all researches under single coordinated supervision and prevent unnecessary duplication. Failing that, the government should at least be regularly advised by a permanent commission, part civilian, part military. Nothing, said the academy, needed to be changed within the Geological Survey. Although in Europe topographic maps were commonly the responsibility of war departments, the U.S. civilian approach under Powell was working well.[74]

Illness prevented Powell from making a full statement before the academy's committee, but in early December when the Allison commission opened hearings he was the first to show up, eager to defend and enlighten. For hours they went over the distinction between the Geological Survey's kind of mapping and the Coast Survey's (which tried to measure the overall shape of the earth) or the General Land Office's. Powell reviewed the legislative authority he had for his operations. On a second day he came back to ask that bureaus like his own "be left free to prosecute . . . research in all its details without dictation from superior authority in respect to the methods of research to be used." If supervision was necessary, it should come from the wise old heads at the Smithsonian, not a new board, a cabinet officer, or the military. Such an independent institution, run by scientists but depending on federal appropriations, was the best solution to the modern demand for governmental research support, one that was gaining ground even in the older countries of Europe.[75]

Years earlier, in an obituary for an obscure student of the Colorado mountains, Powell had complained that too much bad science was being done, competing against the good. "Some of our geological literature," he admitted, "could be burned and no harm done. O that a pope would rise in the holy catholic church of geologists — a pope with will to issue a bull for the burning of all geological literature unsanctified by geological meaning." But administrative experience had taught him that research "cannot be controlled by some central authority, as an army by its general, from the fact that scientific men, competent to pursue original research, are peculiarly averse to dictation and official management."[76]

In a reappearance before the Allison commission in February, 1885, Powell reiterated the point: "Scientific men are, as a class, the most radical democrats in society — patient, enthusiastic, and laborious while engaged in work in which they are thoroughly absorbed, by methods which command their judgments, but restive and rebellious when their judgments are coerced by superior authority."[77] The clear message was that congressmen should let the scientists themselves, and the scientific administrators who understood them best, do any pruning that this bush needed.

He threw both basic and applied science at them, denying any rigid distinction —"there is no scientific research which is not for the general welfare." He granted that government should not take over all research, but added that "private research is very greatly retarded in America because certain lines of research which only the Government itself can pursue have been largely neglected."[78] He defined for them, in short, an ideal of what government should do or not do.

The survey's topographic maps were that positive ideal captured on paper. They were "a plain representation" of the facts of geology, which was "the most comprehensive science studied by man." They drew on advanced knowledge but spoke to the public in symbols they could understand. The maps laid out the very order of the natural world. "It is as important to study the topography and to prepare topographic maps," he told the senators and congressmen, "as it is for the physician or the physiologist to study the anatomy of the human system." Such a contribution to human understanding could only be provided by the federal government; no private interests would go to the expense. That was why he had brought into the Geological Survey the finest corps of topographers that any country had ever seen, a corps that was helping Americans make better use of the earth.[79]

Powell could see his maps one day helping America carry out vast undertakings, most of them involving water and the flow of rivers. His interest in topography had grown out of experiencing the West, he told the commission, where settlers needed "some economic but simple and practical means of learning how the streams of that country could be utilized" for irrigation. Now he could see the fuller dimensions of that need—"the control of great rivers" everywhere in the country. The survey's maps could instruct people living in the lower Mississippi Valley, among the most fertile of agricultural districts but periodically overflowed by flood waters, on how to solve their problem. Trap those waters near their origins, the melting snow fields of the Rocky Mountains, use them for irrigation, and the lower valley could be saved from destruction. "The interests of those two districts of country are bound together, and the only practical way of redeeming the Mississippi valley is by redeeming the deserts of the great plains."[80] You want utility, practicality, science for profit? I offer utility on the grandest scale imaginable. I have only just begun to dream of the possibilities.

The commissioners asked questions, they sought clarification, they called for employment records, publication accounts, and cost comparisons with other agencies. Powell gave them all that over the next twelve months. And he gave them more—150 pages comparing governmental science in Europe, tables detailing the bookkeeping procedures he had put in place, samples of disbursement forms and vouchers, account books that spelled out the expense of a day's supply of hay in North Carolina, a night's lodging in Texas, a cook's wages in California. He showed them how he had tried to cut publication costs by adopting the newest techniques of photoengraving and printing. In March he commenced sending in monthly reports to the Secretary of the Interior on what he and his staff had been doing. If he had grandiose vision, he also wanted his interlocutors to know that he paid attention to details. He had a sense of fiduciary responsibility. His books were open for minute scrutiny.

Outside the commission hearings the capital was going through a much debated shift in party administration. The first Democrat had been elected to the presidency in nearly three decades, since before the Civil War. Grover Cleveland, a short, chunky man of firm ideas, was that victor, though he won by almost as thin a margin as had Garfield. For all the partisan wrangling, however, little distinguished the Democrat from his Republican opponent or predecessors. Like them, he was an advocate of business, the tariff, and low-cost, minimalist government. He meant to reduce the size of the federal budget. A commiserating message came to Powell from Cleveland's home state of New York: "Hope the new President will not send in a message denouncing the U.S. Geological Survey & U.S. Coast Survey as drain pipes for wasting the peoples money. Who knows? He may cease to be a demagogue when he reaches the White House."[81]

As it turned out, once in office Cleveland appeared to take little interest in the investigation going on into government science. His campaign rhetoric against corruption and waste, nonetheless, seemed to inspire others to become more aggressive in looking for scandal. Rumors began to circulate in the spring of 1885 that the USGS director was falling into disgrace and indeed was finished.[82] The *Boston Daily Advertiser* carried on its front page a news item: "Professor Shaler of Harvard College is talked of to succeed Major Powell at the head of the geological survey. There are some charges that this bureau has been extravagantly managed, and a change would be beneficial to the service." Nathaniel Shaler, the Kentucky-born professor of paleontology and geology, wrote to his sister that "nothing could induce me to take the place of Director U.S. Geological Survey. . . . Besides, Powell is doing very well and should be kept in office."[83] Quickly, the rumor died away, though not the scandalmongering.

A few weeks later came new gossip, this time from the *Cincinnati Commercial Gazette*. Now Powell was charged not with financial excess but with spreading the godless doctrine of evolution. To get a job in his agency, the paper reported, a scientist reputedly had to believe that "man has been evolved from mol[l]usks and baboons." Powell denied the charge: "The scientific men in the bureaus under my charge are evolutionists; that is, they accept some form of evolution.

All scientific men do." But it was not a requirement of the job, nor had anyone been denied a place because of his religious views. "Quite a number are members of orthodox churches," he pointed out. Any agency true to the standards of science would not put up either a religious or an antireligious test for admission. "Scientific men can not be bigots, and the only test applied to applicants for places is one of fitness."[84]

The Cincinnati paper was not finished with making trouble, for in July it carried still another accusatory article on "the brazen and persistent lobbying" that Powell supposedly had done to get his empire launched. The article told how the Geological Survey had come into being through "one of the most disreputable exhibitions of lobbying ever carried on about Congress," with the design of getting the General Land Office and Army Corps of Engineers under Powell's thumb. Although some of the Survey's research was valuable, "much of it is utterly useless, much is trash, much is unreliable, and all of it exceedingly costly." An auditor from the Treasury Department, the writer added, was going over all the survey accounts, suggesting that something there must be rotten.[85]

Still more rumors spread about what was turning up in the Treasury audit. The *New York Times*, along with the *Boston Advertiser,* claimed that it made "some very serious and explicit charges" against Powell's management. He had ignored Congress's spending guidelines, for instance, and allowed certain scientists to keep public property as their own.[86]

The scientist Simon Newcomb felt his gorge rising with such false information and "flaming headlines." In truth, he declared, the journalists did not have all the facts. "So far as Auditor Chenowith has examined the accounts of the geological survey, he has found no illegality in its expenditures." Newcomb's defense left open the question of whether Powell had been a little extravagant at times. But apparently the director was not worried about being hauled up for fraud, for Newcomb reported that he had left for a month's tour of inspection in the West.[87]

Rumors had spread all the way to California, where George Becker was getting nervous if Powell was not. A letter he received from Clarence Dutton tried to allay those fears. Auditor Chenowith and his accountants had sniffed around the office for three months, Dutton reported, but in the end they were forced to own that the survey "presented a splendid & creditable showing." Several eastern congressmen had warned the auditor that he was not to report what was not true; Powell had acted lawfully by expanding into their states. Higher up, neither President Cleveland nor Interior Secretary Lucius Lamar had countenanced the attack on Powell, "as far as can now be seen & judged."

> The attack arises from a gang of cheap newspaper men backed by
> a few politicians who want to break down the barrier which keeps
> the petty patronage of the scientific bureaus from their reach.
> They have undertaken to poison public opinion & may have
> temporarily produced some effect in that direction. But I think
> no serious harm beyond that will befall.[88]

As an expression of his own confidence in Powell, Dutton managed to get his leave from Army duty extended so that he could continue working for the survey.

More seriously in trouble was the director of the Coast and Geodetic Survey, J.E. Hilgard, who had been far more lax than Powell in dispersing funds. Eventually, it would be Hilgard, not Powell, who would resign his office. But not before Hilgard's good friend Alexander Agassiz of Harvard denounced the whole accusatory atmosphere that had settled over the country, polluting the reputation of good scientists with innuendo and one-sided summaries of unpublished material. "In this jury," Agassiz complained, "called for the express purpose of deciding upon the value and efficiency of scientific work, men of science have had no voice." If there was waste and duplication, he blamed it on the politicians in the Cabinet and Congress who had not been doing their job with vigilance.[89]

Ironically, then, it was Agassiz who turned out to be Powell's most dangerous enemy in the months that ensued. Son of the famed Harvard biologist Louis Agassiz, a child of academic privilege, Agassiz had proved his mettle by making a fortune in the Michigan copper fields before returning to a professor's life in Cambridge.[90] He was a fiscal conservative who believed that scientists (Hilgard excepted) should stay out of government and confine themselves to academic institutions endowed with large private means.

Here was a scientist with right-thinking views, concluded Hilary Herbert, the most critical member of the Allison commission. Needing ammunition, Herbert wrote to Agassiz in late November for advice on how to bring the Geological Survey "within proper bounds," or even abolish it altogether. Agassiz, who previously had only distant and polite communication with Powell, now answered Herbert that he was shocked "to see how much power a man in Powell's place attains when he knows what he wants" and is prepared "to dole out his patronage."[91] He allowed Herbert to print a letter that rapped not only the current director but his predecessor King, indeed the whole idea of government science.

Agassiz in particular criticized the "wasteful and extravagant" publications of the survey, books that few people read or would pay money to acquire. Among his targets was a history of the Comstock lode that King had authorized. Agassiz could not see "why men of science should ask more than other branches of knowledge, literature, fine arts, &c.," in support of their research and writing. Paleontology, like poetry, should be left to private individuals and learned societies. Topographical or geological maps should be left to the states. If the dissidents within the survey liked the sound of that hard knock he gave Powell's pet project, Agassiz disappointed them by also denouncing all the work done in economic geology—the Comstock, Eureka, and Leadville studies, all useless to the mining industry and more properly done by those in the business.[92]

While Herbert and Agassiz were conspiring for a way to embarrass Powell, the Allison commission resumed its public deliberations, with all but two of its original members back. Although the commissioners had been impressed by Powell's masterly performance a few months ago, they could not help being affected by the subsequent controversy in the press or the panic that was spreading through the scientific bureaus or the censures by the great Agassiz. Fearing the impact of Agassiz's diatribe, Powell rushed to answer him point by point, but it was not his finest moment. If Agassiz had been tersely reactionary, Powell was verbosely scattershot. He defended economic geology with a born-again passion, declaring it to be the "primary" purpose of the survey and an activity that had produced great wealth for the nation. Then pivoting about, he asserted the importance of basic science. "Knowledge is a boon in itself," he told the commission, and "wisdom is exalting." As his critics said, he was good at being all things to all people.

Agassiz's personal wealth was his weak spot, distorting his judgment, and Powell hammered hard on it. Science, he argued, should not be turned into a rich man's hobby or confined to elite institutions supported by private wealth, institutions that excluded the majority of citizens. Scientific research should be open to all. Results should be available in every public library, where the poor but intelligent scholar might get an education. That was why he produced so many government reports at public expense.

There is a sentiment, rarely found in America but more common
in Europe, that would exclude the people at large from a
knowledge of the progress of scientific research. In the lands
where this sentiment has its home it is desired to establish, in
emulation of the hereditary aristocracies, scientific aristocracies,
which, it is claimed, should have official recognition.

The survey was not like Harvard. Its very existence was a triumph of
the people over privilege. "The revenue of new discovery," Powell
told the commission, "is boundless." But that revenue should flow to
the many, not the few.[93]

Behind those words lurked a shivering boy walking along a snow-
packed road in Wisconsin, seeking a high school to attend. A boy
who had struggled to patch together a modest scientific education in
small Midwestern church colleges. A young man who had vaulted
over all the obstacles to reach Washington and a place of eminence
among the nation's scientists. A now powerful figure who was always
ready to help another climb the ladder of achievement. A man for
whom governmental research had become that ladder.

Some observers, watching the contest going on, feared that the
ladder might be collapsing, taking Powell down with it. Hague, in a
confidential note to King, worried about the effectiveness of Powell's
defense. Although he accused Agassiz of playing a nefarious role, he
blamed Powell as well for miscalculating his support. The director
had "felt a little too sure about the Commission and has assured
everybody that they would not interfere with him in any way. If he
had the Commission in his pocket it certainly could not have been in
the pocket of the coat he was wearing."[94]

Powell, for all his public calm, was reported to be feeling the strain
of controversy. He had fallen ill again and seemed to lack his old
nervous force. Hague appealed to King for assistance, but King
stayed well out of it, offering no word of support, waiting like others
in the scientific community for some indication of how the politicians would react.

One of the few scientists who rushed to support Powell in this
tense waiting time was C.S. Pierce of the Coast and Geodetic Survey,
one of the founders of the philosophy of pragmatism. He assured
Powell that everyone in his agency (demoralized and battered
though it was) despised "this abominable & scandalous attack upon
you." Agassiz's behavior was "both idiotic and base." What was going
on was "the first brush of a war upon science, and it is high time that

the whole science of the country should rally for its own defence." Pierce was ready to organize scientists into an interest group, demanding a liberal share of the federal appropriations and bringing pressure from every college faculty in the country."[95] Such academic politicking turned out to be unnecessary. On 10 June the Allison commission finally submitted its recommendations to Congress. Although they were not unanimous, the majority of the commissioners, mostly Republicans led by the chairman, backed Powell with a resounding thump of approval. They reported that the Geological Survey "is well conducted, and with economy and care, and discloses excellent administrative and business ability on the part of its chief." The topographical mapping should continue, they said, though they acknowledged that it would take another twenty-four years to complete the national map. Paleontology should also continue, along with the more utilitarian branches. Only the funding of the publications needed any reform. All future monographs, bulletins, and annual reports should be cost-estimated and submitted for approval by Congress. "The Commission are of opinion that this restriction will not impair the efficiency of the Survey in any way, but will exert a restraining influence upon the expenditures for its publications."[96]

No better vindication of Powell's five years in the directorship could have been asked. The pessimist Hague had to eat his words of doubt and criticism, writing to King that "the majority report is in every way very acceptable to Powell, and I do not see how he could ask for a stronger document. . . . [He] feels in great glee . . . and took pains to say that he had never gone back on anything which you had done while in office and seemed to take great credit to himself for this." Writing to Marsh in New Haven, Hague described the triumphant director reading parts of the commission's report aloud to his office staff. "Powell justly feels in very good spirits today, as he has had a pretty long fight over the matter."[97]

The fight was not quite over, for there was still the full Congress to face. A minority report existed, and its author, Congressman Herbert, was intent on shoving it forward. He had submitted his own bill that would stop virtually all survey publications and prohibit all "discussion of geological theories."[98] The bit about publications was particularly aimed at slapping down O.C. Marsh and his fossil work. But Herbert was dead against Powell's leadership in general. "No such ambitious scheme of geology as that we are now pursuing," he snorted, "was ever mapped by man."[99]

Professor Marsh was not one to take lightly any criticism of his work or his independence of judgment or his USGS salary, and he remonstrated with Herbert. Quickly and apologetically, the congressman retreated to the higher ground of political principle. "I am radically Democratic in my views," he explained. "I believe in as little government as possible — that Government should keep hands off and allow the individual fair play." It was doctrine he had learned from Adam Smith, Henry Buckle, Thomas Jefferson, and John C. Calhoun — his intellectual heroes in the school of laissez-faire. Together, they told him that government had no business messing with "pure science," implying that messing with "practical science" was acceptable. When government attempted to control science and art, as it had under Louis XIV, it "stifled independent thought." This was what Herbert saw developing in Washington — a return to the old despotism — and he opposed it vehemently. Powell was arrogating to himself powers of monopoly, forcing all scientists, in the language of the beloved Buckle describing the ancien régime, to scramble "in miserable rivalry for the sordid favors of a court."[100]

Congress did not listen to Herbert's fears, however, and followed the majority recommendations exactly. They rejected the argument that science should be left to private enterprise, as they rejected the limited-government ideology of Adam Smith and Old South Democrats. Wait of Connecticut characterized the survey's work as among the most important ever done by the government, enabling Americans to become "the richest, most powerful, and the most intelligent people on the face of the earth." Representative Symmes from Colorado, though admitting that aid to mining was his pet interest, added that "this Government can well afford to expend some money in the pursuit and development of those branches of science which may not be of any particular economic value, but which is of very great value from a scientific standpoint."[101]

Such support for the survey did not reflect any deep-probing philosophical position; it bordered on simple faith. Science, by some magic, would bring material benefit to the American empire and the cause of human enlightenment. "What I do not know on this subject," quipped Cannon of Illinois, "would make a pretty large library [laughter]. . . . I know so little about scientific subjects that I am willing to take many things upon the faith of men of character and knowledge."[102] Powell was such a man in congressmen's eyes. They trusted him to run his agency in the public interest. Some of them, to

be sure, tried to follow closely how and why he spent his appropriation, tried to understand what he was doing, and they were impressed. Most did not bother. This kind of work, they agreed, was
properly the work of government for it would make the nation great.

Herbert came away from his defeat discouraged and bitter. To
Agassiz he wrote that he was disappointed that "my honest attempt to
do something toward reforming the abuses of the Geological Survey
. . . should have come to naught." He boasted that at least he had
stopped its runaway momentum; the appropriation had not gone up
any 30 per cent this time, as it had been doing in the past. But still his
colleagues seemed unable to see through Powell's mask of authority
and discern the "unequalled" scientific demagogue lurking under-
neath. Powell had won only because he had spread dollars around
the country, stifling criticism from fellow scientists and creating
around himself an aura of infallibility. Herbert had been unable to
challenge that authority, but he was not through with this man and
would be back for another confrontation.[103]

Once again Powell had come out of a canyon filled with hard
rapids, looking like a hero. Those who had all but given him up for
dead watched him came sailing through, his boat a little battered but
his provisions intact and his hand still on the rudder. Herbert's accusations about dictatorship and bribery were wrong and unfair. Powell
had his powerful enemies, and they had not been silenced. Yet he
had come through the dangerous waters of misinformation, rumors,
ideological opposition, and jealousy by careful navigating and some
heavy portaging. He had gotten past the large rock Agassiz. He had
scraped over the shoals of Herbert. No one else, certainly not
Clarence King, could have done so well. The survey was still afloat.

In early November, Powell received an invitation to join the 250th
anniversary of Harvard University, the oldest and most prestigious
university in the country, the academic home of Agassiz. The university wanted to give the Major an honorary degree, Doctor of Laws.
Was the institution making amends for their misguided faculty member, or was it simply recognizing that John W. Powell deserved its
highest recognition for his contributions to American exploration
and science?[104] Never mind the reason; Powell accepted, and accepted with delight.

Over two thousand alumni came to Cambridge for the event, and
three hundred special guests. Learneds gathered from elite institutions — the presidents of Yale, Columbia, Tufts, Johns Hopkins, Princeton, Amherst — to pay their respects. Foreign dignitaries donned their

J.W. Powell, circa 1880s.
(Courtesy: Marriott Library,
University of Utah)

robes. President Grover Cleveland was there, leading an entourage of cabinet secretaries. The procession wound its way from the severe and somber old Yard where so many generations of students had lived and crossed the street to the new plug-ugly Memorial Hall, commemorating the lives Harvard had lost in the Civil War. They filed in under the patriotic bunting, the brilliant flowers, the sound of chorale music. Oliver Wendell Holmes stood to read an occasional poem, and James Russell Lowell delivered the afternoon's oration. Then Harvard's renowned president, Charles W. Eliot, arose to confer no less than forty-two honorary degrees, one of them on the maimed veteran from Washington, his fierce face tanned and seamed by the western sun.[105]

By this point Powell had several other honorary degrees attached to his name. They compensated for the fact that he had never actually finished his undergraduate studies. Illinois Wesleyan had bestowed on him both a master's degree and a doctorate, the latter in 1877. The Columbian University (later called George Washington University) had made him doctor of laws in 1882, and in this year of personal triumph, 1886, one of the more distinguished universities of Europe, Heidelberg, had given him their Ph.D. in absentia. Harvard's was the last and most important of those honors, and nothing more emphatically signified his high standing among his peers.

As he sat among so many eminent figures, listening to sonorous words, what thoughts or memories flashed through his mind? Did he recall his first tutor, the backwoods savant Crookham, setting him down as a child to read Hume and Gibbon? Or did he remember reading John Bunyan as a teen-aged lad bumping along a wagon road with a load of wheat? Or did his mind flash back to his first sight of the Rocky Mountains, about which he had read in Frémont's writings? Or did he think about the slow, difficult process of self-education that had opened to him the scientist's world of geology and ethnology, evolution and cosmology?

He now had in his charge two comprehensive sciences — the science of man and the science of the earth. Did he relive the political battle he had been through to save them as part of the proper function of the national government? Or did he exult in the power he now had, through science, to bring the American nation to redemption and greatness?

CHAPTER 11

Redeeming the Earth

S lender white spires and stained-glass windows said that Washington was a city of churches. But churches were not where Powell spent time outside of work. He turned to competing institutions—scientific societies and gentlemen's clubs, several of which he had a hand in founding. They provided a sanctuary where he met other men of like interests and where together they could let their imaginations soar to the most grand and esoteric ideas of the day. Several nights a week they listened, held forth, and took their ease among comrades who shared their need for an alternative to religion. Together, they sought a more secular future for America.

True to his parents' example, Powell was saturated with moral fervor. Like them, he aspired to transform the world into a better place. Instead of the Protestant doctrines of Wesleyan Methodism, however, he turned to those other great nineteenth-century gospels of salvation, the nation-state and natural science. His clubs and societies were populated by scientific men who believed as he did that science held out the prospect of radical improvement. Science was to be a means of redemption. That redemption should begin with the nation they loved, cleaning out the cobwebs of its past—the sectional rivalries, the outworn creeds, the destructive greed. Thus redeemed, America could lead the world toward enlightenment.

On 16 November 1878 Powell called several friends to his home to organize a social club for "men devoted to or interested in Science, professionally or otherwise." The inspiration was Clarence Dutton's, who upon returning from the Century Club in New York had laid before Powell and Garrick Mallery the prospect of a similar institution for the capital. The friends gathered in the Powell parlor agreed that such an institution would fill a gap in their lives. Its rooms would be open afternoons and evenings for "temperate, simple, and thrifty" recreation. A few weeks later the Cosmos Club was incorporated. Rational order and harmony, the universal principles, were written into its very name.[1]

Many of the founding members, Powell included, had first met through the Philosophical Society of Washington, established by Joseph Henry. For years they had sat through interminable papers in the old Ford Theater (converted to the Army Medical Museum and Library), chambers filled with the "musty odor of ancient leather and book binder's paste, their monotony relieved by a few colored chromos of human anatomy." As Dutton recalled, the place might have been suitable for "studies of Dr. Dryasdust," but was not appealing to a younger group "just beginning our scientific careers and in whom the love of science did not diminish the love of good fellowship."[2] In reaction, they rented a handful of rooms in the Corcoran Building, where Pennsylvania Avenue bends around the Department of the Treasury, and invited others to join the new club. Some sixty did, including government scientists, professors, physicians, military men, and the sui generis Henry Adams.

The incense that went up from the Cosmos Club was the dense, curling smoke of Cuban cigars and Turkish cigarettes. Powell, like others, was a prodigious smoker. His tobacconist furnished him a hundred Favorites, Almas, or Operas a week, many of them passed out to friends and fellow employees, but he consumed plenty on his own, working and socializing with a constant cigar in his mouth.[3] It was the manly thing to do, and the Cosmos Club was nothing if not manly. Women were not permitted on the premises. Alcohol, on the other hand, was permitted — claret, sherry, brandy, and whiskey with lemons and sugar — though temperance was the motto and intelligent self-control the standard of behavior.

Within three years the club was prosperous enough to move its quarters to Lafayette Square, near the Adams residence, and eventually they owned an entire row of houses there. They put in a billiard table, and Powell starred as the best one-armed player in the bunch, though he kept faith with his Methodist past by supporting a resolution to disallow billiard playing on Sundays.[4] Otherwise, he lived far removed from the small, severe churches of backwoods Ohio and Wisconsin where the hymns of Wesley were uncorrupted by worldly pleasures. But under the slightly decadent pall of smoke and brandy fumes throbbed a serious-mindedness that set this club apart from its contemporaries, clubs organized by men of business and finance.

A "prime function" of the Cosmos Club, according to one of the founders, G.K. Gilbert, was "to bind the scientific men of Washington by a social tie and thus promote that solidarity which is important to their proper work and influence."[5] At the time of the club's founding the atmosphere among the capital's scientists was poisoned by suspicion, jealousy, and dissension. Dutton, Gilbert, Powell, and company wanted to uplift their colleagues. Science, as they conceived it, required men to refrain from selfish competition. Otherwise, science would fail in its effort to win greater support from government and to lead public policy.

If Powell aimed to usurp Joseph Henry's position as leading scientist in Washington by setting up a rival institution to the Philosophical Society, he modestly restrained himself. As candidate for first president of the Cosmos Club, he put forward Henry's successor at the Smithsonian, Spencer Baird. But in 1881, after a decent interval, he came out of the wings to serve as club president, with Mallery as vice president. By then he hardly needed any such office to achieve recognition. No one else in the city could match his reputation for organizing the evening hours of the intelligentsia.

Besides the Cosmos Club, Powell was a founder of the Anthropological Society, incorporated in late 1879. He was elected its first president and served nine terms in all, missing only one year, 1883, due to illness. Here the reading of long papers under flickering gas lights was once more endured. Nearly five hundred persons had joined by century's end, though most meetings drew smaller numbers of the devoted. A women's auxiliary came into being, along with a scholarly journal, *The American Anthropologist*, the first issue of which appeared in 1888. Each year of his presidency Powell gave an address, which was published in the society's *Transactions*, and for more than two decades he was the institution's most resonant voice. Other noted speakers included the British cultural anthropologist Edward B. Tylor, the codiscoverer of evolution, Alfred Russel Wallace, and the crowd-pleasing Frank Cushing.[6]

Nor was this all. A Biological Society took form, and a Chemical Society, an Entomological Society, a Geological Society. All looked to the Cosmos Club for a meeting place: the Anthropological on alternative Tuesday nights from November to May, the Geological on alternative Wednesdays, the Philosophical (abandoning the Army Medical Museum) on alternative Saturdays. Then came consolidation into the Washington Academy of Sciences, and again Powell was in the thick of it, serving as one of the new superorganization's vice presidents.

On still another winter evening still another link in the institutional chain was forged. Thirty-three men gathered at the Cosmos Club in January 1888 to establish a National Geographic Society. Powell was, of course, prominent in that group too, along with Dutton, Gilbert, Gannett, Marcus Baker, Harry Thompson, and Arthur Powell Davis from the Geological Survey and William Dall and Henry Henshaw from the Bureau of Ethnology. A New England lawyer of large means, Gardiner Hubbard, agreed to serve as president, and he brought along the inventor Alexander Graham Bell, whose telephone device Hubbard had financially backed. The capital had one more magazine to promote the cause of science (this one to a more popular audience), and the scientists had one more bond of solidarity to proclaim.[7]

And there was more. Powell sent in dues, not only to all of the above, but to the American Institute of Mining Engineers, the Military Order of the Loyal Legion of the U.S., the University Club, the American Meteorological Society, the American Antiquarian Society, the Society of the Army of the Tennessee, the Choral Society, the Society of Naturalists of the Eastern United States, and the American Historical Association. He was a member of the National Academy of Sciences. For over a quarter-century he paid dues to the American Association for the Advancement of Science (AAAS) and was its president. He was on the editorial board of *Science* and of *Johnson's Cyclopaedia.* His annual subscription list included the *Washington Post,* the *Daily National Republican,* the *Journal of Philology,* the *American Naturalist,* and the *Geological Record* (U.K.). Secular institutions of every sort were his bread and butter, his instruments of change, his source of recreation.[8]

In the latter decades of the nineteenth century Washington became one of the country's most important intellectual centers, perhaps the most important of all. What it lacked in distinguished universities or publishing houses, it made up in the richness of its scientific and other scholarly agencies and institutions. The Smithsonian stood at the core, but radiating from it like avenues from L'Enfant's circles were many lesser organs, clubs, and offices for serious minds. Together, they sought to create in the capital a more highbrow atmosphere that would improve public legislation, administration, and welfare. Powell was among the most dedicated architects of that city of science, the emergent capital of American hope.

Inspiration for scientific clubs and societies came to Washingtonians from elsewhere, mainly Philadelphia, New York, and Boston, but also from Manchester, Edinburgh, and London. Ideas came from the same places, and the American capital sent back its own thoughts in the form of reports and transactions. Wherever English-speaking intellectuals gathered, they shared a common set of ideals and read a common set of books.

The writings of Britain's Charles Darwin stood above all others in significance. Although there were still those who, in Powell's phrase, saw Darwinism as "the name of something wicked that good people must disavow," by the 1880s the weight of opinion in every company of secular thinkers had shifted toward enshrining the British naturalist as the reigning genius of the age. As O.C. Marsh put it, "the battle has been fought and won. A few stragglers on each side may still keep up a scattered fire, but the contest is over, and the victors have moved on to other fields. . . . Evolution is no longer a theory, but a demonstrated truth, accepted by naturalists throughout the world."[9]

Darwin's theory of the evolution of species through natural selection had cracked apart some of the oldest assumptions in Christian cosmology. That humans had divine souls while the rest of creation did not was no longer an acceptable premise in advanced intellectual circles. Fierce arguments followed the new skepticism: How should humans think about God? Did God even exist? What was their place in nature? How should they treat their animal kin? How should they behave toward one another? Were some societies closer to the apes than others? Was nature the best model for man to emulate, and if so, what did that mean?

Evolution confirmed what perceptive men and women understood to be the fundamental reality: the world is characterized, not by stability, but by change. One did not need Darwin to see that fact. It was obvious on any street corner where one could find change in the form of newspapers, horse cars, telephone wires, emancipated slaves, shipping offices. Change was normal. A man was born in one place but died in another. All his life he had to adapt, learn new ways, throw out the old. One could not hold on to the past. One could only press onward, setting doubts and bewilderment aside.

Powell absorbed that idea of evolution completely. In his 1889 presidential address to the AAAS meeting in Toronto, delivered in his absence by his good lieutenant Gilbert, he took the development of music as illustrative of evolution. Music was a tradition handed down to him by his Welsh ancestors. Yet when he looked across the long span of human existence, he heard rhythms of change even here. Primitive dances and chants had given way to folk songs and then to anthems, oratorios, cantatas, the opera, the fugue, the madrigal, the sonata, and the symphony. It had taken thousands of years to produce a Wagnerian prelude or chorus. In every age music had brought joy into people's lives, but the music of the modern age was driving out "the music of our fathers."[10]

"Whatever is, changes," Powell wrote, "and no repetition comes through all the years of time." History was not an endless returning to the same point; it was an endless creation of the new and unfamiliar. Thankfully, change was never sudden or abrupt. It occurred at a steady pace that did not threaten. "This slow but sure metamorphosis is called evolution, and the scientific world is engaged in the formulation of its laws." Scientists in every country and every discipline had the same basic law of change to study. Their researches reinforced one another by "a consilience of many inductive methods."[11]

Nevertheless, Powell was only slightly interested in the evolution of plants and animals, the core of Darwin's work, and he grew less interested in the evolution of the earth's surface, his first enthusiasm. What especially excited him was the notion that societies and cultures evolve. And there he could get little direct help from Darwin or any natural scientist in England or America. He needed different mentors. Two such figures emerged within his own country. One of them, Lewis Henry Morgan, was sixteen years his senior. The other, Lester Frank Ward, was seven years younger. Morgan became Powell's intellectual father, while Ward became more of a brother with whom he sometimes argued intensely.

Morgan was residing in the city of Rochester, New York, when Powell first corresponded with him in the fall of 1876. They had a common origin in the rural villages of that state. Morgan had made a career of the law, accumulating a small fortune by advising Michigan railroads, and had served briefly as a Republican politician in the New York state assembly and senate. When he joined a secret society of young white males who fancied themselves descendants of the Iroquois Confederacy, dressing up as Indians and dancing around the campfire, his mental life took a sudden turn. He became a serious student of the people who heretofore had been only a romantic curiosity. Powell, in a sketch of Morgan's life, called his 1851 publication, *The League of the Iroquois*, "the first scientific account of an Indian tribe ever given to the world."[12] It opened a new career for Morgan, one that eventually earned him an international reputation as an anthropologist.

Having looked into Iroquois ways, Morgan became excited about all Indian tribes and, indeed, all tribal societies. As Powell explained, the senior man collected a vast array of data on kinship and marriage from the far corners of the globe, arranging them into a massive comparative study, *Systems of Consanguinity and Affinity of the Human Family*. Its publication by the Smithsonian in 1871 marked "a most important epoch in anthropologic research."[13]

Morgan had encouraged Powell back in his Paiute days, calling his talk on Indian philosophy to the Geographical Society of New York "the best generalization of Indian beliefs and of their religious system I have seen." The two men came at the Indian, however, from different points on the horizon. Powell approached from religion, interested in Indian belief in the supernatural; Morgan from social organization, following the ties of kinship that defined tribal identities. But it was Morgan's great book *Ancient Society*, coming in the mail one spring day in 1877, that illuminated for Powell more than anything else the long, slow path leading from the past to the present. He stayed up late reading it. When he had the bureau organized and running, he made sure that every assistant or collaborator had a personal copy.[14]

The origins of humans lie in "a vast and profound antiquity," wrote Morgan in his magnum opus, farther back in time than anyone had imagined just a few decades earlier. He identified three broad stages to that history, each with subdivisions: the savage, the barbaric, and the civilized. The first was longest in duration, the last relatively short. Savage societies had lived for hundreds of millennia on fruits and nuts or whatever they could kill with a bow and arrow. Their greatest achievement was the taming of fire. The barbarians appeared some thirty-five thousand years ago, he estimated, and quickly outdistanced all their neighbors in innovation. They crafted pots and adobe bricks from clay, domesticated wild cereals and animals, and in their late stages made tools from iron. Then civilization emerged some five thousand years ago with the phonetic alphabet and the keeping of written records, and it went on to produce gunpowder, the compass, the printing press, the steam engine, and photography. It was a thrilling story of heroic achievement—the self-made man writ large. "Mankind commenced at the bottom of the scale," Morgan noted, "and worked up."[15]

Driving that cultural evolution were hard, tangible novelties ("inventions") and experimental knowledge ("discoveries"). They forced ancient peoples to change their ideas of government, the family, and property. Societies evolved from a local set of kinfolk, the "gens," bearing a common name, into the modern nation-state, where large numbers of unrelated people lived under one common authority. Families shifted from matriarchy to patriarchy, from promiscuity to monogamy. Most astonishing, the progress of science and technology altered the very structure of the human brain, "particularly of the cerebral portion." The species grew more intelligent. Through inheritance it accumulated the biological capacity to carry on civilization, so that there was no danger it would ever be lost.

Morgan was not a Pollyanna in his views of cultural evolution, for he allowed that serious moral flaws had emerged alongside the technology. Slavery was an example. Invented by the barbarians, it had survived down to the most recent past of civilization. Another flaw was the institution of social class based on hereditary wealth, dividing people into aristocrats and paupers. He was confident that the world would follow the American lead in overthrowing the class system, which had been a galling burden for several thousand years. Next to fall would be the concentration of private property in a few hands. "A mere property career," Morgan wrote, "is not the final destiny of mankind. . . . Democracy in government, brotherhood in society, equality in rights and privileges, and universal education, foreshadow the next higher plane of society to which experience, intelligence and knowledge are steadily tending. It will be a revival, in a higher form, of the liberty, equality and fraternity of the ancient gentes."[16]

Those predictions for democracy made the New York lawyer a prophetic hero to the founders of European Marxism. John Powell, though no Marxist, counted himself among the admirers. In reviewing his mentor's work, he singled out for attention the lesson that "government of the people is the normal condition of mankind." Agreeing that temporary "pathologic conditions" of hierarchy had come to dominate "the body politic," he warned that such "diseases must be destroyed or they will destroy." Morgan was gratified by this apt and ready pupil: "I like what you have so well said about the 'survival of the fittest' in political institutions. . . . It is a tremendous thrust at privileged classes, who have always been a greater burden than society could afford to bear."[17]

Morgan died in December 1881, just a few months after Garfield, leaving Powell doubly devastated. As consolation, he held on to a letter from Morgan in May, congratulating him on "promotion to the National Chair in Geology. It is higher in pay and honor than Ethnology," the older man had written, "but not as important a field just now."[18] Powell was bound to agree, and he determined to carry on his Indian studies as Morgan's anointed successor.

Had Morgan remained the primary influence on Powell's thinking that might have happened in an uncomplicated way. Such was not to be. As Morgan's life was ending, the career of another brilliant mind was rising, one who would also leave a profound impact on Powell. A tall, sunburned athlete with intellectual aspirations, Lester Ward had little interest in native Americans or in ancient societies but much in the crisis facing his own civilization. Where Morgan had been an evolutionist without Darwin — there was no biology or competitive struggle among organisms in his writings —Ward was a Darwinian through and through. But Ward was a fearful Darwinian. Trained as a natural scientist, he demanded to know what evolutionary biology implied for the human condition.

Ward had been born in Illinois and raised in Buchanan County, Iowa, the youngest of ten children in a farming family. Four years of service in the Civil War had left him wounded, penniless, barely educated, but, like Powell, married. The Treasury Department hired him because he was a veteran. Nights he devoted to studying for a degree at Columbian University. He earned three degrees in quick succession, the last an M.A. in botany. The death of his wife and infant son sent him reeling, but he soon remarried. Then he began looking for more stimulating work. Powell hired him to collect plants in the Wasatch Mountains of Utah and borrowed heavily from Ward's forest and grass studies for portions of the *Report on the Lands of the Arid Region*.[19] In spring 1881 Powell found a place for him at the Geological Survey as chief of the new Division of Fossil Plants. Ward became one of the country's first paleobotanists, publishing his first systematic treatise under the title "Types of the Laramie Flora" (1887). It was a career that Powell nurtured gladly, sensing as he did that here was a man like himself, filled with diverse possibilities.

The protégé gave back in full measure. Shortly after being hired as assistant geologist, Ward approached Powell with the proposal that he write a sketch of his life and career, which appeared in *Popular Science Monthly*. "Professor John W. Powell, better known as Major Powell, . . . is a pattern of the American self-made man," wrote Ward, "and well illustrates in his life and achievements what may be accomplished with honest, steady adherence to a definite purpose."

Personally, he is of most agreeable manners, frank, genial, and cordial under all circumstances, and possessed of great individual magnetism. Though social by nature, he has a strong preference for persons of culture, and especially of independence of thought, as his friends, and seems to possess the tact of securing such with-out giving offense to others. It is a favorite theory of his that, to observe well, one must also think deeply, and that observation without theory is necessarily sterile; and these ideas he carries into practical affairs in the selection of his assistants in all branches of his service. His mind is in the highest degree realistic, and he looks upon all classes of phenomena from the objective point of view. In anthropology he belongs to the strictly scientific school, represented by Mr. Lewis H. Morgan, which rejects the imagina-tive and poetical accounts of the lower races. He accepts the doc-trine of evolution, but has not failed to perceive inadequacies in the systematic developments which some of its disciples have sought to make of certain of its minor details.[20]

Aside from its cryptic ending, the encomium expressed precisely Powell's strong appeal for the younger men around him.

There was another, more immediate advantage in being included in Powell's genial company. Ward had under preparation a massive manuscript wholly unrelated to his botanical work at the survey. "Major Powell was very liberal in his ideas of official duty," he re-called; "with him it was all for science and the public good." Often he would come into Ward's room to discuss the work in progress and "all manner of subjects."[21] Neither man, it must be said, was any slacker. The $150-a-month salary that Ward earned was, however, regarded as something of a sinecure to allow him to finish the great work. Through Powell's intervention he secured a contract from the pub-lisher D. Appleton. The book appeared in 1883 under the title *Dy-namic Sociology* in two volumes totaling fourteen hundred pages. Appropriately, it was dedicated to "Major Powell, Explorer, Geologist, Anthropologist, and Philosopher, whose generous aid, warm words of encouragement, and friendly intercourse have sustained me in my prolonged effort."[22]

Now it was Powell's turn to be instructed and led by one he had been leading. Borrowing the French philosopher Auguste Comte's "sociology," a word coined to signify a new science of society, Ward dove into dark, unfathomed seas that Comte had never dared: the origins of matter and life, the first appearance of vital relationships among organisms, the genesis of man, the formation of social groups. "No thought, no idea, no plan, no purpose," he wrote, "has entered into the great cosmic movement" called Nature.[23] The waters of the earth roiled, and out of them rose, wet and dripping, that amazing entity called Society. Like Nature, Society was not designed by any intelligent being. No god lurked anywhere in Ward's universe, not even in a footnote. All was Nature — until there was Society coming out of Nature, emerging as "an integral part of the universe." Nature and Society alike should be studied with unblinking materialism.

Because there was no intelligent plan that evolution followed, the world was filled with irrationality. Here Ward struck out against another illusion. Nature has not been carefully arranged or wisely ordered, he argued, either for the benefit of humans or other creatures. Nature is in fact badly designed. Bark grows too tightly on trees, restricting their growth. Insects foolishly die in stinging their attackers. Moths fly stupidly into flames. A cod lays a million eggs a year in order that two may survive. An eel carries around nine million eggs simply to reproduce itself. The mother opossum gives birth to more babies than she has teats for feeding. Where Darwin had discerned a fine adjustment of one organism to another, Ward saw only cases of terrible waste. Life had not been easy as the runt of the litter on that Iowa farm.

Where this argument was heading was toward repudiating nature as a model for human society. "True progress," he maintained, "springs from that restless skepticism which dares even to question the methods of nature."[24] Study nature, yes, and accept the natural origins of humans and society. But do not fall into the trap of "nature worship." Nature must not assume the place of the missing gods.

Like Powell, Ward was a lover of the sublime in nature, an ardent hiker and outdoorsman. In Washington he often rambled through Rock Creek Park, grateful that it had not been laid waste by the ax and plow. Nature offered much to the emotions and inspired the poet and the painter. Nature did not, however, offer any lessons for organizing economic and social life. For that work one needed cold reason. "There is beauty, there is grandeur, there is activity, there is even life," he wrote, "but mind there is none. Nature has no soul, although within her are all the elements of sensibility and all the materials of intelligence."[25]

The second volume of Ward's treatise was a plea for applying human intelligence to the problems of society. Science could show how to lift Americans out of their miserable condition and secure a true happiness for one and all. Rational man must assume "the attitude of a master, or ruler," over the whole continent, subjugating nature's energies to his own ends. Inefficiency must give way to efficiency, laissez-faire to intelligent planning, self-interest to the common good. Rivers must be made to run more directly to the sea, fish to spawn only the fry that humans want to eat. The human mind must take over the management of all evolution.

Science should not stop with imposing a more rational order on nature. Next must come a rationalizing of society as well. "All the functions of society are performed in a sort of chance way, which is precisely the reverse of economical, but wholly analogous to the natural processes of the lower organic world. . . . they are not the best."[26] Narrow, crooked streets of cities must be set straight, and filth and disease swept away. No famines must be permitted. No bitter partisanship in politics. The open hostility between capital and labor, now reaching dangerous proportions, must give way to harmony. Manufacturing must be reorganized to produce and distribute only what is truly needed. Wealth must be more equitably distributed.

The scientific redesign of the nation had, for Ward, a promising beginning in such government agencies as the Geological Survey. Here science was showing its potential for stable, rational leadership. "The scientific mind," he observed, "appears to be peculiarly adapted to faithful service in situations where great practical interests are involved. Scientific men are, from their very education, earnest men, and fully aroused to the importance of putting their knowledge to the best practical use." If such men had charge of drafting legislation and organizing the system of production, the welfare of every American citizen would be secured. Left in the hands of businessmen, on the other hand, a class noted more for their "coarse cunning inspired by avarice," the nation was drifting toward instability and social unrest.[27]

Powell knew perfectly well what a radical young man he had working down the hall. In a four-part review in *Science* he analyzed Ward's book in detail, offering a few mild criticisms but overall proclaiming it to be "America's greatest contribution to scientific philosophy."[28] Where Morgan had helped him understand the past of the species, Ward helped clarify where the future of the nation must lie. The story of evolution now had an end as well as a beginning.

It was not the ending that many other Americans, particularly in the business community, saw promised in the theory of evolution. Naturally, they saw themselves as the finest product of cultural as well as biological evolution and were not eager to turn power over to the scientists. Taking up the British philosopher Herbert Spencer's phrase, "survival of the fittest," businessmen claimed to be the fittest. Experience clearly showed that they had survived better than anyone else by making gobs of money.

No one after Darwin did more to win acceptance of evolution than Spencer.[29] It was significant then that Spencer's version of evolution, if it did not quite enshrine the capitalist, did agree with him that the ideal society was one modeled on capitalist ideology, where every individual should be as free as possible to pursue his own ends. Spencer's distrust of all government had discovered in the doctrine of evolution new scientific support for ideas going back to Adam Smith and Thomas Malthus. Man must not interfere with the natural outcome of evolution. That was the warning drawn over and over in such works as *The Principles of Biology, The Principles of Sociology, The Principles of Ethics* in which Spencer called for a strict and rigorous libertarianism.

In November 1882 Spencer was feted at Delmonico's restaurant in New York, with many of the nation's leading scientists and intellectuals toasting his brilliance. Professor Marsh was there, with his Yale colleague William Graham Sumner, along with Carl Schurz, E.L. Youmans, Henry Ward Beecher, and Lester Ward. (Powell was not present, though he had received Spencer in his Washington office.[30]) Spencer was a more complicated man than these Americans often realized, but they grasped his main idea well enough: evolution taught laissez-faire in public policy. Either they lionized him for that idea or they did not. Ward and Powell did not. For them "Spencer worship" was just another form of "nature worship." If capitalism was natural, as the Englishman taught, then capitalism was not by that fact made good. If evolution had to be accepted as explaining the origin of life, society should not take natural evolution as its moral standard. There was a better guide on offer.

A bureaucrat by day and a club member by night, Powell did not enjoy much leisure for writing. He never learned to write easily with his remaining left hand. His signature remained a jerky scrawl. What he did write had to be done at the office, where he had a stenographer on duty, and it had to be dictated out of his head. Not surprisingly, he published only two full books in his lifetime, neither of them as long as the volumes by Morgan, Ward, or Spencer. All the same, his lifetime output in the form of short essays, addresses, papers, Congressional testimony, and government reports was prodigious. A catalogue of his published writings lists 251 titles and is not complete.[31]

His most prolific decade was his sixth (the years 1884–93), when over half of his publications appeared. Only a few of his topics in that period were geological, though they included a masterful discussion of the natural processes of soil erosion. Aside from the yearly reports that he had to make on his agencies' activities, he wrote mainly on anthropology for such journals as *Science, Forum, American Anthropologist,* and *Popular Science Monthly.* His leading theme was "the story of human evolution," which he described as "the essence of the history of mankind."

Historians had so far failed, according to Powell, to capture that essence. Retelling the exploits of kings, politicians, and warriors was what most historians had taken to be their profession. Even one of the best among them, Henry Adams, whose nine-volume work, *The History of the United States of America,* began appearing in 1889, still conceived of the past in narrow terms—the history of presidential politics. History, therefore, had to be reinvented and put on a scientific basis "to exhibit the growth of culture in all of its great departments" and to discover the laws governing social progress.[32]

History as the growth of culture should not be confined to a few modern, advanced societies, for all peoples in all eras were bearers of culture. Science had established a very long record for humanity, going back into late Tertiary times, more than two million years ago. Already by the Quaternary people were widely distributed across the earth. A genuinely scientific history would take as its province the full diversity of humans living across the full geological record.

North America's native peoples deserved to be part of that more broadly conceived story. Relative newcomers to the continent, appearing only at the end of the glacial period, they nonetheless had experienced thousands of years of cultural development before the coming of the white man. The records for that history lay in "books" that had not been adequately consulted—settlements buried in sand or under lava flows, heaps of rubbish, deserted cliff dwellings, myths of creation. Powell never stopped emphasizing the extraordinary diversity of Indian cultures, sensing as he did that most Americans looked on all Indians as one and the same. When Columbus arrived in the New World, "several thousand languages were spoken, which belonged to many different stocks wholly unlike one another. . . . Often a very small tribe spoke a language which no other people in the world could understand. Thus, tribe was isolated from tribe by barriers of language which could not be overcome."[33]

Finding one's direction through that long, complicated past, though staggering, was possible. Start with that great maker of anthropological maps, Lewis Morgan, and his three main stages in cultural evolution. Take that map into any human group and one would know right away where one was standing. Detailed work on the ground might adjust the boundaries here and there, but they were as real as the contrast between plains and mountains or deserts and forests. Inaccuracies, to be sure, were to be expected. But the scholar could rely on such a cultural map as confidently as the traveler could rely on the Powell Survey's topography of the Plateau Province.

Powell followed his mentor in ranking the three stages of savagery, barbarism, and civilization in a hierarchical scale from "lower" to "higher," with civilization clearly qualifying as the latter. To him that was a fair and objective judgment, no more suspicious than calling a one-celled bacterium a lower organism and a multicellular human being a higher organism. Evolution, every biologist knew, proceeds from the simple to the complex. Cultures likewise change over time from the simple to the complex, or from a lower level of human organization and understanding to a higher one.

Nor did he hesitate to say that the higher societies were all found in Europe and such cultural offshoots as North America. It was perverse to deny that a gap yawned between Europeans and others or to insist that Indians were as highly evolved as the white man. Although sentimentalists might balk at such a conclusion, anyone who had spent time among the Paiutes and Hopis, as Powell had done, could not overlook how far they were from the white man's nation-state, his sophisticated arts and technologies, his well-tested knowledge of how the world worked. Those differences explained why Indians were losers in the struggle for possessing the continent. No amount of sympathy for their plight should obscure their lowly place on the map of cultural evolution.

When it came to explaining why such differences existed among the world's societies, Powell was more ambiguous. Geographical isolation seemed to account for the fact that so many languages were spoken. Yet he resisted giving so much power to the environment, diminishing the power of humans to overcome the limitations that nature put on them. Humanity was a spectacularly creative force on the earth. Its rise from savagery to civilization could not be explained by geographical isolation or any other natural factors forcing people to become different from one another.

Morgan's answer to the question of what made cultures different was invention, technology, and science, and that is about where Powell left it too. In an 1882 address before the annual meeting of mining engineers he singled out technology as the greatest force for change in history. Among human institutions "those relating to industries have been most efficacious, most beneficent. Technology has done more for mankind than sociology, institutions of art more than institutions of government." By "art" he meant not the fine art of Thomas Moran or James Russell Lowell but the skill of the artisan or craftsman. Even philosophy, for which he felt a warm passion, had in the past done less for human advancement than technology. "Philosophy would today be soaring in the absurdities of mythology or wading through the mire of metaphysics but for science, which was born of technology. . . . Technology is the father of science, and science again is the father of technology. Arts give birth to sciences and sciences give birth to arts, and thus in alternating generations they multiply to bless mankind."[34]

Hovering on the brink of technological determinism, Powell pulled himself back to more noncommittal ground. Technology, like environment, was too simple an explanation. Morgan's method of "basing his stages on the arts" would not altogether do because "social organization" was a strong force too. In fact, it was technology and society interacting, each one influencing the other, that seemed more nearly to describe what had happened in history, just as it was technology and science interacting that drove their evolution. Drop an invention like the gun into a society using bows and arrows, and the people might quickly shift their choice of weapons from the old to the new—but not their whole way of life. They still would not be equipped to make and distribute guns or ammunition. To do that they must learn metallurgy and organize gun factories. Otherwise, they remained savages with guns.

Saying that left Powell with a story of human evolution that had no single force behind it, but, rather, was driven by a set of causes, material and immaterial. Precisely because of their interdependence, it was extremely difficult to bring a lower-level society quickly to a higher level. No single factor could guarantee the change. Many interacting factors were necessary, and even then change was bound to be slow and incremental. Savages could not become civilized men and women overnight.

His own tendency, however, was to single out the mental world of humans for closer study. He granted the formative power of technology, but most of his research was into what he called "opinions and philosophies." Man makes himself better, he believed, by thinking better thoughts. Native Americans were savages largely because they perceived the world through a fog of misunderstanding. They had not yet discovered the true causes of things or learned to relate causes to effects.

The paper that Morgan had liked so well, "A Discourse on the Philosophy of the North American Indians," was Powell's earliest effort to penetrate the savage mind, a paper written when Chuar and his other Paiute informants were still fresh in his memory. He was astonished at what he had heard from them and perplexed about how to represent it to a white audience.

> In English I say "wind," and you think of atmosphere in revolution with the earth, heated at the tropics and cooled at the poles, and set into great currents . . . ; the word suggests all the lore of the weather bureau — that great triumph of American science. But I say *neir* to a savage, and he thinks of a great monster, a breathing beast beyond the mountains of the west.

To enter into the savage mind one must somehow suspend scientific reason and try to perceive the sun as a little beast that could be cowed — a rabbit that, through fear, could be "compelled to travel along in an appointed trail, through the firmament, like an ass in a treadmill." It was to reenter a myth-enshrouded world where "the wind is but breath, foul or fair, ejected from the belly of a monster; and where the falling star is but dung."[35]

The savage lived more at the mercy of powerful elements of nature and, consequently, deified them. Gods controlled everything that happened in the world. Those gods were animals running loose through the country, able to think and speak. Every event had an animal personality behind it, acting out motives of revenge or generosity. Even gravity was an animal-like force. Powell recalled traveling with Chuar and other Paiutes along the edge of the Grand Canyon in the early winter of 1882. They amused themselves by trying to throw stones across a smaller gorge, but no one could do it. It was Chuar's belief that the canyon itself "pulled the stones down." He had missed out on Isaac Newton.[36]

That was the savage mind in operation. Everything was known or had a ready explanation, and everything was alive and conscious. To one trained in science such a view of nature amounted to "a mass of nonsense, a mass of incoherent folly, . . . but ethnographically a system of great interest."[37]

The savage's inability to grasp the world in scientific terms, his tendency to deify rather than analyze nature, did not make him a degraded or brutal person. Savages had created clever tools of stone, boats of bark, and elaborate systems of kinship. Though not far removed from animals materially, they were not animals in their intellectual or moral potential. Nor was their life cruel and harsh. They enjoyed a rich bounty of food, for their numbers were never large (Powell estimated that at the time of Columbus's first voyage some five hundred thousand to one million natives lived in what had become the United States). Theirs was not a vicious struggle where every man's hand was raised in self-defense against his neighbor, but neither was it a life that had discovered the principles of universal justice or felt the pull of ambition.

The second stage of barbarism Powell left more faintly defined, for he had no direct experience with it. No barbarians dwelt in the country he had surveyed, though he noted that in a few places the New World was beginning to pass into barbarism "when the good queen sold her jewels."[38]

Relying on Morgan as his authority once more, he listed the distinguishing marks of barbarism. It was an age of clay, of boats with oars, of cities with walls, of music with melody as well as rhythm, of textiles and metal tools, of legal codes and money, of patriarchy. The invention of agriculture was a critical marker too. Particularly where agriculture depended on irrigation, as in the valley of the Nile, the barbarians created impressive systems of production. With their new wealth, they expanded their power far beyond the old tribal limits to establish the first empires.

Philosophically, the barbarians still looked on nature as the home of powerful gods, though the gods no longer assumed the shape of animals. They now represented more elemental forces such as fire or water. When primitive mythology gave way to metaphysics, barbarism was born. Somewhere beneath all the mythologies created by their savage ancestors, the barbarians reasoned, lay universal truth. Its discovery depended on "the development of *formal logic* as a testing machine into which opinions were put for the purpose of sifting truth from error."[39] Unfortunately, logic was not a machine for detecting factual errors or discovering new information. It had the fatal flaw of assuming that the great truths were already known, if they could be distilled out of the savage mind. Until science arose to smash that logic machine and carry out empirical research into nature, barbarism ruled the history of philosophy and opinion.

Powell's timeline for these cultural stages was fuzzy. Two major essays in which he tried to clarify them, "From Savagery to Barbarism" (1885) and "From Barbarism to Civilization" (1888), left the middle stage of barbarism particularly vague and wandering. Were the

Greeks civilized or barbarian? Was feudalism the beginning of civilization or the end of barbarism? Morgan said that Europe had left barbarism behind some five thousand years ago. But when Powell looked at philosophy, he could not follow his mentor. The barbarian reliance on formal logic had held firm down to very recent centuries. Only with the triumph of science over metaphysics could civilization emerge, and that had happened not so long ago. Indeed, science was still struggling for its freedom.

But on one theme Powell was always clear and emphatic. Cultural evolution had nothing to do with biological differences among humans. Indians were whites without science. They were not a different species altogether, doomed by their nature to perpetual backwardness. In his review of Ward's book Powell wrote approvingly:

> The author shows that the chasm which in fact separates the intelligence of the lowest and the highest classes of mankind is chiefly due to inequality in the possession of the data for thought. He shows that the capacity of the mind is, in any particular class of society, practically equal; that, even in what are known as semi-civilized or barbarian races, the capacity exists for a far greater amount of knowledge than is ever obtained.

Years later he was still making the same point. "The unity of the human race is one of the best-established facts of science, and it rests mainly on biologic data."[40]

Not every scientist of the day agreed with that conclusion. Many in fact were ardently looking for data that would divide humans, if not into separate species, at least into biologically fixed races that were very unequal in their abilities. Such scientists mainly came out of physical anthropology or comparative anatomy—Samuel Morton, Josiah Nott, and George Glidden, for example. They spent their time measuring the cranial capacity of black Americans, hoping to find some difference from European skulls. Like Powell, they wanted to establish a hierarchy of "higher" and "lower" people, but one based on racial features—and one justifying slavery, racial segregation, or laws against miscegenation.

Powell, the son of abolitionists, stood firm against that school of scientific racism. His anthropology would have nothing to do with measuring skulls and brain sizes. In one of his late essays, he decried those who interpreted human evolution as a struggle between biological types. "It is in vain that we study skulls," he declared; "it is idle to study the color of the skin, it is folly to study the structure of the hair, it is inane to study the attitude of the eyes, for man is more than the animal; his distinction is discovered in his intellect. To study men, therefore, we have to study mind, and to study human evolution we are compelled to study the development of the mind."[41]

It might seem inconsistent then that Powell sometimes referred to the "Aryans" as the most advanced people on earth. "The Aryan race," he wrote, "has steadily moved forward in the march of culture, leaving savagery behind, borrowing from other races whatever they could, and emerging into the light." Morgan had employed the same term, identifying the Aryans and the Semites as two competing "families" that had invented civilization, though the Aryans had gone on to dominate. Neither Powell nor Morgan, it must be said, had in mind the blonde, blue-eyed Aryan who became notorious in the twentieth century. Neither was very clear whether Aryan was primarily a biological or cultural identity. The word "race" was not a well-defined concept then (or later). Powell in fact argued that the various "ethnic" groups, by which he meant biological races, had no deep or coherent history. As one went back in time, humanity grew more and more varied in character. "Multifarious streams have rolled down from high antiquity to the present, coalescing and parting again and again, until the world has been covered with a network of streams of blood which science cannot unravel." If that was so, then science was better advised to focus on cultural rather than biological distinctions among the species.[42]

Powell was much more clear about the future of the human species. Biological integration, like cultural integration, was the irresistible trend. All races of the human race were becoming one, and uniformity was replacing difference here as in other aspects of modern life. "Distinctions of biologic varieties of mankind, of which we now have but hints in the biologic characteristics remaining, are gradually being obliterated; and we may confidently predict that in the fourth stage, yet to be reached, race distinctions will be utterly lost."[43]

White supremacist, no. Ethnocentrist, yes. That whites would design the future seemed obvious. Because they were the most advanced people, it was their role in history to lead the way forward for everyone else. Had another people converted from mythology to science first, then they might have had the privilege of defining what civilization should be. They had not done so, and Powell was unapologetic that it was his own European and American culture that had discovered progress and now imposed it on the rest of the world.

Virtually the only anthropologist in the United States who rejected such ethnocentric thinking was the shock-haired immigrant Franz Boas, who arrived in the United States in 1887 at the age of twenty-nine. Born into a liberal Jewish-German family, he immigrated to America, where he soon made contact with Powell. Whether he was a victim of discrimination or simply a hard person to get along with, Boas did not find jobs easy to obtain or hold onto. Powell proved willing to fund his summer travels to study Pacific Northwest tribes and, in 1895, offered to make him editor of the bureau's publications.[44] By that point Boas had secured a position at the American Museum of Natural History in New York, which led eventually to a faculty appointment at Columbia, and he refused the offer. He may have been grateful, but he was thoroughly opposed to Powell's evolutionary anthropology.

A short while after coming into the country, Boas published a critique of an exhibit at the National Museum organized by Powell's associate Otis Mason. Out of the extensive holdings of the Smithsonian, Mason had selected artifacts to show the progression from savagery to civilization. Boas thought it was a bad idea. Better to show each culture as separate and unique, with no judgment about where it ranked on the evolutionary scale. Powell came to Mason's defense by arguing that Indian cultures had undergone much shifting through time, making it impossible to display them as static or coherent. Without the map of evolution, one was thrown back on a racial or linguistic or environmental classification, all of which posed serious problems. For Powell, the issue was whether all peoples were one or not; ranking them on a single scale of evolution made them so. Boas, on the other hand, in rejecting that single scale risked dividing the species into segregated fragments.

Both men saw themselves as defending a more enlightened attitude toward race. They agreed that racial minorities should not be judged as naturally inferior when they failed to match the whites in wealth and power. They agreed that all peoples shared a common biological heritage, though Boas paradoxically could not resist trying to discover how racial differences might influence body and mind. Where they clashed was over the ranking of human cultures on a scale of progress. For Boas, such a scale was "not founded on the phenomenon, but in the mind of the student."[45] Accusing Powell and Mason of blindly setting up their own culture as the world's ideal, he called for an anthropology that examined each society in its own terms. All judgment about "higher" or "lower" was biased, and all judgment should be avoided.

Boas's cultural relativism swept the field of anthropology after Powell's death, relegating the old evolutionary approach to the ashheap. Journals stopped using the labels savage or barbarian, not only because they seemed unscientific but also because they smacked of elitism and arrogance. The cultural relativists insisted that all cultures be viewed as equal, no matter how abhorrent or benighted their practices or beliefs might seem to outsiders. To be sure, the relativists had their own fixed moral values to preach — equality, tolerance, the beauty and goodness of primitive ways of life. In pursuit of those values they questioned science itself. Science became a "western myth"— just another way of making sense of the world, no better or worse than the stories told in the flickering light of a cave or wickiup.

Powell could not have disagreed more. He was convinced that science and its methods were superior in every way to the dark superstitions of a shaman or priest. Their perception of nature, though interesting, was not equal in truth value to that of the modern scientist's. By refusing to see the limitations of the primitive mind, Boas was in effect refusing the superior authority of science. By celebrating cultural difference, he was blocking the search for laws governing history. By idealizing premodern cultures, he was condemning civilization. The twentieth century, which often has been hard on the self-confidence of both science and civilization, has been good for Boas's reputation. But during the last quarter of the nineteenth century, self-confidence among the evolutionists was high, and Powell's cultural evolutionism ruled.

The story of progress told in the rooms of the Cosmos Club did not originate with Powell. Civilization's rise was a story that came out of the Renaissance, the Age of Discovery, and, most importantly, the Enlightenment. Powell, when he stepped out of the Methodist chapel, stepped into that well-established narrative. At its core lay a dream of human liberation through reason. Science would replace superstition, virtue would flower, and "happiness" would spread across the earth. Man Thinking was the story's hero, bringing liberation to all races. Humanism, which made the human species the measure of all things, supplied its moral philosophy. Its central plot was the domination of nature, on a material as well as spiritual plane.

It was a nice trick to make liberation depend on domination. Examine it closely, and it had a darker face. The fate of nature, conquered and managed, might become the fate of humankind. Once nature was brought under control and all the world's peoples brought under the centralizing rule of civilization, no check would exist on those in power. Still, the Enlightenment ideal survived through the nineteenth century—indeed survived well into the twentieth—survived so well that it has become identified with modernity.

Civilization, in the eyes of its champion on M Street, brought the blessings of advanced metallurgy, steam locomotives, and electricity. It put sails on ships and sent them to the ends of the earth. It added harmony to music. Increasingly, it promoted republican government that recognized the rule of law. Patriarchy was giving way to a more egalitarian family. God was no longer needed and should give way to Man. As Powell understood his moment in history, humankind was poised on the edge of a glorious era, the "fourth stage of enlightenment," when the "beast" would be completely routed. The human being would soar "away to the goal of his destiny on the wings of higher laws."[46]

To achieve that breakthrough to a higher stage, humans must obey the law of social, not natural, evolution. Nature's method was the one described by Darwin: a ruthless struggle for existence among organisms in an environment that was too limited and impoverished to support them all. Competition must follow, and though the results of that competition were often marvelous to behold, they violated the laws of morality. A better method was possible: evolution steered by scientific ethics. "Egoism" must give way to "altruism." The "moral sentiments" must become "the guiding principles of mankind. So morality repeals the law of the survival of the fittest in the struggle for existence, and man is thus immeasurably superior to the beast."[47]

Thomas Huxley sounded the same theme in his 1893 book *Evolution and Ethics*, though more melodramatically, portraying nature as a writhing pit of vipers lusting for blood. Lester Ward repeated the same theme, though he was more apt to denigrate nature as a stupid system of waste and inefficiency. Powell stood somewhere in the middle of those two ethicists. What all three agreed on was that accepting evolution need not imply holding nature up as the moral standard for civilization. Humans must fight hard against the biotic kingdom. The war for survival must give way to a war on nature.

Such a war meant driving the wildness out of the land, turning the continent into a more productive garden. Although nature had put severe limits on every other species, making life a battle for survival, that need not be the case for humans. For the ingenious species, the earth posed few limits.

One of Powell's comrades, James Welling, president of Columbian University, led the Washington intelligentsia in an attack on the pessimistic doctrines of Thomas Malthus, the British economist of scarcity. In a paper before the Anthropological Society, entitled "The Law of Malthus," Welling identified the pressure of population on resources as a spur that drove humankind forward, not a drag that defeated its best efforts. Civilization had escaped from the Malthusian trap of immiseration. "There is a limitless vista opened (though not an absolutely unlimited one)" to a people who have good laws, wise economics, richly endowed science, and a higher morality on their side. Powell, in the discussion that followed, agreed with Welling's optimism. Malthus was a false prophet. The capacity of the earth to produce food had hardly been tapped, and humans need never fear running out of resources.[48]

Man "adapts the natural environment to his wants, and thus creates an environment for himself," Powell observed. He lives in the desert "by guiding a river thereon and fertilizing the sands with its waters, and the desert is covered with fields and gardens and homes." When winter sends a blast of cold to defeat him, he gathers his family around the blazing heat of a coal-fired stove and "sings the song of the Ingleside." He discovers cures for every disease, "nepenthe" for every pain. "He has organized a new kingdom of matter, over which he rules. . . . the powers of nature are his servants, and the granite earth his throne."[49]

That positive course of human evolution was summed up in two stories Powell told about the danger of lightning. The first was a tale of a young friend's tragic day of boating on Yellowstone Lake. As the boat neared the shore, a bolt of lightning flashed, setting the sail and mast aflame. The vessel, with a hole burned into its hull, began to sink. Two companions were both victims of the bolt, one struck dead and the other paralyzed; only the friend was unharmed. Powell contrasted that terrible day in nature with another friend's effort to send his invalid daughter home to Italy for recuperation. Fearful that she might be lost at sea, he waited anxiously for word of her arrival — until one day another flash of "lightning" came through the ocean depths, a telegram sent via a deep-ocean cable, with a message of safety. "So the genius of man," he wrote, "has transformed the very lightning of destruction into a messenger of love and joy."[50]

A miracle like that could never be wrought by a single individual. It took an entire nation working together to lay the oceanic cable. It would take similar cooperation to escape the Malthusian specter of overpopulation pressing harder and harder on the earth. Against pessimism Powell threw the massed force of a nation and a species that had begun to organize. "Evolution is progress in systematiza-tion," Powell told the Philosophical Society. A system is an "assem-blage of interdependent parts, each arranged in subordination to the whole so as to constitute an integer."[51] His image was deliberately mechanical. The American nation was not only a producer of ma-chines and technological systems but was itself becoming a machine for forcing nature into submission.

Life in the nation's capital was only possible, he pointed out, by an exquisite system of economic coordination, in which "every man works for some other man." Hardly anyone in America produced for himself only. Everyone produced first for others and then indirectly was benefited. Such was the principle of modern political economy. By personal examples Powell tried to thrust home the "vast extent" of interdependence that had grown up.

> For the glasses which I wear, mines were worked in California, and railroads constructed across the continent to transport the produce of those mines to the manufactories in the East. For the bits of steel on the bow, mines were worked in Michigan, smelting works were erected in Chicago, manufactories built in New Jersey, and railroads constructed to transport the material from one point to another. Merchant-houses and banking-houses were rendered necessary. Many men were employed in producing and bringing that little instrument to me.

With so much labor standing behind him, "I am the master of all the world." Yet he realized that he was also "every man's servant; so are we all — servants to many masters and masters of many servants."[52]

One of the most powerful forces working to elevate humans above nature was the corporation. A voluntary association of people, the cor-poration was for Powell a remarkable innovation. It was system exem-plified. It demonstrated what people could accomplish working together. Modern life, he pointed out, was being reorganized by cor-porations, and likewise nature was being incorporated, transformed, and redistributed by the power of the corporation. "These agencies," he enthused, "have been more potent in the civilization, and more po-tent in the culture of mankind, than all the agencies of government."[53]

The corporation need not be "antagonistic," however, caught in a war for subsistence in which one creature must die in order that an-other live. Instead, it might become "emulative," striving "to perform better service" for society. Farmers had learned not to compete against each other; they worked for their common good by organizing agricultural societies and colleges. "The asperities of industrial life," Powell pointed out, "scarcely exist among agricultural people." Nor among artists, who were gladdened by the success of their colleagues. Nor increasingly among the professional classes, who likewise were organized into societies for mutual aid. Only the capitalist, though beginning to realize the same lesson of cooperation through the workings of the corporation, still lagged behind those other groups.

In one of his most remarkable essays, "Competition as a Factor in Human Evolution," Powell blasted the brutalizing of labor he saw in American industry. Driving wages lower and lower, forcing worker to compete against worker for a job, business was dragging the nation back into barbarism. "One of the great questions of the day" was how to end the industrial struggle going on between capital and labor. Few seemed aware of how dangerous it was. The professional classes deplored it, but they stood aloof and did not interfere. As workers became more resentful over their unjust treatment, they tended to ignore "all the evils of their own intemperance" and improvidence and see only their exploitation. Someday they would explode in violence, bringing down the whole country. "Injustice is of such a nature," Powell warned, "that it must be destroyed by society or it will destroy society."[54]

Advertising was another atavism that needed to be rooted out by collective action. Where an honest company simply announced what goods it had for sale and where they might be found,

> in advertising as it now exists, exaggeration is piled on exaggeration, and falsehood is added to falsehood. The world is filled with monstrous lies, and they are thrust upon attention by every possible means.

In the morning's post a letter from a friend lay buried under a pile of sales pitches. Newspapers seemed taken over by advertising, shoving aside the more important events of the day. Advertisers pasted their messages "on walls and on the fences and on the sidewalks and on bulletin boards, and the barns and house-tops and fences of all the land are covered with them, and they are nailed to the trees and painted on rocks. Thus it is that the whole civilized world is placarded with lies, and the moral atmosphere of the world reeks with the foul breath of this monster of antagonistic competition."[55]

How such primitive survivals in the business realm were to be eliminated was obvious to Powell. They must be removed by government. In remarks before the Anthropological Society he poked hard at the laissez-faire principles of Herbert Spencer, who regarded most legislation as pernicious and meddlesome. Powell looked on legislation differently. Laws, he countered, must confine business within moral bounds. As corporations grew in size and power, so must government grow. Eventually a hierarchy of corporations would evolve, the highest of which would be the nation-state, set up to regulate all the rest. Representing the will of the people, it would be a great influence for advancing cultural evolution.[56]

Lifting the wages of working people and shutting down the excesses of advertising were places to begin, but Powell followed Morgan and Ward in prophesying an even more comprehensive role for government in the future. Contrary to what Spencer and his free-enterprise disciples maintained, people were demanding more government, not less. Private property must decline, and property in common must return, though on a higher plane than before The distribution of wealth must become more equitable. As the nation evolved into "one vast body-politic" in which everyone worked for the common welfare, the old individualism must be "transmuted into socialism."[57]

What Powell had in mind by "socialism" was not a Marxist state or worker's commune. He envisioned rather a spirit of brotherhood suffusing America, spreading through government and the economy. A nation animated by generosity, sharing, and kindness. A nation in which men and women "will vie with one another to serve a maimed man." Already he could feel that America stirring around him, and he knew, through his study of the past, that its victory was assured by the law of evolution.

If not exactly in Karl Marx or Friedrich Engels, one could find echoes of Powell's social vision among other contemporaries in both England and the United States. The Fabian Society, for example, founded in London in 1883 and led by Sydney and Beatrice Webb and George Bernard Shaw, had a similar trust in the gradual evolution of a more collectivized society. So did the Danish immigrant to the United States Lawrence Gronlund, whose *Cooperative Commonwealth* (1884) introduced European socialism to American readers. So too did Edward Bellamy, whose utopian novel, *Looking Backward, 2000–1887*, published in 1888, could have been written to illustrate Powell's fourth stage of enlightenment. As these and other writers sensed, the air of industrial society was as heavy with foreboding as promise. Reflecting on the begrimed and angry faces of the proletariat, they deliberately chose hope over despair.

At the same time Powell's utopian outlook had echoes going back into the past, to eighteenth-century visionaries who called for a new order of the ages and even to Christian millennialists who awaited the coming redemption. Among the latter was Emanuel Swedenborg, the Swedish ecumenist whose writings had so moved Powell's mother, Mary, that she continued talking about them until her death. Although he had outgrown the need for theology, Powell still admired the moral side of Christianity, particularly "the doctrines that were uttered by the voice on the Mount." Religion as sorcery and fetishism he had no use for, but religion as "the yearning for something better, something purer" still fired his mind.[58]

The glaring difference between Powell and his Christian forebears was the extraordinary confidence he placed in science as a redeeming agent. More than a means to knowledge, science, he believed, was the greatest moral force in history. In an address given at the inauguration of the Corcoran School of Science and Arts of the Columbian University, he put science at the very core of education. The highest mental training "means a training in modern scientific culture." Law, history, the fine arts, literature must all look to that "culture" for inspiration. From science they might draw a sense of the glory and beauty in the natural world. By immersing themselves in the culture of science students might also learn industry, integrity, modesty, and charity.[59]

"Let us not gird science to our loins as the warrior buckles on his sword," Powell wrote in his tribute to Charles Darwin. "Let us raise science aloft as the olive branch of peace and the emblem of hope."[60] For this wounded veteran the war of man against man had lost all romance, and he had become a deep-dyed pacifist. That science could furnish an olive branch to contending parties was the highest tribute he knew. Yet even as he celebrated science the peacemaker, he remembered a sobering countertruth. In his day war had become more deadly than ever.

It was not the savages or even the barbarians, armed with bones or spears, who killed one another on a wholesale scale. Such slaughter was reserved for civilization.

> The great wars began with civilization, and have continued to the present time. . . . Maybe the nineteenth century has had greater armies than ever before existed; and these forces have been

armed with more terrible implements of destruction than ever before known, and the sacrifice of human life in the nineteenth century has been greater perhaps than in any other such period of the history of the world.[61]

The Gatling gun and the Krupp rifle had to be weighed against the moral influence of scientific training. It was a contradiction in progress that Powell raised but could not resolve.

He was not alone. Others in the final two decades of the century also saw in the deadly new instruments of war the potential defeat of their hopes for a more humane world. For every flash of optimism there was a nervous moment when they had to wonder whether modernity would tear itself apart. Mark Twain, in his novel *Connecticut Yankee in King Arthur's Court*, published just one year after Powell's observations on how civilization had made war worse than ever, gave the contradiction a macabre twist. His hero, the superintendent of a modern American munitions plant, awakens after a blow on the head in the medieval world of Camelot. Barbarism might well describe the beliefs and practices of Twain's ancient fair-haired Saxons. Despite their glamorous reputation, Arthur and his minions prove to be a superstitious and ignorant lot, living in wretched squalor. When the American's efforts to bootstrap them into industrial civilization fall apart, he turns his Gatling guns on them, mowing down ten thousand knights in a few minutes. Liberation becomes annihilation. Civilization proves to be more deadly than barbarism.

The prevailing wisdom told Twain, as it told Powell, that science was ushering in a better life than humankind had ever known. Evidence to the contrary was hard to deal with. Twain, overcome by pessimism, turned darker and darker in his writings. Powell, on the other hand, kept his faith in scientific civilization, though he too was compelled to recognize the cracks. Strikes, riots, labor exploitation, the threat of social chaos, crass commercialism, the mass destructiveness of war, even petty bickering among the scientists who were supposed to stand for higher principles — all that had to be acknowledged. How civilization could transcend its flaws was not clear to him. Faith was all he had to offer: "Faith in my fellow-man, towering faith in human endeavor, boundless faith in the genius for invention among mankind, and illimitable faith in the love of justice that forever wells up in the human heart."[62]

How ironic to fall back on faith in an age of science! Nonetheless, it was all that Powell could do. In an essay written in 1895, just after he passed the age of sixty, he expressed a chastened but still optimistic confidence. He made no sweeping claims to his nation's originality. Every society had been original and creative in its way, contributing something to those who followed.

> We cannot dissever our life from that of the past. We inherit its arts and improve that a little; we inherit its pleasures and make but a slight change; we inherit its speech and improve our expression only to a slight degree; we inherit its institutions and modify the forms of justice only in small particulars, and we entertain new ideas only as we have discovered a few new facts. So we are indebted to the dead for that which we are, and are governed by the dead in all our activities. Yet the past is not a tyranny on the present, but an informing energy which evolves through us that the future may be improved. Science endeavors to guide the way by a study of the past and to conserve and direct our energies in a legitimate course of development.[63]

That last phrase captured his hopes precisely: to discover "a legitimate course of development." Once discovered, science should "direct our energies" to carry forward that development.

The secular religion of American nationalism, revived and reunited, had replaced that of the church. Science had replaced divine inspiration. The conquest of nature through cooperation had replaced an inner moral redemption. Such was Powell's mature faith. It was what he worked for in his clubs and societies. It was why he stayed in Washington.

Such faith, however, would be severely tested in the years 1888 to 1894, his most critical period, when once more his attention turned back to the West. In the West as in America he looked for a "legitimate course of development." But what he found actually unfolding there was hard to call legitimate. That land, so heavily invested with American dreams, was in danger of being overrun by atavistic forces, and Powell realized that he had to confront them. He set out to discover whether the West was redeemable. If it was not, was the nation as a whole redeemable?

CHAPTER 12

The Problem of the West

Twenty years had passed since the first expedition down the Colorado River, and nobody after Powell's men had risked it again—until 25 May 1889, when a new party put their wooden boats in at the old Gunnison's Crossing (now Green River, Utah), below a shiny new railroad bridge, and pushed off into the muddy current. Their leader was a Denver real estate investor, Frank Brown, who conceived the idea of constructing a railroad line on the banks of the river through the Grand Canyon down to the Gulf of California. His second-in-command was an Ohio engineer, Robert Stanton. Their six light boats took a beating, and in Marble Canyon, just below Soap Creek Rapid, Brown was upset and drowned. Five days later two more of the party drowned. Stanton called a temporary halt to the expedition.

A reporter for the *New York Tribune* asked Major Powell why Brown had failed. "He underestimated the perils to be encountered," was the reply; "nobody has ever successfully traversed the Colorado Canon but my parties." But Powell did it without an arm. "I was lucky," he said with a smile.[1]

Brown had consulted the Major in Washington and been told that his scheme was impracticable. A railroad track would have to hang suspended on the canyon walls. Not so, the surviving Stanton responded in an engineering newspaper; construction crews had mastered more difficult challenges than the Grand Canyon. He resented not only Powell's dismissal of the project's feasibility but even more Powell's failure—it was a disputed point—to warn Brown that life preservers would be needed. Stanton would go back to complete his river trip successfully, but for the rest of his life his consuming purpose became one of exposing Powell as a deceitful and unjust man. Powell, in his view, had deliberately avoided any mention of life preservers, had exaggerated some of the rapids and the heights of canyon walls, had never given his crews sufficient credit, and seemed to think that he owned the Colorado River.

"President Brown was a martyr to what will be in time a successful cause," wrote Stanton, "and as we and our children shall ride in safety and luxury through [the Grand Canyon], that most wonderful of rivers will sing, in the roar of its mighty waters, everlasting requiems to his memory."[2] Thankfully, that desecration never happened, though Powell himself was not offended by such a prospect. A railroad that would connect the vast coal fields of Utah and Colorado to tidewater seemed to him "a most desirable thing to accomplish." Nor was it offensive to many other Americans, for it was an age of railroad building and there was no place that railroads did not try to go. In the two decades following the completion of the first continental railway the West laid over seventy thousand miles of track through grasslands, deserts, mountain ranges, and canyons. The Southern Pacific connected Portland, Oregon, to El Paso, Texas. The Atchison, Topeka & Santa Fe connected Chicago to Los Angeles. Why then not a track through the Grand Canyon?

In the two decades since Powell and his men had begun to explore the last hidden part of the West, economic development had roared across the region in a cloud of smoke and ash. The speed and ferocity of that development were amazing. But of course the railroads were only the outward manifestation of a force more powerful than any technology—human desire. Americans fell on the West with a hunger that could not be satisfied. Land, property, money, security, profit were all sought, and few called the search greedy, for all of it was needed and all of it was deserved.

Development hastened the end of the Anglo frontier. The census of 1890 announced that "up to and including 1880 the country had a frontier of settlement, but at present the unsettled area has been so broken into by isolated bodies of settlement that there can hardly be said to be a frontier line." Powell made a similar observation, declaring that "now . . . there is no frontier; railroads and telegraph lines traverse the whole country, and thickly-settled towns are found at short intervals throughout the length and breadth of the country."[3] By 1890 the seventeen western states and territories counted 6,451,000 inhabitants. The biggest city in the region was San Francisco, with 298,000 residents; other sizable urban centers included Denver (107,000), Salt Lake City (45,000), and Seattle (43,000).

Several new states came into the union at this point, including North and South Dakota, Montana, and Washington in 1889 and Wyoming and Idaho in 1890. That left a southern tier, where substantial numbers of ethnic minorities lived, still in a territorial status—Oklahoma, New Mexico, and Arizona. And then there was Utah, land of the Mormon polygamists. No statehood for them until they learned to conform to national standards. But those exceptions did not alter the fact that suddenly the West had acquired not only railroads and cities but also, through statehood, considerable power in Washington—power to pursue economic development more fiercely than they had done before.

The era of military conquest was complete. Indians were confined to reservations, which were being steadily whittled away and sold to whites. Hispanics lived under the control of the Anglos, and much of their land also had been appropriated, legally or fraudulently. The West was now firmly a white man's country. As a new era commenced, when civilization must take the place of savagery, Powell was among those contemplating what that postfrontier civilization should look like. For him as for others the next problem of the West was how best to pursue economic development. What should be the region's role in an industrial nation? Could an arid land be made to feed itself, or the rest of the country? Who should benefit and who should control? Who could furnish the capital to build a civilization?

Urban entrepreneurs like Brown and Stanton had one clear, loud answer to give: capitalists should have charge of the West for they alone could finance its development in the most rapid and efficient way possible. Give us access and right of passage, and we will soon have the place looking like the East. Stanton envisioned a new Pittsburgh rising on the banks of the Colorado, burning coal to make steel, shipping it across oceans. In fact most of the railroads ran at some point to a mine or smelter where businessmen were extracting wealth. They brought in vast sums of capital, and in their dreams they saw a West that furnished the iron, coal, and copper needed to expand an industrial America.

The railroad corporations, which had far more to say about the future of the West than anyone else, were highly enthusiastic about digging as many mines as possible and turning the land into a supplier of raw materials. But they also realized that a mining economy alone could not keep their rails hot. A lively agricultural sector would bring in far more people to settle permanently, raising commodities to sell and ship. So the capitalist plan of economic development included, along with the extractive activity of mining, the extractive activity of farming and ranching. Food must join coal and copper on the steel rails that led to the city.

By 1883 all the bison had disappeared from the northern as well as southern range; fewer than a thousand of the animals remained where there had once been tens of millions. Pushing into their place were the white man's cattle, trailing up from Texas to the Kansas and Nebraska railheads, spreading across the vast grasslands. Although the politicians had not followed Powell's advice to grant lands for "pasturage farms," the cattlemen and sheepmen took over the public domain anyway, filing on scattered waterholes as "homesteads" and controlling all the surrounding country.

Along with the white man's stock animals came plows, seeds, and barbed wire. Farmers were bringing millions of acres into agricultural production, up and down the West Coast and in valleys scattered throughout the interior. They were rapidly advancing across the plains; Kansas counted a million people by 1880, Nebraska a million by 1890. They were pressing hard against Powell's one-hundredth meridian, the approximate limit of twenty-inch rainfall. Nature, to be sure, was proving quite as tough as Powell had predicted. Severe winters had devastated the livestock industry on the Southern Plains (1885–86), on the Northern Plains (1886–87), and in the Great Basin (1889–90). Then drought came along, putting a dismal end to the hope that, as the popular slogan promised, rain would follow the plow. Yet the promoters of development did not give up on the dream of turning the West into an agricultural land of plenty.

As the frontier era ended and the era of civilization opened, a few individuals called for saving the most spectacular remnants of the once wild West. John Muir was the most prominent of these. After leaving Wisconsin, he took a very different route than Powell, rambling through the mountains of California before settling on a fruit farm near San Francisco. Development, he feared, meant the destruction of his beloved Yosemite Valley and Sierra high-country. In 1890 he published two articles, "Treasures of the Yosemite" and "Features of the Proposed Yosemite National Park," that aroused concern among preservationists, including President Benjamin Harrison and his secretary of the interior, John W. Noble. That same year, Yosemite National Park was established, along with Sequoia and General Grant national parks. Those parks represented, if not a repudiation of development, at least a movement to restrain it from spoiling everything in its path.

The nation's first national park, Yellowstone, established in 1872, was likewise under assault by economic interests. Railroad builders were eager to cut a line across the northern part of the park to reach mineral deposits, and market hunters wanted to kill the wildlife that had found refuge in the park. They were stopped by a coalition of eastern sport hunters, military men, and politicians, including the Geological Survey's own Arnold Hague, resident scientist to whom Powell gave considerable freedom to fight for park preservation. Setting aside his geological projects from time to time, Hague picked up his pen to defend the park as "a zoological reservation where big game may roam unmolested by the intrusion of man."[4] He lobbied especially hard to establish a permanent forest reserve around the park as a buffer against civilization.

Powell himself was no match for Muir or Hague in love of wilderness. Indeed, wilderness for him was, like savagery, a condition to be overcome. Yet he took some pride in being among the first to support making a national park of the Grand Canyon. Benjamin Harrison, while serving as senator from Indiana, first proposed such a park in 1882, including part of the Kaibab Plateau and Marble Canyon as well as the Grand Canyon itself. Powell's support was sought, but Congress took no action. When Senator Henry Teller raised the same idea four years later, Powell again offered encouragement. Although the chasms of the Colorado were generally protected by their remoteness and desert condition, he believed, the most sublime portions were threatened by railroads and ranchers. Already the railroad builders talked of running a narrow-gauge line for tourists to the south rim of the Canyon. And the Kaibab Plateau, graced with a "really beautiful tract of timber," was being invaded by sheep and cattle grazers. "The herding of sheep and cattle would, in my judgment," he wrote, "be incompatible with the purposes of a National Park." He added that the Havasupai had a reservation adjoining those scenic lands, and in establishing a park "the rights of the Indians would have to be preserved."[5] No protection came, however, until 1906, when President Theodore Roosevelt proclaimed the Grand Canyon Game Preserve (and a Grand Canyon National Monument in 1908). Due to powerful mining and livestock interests, a fullfledged national park would have to wait until 1919.

Development along capitalist lines was one possibility for the West, and indeed the predominant one as the frontier era came to an end.

Entrepreneurs like Brown and Stanton expected to have the largest say in civilizing the country. Preservation of the wild in national parks was another, but severely limited, possibility. Powell responded enthusiastically to both groups, but closest to heart he had still another vision: a West where scientists carefully plotted development, where agrarian values and independent communities thrived, and where irrigation made the dry soil blossom and flourish. He would be allowed a very short time to make that alternative vision come true.

Big Bill Stewart blew into Washington in 1887, ready to resume his old seat in the Senate, representing Nevada, and to reinhabit his mansion at Dupont Circle. Many of his former colleagues remembered him well, either as the man who had almost been lynched by angry workers in Virginia City or as the crony of President Grant or as the "Father of the Mining Laws of the United States." Stewart had been the chief architect of the law of 1872 that threw the public lands open to any mining operation, free of all royalties to the government. A lawyer by profession, he had gone home intending to augment his fortune in the mining business but instead had made some bad investments. Still bristling with self-confidence, he was a formidable opponent, fully convinced of his rightness, utterly ruthless in a fight.

One issue that brought Stewart back into politics was the demonetization of silver, which hurt his state and his personal interests, though it also hurt, he pointed out with a great show of sympathy, the economic well-being of working people. The country needed to expand the money supply, and the best way to do that was to coin silver. But Stewart also had discovered irrigation — the magic of water artificially applied to land, which could turn his region into gold. Aware that Nevada's own potential for irrigated agriculture was small, he was nonetheless eager to see it fully exploited. Within months he was writing resolutions that would commit the federal government to promoting water development.

The federal census of 1890 counted 3.6 million irrigated acres in the West, almost two-thirds of them in California and Colorado. Both cold reason and fevered imagination said more was possible. In his 1878 report on the arid lands Powell had estimated that 2.8 percent of Utah might be irrigated, if every stream was fully utilized. By 1888 he had better news to tell. The portion that could be "redeemed" had increased to an average of 15 percent across the region, or 150,000 square miles, nearly a hundred million acres. That was half of the

Senator William Stewart of Nevada.
(Courtesy: National Archives)

area currently under cultivation in the country. The western land was worthless without water, supporting only sagebrush and bunch grass; but with water its market value would soar to $30 an acre, adding $3 billion to the wealth of the nation. Powell had joined the boomers.[6]

Led by Stewart, the Senate asked the Director of the Geological Survey on 27 March 1888 to estimate the sum needed for an irrigation survey that would investigate the practicability of constructing reservoirs for the storage of irrigation water in the arid region, "segregate the lands susceptible of irrigation . . . from other lands," and designate "places for reservoirs, canals, and other hydraulic works." Powell's swift reply was $250,000. In hearings, he explained that topographical mapping was the first step in such an investigation. Eventually a thorough investigation would require $5.5 million, most of it for completing the topographical map of the West. The map would provide a systematic overview of the region's drainage system, indicate all the potential reservoir sites, and show which lands could make the most efficient use of the limited water supply. Once again, Congress could see the Major's far-sighted, organizing mind at work.[7]

Legislators, however, were divided in opinion, with those from east of the Mississippi generally skeptical about the wisdom of spending money on western development. On the floor of the Senate the champion from Nevada tried to overcome their resistance. Stewart agreed with Powell that the government should not build irrigation works but only make maps and mark off arable land and canal routes so that the people could know where to focus their energies. He warned that the cattlemen were seizing on the best mountain reservoir sites for summer ranges — monopolizing them and closing off irrigation opportunity. Powell he praised as "a very competent and enthusiastic man, who goes into [the mapping] with all his soul; and he has so acted that there is a general recognition of the usefulness of his work."[8] Other westerners added to that accolade. Powell was their instrument of deliverance from aridity, monopoly, and ignorance.

The most negative voice in either house was Republican Senator Preston Plumb of Emporia, Kansas. Calling the arguments for an irrigation survey "trash," he denied that the country needed any more cultivable land, for there were millions of acres in Kansas, Nebraska, and Minnesota still wanting settlers. "I am not willing now to do anything which will induce the population within the present areas to go out into these great altitudes upon the roseate anticipations which will be excited by the reports we shall get." He accused Powell of promoting irrigation as a way of increasing his budget. "I suppose the Chief of the Geological Survey wants another job."

> We shall hear all about it on the finest letter-press; there will be
> the finest pictures the mind of man ever conceived of or the
> photographer's ever produced as the result of it; there will be
> endless volumes and cart-loads of books, . . . and there will
> be employment for Congressmen's sons and relatives and friends.
> The Geological Survey is the lying-in hospital of the Government.

Powell, he charged, had given employment anywhere it helped to win votes for his appropriations; consequently, he always got what he asked for. The money that had been spent by the survey "has been the worst expenditure since the Government was made." Powell was the conniving mind behind this extravagant scheme, and "I am opposed to giving him any further privileges with the public Treasury."[9]

The charges were true but distorted. Powell was indeed besieged by congressmen to hire their friends or constituents, and though usually he pleaded insufficient funds, he did hire the occasional politician's son or friend. He did indeed want to see irrigation go forward and the USGS to have a commanding role in it. But his agency's publishing had been curtailed by Congress, and he had less power over the purse than Plumb supposed. Not until 2 October did Congress finally agree to fund an irrigation survey, and then because the fiscal year was well advanced the sum added to Powell's budget was only $100,000.

The funding authorization contained a clause reserving all irrigable lands, reservoir sites, and ditch sites from entry. The public land laws were suspended in those places until the survey was complete. As Powell and his surveyors went about the West identifying the best reservoir sites and most irrigable lands, congressmen feared that the speculators would be one step behind, filing on those places and holding them to sell at a stiff price. The reservation clause prevented such speculation, although the legislation allowed the president to reopen any reserved lands at any time, under the terms of the Homestead Act and its 160-acre limit per family.

Representative Symmes of Colorado was the main author of the reservation clause, for he had watched speculators in his state deprive the small farmer of a chance at an inexpensive, watered farm. Countering him was Holman of Indiana, who warned that reservation would lead to injustice. Suspending the land laws for the five years that it would take to complete the irrigation survey (he was sure it would take more time) would hurt the legitimate settler. "Are gentlemen aware," he asked, "of the rapidity with which these so-called desert lands are being taken up and improved under the present laws by private enterprise?" He would leave all the land open to entry, fearing as he and others did, that any reserved land might someday end up becoming a grant to a powerful corporation. The precedent of Congress reserving and granting land to the railroad corporations was the specter they feared. Holman worried too that the next plea from the West would be for the government itself to build storage reservoirs, and then those reservoirs would become another subsidy to the rich and powerful.[10]

A few made no secret that they wanted the federal government to pay for irrigation in the West, a fair balance they thought for the dollars that had been spent on dredging rivers and harbors in the East. But the majority of the region's representatives insisted that they had no larger designs on the federal treasury than making a survey, and they were determined not to let Powell's investigation turn into a bonanza for the speculator. The entire purpose, Stewart and others repeated, was to prevent monopoly. Withdrawing designated reservoir sites and irrigable lands from settlement was necessary, and then Congress could decide how it wanted to see those lands disposed of and settled.

Quickly, as the season was late, Powell wheeled his troops into action. He now had the Irrigation Survey to run, almost a separate agency with two divisions to fill and equip: Topography, which he put in charge of the old warhorse and family member, Harry Thompson; and Hydrography, including engineering, which he assigned to the forever-on-leave Clarence Dutton. Wanting something impressive to show Congress before the next appropriation hearings, Powell concentrated them in the most appealing sites: the Truckee, Carson, and Walker River valleys of Nevada; the South Platte and upper Arkansas River valley of Colorado; the Rio Grande valley; and the headwaters of the Snake and Missouri Rivers in Wyoming and Montana. Snow was already falling in the high country when the men went out.

Thompson faced the challenge of mapping the 90 percent of the arid region that had never been mapped by topographers. Dutton's division had an even more daunting task: to measure the flow of water across a billion acres. They must gauge the volume of rivers large and small, volumes that could dramatically change over the course of a year, and calculate how much water could be stored that was otherwise running unused to the sea. They must determine the "duty" of that stored water, that is, how much land it could irrigate. They must measure the loss of water by evaporation and the amount of sediment carried downstream, calculating the time it would take before a storage reservoir filled with mud. Dutton was not to rely on opinions that were unsupported by careful measurement.

Captain Dutton chose a winter encampment site at Embudo, some forty miles north of Santa Fe on the Rio Grande, to train his young recruits in the technique of stream gauging. "All are very ambitious to distinguish themselves," he wrote, as if zeal could keep them warm.[11] Nights they slept in tents with outdoor temperatures of 15 or 20 degrees. Days they spent putting current meters and nilometers (depth gauges derived from the Nile River of Egypt) into icy water.

The most talented recruit to the hydrographic division was a civil engineer out of the Massachusetts Institute of Technology, Frederick Newell, whom Dutton had hired to run the Embudo camp. "A good Yankee as well as a scholar," he had been born in Pennsylvania of old New England stock. Newell's narrow, ascetic face hardly suggested the passion he felt for controlling the flow of water. Abandoning his first interest in oil and gas resources, he started small with the Irrigation Survey but eventually became one of the nation's most influential hydraulic engineers. "Unless something was done to convert these barren and arid tracts into fruitful and habitable lands," he later wrote, "many of these [western] territories would never gain populations large enough to become states, but would continue for all time to remain territories."[12] That passion for maximum development he shared with other young water technicians brought into government service.

Powell and his agency created language as well as techniques. They coined the terms "runoff" and "flyoff" to denote the rainfall that was not absorbed by the soil, either draining into waterways or evaporating. Needing a measure of water volume, they came up with "acre-feet," the volume of water covering one acre one foot deep. On average, they determined that one acre-foot of water could irrigate an acre of land so that a reservoir containing twenty thousand acre-feet could irrigate twenty thousand acres of land.

Their most important innovation was to envision the West as a series of "hydrographic basins," or watersheds. Every stream, regardless of its size, had a natural terrain that produced it, a set of slopes that collected falling water and concentrated it. The landscape had never been systematically analyzed in that way except by the old Powell Survey. The purpose now was to see the entire region as a mosaic of interconnected watersheds, as integrated units of water and land, not to deepen geological understanding so much as to guide settlement. Each of those carefully mapped and measured watersheds furnished the natural boundaries for a series of "irrigation districts" into which settlers could come and work out their problems together.

The district or colony idea had long appealed to Powell. It came out of Mormon colonization in Utah and mining camp life in California. The latter state's Wright Act, passed in 1887, which allowed such districts to form, own water in common, and sell bonds to finance canals and headgates, was a step in the right direction. But Powell saw that without scientific guidance the irrigation district was a hit-or-miss proposition, as homesteaders new to the West would be unsure how to draw the boundaries of their communities and derive the most efficient use of their most vital resource. Even in New Mexico, where the Hispanic community had been irrigating for a century, the full potential of watersheds had never been realized.

The Irrigation Survey was thus to serve as "a Bureau of Information" for thousands of private citizens looking for secure homes as well as for Congress, the states, and the territories trying to devise new settlement laws. Surveyors, in addition to mapping and measuring, marked reservoir sites and estimated the cost of constructing dams and water delivery systems. Powell told Dutton to aim at the

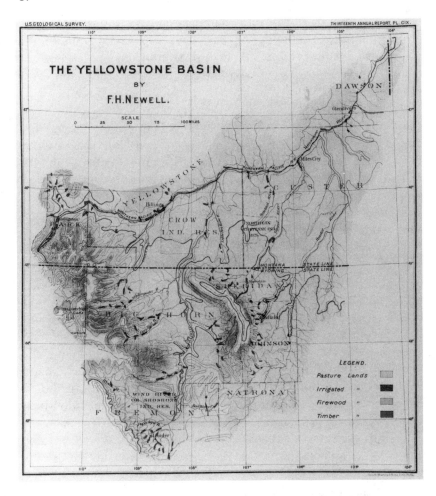

F.H. Newell, "The Yellowstone Basin." From U.S. Geological Survey,
Thirteenth Annual Report.

most practicable, inexpensive, and maintainable systems. They
should start with existing mountain lakes or depressions, which were
natural reservoirs that could be cheaply improved by raising small
dams at their outlets. Wherever streams came falling out of the
mountains onto a plain other reservoirs could be located; these too
could be constructed by people with limited capital. "It should be remembered," Powell instructed, "that the ends in view are not actual
construction by the Government but plans and estimates for the use

of the people and Reports should be prepared in the simplest manner possible."[13]

By those criteria Powell was not projecting massive dams on major rivers such as the Colorado or Columbia. Only rarely did any of the dams he imagined rise higher than one hundred feet. Most were on the small scale suggested for the Sun River of Montana — dams 23, 36, 58, or 84 feet high, with storage capacities below fifty thousand acre-feet. Meted out to small farms of not more than eighty acres, as Powell had proposed in 1878, the water from each dam and reservoir could support a rural community of at most a thousand homesteads. Hundreds of such communities were possible, each sufficient unto itself and indefinitely sustainable within its watershed. So efficiently would they capture and use the flow of the small, manageable tributaries that they would never have to tackle the more powerful mainstreams. In fact the great rivers would diminish or disappear. Much or all of their water would be taken out before they became a roaring dynamo.

By the end of the 1888 fiscal year the Irrigation Survey had mapped 22,230 square miles on a scale of one inch to one or two miles, and in the next fiscal year they added an equivalent area. They had selected 127 reservoir sites, 34 of which had been surveyed. And they had segregated over thirty million acres of irrigable lands in the Snake River, Bear River, Upper Missouri and Yellowstone, Owens River, and Rio Grande basins. All of those acres had been identified by township and section numbers, with recommendation to the General Land Office that no filings be allowed on them until Congress decided upon "the best method for their disposition to actual settlers." Pleased with the results, the legislators gave Powell $250,000 for his second year of operations, after he explained that he was not yet ready to use more than that.[14]

Overnight the USGS had swelled like a bubble, with every floor in the Hooe Building now occupied and an annex established across F Street in the Adams Building. Thirty more employees had quarters in the National Museum, and more were spread from Cambridge and New Haven to Denver, Boise, El Paso, and San Francisco. Even the lively Major could not keep up with all the inquiries afoot or speak the languages of all the specialists he had on the payroll. He concentrated on what excited him most — scientifically guiding the economic development of the West. Geology as the study of earth history or of mineral deposits had little personal appeal, and he turned over such work to Gilbert's astute oversight.

The carpers-within carped about the new responsibilities. Hague took time from his Yellowstone studies to write Becker that "Powell is wholly given over to Indians and irrigation. The irrigation of the arid lands is a most important matter but hardly a question for the Geological Survey to take up." A few months later he wrote again: "The Major is head over ears in irrigation problems. . . . It looks now as if the Survey would be transformed into a bureau of public works." Emmons was also unhappy with the new direction. In the throes of a divorce and with his private investments failing, he was more cranky than ever. Powell is "following the old tendency—only more so," he complained. Out of an annual budget of $850,000, only $100,000 was devoted to what Emmons regarded as "proper" geology, a concept that decidedly did not include topographic mapping or irrigation and water-supply studies but did include underground mining.[15]

Ignoring the few dissenters within the ranks, Powell moved confidently ahead. Support for western irrigation was growing at the primary seat of power in Washington, the legislators on Capitol Hill. Senator Stewart persuaded his colleagues to set up a Select Committee on Irrigation and Reclamation of Arid Lands, with himself as chair and six other members: Lyman Casey (Republican of North Dakota), Arthur Gorman (Democrat of Maryland), James Jones (Democrat of Arkansas and Powell's neighbor on M Street), Gideon Moody (Republican of South Dakota), Preston Plumb (Republican of Kansas), and John Reagan (Democrat of Texas). Stewart invited Powell to accompany them on a fact-finding tour of the West, and he agreed to go along, sure that most of his companions shared his views.

On the first day of August the Select Committee, with Powell in the party, entrained from St. Paul in special railway cars to Sioux Falls and on to Bismarck, passing through wheat fields dying for lack of rain. A North Dakota constitutional convention had convened in Bismarck, and on August 5 Powell addressed them briefly and in plain terms. "I was a farmer boy," he told the agriculturists and lawyers before him. He knew first-hand the problems of settling and cultivating a new land, for he had been a participant in the "march of progress" through the wilderness. He knew a little history too, and what it taught him was that they need not be reluctant to look the problem of aridity squarely in the face, for "civilization was born in arid lands." Four thousand years of experience proved that it was possible to turn a deficiency of water into a promise of prosperity. Then he turned blunt and exhortative. "You hug to yourself the delusion that the climate is changing," but you must accept the facts of nature and adapt. Above all, you must realize that whoever controls water in an arid country controls society. "Fix it in your Constitution," he urged, "that no corporation—no body of men—no capital can get possession and right to your waters. Hold the waters in the hands of the people."[16]

The Senate committee, now joined by Powell's critic Senator Plumb, rolled on to Helena, Montana, where another constitutional convention was meeting in the ornately Romanesque county courthouse. Again Powell was asked to speak to the delegates, and again he identified himself as a son of the soil—"one of the old pioneers" speaking to a room full of "tenderfeet." The tone was too condescending, but Plumb's presence seemed to fire up his determination to speak his mind. When he told them that eastern institutions were not well adapted to western conditions, they applauded. "All the great values of this Territory," he reminded, "have ultimately to be measured to you in acre feet." Then he proceeded to tell them how they should write their new constitution. If they faced their environment rationally, they would make drainage basins the primary units of Montana's political system. The boundaries of their counties would conform to those of nature. Agriculture, not mining, would become the basis of the state's economy, and securing that agriculture required them to tie together the water, land, and forests in a system of community ownership.[17]

As a lesson in civics, the speech was a muddled and sketchy disquisition, one that failed to explain clearly to the delegates the sweeping institutional changes Powell had in mind. He had little chance of persuading them to alter entrenched American traditions without going into far greater detail and laying out simply and clearly what a new polity would look like. Compared to the traveling senators' speeches, which were full of bombast and made little attempt to connect the purpose of their tour with the serious constitutional work at hand, Powell was brilliantly provocative. But he needed time to work out his still-emergent thoughts on resources, property, and politics. As it was, he startled the delegates with radical notions of how Montana might organize its life on the land. He raised Stewart's eyebrows a few inches, and he confirmed Plumb's view that he was not to be trusted with any amount of money.

The senatorial train rolled through the Pacific Northwest, Utah, and Nevada, arriving in Carson City on 22 August. A few days later they were in San Francisco, and then Bakersfield, Los Angles, San Diego, Yuma, Phoenix, Tucson, El Paso, southwestern Kansas, Colorado, Cheyenne, and Nebraska. In all they covered fourteen thousand miles in fifty days, traveling in the full heat of summer, sitting together in bake-oven hotel dining rooms, listening to the flies and witnesses droning in dozens of little court houses. Nearly four hundred people appeared before them; for the most part they were the same people saying the same thing — boosters and investors who wanted government help in their schemes of development. What Stewart expected to get from the exercise was never clear. Perhaps he did not know himself, except to have confirmed his urgent sense of opportunity. Inevitably, he and Powell became sick of one another's company, though more aware than ever of where they differed.

Weeks after their tour, Stewart sent a letter to Powell expressing anxiety that the Major was neglecting Nevada's interests in his irrigation survey. "I fear that we will not be in a position to make a good showing as to my State." Apparently, Powell was less the consummate "political scientist" than some charged, for he had already begun to disappoint a crucial sponsor in the Senate. Stewart let him know that he would be putting together a committee report before the next session of Congress. "I hope you are well," he concluded, "and that your long journey did you no harm."[18] It was an open question.

The Select Committee had missed Idaho's constitutional convention, where they might have heard an earful on how speculators were still trying to get control of water supplies. In early July that convention sent a message to Secretary of Interior Noble, protesting that as Powell's survey team finished investigating the Bear Lake vicinity, located in the southeast corner of the territory and shared with Utah, an army of speculators moved in, staking out land claims for an irrigation project. The claims were illegal, Noble declared to the governor of Idaho, and "the Government must have and will take, eventually, absolute control of every acre of arid land that may be redeemed."[19] He notified the Commissioner of the General Land Office to enforce the prohibition of any entries on reserved land. (Despite the 2 October law, the GLO had been allowing them, with a few words of warning.)

Noble then asked his soliciter general, William Howard Taft, for a ruling, and when it came in May 1890 it came with a stick of dynamite. Not only were the irrigable lands designated by the Irrigation Survey off-limits to any entry, *all public lands* throughout the West were off-limits. Nowhere could anyone file on or acquire title to a piece of the public domain within the arid region (defined by Congress as land beyond the 101st meridian). The reasoning was simple: Congress intended to set aside irrigable land for special treatment, but no one could say where that land was until Powell's men had gone over the whole country. Hence, everything had to be reserved until he was finished.[20]

The full import of that legal interpretation took a while to sink in. Thousands of individuals had been fanning out, in the time-honored way, looking for cheap real estate and expecting government to honor its generous promises. In 1888 more than twenty-two thousand people entered a claim under the Homestead Act on a total of three million acres, many of which claims lay within the arid region. Also, under the Desert Land Act thousands of more acres were entered, all of it in that region. Any such entry made after 2 October 1888, must be thrown out. No one could say when, if ever, the entrants could try again. It was up to the Director of the Geological Survey to decide which lands were irrigable and which were not, and until he did so the land office was closed for business.

Those wanting to acquire land and its resources could, of course, go into the private real-estate market—the railroads had a great deal of land to sell—or they could take up government land east of the 101st meridian. For nearly half a century, however, citizens had enjoyed an open access to public property, and they resented the sudden closing of the door. Many did not want to wait for Congress, the president, or Major Powell to sort things out. They set up a howl of outrage that grew louder as the year ended and a new one began.

As a schoolmaster in Illinois, Powell had led his students in singing the popular words, "Our lands are broad enough—Have no alarm—For Uncle Sam is rich enough to give us all a farm." The song did not actually promise to give away a valuable stand of timber or a lucrative mining claim or a right to build canals across alkali flats—only a farm. It made a certain sense in an earlier time and place. But now facing the end of the frontier and the harsh conditions of the remaining western lands, Uncle Sam was no longer as rich or as generous as he had been. He was rethinking his policies and generating plenty of alarm. Some of that alarm was real and poignant. Some of it was as phony as the tears on a spoiled child's face. In either case westerners suddenly felt thwarted and angry, and they went looking for someone to blame.

"Development" was a word used to explain the changes brought to the land by railroads, farms and ranches, and cities. It meant the land was experiencing a natural unfolding of its economic potential, like a butterfly emerging from its drab cocoon. "Conservation" was similarly a broad and protean word, one however that implied a critique of development. Conservation meant restraint, control, and limitation in people's use of the earth. During Powell's tenure in office, conservation became a national movement of reform. And because the West was the land undergoing the most dramatic new development, the region inevitably became a battleground for the rising conservation spirit.

Among the leaders in the conservation movement were poets and painters, big-game hunters and magazine editors, and a number of scientists and naturalists. All agreed on the need for restraint, though what kind of restraint and for what ends remained open and debatable. One of the prophetic texts of American conservation was George Perkins Marsh's *Man and Nature*, first published in 1864, which called for a new kind of pioneer—"a coworker with nature in the reconstruction of the damaged fabric which the negligence or the wantonness of former lodgers has rendered untenantable."[21] For Marsh, and for many others, science must begin to inform the pioneer's use of the earth, revealing laws that must be obeyed. However discordant their aims, most conservationists shared a hope that science could restrain development.

As the government's leading scientist, Powell was thrust into the new movement and became a powerful figure in defining its aims. Many of the Geological Survey's programs had the wise and prudent use of natural resources as either an immediate or distant goal. Minerals and water were the main resources addressed, but from its founding the survey assumed broad responsibilities for improving American understanding of "the land" as a whole. Land classification and Powell's topographic maps were part of that responsibility, even if they were meant to help civilization establish a more secure control over nature. Marsh had identified the first step in conservation as "a more exact knowledge of the topography," and for both men the end of that knowledge was to achieve "a better economy" and a more exalted life for the noblest of species.[22]

All the same, Powell felt himself being pushed by conservationists to include more natural resources in his agency's purview and to take a bolder stand. Soils and forests in particular became significant new issues during the 1880s, and the survey and its director were pressured to speak up for their conservation. He came to do so but slowly, with some reluctance and independence. Consequently, forest conservationists ended up resenting him and challenging his authority. He made a few enemies among them, and they hurt him politically when he could ill afford it.

First, the soil. Despite the fact that soil was a prominent part of the earth's history and structure and of vital interest to humans, the

Geological Survey paid it little attention. It was left to the Department of Agriculture, which was more interested in what the soil could produce than in the soil itself. A distinguished critic of that attitude was the German immigrant Eugene Hilgard, raised on an Illinois farm and trained at Heidelberg where he took his Ph.D. in 1853. For years he served as state geologist in Mississippi, integrating geology and agriculture in his researches. In 1874 he accepted the chair in agriculture at the University of California, recently established in Berkeley, and directed agricultural experiment work across the state that was already promising to become one of the richest agricultural producers in the nation. He watched farmers trying to irrigate their lands and observed how irrigation brought salt up from below and deposited it on the surface in a white crystalline crust, poisoning the crops.

In 1885 Powell offered Hilgard a job as head of a new agricultural geology division in USGS. Hilgard chose to stay put, but two years later he began lobbying his congressman, W.W. Morrow, to push an "agricultural survey" of the West, with Powell in charge. "When we inquire what has been done to benefit the agricultural industry, or to give to the farmer and immigrant the needed information so freely bestowed on the miner," Hilgard wrote, "we quickly come to the conclusion that the agricultural side of the work has not progressed" beyond where the indifferent Clarence King left it. The Department of Agriculture, on the other hand, was not a scientific research agency, had no geologists on its staff, and was unsuited for the work. In December 1887 Morrow went to see Powell, who expressed interest but felt that the project needed Hilgard himself to give it direction. The congressman suggested that adding soil studies to the survey's program would render it "forever safe against attack." They must win the support of farmers for the agency.[23] Powell still seemed hesitant, though he drew up an appropriation request for the next fiscal year.

The proposed agricultural survey was buried by the irrigation crusade started by Senator Stewart and others. Soils were included in that investigation, to be sure, though not the full science and conservation of soils that Hilgard had in mind. In that same year of 1888, however, Powell began to look more seriously at the Department of Agriculture as it was upgraded to a cabinet-level agency with a secretary of its own. Henry Alvord, director of Maryland's experiment stations, reported to Hilgard: "The world moves! Powell is *hot* to get into the 'enlarged' Dept of Agr. . . . He really tried to move in, before the roof was on the house, but Congress told him to wait a year or so."[24] A transfer of USGS out of Interior was never to take place, though Powell came to feel that the survey could never fulfill its mission until it was firmly rooted in an agricultural context. In the meanwhile he tried to get Hilgard named as assistant secretary in the Department of Agriculture, which failed when Hilgard discovered that he could not get the salary for which he had hoped. It would take another half century before soil research and soil conservation became a significant part of the federal establishment.

Forests excited a great deal more attention than soils, for their destruction left a more visible, emotional scar on the landscape. The longest section of George Perkins Marsh's book was on "The Woods," and it concluded: "We have now felled forest enough everywhere, in many districts far too much. Let us restore this one element of material life to its normal proportions . . . and become, more emphatically, a well-ordered and stable commonwealth, and, not less conspicuously, a people of progress."[25]

The American Forestry Association (AFA) was established in 1875 to promote that more stable nation. By the late eighties it was agitating for federal forest reservations in the West. Among its leaders was another German immigrant, Bernhard Fernow, head of the Forestry Division in the Department of Agriculture, and Charles Sprague Sargent, director of Harvard's Arnold Arboretum and editor of the magazine *Garden and Forest*. They, like Eugene Hilgard, looked to the Director of the U.S. Geological Survey for an ally. What they found instead was a Powell who claimed to support forest conservation, but insisted on doing so in his own way.

Among the conservationists' maxims was the belief that forest destruction had a calamitous effect on the flow of water. Springs dried up, streams shrank, yet flood waters increased without the trees to capture and store rainfall with their roots. They cited scientific studies from Europe to prove that effect. When Congress went crusading for irrigation, the conservationists argued that deforesting the western mountains would decrease the supply of water for farming the arid region. As Sargent wrote, the advance of irrigation "is like the march of a triumphant and liberating army," awakening "fertility where all had been inert and lifeless before." But, he warned, "the destruction of the mountain forests results in the destruction of the mountains themselves, and in that of the streams which have their sources in them."[26]

The Great Lakes states and provinces, not the West, were still the chief source of American lumber. Most of the threat to trees in the arid region came not from rapacious lumbermen but from livestock grazing and, especially, from forest fires burning out of control. A report from California in fall 1889 described a heavy destruction of coastal redwoods, ranchers being forced out of their houses, smoke hanging over the San Francisco Bay area. "The upper Sacramento valley, for a hundred miles, is under a thick cloud, and at night the red edges of fires can be seen on the hills of both Coast Range and Sierra."[27] Putting the forests of the public domain under the protection of the Army seemed the best way to protect the trees, and thus the water supply, from runaway blazes.

Powell had seen plenty of forest fires in his travels through the West. In fact, he confessed to accidentally setting one himself while camping in the Rocky Mountains two decades earlier. He had kindled a blaze at the base of a great pine as snow was threatening, and it had escaped to ignite the forest. "On it swept for miles and scores of miles, from day to day, until more timber was destroyed than has been used by the people of Colorado for the last ten years." In Colorado alone he had witnessed more than a dozen such fires, often producing so much smoke that his men had been unable to carry on their triangulations. Such conflagrations were not the work of nature. They were the work of man.

In his 1878 report Powell had blamed the increased incidence of fires on the Indians. Twelve years later, however, he pointed to "civilized men" who, by protecting the forests from small natural fires caused annually by lightning, ended up creating larger fires than ever. Powell called this "a calamity that cannot well be overestimated." The loss of the beauty and grandeur of the forests, and the loss of a valuable economic resource, he acknowledged, had stirred a rational demand that the government protect its western forests. [28]

Nonetheless, Powell and his associate Henry Gannett denied the argument, made by Fernow and Sargent, that forests were always necessary for generating stream flow. Data were skimpy, they said, but particularly for the arid West, where conditions were different than in Europe or eastern America. In the West, preserving high-elevation forests might produce less, not more, runoff. Forests did not allow the heavy snowpack to melt, and the moisture in it evaporated before it could flow downhill. On the other hand, they agreed with the forest conservationists that the lower slopes needed trees to slow runoff and prevent soil erosion. It was important to prevent destructive fires at the lower elevations, which could be done best by grazing cattle and sheep among the trees, keeping down the inflammable grasses.[29]

On his trip west with the Select Committee, Powell met with the forest commissioner of Colorado on 14 September 1889, assuring him that he would draw up his own forestry bill to present to Congress. Events got in the way, and that bill never appeared. Two months later Powell met the Colorado commissioner, Bernhard Fernow, and other representatives of the American Forestry Association in Secretary Noble's office to talk trees. By his own report Fernow, who was never one to yield the floor easily, was completely silenced, as Powell held forth during the whole meeting, challenging the AFA's science. Fernow came away angry, charging that Powell was a forest vandal and no friend to conservation.[30]

Then Sargent weighed in with a few editorials accusing "my friend Major Powell" of "criminal incendiarism" in personally setting fire to the mountains and doing little to stop the extermination of forests. "It is a matter of regret," Sargent wrote, "that Major Powell and the admirable young men associated with him are not more vitally interested in the preservation of these important forests. Their indifference gives aid and comfort to the enemies of their own work, and of our national civilization."[31]

The immediate stimulus for that charge was an article Powell had written on the horrifying collapse of the South Fork dam at Johnstown, Pennsylvania. Built for a summer resort community whose members included Andrew Carnegie and Henry Frick, powerful executives of the Pittsburgh steel industry, the poorly constructed dam had given way under heavy rain on 31 May 1889. Sixteen million tons of water smashed down the Conemaugh valley, killing over two thousand people and destroying several towns in its way. The tragedy turned many Americans against building reservoirs, threatening an end to irrigation development in the West. Powell, in one of his most important essays, leaped to technology's defense and opened another rift between himself and the forest conservationists.

He sketched a future in which dams plugged every rivulet, capturing their energy for hydropower and their water for urban supplies and rural irrigation. Masonry dams, earthen dams, thousands and thousands of every kind of dam would allow control over nature—a new hydraulic civilization. "All the highland streams of America will be controlled and utilized, and . . . the floods will be bridled and become the trained servants of man, as wild beasts have been domesticated for his use."[32] It was irrational to let one disaster spoil that future. No rational person would do away with railroads because of a single horrible train accident. Civilization was full of danger and risk, but civilization must go forward.

Powell suggested a way to make a water-controlling civilization as efficient and safe as possible. Careful topographic and hydrographic surveys must be made so that engineers could carefully adapt their dams to each site. The South Fork dam had not been constructed with adequate knowledge of its surrounding watershed. "To neglect the essential facts is to be guilty of criminal neglect."

> Modern industries are handling the forces of nature on a stupendous scale. The coal-fields of the world are now on fire to work for man; chemical forces, as giant explosives, are used as his servants; the lightnings are harnessed and floods are tamed. Woe to the people who trust these powers to the hands of fools! Then wealth is destroyed, homes are overwhelmed, and loved ones killed.[33]

The way to avoid disaster then was to demand more, not less, of human intelligence and engineering.

Trust in man's technology was fainter in Professor Sargent, John Muir, and others in the forest conservation movement. In their eyes the forest was a marvelous creation of nature, not to be destroyed anywhere on the assumption that human intelligence might design a superior environment. Sargent disagreed that a man-made reservoir might serve better than a forest in conserving water. "The splendor of the achievements of inventive and mechanical genius during our own time," he noted, "seems to justify the most daring and audacious expectations for the future, and it is not wonderful that men should imagine that nature imposes no limitations which may not be removed or overcome." Engineers, he observed in another editorial, were too fascinated by dams. They placed too much faith in their own ingenuity, not enough in nature's.[34]

Conservationists had, from their earliest appearance, rival views on the relative merits of nature and technology. It would be too simple to say that Powell, with his deep love of topography, saw nothing to respect or emulate in nature. Despite his paeans to industrial progress, he too looked to the natural environment as a template for reconstructing American life. Yet Sargent was right to see in Powell a greater faith in human interventions in nature than others in the conservation movement had. What Sargent might have asked, but did not, was who would end up making decisions in a civilization that exercised so much control over nature. If fools were not to be allowed any power, then who would be left to rule? And how would those rulers be made to answer for *their* failures?

If Powell had wanted to find examples of pride, arrogance, jealousy, and folly corrupting the pursuit of science, he needed to look no further than the field of geology. It was not so much a field of fools as it was a field of foolish squabbles over reputation and ego. Some of the ugliest rivalries in the history of American science could be found there, and Powell came to know them intimately for he was caught in their coils. Those unseemly wrangles among scientists, like his differences with the forest conservationists, damaged him personally as he tried to keep up his governmental support. They helped bring him down to defeat.

The ugliest rivalry came out of Philadelphia, the city of brotherly love. That well-ordered home of pious Quakers had become the seat of some of America's most distinguished scientific institutions and scholars. Powell, however, had never given the city's scientists their due, other than keeping Hayden on the survey payroll, and resentments had burned deep. They burned particularly in the heart of Edward Cope, professor of geology and mineralogy at the University of Pennsylvania after 1889, and they burned in the heart of Persifor Frazer of the Franklin Institute.

The Centennial Exhibition held in Philadelphia brought a number of European geologists to the United States, prompting Frazer and others to propose an International Congress of Geologists (ICG) where the North Americans and Europeans could discuss mutual interests and iron out differences in nomenclature and cartography. Some countries, for example, called the oldest rocks "Archaean," others "Precambrian." The first such congress assembled at the Paris Exposition of 1878, the second in Bologna in 1881, the third in Berlin in 1885, and the fourth in London in the fall of 1888.

Powell gave little attention to those gatherings and never attended any of them. His understudy William John McGee, the self-taught farm boy from Iowa who had taken to calling himself "WJ" McGee (often mocked as "No-Points McGee"), urged Powell to become involved. The survey, he argued, "is by far the most important geologic institution in any country; it is the only geologic institution dealing with a continental area," and a failure to attend the congresses would be regarded as an insult. McGee offered to go himself as "your accredited representative," and when Powell gave no sign of disapproval, he packed his bags and sent a telegram from Flagstaff: "I start this evening for Berlin." Pilling objected to that show of cheeky self-importance but noted to Powell that "the slightest word from you received by him prior to the opening of the Congress will be sufficient to bottle him up." [35] McGee went, but with little command of German, he was effectively bottled.

In 1887 Powell was elected to the American Committee of the ICG and assigned the task of identifying national standards of nomenclature and classification for the Quaternary period. He joined Frazer, Cope, and New York's grand old man of geology, James Hall. When the majority of the committee, led by Frazer, designated themselves final authorities on American usage, Powell resigned in protest. "There is no body of men so wise or so powerful," he offered as explanation, "that it can establish the science of geology by authority." The eminent James Dwight Dana joined him in resisting the attempt to impose a taxonomic scheme on the whole country. Powell's resignation was not accepted, however, and he was further irritated to see his name attached to committee documents circulated in London. On his side, Frazer concluded that the director of the Geological Survey was attempting to make himself czar of science. The air was rife with charges of plagiarism, ungentlemanly conduct, and malicious politicking. Even the mild-mannered Gilbert, to whom Powell delegated the job of correlating survey nomenclature, came in for a few brickbats. At the London meeting it was announced that the next congress would assemble in Philadelphia, but Powell went to work to get the venue changed to Washington.[36]

If the flap over the ICG seems in retrospect to have been a big fight over small matters, then the feud that Powell fell into with Cope was an all too familiar story of petty vanity. It began with Cope's visceral hatred for Othniel Marsh, a passion that was returned with full venom. Cope, a handsome Quaker born to affluence, had gone west to seek glory when he encountered Marsh ahead of him on the trail to fossil deposits. Thwarted, he proceeded to hire away Marsh's assistants, a few of whom were only too glad to leave the portly tyrant and sell the secrets of where he found so many stunning skeletons. The two paleontologists quarreled bitterly over who should get credit, who was a fraud, who had stolen whose ideas, et cetera. None of this sordid rivalry affected Powell until, in his desire to please Spencer Baird, he agreed to put Marsh on the federal payroll and secure some of his old skeletons for the National Museum. Then Powell too became a target of Cope's reckless jealousy.

Relations were tense from the beginning. In assuming the survey directorship, Powell found himself obliged to publish Cope's long overdue work on fossil vertebrates, based on field studies done with Hayden. He could not, however, get the manuscript out of Cope and then he could not stop him from making extensive last-minute changes that drove the printer wild. In spring 1886 Cope went directly to the Secretary of the Interior to complain that his work was being suppressed in favor of his rival's. Two years later he returned with the same accusation, whereupon Secretary Vilas threw the whole matter back to Powell to settle. Over lunch Cope agreed to turn over the fossils he had collected at government expense to the National Museum, and Powell offered to pay him a salary to get the book, now more than a decade in the writing, finished. "I feel much relieved," Cope wrote, but he did not stay in that mood for long. A year later he received a letter from Secretary Noble asking that the government fossils in his possession be turned over before any salary or publication could be contemplated. In a fit of outrage Cope immediately called in a scandal-seeking reporter.[37]

W. H. Ballou, a stringer for the *New York Herald*, made the front page for 12 January 1890 with shrieking headlines: "Scientists Wage Bitter Warfare . . . Serious Charges against Director Powell and Prof. Marsh . . . Corroboration in Plenty . . . Red Hot Denials Put Forth . . . Will Congress Investigate?" The spectacle continued for days, affording much entertainment to a public not used to seeing renowned scientists throw punches at each other.

The charges against Powell were a mix of old rumors going back to the consolidation of the western surveys and of Cope's paranoid fantasies of suppression. They were riddled with contradictions. Powell was accused of setting up "a gigantic politico-scientific monopoly, run on machine political methods" like the notorious Tammany Hall. He had given out "pap" to college professors to silence their criticisms of the Survey. He had "fastened upon the government a department of irrigation, by which he proposes to dam the grand canyon of the Colorado River." He had manipulated the National Academy of Sciences. Yet strangely this boss of bosses exercised no control over the survey, was duped by the scoundrel Marsh, and was "lost and demoralized" by a job that exceeded his abilities. Ballou proceeded to list scientists who could offer evidence of these charges, but only three beside Cope actually spoke to the reporter—Persifor Frazer, William B. Scott of Princeton, and F.B. Endlich, one of Hayden's original party. That might be enough, Ballou surmised, to send Powell down to "official destruction." A "volcano has been slumbering under the Geological Survey," and it was now ready to erupt.[38]

Powell's defense was published near the end of the first day's article, after he had been thoroughly condemned and ridiculed. Four men only, he pointed out, had concocted those charges, and all aspired to run the Geological Survey. Cope, he showed, had been trying for years to foment disloyalty among the survey staff. Marsh, in contrast, was a man of scrupulous honesty. The great crime he and Powell had committed was simply "to put under a bushel the light of the genius of Professor Cope." Cope was unfitted for any position of trust or responsibility by his "hysterical temper" that saw enemies where there were none. He was one of those "species fiends" who cared nothing about important issues in biology but were interested only "in the number of times which their names are quoted in barren catalogues."[39]

The director's defense of his fitness for the job struck one of the few humble notes in this fusillade of denigration:

I am not so egotistic as to claim for myself the credit of the
scientific work which has been done. It has been accomplished
by a large corps of able men working together for a common
purpose, with harmony, energy and genius never excelled. My
labor has been mainly administrative. Theirs has been one of
brilliant discovery, and when these scores of men return to the
office, driven by winter snows from the field, I rejoice at their
success and am proud to be their servant, and then feel that I am
gloriously compensated for my labors at the desk over routine
and official matters relating to ways and means, instruments and
supplies and the general business correlation of the work. And
when I see them toiling from year to year for the increase of
knowledge which is a practical and industrial benefit to mankind,
and know that they do all of this work without jealousy and without feud, generously aiding each other in their several problems,
I rejoice that no incongruous element, no man of petty jealousy,
no blatant disputant, has crept into the corps.[40]

That had the ring of sincerity to it, and it demonstrated precisely why Cope was unfit to run the Geological Survey. His vanity would have made him a poor administrator. Science, despite its ideal of humility in the search for truth, was often corrupted by rotten little men.

In the same week that the *Herald* broke its story of scandal and incompetence, Powell was summoned to testify before the Select Committee on Irrigation and Reclamation of Arid Lands, William Stewart presiding. Not a word was said by anyone about the newspaper articles, but no one could avoid knowing that their very first witness, the man in charge of the Irrigation Survey, was being pilloried in the press. Powell came loaded with tables of data, maps of the arid region, and a visionary plan, expressed in the form of a bill, for settling the country. He had worked out more coherently the ideas he had thrown at the Montana constitution makers—ideas he wanted to present in detail, if he could keep the conversation free of distracting disputes.

A map was always a vital tool of instruction, and on this occasion Powell set up four maps: one showing the irrigated areas of the West, one displaying its forests in shades of green, one outlining its drainage basins like a patchwork quilt of many colors, and one depicting the basin of the Rio Grande, a case study of typical western problems. Here as elsewhere, the water ran clear and deep in mountain canyons, where there was little irrigable land. The best soil was on the low-lying plains where the rivers turned broad, shallow, and silty—less usable for irrigation. Under the anarchy of American settlement, farmers started taking out water where it was easiest and the land was good, then watched others jump in above them, diverting better water on to more marginal lands.

Western state laws allowed that whoever got to a river and "appropriated" it had first claim—the doctrine of appropriation—even if they lived a long way from the river. The scramble for water rights that this law encouraged recognized no greater logic than one of grab and hold on if you can. Individualism was the leading principle. Downstream interests fought against upstream interests, with lawyers taking much of the profit. Even when states such as Colorado and Wyoming asserted that ultimately the water was public property, litigation of one claim against another was common. "Serious troubles are arising in the Rio Grande Valley," Powell pointed out, "and the valley is all aflame. The people are petitioning the Secretary of the Interior and the Secretary of War for troops to protect the old rights from invasion by those who are developing new systems in the country."[41] Time and money might eventually yield a measure of peace, but by then many small farmers would have seen their hopes and fortunes crushed.

Powell's solution was to segment the major rivers into a series of "natural districts" or "hydrographic basins," each of them "a unit in which all the problems must be solved." Eventually some 150 such districts might be identified, each requiring a separate plan, but for now he presented a list of 129 of them, all located beyond the Great Plains. Some were situated at the headwaters of major rivers, others along river trunks, still others on "lost rivers" such as the Humboldt that had no outlet to the sea. In New Mexico the area around Taos was a district of the first type, the area around Albuquerque of the second type.

Nature in the West had drawn the lines that law, politics, land and water use, and economic development must obey. Until the government recognized that fact in its disposition of the public domain, the region would be plagued by unstable settlements, conflict, waste, and frustration. Under Powell's bill each irrigation district would own all the water within its boundaries and have no rights to any other water. Each landowner in the district would have a share of that common water and a voice in its use. Each district would make its own laws, build its own system of irrigation, and raise its own capital to pay for it. All existing landowners would be absorbed into the district. By 1890 nearly half of the irrigable land in the region, Powell estimated, had already been privatized. The remaining irrigable lands, exclusive of mine and town sites, would be divided into eighty-acre homesteads, and the new owners would become members of irrigation districts as they moved in.

In a series of three articles for the *Century* magazine, published in spring 1890, Powell put his proposals into popular form. The last of them, "Institutions for the Arid Lands," acknowledged his indebtedness to Mexican and Mormon models of communitarian settlement. "The plan," he wrote, "is to establish local self-government by hydrographic basins," each of them to be "a commonwealth within itself." Democracy, localism, community self-reliance were to be the touchstones. Westerners should be given the power to determine their own destiny and then told, "with wisdom you may prosper, but with folly you must fail."[42]

The federal government, according to his blueprint, should reserve in perpetuity the remaining public domain — all but the irrigated homesteads, mines, and town sites — and turn it over to local residents to manage. The irrigation districts would supervise the forests and grazing lands as they did the water. "I say to the Government: Hands off! Furnish the people with institutions of justice, and let them do the work for themselves." Government must not build any dams or canals, nor decide who should harvest forests or protect them from fire, nor manage the grazing of livestock on the open range. "If the forests are to be guarded, the people directly interested should perform the task. An army of aliens set to watch the forests would need another army of aliens to watch them, and a forestry organization under the hands of the General Government would become a hotbed of corruption."[43]

As for capitalists, they too should be kept out by placing all land and water under community control. Powell allowed that his districts might want to contract with a corporation to build a water system, but the corporation should never own the water right or the engineering works or the land. "There is a war in the West," he observed, between capital and labor—"a bitter, relentless war, disastrous to both parties." His plan promised peace by opening to capital "a field for safe investment and remunerative return" and yet secure "to the toiling farmers the natural increment of profit which comes from the land with the progress of industrial civilization."[44]

The "progress of industrial civilization"? Powell was either deliberately concealing his social ideals under a veil of standardized rhetoric or, more likely, was unaware of how deeply agrarian his blueprint for the West really was. It owed little to his lofty discussions at the Cosmos Club with cultural evolutionists. He would save the region for the small farmer, small grazer, and small timber cutter, not for industrial civilization. Nor was he dreaming here of a country ruled by scientists or other experts, as Lester Ward proposed. The USGS scientists would have only a very limited role—"the accumulation of facts for the people." What people did with those facts was their responsibility. Thus, when he came to propose a plan to settle the West, this evangelist for progress, science, and technological expertise turned out to be an agrarian looking back to a small-scale way of life.

Besides the Mormons and Hispanics, Powell's ideas may have been influenced by the agrarian protest movement that had, by 1890, begun to achieve political visibility across the South and West. Indeed, the various Grangers, Farmers' Alliance members, and Populists might well have written his bill, for they too shared his ambivalence about industrial progress. All of them had been crying loudly that the yeoman farmer was being squeezed to death by the railroads, grain elevators, and manufacturers. A new political party was needed, they argued, to represent the real producers of wealth in the country—poor, deserving whites and blacks, men and women, laborers and farmers who worked harder and harder for less and less. Like Powell, they looked to government for help in their struggle against capital, but like him they placed more trust in the people than in government. Grassroots cooperation in production and marketing was to secure their salvation.

Powell did not have to go far within his own family to find that agrarian critique of industrialism brilliantly articulated and defended. In the very year that he was putting forth his vision to Congress and the public, his brother-in-law John Davis, husband of sister Martha, was running for a seat in the House of Representatives as a Populist. Davis had been like a brother to him back in DeKalb County, Illinois, and his advisor on where to go to college. In 1872 the Davises had relocated to Kansas, and John was elected president of the first farmers' convention held in the state, then president of the Grange, and then candidate for Congress on the Greenback Party ticket in 1880. This gentle, bearded man started up an agrarian newspaper, the *Junction City Tribune*, which lambasted monopolies, banks, and land speculators and advocated the income tax, unrestricted coinage of silver, women's suffrage, and public ownership of railroads.[45]

Along with William Peffer, "Sockless" Jerry Simpson, and Mary Ellen Lease, Davis founded the People's Party of Kansas and helped write its platform. A copy of that document found among the Director of the Geological Survey's papers claimed the earth as "the common heritage of the people." Every person, it went on, had an equal right "to a place to live and earn a living." It demanded that all land held by corporations, foreign or domestic, that was not in use be redistributed to "actual settlers only." Elected to Congress in November as a Populist, Davis served two terms (1891–95). On the floor of the House of Representatives he continued his campaign to restore agrarian values, frequently comparing the banks and corporations of late nineteenth-century America to the slaveocracy of another era. We live under "a colossal money power," he declared, "which is seeking with merciless greed to dominate a world and to garner in the profits of all labor in all lands."[46]

Populist agrarianism was not, however, what William Stewart wanted to listen to in the Senate hearings. Growing more and more impatient as the days went on, he jabbed and prodded Powell to "do something right away. The people are there and want immediate relief." He was referring specifically to North and South Dakota, where so far no money had been spent by the Irrigation Survey. Couldn't the government drill a few experimental holes to determine the artesian well possibilities there? Theorists held that there was a great river flowing under the plains that could be tapped for irrigation. Senator Casey of North Dakota agreed with Stewart that the people should not have to wait several years for Powell's topographers to map his state and explore its water resources. Get to the "essential facts" now, he demanded, give the people "courage" to go forward on to the plains without delay. Senator Moody of South Dakota chimed in: "What these people want is courage. . . . and if the Government will give them sufficient money to dig experimental wells they will take care of the rest." Stewart told of getting a letter from a New Yorker who had land to sell in the Dakotas and wanted to know what hope the government could offer his prospective buyers that there was plenty of water available. "They want immediate knowledge in order to give them courage."[47]

"Courage": it had been a familiar word among hustlers seeking investors in Stewart's mining-camp days. Have faith, buy my shares, don't run away to another hole. Powell countered, "I do not wish to give people courage to lead them on to failure, to waste their energies in seeking disaster." The settler would benefit by a survey done in a "careful, scientific manner," one that would not raise false hopes or give false advice. "I am not willing," he told the committee, "to deliberately face the facts before me and encourage the people as you desire. . . . Is it wise to encourage the people to gamble for water with the dice loaded against them?" But his slow, deliberate approach, which in his view saved money, gave the most reliable advice, and secured local control over the vital resources, was not persuasive to some on the committee. After Powell's last words, Stewart declared that they had spent enough time on "generalities." What we want now "is to hear from any person present who has practical ideas as to what can and ought to be done to facilitate irrigation."[48]

No one who came forward after that point discussed Powell's proposal for watershed-based commonwealths, and Stewart himself made no direct comment on it. In the four fat volumes of the committee report, packed with thousands of pages of testimony taken on the summer tour, with expert opinion, and with consular reports on overseas irrigation, Stewart tried to avoid any broad discussion of the kind of society the West ought to become. Instead, he worked to discredit Powell by attacking his topographical mapping as "pure science," useless and time-consuming.

On 13 March providence delivered into Stewart's hands Captain Clarence Dutton, head of the hydrographic and engineering division. Under Stewart's questioning Dutton readily admitted that he had been given less than half of the Irrigation Survey's appropriation, the rest going to the topography division. The topographical maps on which Powell placed so much importance were useful, he allowed, but they were "not indispensable" to engineers when they came to design a dam or lay out canal lines. "The Director was under a misapprehension as to the degree of accuracy in his maps," Dutton said. Their scale was too small to be usable for actual, on-site construction work. What then was the value of those maps that were taking so long to complete, asked Senator Reagan. "To furnish general information about the country and a knowledge of the laws of distribution," Dutton answered. "I think no money has been better spent."[49]

That last sentence in his testimony saved Dutton from utterly contradicting and undermining his boss, a friend who had for so long nurtured his interest in the western landscape and relied on him for faithful service. Powell came back to the witness table to point out that this subordinate tended like all the division heads to exaggerate the importance of his own work and that other staff might be questioned who supported the Director's sense of priorities. Stewart, gleeful that he had found his damaging witness, waved off all the others. But Senator Jones broke in to complain that hearings had become "a one-sided affair. . . . It is not right. I want to get the whole truth." Stewart was forced to back down to the extent of allowing testimony from a topographer, Willard Johnson, who pointed out that Dutton's own men had been "annoyingly persistent" in demanding topographical maps. The maps said to the irrigator: "Here spend your money; it will be wasted elsewhere." By that point, however, Stewart was not listening, and the hearings soon drew to a close. Although Powell had demonstrated his old sure command of detail and had offered the politicians a vision of a more securely agrarian and democratic West, only a few were interested, least of all the man who had led the fight for the Irrigation Survey in the first place.[50]

What did Stewart want? He had known all along that Powell believed in the necessity of topographical mapping; the senator had even praised such work earlier. During the hearings Stewart did not seem at all bothered by what later became a bone of contention: the fact that, since last August, no settler or entrepreneur had been able to file on any public land in the arid region. Millions of acres were available for settlement, Powell repeatedly pointed out, and more could be opened with a presidential signature. There was only one plausible motive for Stewart's opposition. Once he saw the anticorporate, agrarian ideals animating the small, one-armed man in front of him, he was determined to crush him. The "Silver Senator" whose ideal of the West had been inspired by the gold rush of '49 and the riches of the Comstock lode, where the strong came to the fore and the weak went to the wall, had decided he would rather have no irrigation program at all than have it continue under the populist Powell.

Three weeks after the hearings ended, Stewart commenced a campaign against Powell of personal slander and defamation that would last through the ensuing summer. Any dirt, any distortion, any lie he could lay his hands on became a piece of ammunition, not to be wasted. Powell fought back gamely, enraging the senator even more. All of Washington was transfixed by the struggle between them. Irrigation and the character of the Major became, for a moment, the most fervid controversies wracking the capital.

On 8 May the Select Committee's report came out, but in two parts: a majority report, written by Stewart and supported by all the other Republicans, calling for irrigation to be put it in the hands of the Department of Agriculture, giving "full play to the enterprise of the pioneers of the west"; and a minority report, prepared by the three Democrats (Reagan, Jones, and Gorman) who supported Powell's administration and wanted to adopt in full his revolutionary blueprint for settlement. The latter report warned that unless Powell's district system was implemented, "the lands and waters of the arid West will be aggregated in the hands of the wealthy few and the farmers themselves will be but hired laborers."[51]

On 26 May Stewart propelled a resolution through the Senate demanding to know how much of the irrigation appropriations had been "diverted and used for topographic surveys." Secretary Noble responded that the appropriations "have not been diverted from their purpose, but have been strictly used as contemplated in the act." Both the Senate Committee on Public Lands and on Appropriations, he reminded, had been exactly informed of what Powell was doing and had repeatedly approved his plan of action.[52]

Two days after the resolution Powell, stung by the attacks on his integrity, gave an interview to the *Washington Star.* "The struggle that I am at present engaged in with relation to the irrigation question," he told the reporter, "is a fight against the speculators pure and simple. I am doing what I can to prevent moneyed sharks from gobbling up the irrigable lands of the arid belt, together with the waters upon which they will depend for fruitfulness, and so establishing a sort of hydraulic feudal system, to which American farmers would be helplessly subject." Lobbyists, he noted, were at that moment stalking the halls of Congress to get the 1888 act repealed and the West reopened to their machinations to monopolize the water and sell it to thirsty settlers.[53]

Powell might have had in mind a few letters he had seen over the preceding months, illustrating private capital working to get water for its own enrichment. A Mrs. Fumey had written him from Fresno, California, in broken English, complaining about a water company that had dug an illegal twenty-foot wide ditch through her town to deliver irrigation water. "If the persons at the head of the American G[o]vernment were informed of such felony I am certain it will not be tolerated, but it seems in California, that only money can win."[54] Across the San Joaquin Valley bigger moguls yet were active, seeking to turn the Irrigation Survey to their advantage. Before their falling out, Stewart had shown Powell a message from "Friend Huntington" (Collis P. Huntington, president of Southern Pacific), who was eager to have the government reveal how his company's immense land grant on the west side might be irrigated.[55]

All over the West investors complained about the delay forced on them by the Irrigation Survey. The president of the Idaho Canal and Land Company, who lived in Canon City, Colorado, wrote Powell to find out whether or not he was able to take water out of the Snake River for land development purposes. (He was not.) A Greeley, Colorado, banker, protested that his company was being prevented from investing in ditches and reservoirs by a government that, "while nominally seeking to develope [sic] its resources," was placing "stumbling blocks in the way of legitimate work, in good faith, done in that direction." Secretary of War Redfield Proctor indicated that he had been ready to grant permission to capitalists wanting to construct reservoirs and canals on New Mexico military lands until Powell had warned him that Congress had decided that "these properties should belong to the people as communities and not to individuals or corporations."[56]

Despite Stewart's repeated assertions that the reservation clause in the 1888 act had been put there deliberately by Powell, the Major had in fact had nothing to do with it. The land had been closed by congressmen and by the Secretary of the Interior, acting on legal advice. In a press release aimed at clarifying his views, Powell professed that the withdrawal of all lands from sale "was wholly a surprise to me." However, he admitted that he believed the withdrawal was "wise" because it "would direct settlement where it ought to go."[57] That principle of guided settlement (or "legitimate development") he was ready to fight for in the interest of poor, land-seeking farmers.

Stewart joined the fight on behalf of the frustrated capitalists, and he joined with no holds barred, sending poisonous letters right and left, putting the worst possible interpretation on Powell's behavior. It was the director, not the capitalists, who was trying to plunder the West. To a Washington lawyer he wrote that "the repressing hand laid upon the settlement of the country is the hand of John W. Powell. He desires to use the irrigable lands of the West as a means of depleting the Treasury for the benefit of lobbyists and favorites." To a Yuma man he described Powell as "drunk with power and deaf to reason." Powell was "a great failure" who must be beaten "for the sake of the pioneers who are developing the country." His ambition "is unlimited; his greed for office and power unsurpassed. He is the king of the lobby. . . . He is a marvel in his way, a political boss, with the same daring and unscrupulous qualities as those found in large cities, who revel in public plunder." In still another letter Stewart soared into even greater hyperbole: "I have never met so unscrupulous and extraordinary a man, ambitious to the last degree, and the most artful, insinuating, and persevering lobbyist known in the annals of this country." And then to Powell's self-avowed enemy, Persifor Frazer, he charged that the director was "ruining the West . . . and is using the necessities of the people as an excuse for plundering the Government."[58]

Long after the battle was over, Stewart continued to solicit damaging information on Powell's private life. To John Conness, former congressman from California, he sent a conspiratorial note: "Since the receipt of your letter I have made some inquiry and find that his habits with women are scandalous."[59] What, if anything, had the senator discovered? Did Powell keep a mistress hidden away in the city? Was he a prowler of bordellos? Were ladies not his wife seen leaning on his empty sleeve around the punch bowl? Whatever embarrassing facts Stewart had come across remained tucked up his own sleeve, stored for a day of "investigation" when this dishonorable public servant would be unmasked.

When Stewart published some of his charges in a widely distributed newspaper article, Powell again felt compelled to reply. Stewart's claim that he was a law unto himself was completely false; "such language is born either of utter recklessness or of a disordered mind." Every individual hired had to have the approval of the Secretary of the Interior and obey the rules of the Civil Service Commission. All salaries, all expenses were set by law—facts that Stewart had to know. "He knows there is no truth in the innuendo" that the director courted political favor in his hiring practices. "In this Bureau of over three hundred appointees there is only one Congressman's son, and he was appointed by a former Secretary of the Interior, on the high testimonials of his college professors, when his father was

Major Powell, circa 1890s.
(Courtesy: U.S. Geological Survey)

not a member of Congress." The reason why Powell had "'the freedom of the Treasury,' if, indeed I enjoy that coveted relation, may possibly be because, during my entire incumbency, no violation or
misinterpretation of law has ever been discovered by the officers of
the Treasury Department in any of the accounts of the Survey,
amounting to many millions of dollars, and not one of our vouchers
has ever been disallowed." "Mr. Stewart assumes," Powell continued,
"that anybody who has a chance to steal does steal, that a man who is
at the head of a bureau of the Government of course bribes Congressmen to grant his appropriations; that Congressmen will not be likely
to vote for bills without a quid pro quo of some sort, and that nobody
obeys the law without compulsion. . . . It is always a public misfortune
when a really great man loses his faith in honesty, and takes it for
granted that everybody plunders who has an opportunity. . . . I am inclined to defend myself and the Bureau of which the U. S. Government has placed me in charge, but I hope I am not malicious or
wantonly cruel."[60]

Despite all the heat in that spring's air the House Committee on
Appropriations remained friendly to Powell and more than doubled
his funding for the next fiscal year to $720,000, with a large part of
the increase targeted for the Great Plains. He wrote to a supporter,
the state water engineer of Wyoming, Elwood Mead, that he had got-

ten all that he had asked for and expected to have a job to offer him.[61] But he was counting his chickens too soon. On 2 July, Senator Allison convened his appropriations committee, where Powell found himself on trial by a battery of prosecuting attorneys—Stewart and several other western senators who, along with a sole defender, Senator Reagan, had been invited by Allison to join the proceedings. Whether by design or not, the Major was dangled from a canyon rim, and heavy boots were ready to kick him over.

The principle behind his Irrigation Survey was clear, Powell told the crowded room: "I think it would be almost a criminal act to go on as we are doing now, and allow thousands and hundreds of thousands of people to establish homes where they can not maintain themselves." Stewart cross-examined him for an hour, ending with a question that showed how little attention he had been paying: "What is your plan for settlement? . . . by the General Government or by private enterprise?" Powell's answer: "By private enterprise."

They would come back to that plan later, but first the senators from the Dakotas and Montana protested that their states had been libeled as "arid" when they were the best garden the earth had to offer. They were upset, nonetheless, that he had not investigated their artesian well prospects. Powell objected, "with a small appropriation I can not go everywhere, and then they tear me to pieces because I don't go." He would not, however, encourage any panaceas, and by that lost the support of the politicians from the northern plains who wanted to believe that nature had endowed them with God's own plenty of resources, if the federal government would find them.

Back to the main issue facing the West. Was a pause in settlement, accompanied by thorough scientific planning and by a new communitarian ownership of the natural resources, the best policy or not? Senator Sanders, from Helena, Montana, rumbled that it was not.

> This whole law [establishing the Irrigation Survey] proceeds upon the hypothesis that the Government shall become paternal and form a kind of Procrustean bed upon which it will lay down these two gifts of irrigation and settlement, and compel settlers to take both or have neither, and that, too, upon the painful doubt or solicitude that haunts the gentleman [Powell] that somebody will locate himself out there unwisely. I do not believe that the Government can do any better for these people than to leave it to their instincts and sagacity and their own care for themselves.

Senator Reagan, on the other hand, warned that such laissez-faire was producing a country controlled by powerful capitalists, and he submitted a list of corporations formed in New Mexico to gain control of the water; the largest of them, the Pecos Valley Irrigation and Investment Company, had sunk a million dollars into two "immense canals." He warned that "there are very powerful interests at work— not for the benefit of the public but for the protection of individual interests—seeking the defeat" of the Irrigation Survey. Sanders then accused Reagan of being a disciple of Henry George, the agrarian reformer who wanted to break up land monopoly by concentrating all taxes on private property.[62]

Debate opened before the full House and Senate on 15 July and lasted for several days, overshadowing the Sherman Anti-Trust bill that was being considered in the same month. Once again the Senate became the bloodier battleground, for here the opposition to Powell, inflamed by Stewart's rhetoric, had become white-hot. Well into August they wrangled, stating and restating the same arguments made in committee earlier. The tone of the debate may be measured by the speech given on the Senate floor by Preston Plumb. Alleging that Powell had contrived so that "not one single acre" in the arid two-fifths of the country "shall ever be settled by any one," he went on, throwing consistency to the winds, to denounce the director's plan of settlement. "There is nothing, in my judgment, that is further from the genius of the American people than [Powell's proposal]. The average American citizen wants what he owns segregated and separated from the holdings of every other person in the world."[63] Powell, his critics thundered, was foisting on the public a profoundly un-American idea, one that would discourage capitalists from investing in western development.

On whose side stood the common man or woman of the West? The evidence is inconclusive, though both sides in the dispute claimed to be speaking for the "people." Stewart and his allies were sure that the people needed private capitalists to develop land and bring water to them. Those senators were often capitalists themselves, and their trusted friends were capitalists who thought as they did about the means and ends of growth. The West had benefited by opening itself wide to capital, they believed, and it must continue to keep itself open.

In contrast, Powell's supporters—Reagan, Jones, and Wilkinson Call of Florida in the Senate; William Morrow and William Vandever, both of California, among others in the House—wanted planned settlement that secured power in the hands of the people who were actually farming and grazing cattle and sheep. They looked on the West as the last chance to preserve democracy in a corporate age. They had no doubt that Powell's commonwealth idea was perfectly consistent with American ideals — and consistent with the needs and demands of the people.

Arnold Hague, touring the New England resorts, wrote on 19 August to his assistant that the bitter fight in Washington continued. "They not only attack Irrigation, but attack Powell all along the line. . . . It is very curious to see that all the men who went into this irrigation scheme are now the ones who are attacking it most strenuously." Eight days later he reported that the fight was over and Powell had lost.[64]

When the eastern politicians who had opposed irrigation spending all along saw that so many western politicians were now willing to throw away the whole project if it meant getting rid of Powell, they formed a majority. Acting contrary to the House, the Senate killed the Irrigation Survey. A conference committee was necessary to resolve the differences, and in late August it emerged with a bill that followed the Senate completely. The House could not summon the will to fight, and no appropriation was made. The entire project came to a crashing halt. Powell found his regular USGS appropriation increased, with more money than before to continue topographic mapping in the West, but all the western lands were restored to the old system so riddled with fraud and conflict and so ill-fitted to the conditions of nature.

It was the worst defeat Powell had ever suffered at the hands of Congress. Two years of intense work had been destroyed, dozens of employees had to be fired. Stewart had thoroughly beaten him, without scruple or regard for the truth.

Stewart had also lost something. He never saw his preferred irrigation scheme transferred to a more compliant Department of Agriculture. Indeed, irrigation was dead at the federal level and remained dead for a dozen more years. During that period capitalists tried to discover their own facts about water and where to invest safely in reclamation, but within another three or four years it was clear that they were failing. Few private water companies managed to survive. If Stewart had supported the Powell investigation, irrigation might have advanced more quickly in the long run, avoiding many bankruptcies and bringing in more people to settle, just as Powell promised.

But then the West might have turned out differently: a mosaic of independent, self-determining commonwealths where water, land,

and forest were united in the body politic. A West where harmony with nature became the foundation for preserving democracy within the region and the nation.

If Stewart spit in his own face, Powell hurt himself by unresolved conflicts in his thinking. He never seemed to realize how much his blueprint for the arid region contradicted his repudiation of nature as a guide to human affairs. When he came down from the heights of cosmic progress, when he looked closely at the land and its rivers, he found, if not a guide to ethics at least a guide to adaptive settlement. While he echoed the idea of conquest, he tried to preach adaptation to place. He called for the liberation of humanity from the constraints imposed by nature but then turned around to advocate a sense of natural limits, a skepticism toward industrial progress, and a populist program of agrarian democracy. It was confusing and ambiguous. For all his brilliance, his message contained fatal flaws.

Now came a lull in the storm, when life seemed almost to return to normal. Powell went back to business as usual at the Bureau of Ethnology and the Geological Survey. Rumors flew that he was eager to resign one or the other responsibility but could not decide which. Nevertheless, each day he made his customary way from M Street to F Street, trying to put the baleful glare of William Stewart out of mind.

He could not, however, put the irrigation question aside so easily. Although he was out of that work now, public and public officials continued to badger him for advice. On 29 September 1890 he sent a long reply to an Aberdeen, South Dakota, citizen explaining why artesian wells could never supply the water needed to farm the droughty plains. He knew drought from personal experience, and he sympathized with the vulnerable settler.

> In wet years the country is settled in great numbers, and at first the farmers are successful and highly prosperous; but when years of small rainfall occur, disaster comes, the crops burn up, the stock must be killed or sold, and often wives and children are without bread. . . . In some portions of Kansas I have known districts of country to be settled three times and almost depopulated three times, and in each case, when the time of exodus came the sufferings of the people were heartrending.

Were it in his power, he would carry on the irrigation investigation to aid the settler, but "the measure was antagonized in the Senate."[65]

Indians as well as whites sought information on diverting rivers to their crops or on storing spring floodwater. Commissioner of Indian Affairs Thomas J. Morgan wrote letters on behalf of the Pimas, the Papagos, the Navajos, the San Carlos Apaches, and the natives on the Fort Hall and Pyramid Lake reservations. As their land base dwindled, those tribes were all forced to intensify food production. Powell hoped the Indian peoples would get their share of the water and be able to use it to advance their condition, but his aborted survey had only sketchy information to offer them.[66] Meanwhile, his pared-down staff continued to assemble the data they had gathered on reservoir sites and to report the same to Congress.

Powell's reputation as an arid-lands expert was now international, and inquiries came from far away. One reached him through the U.S. Legation at St. Petersburg, and in reply he sent along his agency reports and a trenchant judgment on the American experience. Allowing "unrestrained and unregulated" individual enterprise to plan irrigation systems had proved inefficient. The systems built in the West, he wrote, "have not been laid out to give the greatest economy of water, or the widest benefits to the country as a whole. . . . Our system, or rather lack of system, while suited to the demands of a progressive, energetic people, is by no means the best. Advantage can be taken of our mistakes, rather than of our achievements."[67]

Months after one conference committee stripped Powell of his authority to designate irrigable lands for reservation, another gave President Harrison the power to set aside forest reservations on the public lands. The latter committee produced the General Revision Act (later known as the Forest Reserve Act), which went into effect on 3 March 1891. It included a short, poorly understood section that became the opening wedge for establishing a national forest system. Harrison's first reservation was for the lands that Arnold Hague had lobbied to protect adjoining the Yellowstone park. Before his term was over the President had withdrawn twenty-two million acres, including forest lands at the Grand Canyon.

Shortly after the act was signed Powell, despite his notoriety on forest conservation, was asked to make a few suggestions on how those reservations might be mapped and managed. He made another pitch for his languishing "commonwealth" idea. The forest reserves should conform to the natural drainage basins, he wrote to the Secretary of the Interior, and the community of irrigators in each basin should be put in charge of protecting them "from spoliation by choppers and destruction by fire." Although the reserves were intended to safeguard the watershed, he recommended that the land office mark off small tracts that could supply local timber needs. Farmers needing a load of wood or other lumber for use on their farms should be given free access to those tracts, but the commercial saw mill owner should have to make his case to the local community before getting permission to cut. Again, Powell's recommendations went nowhere. Decisions about who should use the national forests remained firmly in the hands of the federal government.[68]

He was more successful in persuading the International Congress of Geologists to change their next venue from Philadelphia to Washington. It was a reasonable decision; when the Congress assembled, 53 of the 148 American delegates were from the Geological Survey alone. No single university, no other metropolis on the North American continent, rivaled the survey as a center for scientific geology. The passed-over Philadelphians could not be expected to swallow that fact gracefully, however, and Persifor Frazer and company resigned in protest from the planning committee.

The congress convened on 26 August in a large lecture hall at the Columbian University. Scientists from Germany, Russia, Sweden, France, Great Britain, Mexico, and Peru mingled among the Americans, who had come from as far away as California, Nebraska, Vermont, and Florida. Among the foreign notables were Karl von Zittel, Charles Barrois, and Emmanuel de Margerie. Professors Cope and Marsh were there, eyeing each other balefully across the hall. The delegates elected John Newberry, the early scientific explorer of the Colorado River, as their president, and Powell was named one of the vice presidents. Emmons of the USGS had been put in charge of organizing the whole affair.

The social events glittered more brightly than the precious ores on display. Clarence King came down from New York City and, with George Becker, hosted a different dinner party every night of the week, spending over $250 on their guests. Not to be outdone, Powell sponsored a dinner for twenty-four at the La Normandie Hotel. The wine and spirits menu included bottles of sherry, rosé, Chablis, Mumms Extra Dry, brandy, creme de menthe, and Benedictine, with thirty-eight cigars and three boxes of Turkish cigarettes. The bill was $219, smaller than King's but still a month's salary for many of the agency's scientists.[69]

After days of discussing the clastic rocks, the classification of Pleistocene deposits, and the correlation of terms, many of the international visitors boarded an excursion train, with Powell as their guide, for a twenty-five-day tour of America's "finest scenery and most important geological phenomena." They spent a week among the wonders of Yellowstone National Park, and they visited Powell's own former domain, the Grand Canyon.[70]

The USGS seemed to some of the foreign visitors to be as impressive in its way as the North American landscape. Emmanuel de Margerie wrote that "we have nothing comparable to that wonderful display of labor in every direction of geological science; the union of topography and of geology seems specially wise and expedient."[71] In December 1891, a few months after the Congress had ended, the Institute of France informed Powell that his survey had been awarded the coveted Cuvier Prize for scientific excellence. He suggested the award of a medal instead of the usual sum of cash, with the unspent funds going back into the prize endowment.[72]

Standing on the sidelines, watchful and resentful, during these international triumphs was an immigrant geologist from Zurich, Switzerland, Jules Marcou, a friend of the Agassiz family. In April 1892 he published a pamphlet savagely attacking Powell, King, and the entire Geological Survey. King's appointment he regarded as "profoundly regrettable," setting a bad precedent of placing poorly trained men in the directorship. Powell was even worse—"formerly a schoolmaster in a village of Illinois," Marcou sniffed. Powell was like a mere "house and sign painter" trying to make pictures as perfect as those of a Millet or Courbet. He ran the agency as a dictator. He had allowed it to fall into a "state of anarchy." The geological congress had been a fiasco. Neither Canada nor Great Britain had sent their national director to the meeting, an obvious expression of disdain. Powell's remarks to the gathering of experts had been an embarrassment and a "blunder." The Cuvier Prize was a farce.[73]

Clearly, despite acclaim and respect, enemies still lurked in the shadows of the scientific community, eager to see Powell brought low and more competent men (themselves) appointed. They watched tirelessly for an opening—an unguarded moment when the "schoolmaster" might overreach himself and fall. But it would be Congress that determined whether he rose or fell. His standing there might be influenced by scientific accolades or be damaged by accusations or controversy from the likes of Cope and Marcou. In the end, however, the Congress would decide whether the survey served the national interest as they understood it. So far they still seemed to favor Powell as they had favored him for over a decade. Despite cutting off the irrigation work, they had given him $719,440 to spend in the fiscal year ending on 30 June 1891, which was more money than he had ever had before to run his other divisions. Beyond any honor or medal, that was the kind of commendation that had to matter most to a civil servant. Would it last?

The new year 1892, marking the four hundredth anniversary of the European discovery of the Americas, opened on a nation drawn taut by anxiety and fear. John Davis's "money power" was everywhere under attack, and to many, another civil war seemed imminent. Dangerous radicals, the newspapers warned, were roaming the streets with bombs concealed under their shabby coats, threatening mayhem. Six years earlier a band of anarchists in Chicago had been convicted of killing a policeman and conspiring against law and order. Anger was rising among iron and steel workers toward the baron Carnegie and his manager Frick, and in July 1892 violence erupted at their Pittsburgh plant between a hired private army of Pinkerton agents and trade unionists. Longer hours and lower wages for workers, higher profits for capitalists, had turned America's industrial cities into a battleground of violent strikes and warring classes.

Also in that same July, the agrarians brought their revolt to Omaha, where they formed a national People's Party and nominated James Weaver of Iowa for the presidency of the United States. They too challenged corporate America — its ties to government, its rhetorical cloak of progress and prosperity. In the fall elections Weaver polled over a million votes. Populists carried six mountain and plains states, electing governors, senators, and congressmen (and reelecting John Davis). Considering it was their first full-scale effort at national politics, it was a bold showing, sending dread through conservative circles.

Democrats, however, won the White House that year, putting Grover Cleveland back in charge of the nation's purse strings. All during the election year he and his party, many of them fiscal conservatives from the South, railed against the "billion-dollar Congress" that had outspent all its predecessors. Frugality, they said, must drive out waste and luxury. Tariffs must come down, even if the government loses revenue. An observer might have thought she was back in 1884, when civil servants had quaked in their boots as Cleveland ran for office, rumbling about cuts in the budget and vetoes for the extravagant.

It was not a propitious time to be defending federal support for the sciences. Anarchists and farmers, businessmen and reformers all had their minds on impending war between the haves and have-nots.

Or on silver or the tariff or immigration. As the time for new appropriations approached, Major Powell was facing the toughest sell of his life.

None of the parties in Congress could be counted on for reliable support. The Republicans had few Garfields left these days, but plenty of Stewarts. On the positive side at least one enemy, Preston Plumb, was gone — dead of a heart attack. The Democrats, who now had overwhelming control of the House and were breathing hard on the Republicans in the Senate, offered some scattered hope. But the friendly John Reagan had resigned to regulate the railroads in Texas, while old nemesis Hilary Herbert was still sitting in his Alabama seat, at least until Cleveland made him Secretary of the Navy — a move that left the military contractors happy. As for the Populists, no one knew where they stood on government science, topographical mapping, or expensive books on paleontology.

During the winter months Powell, sensing it was time to make his case more persuasive to the public, wrote a series of articles on "National Agencies for Scientific Research" for the popular magazine *The Chautauquan.* He appealed to the example of Franklin, Jefferson, and Gallatin who first understood the contributions that science made to "the welfare of the republic." He told the story of Ferdinand Hassler, who as an immigrant to the young nation, had won Jefferson's support for launching a coastal survey; but then ten years later, because people did not understand the importance of his work, found his appropriations stopped completely. Hassler bore the expense himself until 1832, when commercial interests persuaded the politicians to restore his funding. The Coast and Geodetic Survey had grown up from those shaky beginnings, admirably serving the needs of commerce and national defense.[74]

The Geological Survey likewise claimed Jefferson as its progenitor, for it was he who had sent Lewis and Clark on their legendary mission of exploration. "The history of the United States," Powell wrote, "is largely the history of exploration . . . a marvelous story of wild adventure, of courage and cowardice, of triumph and disaster, or religious enthusiasm and cruelty to the natives." He traced that story down to the present work of the USGS, emphasizing the value of earth knowledge to "the great mining industries" on which manufacturing and transportation depended.[75]

But science, he insisted, had more than utilitarian value; it was an index to "the state of civilization reached by any nation." It expressed "the intellectual aspirations of man to understand the marvelous works of creation." Powell described a reptilian skeleton arrayed before him as he wrote, "looking in many respects like the horned-toad of the plains, but of a magnitude equal to that of the elephant." The survey had brought such marvels before the public in 125 volumes, including four large atlases. "The continent is under process of dissection," he concluded, "and the characteristics of its anatomy are being revealed." Government science was translating "the language of nature," he said in a shift of metaphor, and when it was through "a body of useful knowledge and a library of philosophic grandeur will be given to the people worthy of the greatest efforts of the greatest nation."[76]

On 26 March Arnold Hague wrote Captain Dutton that the House appropriations committee had cut the Geological Survey by only $45,000. "This is much better than I had any reason to expect, and so much better than they have treated the National Museum, Coast Survey, and other scientific bureaus." Some weeks later Hague made a more doleful report to O.C. Marsh: the full House had struck out all funds for paleontology. This occurred after Herbert "made a violent speech . . . and no one came to the rescue. He brought up the whole subject of the [Allison] investigation of years ago and used Agassiz's letter, written at that time, with great effect." A few days later Hague wrote to H.S. Williams at Cornell University that "it has been rather a cold day for bones, in which I think shells have participated, although the attack was mainly on the former and directed against Marsh."[77]

The assaulted Marsh wrote to his cousin, Joseph Outhwaite, congressman from Ohio, that "Herbert's animosity is partly personal. . . . He was badly beaten in his previous attempt to injure the Survey, and has waited all these years for his revenge." To the well-worn charges made against himself Marsh answered that paleontology was no waste of money; it was "the foundation of all geology of the stratified rocks, and this every civilized nation recognizes." He furnished his cousin ammunition to defend his credentials, his salary, his record of publications. But he gave him nothing that could counter Herbert's devastating epithet for the Survey — an agency that wasted tax dollars on "birds with teeth."

Cousin Outhwaite proved an ineffectual ally, pleading that the cost-cutting mood was irresistible. "The rage for economy is so great," he lamented, "that nothing can stem it, unless the Senate can." Again he wrote: "The House is extremely utilitarian and has its teeth sharpened for everything simply scientific."[78]

While Herbert was back at his old game of ridiculing the paleontologists for their extravagance, Powell fell into a lethargy he could not shake off. Marsh wrote his cousin, "I heard various rumors in Washington about a change of Directors, as Powell has had about enough of it, and wishes to give it up, and confine himself to the Ethnological Bureau." Hague told Dutton in mid-May that Powell was not well; "in fact, I think his health is very poor."[79] Precisely what was ailing him is unclear. It seems that he had become easily fatigued, his heart was not strong, and his mutilated arm gave him constant pain. He appeared subdued and unusually quiet as House members stormed against the useless *Odontornithes* flapping their wings over ancient seas.

Other than Herbert and a few of his southern conservative friends, no House members expressed any personal hostility toward Powell or any reservations about the achievements under his directorship or any doubt about his fitness for the job. William Holman of Indiana, chairman of the Appropriation Committee that was slashing budgets of all the scientific agencies, called Powell "one of the most accomplished scientists that our age has produced." "No question has been made as to the efficiency and ability with which he has carried on these scientific inquiries." Charles Hooker of Mississippi defended him as "one of the most unselfish officers in the public service." He is "open, frank, and manly. He does not need to do any lobbying." The contribution he had made to opening the arid West made the Geological Survey "one of the most valuable bureaus in the history of our Government." Willis Sweet of Idaho declared that "throughout the West Maj. Powell is doing a splendid work." Even William Dickerson of Kentucky, who wanted the agency abolished as inappropriate expenditures by government, had no intention of discrediting "the character of the work done by Maj. Powell. . . . He is a splendid scholar."[80]

Yet when the House finished debating, Powell's budgets for both the Bureau of Ethnology and the Geological Survey had been reduced, the latter by over $200,000. Henry Bingham of Pennsylvania accused his colleagues of having "no sympathy with those scientific labors which the Government has been wisely aiding for many years, built up and developed to the highest condition of efficiency and usefulness."[81]

On the very day that the full House took up Powell's appropriations the Colorado river explorer and railroad engineer Robert Stanton called at the Hooe Building. Powell received him cordially, but Stanton noted that he was "a very nervous man." Not surprisingly, since his agencies' lives were hanging in the balance at that moment on Capitol Hill. Stanton was offended by Powell's conversation, which seemed to glorify his own expedition and to belittle Stanton's. "Not one word did he express of compliment at my final success — but rather sneered at any value in my work."[82]

The engineer had gone looking for Powell's old river mate, Jack Sumner, to find out the truth of what really had happened at Separation Rapid in 1869, distrusting Powell's account. He found Sumner scratching out a meager living in Utah, still prospecting for mines, and heard an earful about who had really led the trip down the Colorado and who deserved the credit. "This man Sumner is the one man who made Powell's first journey a success," Stanton recorded, "so everyone says. Sumner feels sore towards Powell. He complained to me of P's treatment." When Stanton mentioned seeing "one of his old friends," the Major answered "in a perfectly indifferent voice and manner 'Is he alive yet?'" It was an extraordinary reaction, thought Stanton, and he came away confirmed in his view that Sumner had indeed been mistreated and that the disappearance of the three men must have been Powell's fault.[83]

An arrogant pup like Stanton challenging an aging man's memory of his past glories should have expected to get the cold shoulder. Powell had more immediate troubles to think about. Somehow he must persuade the Senate to restore the funds that the House had cut. Another hot, muggy summer lay ahead, another encounter with Senator Stewart, and if the Major seemed nervous and defensive, then so was the whole city in a nervous mood, with tempers running high and unease creeping from one chamber to the other.

Once again the first hurdle was Allison's appropriation committee, which as before proved friendly to Powell and his agencies. The committee increased the House allocation by $47,000 to a total of $562,000, which was still a reduction. They did so despite a strenuous effort by Cope and his protégé Henry Fairfield Osborn of the American Museum of Natural History to impugn Marsh's paleontology division. Powell defended Marsh, now in his second term as president of the National Academy, by suggesting that Osborn was a young man of no achievement, that Cope was still nursing an old grudge. Someday the two critics would learn "that these controversies are petty and will soon be forgotten." Marsh's investigation of the vertebrate fossils was helping government geologists identify and classify rocks, even discover coal beds. It was not aimed, as some complained, at addressing theoretical problems in evolution. "The energies of the Survey are never diverted from practical geology to take up the speculative, though profoundly interesting, subject of biology."[84]

Marsh enlisted the president of Yale, Timothy Dwight, to make a direct appeal on behalf of the science appropriation to a famous alumnus who had left the college before finishing his degree, William Stewart. The senator's reply was a study in dissimulation. He expressed the most tender feelings for dear old Yale and, if work did not prevent, he wanted to attend the commencement and enjoy a reunion with his class of 1852. "I shall do all I can to secure the appropriation [for paleontology]," he promised, "but it is very difficult at this session of Congress to obtain needful appropriations to carry on the Government. The Democratic party seem determined to make a record for the fall election without regard to the merits of any particular appropriation. They are striking in the dark for the purpose of reducing the aggregate amount, without regard to the effect upon the business of the country, or matters of educational or scientific importance."[85] But it was Stewart as much as the Democrats who was preparing to lead a fight on the Senate floor to cripple paleontology and, above all, to wound and destroy Major Powell.

Several times during the month of July the Senate discussed the Geological Survey and its director, each time leaving sharp little tooth marks on his reputation. Stewart was determined to cut the appropriation to the bone. "This Bureau has grown to enormous proportions," he pounded. "It has an immense patronage; the Director has discretion in the use of this money that gives him a power in legislation that no man can resist." He exaggerated Powell's budget to "one million dollars" a year and charged that the money was all wasted, the field work was "all nonsense," the agency was "a mockery of science." Fifty thousand dollars should be enough money for it. Lieutenant George Wheeler of the defunct Wheeler Survey had scraped by with such sums and produced more results. "The real science of geology has been produced by such men and not by Government clerks and employees who go out in the summer and do a little airing."[86]

Despite his smooth words to President Dwight, Stewart went on to lambaste Marsh and his "birds with teeth." He attacked Clarence King too, and Emmons and Becker, asserting that all the economic geology they had done in the West had not resulted in a single mine. "Never was a geologist sent to that country who knew enough to help on anything of the kind. Never a man was fool enough to put a dollar on the opinion of one of them. . . .They are laughed at. They are scientific tenderfeet, and nobody would think of acting on their advice about mines."[87] If he had his way, the survey would be abolished and its few useful functions put under the Army Corps of Engineers.

Other senators from western states joined the fray, including Republican Edward Wolcott of Colorado. But it was Stewart who held the floor longer than anybody else, and his hostility toward Powell and his supposed "machine" had not lost an ounce of malice. Accused by colleagues of opposing "Prof. Powell because he knows too much," Stewart threw sarcasm back at them:

> He knows too much for the two Houses of Congress; he knows too much for the economy of the country; he knows too well how to bleed the Treasury; he knows too well how to buy laudation; he knows too well how to fool the people; he knows too well how to hire admirers. He knows too well how to get all those things, how to run geology in Washington. He knows too well the geology of the District; and he knows too little of the geology of the earth, and he has recorded too little of it to satisfy me.[88]

Stewart roared like a mountain lion, he cracked wise, he drew big laughs, and he tossed any sense of justice or decency into a brass cuspidor.

The shameless exhibition put on by the western senator compelled a few senators to rise to Powell's defense. The elderly Henry Dawes of Massachusetts deplored the personal antagonism between Stewart and Powell that poisoned the air every time an appropriation bill came forward. He pointed out that "my distinguished friend here never thought of the great extravagance and useless expenditure until he thought one way should be adopted to irrigate the arid lands and the distinguished Director of the Geological Survey thought another way was wiser." And once more Wilkinson Call of Florida, who was proud to be Powell's friend of fourteen years, praised his character: "I have never known a more modest, amiable, devoted enthusiast in the pursuit of learning than Maj. Powell. I do not believe a more honorable man exists upon the face of the earth than he is." If there were charges to be made against him, they should be backed up with evidence and presented before a committee where Powell could vindicate himself.[89]

The attentive scribe Hague dashed off a letter to Marsh in mid-July to let him know, first, that the paleontology division would survive in some form and, second, that Senator Wolcott had just introduced a resolution calling for an investigation of Powell by the Civil Service Reform committee he chaired. "Something has gone wrong with [Wolcott] so far as Powell is concerned," Hague wrote; "I think his feeling is all against Powell."

On 20 July Hague sent another letter to New Haven, this one full of bad news. "The game has been played and we are badly out. Much to the surprise of everybody, the House yesterday afternoon concurred in the Senate amendments regarding the Geological Survey." Paleontology had been "badly damaged," and geology was "equally badly hurt." The next morning the mood in the Hooe Building was grim. "Order has not yet come out of chaos, and we do not know exactly where we stand."[90]

The Senate, rejecting its own appropriation committee's recommendation, had knocked Powell's budget down to $376,100, and the House had meekly gone along. The paleontological division was cut by 70 per cent, geology (including both basic and applied work) by almost 60 per cent, chemistry by more than 60 per cent, printing and engraving by more than 80 percent. Moreover, Congress specified that fourteen positions must be eliminated, eight of them in geology. The fact that those reductions in force and expense were spread across the divisions suggests that it was the overall size of the survey that Congress felt compelled to trim, not Powell's sense of priorities. The one exception was the geology division, and here the transparent message was that underwriting broad scientific research on university campuses, as he had been doing, was not a popular idea.

The staff had been braced for a substantial downsizing for months, though not for the abrupt nose-dive they experienced during the torrid weeks of July. Within hours of the appropriation vote Powell sent brusque telegrams to those whom he had decided to let go. Professor Marsh led the list: "Appropriation cut off. Please send your resignation at once." Also to go were Professors Shaler and Pumpelly at Harvard, Professors Chamberlain and Van Hise in Wisconsin. The two holdovers from the King era, Becker and Emmons, received similar telegrams. All those fired agreed to continue their work without compensation while they put their results in permanent form. Lester Ward was the other geologist who lost his position, but he was transferred to paleontology. Gilbert, Gannett, McGee, Hague, Charles Walcott, Newell, Davis, Thompson, and Dall remained in place.

Compared to what was going on in Pittsburgh, where steel workers were being driven off the job by militia guns, this was not a national tragedy. The disemployed scientists had other financial resources. Nonetheless, the survey was left devastated, and the director left demoralized once again by stinging attacks on his character. If the summer of 1890, when they lost the irrigation project, had been the survey's crackup at Lodore Canyon, then the summer of 1892 was their Separation Rapid. Men who had been associated with the agency for years suddenly faced departure for destinations unknown.

Was Powell personally to blame for the disaster? Some in Congress and the scientific community and even among his friends and staff felt he was. Senator Wolcott went to New York City to ask Clarence King to guide a reorganization of the survey. King wrote to his friend and benefactor John Hay, "You have seen of course the crack of the Geological Survey. It is cut to pieces." Wolcott had predicted that Powell would be "overwhelmingly legislated out of office if he don't resign and is just now in the bull in a china shop condition of mind." King was raring to take command. "I shall get a ring in his nose gradually & finally straighten out the institution. I have gone to the verge of indecency for the past six months with Powell urging him to get out before the storm broke but he cannot realize that the tide of his popularity is swiftly ebbing."[91]

Powell had no reason to trust his predecessor's advice, who had made such a mess of his own life. In the same letter to Hay the once ebullient King admitted that "I feel the need of much and frequent apology for what looks like a fruitless life." He was flattered to be asked back to Washington, like Napoleon returning from exile. But the bull would not budge from his path. The investigation never took place, Congress did not try to force Powell out, and he would not resign.

Undoubtedly Powell must bear some responsibility for his second great budget defeat. Repeatedly, he had thrown himself into the thick of battle, risking his agency's economic health. Never truly foolhardy, he nonetheless was a person who held strong views and expressed them strongly, sometimes bluntly, antagonizing those who disagreed with him. For all his effort to discipline his temper, he remained a controversialist. Like his father before him, who had stood bravely on the steps of the Jackson County courthouse defying his pro-Southern neighbors, the younger Powell believed in standing firm for what he believed was right. Congressmen and others who did not share his views often sensed in him a streak of self-righteousness.

Although Powell never went to war against the corporate elite as he did against the slaveocracy, he did work himself up to a critique of the moneyed classes that was uncommon among high government officials. His political views were bound to get him into trouble, particularly in what contemporaries called the "rich man's club" of the U.S. Senate. He spoke too enthusiastically of "socialism" and, at least briefly, he aligned his agency with the interests of the small producer class looking for secure homes in the West. A more complaisant man, keen on job security and bureaucratic survival, would have presented a more smiling face to those holding wealth and power. By failing to act the obedient servant of money, especially in a time of high social tension, he risked defeat and it came.

It is impossible to calculate how Powell might have fared among the politicians had he been younger and healthier when his crisis came. Always before he had triumphed over his critics with an impressive demonstration of expert knowledge. But by the 1890s he was ailing more than ever and looking toward retirement. His poor physical condition must account for some of his inability to defend himself and his agency against invective and misrepresentation.

Still another factor in his defeat was the weak support he had from the scientific community. He stood up for Marsh, but Marsh did not stand up for him. Nor did any other scientist make a public plea on his behalf, even those whose research he had supported, giving the lie to Stewart's assertion that the director was buying allies all over the country. Quite the contrary, his cause was damaged severely by the long association with Marsh, whose name was tainted by the endless wrangle with the demoniac Cope. Had Powell dropped the paleontologists early on and distanced himself from the Marsh-Cope donnybrook, he might have avoided some of the criticism in Congress.

To be sure, Powell's days as a geologist were well behind him when he tried to sustain the scientific reputation of his agency against its detractors. Science had come to be for him a broad philosophy and an ethic that America needed, one that he used his office to promote, but science had ceased to be a profession that he followed closely. For a decade he had tried to broaden the research program of the survey to touch more people's lives, and to touch them intellectually as well as materially. But by the nineties the science of geology had become more highly specialized than ever, and he had become outmoded and unsuited to direct an agency oriented toward research.

Simply turning the survey back toward economic geology, however, as King or Emmons wanted to do, would not have saved Powell's budget from Stewart and company. If anything, Stewart was more contemptuous of the mining experts than of the topographers, paleontologists, and glacialogists. Through Powell's leadership the agency had moved toward a better balance between basic and applied science and a wider notion of what was useful to the country. The cuts that Congress mandated cannot be read as a demand for more attention to the western mining industry.

There was no single reason why the Geological Survey was "cut to pieces" on the floor of Congress, but probably the most important was the social and political climate of the day. In this fiercely contested election year, politicians were scrambling to look fiscally responsible. Reducing the expenses of government seemed to offer relief to a tense, volatile people who had lost their native sense of optimism and were afraid of what the future might bring. What Senator Dawes called "a spasm of economy" passed through the political body, leaving no science agency unaffected. As one representative explained to Powell, "Our parsimonious House has cut your appropriation but not with my approval."[92]

The mopping up of the breakage took much of August. Then Powell left office matters in the hands of his clerk, H.C. Rizer, and sailed for Nova Scotia for recuperation. He had been invited to spend a few weeks at the summer cottage of Alexander Graham Bell and his wife, Mabel. Born in Edinburgh, Scotland, Bell had arrived in the United States two decades earlier and, in 1876, had demonstrated his recently patented telephone at the Philadelphia Centennial Exhibition. He was rich and intellectually curious. For several years he and Powell had frequented each others' weekly "evenings," when they invited into their homes a coterie of friends to discuss philosophy, invention, literature, or travel. They rode together in Rock Creek Park — an oddly matched pair, the one a massive figure with leonine head, the other short and thickening with unkempt beard. To escape the oppressive Washington heat, Bell retreated each summer to the saltwater village of Baddeck on Cape Breton Island, reminiscent of the cold blue lochs and green headlands of his home country, and here the much battered Major came to take his cure.

By mid-September Powell was in Washington again with his health much improved. "I look back to my visit at Baddock [sic] with great feelings of regard and gratitude to Mrs. Bell and yourself for your unstinted kindness. My visit to your home is an epoch in my life long to be remembered."[93]

Early October found him staying at the Occidental Hotel in San Francisco, attending to survey business. He was still away from the capital at Thanksgiving. "The latest news received from the Major," Charles Walcott wrote to Marsh, "is that he is gaining in health rapidly and feels better than he has during the past five years." Yet Walcott also believed that a restoration of health would not solve all of Powell's problems with Congress. "There is trouble ahead for the Survey," he wrote to Charles Van Hise, "unless the Director succeeds in over-coming the strong feeling against his administration." Walcott, who might be suspected of wanting Powell's job for himself, reported "a wide spread belief that he has used political methods in obtaining appropriations, and been extravagant in the expenditure of them." Some congressmen felt he had not been fair to Cope. "I should not be surprised if there should be a change of Directorship."[94]

By year's end the still surviving and much healthier director was home once more and, according to a rueful Emmons, was ready to fight for a restoration of his appropriation "along the old lines." Powell was now explaining his last summer's defeat as the consequence of his refusal to let the USGS chase after underground rivers on the plains or make rainfall by explosions, "thereby incurring the enmity of the western members who had formed their wild schemes."[95] That explanation, if Walcott was right, ignored the darker corners of hostility toward him — hostility that would not be sated until he was driven from office.

In truth the old restless, driving energy was fading, and Powell was losing interest in his work. His heart was not in it anymore. He found it increasingly difficult to care about the agency he had once fought to establish.

The national scene could not have inspired him with any great expectations. By 1893 the widespread malaise and discontent of the previous year had deepened into the worst economic depression in the country's history. Nothing like it had ever been seen for bank failures, factory closings, farm abandonment, or unemployment. President Cleveland could not fathom what was wrong or how to correct it, offering only fiscal restraint and the gold standard. Throughout his second term in office the poor eked out the barest survival, helped by sporadic charity; the federal government ignored them; and city armories, expecting the worst, stockpiled guns and bullets.

Remarkably, under the circumstances, the Major was able to get his appropriations back on an upward track. Congress, getting over the feuding of its most recent session, increased his survey allocation to $414,100, and with salaries added to that sum he had a half million to spend, about where his funding had been during Cleveland's first administration. Hague wrote to the former employee Marsh that "we came out fairly well. . . .We had no investigation, no trial by newspaper, and [Senator] Wolcott's speech, while it was an attack upon Powell and the Survey, gave everybody to understand that he believed in the Survey and that it must be sustained."[96] A few positions in geology and paleontology were restored. Chief geologist Gilbert, who had been contemplating moving to Columbia University, decided to stick it out with Powell.

The director, however, according to Hague's information, was "by no means well." He wanted "very little to do with the administration of affairs; at best, he seems to shirk his duties as much as possible." To be sure, as long as Congress was in session, he could not attend closely to office routine. But Hague noted a few weeks later that "Powell is apparently busy with his great work on the Elements of Psychology, and sees very few people. Most of the details of geological work are left to [Charles] Walcott who seems to handle them fairly well, but complains of not being able to get authorization from Powell or get him to discuss matters." Walcott was soon promoted to Geologist in Charge, essentially taking command of all but the topographical surveying.[97]

The "great work" on psychology that Hague mentioned was better described as an effort to discover the foundations of scientific truth and clear away the distortions of misperception. It would occupy Powell for several years, pulling him farther and farther from the quotidian life. The other distraction he allowed was travel. For extended periods he left the capital, heading west where hope was still the prevailing spirit. Back to the West that had been his boyhood home, where the great river flowed that had made him famous, where the slant of light and the open sky still could be found that once had quickened his imagination.

Chicago put on a world's fair that summer, officially called the Columbian Exposition, celebrating one year late Columbus's first voyage to the New World. When Powell arrived in July the streets were packed with gaping crowds, dazzled by the nation's wealth and ingenuity on display. Fairgoers wandered through dozens of state and international exhibition buildings, clustered together under strings of electric lights on what had been a mosquito-infested marshland along Lake Michigan. The most popular element of the fair was the Midway Plaisance, where the new Ferris Wheel rotated above the astonished heads of farmers and immigrant laborers. From its heights one could look down on a Dahomey village, a Brazilian music hall, a Cairo Street complete with belly dancer and camel. Nearby was Buffalo Bill's Wild West show. But the most acclaimed feature was the White City, a full-scale mockup of Chicago's architectural future, when a new Venice-Athens-Rome would arise on man-made lagoons and the lake become another Adriatic Sea.

America's literary and intellectual notables came to see what the prairies were getting up to, and most went away with stars in their eyes. Even the morose Henry Adams, drifting in what he called "the dead water of the *fin de siècle*," was stirred by the fair, though he came away more convinced than ever that the country had lost all purpose or coherence, other than what a triumphant industrial capitalism and its machinery provided. Another vaguely pessimistic note came from the young Wisconsin historian, Frederick Turner, who told a meeting of his colleagues at the fair that "the frontier has gone, and with its going has closed the first period of American history." Others, including Powell, had noted the same, but the historian went on to pose the harder question of how democracy could survive in a frontierless future, when there was no empty land to the west promising escape from bondage to the past.[98]

Back in the state that had been his place of residence as a young man, Powell left no record of what he thought of the gleaming White City or the more desperate streets of the real Chicago. He was there to review his agencies' exhibits in the Government Building, including a selection of John Hillers's photographs from the Southwest and a life group of a Comanche family on horseback. He had sent William Henry Holmes ahead to supervise the Bureau of Ethnology's exhibit, and in late July the Powells arrived to camp in Holmes's lodgings. For four days Holmes piloted the director around the fair grounds. "We saw all the anthropological exhibits and studied them with care and naturally landed occasionally in Old Vienna which place the Major enjoyed very much. He is quite weak and I had to take great care not to let him get tired out."[99]

The Bureau of Ethnology mounted a large map delineating the distribution of indigenous languages, based on Powell's 1891 report, "Indian Linguistic Families North of Mexico." The map identified fifty-eight families as they were dispersed when the Europeans first encountered them, ranging from such large, widely spread groups as the Eskimoan, the Algonquian, and the Siouian to the Zunian, limited to a single pueblo in New Mexico. The classification and map were Powell's most important achievement as bureau director, aided by Pilling and Henshaw, and they set the standard for linguists well into the twentieth century. No one viewing the exhibit would be troubled by any challenge to the notion that Indians in their native state were savages. For all the complexity of their tongues, the bureau still insisted that the native peoples, before contact with the white man, had lived under hard material conditions and primitive superstitions and needed progress.

J.W. Powell, "Map of Linguistic Stocks of American Indians."
(From *Annual Report of the Bureau of Ethnology, Vol. 7*)

The story told of geology was no less progressive. Months before the fair opened, Powell had corresponded with exhibit organizer F.J.V. Skiff over a special USGS project in the Mining Building, which the director himself designed. The idea was to show the actual amount of various minerals mined in any one second of time, arranged in a tall column. A single gold coin, a couple of silver dollars, two barrels of petroleum, and a huge block of black coal were among the commodities on display, suggesting how much wealth American enterprise dug or pumped from the ground around the clock.[100] Government scientists, the exhibit insinuated, were out there on the land contributing to national prosperity, even if many of the mines were temporarily closed by the depression.

From Chicago Powell went by train to California, where he joined hundreds of other delegates in Los Angeles at the International Irrigation Congress. Boosters in the West Coast city were as zealous as those in Chicago. They saw a great metropolis arising on their desert plain, a paradise made possible by the control of water. So far the city of Los Angeles counted only fifty thousand souls, with another fifty thousand in the rest of the county. But there was Anaheim, a colony of irrigated vineyards established by Germans, and there was Riverside, where oranges and apples grew in irrigated orchards. Riverside had shipped 2,500 carloads of oranges in the previous season, worth $500 a carload. There was plenty of water if people would go to the mountains to get it, there was the extraordinary sunshine and, after 1892, there was oil. Growth must naturally follow.

Although Congress had ended the Irrigation Survey under Powell, the whole arid region was buzzing with new excitement over what might be done to find water and rescue the land from sterility. Powell had been preaching irrigation for twenty years, but it took the severe drought of 1890 on the Great Plains to ignite a popular crusade. A newspaperman in Omaha, William Smythe, discovered that the secret of prosperity lay in irrigation, and it became for him "a philosophy, a religion, and programme of practical statesmanship rolled into one." Resigning from his paper, he moved to Salt Lake City, founded a new journal, *The Irrigation Age,* and began to crusade. This sad-faced man with his hair parted precisely down the middle dreamed of nothing less than "the conquest of arid America," a dream that took Powell's old cause to new levels of fervor and optimism.[101]

Smythe organized a first Irrigation Congress in Salt Lake City, which ended by resolving that the arid lands should be ceded to the western states and territories, an idea supported particularly by Francis Warren and Joseph Carey of Wyoming, who saw nothing helpful coming out of Washington. The second congress opened in Los Angeles on 10 October, with feeling now turning against a policy of cession. All the prominent figures were there: Smythe; C.C. Wright, author of the Wright district law in California; Richard Hinton, formerly an irrigation specialist in the Department of Agriculture, now a broker looking for investors in reclamation; C.R. Rockwood, who was attempting to divert the lower Colorado River into the Colorado Desert (later renamed Imperial Valley); Elwood Mead, state water engineer of Wyoming; and a delegation from the Geological Survey, led by Frederick Newell and including Powell and his nephew Arthur Powell Davis.

The congress assembled in the Grand Opera House, rented by the city's chamber of commerce for the occasion. Outside stood a display of mechanical water pumps and ditch dredgers, echoing the industrial exhibits in Chicago. Sixteen-foot cornstalks, grown tall by irrigation, flanked the entryway. Inside, a long banner reading "Irrigation: Science, Not Chance" stretched across the proscenium arch. Below it on the stage were covered tables for the speakers backed by a painted scene of California mountains and oaks. The opera boxes, draped in foreign colors, were reserved for delegates from Russia, France, Mexico, Canada, and other countries, while the balconies were opened to local spectators. On the floor sat the delegates, ribboned off state by state like a political convention — seven hundred of them, all male except for a half-dozen women. The governor and mayor offered their welcomes, and for the next five days the house rocked with orations on the imminent blooming of the desert.

The second night Powell delivered a public address, sponsored by the Los Angeles Science Association, on "The Grand Canyon of the Colorado." He recalled how, twenty-six years ago, he and a small band of men had traveled through the sublime wonder of the Canyon, experiencing many thrilling episodes of danger and rescue.[102] The speech left him too exhausted the next day to give his regularly scheduled talk on water supply, and it had to be postponed. Instead, Newell gave a report on the government's scaled-back water studies. He cautioned the delegates that men without capital could no longer divert any water, because all the smaller streams had been taken up. Even for those who had plenty of capital, he added, the arid West could water no more than forty million acres out of its nearly one-billion-acre expanse.

Robert Stanton was on hand to link his Colorado River railroad project to the irrigation crusade. In a long address he chided Powell for neglecting, in his nostalgic look backwards to the days of exploration, the possibilities for future wealth. Now the engineer wanted to construct a dam in the Grand Canyon and, with Thomas Edison's assistance, install a dynamo to generate electricity to power his railroad. Powell had not dreamed big enough; he had missed the industrial potential of river, plateau, and canyon. "When your great irrigation empire is completed," Stanton told the applauding delegates, mining and railroading will provide the "foundation to stand on."[103]

Like Stanton, most speakers expected irrigation to open a new phase of American imperial expansion. The frontier need not end after all. If the small producer could not dam the rivers, then large capital could. Stanton offered to provide his own expertise, to engage the country's most inventive minds, while men such as Hinton were ready to back him up. No market for irrigation projects existed at the moment, because of the depression, but they were confident that one would soon appear. The American march westward, stymied momentarily though it might be, was to be revived among the arid wastes.

The delegates heard in the speeches another, not altogether consistent, message that told them the West must be the last refuge for the down-and-outs of society. The nation was running out of its patrimony. Speakers cited the British historian Macaulay, who had warned that when the new nation became old, when its frontier was finally gone, then would come the test of its democratic institutions. They saw irrigation as a postponement of that day of reckoning. The disgruntled, abused, and unemployed workers of the East might find a small farm with a ditchful of water and raise all the oranges and independence they could want.

Three years later the historian Turner described in an article for the *Atlantic Monthly* "the problem of the West." It was, he explained, "nothing less than the problem of American development." The nation had evolved in its own unique direction, away from European models and toward freedom, equality, and individualism. The West, which was "another name for opportunity," had made that evolution possible. Now, he feared, opportunity was gone, and "discontent is demanding an extension of governmental activity in its behalf."[104] Had Turner been at the Los Angeles congress, he would have heard a similar reading of the national condition, but he would also have heard a bold solution: give us water and we will make opportunity anew.

On the final day the delegates approved a platform proposing that the federal government reenter the irrigation business, this time to build reservoirs and guarantee water for the landless millions. It was the first drumbeat that, nine years later, drummed into being a federal reclamation program with many disappointing social and environmental consequences. But the delegates were already fooling themselves with rhetoric: landless people would never come, not in anything like the numbers projected, to their promised land. Even in that hard year of 1893 the urban poor and working class were not in-

terested in moving off to the desert to learn how to grow alfalfa,
wheat, and melons. They did not look to the arid lands for opportunity; they looked to the unions, the eight-hour day, and the federal
laws to protect them against exploitation. But if the fantasy of solving
economic depression and poverty through a program of federal
reclamation was never to be a realizable hope, then all that remained
was the dream of empire. In the end that was all the congress truly
had to sell.

Even that water empire must have its limits. Powell was fit to speak
again on 13 October. He came to the podium as the grand old man
in their midst, the nation's greatest authority on the arid West. Toss-
ing aside his more technical speech, he gave them instead a brief, off-
the-cuff, sober appraisal of their ambitions.

> When all the rivers are used, when all the creeks in the ravines,
> when all the brooks, when all the springs are used, when all the
> reservoirs along the streams are used, when all the canyon waters
> are taken up, when all the artesian waters are taken up, when all
> the wells are sunk or dug that can be dug in all this arid region,
> there is still not sufficient water to irrigate all this arid region.

While delegates had prattled on about transforming the whole desert
into paradise, he denied that it could be done.

Even more startlingly, he declared that "not one more acre of land
should be granted to individuals for irrigating purposes." The homestead and desert land laws should be repealed immediately, except in
a half-dozen small places. All land still in the public domain should
stay there forever, preserved as forests or pastures. By his calculation
the government had already disposed of more land to individuals
than the available water could irrigate — three times as much land in
fact. Every new entry added another competitor for a limited supply.
"What matters it whether I am popular or unpopular? I tell you, gentlemen, you are piling up a heritage of conflict and litigation over
water rights, for there is not sufficient water to supply these lands."[105]

Now he was speaking like a heretic in a church full of believers. Instantly they were on their feet, waving hands, interrupting, blurting
out angry questions. The *Los Angeles Times* characterized the speech
as the most remarkable event of the day, one that touched off a
"breezy debate." The paper might have called it the most remarkable
event of the week, for it continued to reverberate during what remained of the congress.

Smythe, who like most of the protesters misunderstood Powell's point, charged him with calling their platform a lie. It was not a lie, he insisted, there was indeed room for millions more to settle. Hinton, claiming expert knowledge, had seen many valleys where there was land that could be irrigated and plenty of unused water at hand. Others too could not accept the Major's supply figures or his pessimistic conclusions. Newell tried to excuse his boss as imperfectly informed. Wright wanted the outrageous remarks expunged from the record because of the harm they might do the cause. Governor Gosper of Arizona alone called for a fair hearing; perhaps Mr. Powell erred because he did not have all his figures written out before him. Let him have a chance to revise and amend. We delegates know that "there is an abundance of water" to irrigate "all, or nearly all, the arid lands of this Nation." Within a few more hours the congress, with its tail a little twisted, adjourned.

Newell sent a telegram to the Washington office, reporting on how Powell had riled up the delegates. "The whole crowd jumped on him for some general statements. The Mexican delegate says he liked that—it was the only bullfight he had yet seen in this country."[106]

The vehement reaction disturbed Powell, and he left town hoping to make his cautionary message clearer. He was not saying that the region did not have any potential for growth. His point was that the boosters should concentrate their attention on lands already privatized and accept the fact that by far the greater part of their country could never be supplied with water.

On 22 November he appeared briefly (before being summoned back to Washington to testify on his appropriations) at another irrigation conference in Wichita, Kansas. The delegates there, all from the Great Plains, heard explained to them the facts of evaporation and runoff. If there was any rainfall that seeped into the underground rocks, he explained, it was scanty and could be pumped out only as it was replenished.[107] He was right about that slow process of aquifer replenishment, and right about the scanty accumulation of water in the shallower soil layers. But neither he nor any of his scientists conceived of how much water had seeped down through the two million years of the Pleistocene, accumulating in deep aquifers that only the most powerful pumps could extract.

A century later Powell and Newell's estimate of forty million acres of irrigated land in the West would prove amazingly close to the mark—but only if one included the unexpected explosion of deepwell irrigation on the Great Plains. Nebraska would one day pump up enough fossil water to irrigate over six million acres a year; Texas, five million acres, far outdistancing any other states except California (7.6 million acres).[108]

The soulful-eyed Smythe was at the Wichita convention, where he took Powell to task again for his Grand Opera House offense. On later consideration, however, he decided it was best to restore this "splendidly equipped public servant" to the cause, and he invited him to prepare his thoughts for publication in Smythe's journal. This open-handedness he explained in the January issue, where he also reprinted a letter from Elwood Mead defending Powell "against the extreme severity of the criticism" unleashed in Los Angeles. Mead reminded readers that the director had a long career of friendliness to the West, that he was the author of the famous 1878 report that had provided "a model land system" for the region. If Powell's warnings added up "to a conservative view, it is only a fair offset to the exaggerated estimate in which the convention so freely indulged. As between the dangers of the two there is no question."[109]

In the February and March issues (1894) of *The Irrigation Age* Powell laid scientific data before his friends in the West, while carefully muting the call he had made to close the public domain. He allowed that the overall "catch" of rainfall might, under the most efficient application, water more land than he had estimated, but it was not possible, without great expense, to prevent a great deal of waste in the form of evaporation and seepage. Most of the western states, he showed in tables, had more land in private ownership than their water supply could irrigate. California, Colorado, the Dakotas, Kansas, New Mexico, Oregon, and Washington all had created more demand than the supply could satisfy. Only Idaho, Montana, and Wyoming had not. He left it to the public to decide how to strike a balance.[110]

Time would prove him correct about the lack of water for the public lands, though Congress would not close them to homesteading until 1935. The hope of carving a vast irrigated farm for poor folks from what remained of the public domain was a pipe dream that refused to vanish. It affected even nephew Davis, who pointed to fifty million Americans lacking any piece of land, condemned to death and starvation by the industrial economy. Send them west, he urged; "we have here a vast empire, more productive than any similar area on the globe, which we have scarcely begun to scratch. A continent capable of supporting in ease and opulence at least twenty times its present population."[111] But in truth the millions never got that food or opulence. Not at least from federal reclamation, which would serve those private owners who had already acquired holdings ranging up to hundreds, even thousands, of acres—an outcome of dubious principle.

Once a radical and an optimist about a new American society rising in the West, Powell had now become, in the eyes of detractors and defenders alike, "a conservative." Earlier in his career he had been a utopian, but one with his feet on the ground, his idealism tempered by science. Now he had given up expecting much from the West. The chance to plan a truly different society there had come and gone.

He did not altogether give up on America or on the small farmer. If the public domain no longer offered much opportunity for agrarian democracy, the cities might. In an address to New York farmers, Powell predicted that the trend in agriculture was toward raising more food on smaller parcels of land. Farmers were intensifying their production, often in greenhouses, controlling the elements of nature to improve yields. So far this trend was limited to cultivating vegetables for local markets, but in the future farmers would grow even the cereal crops on very small plots, and under glass. Irrigation offered vital support to that trend all over the country, for it was capable of increasing every farmer's output by five-fold. "The whole body of the agricultural world will gather in the suburbs of the cities and towns," he declared, leaving the vast hinterland to livestock and forests. "There appears now to be no practical limit to the amount of food which can be produced by mankind."[112]

A shift to urban farming lay farther off in the future than Powell reckoned. He raised the prospect but did not examine it closely. Nonetheless, that fleeting image of an agrarianism moving to the city represented a significant shift of emphasis, away from the West and toward the East. To be sure, the vision was close to what the Los Angeles boosters had in mind for their own metropolis—a city embowered in orchards and grain. But the interior West, with its achingly empty spaces, no longer seemed to Powell the home of the future. He had nothing more to do with its development and, in what remained of his life, never returned.

CHAPTER 13

Journey's End

"Turn," a rotation or change of direction. "Century," a period of one hundred years, measured from the birthday of the founder of the Christian religion. As the 1890s drew to a close, Western nations began to buzz with excitement over the "turn of the century." The Nineteenth was passing into history, the Twentieth was about to commence. Arbitrary though it may have been, the "turn" generated talk on both sides of the Atlantic. The world, it was said, was approaching a momentous change of direction from good to better, or from good to worse.

For those who had gained in wealth and power during the preceding years, or for those who had seen their personal hopes realized, the future looked exceptionally bright. Turn did not portend decline. The new century would surely build on the unparalleled success of the last in invention, enlightenment, and prosperity. For others, however, the mood was more pessimistic. Some, particularly among those whom the French called *les intellectuels*—Emile Zola, Henry Adams, Friedrich Nietzsche — had doubts about the sacred verities of progress. They had discovered a few flaws in the modern gods of rationality, science, and technology. Alienated in different ways were those experiencing a decline in their freedom or security, America's rural and minority people among them, who were suffering at the hands of lynch mobs, segregationists, urban capitalists, poor prices, and poor weather. Optimism had never been a universal feeling, but by century's end a growing number of disenchanted people were challenging Herbert Spencer's observation that progress "is not an accident, but a necessity. . . . It is part of nature."[1]

Those rising hopes and those anxieties of the fin-de-siècle surfaced just as Powell was ready to retire from active life and seek a more contemplative place to sit. With others of his generation he faced all the big questions agitating the air: Whither the human species? Whither his native land? Whither the industrial behemoth that was bestriding the oceans? Born in the antebellum period and surviving into the nineties, he had experienced some of history's most wrenching changes, and they required sorting and evaluation. But he also had to weigh his personal life and career as they were winding to a close. What had he accomplished and, in the end, was it worth doing and would it last? What did he have left to do, and why was it important?

In the spring of 1894 he announced his resignation from the Geological Survey, effective at the end of the fiscal year. "I am impelled to this course," he wrote President Cleveland, "by reason of wounds that require surgical operation."[2] The problem was the old one — the severed nerves in his mutilated arm that refused to heal. On 16 May clerk Rizer wrote to Captain John Bourke, a cavalry officer stationed at Fort Riley, Kansas, that Powell had undergone a successful operation that day at the Johns Hopkins University hospital in Baltimore. "It was not an amputation, but consisted in dissecting the abnormal nerve growth which caused all the trouble."[3] But if illness was the ostensible reason for his resignation, Powell had plenty of supporting reasons: weariness, disillusionment, hostility from certain members of Congress, disgust with the politics of science, advancing age. He was now sixty, an old man in his time.

In a farewell letter "to my collaborators," Powell noted that, "under different organizations I have had charge of the work for twenty-five years. In the beginning it was largely exploratory, but gradually, as the Survey expanded, it became more and more administrative, affording less time for research." Reason enough to quit. He singled out five men as his most intimate colleagues in that long career: James Stevenson, "my first executive officer," now deceased; James Pilling, who had progressed from stenographer to supporting scholar (and would be dead a year later); A.H. Thompson, "my first associate in exploration"; Grove Karl Gilbert, "ever my wise adviser"; and Charles Walcott, who took over as USGS director. And there was still another to be thanked: Jack Hillers, who "was with me in the wilderness life of early years" and had enriched the survey's publications with his photographs.[4]

Under Walcott, the agency's budget continued to rebound from the nadir of '92, though he found the funding still dicey, first hiring the geologist Becker back and then letting him go. Walcott had more

Dinner portrait taken on the occasion of Powell's retirement from the Geological Survey, 1894, which was also the tenth anniversary of the "Great Basin Mess," an informal dining group at the Survey. Among the associates gathered here are (seated on Powell's left) William J. McGee, Grove K. Gilbert, and J.C. Pilling, and (seated on his right) Charles Walcott, W.H. Holmes, and J. Stanley Brown. (Courtesy: U.S. Geological Survey)

up-to-date scientific research credentials than Powell, and he was a more popular man with many in Congress. Under his command the survey survived, and Powell's legacy remained intact.[5]

Although some were delighted by this shift in leadership, others were discouraged. Lester Ward, who had worked alongside Walcott in the paleontology division, was not dazzled by his new chief. "The Geological Survey," he recalled, "had fallen into the hands of small men, and was no longer the grand institution that it was in the days when Major Powell was its Director. The policy seemed to be to set up captious criticism and obstruct the scientific work of members of the staff. It was a case of bureaucracy. There was no longer any *esprit de corps,* and no one was certain that his work would be approved by petty officers at headquarters."[6]

Powell did not go far away when he retired from the USGS. He moved just across the street, retaining his position as director of the

Powell with the man who succeeded him as director of the Geological Survey, Charles Walcott (on his right), and the visiting Scottish geologist, Archibald Geikie. Taken at Harper's Ferry, Va., May 1896. (Courtesy: U.S. Geological Survey)

Bureau of Ethnology (renamed the Bureau of American Ethnology [BAE]), which had its quarters in the Adams Building, spreading over several floors.[7] Coming with him across the street was W.J. McGee, a man that the geologists were happy to see the back of. He assumed the air of a great scientist, a national intellectual force, a renaissance man, Powell's alter ego and anointed successor. Emmons in particular had wanted to prick McGee's bubble. Now it floated high among the ethnologists.

McGee later gave Emma an assessment of her husband's physical condition in his last years. After 1894, perhaps even earlier, Powell's administrative obligations were effectively delegated. He held his bureau directorship in name only. After his surgery, McGee noted, he remained "ever afterward an invalid," only rarely showing the physical and mental vigor he had once shown in abundance.

> Of course this condition was well known to you so far as his home life was concerned, and you, in your own way, concealed it from the curious; but in his office life I knew the condition better than anyone else, and sought in every way to have his best side kept outward. The fact remains that since the final operation on his arm in Baltimore the Major never wrote a report or any other

important official paper; for while sometimes he was undoubtedly able to do so, he was oftener unable, and even in his best hours the strain of the work and the need for gathering half-forgotten details would have been injurious. This does not mean that his large experience and broad grasp of administrative policy were useless; for, on the contrary, they were a constant guide during his later days in the Geological Survey as well as throughout the entire history of his Bureau. As illustrative of his condition even before he left the Geological Survey, I may mention that he was unable to prepare his administrative report for the fiscal year 1892–93, despite the fact that he had designed the document to cover the general scientific results of the Survey under his direction for a dozen years; he entrusted the duty to me, and after preparing the copy I forwarded it to him in Chicago [at the World's Fair], where he was then recuperating; but after retaining it several days, he returned the copy for publication with no other change than the striking out of a single clause. It may be added that during later years in this Bureau he seldom saw the reports until they were shown him in printer's proofs.[8]

Although he continued to come into the office, Powell freed himself from the daily operations of the bureau. No longer did the staff have such ready and easy access to his counsel.

Whatever Walcott may have lacked in imagination, he was a competent administrator. The same could not be said of McGee. After he was put in de facto charge of the Bureau of American Ethnology, it deteriorated in almost all respects. The budget did not decline, but the efficient use of funds did. An investigation carried out by Smithsonian officials in 1903 discovered a record of slipshod management during McGee's watch. He signed blank vouchers on a wholesale basis. He kept accounts in his head instead of in the books. He allowed the staff, including his friend Franz Boas, to take valuable manuscripts home to study without proper supervision. So badly run was the agency that one of the clerks, Frank Barnett, was able regularly to open official letters, steal checks from them, forge endorsements, and have them deposited to his private bank account. Secretary Langley was not happy with this state of affairs, but he had not known how bad it was nor had he wanted to override Powell's trusting arrangement.[9]

Most of the old staff remained on at the bureau, including Gatschet, Cushing, Mooney, Thomas, Fewkes, Tilly Stevenson, and F.W. Hodge.

William John ("WJ") McGee.
(Courtesy: U.S. Geological Survey)

They continued to enjoy their customary intellectual freedom in choosing their work, but they exercised no voice in the agency's direction. It was solely up to McGee to set a course for the future. In contrast to Powell, he was impressed by physical differences among the races, which he believed explained differences in achievement, and wanted to bring such research forward. "The average white man," he wrote, "is stronger of limb, fleeter of foot, clearer of eye, and far more enduring of body under stress of labor and hardship than the average yellow or red or black."[10] He tilted the bureau toward comparative studies of musculature, phrenology, and brain size among the races, a research program that Boas encouraged but that Powell had always eschewed because of its racialist tendencies.

Powell tolerated that tilt in the Bureau's research, though he paid it little attention. He even accepted a friendly bet with McGee over whose brain was larger. Only autopsies could decide that question, of course, and when completed they showed Powell the clear winner in the competition for biological superiority.[11]

That large old head was crammed full of the accumulated knowledge of an exceptionally diverse career. Now Powell wanted to sift through his fund of knowledge and reflect on its meaning. Invalid he may have been, but his mental powers had not completely failed him.

Incapacitated he may often have been, but he was used to cycles of illness and recuperation. Like a tenured senior professor, he now assumed a high degree of freedom from institutional responsibility to gather his life's work into its final form. No one challenged that assumption; quite the contrary, he was given considerable license by his superiors to come and go as he pleased.

A photograph taken of Powell late in life shows him sitting at his desk in the Adams Building, seemingly out of sorts or frowning at

Powell at his desk in the Adams Building, circa 1896.
(Courtesy: U.S. Geological Survey)

some unpleasant memory passing before him. A wall of books rises behind his desk, a few Indian artifacts lie on his desktop. He is dressed in his normal garb of rough tweed coat and vest, his right sleeve hollow. His once auburn hair has thinned and grizzled. Unkempt whiskers flow down over his cravat, reeking of tobacco and flecked with ash. Heavy eyebrows slant over his glowering eyes and bulbous nose. He is poised to write.

The portrait is deceptive in two ways. First, writing for him was still really a matter of dictating, so that the writing instrument in his left hand was something of a prop; sitting before a secretary with pencil poised over *her* notebook would have been a more accurate picture of Powell at work. Second, however gloomy his expression, what he "wrote" in his late years proved to be never bilious or world-weary or pessimistic. Mostly his thoughts inclined toward philosophical subjects that had no connection to the passing controversies agitating the day. He became more abstract. If his mind ran over any of his personal grievances, he put them aside. He rose above politics and personalities to focus on matters that had always concerned him more: Indians, the earth, the promise of science, the faith of an evolutionist that the future will be better than the past.

At this point the most important person to Powell professionally was his personal secretary, May Clark. She was another native of the Midwest, though living in Denver when first hired by the Geological Survey in 1889. She moved over to the bureau offices when Powell did and labored faithfully for him the rest of his days. The proverbial office wife, she assisted his research, arranged his daily schedule, took endless hours of dictation, and even helped with parties at his home. Loyal to the point of worship, she left no complaint or charge against their relationship.

The same cannot be said for another bureau amanuensis, William McDevitt, who was assigned briefly to work with the Major on his projects. In a 1950 interview, McDevitt, then at the California Academy of Sciences, had nothing to give but bad memories. He would rather have stayed with his old superior, Walcott, in the survey, he said, but had been tossed for and lost to the bureau. Fortunately for any stenographer, Powell dictated his thoughts at a slow, deliberate speed and was easy to follow, though not always easy to understand. On the other hand, Powell, after his resignation from the survey, tended to take his residual anger out on his subordinates. Seldom coming into the office, he was a dictator when he was there—stern-faced, sneering, humorless, inelegant, impolite. "Powell would be the last man in the world I would want to go on a fishing trip with," McDevitt snapped.[12]

So Powell was not in his late years, any more than in his early ones, universally beloved. He drove his assistants, as he drove himself, and some of them resented that driving while others looked on him with awe. Mainly, he drove to organize a lifetime of accumulated knowledge into broad, coherent syntheses, especially in his great work in progress, the so-called "Elements of Psychology" that Arnold Hague had referred to in the spring of 1893. As it slowly took shape, he filled up his assistants' idle moments by dictating a few shorter pieces that likewise encompassed the world. If he was confined to a desk, he still meant to command the field, pressing all his available forces into action.

For years he had neglected his commitment to the indigenous peoples, whom he sometimes now referred to as the "Amerinds" to distinguish them from the people of India, and now he intended to repair that neglect. He was the most widely informed authority in the field. While other scholars may have probed more deeply into specific tribes or known more about anthropological specializations, Powell was more encyclopedic in his knowledge. Fittingly, when an ambitious new publication, *Johnson's Universal Cyclopaedia*, appeared under the general editorship of Charles Kendall Adams, president of the University of Wisconsin, Powell was listed among the associate editors, in charge of archaeology and ethnology. He joined a distinguished group that included Grove Karl Gilbert, editor for geology; Simon Newcomb, astronomy and mathematics; Cornell's Liberty Hyde Bailey, agriculture; Stanford's David Starr Jordan, zoology; and Yale's Theodore Woolsey, international law and relations. Powell recruited several of his bureau staff to write articles for the project, which they did for a fee while on the public payroll, as Powell himself did. No one saw anything wrong with that practice under the liberal policies of Congress to promote scientific research and public understanding.

No better summary of the state of Indian research in the period exists than Powell's long essay, "Indians of North America," written for the *Cyclopaedia*. It brings together a century's effort on the part of whites to understand the indigenous peoples whom they had invaded and largely displaced. Since Gallatin and Schoolcraft, scholars had learned a sizable amount about the first appearance of Indian immigrants in the New World and the subsequent evolution of their ways of life. Powell expertly reviewed that knowledge, ranging from village architecture, clothing, tattooing, food, domestication of animals, stone and metal tools to amusements, social institutions, totemism, mythology, and language. But it was knowledge about the human past, readers learned, a past that must surely fade away. "The primeval life of the Indian was inexorably doomed."[13]

For all the knowledge that he had accumulated, nothing had altered Powell's view that the native peoples could and should be assimilated into American life — that is to say, be transformed into white people. Already he saw a racially integrated society shining on the horizon. In his 1893 essay, "Are Our Indians Becoming Extinct?" he admitted that their numbers had declined precipitously, down to 250,000 by the last census, and that the difficulty of bridging the cultural gap remained enormous. Yet he also saw impressive gains. During his lifetime he had seen an astonishing conversion. "Young Sioux that fought Custer now drive teams at the Government agency; Navajo that fought Kit Carson are now digging ditches; and Apaches that fought Crook are now husking corn." More than two-thirds of the surviving Indians had abandoned a hunting and gathering life to engage in "civilized industries, and are fighting their industrial battles with success." Half of them spoke English well enough for practical purposes; "in a generation or two the pristine tongues will all be gone." Remarkably, a condition of savagery had completely disappeared from the United States, though not everyone had made equal progress. "The lowest tribes are still children," he cautioned, "and must be managed by a kindergarten system, or we shall still have outrages and wars." A "wise middle policy" that did not push too far or too fast would eventually put all Indians on an equal basis with whites.[14]

The government's top ethnologist thus found nothing substantial to criticize in federal Indian policy. According to him, that policy had generally been enlightened in concept and directed by men of "high character." The government had consistently paid the natives, and paid them generously, for their lands, leaving them spacious reservations that abounded in natural resources. Those lands had gained in value by unearned increment, making many tribes "comparatively wealthy and nearly all are well-to-do." The current federal support for the reservations was costing nearly $11 million per annum, and the cumulative transfer of wealth from whites to Indians now totaled over $300 million, a testimonial both to native people's skill in asserting their rights and the white man's sense of justice. "Treated in this manner the Indians have not become mendicants and criminals," Powell wrote; "they have retained their self-respect."[15]

Few native Americans were so sanguine as Powell about their future under white dominion. They pointed not only to widespread hunger and a shrinking land base but also to demoralization and cultural loss. Most told a story of tragedy in which they suffered as victims of injustice and even murder. But Powell believed that to read history thus was to take the gloomiest possible view of their situation. It ignored the fact that the Indians had made peace among themselves as much as with the whites and now for the first time in their long history lived free of warfare, free of the old violence and insecurity. They had food, clothing, and shelter of a higher quality than ever before. Sorcery was giving way to rational treatment for disease. The blessings of citizenship must follow in due course.

By emphasizing those positive trends among the conquered peoples, Powell was also affirming the essential virtue and wisdom of the American nation. Nothing in his lifetime, nothing in his long career in government, had shaken his bedrock faith in his country's essential benevolence. The United States was still the promised land. Its promise, he was sure, was made to all its peoples, Indians included — a promise that would, if they were patient, be delivered by and by.

For all the pain that he had been through, political as well as medical, Powell's life in Washington remained fairly serene and comfortable, a daily corroboration that the nation was writing a story of success. He could count the pleasures of his club and professional societies, the museums, steam heat and electricity, the streetcars for when he was weary of walking, his old friends of the Great Basin Mess, and his family and house on M Street. Little of the urban or rural hardship felt around the country ever touched him personally. Jacob Coxey's "army" of five hundred unemployed workers caused a small stir when they marched on the Capitol in the year of Powell's resignation, but for a middle-class white man on a government salary the city provided a quiet, stable round of work and leisure.

Powell had gained a little weight over the years; at one point he tipped the scales at 190 pounds, but normally was closer to 170. For physical exercise he liked nothing better than a horseback ride, and at age sixty-two he bought a Victor Bicycle to wobble through the parks. More sedentary recreation included a game of whist or cribbage. Poor eyesight had forced him to give up playing billiards at the club, but his eyes were good enough for reading, which he indulged through regular orders for French novels or the poems of Robert Browning and Robert Burns from the local book shops. Always he had a book at hand. While sitting for a bronze bust, his aide Marcus Baker read aloud to him from a favorite, John Ruskin's book of essays, *Sesame and Lilies*. In a century that had learned how to mass-produce books in extraordinary abundance, he was the gratified consumer, the omnivorous collector. If he could forget the wounds inflicted by Stewart and the ailments of an aging body, he could say that America, modern urban life, and industrial civilization had all been good to him.

Congress, in its new mood of stringency, cut Powell's salary down to $4,500 a year, a substantial reduction over what it had been. Still, it was enough to maintain a decent bank account at Bell and Company and to pay out a generous policy with the New York Life Insurance Company. There was even enough left over from household expenses to invest in real estate, though never on a grand scale. He bought a couple of house lots in Colonial Beach, Virginia, not far from George Washington's birthplace on the Potomac. He invested in a house at Chilmark on Martha's Vineyard but spent little time there, renting it out for the summer before selling. Another property he held for a time was a house in Winfield, Kansas, in which brother Walter lived. And in 1899 he was renting out a piece of bottom land he had acquired along the Des Plaines River in suburban Illinois, in the town of Lyons, directly across from the successful suburb of Riverside, designed by Frederick Law Olmsted. The son of a man who had done modestly well in real estate ventures followed the paternal example, though it did not generate for him any substantial wealth.[16]

Requests for copies of the *Exploration of the Colorado River of the West and Its Tributaries* continued to come in regularly, but that report, published in 1875, was long out of print. On its twentieth anniversary Powell arranged with a publisher, Flood and Vincent of Meadville, Pennsylvania, to bring out an elegant new edition to be sold by subscription. The book was retitled *The Canyons of the Colorado*. Undoubtedly, he hoped the new edition would sell by the thousands, augmenting his income; after all, he had received not a dollar from the original report, for all its steady demand. In this he was disappointed. *The Canyons of the Colorado*, though it would endure as Powell's literary masterpiece, going through several printings in the twentieth century, was not a popular success in his own lifetime. Expensive to produce, it found few subscribers. Five years after its appearance, the publisher declared bankruptcy, leaving the author with the stereotype plates. No other commercial house could see any profit in it, and for many years the new edition also remained out of print.

No immense royalties then, no highly profitable investments, no corporate job offers. Materially, the Powells carried on domestic life at their townhouse much as they had done over the previous two decades. All may not have continued harmonious within, however; rumors floated about that Emma had increasingly become a termagant who abused and upbraided her husband. Most of the rumors came from Powell's sister Nellie and her husband Harry. Harry wrote to old boat mate Fred Dellenbaugh that Emma's "treatment of the Major in the later years of his life has been damnable. Sometime I'll give you *facts* which will make your blood boil."[17] Whatever those facts were, they never were spelled out on paper. Emma seems to have retaliated by shunning the Thompsons. After the Major's death, she was adamant against any effort to link her husband's name with Harry's on any monument. Harry, in her view, had always been "distinctly disloyal" to the Major. Whether she too was "disloyal" cannot be confirmed, but relations within the M Street house do not seem to have been warm or intimate.[18]

Other rumors against Emma passed down through family memories, most of them religious in nature. It was whispered by some of the Powell descendants that she was a Catholic, which would have put her at odds with their Protestant inclinations.[19] Although Emma's family, the Deans, had been Catholic in England, her parents were no longer so after immigration. She and Wes had been married by a Baptist preacher in Detroit. In fact, no firm evidence exists of any religious feelings or church affiliation on her part. Moreover, for forty years she put up with a husband who inclined toward agnosticism and free thought. The vague rumors of religious incompatibility between husband and wife and between husband's family and wife cannot be substantiated, but they do reinforce the impression that Emma, though a half-cousin to them all, was never on close terms with any of the Powell clan.

And now that clan was near at hand, many of them living in Washington at the time the Major retired from the Geological Survey. Two of his sisters (Martha and Nellie) and one of his brothers (Bram) had moved to the city in his wake, and another brother (Walter) was later brought there in a state of collapse. Always a devoted family, they looked out for one another. They pulled Brother Wes away from his less than successful marriage and into their warm-hearted parlors, into their children's lives, and into their careers. Though he had won the greatest distinction among them and stood at the center of the clan, several of the other Powell siblings had achieved some distinction too.

Powell and his siblings, taken late in his life. Left to right: Mary Wheeler, JWP,
Bram, Bram's son Billy, Nellie and Harry Thompson.
(Courtesy: Utah State Historical Society)

They were an unusually accomplished family, many of them marching in the forefront of social reform, and they shared with Wes many
ideals as well as memories.

Sister Nellie, after following her husband into the western field and
making a small mark in botany, had found in Washington a passionate
cause, female suffrage. In 1890 the two major woman's rights organizations united to form the National American Woman Suffrage Association, making full political equality its goal. Under presidents
Elizabeth Cady Stanton, Susan B. Anthony, and Carrie Chapman Catt,
the association led the long struggle that ended in 1920 with the
Nineteenth Amendment, giving women the right to vote. Ellen Powell
Thompson was one of the more prominent leaders in the Washington
branch of the organization, and during 1896–97 she supervised a
project to get senators and representatives to commit to paper their
views on suffrage, pro or con, for distribution to the public.[20]

Sister Martha, married to the Populist congressman John Davis and mother of seven children, remained in residence in Washington through 1894. When John was defeated for reelection that year, they returned to Kansas, settling in Topeka, where they continued to work for agrarian principles. The bruising defeat of the Populists's candidate for President, William Jennings Bryan, in 1896 ended their hopes for any effective challenge to the growing concentration of economic power.

Then there was Powell's younger brother Bram, who became one of the most famous public school reformers and educators in the nation. He made his early mark as superintendent of schools in Aurora, Illinois — a man of "extraordinary executive ability," according to the local paper.[21] An outspoken critic of poor teacher preparation and rigid, outdated curricula, he instituted sweeping changes that attracted wide attention. In 1885 he was appointed superintendent of schools in Washington, D.C., where he became an even more outspoken advocate of reform. Outdoor nature study was one of his projects, along with vocational high schools, intense teacher training and supervision, new methods of teaching writing and reading, and a more simplified and rational grammar of the English language. Any of that could produce controversy, but a firestorm broke out when he announced that he no longer supported standardized examinations or rigid disciplinary methods, all of which landed him in serious trouble with conservatives in the nation's capital.

Both the Powell brothers came to find their archenemy in the conservative senator from Nevada, William Stewart. After the satisfaction of seeing the Major leave the Geological Survey, Stewart went to battle against Superintendent Powell, employing all of his familiar cutthroat tactics. Stewart got himself appointed chair of a senatorial investigation into the superintendent's liberal philosophy of education. Like brother Wes, Bram defended his views and administration with no evasion or apology: "We have sought to make the child love his school, and like to come to school . . . not by credits, not by rewards, prizes — training to selfishness, every one of them — but . . . by making learning delightful to him."[22] Stewart and his colleagues were not impressed by that philosophy; they wanted to know whether the students could do their sums correctly or knew how to use proper punctuation marks. By 1900 they succeeded in driving Bram from office. After resigning from the District superintendency, he went to the Philippines to study its educational needs after which, weakened by his travels in the tropics, he took up residency in White Plains, New York.

Then there was the Major's other brother, Walter, who likewise ended up in the capital. But for Walter the city offered only a care-taking asylum for the insane. After residing independently for many years in Kansas, this unfortunate man, who had never recovered from his Civil War imprisonment, was passed from sister to sister, until at last no one felt competent to deal with his severe mental disorder. He was committed to professional care and died in an asylum in 1915.[23]

Two other sisters of Wes came to the city only on occasional visits. The oldest sibling, Mary Powell Wheeler, wife of William, had settled on a farm near St. Paul, Minnesota, where she raised three children. When she came to see her brother, she brought along a sharp tongue, one that may have rivaled Emma's. "Wes," she broke in one day while he was speaking, "I think you're the homeliest man God ever made." The years had not been easy on Wes's features, but they had also toughened his hide — tough enough for a family that spoke its mind bluntly, with more candor than tact. He took the harsh judg-ment in good humor, and whenever he saw her after that would ask, "Well, Mary, so you think I'm homely?"[24]

The two youngest sisters moved away from the rest of the clan. Eliza, or Lida, married Charles Garlick, a wagon maker, and taught school in Chase County, Kansas, staying well out of the limelight. The youngest of the Powells, Juliet, married Lemuel Rice and settled in southern California. She taught music at the normal schools in Santa Barbara and San Diego, then became director of music in the public schools of Corona. Folk dancing and singing were her chief interests, and she became a student of native American songs and chants.[25]

An enthusiasm for music, which they liked to attribute to their Welsh ancestry, persisted into the third generation of Powells. Bram and Minnie's daughter, Maud, was a child prodigy on the violin, de-buting with the New York Philharmonic Society at the age of sixteen. She formed her own Maud Powell String Quartet and, from a base in London, played the leading concert halls of Europe, becoming one of the most renowned string artists of her day. Uncle Wes, immensely proud of this talented niece, followed her career closely. On one occa-sion, at her request, he did ethnological research for a cantata she liked to play, "The Song of Hiawatha."[26] None of his other nieces and nephews showed anything like Maud's musical talent or acclaim, though Arthur Powell Davis rose to become the federal government's commissioner of reclamation. As for Wes and Emma's daughter, Mary, she cut no figure at all in the world; living quietly at home, she suffered through recurrent illnesses and never married or took up a career.

The Powell siblings, born to evangelical, working-class British immigrants with no formal education, had, with the exception of the deranged Walter, all done well for themselves, some exceptionally well. None had become wealthy nor cared much about wealth. Instead, they had devoted their adult energies to the middle-class professions and to progressive causes; and they had won a few important victories. With brother Wes, they had good reason to be satisfied with the progress of their own lives and with the capacity of the nation's institutions to grow and improve. Spread out from one coast to the other, they reflected much of the native American hopefulness that had so animated the century that was passing.

A defining trait in the Powell family, as distinctive as shape of head or color of hair, was a streak of idealism that refused to accept the world as it was. Yet all were staunch realists who kept both feet on the ground, never expecting improvements to come overnight and never calling for a violent or revolutionary destruction of the existing order. Wes Powell resembled his siblings in this trait. Even as an old man, he was a realist who tried to discover and honor the facts and to plan reform carefully.

The late writings of his life continued to express a visionary realism, but they did so with varying degrees of concreteness or abstraction. Sometimes he seemed to be almost completely rooted in the earth — rooted in facts of soil and water, in the problems of getting a living from the land. At other times, however, his head was way up in the clouds, looking for the unseen — the laws that governed the evolution of life. Yet no matter how concrete or how abstract he became, he was always a man who believed that the first requirement is to know the world as it is, honestly and without illusion, before attempting its renovation.

For down-to-earth realism nothing in his late bibliography excelled the three long essays he wrote for the third number of *National Geographic Monographs*, published in 1895, a comprehensive guide to the American landscape. He was in good company once again; Gilbert was a contributor to the issue, with a piece on Niagara Falls; William Morris Davis was also there, writing on southern New England, and so was Nathaniel Shaler, who covered the Atlantic coastal beaches. But Powell was the point man, providing three essays of his own that formed most of the issue: "Physiographic Processes," "Physiographic Features," and "Physiographic Regions of the U.S." They took in the whole of the nation, further evidence that he was no longer focused on the arid West. But as he had done for that region, he drew on the artists Moran and Hillers, as well as other photographers and cartographers, to help Americans understand the continent around them.

Physiography, which Powell defined as the "description of the surface features of the earth, as bodies of air, water, and land," had always been his natural bent in science. Each of those bodies was a "moving envelope," he wrote, interacting with the others to create the ever shifting climate, the meandering rivers, the diastrophic swells and folds called mountains or plateaus. He brought before the public a land undergoing unceasing change, some of it dramatic but most of it slow, steady, and unnoticed. He gave them language to describe that change, some of which was too innovative to have any chance of sticking. He called the Rockies by a long defunct name, the "Stony Mountains," for example, while the Great Plains became the "Great Plateaus" and the Mississippi Valley the "Gulf Slope."

The most provocative feature of those essays was his attempt to break the country down into "natural divisions," or physiographic regions. Expanding on his earlier analysis of the West's principal river basins, he talked about four great "drainage slopes": the Atlantic, Great Lake [sic], Gulf, and Pacific (now relegating the Colorado Plateau and Great Basin to secondary aberrations). A tinted map broke those broad divisions into a complicated assortment of interlocking pieces, enough to challenge any picture-puzzle enthusiast. Here, as in the encyclopedia essay on Indians, was Powell's last effort to sum up the accumulated understanding of a century's worth of exploring, scientific investigating, and mapping — the intellectual harvest of the westward movement.

Nor did he stop with a picture of the land's "divisions" as carved by the elemental forces of nature. He showed examples of how humans had entered this landscape, following the retreat of the glaciers, and changed its dynamics and appearance. Indians had burned over the whole country, he claimed. Then came the white man who stopped the Indian's fires and let the natural forests return, until they covered more acres than at the time of Columbus's first landfall. The civilized plow subsequently destroyed most of the prairies, but it also stopped fires from spreading. Immigrants from Europe proceeded to fence the grasslands with hedges and wire, drain wetlands for crop production, and plant orchards. Powell told a familiar saga of environmental conquest. But he was also telling another story filled with affection and attachment. His essays were an old man's valentine to the richness, beauty, and history of the lands he had spent a lifetime exploring, learning to see and love.

Powell's late geographical essays opened the eyes of at least one reader and gave him a more complicated understanding of the natural environment of the nation. The historian Frederick Turner, after delivering his frontier paper at the '93 World's Fair, had moved on to examine the role of regions, or "sections," in American history. Advancing toward the frontier, he realized, was only part of the nation's historical narrative. The nation did not roll west like a featureless tidal wave, a homogeneity held together by strong centralizing tendencies. America was also a nation responding to many different places—a nation emerging with strong sectional differences. Powell's portrayal of "natural divisions" stirred Turner's curiosity about the impact the physical environment worked on the country's development. Might differences in river basins, soils, and topography have promoted differences in politics, economy, or even psychology? Might environment explain the conflict between the South and the North or the West and the East? In the fall of 1898 Turner enrolled in a seminar on physiography taught by his Wisconsin colleague—and former Geological Survey division head—Charles Van Hise, to learn more about the Allegheny Plateau, the legacy of the Ice Age, and the arid basins of Nevada.[27]

Powell's essays on the complex physiography of the nation expressed one side of his temperamental realism, the side that was earth-bound and brimming with passion for the varieties of landscape. His more ambitious writing of the late years, however, expressed another dimension—a realism that was, ironically, soaringly abstract and had very little of the actual earth in it, and very little passion. That writing consisted mainly of a book, *Truth and Error, or the Science of Intellection*, which was published in Chicago in 1898 by the Open Court Company, whose director Paul Carus had become a personal friend. In its more than four hundred pages Powell tried to discover the mental processes needed to discriminate what was real from what was not. The only book he ever wrote directly for a commercial press, it was read by almost no one, severely criticized by those who did read it, and could not be said to have stirred up any enthusiasm anywhere. A hundred years later it would find even fewer readers than when it first appeared. A dead flop, in other words, yet it throws light on the man and his mental world that should not be overlooked.

Five years of eclectic reading went into the book's preparation, ranging from the ancient Greeks to Bishop Berkeley, Immanuel

Kant, and Georg Friedrich Hegel but strikingly neglecting Powell's own contemporaries in the fields of epistemology and psychology. He seems, for example, never to have looked into William James's pathbreaking *Principles of Psychology*, which came out in 1890, or the writings of the other founders of pragmatism. Like the pragmatists, Powell opposed the notion that truth is a matter of deduction from enduring first principles; truth, he maintained, is experimental, tentative, and imperfect in an evolving world. Yet without the pragmatists' guidance, he was bound to flounder in his attempt to come to terms with the deeper philosophical implications in modern evolutionary science. In fact, in many ways he did not push much beyond the world view of Herbert Spencer and other influential figures of his younger days. His book was more reminiscent of the nineteenth century than anticipatory of the twentieth. It demonstrated how much of a Victorian he was and remained to the end.

The first chapter of the book, "Chuar's Illusion," opens in the fall of 1880, when Powell "was encamped on the Kaibab plateau above the canyon gorge of a little stream." He describes once again the Paiute chief Chuar's conviction that gravity was really a spirit in nature that pulled objects down from the sky. So much of human philosophy had followed in the track of that primitive view, Powell complained, as people preferred the "hashish of mystery" to the plain and simple facts discovered by science. He intended nothing less than to cleanse the senses with a cold, clear draft of scientific realism. "Science," he declared, "deals with realities," and it was science, and science alone, that could bring the human mind out of its age-old fog of misconception, superstition, and metaphysics.

Perhaps the best way to grasp the book's intentions is open its pages to the chapter on "Fallacies of Perception," which also appeared as an article in Carus's magazine, *The Open Court*. Here Powell shows how easily the human eye is tricked by optical illusions. What may appear to the untutored eye to be so is often untrue. For a long time the earth was perceived to have ends, corners, and a level surface. Exploration then revealed that the earth is actually a sphere, though the illusion of a flat earth persisted. So too persisted the age-old illusion of ghosts and other supernatural beings, not only among traditionalists in religion but also among the eager-to-believe audiences that thronged the halls of table-rappers, spiritualists, and psychics. It was an age avid for such antiscientific cults as it was for hypnosis, peyote, and other hallucinatory drugs, all of which sought to transcend the sober facts of science.

The scientist was regarded by philosophers with contempt. His realities were considered "base-born, belonging only to the lower world where men live, while metaphysic is supposed to dwell in a region of sublime thought." Powell's purpose was to raise the truth claims of science over all its competitors, but particularly over philosophical idealists such as Hegel who taught that "the furniture of the world, which we suppose to be external, does not exist, except as fallacy."[28]

A new "science of intellection," that is, a philosophy based on sound, empirically testable ideas about the world's furniture, must begin by discovering the essential properties of matter. Powell thought he had isolated five such properties: "Every body, whether it be a stellar system or an atom of hydrogen, has certain fundamental characteristics found in all. These are number, space, motion and time, and if it be an animate body, judgment." Nothing can be said to exist if it does not have those properties. The fifth property, judgment, was the most difficult to define or explain; it did not help that he threw in such synonyms as "affinity," "consciousness," and "choice" as the book progressed. What he appears to have wanted was to find a property inherent in all nature that was not bound by matter but could evolve eventually into mind.

It is easy to see why the book was a failure. Much of the text is a string of definitions — and often definitions for new terms that Powell himself coined. The earth becomes the "geonomic realm," vegetation the "phytonic realm," animals the "zoonomic realm." Words such as "demotics," "chemism," "metagenesis," "hylozoism," "noumenon," "multeity," and "ideation" lard the text. Then he turns nearly every chapter into a string of enumerations: two kinds of this, four kinds of that. Underlying all else, the fundamental numerical structure of the universe, he argues, is the figure five. The five properties of matter lead to the five orders of animal life and then to the five faculties of human thought. Nature is everywhere and at every level a quincunx. And its grand interpreter Powell begins to seem like a man obsessed with classification and logical symmetry more than scientific discovery.

On the positive side, his book is loaded with everyday examples that try to illustrate the difficult points he is making about perception. "Sitting on a rock," he writes, "I hear a noise." Is it a crow, or does my mind say it is the friend whom I'm expecting to come along? Eating a blackberry turnover, my mind strays, following a stream of consciousness, to blackberry patches picked long ago in southern Ohio and then to "my companion, Charles Isham, who was killed at

the battle of Shiloh," and then to the carnage of that battle. He en-
livens his often impenetrable text with quotes from Milton and
Shakespeare. And if he carries neologism to a fault, his new terms are
no more opaque nor his vocabulary more peculiar than that of many
other nineteenth-century philosophers.

An Enlightenment rationalist to the end, Powell hoped to show, in
this last work, how human reason might break free from superstition
and revelation to discover true order in the world. Unfortunately for
his effort, the intellectual world was already shifting away from that
drive for rational mastery and order and toward fragmentation, inde-
terminancy, relativity, and complexity.

Truth and Error is dedicated to Lester Ward, a repayment for the acknowledgment that fifteen years earlier Ward had paid him in *Dynamic Sociology*. Powell, eager to know what the younger man thought
of his magnum opus, invited Ward over to his office for lunch and
surprised him with an inscribed copy. Immediately Ward began to
read, taking the book with him on vacation. A month later he had
gone through it several times, reorganizing it into a series of tables,
"as Major Powell had neglected to bring his points together in such a
form that his system could be grasped by the reader."[29] In late January 1899 Ward published his review of the book in the journal *Science*, and it was not one calculated to please the author. "As a
specimen of what Kant called 'architectonic symmetry'," Ward
began, "it probably has never been excelled. . . . The temple of philosophy is entirely rebuilt out of new bricks cast in new moulds." He
complained about the excessive series of pentologies — the "magic
number" of five that was supposed to be the ground plan of nature's
temple — and about the excessive introduction of new terms. But
mainly he could not stomach the claim Powell made that he had
found logical order in the natural world.

All along Ward's core conviction had been that nature is chaotic.
Nature has no order or purpose, nor does it offer any model for humankind. Somehow (it was never clear exactly how) mind had
emerged out of that chaos, discovered just badly organized the world
was, and was now engaged in imposing order through the interventions of civilization. "The real world will not fit into our square or
round or oval frames," he lectured Powell; "the mind strains to make
it fit." True science discovers

everywhere irregularity, heterogeneity, amorphism, chaos; and
however laudable the effort to reduce this anarchy to law and this

chaos to cosmos, any attempt in this direction which goes beyond the limit set by concrete facts is, by minds trained to the scientific habit, dismissed at once as not science, whatever else it may be.[30]

In point of fact the whole enterprise of science had been precisely to reduce the seeming anarchy of nature to rational order. But Ward was right to ask whether Powell's peculiar ordering of nature was an imposition rather than a discovery.

A second review in the same issue of *Science*, by W.K. Brooks of Johns Hopkins University, accused Powell of carrying "idealism to dizzy heights where even Berkeley never dared to soar." This reviewer confessed to being no philosopher; clearly he did not know the difference between realism and idealism and ended by hoping that Powell and the rest of the philosophical breed would kill each other off in their fights, leaving the world to "simple honest folks."[31] Such a critic could be easily dismissed, but it was not so easy to ignore a hostile reception from the very person to whom the book was dedicated.

When it came his turn to reply, Powell assumed a dignified, patient tone. What he had tried to do, he explained, was "to make all fundamental doctrines of science congruous." He wanted to identify the common laws and properties that extended from the atom to human society. Yet he wanted to avoid reducing all existence to the mechanical properties of pure matter. Both his critics had attacked the suggestion that nature includes that mysterious self-organizing property "affinity" or "choice." Powell cited authorities in chemistry and physics who used such language in describing patterns of bonding (or "choosing") that operated at the most microscopic level. Then he connected such mindless integrative behavior with the more purposeful joining together of individual persons into societies or corporations. One kind of self-organizing behavior was unconscious, the other was conscious; but both represented a root property in nature. The laws governing social relationships, in other words, were not radically separate from the laws that brought particles together into molecules or organic compounds or bodies of ore or solar systems. It was not "metaphysical" or "idealist" to find those congruities prevailing across all the levels of being, making the various sciences one.[32]

The argument, though difficult to establish empirically, was not altogether old-fashioned or antiquated. Twentieth-century philosophers and scientists, including Alfred North Whitehead, would find similar integrative, cooperative, self-organizing properties in the natural world. Powell's problem was that he was crossing into unfamiliar territory where he was unprepared, by ability or training, to understand or explain fully, even if he may have been right in his general instincts. He had entered a new country where the old fierce dualism opposing matter to spirit, or matter to mind, expressed most powerfully by René Descartes, no longer seemed relevant. He believed he could see congruities stretching across the dualist's chasm, and he was struggling to make others see them too. "I have begun on the attempt to propound a Philosophy of Science," he bravely declared. How disappointing then to encounter, in his first propounding, so much criticism.

Ward may have felt somewhat ashamed of his rough handling of the Major's big project. The day after his *Science* review, he was invited by Powell to talk over his criticisms. "He was the type of true nobleman," Ward wrote, "and easily distinguished between a difference in our views and any personal difference. And this is perhaps the place to say that of all the men I have ever met he seemed to me the most truly great in his personal character." For years Powell had attempted to close the distance between himself and Ward, while Ward had resisted, keeping aloof from the inner circle and scorning all the "chauvinists" who defended everything the Major said or did. Those supporters had been "horrified" when Ward dared to find fault with their hero's philosophizing. "That I should do it in a book that was dedicated to me was considered as in bad taste." To be sure, when they read *Truth and Error* for themselves, they found it "so abstruse, abstract, and profound that it was wholly beyond them." Ward felt he had done the Major the compliment of reading his book carefully and publishing an evaluation of it. He had never intended to hurt, "for if there ever was man whom I could truly say I loved, that man was Major Powell."[33]

A touching tribute, but Ward's negative appraisal of the book seems to have discouraged Powell from pursuing his original plan. He had projected three volumes of philosophy; after disposing of matter and consciousness, the realm of objective fact, he would write a second volume on "Good and Evil," where he would lay out the science of cultural evolution; and then a third volume on the private realm of emotions. Volume 2 never appeared in print, though he did publish several essays in *American Anthropologist*, from 1899 to 1901, that covered most of its content. The third volume did not get even that far.

An adumbration of the second volume appeared in a rambling, disjointed talk Powell gave at the National Museum on 25 April 1896 in the Saturday Lecture series. In it he distinguished between "properties," which are attributes of nature that are fixed and independent of human consciousness, and "qualities," which depend wholly on consciousness. Again he drew examples from daily life. A streetcar passes, and its motion is a natural property, measurable and agreed on by all. But whether that motion is described by onlookers as "fast" or "slow" depends upon the individual observer: to a man fallen across the tracks the car seems moving fast, while to an impatient commuter it may be moving slowly. Similarly, a mussel shell taken from the river has color and form, which are properties on which all can agree; but whether its lustrous nacre is considered "beautiful" or not is wholly a matter of quality, as is the shell's usefulness as a knife, scraper, or scoop, wide open to interpretation. "A book might be written," he hinted, "on all of these properties and their mutation into qualities."[34]

A property becomes a quality, therefore, when a human approaches with "purposes" and places a value of good or evil on it. Powell's projected second volume was to set forth those human purposes as they had evolved over time, from savagery to civilization. It was characteristic of humans, he had been saying all through his professional life, to place such values on nature. The values themselves changed, though the things of nature did not. What had been considered useless by a Stone Age people (iron ore or a waterfall) might become useful to an industrial nation. Science must concern itself not only with properties, therefore, but also with qualities as determined by individuals and societies.

Once again the "magic number" of five structured the philosopher's cosmos. Qualities and purposes, like properties, came in sets of five. Pleasure was one distinct purpose, followed by welfare, justice, wisdom, and expression; together, they covered the sum of human striving. In turn they spurred people into activity, which naturally had five divisions too: the arts (activities of pleasure), industries (welfare), institutions (justice), learning (wisdom), and language (expression). If those activities sounded familiar, they were, with some refinement, the same research guidelines under which the Bureau of Ethnology had operated from its inception.

Powell sought terms to describe the scientific study of each of those activities. Some of them were already circulating among scholars, and he took them over without hesitation, though he might try to sharpen or confine their meaning. Others he invented de novo, and not one of them survived him.

"Esthetology" was his label for a new science that would study activities designed to give pleasure. In the first of his series of articles for *American Anthropologist* Powell brought together under this heading an array of pleasures that might startle, if not offend, any highbrow aesthete by their juxtaposition. The fine arts, music, and dance were all there, but so were games, sports, interior decoration, and the "ambrosial pleasures." Tobacco, one of the latter, ranked with opera in the eyes of science! Both were acquired tastes that many enjoyed though others found unpleasant or even loathsome. Science must discover why such things gave pleasure or pain, and how they had been refined from crude beginnings.

"Technology" was Powell's suggested label for a science dealing with the activity of industries, whose purpose was to promote material welfare. "Do not quarrel with me about my terms," he admonished, "but quarrel with me about my distinctions."[35] Fearlessly, he lumped farming, fishing, forestry, and mining under the subheading of "substantiation" ("the artificial production of substances for human welfare"). Technologists must also cover industries of construction and mechanics, the transition in energy from horse power to electricity, the development of commerce, money, banking, advertising, and the medical arts.

The other new sciences he proposed can be quickly named. "Sociology" was to examine modern institutions—government, property, corporations—and their roots in earlier times, and to examine the search for justice and harmony among competing groups of people. "Sophiology" would be the science of human opinions or ideas, from Chuar and his ludicrous misunderstanding of gravity to Darwin's profoundly true theories, and the means by which those ideas passed from generation to generation. "Philology" meant the science of languages, oral and written, of letters and numbers.

With every one of those sciences the scholar must not only take a comprehensive view but also help reveal the laws of progress. Every science had a story to tell of growth and development—and every scientist had a responsibility to help, through the insights he offered, to write the next chapter in that growth. Powell was doing his best, for example, to make the English language a more precise and efficient instrument of expression.

"Moral opinions cannot abruptly be revolutionized," he declared; "they can only be developed. The past cannot be ignored by the present; the present is ever modifying the past. Healthy change must be evolution, not revolution, though there is an element of revolution in all evolution."[36] If the theme of his late work could be summed up in a single phrase, it was this: science offered humanity's best hope for cultural progress. Progress across the entire spectrum of activities — progress in pleasure, welfare, justice, wisdom, and expression.

Having no fresh, undiscovered landscapes in America left to explore, Powell spent his mature years venturing into the country of philosophy. He came looking for a Colorado River in the realm of epistemology and value, nature and the human emergence out of nature's cradle. Ever the map maker, he wanted to find order in this philosophical landscape and put down its lineaments on paper — its watersheds, elevations, contour lines, geological formations — to identify the best places where one could build a civilization. He would send out field parties to triangulate this cosmic terrain and report back to him. Yet his days of directing any kind of exploration were over. Where he had once masterfully organized the labors of others and synthesized their results, he was now acting alone in the biggest exploration of all. Wandering to and fro over the landscape, he suggested a broad map of scientific philosophy, but could he find his way back to civilization with it? And would anybody after him want to go there and fill in the blanks?

The tropical summers of Washington and other eastern metropolises had simply been endured until the railroad allowed at least a few privileged people to escape. In Grant's day presidents, affluent businessmen, and other dignitaries found relief in the New Jersey shore. As transportation improved, they began trekking farther north and staying for longer times — to Newport, Nantucket, the Isles of Shoals. Among the most elite summering places on the Atlantic Coast was Bar Harbor on Mount Desert Island, Maine, where Charles Eliot of Harvard and the Rockefellers of New York built sumptuous "cottages" with a view to the sea. Wicker chairs, iced tea, sailboats and tennis courts, long idle days, straw hats and white billowy dresses created a culture of summering among the people of quality.

In the mid-nineties Powell, who had given up his summer and fall field trips to the West, began looking for his own place on the shore. In August 1895 he sent a note to McGee, who was stuck at the Bureau with administrative duties: "By reason of the ill health of Dr. [D.W.] Prentiss [Powell's personal physician] I concluded to go no further than Gloucester [Massachusetts]. Here I find I can work; the temperature, especially the sea breeze, is delightful and I spend much time on the water. . . . I have employed a stenographer and keep her at work every day and my book grows apace. . . . My love to all my associates in the office." A week later May Clark joined the party staying at the Harbor View House, and the dictation hummed along. "I find the atmosphere cool and invigorating here," Powell wrote again, "and can work very well as there is no discomfort from the earth."[37]

The next summer he found a retreat that laid a much stronger hold on his affections: the fishing village of Brooklin, Maine, located across Blue Hill Bay from Mount Desert Island. It offered a plain and simple alternative to that fashionable resort. Noah Tibbetts, an employee in the Pension Bureau, had inherited a forty-acre saltwater farm on the western end of the village. Around the federal offices in Washington he advertised summer lodgings in the eighteenth-century farmhouse still standing on the property. Soon he conceived of turning the farm into a small colony, the Haven (for a while it was also known as Castle View), with several cottages clustered around a common dining hall and all meals provided by staff. For as little as $50 one could stay a full month. His brochure held out a tantalizing promise:

> Leave the chains of care that bind you
> for the freedom of the wild.
> Listen to my voices calling
> Once again be nature's child.[38]

Drawn by these promises of natural simplicity, the Major, Emma, and Mary first arrived in July 1896, and they were still there in September, bunking down in the Morris Cottage. Every summer thereafter they came back.

With the other Washingtonian regulars, including a Lutheran minister, two business partners in railroading, Miss Clark, and Dr. Prentiss, the Powells made their way north as the heat arrived. They caught a Fall River steamer from Boston to Portland; a smaller boat brought them down east, crossing Penobscot Bay and heading up Eggemoggin Reach to a landing at the colony. It always arrived at sunrise. The sparkling morning sea stretched away to the south, with low granite-ledged islands in the foreground and Deer Isle and Isle au Haut in the distance. A few dusty roads had been scraped across the disused pastures, now returning to spruce, balsam, birch, and white pine. Walking toward the village center, one passed a sardine cannery, several small hotels, a blacksmith's barn, a general store, a stray lobster pot or two. Nights at the colony were dark, illuminated

Powell in a boat off the coast of Maine, taken during a summer in the late 1890s. Also in the boat are two Geological Survey staff members, Arthur Keith and John D. McChesney; at the tiller is local resident Judson Freethey.
(Courtesy: U.S. Geological Survey)

only by kerosene lanterns, and water had to be fetched in a bucket from a single community well.

Sister Nellie came here to visit on one occasion, and Alexander Bell regularly stopped on his way to Nova Scotia. Otherwise, there was the steady company of the familiars who gathered at the dining hall three times a day, eating the local bread and beefsteak, apples and blueberries, cod, haddock, clams, or lobster, all served in plain style. Powell made a good friend in one of the old-time residents, "Captain" Judson Freethey, whose boat, the Effie, they sailed on many excursions among the islands. Freethey was a yarn spinner who loved an audience. He knew the best fishing sites. When the Major caught a fish, he gaffed it and pulled it aboard for him. Some evenings they stayed out late, sleeping over at a lodge on Marshall's Island where sheep were pastured in the warm months, making tunnels through the lower branches of the black spruce forest.

Freethey's son, Will, remembered that Powell was writing "some kind of a book at that time." Not all was recreation or excursion. Secretary Clark was always on hand to help pick up the thread of the book manuscript. She also took down a stream of letters to McGee, ordering reading material for Powell and asking how things were going in the office and whether the salary check was deposited on time at the bank. "The Major is in most *excellent health*," she added at the bottom of one letter in which she acknowledged the receipt of galley proofs from the publisher.[39]

There was even some anthropological investigation to be done along the nearby coast. Will Freethey told of Powell's "diging Indian Relecks He had 4 men working for three summers and I worked with them diging relecks, used to Row him around four and five hours at a time and git 50¢ for my Pain."[40] Old shell middens at Naskeag Point and on the islands indicated sites where the long-ago natives had encamped, and Powell wanted to see what artifacts they might contain. He summoned Frank Cushing from Washington, and together they supervised the excavations that went on over several summers.

Cushing, meanwhile, had fallen into a great deal of trouble with his diggings in Florida. In March 1897 a Philadelphia newspaperman, William Dinwiddie, accused him of faking some of his finds, the most questionable of which was a jeweled effigy of a toad. Powell pronounced the artifact to be genuine and defended Cushing against his detractors. Two years later he was again quick to back his protégé against the University of Pennsylvania, which charged Cushing with holding on to archaeological collections that did not belong to him. No misdeed, or accusation of misdeed, could shake Powell's loyalty to his younger colleague, for he delighted in his conversation, admired his field skills, and regarded him as a bona fide genius. Their midden prowls did not lead to any important insights into Maine's maritime Indian cultures, but while engaged in the project they were like father and son. When Cushing died by choking on a fishbone in his home, in April 1900, Powell gave one of the eulogies.

In fall 1899 Powell purchased a lot from Tibbetts, fronting the ocean and bordering the wagon path leading down to Steamship Wharf. He hired Captain Freethey to build him a small bungalow on the site. The front door was low and inauspicious, but the back door led onto a wide verandah, standing high on stilts, with a sweeping view of the water. A grassy meadow swept down to a bank where one could look on gray boulders and beating waves. It was a modest place by Bar Harbor standards, almost a shack, but Powell was particular about the details. He wanted two fireplaces, a red roof, yellow board-and-batten siding, blue foundation lattice, and oiled—not painted—floors.[41] There was no water piped in, nor electricity. When it was finished, he brought a toilet seat with him for the privy. (Today the cottage, called the Bungalow, or "Bung," still stands, though the red roof is now gray and trees have crept in along the property's edges.)

The Powells' place was only a short walk from the other cottages and dining hall, an intimate part of the little community. They saw much of neighbor Parson's young son Eric, who left a memoir of those quiet summers. The Major he remembered as willing to listen, "always a kindly, sociable, and wise companion. . . . He spoke softly and always genially, often with half-shut eyes and his large rounded nose wrinkled into deep furrows at the bridge." He sang popular sentimental songs—"Believe me if all those endearing young charms"—with the barest semblance of a melody. Although he loved a good joke, he was not a great story teller and had little to say about his heroic western adventures. "There was not the slightest romantic retrospect in his make-up, and . . . in these final years no wish to relive his active days." Emma certainly had no interest in hearing about them again. "Like Socrates," Eric Parson wrote, "he had his Xantippe in those later years, but like Socrates his philosophy never forsook him. He remained unruffled when a woman's shrill speech was dinning in his ears."[42] Perhaps Emma was not as soothed by the pleasures of the simple life as her husband.

Powell was the most prominent summer visitor the village had in those years (though several decades later the writer E.B. White bought a genteel farmstead at Allen's Cove a few miles from the colony). In his second summer the residents invited Powell to speak on his Colorado River expeditions at the Odd Fellows Hall, and with the ticket proceeds they established a community library. But the great rivers of the West were no longer flowing through his imagination with the old thrilling force. Nor was he any longer preoccupied with dams, irrigation canals, or water for reclaiming the desert. Now he was thinking about water of another kind: the still, silent sea, with the fog rolling in, the fishermen going out in small boats. At the colony he could slip away into a timeless world—becoming "nature's child"—and be part of a close-knit, rooted community. The conqueror of wild rivers, the champion of modernity and progress, became, at least in those summers in Maine, a man slipping back into an archaic past.

O n 1 January 1900, as Americans hung fresh calendars on their walls, they heard repeatedly that in the century to come their nation would win its greatest triumphs. The United States stood first in the world in industrial production. It had driven the Europeans out of the Caribbean and the Pacific, where it proposed to create its own overseas empire. At home the population exceeded one hundred million, with a million new immigrants arriving every year. The Republican party of Lincoln, sober virtue, and business enterprise was back in power, under President William McKinley, who that year easily won reelection, naming as his vice president the governor of New York, Theodore Roosevelt, a hero in the recent war against Spain. Surely the twentieth century must belong to the awakening giants of North America.

It would not, however, belong to John W. Powell, who was sinking fast into incapacity. Politics no longer held his attention, not even the assassination of McKinley months after his reelection—the third such event in Powell's lifetime, a record of violence unmatched anywhere in the civilized world. Little in fact excited him at this point. His mind and body were failing, his creative juices were running dry. The round of daily work was increasingly a ritual, masking a creeping senility.

When he took sick with a winter cold, his physicians advised a long recuperative trip to Cuba and Jamaica, two new American protectorates. During February and March 1900 William Henry Holmes, now curator at the Smithsonian, went along as his companion, and they met Arnold Hague and Secretary Langley in midcourse. Ostensibly, Powell and Holmes went to study the collections of aboriginal antiquities in island museums, while Langley, frustrated by his failures to construct a successful flying machine, went to look at buzzards, hoping they would show him how to get a heavy body off the ground. A steamship took them from Tampa to Havana, then along the leeward coast to Santiago (scene of Roosevelt's charge up San Juan Hill) and over to Kingston. Although he became seasick in the open channel, the warm breezes and coconut palms perked Powell up a little. In Kingston he felt well enough to lecture on his Grand Canyon trip. According to Holmes, "it was first-rate and the old man is so full of enterprise and vigor that it is impossible to keep him in check."[43] By late March they were riding home with a shipload of bananas.

Commencement season brought an invitation to speak at Limestone College in the South Carolina piedmont. He titled his address "Archaeology" in the program and called it "a song" in the text; indeed it was more poetry than prose, and windy poetry at that. To the young, upturned faces before him he talked grandiloquently of ruins, sepulchers, and dead kings of yore:

Capitol wrecked, metropolis crushed,
Palace in dust and temple in ash;
Tyrant in tomb and orator hushed,
The cities are gone in the centuries' crash.[44]

Did he mean to suggest that this was America's future too — a melancholic warning for a bellicose, imperialistic nation — or merely that tyrants and monarchs happily belonged to the past, banished by American democracy?

In October he underwent a hernia operation at the Johns Hopkins University hospital, which left him wearing a truss, unfit for much physical exercise. An invitation the next spring, April 1901, to join the Mazamas Club on a hike up Mount Hood prompted a good-humored decline: "If I yet could climb! There's the rub." These days he could not climb even a modest hill, though twenty-five years earlier he could scramble up a tall mountain in a single morning. "Many years make me a coward, many climbs have made me a cripple," but he cherished memories of all his past ascents. "The very suggestion of mountain climbing almost makes me young again." A gift of trout from New York sportsmen likewise brought back the flavor of the outdoors. "I have always believed that I could distinguish between the taste of the Sierra, the taste of the Rocky Mountains and the taste of the Adirondacks. How!"[45]

News came in late 1901 that a railroad line had been laid down from Williams, Arizona, to the South Rim of the Grand Canyon, promising to bring masses of tourists to view the chasm. Powell welcomed the railroad's contribution to opening this spectacle to the nature seeker: "[F]or stupendous scenery, beauty and variety, the Grand Canyon . . . is unequalled on the face of this earth, and if the traveler has a modicum of scientific knowledge it is a rock-leaved bible of geology."[46] Meanwhile, another technological force was beginning to appear in this once remote country, a force that would one day eclipse the railroad as a mode of tourist travel. A steam-powered automobile, a Toledo Eight-horse, arrived at the Rim on 4 January 1902, after running out of gas and water on the road. Although national park status was still a long way into the future, Americans had begun to blaze a mechanical trail to the canyon where, thirty years earlier, Powell and his men had risked their lives in small wooden boats.

As the railroad and the automobile arrived at the Canyon — nearly simultaneously — books and brochures also appeared to instruct the traveler on what to see and how to see it. Powell's last published essay, "The Scientific Explorer," appeared in the Santa Fe's popular guide, *The Grand Canyon of Arizona* (1902). His companion authors included Thomas Moran, Charles Lummis, Harriet Monroe, Hamlin Garland, and the persistent Robert Stanton; but it was Powell's name, the editor noted, that was "indissolubly linked with that of the Grand Canyon." Powell obliged with rapturous history and science. He reviewed the river's explorers, from Coronado to Ives, Wheeler, and himself. Once again he described the high plateau through which the chasm ran, identified its most prominent geological features, walked the reader through its layers of gneiss, sandstone, and marble. He told of meeting the Mormon renegade John Lee and his wife at the mouth of the Pariah River. Then he warned the casual tourist, "you cannot see the Grand Canyon in one view, as if it were a changeless spectacle from which a curtain might be lifted," but must enter deeply into its labyrinths where "by a year's toil a concept of sublimity can be obtained never again to be equaled on the hither side of paradise."[47]

A more substantial book on the Canyon's history was in preparation by Fred Dellenbaugh, who had been a teenager on the second Powell expedition and was now approaching the age of fifty. In 1891 he sent the Major a copy of his first book, *The North Americans of Yesterday*, an appreciation of the Indians that he dedicated to the old man. The dedication was acknowledged by an encouraging letter: "I always delight in your successes and your prosperity and I ever cherish the memory of those days when we were on the great river together." It was time, Dellenbaugh maintained, to give "those days" full historical treatment. Powell agreed: "I am pleased to hear that you are engaged in writing a book on the Colorado Canyon," he wrote in January 1902. "I hope that you will put on record the second trip, and the gentlemen who were members of that expedition. I shall be very glad to write a short introduction to your book."[48] The opportunity to do that, however, would never come, as soon after Powell went into sudden decline.

Sometime late in the month of January, he suffered a severe stroke, which impaired his speech and memory and sent him to bed for the next six weeks. His physician called in another opinion, which confirmed a diagnosis of arteriosclerosis; the walls of Powell's arteries had become hard and thick, interfering with blood circulation. The prescription was moderate work and carriage drives, "freedom from emotions," and small doses of nitroglycerine. "Further, that he be warned not to walk on the street alone. Apoplexy may come on at any time or may never appear, the more he is freed from excitement and bodily stress, especially sudden movements, the better his chance of escaping." The Major, they added, would run less risk of a fatal cerebral hemorrhage if Emma and Mary were with him. They were not at home, however; Mary, stricken by nervous illness, had been taken by her mother to France for recovery, and news of her father's breakdown, the doctors feared, might push her over the edge.[49]

For Dellenbaugh, who now saw himself as Powell's Boswell, eager to record the fading memories of the great explorer, the turn of events was catastrophic too. There was so much he wanted to ask about both the first and second expeditions. Where, for example, was Jack Sumner's journal, from which the boys had read in 1871–72? Brother-in-law Thompson rummaged through old papers with May Clark but could not find it. For years it had been in Thompson's possession; he had turned it over to Powell for use in *The Canyons of the Colorado*, but then it had disappeared. He reported that the Major was "in a very precarious condition," unfit to talk, with no hope of a full recovery. "I will help you to all I can," Thompson offered. "Perhaps I am the only person who knows the history of the Expeditions that led to the first voyage — and the *true* history of the same."[50]

A few weeks later Thompson reported that "the Major is quite improved, but cannot talk much." He was taking a carriage drive every day and was more comfortable than he had been. "But Fred," Thompson went on, "why do you want to talk with him very much[?] You have got to say things about the Second Expedition as well as the First that will not put the Major in a very favorable light as a fair generous man — to put it mildly."[51]

By April Powell was able to leave his bed and venture into the open air, though he was not well enough to speak at a fortieth anniversary commemoration of the Battle of Shiloh, held in Washington. He

The Powell cottage in the Haven colony, Brooklin, Maine,
taken by the author in May 1999

needed assistance wherever he walked. It was probably about this time that the novelist Hamlin Garland passed him on the street, describing him as "gray and feeble, shuffling along on the arm of a colored attendant." The Major knew Garland's face but could not recall his name. "I've lost my memory," he said. The attendant was probably Tolly Spriggs, born a slave in Maryland and employed by the bureau, serving at this point as Powell's constant companion. Garland was moved by the encounter to write a poem, "The Stricken Pioneer," a tribute to all those men (white men was implied) who had carried the country west: "Our velvet way his steel prepared / He died without a curse or moan. / Then bury him not here in city soil / Where car-wheels grind and factories spill their acrid smoke on those who toil." Bury him on a high hill overlooking a great river, the pathway of the westward movement.[52]

After Emma and Mary returned from France, the family prepared to leave for their colony in Maine. They arrived earlier than usual, on 28 May, while spring was still arriving in the northern clime. Powell was not, alas, in a condition to go on fishing excursions, or for smoking cigars on the bench outside the dining hall, or for taking on new writing projects. Under watchful eye he could manage only to sit on the cottage verandah or make his way down to the water's edge to keep track of the rising and falling tide.

On 17 June President Roosevelt signed into law the National Reclamation Act, which put the federal government into the irrigation business. Back in March, Congress had reached a long-resisted consensus that reclaiming the arid West ought to be the government's responsibility. Private capital had failed whenever it tried to build on the grand scale; the economic return from irrigation was not enough to induce investors to shift their dollars into dams, canals, or western farm lands. Senator Stewart, still a power in Washington, had come around completely to federalization. "Here is a vast store of wealth, almost incomprehensible if irrigation can be carried on," he promised, though businessmen had said otherwise; a federal reclamation program will "increase the grandeur and power of this Republic."[53] But it was the junior senator from Nevada, Francis Newlands, and President Roosevelt who together pushed the bill through, against only half-hearted opposition. The bill set up a "reclamation fund" with proceeds from the sale of public lands in sixteen western states and territories. Drawing on the fund, a new Reclamation Service (later renamed the Bureau of Reclamation) in the Department of the Interior, staffed by Powell men, set about constructing irrigation works for the storage, diversion, and development of waters for reclaiming the arid and semiarid lands. No family could get water for more than 160 acres (twice as high as the limit Powell had proposed). Nowhere was any "commonwealth" system of governance mentioned, as Powell had recommended, nor any local community control over forests or grazing lands within each watershed.

All of that legislating and constructing was far away and long ago for the damaged man gazing vacantly at Eggemoggin Reach. The summer passed, the nights grew colder, the colors on the trees began to turn. In mid-September Powell suffered a cerebral hemorrhage, rendering him senseless. At six P.M. on Tuesday, 23 September, he died in his bungalow bed.

The body was returned by boat and rail to Washington, accompanied by Emma and Mary, who were joined in New York by Bram. When they arrived in the capital on the evening of 25 September, Jack Hillers met them at the station, and together they carried the corpse home to M Street. Next day, the day of the funeral, the offices of the Bureau of American Ethnology and Geological Survey were closed; crepe was tied to the doorknobs and Powell's picture was put on display.

Preceding the funeral a memorial meeting took place in the National Museum, with McGee presiding. Among the speakers was President Daniel Gilman of Johns Hopkins University, who recalled how skillfully Powell had presided over the American Association for the Advancement of Science and how he had won many friends among scientists. Commissioner of Education William T. Harris noted that Powell had "worked little less than a revolution" in getting congressional committees to listen to the scientific expert. On a more personal note, Charles Walcott recalled that, upon his resignation, Powell had only one touching request of his successor: "Look after Jack"—that is, Jack Hillers, the man who had nearly drowned with him in the Canyon. McGee concluded the somber proceedings by calling Powell "a moral giant. . . . The greatest of scientific men is gone; our warmest friend of scientific progress has passed away; our brightest exemplar of human knowledge is no more."[54]

They buried him in Arlington National Cemetery. A friend, the Reverend H.D. Sterrett, pastor of All Souls Memorial Church, presided over the internment, though Powell had not been a member of his church. A tall, tapered shaft of granite marked the grave, the upper part highly polished, the lower left rough and dark gray, speckled with black grains. Beneath a bronze portrait, a chiseled name, and the dates of birth and death (1834–1902), they carved an inscription reading, "Soldier. Explorer. Scientist."

At her husband's death Emma was left with no income, other than the small Civil War disability pension of $30 a month the couple had received for years. She looked to the Major's associates to get that sum increased. On 9 December she sent a small, black-edged note to Alexander Bell, soliciting a letter affirming "your appreciation of and friendship for my husband. . . . You know better than others how faithfully he worked in the service of this government, and how much he suffered in the loss of his good right arm—on the battle field, of his country. The committee on pensions, are inclined favorably to me—but I want all the Major's friends to help me."[55] Bell gave assistance, and in February 1903 the pension was raised to $50 a month. On that meager sum Emma lived until her death on 13 March 1924, staying quietly within her own circle of friends and withdrawing from much contact with Wes's friends and relatives.

Newspapers across the country noted the Major's passing, most often harking back to his dramatic outdoor achievements. The *Denver*

Times, for example, ran the headline, "Explored Canon of Colorado," and emphasized his early career in the West. The expedition of 1869 was extolled as "one of the most notable geographical, geological, and ethnological explorations and surveys in the history of North America." More expansively yet, the *Washington Post* called him "one of the most stalwart figures of that great band of explorers to which we are indebted for our knowledge of the two Americas." He ranked with Columbus, Magellan, Pizzaro, LaSalle, Raleigh, John Smith, and Lewis and Clark in the exalted pantheon of the western hemisphere's discoverers. The same paper asked for an appraisal from David T. Day, chief of mining and mineral resources of the Geological Survey, who emphasized more what Powell had done for the modern nation. "If we were called upon to select ten of the most influential men in the development of the United States," he declared, "a scientist would be one of them, and he would be Major Powell."[56]

In the months following the funeral, obituaries and tributes appeared in several national magazines. Gilbert Grosvenor wrote that "few men in the history of the United States have left behind them such a deep and lasting impression on the practical scientific work of the nation." The Yale geologist William H. Brewer said of Powell's 1869 expedition, "Never was a bolder voyage planned and executed. I know of no equal in the annals of exploration and navigation." Grove Gilbert also praised the boldness of his friend's Colorado River trip, adding, however, that it was "an adventurous episode by no means essential to his career as an investigator." In contrast to these, Alexander Chamberlain of Clark University singled out the Bureau of American Ethnology as Powell's greatest "monument." And William Dall, for whom Powell was "the ideal Western spirit," judged that his contributions to the understanding of the American Indian, "though largely developed through other workers, are his best gift to the store of modern science and that upon which his scientific reputation will chiefly last."[57]

Months after his death, on 16 February 1903, the Washington Academy of Sciences arranged still another memorial meeting, this one held at Columbian University where Powell had been a trustee. Walcott took the chair this time, as several notable speakers addressed different sides of Powell's manifold career. Congressman David Henderson of Iowa, formerly a general in the Civil War, a veteran of Shiloh and wounded at Corinth, described their mutual hatred of war. Professor Charles Van Hise of Wisconsin reviewed the western explorations, while Gilbert and McGee examined "Powell as a Geologist" and "Powell as an Anthropologist." He was the founder of the "new geology," Gilbert noted, the science that read history "not only in the rocks but in the forms of the land and the arrangement of streams." Only McGee touched on the congressional reversals that Powell had endured — a failure of fortune that "gradually broke the Old Man's sturdy spirit, embittered his later years, and undoubtedly shortened his life." Secretary Langley quickly drew a veil over that unhappy episode in his concluding remarks, calling Powell generous, brave, self-contained, a stoic. He was "a truthful and steadfast man, and one who never deserted a friend. We shall not often look upon his like."[58]

To Harry Thompson, sitting impatiently on the sidelines of so many eulogies, the Washington Academy meeting "was a good deal of a farce." Henderson "was full of whiskey"; the others, except for Gilbert and McGee, knew little about their man.[59] Perhaps so, but Harry's information was not always reliable either, and his long-standing resentments against Powell always distorted his judgment. Those resentments survived their object by four years, after which Harry died also, of stomach cancer, and took his place in the national cemetery.

In the aftermath of his death both admirers and detractors agreed that Powell ranked as one of the century's colossal figures in western exploration. Many noted that he had been a pivotal figure in securing for the indigenous people a wiser, more generous policy of tolerance. Many understood how crucial a role he had played in organizing federally supported science and making research a permanent part of the government's duty to its citizens. Many were aware of how important he had been in confronting the challenge of the arid West, though they did not agree on how valid his advice had been for designing institutions better adapted to their environment.

But there was still more significance to his life. From his birth in the back country of New York through his migration westward to the prairies and deserts of the West to his last years in Washington, D.C., and the coast of Maine, Powell participated in one of the great sagas of modern history — the rise of the American nation out of the raw materials of a diverse land and the hard labor of its people. He witnessed not only that impressive creation but also a revolution in the direction of the nation's development — from agrarianism to industrialism, a change that brought a deep shift of power and a profound redefinition of values.

He was born in an era that throbbed with religious faith, and he died in one that was distinctly more secular in its concentration on the seen and the material. Where his parents had brought to the New World a quest for spiritual regeneration, he chose another mission for himself. He served as pathfinder for a nation finding its way out of the territory of God—where belief in a benevolent supernatural power was all but unquestioned—and toward the territory of Science, where human reason would assume more and more authority to describe reality and even define secular ideals.

He stood also at the center of a change that began late in the last century and is still inching forward today, away from a careless, unplanned exploitation of nature and toward a more thoughtful, scientifically informed ethic of conservation. He had learned that ethic as he had learned the natural contours of the continent, by days and years spent traveling on foot, by mule, and by rail—learned it through the soles of his feet, learned it through acquiring calluses on his hands as well as from storing up vast knowledge in his large, bearded head. A utilitarian at core, he nonetheless appreciated the land for its wild beauty as well as for its economic potential. Conservationists and environmentalists would rightly look back on him as one of their founding giants.

Finally, and perhaps most essentially, he was a man of unstinting confidence in his country's basic goodness. Another century has not been easy on that spirit of confidence. We have come into still another territory, where doubt and skepticism are more common, where the land has become more overburdened and despoiled, where the very ideal of the nation is fading away, to be replaced by a more private, and yet more global, sense of identity, and where many fears and disappointments have accumulated. We will not bring back that old exuberant confidence. But as we struggle to discover and accept a less exalted notion of our place among the peoples of the earth, we may well look back on Powell as a measure of where we have been and what we have lost. Dogged in hope, driving in energy, he remained to the end incapable of imagining that his native country would ever fail in its promise.

Notes

PROLOGUE: GREEN RIVER STATION, 1869

1. *Deseret News*, 19 May 1869.
2. *New York Times*, 8 June, 7 and 13 Aug. 1869.
3. Gilbert to Robert B. Stanton, 5 Mar. 1907, Stanton papers, New York Public Library, box 5.

1. A MISSION TO AMERICA

1. Chevalier, *Society, Manners, and Politics*, 97, 182–83.
2. *Works of John Wesley: Sermons III*, 354–58.
3. Parish Register RG4–3686, East Riding County Archive Office, Beverley, Yorkshire. Family genealogies in America inaccurately give her date of birth as 1805, but she was born two years earlier than her husband.
4. *Battle's Hull Directory*, 4th ed., and *Battle's New Directory*, 6th ed.
5. *A Modern Delineation of Kingston upon Hull*, 11. See also *City of Kingston upon Hull*.
6. *Arcana Coelestia*, no. 2284; quoted in Synnestvedt, ed., *The Essential Swedenborg*, 85. Swedenborg died in London in 1772, and in 1810 a society organized to publish his works in English.
7. Because centralized registration of births, marriages, and deaths did not begin in England and Wales until 1837, the records for this period are incomplete. The *International Genealogical Index*, nonetheless, provides a fairly comprehensive listing of personal names found in parish records.
8. *History of Shropshire*, vol. 2.
9. Brown, *Charles Darwin*, vol. 1, 3–35.
10. Tocqueville, quoted in *City of Birmingham*, 223.
11. Parish Register for St. Martin's, Microfilm M114, entry no. 539, Birmingham Public Library.
12. One of Methodism's strongholds developed downstream from Shrewsbury in Severn Gorge, the world center of iron production in the eighteenth

century. See Trinder, *Industrial Revolution in Shropshire*, 157–65; and, *History of Shropshire*, 71–75.

13. The historians' debate over whether Methodism was repressive or liberal, reactionary or progressive, is presented in the following: Thompson, *Making of the English Working Class*, 36–54, 350–400; Hobsbawm, "Methodism and the Threat of Revolution in Britain," 23–33; Semmel, *Methodist Revolution*; and Hempton, *Methodism and Politics in British Society*.

14. Chidlaw, *The American*, 32–37.

15. Wilentz, *Chants Democratic*, 23–60, 107–29.

16. Ellen Thompson to Frederick Dellenbaugh, 3 Nov. 1902, DC, box 5, folder 17.

17. On the effects of and debate over the canal, see Sheriff, *Artificial River*.

18. Sellers, *Market Revolution*, 240. An average married woman in 1800 had 6.4 children, but by 1850 that number had dropped to 4.9.

19. P.E. Johnson, *Shopkeeper's Millennium*, 137.

20. Arrington and Bitton, *Mormon Experience*, 1–19.

21. *Mt. Morris Spectator*, 5 Mar. 1834. The town's history is told in Doty, *History of Livingston County, New York* and *History of the Genesee Country*, vol. 2, 911–16; and in Parsons and Rockfellow, *Centennial Celebration*.

22. Hudson, *Narrative of John Hudson*, 142–43.

23. *Mount Morris Spectator*, 1 June 1834.

24. McIntosh, *History of Wyoming County*, 163–72. The county had been part of the Holland Purchase, which Robert Morris had sold to a group of Amsterdam investors; see Wyckoff, *The Developer's Frontier*.

25. Clarke, *James Hall*, 68–71.

26. D. Williams, *Cymru ac America*, 11–19. Also, DeVoto, *Course of Empire*, 68–73.

27. Evans, *History of Welsh Settlements*.

28. Chidlaw, *The American*, 10–14. See also Chidlaw, *Story of My Life*.

29. Darrah, *Powell of Colorado* (p. 6), gives the date of Joseph and Chidlaw's meeting as 1836, but Chidlaw dates his trip along the Erie Canal in Aug. 1839, which was after the Powells left the area.

30. Jakle, *Images of the Ohio Valley*, 25 ff; Scheiber, *Ohio Canal Era*, 18.

31. R. Jones, *Early Jackson*.

32. Their house site was later occupied by the Crescent Opera House, then by an ice-skating rink, and then by a restaurant's parking lot. A small memorial museum to John Wesley Powell was dedicated in 1934, next to the courthouse.

33. *History of Lower Scioto Valley*, 458.

34. Ibid., 465.

35. Howe, *Historical Collections of Ohio* vol. 2, 245; Jackson *Standard-Journal*, 15 Oct. 1893.

36. D.W. Williams, *History of Jackson County*, vol.1, 166.

37. In 1840 a full-time Ohio circuit preacher, serving thirty "stations," received about $300 a year. Weisenburger, *Passing of the Frontier*, 152–53.

38. See the Jackson County registry of deeds from 1838 to 1846. No deeds were recorded for Walter Powell.

39. *Ohio 1840 Population Census* (ms.), Jackson County, Lick Township, sheet 58. This first comprehensive national census does not give names or exact ages

of individuals but puts them in age groups ("males under age 5," etc.). It records Uncle Walter and the two older girls as younger than they were.

40. Robert Ervin, "George L. Crookham" (unpublished manuscript). The author thanks Ervin for sharing his research. See also Jackson *Journal-Herald*, 15 and 29 June 1990, for a biographical sketch of Crookham.

41. Willard, *History of the Hanging Rock Iron Region*, 369–70.

42. Weisenburger, *Passing of the Frontier*, 40–46. In 1850, Jackson County counted 391 blacks.

43. Cartwright was of an older generation than Joseph Powell, and more of a backwoods figure, but his *Autobiography* gives a vivid picture of the itinerant's life. See also Eggleston's novel, *The Circuit Rider*, and Weisberger, *They Gathered at the River*, 45–50.

44. Hatch, *Democratization of American Christianity*, 3, 220.

45. Wesley, "Thoughts upon Slavery," 97–98.

46. Mathews, *Slavery and Methodism*, 166–68.

47. *History of Lower Scioto Valley*, 531–33.

48. The best account of this episode remains Barnes, *Antislavery Impulse*, 64–78.

49. Fladeland, *James Gillespie Birney*, 117, 121, 129, 264–65; Birney, *Letters*, xii-xvii.

50. T.C. Smith, *Liberty and Free Soil Parties*, 46–47, 80; McKivigan, *War Against Proslavery Religion*, 149.

51. William Bramwell Powell, letter to *Jackson Standard Journal*, 14 Jan. 1903.

2. RISING ON THE PRAIRIE

1. Garland, *Son of the Middle Border*, 133.

2. Unruh, *The Plains Across*, 120.

3. Lapham, *Wisconsin*, 137. See also Beckwith, *Walworth County, Wisconsin*, vol. 1, 29–37.

4. See Gates, *Farmer's Age*, 51–98.

5. These details come from the grantor and grantee indices to deeds, County Clerk Records, Walworth County Courthouse, Elkhorn, Wisconsin.

6. Wisconsin became a state in 1848, when its population reached nearly 250,000; it had been less than 45,000 just three years earlier. See Current, *Wisconsin: The Civil War Years*, 3. The population of Walworth County was 2,611 in 1840 and 17,832 in 1850.

7. *History of Walworth Co., Wisconsin*, 755–56. South Grove disappeared as a village after the railroad came through Sharon, a competing center only a couple of miles south, in 1856. The Powell farm, however, has remained in production to this day.

8. *The Combination Atlas Map of Walworth County* shows the piece of land that Joseph bought from Larkin as still partially wooded in 1873. There were some fifteen houses at the crossroads then, though today only two survive.

9. JWP, "Proper Training," 622.

10. "By 1847 Milwaukee, Kenosha, and Racine were shipping some 1.3 million bushels of wheat and 40,000 bushels of flour." Clark, *Grain Trade*, 98.

11. Margaret Whittemore to William Culp Darrah, 5 Oct. 1946, DarC.

12. Muir, *Boyhood and Youth*, 162, 175.

13. "On Riches" (1788), *Works of Wesley: Sermons*, vol. 3, 520.

14. "Governor's Message," *Dewitt Courier*, 5 Jan. 1855.

15. *Oberlin Evangelist* 17 (1855), 159.

16. Ibid. 12 (1851), 199.

17. Jesse Wheaton, a carpenter from New England, was the main force behind the founding of the town; he had shrewdly bought up the land before the railroad arrived in 1850 and divided it into twelve blocks for urban development. Today, the town is famous for its world evangelism center honoring Billy Graham. See Richmond and Vallette, *History of DuPage*.

18. Joseph did not buy his college lots until 1854–55 so the move may have come later. See the grantee index to deeds in the DuPage County Courthouse. He did not begin selling any of their Boone County land until April 1855, according to courthouse records in Belvidere.

19. David Maas, "Wheaton College's Forgotten Heritage." The author thanks Professor Maas for the loan of this unpublished manuscript.

20. For brief mention of the Powells in his early correspondence, see letters dated 27 Aug., 15 Oct. 1839; 19 May; 9 June 1840, in Jonathon Blanchard Papers, Wheaton College Archives.

21. Joseph Powell to Board of Trustees, Illinois Institute, 15 April 1857, ibid.

22. *Population Schedules of the Eighth Census of the United States, 1860*, Roll 175, vol. 12, DuPage County, Illinois.

23. Doyle, *Social Order of a Frontier Community*, 263–64.

24. Foner, *Free Soil*, 11–39.

25. Merrill, *First One Hundred Years*, 194–99.

26. According to Goetzmann (*Army Exploration*, p. 311), the most important achievement of the surveys was Lieutenant G.K. Warren's map of the West, over four feet wide and four feet tall, a map to guide all later explorers, cartographers, and naturalists.

27. Wesley, *Survey of the Wisdom of God* I, 2.

28. For background on Lyell, see Rudwick, *Meaning of Fossils*, 164–217; Carey, *Theories of the Earth*, 57–62.

29. Oldroyd, *Thinking about the Earth*, 119.

30. Lyell, *Travels in North America*, vol. 2, 47, 62–65; Wilson, *Lyell in America*, 104–8, 261–62. In Ohio Lyell went to hear a minister preaching to a Welsh congregation, but probably it was not Joseph Powell.

31. Darwin, *Correspondence of Charles Darwin*, vol. 6, 432.

32. JWP, "Darwin's Contributions to Philosophy," 65–66.

33. Bessie M. Lindsey, "Long Creek Township in Macon Co., Illinois," typescript ms., Decatur Historical Society, 119–20.

34. Periam, *Origin, Aims, and Progress of the Farmers' Movement*, 377–81.

35. *Dewitt Courier*, 22 June 1855.

36. Ibid., 30 Mar. 1855.

37. This episode is recorded in both Lincoln and Darrah. The latter got much of his information about the Decatur interlude from John and Martha's descendants, but his documentation is missing. Apparently, he saw the letters from Joseph (dated March 1855) and Mary to Wes, and I am relying on his report.

38. Davis, "Notes of Travels," *Dewitt Courier*, 6 April 1855.

39. Rammelkamp, 137–94.

40. Davis, "Notes of Travels," *Dewitt Courier*, 6 April 1855.

41. "J.W. Powell" is listed as a new student from Decatur in *Catalogue of the Officers and Students of Illinois College*, 8.

42. Gibson, *Sigma Pi Society*, 105.

43. College records show JWP enrolled in 1857–58 in the "preparatory" department, which would have been a demotion if true. I suspect that it was an error in recording his status, which should have been second-term freshman. H. Gary Hudson, president of Illinois College, to William C. Darrah, 22 Oct. 1946, DarC.

44. Harper, *Development of the Teachers College*, 6.

45. The society was formed in fall 1855. JWP's name is on the fly leaf of the first volume of minutes, but he was down in Jacksonville at that time, so could not have been one of the organizers.

46. Quoted in Brandt, *Town That Started the Civil War*, frontispiece.

47. C.W. Williams, *Medina, Elyria & Oberlin City Directory*, 96.

48. *Annual Catalogue of Oberlin College*. This catalogue is for the year succeeding JWP's period in residence, but the curriculum did not change much. For his courses, see Records of the Office of the Registrar, 1859–1995 (RG 27), SG III: Student Grade Records, 1859–1939, Oberlin College Archives.

49. Philip James Bailey, *Festus: A Poem*, 123–24.

50. C.A. Kenaston to L.D. Harkness, 8 June 1903, Oberlin College Archives. Kenaston became a railroad engineer, then in 1882 a professor in Howard University in Washington, D.C., when he met Powell again and renewed their friendship.

51. Twain, *Life on the Mississippi*, 48–49.

52. Ibid, 82–85.

53. Powell's brother-in-law Almon Thompson questioned whether Powell made any of the long river trips. See Thompson to Fred Dellenbaugh, 27 Oct. 1902, DelC, box 5, folder 17. But Thompson did not meet Powell until two or three years after the Mississippi trips were supposed to have occurred.

54. Darrah apparently saw this letter and summed up its contents (Darrah, *Powell of the Colorado*, p. 43), but its location is now unknown.

55. See the frontispiece of Twain, *Life on the Mississippi*.

56. Harper, *Development of the Teachers College*, 362–63.

57. Lincoln, "John Wesley Powell," part 1, 714.

58. The author is indebted to Sharon Clausen of the Putnam County Historical Society (Ill.) for background on Hennepin. She has found Powell's school pay recorded in the County Treasurer's Book until April 1861, after which brother Bram took his place.

59. See *U.S. Census Office, Eighth Census, 1860: Population Schedules; Wayne County, City of Detroit, Wards 6–10*, 914, where Emma is listed as twenty-three years old, the oldest of four children. Joseph Dean's obituary appeared in the *Detroit Free Press*, 12 Oct. 1879; he died from the lingering effects of a Fourth of July skyrocket stick that struck him in the eye.

3. THE HORNETS' NEST OF WAR

1. McPherson, *Battle Cry of Freedom*, 232, 234–75.

2. Benjamin J. Radford, who had enlisted with a group of students from Eureka College, Illinois, and later went on to Shiloh, gives a vivid description of their time guarding the siege guns. See *The Community* [Cape Girardeau], 27 Aug. 1936.

3. McFeely, *Grant*, 77–110.

4. Grant, *Papers of Ulysses S. Grant*, vol. 3, 30.

5. *Detroit Free Press*, 1 Dec. 1861. The officiating minister was Reverend John Herbert Griffith of the First Baptist Church, and they paid him $10, or twice his normal fee. His presence suggests that the Deans were not by this point Catholics, though Joseph, like his sister Mary, had been raised Catholic in Hull. See also *Marriages Performed by John Herbert Griffith, D.D.*, photostat of original record book, Burton Historical Collection, Detroit Public Library.

6. Grant to Captain John C. Kelton, 2 Dec. 1861, *Papers of Ulysses S. Grant*, vol. 3, 248–50. Grant explained that Powell's battery would be formed around a core of Missouri Home Guards that had been authorized by Frémont. For a list of names and occupations in the 2nd Light Artillery, Battery F, see Adjutant General Records, Muster Roles for Illinois Regiments in Civil War, Illinois State Archives, Springfield, Microfilm Roll 27. Walter had enlisted at Decatur on 8 April 1861 and served three months in the 8th Illinois as a captain before returning to teaching. He then signed up for a three-year term in March 1862 as a private in Battery F.

7. "The relations between officers and soldiers in the war depended heavily on the institution in which men were most used to issuing orders and receiving them, the[ir] model for authority . . . the family." Mitchell, *The Vacant Chair*, 43.

8. This famous battle has been written about in numerous books, including Grant, *Memoirs*, 227–47; Sword, *Shiloh*; Luvaas, Bowman, and Fullenkamp, *Guide to the Battle of Shiloh*; and Daniel, *Shiloh*.

9. Their encampment was only a few hundred feet from the present visitor center of Shiloh National Military Park and is marked by signs and five field guns.

10. Reed, *Battle of Shiloh*, 61.

11. Leonard B. Houston, quoted in Throne, ed., "Letters from Shiloh," 265.

12. Powell to Colonel Cornelius Cardle, Chairman, Shiloh National Military Park Battlefield Commission, 15 May 1896, Shiloh National Military Park.

13. Darrah (*Powell*, 58) describes Medcalfe as a druggist in civilian life, but his military record indicates he had been a physician. He was mustered into the 49th Illinois at age forty as a "surgeon." See Adjutant General Records, Muster Roles for Illinois Regiments in Civil War, Illinois State Archives, Springfield, Microfilm Roll 8.

14. For Emma's recollections as related to friends over the years, see Darrah, *Powell*, 58–59. She continued serving as a field hospital volunteer nurse during the duration of the war.

15. Quoted in Lincoln, "John Wesley Powell," part 2, 14–15. The original of the letter has disappeared, and the year of writing is uncertain.

16. Henderson, "Powell as a Soldier," 101.

17. Almost two hundred thousand blacks joined the Union army, out of about two million soldiers in all. Wiley, *Life of Billy Yank*, 313–16.

18. Xavier Picquet, deposition taken at Walter's pension hearing, 1896, Veterans Records, NARG 15, no. 922,237.

19. O.O. Howard to George H. Thomas, 3 Nov. 1864, *War of the Rebellion*, ser. 1, vol. 39, part 2, 618–19.

20. Z. B. Tower to George H. Thomas, 15 May 1865, ibid., ser. 1, vol. 49, part 2, 780.

21. *Chicago Tribune*, 18 April 1865.

22. *Chicago Tribune*, 4 May 1865.

4. WESTWARD THE NATURALIST

1. Gilpin, *Central Gold Region*, 194.

2. Ibid., 79.

3. Bowles, *Our New West*, viii. Bowles was editor of the Springfield *Republican*, for a while one of the most popular, influential weeklies in the country.

4. Ibid, 156–58.

5. Watson, *Illinois Wesleyan Story*, 60, 73.

6. Taylor, "In the Wesleyan," 68.

7. Illinois Wesleyan University, *Ninth Annual Catalog*, 18–20, lists his courses. Powell is well remembered on this campus by the library's Special Collections, which includes faculty and trustees' minutes that track some of his local activities; by a display of his Indian pottery collection; and by an outdoor stone monument.

8. *Proceedings of the Board of Education*, 10–11.

9. Letter by Milton Titterington, 8 May 1928, Special Collections, Illinois Wesleyan University. Titterington later became a schoolteacher in Lawrence, Kansas.

10. *Chicago Republican*, 15 July 1867.

11. Dorsett and McCarthy, *Queen City* 27–53; Abbott, Leonard, and McComb, *Colorado*, 50-100.

12. "So far as I know," Almon Thompson wrote, "the Major never had any idea of exploring the Colorado before 1868–9[,] although we had the interview with Ex Gov Gilpin of Colorado in 1867." Thompson to Fred Dellenbaugh, 21 Oct. 1902, DelC, box 5, folder 17. In fact, late in 1867 Powell announced his plans to explore the river.

13. *Bloomington Daily Pantagraph*, 19 Aug. 1867.

14. Ibid., 26 Aug. 1867.

15. *Chicago Republican*, 3 Sept. 1867.

16. *Daily Colorado Tribune* (Denver), 6 Nov. 1867.

17. "Jack Sumner's Account," in Stanton, *Colorado River Controversies*, 167–70. Sumner gave this account six months before his death in 1907.

18. "Report of Professor Powell," *Proceedings of the Board of Education*, 9–13.

19. *Bloomington Daily Pantagraph*, 7 Jan., 26 Feb. 1868.

20. *Congressional Globe*, 25 May 1868, 2563–2566.

21. "Reports of Explorations and Surveys," 33 Cong., 2 sess., House Ex. Doc. 71. This document includes Lieutenant Warren's 120-page summary of all western surveys and explorations after 1800.

22. Pyne, *How the Canyon Became Grand*, 4–10.

23. Smith, "Before Powell," 106-8; Warner, *Dominguez-Escalante Journal;* Bolton, *Pageant in the Wilderness*. Other Spanish-Mexican explorers also came into the middle Colorado River valley, as well as various slave traders.

24. Julien was a Frenchman, born in eighteenth-century St. Louis and active in that city's fur trade; he carved his name in at least five places along the Green and Colorado rivers. See Charles Kelly, "Mysterious 'D. Julien.'"

25. Goetzmann, *Army Exploration*, 378–94.

26. Woodward, *Feud on the Colorado*, 80–104.

27. The Utah, or Mormon, War broke out a few months before Ives arrived and gave his survey a more immediate military purpose. President James Buchanan sent troops to Utah under Albert Sidney Johnston to put down an alleged rebellion. Brigham Young responded by mobilizing the Nauvoo Legion, a church militia, fortifying passes, and looking for Indian allies along the Colorado River. On 11 Sept. 1857 Mormon militiamen and Indians attacked a Missouri-Arkansas wagon train at Mountain Meadows, in southwestern Utah, and killed more than one hundred men, women, and children. Ives had reason to fear that he was entering a war zone. See M. Smith, "Colorado River Exploration and the Mormon War."

28. "Report upon the Colorado River of the West," 36 Cong., 1 sess., Sen. Ex. Doc. 90, 107.

29. "Report upon the Colorado River of the West," 101.

30. Macomb, *Report of Exploring Expedition from Santa Fe*, 6.

31. White to brother, 26 Sept. 1867, in Stanton, *Colorado River Controversies*, 10. See also Thomas Dawson's "The Grand Canyon," 65 Cong., 1 sess., Sen. Doc. 42.

32. Parry, "Account of the Passage Through the Grand Cañon."

33. Stanton, *Colorado River Controversies*, 93.

34. Ibid., 39–41.

35. There is no reliable roster of the 1868 party; the reported numbers varied from twenty-one to twenty-five, and some of the names are uncertain. The *Chicago Republican* (30 June 1868) lists, in addition to the names given here, a Mr. and Mrs. Woodward, James Taylor, and Dr. A.M. Todd. All but Mrs. Woodward, who would have been the second woman in the expedition, can be corroborated in the various diaries and newspaper correspondence the party kept or published. Rhodes Allen, Lyle Durley, and the Reverend Daniels all kept journals, and Lewis Keplinger left some correspondence and published several articles, all of which are noted below. Reverend Healy sent in an account to the *Chicago Journal*, which has been reprinted in Watson, *The Professor Goes West*, 14–22. W.C. Wood also kept a journal, now in the Huntington Library, with notes added later by his son Henry, and he published accounts in the *Chicago Republican*. Finally, Taylor wrote a reminiscence in 1902, which is republished in Watson, 26–27. Taylor is the only person to claim that Harry and Nellie Thompson were in the party; but the Thompsons had gone to Greenwood County, Kansas, in 1867, after the first Colorado expedition, to raise sheep. The problem of compiling an accurate list of expeditioners is complicated by the fact that some people who joined left en route; for example, L.E. Shinn quit to work as a hotel clerk in Central City.

36. W.C. Wood, entry for 3 July 1868, typescript diary, Huntington Library.

37. "Historicus" [W.H. Daniels], *Chicago Tribune*, 3 Aug. 1868.

38. W.C. Wood, entries for 11 and 16 July 1868, typescript diary, Huntington Library.

39. *Denver News*, 14 July 1868.

40. Daniels, "Journal Leaves from Powell's Expedition," 42–44.

41. Keplinger to his brother, 12 Aug. 1868, Kansas State Historical Society.

42. Keplinger, "First Ascent of Long's Peak," 7.

43. Byers, *Daily Rocky Mountain News*, 1 Sept. 1868. Byers's diary, which gives a more laconic record of the climb than the newspaper account, is in the Western History Collection, Denver Public Library.

44. Keplinger, "First Ascent of Long's Peak," 9.

45. Garman to Friend [Gertrude] Lewis, 28 Aug. 1868, Special Collections, Milner Library, Illinois State University. Garman does not name the abstainers, but it seems likely that they were Powell and himself.

46. Ibid.

47. Hill, *A Dangerous Crossing*, 106–11.

48. "Diary of Lyle Durley," 22 Aug. 1868, DarC, box 3.

49. "Diary of Rhodes Allen," 9 Aug. 1868, DarC, box 3.

50. Garman to Friend Gertrude, 28 Aug. 1868.

51. Sumner, whom the Utes called "Jack Rabbit," had had some tense moments with them. In fall 1867 an Indian put an arrow through his arm and, in return, was shot dead. Sumner confronted the angry tribal leaders while sitting with cocked revolver on a keg of powder. They calmed down and listened to his plea of self-defense. Gease, "William Newton Byers," M.A. thesis, 57.

52. Bowles, *Switzerland of America*, 82–85.

53. Ibid., 84–86.

54. "Diary of Rhodes Allen," 10 and 11 Sept. 1868.

55. Ibid., 12, 18, and 20 Sept. 1868.

56. *Chicago Tribune*, 26 Oct. 1868.

57. Dawson, "Lost Alone on Bear River," 13–20.

58. Ten years after the Powell party camped here, Nathan Meeker, a reformer from Greely, Colorado, was appointed agent to the White River Utes. He tried to persuade the Indians to give up nomadic bison hunting and settle into farming the valley; in fall 1879 he and his assistants were killed by his charges in what became known as "the Meeker massacre." See Emmitt, *Last War Trail*.

59. *Chicago Tribune*, 4 Sept. 1868.

60. The best account of this trip is in the "Diary of Rhodes Allen," 2–16 Nov. 1868. But also see the report on the winter encampment and travel north, probably written by Howland: "The Powell Expedition," *Daily Rocky Mountain News*, 14 May 1869.

61. Powell to Dr. Edwards, 26 Jan. 1869, in Watson, *The Professor Goes West*, 24–25.

62. Garman to Friend Gertrude, 2 April 1869. See also his letter of 27 Jan.: "I can't afford to stay with the expedition as it requires too much of my time & too complete an abnegation of one's own affairs to present very great attractions to a student and traveler who is receiving no pay and not learning enough to pay for the time."

5. DOWN THE GREAT UNKNOWN

1. For other names see Roy Webb, *If We Had a Boat*, 10–11.

2. Powell, "Cañons of the Colorado," 293.

3. Bell, *New Tracks*, 559.

4. I am indebted to Ralph Frese of the Chicago Maritime Society for information on Bagley and the Powell boats.

5. *Chicago Tribune*, 29 May 1869.

6. Biographical sketches of the 1869 party were compiled by William Culp Darrah in the *UHQ* 15 (1947).

7. Billy Hawkins recalled "a young man whom some friends of the Major sent out West" to join the expedition, who may or may not have been Adams; he became the butt of their humor for several days. See Stanton, *Colorado River Controversies*, 145.

8. Powell to McCormick, May 1872, PS letters sent, roll 1, nos. 59–66.

9. A copy of the agreement is in DelC, box 5, folder 9.

10. Powell's bow oarsmen faced upstream, unable to see where they were going, a position that river runners now call "Powelling" through a rapid. In the 1890s, Nathaniel Galloway changed the practice of Colorado River rowing by turning around to face downstream. He also adopted light, maneuverable boats with flat bottoms instead of Powell's heavy, clumsy, deep-bottomed craft. See Webb, *If We Had a Boat*, 86–87.

11. *Chicago Tribune*, 29 May 1869.

12. Sumner, "Lost Journal," 175. This journal, which runs to 28 June and is signed "Jack Sumner Free Trapper," was originally published in a St. Louis newspaper, the *Missouri Democrat*, with an introductory letter by Powell.

13. Powell, *Exploration*, 124–25.

14. Powell's immediate record of the expedition consisted of seven letters published in three separate issues of the *Chicago Tribune* and a couple of personal letters to friends, all penned from 24 May to 23 June. They have been reprinted in *UHQ* 15 (1947): 73–88. Also, from early July to late August, he kept a brief journal on long slips of brown paper, which is preserved in the NAA/SI, and has been published as "Major Powell's Journal," ibid., 125–31. There is also his geological journal, preserved in the same archive and partially reprinted in ibid., 134–39. Powell's first full account of the 1869 expedition was the government report "Exploration of the Colorado River of the West and Its Tributaries," 43 Cong, 1 sess, House Misc. Doc. 300 (1875). The enlarged trade version, *The Canyons of the Colorado* (1895), has been reprinted several times, and I have used here a 1987 reprint (see bibliography).

15. Sumner, "Lost Journal," 176; Bradley, "Journal," 32.

16. Today this gorge is flooded by the Bureau of Reclamation's Flaming Gorge Dam, which generates electrical power for Utah's industrial growth.

17. Powell, *Exploration*, 141; Sumner, "Lost Journal," 178.

18. *Chicago Tribune*, 19 July 1869.

19. Ashley, *The West of William H. Ashley*, 107–15, 269–81. Ashley was on the river for a little over a month, reaching Minny Maud Creek before returning to the Uinta River and proceeding up that tributary to the mountains. William Manly and his party of Forty-niners had also navigated, in a flimsy wooden ferry boat, a long stretch of the Green (Manly, *Death Valley in '49*, 84–125).

20. Bradley, "Journal," 34; Sumner, "Lost Journal," 179. On the Diamond Hoax, see Wilkins, *Clarence King*, 167–85.

21. Sumner, "Lost Journal," 180; Powell, *Exploration*, 148.

22. *Rocky Mountain News*, 17 July 1869.

23. Bradley, "Journal," 38.

24. Ibid.

25. In the 1950s the Bureau of Reclamation proposed to dam this place but was defeated by conservationists. See Harvey, *A Symbol of Wilderness.*

26. Howland, "Letters to the *Rocky Mountain News*," 98; Powell to Henry Wing, 29 June 1869, *UHQ* 15 (1947): 88.

27. Sumner, "The Lost Journal," 188.

28. Goodman settled eventually in the Browns Park area, where he raised sheep and apples, and kept a home in Vernal, Utah. (Personal communication from a descendant, Mary K. Ferguson.)

29. Bradley, "Journal," 43, 45.

30. *Bloomington Pantagraph*, 1 July 1869. Powell's prudence shows in his taking out $5,000 worth of life insurance and putting all his business papers in the hands of a Normal lawyer before leaving.

31. *Chicago Tribune*, 3 July 1869.

32. *Detroit Post*, 4 July 1869; *Chicago Tribune*, 8 July 1869.

33. *Bloomington Pantagraph*, 6 July 1869. Almon Thompson, Powell's brother-in-law in Lacon, Illinois, pronounced Risdon "an arrant liar or a crazy person," and possibly a thief. The idea of making a bark canoe on the Colorado River, he noted, was laughable to anyone who knew the type of trees growing there. See *Chicago Tribune*, 7 July 1869.

34. *Chicago Tribune*, 5 July 1869; *Bloomington Pantagraph*, 12 July 1869.

35. Goetzmann, *Exploration and Empire*, 283, 286–88.

36. Bradley, "Journal," 50–51. One man had boasted to Powell that he had built a town at the junction, but they found no such place.

37. Powell, *Exploration*, 206.

38. Ibid., 116. On some older maps the Dirty Devil is called the Fremont River.

39. Powell, *Exploration*, 23.

40. Edgar Rider to Frederick Dellenbaugh [1904?], DelC, box 5, folder 16. Rider was Sumner's friend in Grand Junction, Colorado, and recorded in this letter the "truth" according to Sumner. There are two Sumner letters to Dellenbaugh in this same folder, but neither mentions the story.

41. Hawkins, in Bass, 23–27. When these disputes occurred is hard to determine; Hawkins may have concocted them out of whole cloth late in life. In any case it seems likely that the good will of the party was sinking under the weather, the monotonous diet, and their weariness with the work.

42. Aton, *John Wesley Powell*, 32.

43. In 1963 the Bureau of Reclamation completed Glen Canyon Dam, which backs the river up into a reservoir named Lake Powell that reaches upstream more than two hundred miles, into Cataract Canyon. Much of the beauty of Glen Canyon now lies buried in mud and water.

44. *Chicago Tribune*, 29 May 1869; Powell, "Cañons of the Colorado," 402.

45. Bradley, "Journal," 63.

46. Ibid., 62.

47. Ibid., 58.

48. Powell, *Exploration*, 247.

49. Soon after the voyage Powell estimated (Bell, *New Tracks*, 564) that they had come 626 miles from Green River City to the mouth of the Little Colorado, and another 299 miles through the Grand Canyon to Callville.

50. Bradley, "Journal," 64.

51. Powell, *Exploration*, 255.

52. Ibid., 259–60. In fact, these buildings dated back well before the arrival of the Spanish in the New World; native peoples had been coming into and living in the Grand Canyon for more than four thousand years.

53. Ibid., 263.

54. Ibid., 274.

55. Ibid., 275.

56. Ibid., 279–80.

57. Bradley, "Journal," 70; Hawkins, in Bass, 28.

58. Bradley, "Journal," 70.

59. Sumner, "Journal," 122. Some time later Powell called the point Separation Rapid. It is located at Mile 239.5 below Lee's Ferry. By 1938 the construction of the Hoover Dam and the filling of Lake Mead put the fateful rapid under deep water. Plaques in memory of the Howlands and Dunn have been placed above waterline on the canyon wall

60. Powell, *Exploration*, 284–85.

61. Sumner, "Journal," 122.

62. Ibid., 123.

63. Sumner to *Denver Post*, 13 Oct. 1902, reprinted in Stegner, "Jack Sumner and John Wesley Powell," 65. Part of Sumner's bitterness may have been due to the mistaken notion that Powell had gotten a $50,000 appropriation from the federal government that he had not shared with the men. He also felt that Powell had not given sufficient credit to the others, except to Walter, who "was about as worthless a piece of furniture as could be found in a day's journey." See Stanton, *Colorado River Controversies*, 211.

64. Bradley, "Journal," 72.

65. Sumner, "Journal," 123.

66. James G. Bleak, "Annals of the Southern Utah Mission: Vol. 2," in Bleak papers, Utah State Historical Society, box 2, folder 6; *Deseret Evening News*, 7 and 8 Sept. 1869.

67. *Deseret Evening News*, 15 and 16 Sept. 1869. See also *Chicago Tribune*, 28 Sept. 1869, for a report of this lecture.

68. *Chicago Republican*, 21 Sept. 1869.

69. "Colorado River Expeditions of Samuel Adams," 42 Cong., 1 sess., House Misc. Doc. 37, 6–9. The original manuscript journal of Adams's exploration is in the Huntington Library.

70. Clippings from *San Francisco Chronicle*, 25 Mar. 1872, PS letters received, roll 1, nos. 68–76.

71. Powell to R. C. McCormick, May 1872, PS letters sent, roll 1, nos. 59–66.

6. SURVEYING THE HIGH PLATEAUS

1. The standard works on the subject are Bartlett, *Great Surveys of the American West*; and Goetzmann, *Exploration and Empire*, part 3.

2. The most thorough study, and a fair-minded appraisal, is Foster, *Strange Genius*.

3. Grant had been a failure before the war, and as president he returned to his norm; unskilled in politics and indifferent to ethical matters, he produced

one of the most corrupt administrations in American history. See McFeely, *Grant*, 400–49.

4. See Merrill, *First One Hundred Years of American Geology*, 407–11; and Josiah Dwight Whitney, *Life and Letters*, 305–12, on the significance of the California survey for future scientific work.

5. Wilkins, *Clarence King*, 89–100.

6. Ibid., 165. King's superior in the Army Corps of Engineers, General A.A. Humphreys, refused his request to explore the Green and Yampa Rivers. So King finished the work he had been appointed to do and by spring 1875 had moved back to New York.

7. Wheeler, *Report upon United States Geographical Surveys West of the One Hundredth Meridian*, 35.

8. "Poem Written by Major John Wesley Powell in Memory of His Mother," J.W. Powell Collection, Grand Canyon National Park Museum.

9. See, for example, *New York Herald*, 11 Jan. 1871. Another description of his platform appearance and style, on the occasion of a lecture at Wheaton College, exudes pride in the local boy who has made good:

> Major Powell is about 35 years of age, rather above medium height,
> erect as a pine, and compactly built, brown hair and whiskers, the
> latter cut in Burnside fashion. In manners affable — his style of delivery
> is free from affectations and display; he expresses his thoughts in
> language forcible, clear, and elegant. He excels in freshness,
> originality and compactness of idea and expressions, rather than
> oratorical finish and flourish.

Reported in the *Naperville Clarion* [1869], Clyde Eddy Scrapbook, American Philosophical Society, 8.

10. "Exploration of Colorado River," 41 Cong., 2 Sess., House Exec. Doc. 280 and 281; *Congressional Globe*, 12 July 1870, 696.

11. Young's entourage included John Doyle Lee, whose description of their travels appears in Lee, *Diaries*, vol. 2, 135–41. For Powell's movements during this time see *Deseret News*, 29 Aug. and 5 Sept. 1870.

12. Dellenbaugh's eulogy is inscribed in the flyleaf of his copy of *Jacob Hamblin: A Narrative of His Personal Experience*, DelC.

13. Powell, *Exploration*, 300.

14. Powell's first name for this geological feature was the Passion Cliffs. See A.M. Musser, *Deseret Evening News*, 21 Sept. 1870.

15. James Whitmore, a Mormon rancher, was the first to file a claim on the Pipe Spring site in 1862 or 1863. After Indian livestock raids defeated him, the church took over the ranch and ran it for thirty years, building a large fortification with thick stone walls that became known as Winsor Castle. The place became an important stopping point for the Powell Survey. See Lavender, *Pipe Spring and the Arizona Strip*; and Olsen, "Winsor Castle."

16. Powell, *Exploration*, 320–23.

17. Belshaw ("The Dunn-Howland Killings") speculates that the motive behind the killing was robbery. Local white tradition fingered a Shivwit man named Toab as the killer (see Ivins, "Mystery of the Grand Canyon Solved"). Others have countered that the men were victims of the "Walapai War," provoked by white incursion into Indian territory across the Colorado River (Dobyns and

Euler, "Dunn-Howland Killings"). If so, it remains unclear why, only a year later, the Shivwits would readily admit to the killing and be eager for Powell's friendship.

18. Sumner to Frederick Dellenbaugh, 7 and 15 Feb. 1904, DelC, box 5, folder 16; Larsen, "The 'Letter.'"

19. Hamblin to Young, 30 Sept. 1870, Brigham Young papers, Church of Jesus Christ of Latter-day Saints, Historical Dept., MS 1234, reel 63, folder 11.

20. Young to Daniel Wells, 16 Dec. 1870, ibid., MS 1234, box 73, folder 33.

21. Powell, *Exploration*, 353. The council, which took place on 5 Nov., was reported by Hamblin to Erastus Snow, the Mormon chief in southern Utah. See Bleak, "Annals of the Southern Utah Mission," Vol. 2, Utah State Historical Society; and Little, *Jacob Hamblin*, 96–103.

22. *Rocky Mountain News*, 19 Nov. 1870. A few months later A.C. Osborn, of Brooklyn, New York, was seeking Powell's support for a railroad project, "the Great Southern," and hoping that Powell would "'go in' with all your forces" to secure a land grant from Congress. A.C. Osborn to Powell, 21 Feb. 1871, PS letters received, roll 1, no. 46.

23. Hamblin to Powell, 20 Dec. 1870, PS letters received, roll 1, no. 19.

24. The Thompsons lived briefly in Greenwood County, Kansas, where they raised sheep; and Harry became active in the Kansas Wool Growers and Sheep Raisers Association. By the mid-1880s none of the Powell siblings remained in Illinois.

25. Clement Powell's was the longest journal, but Jones's was the most literate. Steward revised his notes many years afterwards, so his journal lacks the immediacy of the others. All, including J.W. Powell's very brief journal, are listed separately in the bibliography.

26. Beaman's publisher, *Appleton's*, inserted subtitles that indicate what they thought the public would find most interesting in the Powell expedition: "A Wild Boat-Ride through the Cañons and Rapids," "A Visit to the Seven Cities of the Desert," and "Glimpses of Mormon Life."

27. See Hillers, *"Photographed All the Best Scenery."* Dellenbaugh's notes were deposited in the New York Public Library and incorporated into his book *A Canyon Voyage*.

28. Jones, "Journal," 34–35.

29. Beaman ("Cañon of the Colorado," 483) described their scene thus:
> Imagine a group of rough, unkempt men, surrounded by the
> wildest and grandest solitude, with all the rude appurtenances
> of camp-life about them listening to the musical rhythm of
> Hiawatha's wooing, intelligently read; and afterward, wrapped
> in our blankets upon the hard rocks, lulled to sleep and to
> dreams of the gentle Minnehaha by the roaring cataract at
> our feet, and you should may realize something of the incon-
> gruous charm attending life in the cañons.

30. Dellenbaugh, *A Canyon Voyage*, 73–74. Yet he also remembered how Powell rebuked him. One evening after supper Dellenbaugh found a brood of young magpies floundering in the sand, and he picked one of them up to show the others at the campfire how comical it looked. When he turned it loose to find its way back to the brood, Powell censured him for being cruel to animals.

31. Bishop, "Journal," 170. In the letter published in the *Bloomington Daily Pantagraph*, 7 July 1871, Bishop put it more bluntly: "[Richardson] was not rugged enough for the rough usage of the cañons."

32. Jones, "Journal," 50; Thompson, "Diary," 28–31; Hillers, *Photographed All the Best Scenery*", 54.

33. Rusho, "Francis Bishop's 1871 River Maps." Bishop's personal copies of a few sheets have survived and are in the possession of the Utah Historical Society.

34. Walter Clement Powell, "Journal," 268, 303, 321, 303.

35. "Survey of the Colorado River of the West," 42 Congress, 2 sess., House Misc. Doc. 173, 8. Powell was confused about geography at this point; the Escalante River, whose mouth he had missed on the first expedition and whose existence was unfamiliar to Mormons, lies more than thirty miles upstream of the Crossing of the Fathers.

36. Thompson, "Diary," 46.

37. Steward, "Journal," 248–49.

38. Levi Stewart had been one of the pioneers coming over the Mormon Trail from Nauvoo. Upon arriving in Kanab, he moved his family into the old fort, but on 14 Dec. 1870, a fire broke out, killing one of his wives and five of his children. He built a new two-story brick house, with picket fence, across from the town square, which still stands today. See May, "Utah Writ Small"; Robinson, *History of Kane County*; and Clarice Stewart Anderson, "A Sketch of the Life of Levi Stewart," manuscript, Utah State Historical Society.

39. Dellenbaugh, *A Canyon Voyage*, 166–67, 174–75.

40. Blanche Mace to William Culp Darrah, 17 and 23 May, 10 June 1948, DarC.

41. "Report on the Survey of the Colorado of the West," 43d Cong., 1 sess., House Misc. Doc. 265, 5. See also Olsen, "The Powell Survey Kanab Base Line."

42. Bishop, "Journal," 214.

43. Beaman's version was that he left of his own accord when he saw that Powell was going to Washington and there would be little for him to do. "Cañon of the Colorado," 548.

44. Thompson to Powell, 11 and 18 Mar. and 10 May 1872, PS letters received, roll 1, nos. 116, 119, 124.

45. Thompson described how bad weather had sabotaged the trip: "Could do nothing. Waited and tried for eighteen days—till the last was worse than the first. Got out of rations—used up horses and was forced to pull out for warmer locality." Thompson to Powell, 18 April 1872, PS letters received, roll 1, no. 121.

46. Smith, B.S., "The 1872 Diary and Plant Collections of Ellen Powell Thompson," 124. Ellen's only diary from her sojourn in Utah, it mainly covers the period from 5 March to 16 May.

47. Thompson to Powell, 10 May 1872, PS Letters received, roll 1, no. 123. Later Thompson wrote, "I had rather have Jack (if he had more experience) than Beaman Fennemore & Clem combined—Will work harder and select better more characteristic and artistic views. Clem & Fennemore do not love each other much." Thompson to Powell, 20 May 1872, ibid., no. 126.

48. Thompson to Powell, 10 May 1872, PS letters received, roll 1, no. 125.

49. A Mormon militia under the command of Captain James Andrus had earlier passed through and named this valley. See C. Gregory Crampton, "Military Reconnaissance in Southern Utah."

50. Thompson, "Diary," 83.

51. E.A. Gastman to Powell, 3 July 1872, PS letters received, roll 1, no. 90. Powell had not been receiving his museum salary after going on the federal payroll in 1871. The acting curator, Stephen A. Forbes, would take his place and go on to become one of the founders of American ecology.

52. Thomas Moran to Powell, 24 June 1872, PS letters received, roll 1, no. 98.

53. H. C. DeMotte, cit. in Watson, *The Professor Goes West*, 95.

54. The major sources for Lee's story are Juanita Brooks, *The Mountain Meadows Massacre* and *John Doyle Lee*. Lee had been part of the Powell-Brigham Young party of Sept. 1870, and was present at the consecration of Kanab. In Nov. 1871, while Powell's men were camping in House Rock Valley after their river voyage, Lee received instructions through Jacob Hamblin to make a road down to the mouth of the Paria and to settle there and help Mormon migrants crossing into Arizona. See Cleland and Brooks, vol. 2, 135–39, 175.

55. Dellenbaugh, *A Canyon Voyage*, 212. Hillers recorded that the boys spent 24 July—Pioneer Day, when Mormons celebrate their exodus into the Salt Lake valley—with the Lee family. "Had a splendid dinner, played cards and sang songs. After supper returned to camp without a change of opinion of Mormonism." Hillers, *"Photographed All the Best Scenery"*, 130.

56. Dellenbaugh to Russell Frazier, 17 June 1934, in Crampton, "F.S. Dellenbaugh of the Colorado," 231.

57. Dellenbaugh, *A Canyon Voyage*, 222.

58. Ibid., 232.

59. Walter Clement Powell, "Journal," 446.

60. Jones, "Journal," 151.

61. Hillers, *"Photographed All the Best Scenery"*, 139. River runners today call these high-water conditions "hydraulics," when whirlpools along the canyon walls became especially hellacious, adding to the danger of the rapids.

62. Dellenbaugh, *A Canyon Voyage*, 237.

63. Hillers, *"Photographed All the Best Scenery"*, 142.

64. Hamblin to Powell and Thompson, 27 Aug. 1872. PS letters received, roll 1, no. 94.

65. Powell, *Exploration*, preface.

66. Thompson to Dellenbaugh, 30 April and 23 Oct. 1902, DelC, box 5, folder 17. In another letter in the same file, dated 9 Nov. 1902, Thompson writes of Powell: "He was not all saint—he could lie on occasion—be generous one moment and contemptible mean the next."

67. Steward was another who felt some resentment; later in his life he accused Powell of having stolen his ideas and published them as his own (Steward, "Journal," 236–37). But in fact Powell did give credit to Steward in his *Report on the Geology of the Eastern Portion of the Uinta Mountains*, vi.

68. "Survey of the Colorado River of the West," 42 Cong., 2 sess. House Misc. Doc. 1735, 10; "Report of the Survey of the Colorado of the West," 42 Cong., 3 sess., House Misc. Doc. 76, 2–6.

69. Clem's letter on this trip was printed in the *Chicago Tribune*, 25 Feb. 1873, after he had returned home to Naperville. Although he complained about the filth and stench of the Hopi houses, he was more sympathetic than he had been toward Indians earlier on the Green River. Devastated by smallpox, by the "white man's greed and tyranny," and by their hostile Navajo and Apache neighbors, the Hopis, he feared, were on the way to extinction.

70. President Ulysses Grant had been reelected in November, despite the stench of scandal in his administration. Hamblin brought the news, along with a report that Boston had burned, into their camp on the Uinkaret Plateau. For the

Mormons, who were heavily Democratic in sympathies, it was not good news, for it dashed their hopes for statehood.

7. KAPURATS

1. The most valuable guide to Mormon expansion remains the historian Leonard Arrington; see his *Great Basin Kingdom*, 215–23; "Inland to Zion," 239–50; and *The Mormon Experience*, 117–226. As early as 1849 Brigham Young began to plan the economic development of the entire Great Basin and the Colorado River country.

2. An illuminating example is described by Stoffle and Evans, "Resource Competition and Population Change."

3. Metcalf, "A Precarious Balance."

4. Brigham Young, "Governor's Message to the General Assembly of the State of Deseret," 22 Jan. 1866, in Alter, "The Mormons and the Indians," 65. See also Christy, "Open Hand and Mailed Fist"; and Walker, "Toward a Reconstruction of Mormon and Indian Relations."

5. See Euler, "The Canyon Dwellers"; and "Southern Paiute Archaeology." In the 1930s animal figures, or effigies, made of split willow twigs were found in canyon caverns; these have been dated back 4,200 years before the present, well before the Anasazi arrived.

6. Euler, "The Colorado Plateaus."

7. Fowler, "Notes on the History of the Southern Paiutes and Western Shoshonis." For general introductions see Callaway, Janetski, and Stewart, "Ute," and Kelly and Fowler, "Southern Paiute."

8. JWP to U.S. Agent for Indians of Southern Utah and Nevada, 16 Jan. 1872, BIA, Nevada Superintendency, roll 540, nos. 452–54.

9. A group of white citizens in Lincoln County, Nevada, including a district attorney and a justice of the peace, reported that the Paiutes dwelling there had not received "a single dollar's worth of gratuities" paid for by the federal government in a period of four years. "They were once comfortable, in their way, and contented. Now, a more wretched set of creatures would be hard to find; and that too, as we believe, when the Government has annually made appropriations for their benefit." They pointed to the agent Fenton and his nightly entertainment as the cause. C.W. Wandell, et al., to E.G. Parker, 26 Dec. 1870, BIA, Nevada Superintendency, roll 539, nos. 1038–1041.

10. McFeely, *Grant*, 315–18; Prucha, 152–64. All the churches withdrew from the Indian agencies by 1882.

11. Henry Douglas to Ely Parker, 5 April 1870, Commissioner of Indian Affairs, letters received, roll 539, nos. 132–36.

12. "Report of the Commissioner of Indian Affairs," 42 Cong., 3 sess., House Ex. Doc. 1, part 5, 397; "Report of the Commissioner of Indian Affairs," 44 Cong., 1 sess., House Ex. Doc. 1, part 5, 526.

13. "Report of the Commissioner of Indian Affairs," 43 Cong., 1 sess., House Ex. Doc. 1, part 5, 372.

14. JWP to Senator Henry Teller, Feb. 1880, file 3751, Powell papers, NAA.

15. "Geographical and Geological Surveys West of the Mississippi," 43 Cong., 1 sess., House Report 612, 52.

16. "Indians West of the Rocky Mountains," 43 Cong., 1 sess., House Misc. Doc. 86, 9.

17. Cited in Euler, *Southern Paiute Ethnohistory*, 95.

18. See Murray, *The Modocs and Their War*, and Limerick, "Haunted America."

19. Powell recalled these circumstances to William Seeds, acting commissioner of Indian Affairs, 1 Aug. 1878, PS letters sent, roll 8, no. 105. Other whites, though sympathetic to the Indians, had the same fear. See J.F. Ray to Secretary of the Interior, Feb. 1874, Commissioner of Indian Affairs, letters received, roll 541, nos. 446–50: "[I]f some means are not taken: in my opinion there will be another Modock affair; but on a larger scale, that too at no distant day."

20. Ingalls earned his appointment through working on the political campaign of Senator Shelby Cullom of Illinois. He left behind a sick wife and came, apparently, with good intentions though no experience. While serving as special commissioner, he left his brother in charge at the agency, who proved to be an embarrassment. Ingalls eventually resigned and took a new post in the Indian Territory.

21. Ingalls to F.A. Walker, 1 Nov. 1872, "Condition of the Pi-Ute Indians," 42 Cong., 3 sess., House Exec. Doc. 66, 3.

22. JWP to Commissioner, 9 Feb. 1874, Commissioner of Indian Affairs, letters received, roll 904, nos. 610–11. See also roll 541, nos. 388–89, 901–906, for summaries of their costs, itinerary, and staff. Powell paid for two assistants out of his own pocket: Richard Komas, the Ute college student, and James C. Pilling of Washington, who became one of Powell's longtime staff members.

23. "Indians West of the Rocky Mountains," 43 Cong., 1 sess., House Misc. Doc. 86, 5.

24. The most famous Northern Paiutes in the nineteenth century were Sarah Winnemucca Hopkins, author of the book *Life among the Piutes* (1883); and Wovoka, the so-called "Indian Messiah," a medicine man who inspired the Ghost Dance religion, a revitalization movement that swept from Nevada to the Dakotas.

25. "Indians West of the Rocky Mountains," 43 Cong., 1 sess., House Misc. Doc. 86, 9.

26. "Ute, Pai-Ute, Go-si Ute, and Shoshone Indians." 43 Cong., 1 sess., House Ex. Doc. 157, 5. The early history of the Uintah reservation is discussed in O'Neil, "The Reluctant Suzerainty"; Allen and Warner, "The Gosiute Indians in Pioneer Utah"; and Lewis, *Neither Wolf Nor Dog*, 38–42.

27. Critchlow to E.S. Parker, 4 Feb. 1871, Commissioner of Indian Affairs, letters received, roll 903, nos. 137–40. However, in a later report, Critchlow estimated that only 1 percent of the reservation was tillable, one tenth of 1 percent was wooded, about half was useful for grazing, and the rest was "worthless." "Report of the Commissioner of Indian Affairs," 44 Cong., 1 sess., House Ex. Doc. 1, part 5, 861.

28. Ingalls to E.P. Smith, 16 July 1873, Commissioner of Indian Affairs, letters received, roll 904, nos. 313–15.

29. "Abstract of Report and sundry papers forwarded by U.S. Indian Agent Geo. W. Dodge," 21 June 1872, Commissioner of Indian Affairs, letters received, roll 903, nos. 627–31. A letter to Powell from a Grass Valley resident, George W. Bean, puts a more benign face on this Mormon critique of reservations. He wrote that he was "really anxious to assist in benefitting those natives" by making

it possible for them to stay in the valley. Bean to JWP, 10 Feb. 1874, PS letters received, roll 2, no. 100.

30. Geo. W. Dodge to F.A. Walker, 3 Oct. 1872, "Report of the Commissioner of Indian Affairs," 42 Cong., 3 sess., Ex. Doc. 1, 678–79; Critchlow to E.P. Smith, 25 Sept. 1873, "Report of the Commissioner of Indian Affairs," 43 Cong., 1 sess. House Ex. Doc. 1, part 5, 629.

31. "Ute, Pai-Ute, Go-si Ute, and Shoshone Indians," 4.

32. Fleming, "The Settlements on the Muddy"; Townley, "Conquered Provinces."

33. Bonelli to JWP, 9 Oct. 1873, PS letters received, roll 2, no. 14.

34. JWP to Commissioner of Indian Affairs, 6 Aug. 1873, Commissioner of Indian Affairs, letters received, Roll 904, nos. 467–70.

35. Bonelli to JWP, 9 Jan. 1873, PS letters received, roll 12, no. 12; Bonelli to Commissioner, 23 Oct. 1874, Commissioner of Indian Affairs, letters received, roll 541, nos. 152–55.

36. Henry P. Geib to Commissioner, 26 Oct. 1874, Commissioner of Indian Affairs, letters received, roll 541, nos. 216–20.

37. Ingalls to Commissioner, 25 Jan. 1874, Commission of Indian Affairs, letters received, roll 541, nos. 238–40; "Ute, Pai-Ute, Go-si Ute, and Shoshone Indians," 43 Cong., 1 sess., House Ex. Doc. 157, 30–31.

38. "Ute, Pai-Ute, Go-si Ute, and Shoshone Indians," 25.

39. JWP, "An Overland Trip to the Grand Canyon," 677.

40. JWP to William M. Seeds, 1 Aug. 1878, PS letters sent, roll 8, no. 105.

41. A superb collection of these photographs is Fowler, *The Western Photographs of John K. Hillers.*

42. See Fowler and Matley, *Material Culture of the Numa.*

43. JWP, *Anthropology of the Numa*, 123–25, 129, 163, 210, 250.

44. Ibid., 53–59.

45. "Ute, Pai-Ute, Go-si Ute, and Shoshone Indians," 26.

46. JWP, *Anthropology of the Numa*, 37–38.

47. Ibid., 51.

48. Rydell, *All the World's a Fair,* 10–37.

49. JWP to E.P. Smith, 13 July 1875, Commissioner of Indian Affairs, letters received, roll 541, nos. 965–68.

50. Trennert, "A Grand Failure"; Rivinus and Youssef, *Spencer Baird,* 124–25.

51. JWP "The Ancient Province of Tusayan," 203–4.

52. William R. McAteer to E.A. Hayt, 5 June 1878, National Archives, Pacific Region, BIA, Moqui Pueblo Agency, letters sent; J. H. Fleming to Commissioner of Indian Affairs, 21 Aug. 1882, ibid. See also Dockstader, "Hopi History, 1850–1940."

8. THE SUBLIMEST THING ON EARTH

1. The full story and claim are given in Langford, *Discovery of Yellowstone Park.*

2. Kinsey, *Thomas Moran and the Surveying of the American West,* 43–67; and Foster, *Strange Genius,* 199–239.

3. Moran to Hayden, 28 June 1873, Hayden Survey, letters received. For Moran's relationship to JWP see Wilkins, *Thomas Moran,* 72–94.

4. Bassford and Fryxell, *Home-Thoughts from Afar*, 31–32.

5. Justin Colburn, "The Colorado Canyon," *New York Times*, 4 Sept. 1873.

6. "Utah Scenery," *The Aldine*, 14. On Moran's experiences in the publishing business see Kinsey, *Thomas Moran and the Surveying of the American West*, 79–94.

7. These appeared as "The Great American Desert," *New York Times*, 15 July 1873; "The Land of Mormon," 7 Aug. 1873; and "The Colorado Canyon," 4 Sept. 1873. In the last article Colburn wrote: "The Grand Cañon is, perhaps, the least known, or, rather, known to fewer people than any of the great natural wonders of the country. Probably not more than a thousand or two white men have ever beheld it in any portion of its length, while less than half a hundred have ever visited it at its two or three most interesting points. There is not a published map that gives its proper location in any considerable part of its course. Yet, generally unknown as it is, there is no unsettled portion of our country that has been so thoroughly explored, surveyed, and measured, and so much and such careful and patient scientific investigation as the basin of the Grand Cañon. The results, both topographical and scientific, will be placed in the reach of all mankind within the next twelve months, by the publication of Major Powell's reports, or a portion of them, to the Smithsonian Institution. Furthermore, in the early part of the coming Winter the Major will give to the public, through the regular channels of the trade, a work giving a popular account of his first trip through the cañon and subsequent explorations." In fact, it would be 1875 before *Scribner's Monthly* brought out a series of three articles by Powell on his first trip.

8. Beaman continued to correspond with Powell after being dismissed, offering to make stereographs at $74–$80 per thousand and to act as Powell's visual-aids assistant in giving lectures. Later he offered to sell the negatives he had made of the Hopis on his own after leaving the survey. None of the offers seems to have been accepted. Beaman to JWP, 1 and 19 Feb. 1873; 22 April 1874, PS letters received, roll 2, nos. 3, 102.

9. Fowler, *Western Photographs of John K. Hillers*, 54–55.

10. Darrah, *Powell of the Colorado*, 182, fn. 7.

11. Moran to JWP, 16 Dec. 1873, PS letters received, roll 2, no. 38.

12. [Gilder], "Culture and Progress"; *New York Times*, 18 May 1874; *Newark Daily Advertiser*, 13 May 1874. For more critical reaction see Anderson, *Thomas Moran*, 99–100.

13. Burke, *A Philosophical Inquiry*, xxi–xxii, 36, 53.

14. Stein, *John Ruskin and Aesthetic Thought in America*, 157–85.

15. Agassiz quoted in Lurie, *Louis Agassiz*, 307.

16. One of JWP's correspondents was "the great agnostic" Robert G. Ingersoll, author of *Some Mistakes of Moses* and other works. A letter of 2 April 1877 (PS letters received, roll 5, no. 307) indicates at least a passing friendship between the Ingersoll and Powell families.

17. Moran to JWP, 4 Jan., 7 Mar., 10 May, 4 June 1875, PS Letters received, roll 3, nos. 208–9.

18. JWP, "Some Remarks on the Geological Structure of a District of Country."

19. James D. Dana to JWP, 21 April 1873, PS letters received, roll 2, no. 25.

20. JWP, "Physical Features of the Colorado Valley," 538.

21. Ibid., 390, 399. For an assessment of scientific contributions, see Hunt, "John Wesley Powell: His Influence on Geology"; and Oldroyd, *Thinking about the Earth*, 158–60.

22. JWP, "Physical Features of the Colorado Valley," 670–71.

23. Hansen, W. *Geologic Story of the Uinta Mountains,* 3.

24. JWP, "Physical Features of the Colorado Valley," 397–98, 539, 680.

25. King, "Catastrophism and Evolution," 449–70.

26. King, "The Age of the Earth." See also Merrill, *First One Hundred Years of American Geology,* 658–59.

27. King, "Catastrophism and Evolution," 470.

28. S. F. Emmons to JWP, May 9, 1872, PS letters received, roll 1, no. 86.

29. See PS letters received, roll 2, no. 47; roll 3, nos. 29, 30, 33, 37, 47.

30. Stevenson to JWP, 21 Jan. and 27 July 1876, PS letters received, roll 4, nos. 307, 311.

31. Wheeler, *Report upon United States Geographical Surveys West of the One Hundredth Meridian,* 170.

32. See Pyne, *Grove Karl Gilbert,* 95–103. Pyne draws a distinction between Powell's historical approach to geology and Gilbert's "Newtonian" search for equilibrium, which gave his thinking "a curiously conservative flavor." Gilbert sought, as did eighteenth-century philosophers, for a stable point, a balance between conflicting physical forces in the earth's crust, rather than in Darwinian evolutionary terms.

33. Clem Powell noted on 20 Nov. 1872, that "a Mr. Gilbert of Lieut. Wheeler's party in camp today. Cousin Nellie sold him a Navajo blanket quite cheap." Powell, W.C., "Journal," 472.

34. G.K. Gilbert, *Report on the Geology of the Henry Mountains.* See also Yochelson, *Scientific Ideas of G.K. Gilbert*; and Pyne, *Grove Karl Gilbert,* 83–95. Gilbert's most important western research was on ancient Lake Bonneville, the predecessor to the Great Salt Lake, and was not published until after the Powell Survey ceased to exist.

35. Gilbert, "Powell as a Geologist."

36. Ibid., 116. The most important luminary in this school was William M. Davis of Harvard University. For an example of where he took Powell's ideas see Davis, "The Lessons of the Grand Canyon."

37. As the 1876 field season approached, Dutton was stationed in Omaha, Nebraska, under General George Crook, and eager to avoid getting embroiled in conflict with the Indians, which was reaching a peak. He wrote JWP that the Indians "have 3000 warriors under Sitting Bull all ready. After the Crazy Horse affair I rather think they may give Crook a crack at them & if they do they will get licked." Actually, it was the Army that got licked a few weeks later at the Battle of the Little Big Horn. Dutton to JWP, 5 June 1876, PS letters received, roll 4, no. 89.

Dutton was given leave to join the survey, but he contracted malaria that summer and, by September, was in bad shape. "I want to look into the Grand Canon[.] I have some malaria hanging about me & when the spell is on, it makes me feel wo[e]fully—so much so that I can scarcely reason my self out of the conclusion that I am going to die. It makes me lazy inert & destroys much of my interest in work." He recovered and lived until 1912. Dutton to JWP, 17 Sept. 1876, PS letters received, roll 4, no. 92.

38. Dutton to Marcus Benjamin, 20 Dec. 1886, Marcus Benjamin papers, SA.

39. King to Dutton, Oct. 12 [18?], Clarence King letterbook, James Hague Collection, Huntington Library.

40. Dutton to JWP, 26 Sept. 1877, PS letters received, roll 5, no. 168.

41. Dutton, *Tertiary History*, 260.

42. Ibid., xvi.

43. Ibid., 141-43.

44. For an intellectual history of the Grand Canyon and the changing perception of it, see Pyne, *How the Canyon Became Grand*. Pyne argues that a generation of intellectuals (including Powell, Gilbert, and Dutton) "created" the modern view of the canyon.

45. Dutton, *Tertiary History*, 86.

46. Ibid., 143, 150.

47. Ibid., 155.

48. William Henry Holmes, "Random Records of a Lifetime, 1846–1931," Smithsonian Institution, vol. 5. National Museum of American Art.

49. Dutton, "Mount Taylor and the Zuñi Plateau," *Sixth Annual Rpt. of U.S. Geological Survey* (Washington, D.C., GPO, 1885), 111–98.

50. Letters from to JWP, 6 Mar., 12 and 24 April 1873; R.W. Gilder to JWP, 14 and 23 July 1874, PS letters received, roll 2, nos. 36, 60, 88–89, 190–93.

51. Moran to JWP, 19 Dec. 1874, PS letters received, roll, no. 174.

52. JWP, *Exploration*, 394.

53. Ibid., 397.

9. DEMOCRACY ENCOUNTERS THE DESERT

1. Schuchert and LeVene, *O.C. Marsh*, 145–66. The 1876 impeachment trial of William W. Belknap, former Secretary of War, revealed other ways in which the Indians were being cheated by the selling of trading post licenses and allowing the traders to deal dishonestly with the Indians. See McFeely, *Grant*, 430–36.

2. The GLO was first established in the Treasury Department in 1812, an indication that its early role was to raise revenue through land sales. When the Department of the Interior was created in 1849, the GLO moved in as its most important agency, and over time its role changed to reflect a growing emphasis on distributing land free to promote internal improvements and rural homesteads. It lasted until 1946, when it was reorganized as the Bureau of Land Management. For background see Gates, *History of Public Land Law Development*; Robbins, *Our Landed Heritage*; Hibbard, *A History of the Public Land Policies*; and Dunham, "Some Crucial Years of the General Land Office."

3. "Geographical and Geological Surveys West of the Mississippi," 43 Cong., 1 sess., House Rpt. 612, 16, 63.

4. The first two volumes included a study of the Pacific Northwest tribes, written by W.H. Dall and George Gibbs (1877), and a study of the California tribes by Stephen Powers (1877). Whether "practical" or not, these studies were some of the most frequently requested titles published by any of the surveys; their audience included scholars throughout western Europe as well as the United States.

5. PS Letters received, roll 6, no. 75.

6. PS Letters sent, vol. 1, box 1, nos. 137, 154, 156–58, 159–62.

7. "Geological and Geographical Surveys," 45 Cong., 2 sess., House Ex. Doc. 80, 5, 8; Merrill, *First One Hundred Years of American Geology*, 551.

8. "Geological and Geographical Surveys," 11.

9. Hewitt, *Selected Writings of Abram S. Hewitt*, 152. In this speech Hewitt criticized the recently retired senator from Nevada, William M. Stewart, for Stewart's unethical legal representation of a client embroiled in the Emma mine scandal in Utah, which bilked many British investors. Stewart left Washington in 1875, but he would be back twelve years later to become one of Powell's arch-enemies.

10. "Public Surveys," 45 Cong., 2d sess., House Misc. Doc. 55, 1.

11. A handwritten copy of Powell's instructions from Sec. Delano, dated 1 July 1874, can be found in DelC, box 5, folder 9.

12. Hayden, *Tenth Annual Report*, xxiv.

13. The rain chart is plate 5 in *Statistical Atlas of the United States*. See also Schott, *Tables and Results of the Precipitation*, where the map was originally published.

14. Henry to J.A. Garfield, *Congressional Globe*, Part 3, 26 May 1868, 2564.

15. "Geographical and Geological Surveys West of the Mississippi," 43 Cong., 1 sess., House Rpt. 612, 10.

16. *New York Tribune*, 28 April 1877.

17. Colburn, *New York Times*, 15 July 1873.

18. In 1870 Utah, with a population of 86,786, counted 4,908 farms. Only two of those were larger than 1,000 acres; the most numerous type were 20–49 acres in size (2,019), followed by the 10–19 acre farms (1,660). *Ninth Census*, 340–41.

19. Brigham Young to Orson Hyde, 9 Oct. 1848, in Rollins, "Land Policies of the United States as Applied to Utah to 1910," 243.

20. Jackson, "Righteousness and Environmental Change," 32–33.

21. See Brough, *Irrigation in Utah*; and Thomas, *Development of Institutions Under Irrigation*.

22. By 1885, Utah Territory supported one million head of sheep; by 1900, almost four million. The Mormons eventually shifted into large-scale cattle ranching. The first giant beef operation in Arizona was established by one of Brigham Young's sons on the south side of the San Francisco mountains, with thirty thousand head. See Peterson, "Grazing in Utah."

23. Arrington, et al., *Building the City of God*, 225–63; Ricks, *Forms and Methods of Early Mormon Settlement*, 105–14.

24. Dutton, *Tertiary History*, 78–79.

25. The original edition appeared as "Report on the Lands of the Arid Region," 45th Congress, 2d session, House Exec. Doc. 73. I cite here a reprint based on the 1879 edition. Because it had been rushed into print without the several authors having an opportunity to correct errors, Powell persuaded Congress to issue the revised edition in five thousand copies, including one thousand for the Senate, two thousand for the House, and two thousand for the Department of the Interior. There is little difference between the two editions.

26. JWP, *Report on the Lands of the Arid Region*, 28.

27. Ibid., 8.

28. Ibid., 53–54.

29. Ibid., 54.

30. Over a century later Utah would have only slightly more than a million acres under irrigation; Powell's estimate, therefore was too optimistic. See *Census of Agriculture: 1992*, vol. 1, part 44, p. 18.

31. The minimum of 2,560 acres later in the report became a ceiling, though he recommended adjusting it to experience.

32. *New York Tribune*, 4 April 1878. E.L. Godkin's magazine, *The Nation*, also responded with a favorable editorial, "Our Unavailable Public Lands," on 2 May 1878, one in a series on reforming the land and scientific surveys that began in 1874.

33. JWP to Garfield, undated, Garfield papers, LC, reel 35, vol. 46, nos. 59–61.

34. *Deseret News*, 1 May 1878. Peter Wigginton was born in Illinois and lived in Wisconsin before moving to Merced County, California, in 1862. He took his seat in Congress just a few weeks before Powell's report came out and was retired from office by the time the second edition appeared.

35. In the 45th Congress's 2d session, the Committee on Public Lands had twelve members — six Democrats, including the chairman, William Morrison of Illinois, and six Republicans. They came from such states as New York, Arkansas, Indiana, Pennsylvania, and Alabama. Only four represented states or territories west of the Mississippi. Clearly, the inaction of this committee should not be read as a reflection of grassroots western attitudes.

36. Huntington to JWP, 30 April 1877, PS letters received, roll 5, no. 293.

37. Smith, *Virgin Land*, book 3, shows how the agrarian myth influenced western land laws and settlement.

38. Hayden in *Report of the Commissioner of the General Land Office for the Year 1867*, 135–36; and "Preliminary Report of the United States Geological Survey of Wyoming and Portions of Contiguous Territories," 42 Cong., 2d sess., House Ex. Doc. 325, 6–8.

39. Gilbert, "Water Supply," in JWP, *Report on the Lands of the Arid Region*, 57–80.

40. Stegner, "Editor's Introduction," in ibid., xiv.

41. In his "Biographical Memoir of Clarence King," 43–44, Samuel Emmons gave King credit for this idea.

42. "Surveys of the Territories," 45 Cong., 3 sess, House Misc. Doc. 5, 16.

43. Ibid., 17.

44. Ibid.

45. Ibid., 2-5.

46. Pilling to JWP, 5 Dec. 1878, PS letters received, roll 8, no. 86.

47. Wetherby to JWP, 15 Dec. 1878, PS letters received, roll 8, no. 230; Dutton to Wetherby, ibid., 21 Nov. 1878, roll 7, no. 139.

48. Mike Foster, *Strange Genius*, 301–4. This biographer gives an excellent account of the personal maneuverings behind the academy report. There was, however, no organized conspiracy against Hayden, but there was a widespread lack of respect.

49. JWP to Garfield, 7 Mar. 1879, Garfield Papers, LC, reel 44, v. 59. See also JWP to John Atkins, 4 Mar. 1879, PS letters sent, box 2, vol. 3, no. 223, where Hayden's active opposition to the proposed reforms is pointed out.

50. *CR*, Feb. 11, 1879, 1202–3.

51. Ibid., 221.

52. Ibid., 1197, 1208.

53. Ibid., 1202, 1210.

54. Ibid., 217.

55. Ibid., 1205–6.

56. Marsh to JWP, 6 April 1879, PS letters received, roll 10, no. 12.

57. Meeker to JWP, 12 Dec. 1878, PS letters received, roll 8, no. 50.

58. Hawkins to JWP, 24 Jan. 1879, PS letters received, roll 9, no. 240.

59. Moran to JWP, 18 Feb., 9 and 17 Mar. 1879, PS letters received, roll 10, nos. 34, 36, 37; JWP to Moran, 17 March 17, 1879, PS letters sent, box 2, vol. 3, no. 280.

60. Norris to JWP, 27 May 1879, PS letters received, roll 10, no. 51. On Hague's defense of the Park, see Bartlett, *Yellowstone*, 142–43.

61. Bell to JWP, 19 April 1879, PS letters received, roll 9, no. 47.

62. King to JWP, 2 June 1879, PS letters received, roll 9, no. 316.

63. Donaldson's background is given by Gates, *History of Public Land Law Development*, 430. On Williamson's role in the Maxwell Grant, see Lamar, *The Far Southwest*, 145–46.

64. Wilkins, *Clarence King*, 236–37.

65. Julian, "Our Land Policy," 336.

66. *Salt Lake Tribune*, 16 Sept. 1879.

67. "Report of Public Lands Commission", 46 Cong., 2d sess., House Exec. Doc. 46, 377–79.

68. Ibid., 382–84.

69. Ibid., xxvi–xxviii.

70. Ibid., xxix–xxx.

71. Ibid., xxxi–xxxiii.

72. Ibid., xlvii. Contrary to Paul Gates (*History of Public Land Law Development*, 424), Powell's ideas and philosophy do not "permeate every part of the commission's report."

10. MYTHS & MAPS

1. Adams, *Democracy*, 18.

2. Ibid., 90, 182.

3. Davis, "Biographical Memoir," 11.

4. Logan, *Thirty Years in Washington*, 518–21.

5. Keim, *Washington and Its Environs*, 178–89.

6. Cited in Reps, *Washington on View*, 108, 194.

7. Green, *Washington: Capital City*, 17.

8. Jacob, *Capital Elites*, 80.

9. Boyd, *Boyd's Directory*.

10. Gallaudet's Diary, 30 Mar. 1881, Gallaudet papers, LC.

11. Garfield, *Diary*, 2: 42, 150, 322; 3: 331. See also Leech and Brown, *The Garfield Orbit*, 167.

12. Garfield, *Diary*, 4: 158–59. Brown later changed his name to Stanley-Brown. His post-Garfield career led him to Yale's Sheffield Scientific School and the world of railroads and investment banking. He died in 1941.

13. Manning, *Government in Science*, 69–70. Manning assesses King's brief tenure as "an unfinished performance," with meager accomplishments. For a more laudatory view see Nelson and Rabbitt, "The Role of Clarence King."

14. King to Emmons, 1 July 1881, Emmons papers, letters received, NA.

15. Becker to Emmons, 19 Feb. 1881, Becker papers, LC, box 15.

16. Garfield, *Diary*, 4: 554.

17. King to Becker, 17 Mar. 1881, Becker Papers, LC, box 15; Adams, *Letters of Mrs. Henry Adams*, 276; Hague to Emmons, 12 June 1880, Emmons papers, NA.

18. Stanley-Brown, "An Eventful Career," ms., DarC, 24.

19. JWP to Brown [1881], Garfield papers, LC, reel 106.

20. Newcomb, *Reminiscences of an Astronomer*, 357.

21. Congressman Charles Moses (Ga.), *CR*, 16 May 1892, 4284.

22. Mitchell, L.C., *Witnesses to a Vanishing America*, 162–63.

23. Henry had encouraged anthropology because it was popular with the public, but he had no one on his staff to organize and interpret the linguistic material that came in. In 1876 he put all of it in Powell's charge. See Noelke, "Origin and Early History of the Bureau of American Ethnology," Ph. D. diss., 20.

24. Mainly this referred to the monograph series he had launched, *Contributions to North American Ethnology*, whose volumes eventually included the following: Albert Samuel Gatschet, *The Klamath Indians of Southwestern Oregon* (1890); Stephen Powers, *Tribes of California* (1877); Lewis H. Morgan, *Houses and House Life of the American Aborigenes* (1881).

25. The best account of the Bureau's early decades is Hinsley, *Savages and Scientists*.

26. *First Annual Rpt of BE*, xiv–xv.

27. *Second Annual Rpt. of BE*, iii. The phrase "Science of Man" appeared in *Fourteenth Annual Rpt. of BE*, part 1, xxix. "The immediate purpose in instituting these researches and in organizing the Bureau in 1879," according to the later report, "was the discovery of the relations among the native American tribes, to the end that amicable groups might be gathered on reservations" (p. xxvii).

28. For biographical details on these figures see Judd, *Bureau of American Ethnology*, 10–27, 39–68. In 1894 the Bureau of Ethnology became the Bureau of American Ethnology, and as it such it endured until 1964, when it was transformed into the Smithsonian's Office of Anthropology.

29. Erminnie Smith died of a hemorrhage in 1886, when she was only forty-nine years old. A devout Christian, she credited Powell with opening her mind to more liberal views about Indian religion. See her "Myths of the Iroquois," *Second Annual Rpt. of BE*, 47–116.

30. Fletcher (1838–1923) was also active in women's groups and Indian policy reform efforts; later she founded the School of American Research in Santa Fe. See Mark, *A Stranger in Her Native Land*.

31. Noelke, "Origin and Early History of the Bureau of American Ethnology," 136–44.

32. Pilling's personal letters to Powell and others are playful and bantering, but his reputation for mean-spiritedness originated with Clarence King, who advised, "If you want to do Powell a true service, poison Pilling. On the whole shoot him; poison won't act on his system. He is of the George Hearst kind. You remember that in Tucson, Arizona, Hearst was bitten on the privates by a scorpion. The latter fell dead." King to George Becker, 4 April 1882, King letters, Huntington Library.

33. Quoted in Hinsley, *Savages and Scientists,* 274.

34. JWP, "Address of Major Powell in Memory of Professor Baird," 25–26.

35. Baird to William J. Rhees, 20 Aug. 1883, SA, RU 64, box 1.

36. JWP to Baird, 14 Aug. 1883, NAA, file 4677, 290. See also Rivinus and Youssef, *Spencer Baird of the Smithsonian,* 132–36.

37. JWP to Baird, 4 Aug.1888, NAA, file 4677, 279.

38. "Ethnology of the North American Indians," 46 Cong., 2 sess., House Misc. Doc. 35, 1–2.

39. Baird to JWP, 8 Nov. 1883, SA, RU 7081, box 11.

40. JWP, "Prehistoric Man in America," 491–92.

41. Cushing tells about his unusual experiences in "My Adventures in Zuni."

42. Cushing, *Cushing at Zuni,* 213, 216.

43. Baird to Cushing, 23 Dec. 1882, NAA, file 4677, 27, 204. The full story of the Logan raid on Indian lands is told in Raymond Brandes, "Frank Hamilton Cushing: Pioneer Americanist," Ph.D. diss., 96–107.

44. Powell recalled Cushing to Washington in March 1884. When Cushing failed to write up his research for publication, he arranged for an extended health leave. Several years later Cushing was appointed head of the Hemenway archaeological expedition to Arizona. To help steady Cushing's leadership, Powell arranged for two of his brothers-in-law, Almon Thompson and Charles Garlick (husband of Lida), to go along. But to no avail: Cushing's incompetence as a manager brought it to collapse. See Brandes, "Frank Hamilton Cushing," 116–31.

45. Utley, *Last Days of the Sioux Nation,* 60–84.

46. Mooney, "The Ghost-Dance Religion and the Sioux Outbreak of 1890," *Fourteenth Annual Rpt. of BE,* part 2, 939–44.

47. JWP, "Mythologic Philosophy, II," 63.

48. JWP, *Fourteenth Annual Rpt. of BE,* part 1, lx–lxi.

49. JWP, *Twelth Annual Rpt. of BE,* xxiii; *Fourteenth Annual Rpt. of BE,* part 1, lx; *Sixteenth Annual Rpt. of BE,* lxxxvii. The "needless loss of life" may have referred to the massacre of at least 146 Miniconjou Sioux by the Seventh Cavalry at Wounded Knee Creek on the Pine Ridge Reservation, 29 Dec. 1890.

50. Pilling to Smith, 17 Dec. 1881, NAA, BAE Records, letters sent.

51. "Annual Report of the United States Geological Survey," 46 Cong., 3 sess., House Exec. Doc. 1, 334.

52. Ibid., 389.

53. Manning, *Government in Science,* 63–64.

54. 20 U.S. Statutes at Large, 394–95 (1879).

55. King to H.G. Davis, 15 Dec. 1879, USGS letters sent, roll 1, no. 111.

56. Fred A. Prime to JWP, 19 Mar. 1881, USGS letters sent, roll 1, no. 322.

57. *CR,* 11 July 1882, 5923–30.

58. *CR,* 18 June 1882, 5445–48.

59. Paul, *Mining Frontiers of the Far West,* 127–32. Emmons's monograph *Geology and Mining Industry of Leadville* (1886) was lauded by the local newspaper for reducing "the pursuit of mining to a fixed science"; nonetheless, investors took their gains and left.

60. Hayden to JWP, 22 Mar. 1881, USGS letters received, roll 7, no. 319; 28 June 1882, roll 11, no. 734; 6 Oct. 1882, roll 13, no. 1395. For Hayden's last years see Foster, *Strange Genius,* 328–37.

61. JWP, "Organization and Plan of the United States Geological Survey."

62. Schuchert and LeVene, *O.C. Marsh,* 247.

63. JWP, "Address of Major Powell," 233.

64. JWP, "Organization and Plan of the United States Geological Survey," 93.

65. "Testimony before the Joint Committee," 49th Cong., 1st sess., Senate Misc. Doc. 82, 40.

66. Davis, "Biographical Memoir," 50.

67. JWP to John Davis, 14 Aug. 1882, USGS letters sent, roll 3, no. 301.

68. Williams to Becker, 3 June 1884, Becker papers, LC, box 15.

69. Emmons to George Becker, 1 May 1881, Becker papers, LC, box 15.

70. Emmons to Becker, 29 April 1882; Becker to Emmons, 26 April 1883, Emmons papers LC.

71. Becker to JWP, 4 July 1882, USGS letters received, roll 11, no. 746; Emmons to JWP, Nov. 1887, roll 38, no. 2148; Emmons, "Mining Work of the United States Geological Survey," 412, 414.

72. Emmons to JWP, 17 July 1884, USGS letters received, roll 23, no. 1480.

73. JWP to Becker, 29 April 1884, Becker Papers, LC, box 15.

74. "Testimony before the Joint Committee," 8.

75. A portion of his testimony was reprinted as "Administration of the Scientific Work of the General Government."

76. JWP, "Biographical Notice of Archibald Robertson Marvine," 58; "Testimony before the Joint Committee," 178.

77. "Testimony before the Joint Committee," 381.

78. Ibid., 187.

79. Ibid., 168–69.

80. Ibid., 199–200.

81. Stevenson to JWP, 11 Nov. 1884, USGS letters received, roll 23, no. 2348.

82. Williams doubted that Powell would be replaced because "everybody in the country is already connected with the Survey and therefore debarred from running against the Major. Hague says that the Survey has bought up the scientific conscience of the United States." Williams to Becker, 16 Mar. 1885, Becker papers, LC, box 16.

83. *Boston Daily Advertiser,* 16 Mar. 1885; Shaler to sister, 26 Mar. 1885, *Autobiography of Nathaniel Southgate Shaler,* 328–29. Had he become director, Shaler would likely have given the survey a more pronounced eastward tilt. His work in the survey had dealt, among other things, with the possibilities for reclaiming saltwater and fresh-water swamps along the Atlantic shore for agriculture. See Koelsch, "Nathaniel Southgate Shaler," 134.

84. *Cincinnati Commercial Gazette,* 13 April 1885.

85. Ibid., 27 July 1885. The attack continued on 31 July when the paper claimed that the Allison commission hearings, which had not yet been sent to the printer, made it clear that Powell had no legal authority to expand into the eastern states — a reading that was flatly wrong. The charge that the survey had come about by means of a conspiracy within the National Academy could only have come from one source, Edward Cope, who was Marsh's bitter rival and the lone dissident in the academy vote.

86. *New York Times,* 16 Sept. 1885.

87. [Newcomb], *Science* 4 (1885): 261, 301.

88. Dutton to Becker, 13 Oct. 1885, Becker Papers, LC, box 16.

89. Agassiz, "The Coast-Survey and 'Political Scientists'," 253–55.

90. Agassiz, born in 1835, became superintendent and president of the fabulous rich Calumet copper mine on the Michigan shore of Lake Superior. Later he backed King in his Mexican ventures, with disastrous results. See Agassiz, *Letters and Recollections*, 191–92.

91. Herbert to Agassiz, 27 Nov. 1885; Agassiz to Herbert, 14 Dec. 1885, Agassiz/Harvard.

92. Agassiz to Herbert, 2 Dec. 1885, in ""Organization of Certain Bureaus" 91–92. The total cost of all USGS publications to that point had been nearly $300,000. Abram Hewitt was not impressed: "I never contemplated the establishment of a scientific publication department for original research." Hewitt to O.C. Marsh, 3 May 1886, Marsh/Yale, roll 9, no. 144.

93. "Testimony before the Joint Committee," 1077, 1082.

94. Hague to King, 3 May 1886, Hague papers, letters sent, NA, book 2c, 59.

95. Pierce to JWP, 2 May 1886, USGS Letters received, roll 33, no. 981.

96. "Organization of Certain Bureaus," 52–53.

97. Hague to King, 10 June 1886, Hague papers, letters sent, NA, book 2c, 127; Hague to Marsh, 9 June 1886, Marsh/Yale, reel 7, no. 311.

98. Powell openly criticized Herbert's bill in the *New York Daily Tribune*, 3 May 1886. Stopping the publications would remove much of the incentive for doing good work, he warned, and would mean that "only men of wealth can be induced to share in those labors of the Survey, whose results cannot be sold to interested parties." The prohibition on discussing "theory" would have no effect, he added, because the survey did not spend its time doing that anyway.

99. "Restricting the Work and Publications of the Geological Survey," 49 Congress, 1 sess., House Rpt. 2214, 9.

100. Herbert to Marsh, 13 July 1886, Marsh/Yale, reel 9, no. 116; "Organization of Certain Bureaus," 95. Disclaiming any personal animosity, Herbert collected the names of sixty-nine geologists who had non-survey positions but still collected survey moneys, and who were thus supposedly silenced as critics. They included John Newberry (Columbia), James Hall (state geologist of New York), William Davis (Harvard), E.W. Hilgard (California), George Wright (Oberlin), and E.A. Smith (state geologist of Alabama). Once more the *Cincinnati Commercial Gazette* (4 May 1886) leaped to conclude that all these scientists had been bought for political purposes, "including our own Prof. William L. Dudley among the sinecures."

101. *CR*, 29 June 1886, 6300.

102. Ibid., 6301.

103. Herbert to Agassiz, 5 July 1885, Agassiz/Harvard.

104. Powell's several friends at Harvard included Shaler, Davis, Pumpelly, and Samuel Garman, who was Agassiz's assistant at the Museum of Comparative Zoology. Garman had been part of Powell's expedition to Colorado in summer 1868 and had climbed Long's Peak with him (see chap. 4).

105. The anniversary, which was observed on 5–8 Nov. 1886, is described in Samuel Eliot Morison, *Three Centuries of Harvard, 1636–1936* (Cambridge, Mass.: Harvard University Press, 1936), 361–64.

11. REDEEMING THE EARTH

1. Dutton, in *Twenty-fifth Anniversary of the Cosmos Club*, 29.

2. Ibid., 26–27.

3. Powell mss., NAA, file 4453.

4. Washburn, *Cosmos Club*, 270.

5. Gilbert, in *Twenty-fifth Anniversary of the Cosmos Club*, 40.

6. Lamb, "Story of the Anthropological Society of Washington."

7. Bryan, *National Geographic Society*, 24–25.

8. Powell mss., NAA, file 4453.

9. Marsh, in Youmans, *Herbert Spencer on the Americans*, 49–50.

10. JWP, "Evolution of Music," 5.

11. JWP, "Evolution of Music," 2; "Three Methods of Evolution," xxx.

12. JWP, "Sketch of Lewis H. Morgan," 115.

13. Ibid., 117.

14. L.H. Morgan to JWP, 19 Feb. 1877, Morgan/Rochester, box 8; JWP to L.H. Morgan, 23 May and 17 April 1880, box 9.

15. L.H. Morgan, *Ancient Society*, 12, 19.

16. Ibid., 561–62.

17. JWP, "Sketch of Lewis H. Morgan," 121; L.H. Morgan to JWP, 3 Nov. 1880, Morgan/Rochester, box 10.

18. Morgan to JWP, 11 May 1881, Morgan/Rochester, box 10.

19. Ward, *Glimpses of the Cosmos*, vol. 2, 235–42.

20. Ward, "Sketch of Professor John W. Powell," 390, 397.

21. Ward, *Glimpses of the Cosmos*, vol. 3, 204.

22. Ward, *Dynamic Sociology*, vol. 1, dedication page.

23. Ibid., vol. 2, 5.

24. Ibid., 89.

25. Ibid., 74.

26. Ibid., 89.

27. Ibid., 583; *Glimpses of the Cosmos*, vol. 2, 113.

28. JWP, "Ward's Dynamic Sociology, Part 4," 226.

29. Burrow, *Evolution and Society*, 179–227.

30. After visiting him in Washington, Spencer sent Powell a note: "Take warning against doing too much, and by way of precaution abandon that telephone in your bed-room that you told me of." 2 July [1883?], Powell mss., NAA, file 4024c.

31. Warman, "Catalogue of the Published Writings of John Wesley Powell."

32. JWP, "The Larger Import of Scientific Education," 454.

33. JWP, "Are Our Indians Becoming Extinct?" 343.

34. "Address of Major Powell," *American Institute of Mining Engineers*, 235–36.

35. JWP, "Discourse on the Philosophy of the North American Indians," 253–54.

36. JWP, "Three Methods of Evolution," xxxi–xxxii.

37. JWP, "Discourse on the Philosophy of the North American Indians," 261–62.

38. JWP, "Prehistoric Man in America," 503.

39. JWP, "Darwin's Contributions to Philosophy," 62.

40. JWP, "Ward's Dynamic Sociology, part 1," 48; "Problems of American Archaeology," 638.

41. JWP, "Relation of Primitive Peoples to Environment," 632–33.

42. JWP, "The Larger Import of Scientific Education," 454–55; "The Humanities," 411, Morgan, *Ancient Society*, 38.

43. JWP, "Ward's Dynamic Sociology, part 4," 226.

44. JWP to Boas, 7 June and 3 July 1895; Boas to JWP, 19 June, Franz Boas papers, American Philosophical Society.

45. Boas, "Museums of Ethnology: Reply," 614.

46. JWP, "Evolution of Music," 4.

47. JWP, "Three Methods of Evolution," l.

48. Welling, "The Law of Malthus."

49. JWP, "Three Methods of Evolution," lii.

50. JWP, "Competition as a Factor," 305.

51. JWP, "Three Methods of Evolution," xliii.

52. JWP, "From Savagery to Barbarism," 195–96.

53. "Address of Major Powell," *American Institute of Mining Engineers*, 234–35.

54. JWP, "Competition as a Factor," 320.

55. JWP, "Competition as a Factor," 321.

56. Comments by Powell, 15 Mar. 1881, *Anthropological Society of Washington, Trans.* vol. 1 (Washington: Judd & Detweiler, 1882), 43.

57. JWP, "From Savagery to Barbarism," 196.

58. JWP, "Mythologic Philosophy, part 2," 66.

59. JWP, "The Larger Import of Scientific Education," 452–56.

60. JWP, "Darwin's Contributions to Philosophy," 70.

61. JWP, "From Barbarism to Civilization," 103.

62. JWP, "Competition in Human Evolution," 323.

63. JWP, "The Five Books of History," 161.

12. THE PROBLEM OF THE WEST

1. *New York Tribune*, 18 Aug. 1889.

2. Stanton, "Denver, Colorado Canon & Pacific Railroad Project."

3. JWP, "National Agencies for Scientific Research, part 1," 294.

4. Hague, "The Yellowstone Park as a Game Reservation," typescript, Hague papers, NA.

5. JWP to Teller, 16 Feb. 1888, USGS letters sent, roll 11, no. 467.

6. *Report on Agriculture by Irrigation in the Western Part of the United States at the Eleventh Census: 1890* (Washington: GPO, 1894), vii; "Reservoirs for the Storage of Water," 50 Cong., 1 sess., Sen. Ex. Doc. 163, 5.

7. "Sundry Civil Bill," 50 Cong., 1 sess., Sen. Rpt. 1814, 66–67.

8. *CR*, 30 July 1888, 7014–7016.

9. Ibid., 7021–7022.

10. Ibid., 11 Sept. 1888, 8504–8518.

11. Dutton to JWP, 21 Dec. 1888, USGS letters received, roll 25, no. 2705.

12. *Washington Post*, 25 May 1902.

13. JWP to Dutton, 28 May 1889, USGS letters sent, roll 14, no. 263.

14. *USGS Tenth Annual Rpt.:* part 2—*Irrigation*, viii.

15. Hague to Becker, 3 Sept. 1888, 19 April 1889; Emmons to Becker, 11 May 1889, Becker papers, LC, box 16.

16. "Major Powell's Address," *Official Report of First Constitutional Convention of North Dakota*, 410–12.

17. *Proceeding and Debate of the Constitutional Convention [Montana]*, 920–23.

18. Stewart to JWP, 28 Oct. 1889, Stewart/Nevada, letterbook 2, no. 282.

19. Noble to Gov. G.L. Shoup, 3 Aug. 1889, *CR*, 26 July 1890, 7781.

20. See the full record of correspondence reprinted in *CR*, 26 July, 1896, 7778–81.

21. Marsh, *Man and Nature*, 35.

22. Ibid., 51–52.

23. Hilgard to Morrow, 20 Oct. 1887, Hilgard papers, Bancroft Library, outgoing letters, box 2; Morrow to Hilgard, 13 Dec. 1887, incoming letters, box 16; Hilgard to JWP, 12 Nov. 1887, letterpress, vol. 14

24. Alvord to Hilgard, 11 Feb. 1889, Hilgard papers, Bancroft Library, incoming letters, box 4.

25. Marsh, *Man and Nature*, 280

26. Sargent, "Mountain Reservoirs and Irrigation," 313.

27. Shinn, "The Forest," 502.

28. JWP, *Report on the Lands of the Arid Region*, 17; "Non-Irrigable Lands," 919–20.

29. See "J.W. Powell-Report [1890]," typescript, Irrigation Survey records, NA, box 1. This document appear to be a press release for western newspapers.

30. Edgar Ensign to JWP, 14 Sept. 1889, USGS letters received, roll 46, no. 2672; Fernow, cit. by Rodgers, *Bernhard Eduard Fernow*, 154.

31. Sargent, "The Lesson of Conemaugh, 422.

32. JWP, Ibid., 153.

33. JWP, Ibid., 156.

34. Sargent, "Mountain Reservoirs and Irrigation," 313; "Forests and Irrigation," 293.

35. McGee to JWP, 10, 18, 22 Sept. 1885, McGee papers, LC, box 21.

36. Frazer, "A Short History of the Origin and Acts of the International Congress of Geologists," and "The Geologists' Congress"; "International Congress of Geologists"; Powell, "Communication;" Gilbert, "The Work of the International Congress of Geologists."

37. JWP to Cope, 31 May 1883, USGS letters sent, roll 4, no. 323; Osborn, *Cope*, 362, 368–69, 384–45.

38. *New York Herald*, 12 Jan. 1890. The articles continued on 13, 19, 20, and 26 Jan.

39. *New York Herald*, 12 Jan. 1890.

40. Ibid.

41. "Report of Special Committee," 51 Cong., 1 sess., Sen. Rpt. 928, part 5, 21.

42. JWP, "Institutions for the Arid Lands," 115. See also "J.W. Powell-Report [1890]," typescript, Irrigation Survey records, NA, box 1.

43. JWP, "Institutions for the Arid Lands," 113–14.

44. JWP, Ibid., 116.

45. Jonathan Periam, *A History of the Origin, Aims, and Progress of the Farmers' Movement*, 377-81; "Davis Is Dead," *Topeka State Journal*, 2 Aug. 1901.

46. "Platform of the People's Party," USGS letters received, roll 51, no. 188; *CR*, 1 Nov. 1893, appendix, 550.

47. "Report of Special Committee," part 5, 85–93.

48. Ibid., 90, 95.

49. Ibid., 138, 142, 146.

50. Ibid., 169, 185–86.

51. Ibid., part 1, 135.

52. "Irrigation Survey," 51 Congress, 1 sess, Sen. Ex. Doc. 141, 1.

53. *Washington Star* interview reprinted in *CR*, 29 May 1890, 5419.

54. Fumey to JWP, 26 Aug. 1889, USGS letters received, roll 46, no. 2688.

55. Stewart to Huntington, 27 Mar. 1889, Stewart/Nevada, box 10, letterbook 1, 557.

56. JWP to G.G. Shaver, 7 Jan. 1890, USGS letters sent, roll 16, no. 94; West to JWP to West, 21 Feb. 1890, USGS letters received, roll 48, no. 464; JWP to Proctor, 14 Feb. 1890, letters sent, roll 16, no. 233.

57. "J.W. Powell-Report [1890]," typescript, Irrigation Survey records, NA, box 1.

58. See Stewart/Nevada, outgoing letters, box 9, letterbook 4, nos. 177, 181, 209, 264, 266, 282.

59. Stewart to Congess, 29 Aug. 1890, Stewart/Nevada, outgoing letters, box 9, letterbook 4, no. 476.

60. Typescript, undated, Powell mss, NAA, file 4024e.

61. JWP to Mead, 9 June 1890, USGS letters sent, roll 17, no. 208.

62. "Sundry Civil Appropriation Bill," 51 Congress, 1 sess., Sen. Rpt. 1466, 112–13, 118–22.

63. *CR*, appendix, 16 July 1890, 720-21.

64. Hague to Iddings, 19 and 27 Aug. 1890, Hague papers, NA, book 2F, 278, 290.

65. JWP to E. Bach, 29 Sept. 1890, USGS letters sent, roll 18, no. 151.

66. Letters from JWP to Morgan, USGS letters sent, roll 19, nos. 77, 81, 84, 86, 90, 92, 98.

67. JWP to Department of Domains [Russia], 17 April 1891, USGS letters sent, roll 19, no. 395.

68. JWP to Secretary of the Interior, 21 and 23 Mar. 1891, USGS letters sent, roll 11, nos. 293–307.

69. Powell mss., personal receipts, NAA, file 4453.

70. "International Congress of Geologists," 356.

71. Margerie to JWP, USGS letters received, 21 Feb. 1890, roll 48, no. 588.

72. For correspondence between Powell and the Cuvier Institute see USGS letters sent, roll 21, no. 222.

73. Marcou, "The Geological Map of the United States and the United States Geological Survey" (Cambridge, Mass.: privately printed, 1892).

74. JWP, "National Agencies for Scientific Research," 422–25.

75. Ibid., 668, 670.

76. Ibid., 672–73.

77. Hague to Dutton, 26 March 1892; Hague to Marsh, 19 May; Hague to Williams, 28 May, Hague papers, NA, box 3B, 230, box 2G, 186, 206.

78. Outhwaite to Marsh, 19 and 25 May 19 1892, Marsh/Yale, reel 13, nos. 54 and 58.

79. Marsh to Outhwaite, 30 April 1892, Marsh papers, reel 13, no. 51; Hague to Dutton, 11 May 1892, Hague papers, box 3B, 266.

80. *CR*, 16 May 1892, 4285; 18 May, 4396, 4401; 19 May, 4434-36. Hooker lost his left arm fighting for the Confederacy. After he and Powell met in Washington in later years, they divided up the pairs of gloves they bought — right-handed gloves going to Hooker, left-handed gloves going to Powell.

81. *CR*, 16 May 1892, 4285.

82. Stanton, *Colorado River Controversies*, 109–10.

83. Ibid., 110-11.

84. JWP to Allison, 24 June 1892, USGS letters sent, roll 22, no. 363.

85. Stewart to Dwight, 21 June 1892, Marsh/Yale, reel 16, 60.

86. *CR*, 8 July 1892, 5889.

87. Ibid., 5888.

88. Ibid., 5890.

89. Ibid., 5889–90.

90. Hague to Marsh, 20 July 1892, Marsh/Yale, reel 7, no. 329.

91. King to Hay, 30 July 1892, Hay papers, John Hay Library, Brown University.

92. Compton to JWP, 22 July 1892, USGS Letters received, roll 58, no. 1487.

93. JWP to Bell, 14 Sept. 1892, Alexander Graham Bell family papers, LC, box 127.

94. Walcott to Marsh, 26 Nov. 1892, Marsh/Yale, reel 17, no. 95; Walcott to Van Hise, 10 Dec. 1892, Van Hise papers, State Historical Society of Wisconsin.

95. Emmons to Marsh, 25 Dec. 1892, Marsh/Yale, reel 5, no. 4.

96. Hague to Marsh, 11 Mar. 1893, ibid., reel 7, no. 331.

97. Hague to Marsh, 2 April 1893, ibid., reel 7, no. 334.

98. Adams, *Education of Henry Adams*, 331–45; Turner, "The Significance of the Frontier," in Billington, ed., *Frontier and Section*, 37–62.

99. Holmes to his wife, 27 July 1893, "Random Records of a Lifetime," vol. 7, Smithsonian Institution, National Museum of American Art.

100. Powell to Skiff, 16 Jan. and 22 Mar. 1893, USGS letters sent, roll 24, nos. 30, 149.

101. Smythe, *The Conquest of Arid America*, 265–67.

102. A reporter summed up the talk's contents in the *Los Angeles Times*, 12 Oct. 1893.

103. Stanton, "Transportation Problem," 88.

104. Turner, "Problem of the West," in Billington, ed., *Frontier and Section*, 63, 75.

105. JWP, address, *Official Report of the International Irrigation Congress*, 109, 112.

106. Newell to Rizer, 14 Oct. 1893, USGS letters received, roll 60, no. 1884.

107. For a summary of Powell's remarks, see Hay, "Water Supply on the Great Plains."

108. According to the most recent data, the seventeen western states irrigated 39,074,000 acres. (*1992 Census of Agriculture*, vol. 1, part 51, p. 8.)

109. Mead, letter to editor, *Irrigation Age* 6 (1894): 4.

110. JWP, "Water Supplies in the Arid Region"; and "Ownership of Lands in the Arid Region."

111. Arthur Powell Davis, "The Public Domain in Its Social Aspect," 17.

112. JWP, "Speech before New York Farmers," 75–76.

13. JOURNEY'S END

1. Spencer, *Social Statics*, 80.

2. JWP to Cleveland, 8 May 1894, Department of Interior Appointment Papers, NA, RG 48, file 226–1881, box 159.

3. Rizer to Bourke, 16 May 1894, USGS letters sent, roll 26, no. 272.

4. Letter dated 30 June 1894, *Fifteenth Annual Rpt. of the USGS*, 7.

5. See Yochelson, *Charles Dolittle Walcott*, 293–96.

6. Ward, *Glimpses of the Cosmos*, vol. 6, 218. On 11 May 1894 Emmons complained to Becker, "Walcott has no education, & knows little geology, but he . . . has the confidence of a government mule." Emmons papers, LC, box 26.

7. In 1896 Powell returned to the survey, briefly and with pomp and ceremony, to meet the famed Scottish geologist Sir Archibald Geikie and to accompany him on an official field trip to Harper's Ferry, Virginia.

8. McGee to Emma Powell, 19 Nov. 1902, NAA, BAE Records, letters sent by W.J. McGee, nos. 417–18.

9. Committee Report, Records relating to the investigation of the BAE, 1903, NAA, BAE Records.

10. McGee, "Trend of Human Progress," 413.

11. Spitzka, "Study of the Brain of Powell."

12. Notes of an interview with Otis Marston, Marston Collection, Huntington Library, box 190, folder 41.

13. JWP, "Indians of North America," 544.

14. JWP, "Are Our Indians Becoming Extinct?"

15. JWP, "Proper Training and the Future of the Indians."

16. JWP to various correspondents, 1898–99, NAA, Powell letterbook, file 3322.

17. Thompson to Dellenbaugh, 21 Oct. 1902, DelC, box 5, folder 17.

18. Arthur P. Davis to Dellenbaugh, 10 June 1922, DelC, box 4, folder 1.

19. Mae Jackson to William C. Darrah, 2 July 1946, DarC, box 3.

20. See the Thompson file, National American Woman Suffrage Association papers, New York Public Library, box 1.

21. See *Aurora Evening Post*, 28 Nov. 1894.

22. W. B. Powell quoted in *Washington Evening Star*, 27 June 1900. See also "Public Schools of the District of Columbia," 56 Cong., 1 sess., Senate Rpt. 711.

23. Major Powell explained that "any political or religious excitement has affected [Walter] very much for the past 12 years. At one time, perhaps for two years he claimed to be a prophet. I never knew claimant to be dangerous to any one except once when I was afraid he would kill one of my men. . . . [He] has had occasional attacks of nervous excitement under which he would wander away from home and in solitude as far as possible from these attacks he would recover by exhaustion and would return to his home." Deposition taken at Walter's pension hearing, 1896, Veterans Records, NA, RG 15, no. 922,237.

24. Mae Jackson to William Darrah, 2 Oct. 1946, DarC, box 3.

25. See *Corona Daily Independent*, 7 Mar. 1927.

26. JWP to Maud Powell, 24 Oct. 1899, NAA, Powell letterbook, file 3322.

27. An annotated copy of Powell's *National Geographic* essays is in the Turner papers at the Huntington Library. In his *Frederick Jackson Turner*, Ray Allen

Billington points out that Turner was using the Geological Survey maps to draw his own sectional divisions immediately before reading Powell (526, fn. 11).

28. JWP, *Truth and Error*, 350, 405.

29. Ward, *Glimpses of the Cosmos*, vol. 6, 51–52.

30. Ward, "Truth and Error," 136.

31. Brooks, "Truth and Error," 125–26.

32. Powell, "Reply to Critics," 260–61.

33. Ward, *Glimpses of the Cosmos*, vol. 6, 52–53.

34. Powell, "Relation of Primitive Peoples to Environment," 629–31.

35. Powell, "Technology," 326.

36. Powell, "Sociology," 742.

37. Powell to McGee, 2 and 9 Aug. 1895, NAA, BAE Records, letters received.

38. Advertising brochure cited in Jane Hooper and Sunny Toulmin, "Memories of Haven Colony, Brooklin," typescript in Friend Memorial Library, Brooklin, Maine.

39. JWP to McGee, 26 July 1898, NAA, BAE Records, letters received.

40. Will Freethey to William Culp Darrah, 2 Sept. 1947, DarC.

41. JWP to J. Freethey, 4 Nov. 1899, NAA, Powell letterbook, file 3322.

42. Eric Parson's memoir, Feb. 1947, DarC, box 3.

43. Holmes to his wife, 11 Mar. 1900, "Random Records of a Lifetime," vol. 8, Smithsonian Institution, National Museum of American Art.

44. JWP, "Archaeology," 24. His other philosophical poems, published in *The Monist* and *The Open Court*, include "Immortality," "The Soul," "and "The Books of Primeval History."

45. Letters of 8 and 29 April 1901, NAA, Powell letterbook, file 3322.

46. JWP to F. E. Shellaberger, 21 Feb. 1902, NAA, Powell letterbook, file 3322.

47. JWP, "The Scientific Explorer," 32.

48. JWP to Dellenbaugh, 21 July 1900; 8 April 1901, 6 Jan. 1902, DelC, box 5, folder 9.

49. Prentiss to Langley, 27 Jan. 1902, DarC.

50. Thompson to Dellenbaugh, 10 Mar. 1902, DelC, box 5, folder 17. In 1907 Robert Stanton found Sumner's journal tucked away in Powell's office papers.

51. Thompson to Dellenbaugh, 30 April 1902, DelC, box 5, folder 17.

52. Garland, *Roadside Meetings*, 362–63.

53. *CR*, 1 Mar. 1902, 2278.

54. "In Memory of John Wesley Powell."

55. Emma Powell to Bell, 9 Dec. 1902, Bell Family papers, LC, container 127.

56. *Denver Times*, 24 Sept. 1902; *Washington Post*, 25 Sept. and 5 Oct. 1902.

57. Grosvenor, "John Wesley Powell," 393; Brewer, "John Wesley Powell," 380; Gilbert, "John Wesley Powell," 562; Dall, "John Wesley Powell," 307–8.

58. "John Wesley Powell: Proceedings of a Meeting," 99–129. Appended to these remarks was P.C. Warman's catalog of Powell's published writings (pp. 131–87).

59. Thompson to Dellenbaugh, 14 Feb. 1903, DelC, box 5, folder 17.

Bibliography

ABBREVIATIONS

BAE   Bureau of American Ethnology
BE   Bureau of Ethnology
BIA   Bureau of Indian Affairs
CR   *Congressional Record*
DarC   Darrah collection, Utah State Historical Society
DelC   Dellenbaugh Collection, University of Arizona
GPO   Government Printing Office
JArH   *Journal of Arizona History*
JWP   John Wesley Powell
LC   Library of Congress
NAA   National Anthropological Archives
NA   National Archives
PS   Powell Survey
RG   Record Group
SA   Smithsonian Archives
UHQ   *Utah Historical Quarterly*
USGS   United States Geological Survey

MANUSCRIPT COLLECTIONS

American Philosophical Society Library
      Franz Boas papers
      John Wesley Powell papers
Arizona Historical Society
      Frederick Dellenbaugh collection
Birmingham Public Library, Birmingham, Warwickshire, U.K.
      Parish register for St. Martin's
Brown University, John Hay Library
      John Hay papers
      Lester Ward papers

Church of Jesus Christ of Latter-day Saints, Historical Department
    Brigham Young papers
    Jacob Hamblin's journal
Denver Public Library
    William Newton Byers diary
Detroit Public Library
    Burton Historical Collection
East Riding County Archive Office, Beverley, Yorkshire, U.K.
    Parish registers
Grand Canyon National Park Museum
    John Wesley Powell collection
    Walter Clement Powell journal
Harvard University libraries
    Alexander Agassiz papers
    Nathaniel Shaler papers
Huntington Library
    Otis Marston collection
    Clarence King letters (in James D. Hague papers)
    Samuel Adams's journal
    Henry Ellsworth Wood papers
    Bailey Willis papers
Illinois State Archives
    Adjutant General records
Illinois State University, Milner Library
    Samuel Garman letters
Illinois Wesleyan University Library
    John Wesley Powell collection
Kansas State Historical Society
    Lewis W. Keplinger letters
Library of Congress, Manuscripts Division
    Simon Newcomb papers
    George Becker papers
    Alexander Graham Bell papers
    Henry L. Dawes papers
    S.F. Emmons papers
    James Garfield papers
    Benjamin Harrison papers
    Jed Hotchkiss letterbooks
    Anita Newcomb McGee papers
    William John McGee papers
    Gifford Pinchot papers
    Carl Schurz papers
National Archives I
    Bureau of Indian Affairs, RG 75:
        Commissioner of Indian Affairs, Letters Received (microfilm M234)
        Nevada and Utah Superintendency (microfilm M234)
        Veterans Records, RG 15

National Archives II
    Geological Survey, RG 57:
        S.F. Emmon papers, letters received, 1880–85
        Arnold Hague papers
        Hayden Survey, letters received
        Powell Irrigation Survey records
        Powell Survey, letters received (microfilm M156)
        Powell Survey, letters sent, Entry 6, Boxes 1–2
        Records concerning Othniel Charles Marsh, 1885–99
        USGS, letters sent, 1879–95 (microfilm M152)
        USGS, letters received, 1879–1901 (microfilm M590)
National Archives, Pacific Region
    Bureau of Indian Affairs, RG 75:
        Moqui Pueblo Agency records
Nevada Historical Society
    William M. Stewart papers
New York Public Library
    Almon Harris Thompson's journals
    Robert Brewster Stanton papers
    Frederick Samuel Dellenbaugh collection
    National American Woman Suffrage Association papers
New York State Library & State Archives
    James Hall papers
Oberlin College Library
    College records
Shropshire Records and Research Centre, Shrewsbury,
Shropshire, U.K.
    Parish registers for Shrewsbury and Ludlow
Smithsonian Institution, Archives
    Office of the Secretary records
    Joseph Henry papers
    Spencer Fullerton Baird papers
    Samuel P. Langley papers
    William H. Dall papers
    Marcus Benjamin papers
    William Henry Holmes papers
    Philosophical Society of Washington records
    George Vasey papers
    Washington Academy of Sciences records
Smithsonian Institution, National Anthropological Archives
    Anthropological Society of Washington records
    Bureau of American Ethnology records
    John Wesley Powell papers
    Spencer Fullerton Baird papers
Smithsonian Institution, National Museum of American Art
    William Henry Holmes, "Random Records of a Lifetime,
    1846–1931"

Southwest Museum Library
    Frank Hamilton Cushing papers
    Frederick W. Hodge papers
Stanford University Library
    Wallace Stegner papers
State Historical Society of Wisconsin
    Charles R. Van Hise papers
University of Arizona, Special Collections
    Frederick Samuel Dellenbaugh collection
University of California at Berkeley, Bancroft Library
    Eugene Hilgard papers
University of Rochester, Rhees Library
    Lewis Henry Morgan papers
University of Wyoming, American Heritage Center
    Joseph Carey papers
    Elwood Mead papers
    Francis Warren papers
Utah State Historical Society
    James G. Bleak, "Annals of the Southern Utah Mission"
    William Culp Darrah collection
Wheaton College Library
    College records
Wyoming State Library
    Elwood Mead papers
Yale University, University Archives
    Othniel C. Marsh papers

BOOKS

Abbott, Carl, Stephen Leonard, and David McComb. *Colorado: A History of the Centennial State.* 3rd ed. Niwot: Univ. Press of Colorado, 1994.

Adams, Henry. *Democracy: A Novel.* 1880; New York: Meridian, 1994.

———. *The Education of Henry Adams.* Boston: Houghton Mifflin, 1918.

Adams, Marian. *The Letters of Mrs. Henry Adams, 1865–1883.* Edited by Ward Thoron. Boston: Little, Brown, 1936.

Agassiz, Alexander. *Letters and Recollections of Alexander Agassiz.* Edited by George R. Agassiz. Boston: Houghton Mifflin, 1913.

Alexander, Thomas G. *A Clash of Interests: Interior Department and Mountain West, 1863–96.* Provo: Brigham Young Univ. Press, 1977.

Anderson, Nancy, et al. *Thomas Moran.* Washington: National Gallery of Art, and New Haven: Yale Univ. Press, 1997.

Annual Catalogue of the Officers and Students of Oberlin College for the College Year 1859–1860. Oberlin, Ohio, 1859.

Anthropological and Biological Societies of Washington. *The Saturday Lectures.* Washington, D.C.: Judd & Detweiler, 1882.

Anthropological Society of Washington, Trans. 1–3 (1878–1885).

Arrington, Leonard J. *Brigham Young: American Moses.* New York: Alfred A. Knopf, 1985.

————. *Great Basin Kingdom: An Economic History of the Latter-day Saints, 1830–1900.* Cambridge: Harvard Univ. Press, 1958.

————., and Davis Bitton. *The Mormon Experience: A History of the Latter-day Saints.* New York: Vintage Books, 1979.

————., Feramorz Y. Fox, and Dean L. May. *Building the City of God: Community and Cooperation among the Mormons.* 2nd ed. Urbana: Univ. of Illinois Press, 1992.

Ashley, William H. *The West of William H. Ashley.* Edited by Dale L. Morgan. Denver: Old West Publishing Co., 1964.

Aton, James M. *Inventing John Wesley Powell: The Major, His Admirers, and Cash-Register Dams in the Colorado River Basin.* Cedar City: Southern Utah State College, 1988.

————. *John Wesley Powell.* Boise: Boise State Univ. Press, 1994.

Baars, Donald L., and Rex C. Buchanan. *The Canyon Revisited: A Rephotography of the Grand Canyon, 1923/1991.* Salt Lake City: Univ. of Utah Press, 1994.

Bailey, Paul. *Jacob Hamblin, Buckskin Apostle.* Los Angeles: Westerlore Press, 1948.

Bailey, Philip James. *Festus: A Poem.* 5th ed. Boston: B.B. Mussey, 1847.

Bain, David Haward. *Empire Express: Building the First Transcontinental Railroad.* New York: Viking, 1999.

Bannister, Robert C. *Social Darwinism: Science and Myth in Anglo-American Social Thought.* Philadelphia: Temple Univ. Press, 1979.

Barnes, Gilbert H. *The Anti-Slavery Impulse, 1830–1844.* Reprint. New York: Harcourt, Brace & World, 1964.

Bartlett, Richard A. *Great Surveys of the American West.* Norman: Univ. of Oklahoma Press, 1962.

————. *Yellowstone: A Wilderness Besieged.* Tucson: Univ. of Arizona Press, 1985.

Bass, William Wallace. *Adventures in the Canyons of the Colorado by Two of Its Earliest Explorers, James White and W.W. Hawkins.* Grand Canyon, Ariz., 1920.

Bassford, Amy O., and Fritiof Fryxell, eds. *Home-Thoughts from Afar: Letters of Thomas Moran to Mary Nimmo Moran.* East Hampton, N.Y., Free Library, 1967.

Bates, Ralph S. *Scientific Societies in the United States.* 3rd ed. Cambridge: MIT Press, 1965.

Battle's Hull Directory for the Year 1810–1811. 4th ed. Hull, 1810.

Battle's New Directory, for Kingston-upon-Hull. 6th ed. Hull, 1817.

Beadle, J. H. *The Undeveloped West: or, Five Years in the Territories.* Philadelphia: National Publishing Co., 1873.

————. *Western Wilds, and the Men Who Redeem Them.* Cincinnati: Jones Brothers, 1878.

Bechtel, Paul M. *Wheaton College: A Heritage Remembered, 1860–1984.* Wheaton: H. Shaw, 1984.

Beckwith, Albert Clayton. *History of Walworth County, Wisconsin.* 2 vols. Indianapolis: Bowen, 1912.

Beckwith, E. G. *Report of Exploration of a Route for the Pacific Railroad, Near the 38th and 39th Parallels of Latitude, from the Mouth of the Kansas to Sevier River, in the Great Basin.* Washington, D.C.: A.O.P. Nicholson, 1855.

Bell, William A. *New Tracks in North America: A Journal of Travel and Adventure Whilst Engaged in the Survey for a Southern Railroad to the Pacific Ocean during 1867–8.* 2nd ed. 2 vols. London: Chapman and Hall, 1870.

Bieder, Robert E. *Science Encounters the Indian, 1820–1880: The Early Years of American Ethnology.* Norman: Univ. of Oklahoma Press, 1986.

Billington, Ray Allan. *Frederick Jackson Turner.* New York: Oxford Univ. Press, 1973.

Birney, James Gillespie. *Letters of James Gillespie Birney, 1831–1857.* 2 vols. Edited by Dwight L. Dumond. New York: D. Appleton-Century Co., 1938.

Boas, Franz. *Introduction to Handbook of American Indian Languages;* and John W. Powell. *Indian Linguistic Families of America North of Mexico.* Edited by Preston Holder. Lincoln: Univ. of Nebraska Press, 1966.

———. *The Mind of Primitive Man.* New York: Macmillan, 1924.

Boller, Paul F. Jr. *American Thought in Transition: The Impact of Evolutionary Naturalism, 1865–1900.* Chicago: Rand McNally, 1969.

Bolton, Herbert E. *Pageant in the Wilderness: The Story of the Escalante Expedition to the Interior Basin, 1776.* Salt Lake City: Utah State Historical Society, 1950.

Bowler, Peter J. *Evolution: The History of an Idea.* Berkeley: Univ. of California Press, 1984.

———. *Fossils and Progress: Paleontology and the Idea of Progressive Evolution in the Nineteenth Century.* New York: Science History Publications, 1976.

Bowles, Samuel. *Across the Continent: A Summer's Journey to the Rocky Mountains, the Mormons, and the Pacific States, with Speaker Colfax.* Springfield, Mass.: S. Bowles & Co., 1866.

———. *Our New West: Records of Travel between the Mississippi River and the Pacific Ocean.* Hartford, Conn.: Hartford Publishing Co., 1869.

———. *The Parks and Mountains of Colorado: A Summer Vacation in the Switzerland of America, 1868.* Norman: Univ. of Oklahoma Press, 1991.

Box, Thadis W. *The Arid Lands Revisited: One Hundred Years since John Wesley Powell.* Logan: Utah State Univ., 1978.

Boxeman, Theodore Dwight. *Protestants in an Age of Science: The Baconian Ideal and Antebellum Religious Thought.* Chapel Hill: Univ. of North Carolina Press, 1977.

Boyd, William H. *Boyd's Directory of the District of Columbia.* Washington, D.C.: Wm. H. Boyd, 1880 and subs. eds.

Brandt, Nat. *The Town That Started the Civil War.* Syracuse: Syracuse Univ. Press, 1990.

Brian, Nancy. *River to Rim: A Guide to Place Names Along the Colorado River in Grand Canyon from Lake Powell to Lake Mead.* Flagstaff: Earthquest Press, 1992.

Brockett, L. P. *Our Western Empire: or, The New West beyond the Mississippi.* Philadelphia: Bradley, Garretson, 1882.

Brooke, John L. *The Refiner's Fire: The Making of a Mormon Cosmology, 1644–1844.* New York: Cambridge Univ. Press, 1994.

Brooks, Juanita. *John Doyle Lee: Zealot, Pioneer-Builder, Scapegoat.* Glendale, Calif.: A.H. Clark, 1962.

———. *The Mountain Meadows Massacre.* Palo Alto: Stanford Univ. Press, 1950.

Brough, Charles Hillman. *Irrigation in Utah.* Baltimore: Johns Hopkins Univ. Press, 1898.

Brown, Janet. *Charles Darwin.* Vol. 1. New York: Knopf, 1995.

Bruce, Robert V. *Bell: Alexander Graham Bell and the Conquest of Solitude.* Boston: Little, Brown, 1973.

————. *The Launching of Modern American Science, 1846–1876*. New York: Knopf, Random House, 1987.

Bryan, C.D.B. *The National Geographic Society: 100 Years of Adventure and Discovery*. New York: Harry N. Abrams, 1987.

Burke, Edmund. *A Philosophical Inquiry into the Origin of our Ideas of the Sublime and Beautiful*. Edited by Adam Phillips. 1757; Oxford: Oxford Univ. Press, 1990.

Burnham, John C. *Lester Frank Ward in American Thought*. Washington: Public Affairs Press, 1956.

Burrow, J.W. *Evolution and Society: A Study in Victorian Social Theory*. Cambridge: Cambridge Univ. Press, 1966.

Bushman, Richard L. *Joseph Smith and the Beginnings of Mormonism*. Urbana: Univ. of Illinois Press, 1984.

Calhoun, Alfred R. *Lost in the Cañon: The Story of Sam Willett's Adventures on the Great Colorado of the West*. New York: A.L. Burt, 1888.

Carey, S. Warren. *Theories of the Earth and Universe: A History of Dogma in the Earth Sciences*. Stanford: Stanford Univ. Press, 1988.

Carlson, Vada F. *John Wesley Powell: Conquest of the Canyon*. Irvington-on-Hudson, N.Y.: Harvey House, 1974.

Carothers, Steven W. *The Colorado River Through Grand Canyon: Natural History and Human Change*. Tucson: Univ. of Arizona Press, 1991.

Cartwright, Peter. *Autobiography of Peter Cartwright, The Backwoods Preacher*. New York: Methodist Book Concern, 1856.

Catalogue of the Officers and Students of Illinois College for the Academical Year, 1855–1856. Jacksonville, Ill.: Selby and Clayton, 1856.

Century Association. *Clarence King Memoirs*. New York: G.P. Putnam's Sons, 1904.

Chandler, Alfred. *The Visible Hand: The Managerial Revolution in American Business*. Cambridge: Harvard Univ. Press, 1977.

Chevalier, Michel. *Society, Manners, and Politics in the United States: Letters on North America*. Edited by John William Ward. 1836; Gloucester, Mass.: P. Smith, 1967.

Chidlaw, Benjamin W. *The Story of My Life*. Philadelphia: W.H. Hirst, 1890.

Chugerman, Samuel. *Lester Ward, the American Aristotle: A Summary and Interpretation of His Sociology*. Durham: Duke Univ. Press, 1939.

The City of Birmingham. Edited by W.B. Stephens. Vol. 7 of *A History of the County of Warwick*. London: Oxford Univ. Press, 1964.

The City of Kingston upon Hull. Edited by K.J. Allison. Vol. 1 of *A History of the County of York East Riding*. London: Oxford Univ. Press, 1969.

Clark, Carol. *Thomas Moran: Watercolors of the American West*. Austin: Univ. of Texas Press, 1980.

Clark, John G. *The Grain Trade in the Old Northwest*. Urbana: Univ. of Illinois Press, 1966.

Clarke, John M. *James Hall of Albany: Geologist and Paleontologist, 1811–1898*. Reprint. New York: Arno Press, 1978.

Cochrane, Rexmond C. *The National Academy of Sciences: The First Hundred Years, 1863–1963*. Washington D.C.: NAS, 1978.

Cole, Arthur C. *The Centennial History of Illinois*. Vol. 3. *The Era of the Civil War, 1848–1870*. Springfield, Ill., 1919.

The Colorado River Region and John Wesley Powell. Geological Survey Professional Paper 669. Washington D.C.: GPO, 1969.

Combination Atlas Map of Walworth County, Wisconsin. Chicago: Everts, Baskin, & Stewart, 1873.

Conway, Alan, ed. *The Welsh in America: Letters from the Immigrants.* Minneapolis: Univ. of Minnesota Press, 1961.

Corbett, Pearson. *Jacob Hamblin, the Peacemaker.* Salt Lake City: Deseret Book Co., 1952.

Cosmos Club. *The Fiftieth Anniversary of the Founding of the Cosmos Club, 1878–1928.* Washington D.C.: Cosmos Club, 1929.

Cosmos Club. *The Twenty-fifth Anniversary of the Founding of the Cosmos Club of Washington.* Washington D.C.: Cosmos Club, 1904.

Crampton, C. Gregory. *Land of Living Rock: The Grand Canyon and the High Plateaus; Arizona, Utah, Nevada.* New York: Alfred A. Knopf, 1972.

———. *Standing Up Country: The Canyon Lands of Utah and Arizona.* New York: Alfred A. Knopf, 1964.

Cronon, William. *Nature's Metropolis: Chicago and the Great West.* New York: Norton, 1991.

Crossette, George. *Founders of the Cosmos Club of Washington, 1878: A Collection of Biographical Sketches and Likenesses of the Sixty Founders.* Washington D.C.: Cosmos Club, 1966.

Current, Richard N. *The History of Wisconsin.* Vol. 2. *The Civil War Era, 1848–1873.* Madison: Univ. of Wisconsin Press, 1976.

Cushing, Frank Hamilton. *Cushing at Zuni: The Correspondence and Journals of Frank Hamilton Cushing, 1879–1884.* Albuquerque: Univ. of New Mexico Press, 1990.

———. *My Adventures in Zuni.* Palo Alto: American West Publishing, 1970.

Cutright, Paul R., and Michael J. Brodhead. *Elliot Coues: Naturalist and Frontier Historian.* Urbana: Univ. of Illinois Press, 1981.

Dale, Harrison Clifford. *The Ashley-Smith Explorations and the Discovery of a Central Route to the Pacific, 1822–1829, With the Original Journals.* Rev. ed. Glendale, Calif.: Arthur H. Clark, 1941.

Daniel, Larry J. *Shiloh: The Battle That Changed the Civil War.* New York: Simon & Schuster, 1997.

Darrah, William Culp. *Powell of the Colorado.* Princeton: Princeton Univ. Press, 1951.

Darwin, Charles. *The Correspondence of Charles Darwin.* Cambridge: Cambridge Univ. Press, 1985–.

———. *On the Origin of Species by Means of Natural Selection.* London: J. Murray, 1859.

Davidson, Stanley R. *The Leadership of the Reclamation Movement, 1875–1902.* New York: Arno Press, 1979.

Davis, John, and L.A. Stockwell. *Public Ownership of Railroads.* Girard, Kans.: J.A. Wayland, 1898.

Dellenbaugh, Frederick S. *A Canyon Voyage: The Narrative of the Second Powell Expedition.* 1908; Tucson: Univ. of Arizona Press, 1984.

———. *The Romance of the Colorado.* New York: G. P. Putnam's Sons, 1904.

Derby, E.H. *The Overland Route to the Pacific.* Boston: Lee & Shepard, 1869.

De Voto, Bernard. *The Course of Empire.* Boston: Houghton, Mifflin, 1952.

———. *The Year of Decision: 1846.* Boston: Houghton Mifflin, 1942.

Dictionary of American Biography. 3rd ed. New York: Scribner, 1980.

Dictionary of Scientific Biography. New York: Charles Scribner's Sons, 1975.

Doenecke, Justus D. *The Presidencies of James A. Garfield and Chester A. Arthur.* Lawrence: Regents Press of Kansas, 1981.

Dorman, Robert. *A Word for Nature: Four Pioneering Environmental Advocates, 1845–1913.* Chapel Hill: Univ. of North Carolina Press, 1998.

Dorsett, Lyle W., and Michael McCarthy. *The Queen City: A History of Denver.* 2nd ed. Boulder, Colo.: Pruett Pub., 1986.

Doty, Lockwood L. *A History of Livingston County, New York.* Geneseo, N.Y.: Edward L. Doty, 1876.

Doty, Lockwood R., ed. *History of the Genesee Country (Western New York).* Chicago: S.J. Clarke Pub. Co., 1925.

Doyle, Don Harrison. *The Social Order of a Frontier Community: Jacksonville, Illinois, 1825–1870.* Urbana: Univ. of Illinois Press, 1978.

Dupree, A. Hunter. *Science in the Federal Government: A History of Policies and Activities to 1940.* Cambridge: Harvard Univ. Press, 1957.

Dutton, Clarence E. *Report on the Geology of the High Plateaus of Utah.* Washington, D.C.: GPO, 1880.

———. *The Tertiary History of the Grand Cañon District, with Atlas.* Washington, D.C.: GPO, 1882.

Eggleston, Edward. *The Circuit Rider: A Tale of the Heroic Age.* New York: C. Scribner's Sons, 1920.

Elliott, Russell. *Servant of Power: A Political Biography of Senator William M. Stewart.* Reno: Univ. of Nevada Press, 1983.

Ellis, Elmer. *Henry Moore Teller, Defender of the West.* Caldwell, Idaho: Caxton Printers, 1941.

Emmitt, Robert. *The Last War Trail: The Utes and the Settlement of Colorado.* Norman: Univ. of Oklahoma Press, 1954.

Emmons, Samuel Franklin. *Geology and Mining Industry of Leadville, Colorado, with Atlas.* USGS Monograph 12. Washington, D.C.: GPO, 1886.

Euler, Robert C. *The Paiute People.* Phoenix: Indian Tribal Series, 1972.

———. *Southern Paiute Ethnohistory.* Anthropological Paper 78. Salt Lake City: Univ. of Utah Press, 1966.

———, and Frank D. Tikalsky, eds. *The Grand Canyon: Intimate Views.* Tucson: Univ. of Arizona Press, 1992.

Evans, William R. *History of Welsh Settlements in Jackson and Gallia Counties of Ohio.* Trans. by Phillips G. Davies. Columbus: Chatha Communicator, 1988.

Faragher, John Mack. *Sugar Creek: Life on the Illinois Prairie.* New Haven: Yale Univ. Press, 1986.

Fehrenbacher, Don E. *Prelude to Greatness: Lincoln in the 1850s.* Stanford: Stanford Univ. Press, 1962.

Fernlund, Kevin J. *William Henry Holmes and the Rediscovery of the American West.* Albuquerque: University of New Mexico Press, 2000.

Flack, J. Kirkpatrick. *Desideratum in Washington: The Intellectual Community in the Capital City, 1870–1900.* Cambridge, Mass.: Schenkman, 1975.

Fladeland, Betty. *James Gillespie Birney: Slaveholder to Abolitionist.* Ithaca, N.Y.: Cornell Univ. Press, 1955.

Fletcher, Robert S. *A History of Oberlin College: From Its Foundation Through the Civil War.* 2 vols. Oberlin: Oberlin College Press, 1943.

Foner, Eric. *Free Soil, Free Labor, Free Men: The Ideology of the Republican Party before the Civil War.* New York: Oxford Univ. Press, 1970.

Foote, Mary Hallock. *A Victorian Gentlewoman in the Far West: The Reminiscences of Mary Hallock Foote.* Edited by Rodman W. Paul. San Marino, Calif.: Huntington Library, 1972.

Foster, Mike. *Strange Genius: The Life of Ferdinand Vandeveer Hayden.* Niwot, Colo.: Robert Rinehart, 1994.

Fowler, Don D. *The Western Photographs of John K. Hillers.* Washington, D.C.: Smithsonian Institution Press, 1989.

Fowler, Don D., Robert C. Euler, and Catherine S. Fowler. *John Wesley Powell and the Anthropology of the Canyon Country.* USGS Professional Paper 670. Washington, D.C.: USGS, 1969.

————, and John F. Matley. *Material Culture of the Numa: The John Wesley Powell Collection, 1867–1880.* Washington D.C.: Smithsonian Institution Press, 1979.

Fraser, Mary Ann. *In Search of the Grand Canyon: Down the Colorado with John Wesley Powell.* New York: H. Holt, 1995.

Frederickson, George M. *The Inner Civil War: Northern Intellectuals and the Crisis of the Union.* New York: Harper & Row, 1965.

Gabriel, Ralph Henry. *The Course of American Democratic Thought: An Intellectual History since 1815.* New York, 1940.

Gaines, Ann. *John Wesley Powell and the Great Surveys of the American West.* New York: Chelsea House, 1992.

Gannett, Henry. *The Building of a Nation: The Growth, Present Condition, and Resources of the United States, with a Forecast of the Future.* New York: H.T. Thomas, 1895.

Garfield, James A. *The Diary of James A. Garfield.* Edited by Harry James Brown and Frederick D. Williams. 4 vols. East Lansing: Michigan State Univ. Press, 1967.

Garland, Hamlin. *Roadside Meetings.* New York: Macmillan, 1930.

————. *A Son of the Middle Border.* New York: Macmillan, 1923.

Gates, Paul W. *The Farmer's Age: Agriculture 1815–1860.* New York: Holt, Rinehart, and Winston, 1960.

————. *History of Public Land Law Development.* Washington D.C.: GPO, 1968.

George, Henry. *Progress and Poverty.* 1879; New York: Modern Library, 1938.

Gibson, Harold E. *Sigma Pi Society of Illinois College, 1843–1971.* Jacksonville, Ill.: Sigma Pi Society, 1972.

Gilbert, Grove Karl. *Lake Bonneville.* USGS Monographs 1. Washington, D.C.: GPO, 1890.

————. *Report on the Geology of the Henry Mountains.* Washington, D.C.: GPO, 1877.

Gillispie, Charles C. *Genesis and Geology: A Study in the Relations of Scientific Thought, Natural Theology, and Social Opinion in Great Britain, 1790–1850.* Cambridge: Harvard Univ. Press, 1951.

Gilpin, William. *The Central Gold Region: The Grain, Pastoral, and Gold Regions of North America.* Philadelphia: Sower, Barnes, 1860.

————. *Mission of the North American People: Geographical, Social, and Political.* Philadelphia: J. B. Lippincott, 1873.

Goetzmann, William H. *Army Exploration in the American West, 1803–1863.* New Haven: Yale Univ. Press, 1959.

———. *Exploration and Empire: The Explorer and the Scientist in the Winning of the American West.* New York: Alfred A. Knopf, 1966.

Goode, George Brown, ed. *The Smithsonian Institution, 1846–1896: The History of Its First Half Century.* Washington, D.C.: De Vinne, 1897.

Goodwyn, Lawrence. *Democratic Promise: The Populist Moment in America.* New York: Oxford Univ. Press, 1976.

Grant, Ulysses S. *The Papers of Ulysses S. Grant.* Edited by John Y. Simon. 18 vols. Carbondale: Southern Illinois Univ. Press, 1967–99.

———. *Memoirs and Selected Letters.* Edited by Mary Drake and William S. McFeeley. New York: Library of America, 1990.

Green, Constance McLaughlin. *Washington: Village and Capital, 1800–1878.* Princeton: Princeton Univ. Press, 1962.

———. *Washington: Capital City, 1879–1950.* Princeton: Princeton Univ. Press, 1963.

Greene, Mott T. *Geology in the Nineteenth Century: Changing Views of a Changing World.* Ithaca, N.Y.: Cornell Univ. Press, 1982.

Hafertepe, Kenneth. *America's Castle: The Evolution of the Smithsonian Building and Its Institution, 1840–1878.* Washington: Smithsonian Institution Press, 1984.

Hales, Peter. *William Henry Jackson and the Transformation of the American Landscape.* Philadelphia: Temple Univ. Press, 1988.

Halévy, Elie. *The Birth of Methodism in England.* Edited by Bernard Semmel. Chicago: Univ. of Chicago Press, 1971.

Hamblin, Jacob. *A Narrative of His Personal Experience, as a Frontiersman, Missionary to the Indians and Explorer.* Salt Lake City: Juvenile Instructor Office, 1881.

Hansen, Klaus J. *Mormonism and the American Experience.* Chicago: Univ. of Chicago Press, 1981.

Hansen, Wallace R. *The Geologic Story of the Uinta Mountains.* USGS Bull. 1291. Washington, D.C.: GPO, 1969.

Harper, Charles A. *Development of the Teachers College in the United States.* Bloomington, Ill.: McKnight & McKnight, 1935.

Harvey, Mark W.T. *A Symbol of Wilderness: Echo Park and the American Conservation Movement.* Albuquerque: Univ. of New Mexico Press, 1994.

Hatch, Nathan O. *The Democratization of American Christianity.* New Haven: Yale Univ. Press, 1989.

Hayden, Ferdinand. *Sketch of the Origin and Progress of the United States Geological and Geographical Survey of the Territories.* Washington D.C.: Darby & Duvall, 1877.

———. *Tenth Annual Report of the United States Geological and Geographical Survey of the Territories.* Washington, D.C.: Darby & Duvall, 1877.

Hays, Samuel P. *Conservation and the Gospel of Efficiency: The Progressive Conservation Movement, 1890–1920.* Cambridge: Harvard Univ. Press, 1959.

Hempton, David. *Methodism and Politics in British Society, 1750–1850.* London: Hutchinson, 1984.

Hewitt, Abram S. *Selected Writings of Abram S. Hewitt.* Edited by Allan Nevins. New York: Columbia Univ. Press, 1937.

Hibbard, Benjamin Horace. *A History of the Public Land Policies.* Madison: Univ. of Wisconsin Press, 1924.

Hill, Emma Shepard. *A Dangerous Crossing and What Happened on the Other Side: Seven Lean Years.* Denver: Bradford-Robinson, 1924.

Hillers, John K. *"Photographed All the Best Scenery": Jack Hillers's Diary of the Powell Expeditions, 1871–1875.* Edited by Don D. Fowler. Salt Lake City: Univ. of Utah Press, 1972.

Hinsley, Curtis Matthew, Jr. *Savages and Scientists: The Smithsonian Institution and the Development of American Anthropology, 1846–1910.* Washington, D.C.: Smithsonian Institution Press, 1981.

History of Lower Scioto Valley, Ohio. Chicago: Inter-state Pub. Co., 1884.

A History of Shropshire. Edited by A.T. Gaydon. Vol. 2. London: Oxford Univ. Press, 1973.

History of Walworth, County, Wisconsin. Chicago: Western Historical Co., 1882.

Hodge, F. W., ed. *Handbook of American Indians North of Mexico.* 2 vols. BAE Bulletin 30. Washington, D.C.: GPO, 1907–1910.

Hofstader, Richard. *Social Darwinism in American Thought, 1860–1915.* Boston: Beacon Press, 1964.

Holt, Robert. *Beneath These Red Cliffs: An Ethnohistory of the Utah Paiutes.* Albuquerque: Univ. of New Mexico Press, 1992.

Hoogenboom, Ari. *Rutherford B. Hayes: Warrior and President.* Lawrence: Univ. Press of Kansas, 1995.

Howard, Robert P. *Illinois: A History of the Prairie State.* Grand Rapids, Mich.: W.B. Eerdmans, 1972.

Howe, Henry. *Historical Collections of Ohio.* Vol. 2. Columbus: Henry Howe & Son, 1891.

Hoxie, Frederick. *A Final Promise: The Campaign to Assimilate the Indians, 1880–1920.* Lincoln: Univ. of Nebraska Press, 1984.

Hudson, John B. *Narrative of the Christian Experience, Travels and Labors of John B. Hudson.* Rochester, N.Y.: William Alling, 1838.

Hughes, J. Donald. *In the House of Stone and Light: A Human History of the Grand Canyon.* N.p.: Grand Canyon Natural History Association, 1978.

Huseman, Ben W. *Wild River, Timeless Canyons: Balduin Möllhausen's Watercolors of the Colorado.* Tucson: Univ. of Arizona Press, 1995.

Illinois Wesleyan University. *Ninth Annual Catalog, 1865–1866.* Bloomington: Illinois Wesleyan Univ., 1866.

Jackson, William Henry. *Time Exposure: The Autobiography of William Henry Jackson.* New York: G.P. Putnam's Sons, 1940.

Jacob, Kathryn Allamong. *Capital Elites: High Society in Washington, D.C., After the Civil War.* Washington, D.C.: Smithsonian Institution Press, 1995.

Jakle, John A. *Images of the Ohio Valley: A Historical Geography of Travel, 1740 to 1860.* New York: Oxford Univ. Press, 1977.

James, George Wharton. *Reclaiming the Arid West.* New York: Dodd, Mead, 1917.

Johnson, Hildegard Binder. *Order upon the Land: The U.S. Rectangular Land Survey and the Upper Mississippi Country.* New York: Oxford Univ. Press, 1976.

Johnson, Paul E. *A Shopkeeper's Millennium: Society and Revivals in Rochester, New York, 1815–1837.* New York: Hill & Wang, 1978.

Jones, Greta. *Social Darwinism and English Thought: The Interaction Between Biological and Social Theory.* Brighton, Sussex: Harvester Press, 1980.

Jones, Romaine Aten. *Early Jackson.* Columbus: F. J. Heer, 1942.

Judd, Neil M. *The Bureau of American Ethnology: A Partial History.* Norman: Univ. of Oklahoma Press, 1967.

Karnes, Thomas L. *William Gilpin, Western Nationalist.* Austin: Univ. of Texas Press, 1970.

Keim, De B. Randolph. *Washington and Its Environs.* Washington, D.C.: D.R. Keim, 1874.

Keller, Morton. *Affairs of State: Public Life in Late Nineteenth-Century America.* Cambridge: Harvard Univ. Press, 1977.

Kelly, Isabel. *Southern Paiute Ethnography.* Anthropological Paper 69. Salt Lake City: Univ. of Utah Press, 1964.

King, Clarence. *Mining Industry.* Washington, D.C.: GPO, 1870.

———. *Mountaineering in the Sierra Nevada.* 1874; New York: Penguin, 1989.

Kinsey, Joni Louise. *Thomas Moran and the Surveying of the American West.* Washington, D.C.: Smithsonian Institution Press, 1992.

Koepp, Donna, ed. *Exploration and Mapping of the American West: Selected Essays.* Chicago: Spectrum Orbis Press, 1986.

Lamar, Howard. *The Far Southwest, 1846–1912.* New York: W.W. Norton, 1970.

Langford, Nathaniel Pitt. *The Discovery of Yellowstone Park.* 1905; Lincoln: Univ. of Nebraska Press, 1972.

Lanham, Url. *The Bone Hunters.* New York: Columbia Univ. Press, 1973.

Lapham, Increase A. *Wisconsin: Its Geography and Topography, History, Geology, and Mineralogy.* 2nd ed. 1846; New York: Arno, 1975.

Lavender, David. *Pipe Spring and the Arizona Strip.* Springdale, Utah: Zion Natural History Association, 1984.

———. *River Runners of the Grand Canyon.* Tucson: Univ. of Arizona Press, 1985.

Lee, John D. *A Mormon Chronicle: The Diaries of John D. Lee, 1848–1876.* 2 vols. Edited by Robert Glass Cleland and Juanita Brooks. San Marino, Calif.: Huntington Library, 1955.

Leech, Margaret. *Reveille in Washington, 1860–1865.* New York: Harper Brothers, 1941.

———, and Harry J. Brown. *The Garfield Orbit.* New York: Harper & Row, 1978.

Lessoff, Alan. *The Nation and Its City: Politics, "Corruption," and Progress in Washington, D.C., 1861–1902.* Baltimore, Md.: Johns Hopkins Univ. Press, 1994.

Lewis, David Rich. *Neither Wolf Nor Dog: American Indians, Environment, and Agrarian Change.* New York: Oxford Univ. Press, 1994.

Little, James A. *Jacob Hamblin.* 2nd ed. Salt Lake City: Deseret News, 1909.

Livingstone, David N. *Nathaniel Southgate Shaler and the Culture of American Science.* Tuscaloosa: Univ. of Alabama Press, 1987.

Logan, Mrs. John A., ed. *Thirty Years in Washington: or, Life and Scenes in Our National Capital.* Hartford, Conn.: A.D. Worthington, 1901.

Lurie, Edward. *Louis Agassiz: A Life in Science,* Chicago: Univ. of Chicago Press, 1966.

Luvaas, Jay Stephen Bowman, and Leonard Fullenkamp, eds. *Guide to the Battle of Shiloh.* Lawrence: Univ. Press of Kansas, 1996.

Lyell, Charles. *Travels in North America: With Geological Observations on the United States, Canada, and Nova Scotia.* 2 vols. London: J. Murray, 1845.

———. *A Second Visit to the United States of North America.* New York: Harper and Brothers, 1849.

Mahoney, Timothy R. *River Towns in the Great West: The Structure of Provincial Urbanization in the American Midwest, 1820–1870.* New York: Cambridge Univ. Press, 1990.

Manly, William L. *Death Valley in '49*. Edited by Milo M. Quaife. Chicago: Lakeside Press, 1927.

Manning, Thomas G. *Government in Science: The U.S. Geological Survey, 1867–1894*. Lexington: Univ. of Kentucky Press, 1967.

Marcou, Jules. *A Little More Light on the United States Geological Survey*. Cambridge, Mass.: privately published, 1892.

———. *The Geological Map of the United States and the United States Geological Survey*. Cambridge, Mass.: privately published, 1892.

Mark, Joan. *A Stranger in Her Native Land: Alice Fletcher and the American Indians*. Lincoln: Univ. of Nebraska Press, 1988.

———. *Four Anthropologists: An American Science in Its Early Years*. New York: Science History Publications, 1980.

Mathews, Donald G. *Slavery and Methodism: A Chapter in American Morality, 1780–1845*. Princeton: Princeton Univ. Press, 1965.

McCarren, Mark J. *The Scientific Contributions of Othniel Charles Marsh: Birds, Bones, and Bronotheres*. New Haven: Peabody Museum of Natural History, 1993.

McDannell, Colleen. *The Christian Home in Victorian America, 1840–1900*. Bloomington: Indiana Univ. Press, 1986.

McFeely, William. *Grant: A Biography*. New York: W.W. Norton, 1981.

McGee, Emma R. *Life of W.J. McGee*. Farley, Iowa: privately published, 1915.

McIntosh, W. H. *History of Wyoming County, N.Y.*. Philadelphia: Everts, Ensign & Everts, 1877.

McMath, Robert C., Jr. *American Populism: A Social History, 1877–1898*. New York: Hill & Wang, 1992.

McPherson, James M. *Battle Cry of Freedom: The Civil War Era*. New York: Oxford Univ. Press, 1988.

———. *For Cause and Comrades: Why Men Fought in the Civil War*. New York: Oxford Univ. Press, 1997.

Merrill, George P. *The First One Hundred Years of American Geology*. New Haven: Yale Univ. Press, 1924.

Mitchell, Lee Clark. *Witnesses to a Vanishing America: The Nineteenth-Century Response*. Princeton: Princeton Univ. Press, 1981.

Mitchell, Reid. *The Vacant Chair: The Northern Soldier Leaves Home*. New York: Oxford Univ. Press, 1993.

A Modern Delineation of the Town & Port of Kingston upon Hull. Hull, 1805.

Moore, James R. *The Post-Darwinian Controversies: A Study of the Protestant Struggle to Come to Terms with Darwin in Great Britain and America, 1870–1900*. Cambridge: Cambridge Univ. Press, 1979.

Morgan, H. Wayne. *From Hayes to McKinley: National Party Politics, 1877–1896*. Syracuse: Syracuse Univ. Press, 1969.

Morgan, Lewis Henry. *Ancient Society*. 1877; Chicago: Charles H. Kerr, 1907.

Muir, John. *The Story of My Boyhood and Youth*. Boston: Houghton Mifflin, 1913.

Murray, Keith A. *The Modocs and Their War*. Norman: Univ. of Oklahoma Press, 1959.

Nelson, Lowry. *The Mormon Village: A Pattern and Technique of Land Settlement*. Salt Lake City: Univ. of Utah Press, 1952.

Nevins, Allan. *Abram S. Hewitt: With Some Account of Peter Cooper*. New York: Harper & Brothers, 1935.

————, ed. *The Selected Writings of Abram Hewitt.* New York: Columbia Univ. Press, 1937.

Newcomb, Simon. *The Reminiscences of an Astronomer.* Boston: Houghton, Mifflin, 1903.

Nims, Franklin A. *The Photographer and the River, 1889–1890: The Colorado Canon Diary of Franklin A. Nims with the Brown-Stanton Railroad Survey Expedition.* Edited by D.L. Smith. Santa Fe, N.M.: Stagecoach Press, 1967.

Numbers, Ronald. *Darwinism Comes to America.* Cambridge: Harvard Univ. Press, 1998.

Oldroyd, David R. *Thinking about the Earth: A History of Ideas in Geology.* Cambridge: Harvard Univ. Press, 1996.

Osborn, Henry Fairfield. *Cope, Master Naturalist.* Reprint. New York: Arno Press, 1978.

Paley, William. *Natural Theology.* London: Wilks and Taylor, 1802.

Paludan, Phillip Shaw. *"A People's Contest": The Union and the Civil War, 1861–1868.* New York: Harper & Row, 1988.

Park, Susan, and R.F. Heizer, eds. *Stephen Powers, California's First Ethnologist; and, Letters of Stephen Powers to John Wesley Powell Concerning Tribes of California.* Berkeley, Calif.: Department of Anthropology, 1982.

Parsons, Levi, and Samuel L. Rockfellow. *Centennial Celebration, Mt. Morris, N. Y., August 15, 1894.* Mt. Morris: J.C. Dickey, 1894.

Paul, Rodman W. *Mining Frontiers of the Far West.* Albuquerque: Univ. of New Mexico Press, 1963.

Peffer, Louise. *The Closing of the Public Domain: Disposal and Reservation Policies, 1900–1950.* Stanford: Stanford Univ. Press, 1972.

Periam, Jonathan. *A History of the Origin, Aims, and Progress of the Farmers' Movement.* Cincinnati: E. Hannaford, 1874.

Pisani, Donald J. *To Reclaim a Divided West: Water, Law and Public Policy, 1848–1902.* Albuquerque: Univ. of New Mexico Press, 1992.

Place, Marian T. *John Wesley Powell: Canyon's Conqueror.* Boston: Houghton Mifflin, 1963.

Plate, Robert. *The Dinosaur Hunters: Othniel C. Marsh and Edward D. Cope.* New York: David McKay, 1964.

Powell, John Wesley. *Anthropology of the Numa: John Wesley Powell's Manuscripts on the Numic Peoples of Western North America, 1868–1880.* Edited by Don and Catherine Fowler. Washington, D.C.: Smithsonian Institution, 1971.

————. *The Canyons of the Colorado.* Meadville, Penn.: Flood and Vincent, 1895.

————. *The Exploration of the Colorado River and Its Canyons* [reprint of *The Canyons of the Colorado*]. New York: Penguin, 1987.

————. *Report on the Lands of the Arid Region of the United States.* Edited by Wallace Stegner. Washington D.C.: GPO, 1879; Cambridge, Mass.: Belknap Press, 1962.

————. *Truth and Error: Or, the Science of Intellection.* Chicago: Open Court, 1898.

Proceedings of the Board of Education of the State of Illinois. Peoria: Illinois State Teachers Association, 1867.

Prucha, Francis Paul. *The Great Father: The United States Government and the American Indians.* Lincoln: Univ. of Nebraska Press, 1986.

Pyne, Stephen J. *Grove Karl Gilbert: A Great Engine of Research.* Austin: Univ. of Texas Press, 1980.

————. *How the Canyon Became Grand: A Short History.* New York: Viking, 1998.

Rabbitt, Mary C. *Minerals, Lands, and Geology for the Common Defence and General Welfare.* Vol. 1. *Before 1879.* Washington, D.C.: GPO, 1979.

————. Vol. 2. *1879–1904.* Washington, D.C.: GPO, 1980.

————. *The United States Geological Survey: 1879–1989.* Reston, Va.: USGS, 1989.

Rammelkamp, C. H. *Illinois College: A Centennial History, 1829–1929.* New Haven: Yale Univ. Press, 1928.

Reed, D.W. *The Battle of Shiloh and the Organizations Engaged.* Washington, D.C.: GPO, 1903.

Reps, John R. *Washington on View.* Chapel Hill: Univ. of North Carolina Press, 1991.

Resek, Carl. *Lewis Henry Morgan: American Scholar.* Chicago: Univ. of Chicago Press, 1960.

Richardson, Albert D. *Beyond the Mississippi From the Great River to the Great Ocean: Life and Adventure on the Prairies, Mountains, and Pacific Coast.* Hartford: American Publishing Co., 1869.

Richmond, C.W., and H.F. Vallette. *A History of the County of DuPage, Illinois.* Chicago: Scripps, Bross & Spears, 1857.

Ricks, Joel Edward. *The Forms and Methods of Early Mormon Settlement in Utah and Surrounding Regions, 1847–1877.* Logan: Utah State Univ. Press, 1964.

Rivinus, E.F., and E.M. Youssef. *Spencer Baird of the Smithsonian.* Washington, D.C.: Smithsonian Institution Press, 1992.

Robbins, Roy M. *Our Landed Heritage: The Public Domain, 1776–1936.* Lincoln: Univ. of Nebraska Press, 1942.

Robinson, Adonis Findlay. *History of Kane County.* Salt Lake City: Utah Printing Co., 1970.

Rodgers, Andrew Denny, III. *Bernhard Eduard Fernow: A Story of North American Forestry.* Princeton: Princeton Univ. Press, 1951.

Rudwick, Martin J.S. *The Meaning of Fossils: Episodes in the History of Paleontology.* 2nd ed. New York: Science History Publications, 1976.

Rusho, W.L. *Powell's Canyon Voyage.* Palmer Lake, Colo.: Filter Press, 1969.

————, and C. Gregory Crampton. *Lee's Ferry: Desert River Crossing.* Salt Lake City: Cricket Productions, 1992.

Ruskin, John. *Modern Painters.* 5 vols. New York: John Wiley & Son, 1868.

————. *Sesame and Lilies.* Rev. ed. New York: T.Y. Crowell, 1891.

Russett, Cynthia E. *Darwin in America: The Intellectual Response, 1865–1912.* San Francisco: W.H. Freeman, 1976.

Rydell, Robert W. *All the World's a Fair: Visions of Empire at American International Expositions, 1876–1916.* Chicago: Univ. of Chicago Press, 1984.

Sarles, Frank B., Jr. *John Wesley Powell and the Colorado River: A Special Study of the Colorado River Expeditions of 1869 and 1871.* Washington, D.C.: National Park Service, 1968.

Scheiber, Harry N. *Ohio Canal Era: A Case Study of Government and the Economy, 1820–1861.* Athens: Ohio Univ. Press, 1969.

Schmeckebier, L. F. *Catalogue and Index of the Publications of the Hayden, King, Powell, and Wheeler Surveys.* USGS Bull. 222. Washington, D.C.: GPO, 1904.

Schott, Charles A. *Tables and Results of the Precipitation, in Rain and Snow, in the United States.* Smithsonian Contributions to Knowledge. Vol. 18. Washington, D.C.: Smithsonian Institution, 1873.

Schuchert, Charles, and C.M. LeVene. *O.C. Marsh: Pioneer in Paleontology.* New Haven: Yale Univ. Press, 1940.

Schullery, Paul, ed. *The Grand Canyon: Early Impressions.* Boulder: Colorado Associated Univ. Press, 1981.

Schurz, Carl. *Reminiscences of Carl Schurz.* 3 Vols. New York: Doubleday, Page, 1908.

Sellers, Charles. *The Market Revolution: Jacksonian America, 1815–1846.* New York: Oxford Univ. Press, 1991.

Semmel, Bernard. *The Methodist Revolution.* New York: Basic Books, 1973.

Shaler, Nathaniel. *The Autobiography of Nathaniel Southgate Shaler.* Boston: Houghton Mifflin, 1909.

Sheriff, Carol. *The Artificial River: The Erie Canal and the Paradox of Progress, 1817–1862.* New York: Hill & Wang, 1996.

Shipps, Jan. *Mormonism: The Story of A New Religious Tradition.* Urbana: Univ. of Illinois Press, 1985.

Shor, E.N. *The Fossil Feud between E.D. Cope and O.C. Marsh.* Hicksville, N.Y.: Exposition Press, 1974.

Smith, Henry Nash. *Virgin Land: The American West in Myth and Symbol.* Cambridge: Harvard Univ. Press, 1951.

Smith, Theodore Clark. *The Liberty and Free Soil Parties in the Northwest.* New York: Longmans, Green, 1897.

———. *The Life and Letters of James Abram Garfield.* 2 Vols. New Haven: Yale Univ. Press, 1925.

Smythe, William E. *The Conquest of Arid America.* 1900; Seattle: Univ. of Washington Press, 1969.

Spamer, Earle E. *Bibliography of the Grand Canyon and the Lower Colorado River, 1540–1980.* Grand Canyon, Ariz.: Grand Canyon Natural History Association, 1981.

Spencer, Herbert. *Collected Works.* 18 vols. New York: D. Appleton, 1910.

———. *Social Statistics.* New York: D. Appleton, 1865.

The Spirit of the Earth: Selections from the John Wesley Powell Collection of Pueblo Pottery at Illinois Wesleyan University. Urbana: Krannert Art Museum and Kinkead Pavilion, University of Illinois at Urbana-Champaign, 1993.

Stanton, Robert Brewster. *Colorado River Controversies.* 1932; Boulder City, Nev.: Westwater Books, 1982.

———. *The Colorado River Survey: Robert B. Stanton and the Denver, Colorado Canyon & Pacific Railroad.* Edited by Dwight L. Smith and C. Gregory Crampton. Salt Lake City: Howe Bros., 1987.

———. *Down the Colorado.* Edited by Dwight L. Smith. Norman: Univ. of Oklahoma Press, 1965.

Statistical Atlas of the United States. New York: Julius Bien, 1874.

Stegner, Wallace. *Beyond the Hundredth Meridian: John Wesley Powell and the Second Opening of the American West.* Boston: Houghton Mifflin, 1954.

———. *Mormon Country.* New York: Duell, Sloan and Pearce, 1942.

Stein, Roger B. *John Ruskin and Aesthetic Thought in America, 1840–1900.* Cambridge: Harvard Univ. Press, 1967.

Stephens, Hal G., and Eugene M. Shoemaker, eds. *In the Footsteps of John Wesley Powell: An Album of Comparative Photographs of the Green and Colorado Rivers, 1871–72 and 1968.* Boulder, Colo.: Johnson Books, 1987.

Stewart, William M. *The Reminiscences of Senator William M. Stewart of Nevada.* Edited by G.R. Brown. New York: Neale Publishing Co., 1908.

Stocking, George W. *Race, Culture, and Evolution: Essays in the History of Anthropology.* New York: Free Press, 1968.

Stoffle, Richard W., and Michael J. Evans. *Kaibab Paiute History: The Early Years.* Fredonia, Ariz.: Kaibab Paiute Tribe, 1978.

Sword, Wiley. *Shiloh: Bloody April.* New York: Morrow, 1974.

Synnestvedt, Sig., ed. *The Essential Swedenborg.* N. p.: Swedenborg Foundation and Twayne Publishers, 1970.

Taylor, Bayard. *Colorado: A Summer Trip.* New York: G.P. Putnam, 1867.

Terrell, John Upton. *The Man Who Rediscovered America: A Biography of John Wesley Powell.* New York: Weybright and Talley, 1969.

Thomas, George. *The Development of Institutions Under Irrigation.* New York: Macmillan, 1920.

Thompson, E.P. *The Making of the English Working Class.* New York: Vintage Books, 1963.

Tocqueville, Alexis de. *Journeys to England and Ireland.* 1835; London: Faber & Faber, 1958.

Trachtenberg, Alan. *The Incorporation of America: Culture and Society in the Gilded Age.* New York: Hill and Wang, 1982.

Trefousse, Hans. *Carl Schurz: A Biography.* Knoxville: Univ. of Tennessee Press, 1982.

Trinder, Barrie Stuart. *A History of Shropshire.* Chichester, Sussex: Phillimore, 1983.

———. *The Industrial Revolution in Shropshire.* 2nd ed. London and Chichester: Phillimore, 1981.

True, Frederick W., ed. *A History of the First Half-Century of the National Academy of Sciences, 1863–1913.* Washington D.C.: NAS, 1913.

Twain, Mark [Samuel Clemens]. *A Connecticut Yankee in King Arthur's Court.* New York: Harper, 1889.

———. *Life on the Mississippi.* New York: C.L. Webster, 1874.

Tylor, Edward Burnett. *Primitive Culture: Researches into the Development of Mythology, Philosophy, Religion, Art, and Custom.* London: John Murray, 1871.

Ullman, James Ramsey. *Down the Colorado with Major Powell.* Boston: Houghton Mifflin, 1960.

Utley, Robert M. *The Last Days of the Sioux Nation.* New Haven: Yale Univ. Press, 1963.

Van Hise, Charles R. *The Conservation of Natural Resources in the United States.* New York: Macmillan, 1910.

Vance, Maurice M. *Charles Richard Van Hise: Scientist Progressive.* Madison: State Historical Society of Wisconsin, 1960.

Vrooman, Frank Buffington. *The New Politics.* New York: Oxford Univ. Press, 1911.

The War of the Rebellion: A Compilation of the Official Records of the Union and Confederate Armies. Harrisburg, Pa.: National Historical Society, 1985.

Ward, Lester Frank. *Dynamic Sociology, or Applied Social Science.* 2 Vols. New York: D. Appleton, 1883.

———. *Glimpses of the Cosmos.* 6 Vols. Edited by Mrs. Emily Palmer Cope. New York: G.P. Putnam's Sons, 1918.

———. *Lester Ward and the Welfare State.* Edited by Henry Steele Commager. New York: Bobbs-Merrill, 1967.

————. *Young Ward's Diary.* Edited by Bernhard Joseph Stern. New York: G.P. Putnam's Sons, 1935.

Warner, Ted J., ed. *The Dominguez-Escalante Journal: The Expedition Through Colorado, Utah, Arizona, and New Mexico in 1776.* Provo: Brigham Young University Press, 1976.

Washburn, Wilcomb E. *The Cosmos Club of Washington.* Washington: Cosmos Club, 1978.

Watkins, T.H. *The Grand Canyon: The Story of a River and Its Canyons.* Palo Alto: American West, 1969.

Watson, Elmo Scott. *The Illinois Wesleyan Story, 1850–1950.* Bloomington: Illinois Wesleyan Univ. Press, 1950.

————, ed. *The Professor Goes West: Illinois Wesleyan University Reports of Major John Wesley Powell's Explorations, 1867–1874.* Bloomington: Illinois Wesleyan Univ. Press, 1954.

Webb, Roy. *Call of the Colorado.* Moscow: Univ. of Idaho Press, 1994.

————. *If We Had a Boat: Green River Explorers, Adventurers, and Runners.* Salt Lake City: Univ. of Utah Press, 1986.

Webb, Walter Prescott. *The Great Plains.* Boston: Ginn, 1931.

Weisberger, Bernard. *They Gathered at the River: The Story of the Great Revivalists and Their Impact upon Religion in America.* Boston: Little, Brown, 1958.

Weisenburger, Francis P. *The Passing of the Frontier, 1825–1850.* Vol. 3 of *The History of the State of Ohio.* Columbus: Ohio State Archaeological and Historical Society, 1941.

Wesley, John. *Sermons III.* Vol. 3 of *The Works of John Wesley.* 23 Vols. Nashville: Abingdon Press, 1984.

————. *A Survey of the Wisdom of God in the Creation.* Bristol, England, 1763.

West, Elliot. *The Contested Plains: Indians, Goldseekers, and the Rush to Colorado.* Lawrence: Univ. Press of Kansas, 1998.

White, Leslie A., ed. *Pioneers in American Anthropology.* Albuquerque: Univ. of New Mexico Press, 1940.

Wibberley, Leonard. *Wes Powell: Conqueror of the Grand Canyon.* New York: Ariel Books, 1958.

Wiebe, Robert H. *The Search for Order, 1877–1920.* New York: Hill & Wang, 1967.

Wilentz, Sean. *Chants Democratic: New York City & the Rise of the American Working Class, 1788–1850.* New York: Oxford Univ. Press, 1984.

Wiley, Bell Irwin. *The Life of Billy Yank: The Common Soldier of the Union.* Indianapolis: Bobbs-Merrill, 1952.

Wilkins, Thurman, and Caroline Lawson Hinkley. *Clarence King: A Biography.* Rev. ed. Albuquerque: Univ. of New Mexico Press, 1988.

————. *John Muir: Apostle of Nature.* Norman: Univ. of Oklahoma Press, 1995.

————. *Thomas Moran: Artist of the Mountains.* Norman: Univ. of Oklahoma Press, 1998.

Willard, Eugene B., ed. *A Standard History of the Hanging Rock Iron Region of Ohio.* Chicago: Lewis Publishing Co., 1916.

Williams, C.W. *Medina, Elyria & Oberlin City Directory.* N.p.: C.S.W. , 1857.

Williams, Daniel Webster. *A History of Jackson County, Ohio.* Vol. 1. Jackson, Ohio, 1900.

Williams, David. *Cymru ac America / Wales and America.* Cardiff: Univ. of Wales Press, 1975.

Williams, John Hoyt. *A Great and Shining Road: The Epic Story of the Transcontinental Railroad.* New York: Times Books, 1988.

Willis, Bailey. *A Yanqui in Patagonia.* Stanford: Stanford Univ. Press, 1947.

Wilson, Leonard G. *Charles Lyell, the Years to 1841: The Revolution in Geology.* New Haven: Yale University Press, 1972.

———. *Lyell in America: Transatlantic Geology, 1841–1853.* Baltimore: Johns Hopkins Univ. Press, 1998.

Woodward, Arthur. *Feud on the Colorado.* Los Angeles: Westernlore Press, 1955.

Wyckoff, William. *The Developer's Frontier: The Making of the Western New York Landscape.* New Haven: Yale Univ. Press, 1988.

Yochelson, Ellis Leon. *Charles Doolittle Walcott: Paleontologist.* Kent, Ohio: Kent Univ. Press, 1998.

———, ed. *The Scientific Ideas of G.K. Gilbert.* Geological Society of America Special Paper 183. Boulder, Colo.: Geological Society of America, 1980.

Youmans, Edward L. *Herbert Spencer on the Americans and the Americans on Herbert Spencer.* New York: D. Appleton, 1883.

CHAPTERS AND ARTICLES

Agassiz, Alexander. "The Coast-Survey and 'Political Scientists.'" *Science* 6 (1885): 253–55.

Alexander, Thomas G. "John Wesley Powell, The Irrigation Survey, and the Inauguration of the Second Phase of Irrigation Development in Utah." *UHQ* 37 (1969): 190–206.

———. "The Powell Irrigation Survey and the People of the Mountain West." *Journal of the West* 7 (1968): 48–54.

Allen, James B. and Ted J. Warner. "The Gosiute Indians in Pioneer Utah." *UHQ* 39 (1971): 162–77.

Allen, S. H. "The Grand Canyon of the Colorado." *Parry's Monthly Magazine* 5 (1889): 166–67, 201–06, 241–46, 281–87.

Alter, J. Cecil, ed. "The Mormons and the Indians." *UHQ* 12 (1944): 49–67.

Amundson, Ronald, and Dan H. Yaalon, "E.W. Hilgard and John Wesley Powell: Efforts for a Joint Agricultural and Geological Survey." *Soil Science Society of America Journal* 59 (1995): 4–13.

Anderson, Martin J. "First Through the Canyon: Powell's Lucky Voyage in 1869." *JArH* 20 (1979): 391–408.

———. "John Wesley Powell's Explorations of the Colorado River: Fact, Fiction, or Fantasy?" *JArH* 24 (1983): 363–80.

———. "Artist in the Wilderness: Frederick Dellenbaugh's Grand Canyon Adventure." *JArH* 28 (1987): 47–68.

Arrington, Leonard J. "Inland to Zion: Mormon Trade on the Colorado River, 1864–1867." *Arizona and the West* 8 (1966): 239–50.

Baker, Marcus. "Major J.W. Powell: Personal Reminiscences of One of His Staff." *Open Court* 17 (1903): 348–51.

Bartlett, Richard A. "Clarence King's Fortieth Parallel Survey." *UHQ* 24 (1956): 131–47.

———. "The Hayden Survey in Colorado." *Colorado Quarterly* 4 (1955): 73–88.

————. "John Wesley Powell and the Great Surveys: A Problem in Historiography." In *The American West: An Appraisal*, edited by Robert G. Ferris, 48–57. Santa Fe: Museum of New Mexico Press, 1963.

Basson, Keith O. "History of Ethnological Research." In *Handbook of North American Indians*, vol. 9: *Southwest*, edited by Alfonso Ortiz, 14–21. Washington: Smithsonian Institution Press, 1979.

Beaman, E.O. "The Cañon of the Colorado, and the Moquis Pueblos." *Appleton's Journal* 11 (1874): 481–84, 513–16, 545–48, 590–93, 623–26, 641–44, 686, 689.

Bellomy, Donald C. "Social Darwinism Revisited." *Perspectives in American History* 1 (1984): 1–129.

Belshaw, Michael. "The Dunn-Howland Killings: A Reconstruction." *JArH* 20 (1979): 409–22.

Bieder, Robert E. "Anthropology and History of the American Indian." *American Quarterly* 33 (1981): 309–26.

Bingham, Jay R. "Reclamation and the Colorado." *UHQ* 28 (1960): 233–50.

Bishop, Francis Marion. "Captain Francis Marion Bishop's Journal." *UHQ* 15 (1947): 159–238.

Boas, Franz. "Museums of Ethnology and Their Classification: Reply." *Science* 9 (1887): 614.

Bradley, George Y. "George Y. Bradley's Journal." *UHQ* 15 (1947): 31–72.

Brewer, William H. "John Wesley Powell." *American Journal of Science* 14 (1902): 377–82.

Brooks, Juanita. "Indian Relations on the Mormon Frontier." *UHQ* 12 (1944): 1–48.

Callaway, Donald, Joel Janetski, and Omer C. Stewart. "Ute." In *Handbook of North American Indians*, vol. 11: *Great Basin*, edited by Warren L. D'Azevedo, 336–67. Washington: Smithsonian Institution Press, 1986.

"Centennial Issue, 1869–1969: Colorado River Explorer Powell." *Reclamation Era* 55 (1969): 1–23.

Chidlaw, Benjamin W. "The American." *Historical and Philosophical Society of Ohio* 6 (1911): 7–41.

Christy, Howard A. "Open Hand and Mailed Fist: Mormon-Indian Relations in Utah, 1847–52." *UHQ* 46 (1978): 214–26.

Cloud, Preston. "The Improbable Bureaucracy: The United States Geological Surveys, 1879–1979." *Proceedings of the American Philosophical Society* 124 (1980): 155–67.

"The Colorado River Expedition of 1869." *UHQ* 15 (1947): 1–253.

Cope, Edward D., and J.S. Kingsley. "Editorial." *The American Naturalist* 24 (1890): 460–61, 562.

Crampton, C. Gregory. "F.S. Dellenbaugh of the Colorado: Some Letters Pertaining to the Powell Voyages and the History of the Colorado River." *UHQ* 37 (1969): 214–43.

Cross, Whitney R. "WJ McGee and the Idea of Conservation." *The Historian* 15 (1953): 148–62.

Cushing, Frank. "My Adventures in Zuni." *Century Magazine* 25–26 (1882–1883): 191–207, 500–11.

Dall, William H. "The Origin and Early Days of the Philosophical Society of Washington." *Journal of Washington Academy of Science* 8 (1918): 29–34.

Daly, C. P. "Professor Powell's Exploration of the Colorado River." *American Geographical Society Journal* 4 (1874): 79.

———. "Professor Powell's Explorations." Ibid. 7 (1876): 65.

———. "Professor J. W. Powell's Exploration of the Colorado." Ibid. 8 (1878): 46–48.

———. "Professor Powell's Expedition." Ibid. 8 (1878): 58–59.

Daniels, W.H. "Journal Leaves from Powell's Expedition of 1868." *Illinois Wesleyan Alumni Journal* 1 (1872): 42–44.

Darnton, N.H. "Memoir of Henry Gannett." *Annals of the Association of American Geographers* 7 (1917): 68–70.

Darrah, William C. "John Wesley Powell and an Understanding of the West." *UHQ* 37 (1969): 146–51.

———. "John Wesley Powell, His Western Explorations." *Geotimes* 14 (1969): 13–15.

Davis, William. "Biographical Memoir of John Wesley Powell, 1834–1902." *National Academy of Sciences, Biographical Memoirs* 8 (1915): 11–83.

———. "The Lessons of the Grand Canyon." *Bull. of the American Geographical Society* 41 (1909): 345–54.

Dawson, Thomas F. "Lost Alone on Bear River." *The Trail* 11 (1918): 13–20.

De Forest, John W. "Overland." *Galaxy* 11 (1871): 387–400.

Dellenbaugh, Frederick. "John Wesley Powell: A Brief Review of His Career." In *The Romance of the Colorado River*, 3rd ed., 371–86. New York. Putnam, 1909.

———. "Memorial to John Wesley Powell." *American Anthropologist* 20 (1918): 432–36.

———. "Naming the Grand Canyon." *Science* 77 (1933): 349–50.

Dobyns, Henry F., and Robert C. Euler. "The Dunn-Howland Killings: Additional Insights." *JArH* 20 (1980): 87–95.

Dockstader, Frederick J. "Hopi History, 1850–1940." In *Handbook of North American Indians*, vol. 9: *Southwest*, edited by Alfonso Ortiz, 524–32. Washington: Smithsonian Institution Press, 1979.

Dunham, Harold H. "Some Crucial Years of the General Land Office, 1875–90." *Agricultural History* 11 (1937): 117–41.

Emmons, Samuel Franklin. "Biographical Memoir of Clarence King, 1842–1901." *Biographical Memoirs, National Academy of Sciences* 6 (1909): 27–55.

———. "The Geology of Government Explorations." *Science* 5 (1897): 1–15, 42–51.

———. "The Mining Work of the U.S. Geological Survey." *American Institute of Mining Engineers, Trans.* 10 (1882): 412–24.

Euler, Robert C. "The Canyon Dwellers." *American West* 4 (1967): 22–27, 67–71.

———. "Southern Paiute Archaeology." *American Antiquity* 29 (1964): 379–81.

———, George Gummerman, et al. "The Colorado Plateaus: Cultural Dynamics and Paleoenvironment." *Science* 205 (1979): 1089–101.

"The Exploration of the Colorado River and the High Plateaus of Utah by the Second Powell Expedition of 1871–72." *UHQ* 16–17 (1948–49): 1–508.

Farrow, E.A. "The Kaibab Indians." *UHQ* 3 (1930): 52–59.

Fleming, L.A. "The Settlements on the Muddy, 1865 to 1871: 'A God Forsaken Place.'" *UHQ* 35 (1967): 147–72.

Flores, Dan L. "Zion in Eden: Phases of the Environmental History of Utah." *Environmental Review* 7 (1983): 325–44.

Forbes, Stephen A. "History of the Former State Natural History Societies of Illinois." *Science* 26 (1907): 892–98.

Fowler, Don D., and Catherine S. Fowler. "John Wesley Powell, Anthropologist." *UHQ* 37 (1969): 152–72.

Frazer, Persifor, Jr. "Address of G.K. Gilbert, The Work of the International Congress of Geologists." *American Naturalist* 21 (1887): 841–47.

Frenkiel, Francois N. "Origin and Early Days of the Philosophical Society of Washington," *Bulletin of the Philosophical Society of Washington* 16 (1962): 9–24.

Gannett, Henry. "Do Forests Influence Rainfall?" *Science* 11 (1888): 3–4.

———. "The Influence of Forests on the Quantity and Frequency of Rainfall." *Science* 12 (1888): 242–44.

———. "The Timber-supply of the United States." *Garden and Forest* 6 (1893): 181–82.

———. "The Topographical Work of the National Geological Survey." *American Geologist* 11 (1893): 65–67, 127–28.

Gilbert, Grove Karl. "John Wesley Powell." In *Smithsonian Institution Annual Report. 1902*, 633–40. Washington: GPO, 1903.

———. "John Wesley Powell." *Science* 16 (1902): 561–67.

———. "John Wesley Powell: V. The Investigator," *Open Court* 17 (1903): 228–39, 281–90.

———. "Powell as a Geologist." *Washington Academy of Sciences Proc.* 5 (1903): 113–17.

———. "The Work of the International Congress of Geologists." *American Journal of Science* 31 (1887): 284–99.

[Gilder, Richard Watson.] "Culture and Progress." *Scribner's Monthly* 8 (1874): 373–74.

Godkin, E.L. "Who Shall Direct Our National Surveys." *The Nation* 18 (1874): 328–29.

———. "The War Department and the National Surveys." Ibid. 360–61.

———. "Who Shall Direct Our National Surveys." Ibid. 361–62.

———. "The National Surveys Again." Ibid. 377–78.

———. "The National Surveys Again." Ibid. 22 (1876): 9.

———. "Our Unavailable Public Lands." Ibid. 26 (1876): 288–89.

———. "The Proposed Reform in Our Land and Scientific Surveys." Ibid. 28 (1879): 27–29.

Goetzmann, William. "The Heroic Age of Western Geological Exploration: The U.S. Geological Survey and the Men and Events That Created It." *American West* 16 (1979): 4–13, 59–61.

———. "The Wheeler Surveys and the Decline of Army Exploration in the West." In *The American West: An Appraisal*, edited by Robert G. Ferris, 37–47. Santa Fe: Museum of New Mexico Press, 1963.

Gregory, H.E. "A Century of Geology: Steps of Progress in the Interpretation of Land Forms." *American Journal of Science* 46 (1918): 104–32.

Gressley, Gene M. "Arthur Powell Davis, Reclamation, and the West." *Agricultural History* 42 (1968): 241–57.

Hagan, William T. "United States Indian Policies, 1860–1890." In *Handbook of North American Indians*, vol. 4: *History of Indian-White Relations*, edited by Wilcomb E. Washburn, 51–65. Washington: Smithsonian Institution Press, 1988.

Hague, Arnold. "Samuel Franklin Emmons, 1841–1922." *National Academy of Sciences, Biographical Memoirs* 7 (1913): 309–34.

Henderson, David B. "Powell as a Soldier." *Washington Academy of Sciences Proc.* 5 (1903): 1–6.

Hendrickson, Walter B. "Nineteenth-Century State Geological Surveys: Early Government Support of Science." In *Science in America Since 1820*, edited by Nathan Reingold, 131–145. New York: Science History Publications, 1976.

Hill, R.T. "The Topographical Work of the National Geological Survey." *American Geologist* 11 (1893): 304–10.

Hobbs, William H. "John Wesley Powell, 1834–1902." *Scientific Monthly* 39 (1934): 519–29.

Hobsbawm, E.J. "Methodism and the Threat of Revolution in Britain." In *Labouring Men*, 23–33. London: Weidenfeld and Nicolson, 1964.

Howard, Robert West. "John Wesley Powell: Conqueror of the Colorado." *Conservationist* 33 (1978): 17–19, 48.

———. "Powell of the Genesee." *The Westerners Brand Book: New York Posse* 16 (1969): 25–32.

Howland, O.G. "Letters of O.G. Howland to the *Rocky Mountain News*." *UHQ* 15 (1947): 95–105.

Hunt, Charles B. "John Wesley Powell, His Influence on Geology." *Geotimes* 14 (1969): 16–18.

Hunter, Milton. "Mormons and the Colorado River." *American Historical Review* 44 (1939): 549–55.

"In Memory of John Wesley Powell." *Science* 16 (1902): 782–90.

Ireland, H. Andrew. "History of the Development of Geologic Maps." *Bulletin of Geological Society of America* 54 (1943): 1227–1280.

Ivins, Anthony. "A Mystery of the Grand Canyon Solved." In *Pioneer Stories*, edited by Preston Nibley, 207–10. Salt Lake City: Deseret News Press, 1940.

Jackson, Richard H. "Righteousness and Environmental Change: The Mormons and the Environment." In *Essays on the American West, 1973–1974*, edited by Thomas G. Alexander, 21–41. Provo: Brigham Young University Press, 1975.

James, P.E. "John Wesley Powell, 1834–1902." In *Geographers: Bibliographical Studies*, edited by T.W. Freeman and Philippe Pinchemel, vol. 3, 117–124. London: Mansell Information Publishing, 1979.

"John Wesley Powell: Proceedings of a Meeting Commemorative of His Distinguished Services." *Washington Academy of Sciences Proc.* 5 (1903): 99–187.

Johnson, George A. "Exploration of the Colorado River." *The Golden Era* 37 (1888): 216–18.

Jones, Stephen Vandiver. "Journal of Stephen Vandiver Jones." *UHQ* 16 (1948): 19–174.

Judge, Joseph. "Retracing John Wesley Powell's Historic Voyage Down the Grand Canyon." *National Geographic* 135 (1969): 668–713.

Julian, George. "Our Land Policy." *Atlantic Monthly* 43 (March 1879): 325–37.

Karrow, Robert W. Jr. "George M. Wheeler and the Geographical Surveys West of the 100th Meridian, 1869–1879." In *Exploration and Mapping of the American West: Selected Essays*, edited by Donna P. Koepp, 120–57. Chicago: Speculum Orbis, 1986.

Kay, Jeanne, and Craig J. Brown. "Mormon Beliefs about Land and Natural Resources, 1847–1877." *Journal of Historical Geography* 11 (1985): 253–67.

Kelly, Charles. "The Mysterious 'D. Julien'." *UHQ* 6 (1933): 83–88.

Kelly, Isabel T., and Catherine S. Fowler. "Southern Paiute." In *Handbook of North American Indians*, vol. 11: *Great Basin*, edited by Warren L. D'Azevedo, 368–97. Washington, D.C.: Smithsonian Institution Press, 1986.

Keplinger, Lewis. "The First Ascent of Long's Peak." *The Trail* 12 (1919): 5–16.

King, Clarence. "The Age of the Earth." *American Journal of Science and Arts* 145 (1893): 1–20.

——. "Catastrophism and Evolution." *The American Naturalist* 11 (1877): 449–70.

Kramer, Howard D. "The Scientist in the West, 1870–1880." *Pacific Historical Review* 12 (1943), 239–51.

Lamb, Daniel S. "The Story of the Anthropological Society of Washington." *American Anthropologist* 8 (1906): 564–79.

Larsen, Wesley P. "The 'Letter': Were the Powell Men Really Killed by Indians?" *Canyon Legacy* no. 17 (1993): 12–19.

Larson, Gustive O., and Charles S. Peterson. "Opening the Colorado Plateau." In *Utah's History*, edited by Richard D. Poll, et al., 371–86. Provo: Brigham Young University Press, 1978.

Lavender, David. "James White: First Through the Grand Canyon?" *American West* 19 (1982): 22–28, 30.

Lee, Lawrence B. "William Ellsworth Smythe and the Irrigation Movement: A Reconsideration." *Pacific Historical Review* 41 (1972): 289–311.

Levi-Strauss, Claude. "The Work of the Bureau of American Ethnology and Its Lessons." In *Structural Anthropology*, 2 vols., trans. by Monique Layton, 49–59. New York: Basic Books, 1976.

Limerick, Patricia Nelson. "Haunted America." In *Sweet Medicine: Sites of Indian Massacres, Battlefields, and Treaties*, 119–63. Albuquerque: Univ. of New Mexico Press, 1995.

Lincoln, Mrs. M.D. "John Wesley Powell," Part 1: "Boyhood and Youth." *Open Court* 16 (1902): 705–15; part 2: "The Soldier." Ibid. 17 (1903): 14–25; part 3: "The Professor." Ibid.: 86–94.

Lurie, Nancy O. "Relations between Indians and Anthropologists." In *Handbook of North American Indians*, vol. 4: *History of Indian-White Relations*, edited by Wilcomb E. Washburn, 548–56. Washington: Smithsonian Institution Press, 1988.

Mark, Joan. "Frank Hamilton Cushing and an American Science of Anthropology." *Perspectives in American History* 10 (1976): 449–86.

Marston, O. Dock. "The Lost Journal of John Coton Sumner." *UHQ* 37 (1969): 173–89.

——. "Separation Marks: Notes on 'The Worst Rapid' in the Grand Canyon." *JArH* 17 (1976): 1–20.

Maxwell, John. "John Wesley Powell and Democracy: A Textual Politics for the Arid Region." *Journal of the Southwest* 37 (1995): 482–94.

May, Dean L. "Utah Writ Small: Challenge and Change in Kane County's Past." *UHQ* 58 (1985): 170–83.

McGee, W.J. "The Trend of Human Progress." *American Anthropologist*, ns 1 (1899): 407–47.

Metcalf, Warren. "A Precarious Balance: The Northern Utes and the Black Hawk War." *UHQ* 57 (1989): 24–35.

Miller, David E. "The Ives Expedition Revisited: Overland into Grand Canyon." *JArH* 13 (1972): 177–96.

Miller, Peter. "John Wesley Powell: Vision for the West." *National Geographic* 185 (1994): 86–115.

Muir, John. "The Grand Canyon of the Colorado." *Century Magazine* 65 (1902): 107–16.

Murphree, Idus. "The Evolutionary Anthropologists: The Progress of Mankind: The Concepts of Progress and Culture in the Thought of John Lubbock, Edward B. Tylor, and Lewis H. Morgan." *Proceedings of the American Philosophical Society* 105 (1961): 265–300.

Nelson, Clifford M. "Paleontology in the United States Federal Service, 1804–1904." *Earth Science History* 1 (1982): 44–57.

———. "Powell, John Wesley." In *Encyclopedia of Earth Sciences*, edited by E. Julius Dasch, 887–89. New York: Macmillan, 1996.

———, and Mary C. Rabbitt. "The Role of Clarence King in the Advancement of Geology in the Public Service, 1867–1881." In *Frontiers of Geological Exploration of Western North America: A Symposium*, 19–35. San Francisco: The Division, 1982.

———, Mary Rabbitt, and Fritiof M. Fryxell. "Ferdinand Vandiveer Hayden: The U.S. Geological Survey Years, 1879–1886." *Proceedings of the American Philosophical Society* 125 (1981): 238–43.

Newberry, J.S. "The Grand Canyon of the Colorado." *American Antiquarian* 20 (1898): 114–17.

Olsen, Robert W. Jr. "Clem Powell and Kanab Creek." *Kiva* 34 (1968): 41–50.

———. "Pipe Spring, Arizona, and Thereabouts." *JArH* 6 (1965): 11–20.

———. "The Powell Survey Kanab Base Line." *UHQ* 37 (1969): 261–68.

———. "Winsor Castle: Mormon Frontier Fort at Pipe Spring." Ibid. 34 (1966): 218–26.

O'Neil, Floyd A. "The Reluctant Suzerainty: The Uinta and Ouray Reservation." *UHQ* 39 (1971): 129–44.

Palmer, William R. "Paiute Indian Homelands." *UHQ* 6 (1932): 88–102.

Parry, C.C. "Account of the Passage Through the Great Cañon of the Colorado of the West, . . . by James White." *Academy of Science of St. Louis Trans.* 2 (1868): 499–503.

Peterson, Charles S. "Grazing in Utah: A Historical Perspective." *UHQ* 57 (1989): 300–19.

———. "Imprint of Agricultural Systems on the Utah Landscape." In *The Mormon Role in the Settlement of the West*, edited by Richard H. Jackson, 91–106. Provo: Brigham Young University Press, 1978.

———. "Life in a Village Society, 1877–1920." *UHQ* 49 (1981): 78–96.

Pisani, Donald J. "Forests and Reclamation, 1891–1911." *Forest & Conservation History* 37 (1993): 68–79.

———. "Reclamation and Social Engineering in the Progressive Era." *Agricultural History* 57 (1983): 46–63.

Powell, John Wesley. "Address of Major Powell." *American Institute of Mining Engineers, Trans.* 10 (1881–82): 232–236.

————. "Address of Major Powell in Memory of Professor Baird." *Science* 11 (1888): 25–26.

————. "The Administration of the Scientific Work of the General Government." *Science* 5 (1885): 51–55.

————. "The Ancient Province of Tusayan." *Scribner's Monthly* 11 (1875): 193–213.

————. "Are Our Indians Becoming Extinct?" *Forum* 15 (1893): 343–54.

————. Biographical Notice of Archibald Robertson Marvine." *Philosophical Society of Washington Bull.* 2 (1875–80): appendix, 53–60.

————. "The Cañons of the Colorado." *Scribner's Monthly* 9 (1875): 293–310, 394–409, 523–37.

————. "The Categories." *American Anthropologist* ns 3 (1901): 404–30.

————. "Classification of the Sciences." *American Anthropologist* ns 3 (1901): 601–5.

————. "Competition as a Factor in Human Evolution." *American Anthropologist* 1 (1888): 297–323.

————. "Darwin's Contributions to Philosophy." *Biological Society of Washington Proc.* 1 (1882): 60–70.

————. "A Discourse on the Philosophy of the North American Indians." *Journal of American Geographical Society of New York* 8 (1878): 251–68.

————. "Dualism Modernised." *Monist* 10 (1900): 385–96.

————. "Esthetology." *American Anthropologist* ns 1 (1899): 1–40.

————. "Evolution of Music from Dance to Symphony." In *American Association for the Advancement of Science, Proc., 38th meeting*, 1–21. Salem, Mass.: AAAS, 1890.

————. "The Evolution of Religion." *Monist* 8 (1898): 183–204.

————. "Fallacies of Perception." *Open Court* 12 (1898): 720–29.

————. "The Five Books of History." *Science* 1 (1895): 157–61.

————. "From Savagery to Barbarism." *Anthropological Society of Washington Trans.* 3 (1885): 173–96.

————. "Geological Notes and Sections." *UHQ* 15 (1947): 134–39.

————. "How a Savage Tribe is Governed." *Forum* 25 (1898): 712–22.

————. "The Humanities." *Forum* 10 (1890): 410–22.

————. "Indians of North America." In *Johnson's Universal Cyclopedia*, Vol. 4 544–52. New York: D. Appleton, 1895.

————. "Institutions for the Arid Lands." *Century Magazine* 40 (1890): 111–16.

————. "Irrigable Lands of the Arid Region." *Century Magazine* 39 (1890): 766–76.

————. "James Dwight Dana." *Science* 3 (1896): 181–85.

————. "John Wesley Powell's Journal: Colorado River Explorations, 1871–1872." *Smithsonian Journal of History* 3 (1968): 1–44.

————. "The Larger Import of Scientific Education." *Popular Science Monthly* 26 (1885): 452–56.

————. "The Lesson of Conemaugh." *North American Review* 149 (1889): 150–56.

————. "The Lessons of Folklore." *American Anthropologist* 2 (1900): 1–36.

————. "Letters of Major J. W. Powell to the *Chicago Tribune* [1869]." *UHQ* 15 (1947): 73–88.

————. "Major Powell's Journal." *UHQ* 15 (1947): 125–31.

————. "Major Powell's Report on His Explorations of the Rio Colorado in 1869." In *New Tracks in North America*, William A. Bell, 559–64. New York: Scribner, Welford, and Co., 1870.

————. "Museums of Ethnology and Their Classification." *Science* 9 (1887): 612–14.

————. Mythologic Philosophy." *Popular Science Monthly* 15 (1879): 795–808; 16 (1879): 56–66.

————. "National Agencies for Scientific Research." *Chantauquan* 14 (1891–92): 37–42, 160–65, 291–97, 422–25, 545–49, 668–73.

————. "The New Lake in the Desert." *Scribner's Magazine* 10 (1891): 463–68.

————. "The Non-Irrigable Lands of the Arid Region." *Century Magazine* 39 (1890): 915–22.

————. The Organization and Plan of the United States Geological Survey." *American Journal of Science* 29 (1885): 93–102.

————. "An Overland Trip to the Grand Canyon." *Scribner's Monthly* 10 (1875): 659–78.

————. "Philology." *American Anthropology* ns 2 (1900): 603–37.

————. "Physical Features of the Colorado Valley." *Popular Science Monthly* 7 (1875): 385–99, 531–92, 670–80.

————. "Physiographic Processes," "Physiographic Features," and "Physiographic Regions of the United States." In *The Physiography of the United States*, 1–100. New York: American Book Co., 1895.

————. "Prehistoric Man in America." *Forum* 8 (1890): 489–503.

————. "Problems of American Archaeology." *Forum* 8 (1890): 638–52.

————. "Proper Training and the Future of the Indians." *Forum* 18 (1895): 622–29.

————. "Relation of Primitive Peoples to Environment." In *Smithsonian Institution, Annual Rpt., 1895*, 625–37. Washington, D.C.: GPO, 1896.

————. "Reply to Critics." *Science* 9 (1899): 259–63.

————. "The Scientific Explorer." In *The Grand Canyon of Arizona*, 18–32. N.p.: Santa Fe Railroad, 1902.

————. "Sketch of Lewis H. Morgan." *Popular Science Monthly* 18 (1880): 114–21.

————. "Sociology." *American Anthropologist* ns 1 (1899): 475–509, 695–745.

————. "Some Remarks on the Geological Structure of a District of Country Lying to the North of the Grand Cañon of the Colorado." *American Journal of Science and Arts* 5 (1873): 456–65.

————. "Sophiology." *American Anthropologist* ns 3 (1901): 51–79.

————. "Technology." *American Anthropologist* 1 (1899): 319–49.

————. "The Three Methods of Evolution." *Philosophical Society of Washington Bull.* 6 (1884): xxvii–lii.

————. "Ward's Dynamic Sociology." *Science* 2 (1883): 45–49, 105–108, 171–74, 222–26.

Powell, Walter Clement. "Journal of W.C. Powell." *UHQ* 16 (1949): 257–489.

Powell, Walter Henry. "Letters of W.H. Powell to the *Chicago Evening Journal*." *UHQ* 15 (1947): 90–92.

"The Proposed Reform in Our Land and Scientific Surveys." *The Nation* 28 (1879): 27–29.

Pyne, Stephen J. "Geophysics in the Giant Forest: Grove Karl Gilbert as Conservationist." *Environmental Review* 6 (1978): 2–13.

Rabbitt, Mary C. "John Wesley Powell, His Life and Times." *Geotimes* 14 (1969): 10–12.

Rideing, W. H. "A Chapter of American Exploration." *Lippincott's Magazine* 26 (1880): 393–410.

Rusho, W. L. "Francis Bishop's 1871 River Maps." *UHQ* 37 (1969): 207–13.

Sageser, A. Bower. "Los Angeles Hosts an International Irrigation Congress." *Journal of the West* 4 (1965): 411–24.

Sargent, Charles Sprague. "The Danger from Mountain Reservoirs." *Garden and Forest* 2 (1889): 289.

———. "Forests and Irrigation." Ibid. 3 (1890): 293.

———. "The Forests on the Public Domain." Ibid. 3 (1890): 13–14.

———. "The Forests on the Public Domain." Ibid. 4 (1891–92): 301, 493–94.

———. "The Forests on the Public Domain." Ibid. 10 (1897): 420.

———. "Irrigation Problems in the Arid West." Ibid. 1 (1888): 277–78.

———. "The Lesson of Conemaugh." Ibid. 2 (1889): 421–22.

———. "Mountain Reservoirs and Irrigation." Ibid. 2 (1889): 313–14.

Shinn, Charles Howard. "The Forest." *Garden and Forest* 2 (1869): 502.

Smith, Beatrice Scheer. "The 1872 Diary and Plant Collections of Ellen Powell Thompson." *UHQ* 62 (1994): 104–31.

Smith, Dwight L. "The Engineer and the Canyon." *UHQ* 28 (1960): 263–74.

———. "Robert B. Stanton's Plan for the Far Southwest." *Arizona and the West* 4 (1962): 369–80.

Smith, Henry Nash. "Clarence King, John Wesley Powell, and the Establishment of the United States Geological Survey." *Mississippi Valley Historical Review* 34 (1947): 37–58.

———. "Rain Follows the Plow: The Notion of Increased Rainfall for the Great Plains, 1844–1880." *Huntington Library Quarterly* 10 (1947): 169–93.

Smith, Melvin. "Before Powell: Exploration of the Colorado River." *UHQ* 55 (1987): 104–19.

———. "Colorado River Exploration and the Mormon War." *UHQ* 38 (1970): 207–23.

Sperry, James E., ed. "John Wesley Powell's Address at the North Dakota Constitutional Convention." *North Dakota History* 36 (1969): 369–80.

Spitzka, E.A. "A Study of the Brain of the late Major J. W. Powell." *American Anthropologist* ns 5 (1903): 585–643.

Stanton, Robert Brewster. "The Denver, Colorado Canyon, and Pacific Railroad Project." *Engineering News and American Railway Journal* 22 (1889): 269.

———. "Through the Grand Canyon of the Colorado." *Scribner's Monthly* 8 (1890): 591–613.

Stegner, Wallace. "A Dedication to the Memory of John Wesley Powell, 1834–1902." *Arizona and the West* 4 (1962): 1–4.

———. "C.E. Dutton: Explorer, Geologist, Nature Writer." *Scientific Monthly* 45 (1937): 82–83.

———. "Jack Sumner and John Wesley Powell." *Colorado Magazine* 26 (1949): 61–69.

Sterling, Everett W. "The Powell Irrigation Survey, 1888–1893." *Mississippi Valley Historical Review* 27 (1940): 421–34.

Steward, John F. "Journal of John F. Steward." *UHQ* 16: (1948): 181–251.

Stirling, Matthew Williams. "John Wesley Powell Rediscovered." *Cosmos Club Bull.* 12 (1959): 2–9.

Stoffle, Richard W., and Michael J. Evans. "Resource Competition and Population Change: A Kaibab Paiute Ethnohistorical Case." *Ethnohistory* 23 (1976): 173–97.

Sumner, Jack. "John C. Sumner's Journal." *UHQ* 15 (1947): 113–24.

———. "The Lost Journal of John Colton Sumner." *UHQ* 15 (1969): 173–89.

Thompson, Almon H. "Diary of Almon Harris Thompson, Geographer." *UHQ* 7 (1939): 3–140.

Throne, Mildred, ed., "Letters from Shiloh." *Iowa Journal of History* 52 (1954): 235–80.

Tikalsky, Frank D. "Historical Controversy, Science and John Wesley Powell." *JArH* 23 (1982): 407–22.

"The Topographical Map of the United States." *American Geologist* 10 (1892): 304–10.

Trennert, Robert A. "A Grand Failure: The Centennial Indian Exhibition of 1876." *Prologue: The Journal of the National Archives* 6 (1974): 118–29.

Tylor, Edward Burnett. "How the Problems of American Anthropology Present Themselves to the English Mind." *Anthropological Society of Washington Trans.* 34 (1885): 81–94.

Unrau, William E. "The Civilian as Indian Agent: Villain or Victim?" *Western Historical Quarterly* 3 (1972): 405–20.

"Utah Scenery." *The Aldine* 7 (1874): 14–15.

Walker, Ronald W. "Toward a Reconstruction of Mormon and Indian Relations, 1847–1877." *Brigham Young University Studies* 29 (1989): 23–42.

Ward, Lester F. "Sketch of Professor John W. Powell." *Popular Science Monthly* 20 (1882): 390–97.

Warman, P. C. "Catalogue of Published Writings of John Wesley Powell." *Washington Academy of Sciences Proc.* 5 (1903): 131–87.

Warren, Lt. Gouverneur K. "Memoir to Accompany the Map of the Territory of the United States from the Mississippi to the Pacific Ocean." *Pacific Railroad Reports*, vol. 11. Washington, D.C.: GPO, 1861.

Welling, James C. "The Law of Malthus." *American Anthropologist* 1 (1888): 1–23.

Wesley, John. "Thoughts upon Slavery" (1774). In *Views of American Slavery*. New York: Arno Press, 1969.

White, James. "Passage of the Great Canyon of the Colorado." In *New Tracks in North America*, edited by William A. Bell, 435–53. New York: Scribner, Welford, and Co., 1870.

Whitney, J. Dwight. "Geographical and Geological Surveys." *North American Review* 121 (1875): 37–85, 270–314.

Wilkins, Thurman. "Major Powell and Thomas Moran in Canyon Country." *Montana* 19 (1969): 16–31.

Wilson, Leonard. "The Emergence of Geology as a Science in the United States." *Journal of World History* 10 (1967): 416–37.

Zegas, Judy Braun. "North American Exhibit at the Centennial Exposition." *Curator* 19 (1973): 162–73.

GOVERNMENT DOCUMENTS

Annual Reports of the Bureau of Ethnology, 1879–1902.

Annual Reports of the U.S. Geological Survey, 1879–1894.

Biographical Dictionary of the United States Congress, 1774–1989. Washington, D.C.: GPO, 1989.

Congressional Globe.

Congressional Record.

Gannett, Henry. *Topographic Atlas of the United States: Physiographic Types.* Folios 1 and 2. Washington, D.C.: USGS, 1898–1900.

Hayden, Ferdinand V. *Tenth Annual Report of the United States Geological and Geographical Survey of the Territories.* Washington, D.C.: GPO, 1878.

Ives, Lt. Joseph C. *Report upon the Colorado River of the West, Explored in 1857 and 1858.* Washington, D.C.: GPO, 1861.

"List of Publications of the Bureau of American Ethnology." BAE Bull. 49. Washington, D.C.: GPO, 1911.

Macomb, Capt. J. N. *Report of the Exploring Expedition from Santa Fé, New Mexico.* Washington, D.C.: GPO, 1876.

Ninth Census of the United States: Statistics of Population. Washington D.C.: GPO, 1872.

Powell, J.W. *Exploration of the Colorado River of the West and Its Tributaries.* Washington, D.C.: GPO, 1875.

———. *Introduction to the Study of Indian Languages.* 2nd ed. Washington, D.C.: GPO, 1875.

———. *Report on the Geology of the Eastern Portion of the Uintah Mountains.* Washington, D.C.: USGS, 1876.

Wheeler, George M. *Chronological Account of Explorations of the Colorado River of the West.* Washington, D.C.: GPO, 1880.

———. *Report upon United States Geographical Surveys West of the One Hundredth Meridian.* Vol. 1: *Geographical Report.* Washington, D.C.: GPO, 1889.

U.S. Congress, House of Representatives

"Reports of Explorations and Surveys." 33 Cong., 2 sess., Ex. Doc. 91. Serial 797.

"Exploration of Colorado River." 41 Cong., 2 sess., Ex. Doc. 280 and 281. Serial Set 1426.

"Communication from Captain Samuel Adams Relative to the Exploration of the Colorado River and Its Tributaries." 41 Cong., 3 sess., Misc. Doc. 12. Serial 1462.

"The Colorado River Expeditions of Samuel Adams." 42 Cong., 1 sess., Misc. Doc. 37. Serial 1472.

"Survey of the Colorado River of the West." 42 Cong., 2 sess., Misc. Doc. 173. Serial 1526.

"Report of the Commission of Indians Affairs." 42 Cong., 3 sess., Ex. Doc. 1, part 5. Serial 1560.

"The Condition of the Pi-Ute Indians." 42 Cong., 3 sess., Ex. Doc. 66. Serial 1565.

"Report of the Survey of the Colorado of the West." 42 Cong., 3 sess., Misc. Doc. 76. Serial 1572.

"Report of the Commissioner of Indian Affairs." 43 Cong., 1 sess., Ex. Doc. 1, part 5. Serial 1601.

"Ute, Pai-Ute, Go-si Ute, and Shoshone Indians." 43 Cong., 1 sess., Ex. Doc. 157. Serial 1610.

"Indians West of the Rocky Mountains." 43 Cong., 1 sess., Misc. Doc. 86. Serial 1618.

"Report on the Survey of the Colorado River of the West." 43 Cong., 1 sess., Misc. Doc. 265. Serial 1621.

"Geographical and Geological Surveys West of the Mississippi." 43 Cong., 1 sess., Rpt. 612. Serial 1626.

"Report of the Commissioner of Indian Affairs." 44 Cong., 1 sess., Ex. Doc. 1, part 5. Serial 1680.

"Exploration of the Colorado River of the West and Its Tributaries." 43 Cong., 1 sess., Misc. Doc. 300. Serial 1622.

"Report on the Geographical and Geological Survey of the Rocky Mountain Region." 45 Cong., 2 sess., Ex. Doc. 1, part 5. Serial 1800.

"Report of the Commissioner of Indian Affairs." 45 Cong., 2 sess., Ex. Doc. 1, part 5. Serial 1800.

"Report on the Lands of the Arid Region." 45 Cong., 2 sess., Ex. Doc. 73. Serial 1805.

"Geological and Geographical Surveys." 45 Cong., 2 sess., Ex. Doc. 80, 81, 88. Serial 1809.

"Public Surveys: Testimony before the Committee on the Public Lands." 45 Cong., 2 sess., Misc. Doc. 55. Serial 1818.

"Report of the Secretary of Interior." 46 Cong., 3 Sess., House Ex. Doc. 1, part 5. Serial 1951.

"Annual Report of the United States Geological Survey." 46 Cong., 3 sess., Ex. Doc. 1. Serial 1960.

"Surveys of the Territories." 45 Cong., 3 sess., Misc. Doc. 5. Serial 1861.

"Report of the National Academy of Sciences." 46 Cong., 1 sess., Misc. Doc. 7. Serial 1876.

"Report of the Public Lands Commission." 46 Cong., 2 sess., Ex. Doc. 46. Serial 1923.

"Ethnology of the North American Indians." 46 Cong., 2 sess., Misc. Doc. 35. Serial 1931.

"The Existing Laws of the United States" and "The Public Domain: Its History with Statistics." 46 Cong., 2 sess., Ex. Doc. 47, parts 1 and 4. Serial 1975.

"The Public Domain." 47 Cong., 2 sess., Misc. Doc. 45. Serial 2158.

"Restricting the Work and Publications of the Geological Survey, and for Other Purposes." 49 Cong., 1 sess. Rpt. 2214. Serial 2441.

"Limiting the Printing and Engraving for the Geological Survey." 49 Cong., 1 sess. Rpt. 2740. Serial 2443.

"Sundry Civil Appropriations Bill." 51 Cong., 1 sess., Rpt. 2407. Serial 2813.

U.S. Congress, Senate

"Report upon the Colorado River of the West: Explored in 1857 and 1859." 36 Cong., 1 sess., Ex. Doc. 90. Serial 1058.

"Petition of Samuel Adams." 41 Cong., 2 sess. Misc. Doc. 17. Serial 1408.

"Washburn Report." 43 Cong., 2 sess., Rpt. 662. Serial 1632.

"Letter from O.C. Marsh." 45 Cong., 3 sess., Misc. Doc. 9. Serial 1833.

"United States Geological Survey." 46 Cong., 2 sess., Misc. Doc. 48. Serial 1890.

"Testimony before the Joint Committee." 49 Cong., 1 sess., Misc. Doc. 82. Serial 2345.

"Irrigation in the United States." 49 Cong., 2 sess., Misc. Doc. 15. Serial 2450.

"Letters from the Secretary of the Interior." 49 Cong., 2 sess., Misc. Doc. 22. Serial 2450.

"Letter in Response to Senate Resolution by J.W. Powell." 50 Cong., 1 sess., Ex. Doc. 134. Serial 2513.

"Reservoirs for the Storage of Water in the Arid Regions of the U.S." 50 Cong., 1 sess., Ex. Doc. 163. Serial 2513.

"Report of the Select Committee. . . . to Enquire into and Examine the Methods of Business and Work in the Executive Departments." 50 Cong., 1 sess., Rpt. 507. Serial 2522.

"Sundry Civil Bill." 50 Cong., 1 sess., Rpt. 1814. Serial 2525.

"Preliminary Report on the Organization and Prosecution of the Survey of the Arid Lands for Purposes of Irrigation." 50 Cong., 2 sess., Ex. Doc. 43. Serial 2610.

"Letter of J.W. Gregory in Relation to Irrigation and Reclamation of Arid Lands." 50 Cong., 2 sess., Misc. Doc. 84. Serial 2615.

"Sundry Civil Appropriations." 50 Cong., 2 sess., Rpt. 2613. Serial 2619.

"Irrigation Survey." 51 Cong., 1 sess., Ex. Doc. 141. Serial 1688.

"Report of the Special Committee on the Irrigation and Reclamation of Arid Lands." 51 Cong., 1 sess., Rpt. 928. Serial 2707.

"Report of the Special Committee on the Irrigation and Reclamation of Arid Lands." 51 Cong., 1 sess., Rpt. 928. Serial 2708.

"Sundry Civil Appropriation Bill." 51 Cong., 1 sess., Rpt. 1466. Serial 2710.

"Public Schools of the District of Columbia." 56 Cong., 1 sess., Rpt. 711. Serial 3889.

"The Grand Canyon." 65 Cong. 1 sess., Doc. 42. Serial 7264.

NEWSPAPERS

Bloomington Pantagraph (Ill.)
Chicago Tribune
The Community (Cape Girardeau, Mo.)
Daily Colorado Tribune (Denver)
Denver Post
Deseret News and *Telegraph* (Salt Lake City, Utah)
Detroit Free Press
Dewitt Courier (Ill.)
Jackson Journal-Herald (Ohio)
Jackson Standard-Journal (Ohio)
Mt. Morris Spectator (N.Y.)
New York Evening Post
New York Herald
New York Times
Salt Lake Tribune (Utah)
Washington Post
Washington Star

UNPUBLISHED THESES AND DISSERTATIONS

Berstein, William Samuel. "Lewis Henry Morgan, John Wesley Powell, and Henry George: A Study in the Relation between Nineteenth-Century Intellectual Thought and Social Reform." Brown Univ., 1979.

Brandes, Raymond S. "Frank Hamilton Cushing: Pioneer Americanist." Univ. of Arizona, 1965.

Gease, Deryl Vaughn. "William Newton Byers: Promoter of Early Colorado Agriculture, 1859–1870." Univ. of Denver, 1966.

Jones, Daniel H. "Science, Society, and the Myth of Objectivity: The Geology of Clarence King and John Wesley Powell." Utah State Univ., 1991.

Lacey, Michael J. "The Mysteries of Earth-Making Dissolve: A Study of Washington's Intellectual Community and the Origins of American Environmentalism in the Late Nineteenth Century." George Washington Univ., 1979.

Morris, Lindsay Gardner. "John Wesley Powell: Scientist and Educator." Illinois State Normal Univ., 1947.

Noelke, Virgina Hall McKimmon. "The Origin and Early History of the Bureau of American Ethnology, 1879–1910." Univ. of Texas, 1974.

Rindge, Debora Anne. "The Painted Desert: Images of the American West From the Geological and Geographical Surveys of the Western Territories, 1867–1879." Univ. of Maryland, 1993.

Smith, Melvin T. "The Colorado River: Its History in the Lower Canyons Area." Brigham Young Univ., 1972.

Steinbacher-Kemp, William F. "The Illinois Natural History Society: 1858–1871." Illinois State University, 2000.

Townley, John M. "Reclamation in Nevada, 1850–1904." Univ. of Nevada, 1976.

Zernel, John Joseph. "John Wesley Powell: Science and Reform in a Positive Context." Oregon State Univ., 1983.

Acknowledgments

I owe heartfelt thanks to a long list of individuals who have helped make this book possible. High on that list stand my wife Bev, the world's most generous and cheerful companion, to whom this book is dedicated, and my students and colleagues at the University of Kansas who have enriched my social and intellectual life immeasurably. A special debt is owed to four exceptionally fine scholars, James Aton, Peter Mancall, Adam Rome, and Paul Salstrom, who read chapters of the manuscript-in-process and made many superb suggestions, and to those many lecture audiences that responded with penetrating questions and comments. Over the years my indispensable research assistants have included Karl Brooks, Jeffrey Crunk, Mark Frederick, Michael Grant, Mark Hersey, Nancy Scott Jackson, and Dale Nimz. Don Fowler, an eminent anthropologist and Powell scholar, and Clifford Nelson, historian at the U.S. Geological Survey, have been models of generosity and copious founts of information on many occasions. Others who have supplied valuable research assistance are Victor Bailey, Michael Brodhead, Sharon Clausen, Mark Davis, William de Buys, Robert Euler, Kevin Fernlund, Mary Ferguson, Ralph Frese, Gordon Holland, Donna Koepp, David Maas, Christian McMillan, Jim O'Brien, and William Steinbacher-Kemp. A number of research institutions and their staffs deserve particularly to be mentioned: the American Philosophical Society, the Brown University libraries, the Church of Jesus Christ of Latter-Day Saints' Historical Department, the Denver Public Library's Western History Collection, the Huntington Library, the Manuscript Division of the Library of Congress, the National Archives, the Smithsonian Institution libraries, the Utah State Historical Society, the Wheaton College Library, and the libraries of the University of Arizona, the University of Kansas, and the University of Utah, along with others noted in the Bibliography. Not least, I have been blessed to have Gerard McCauley as my literary agent and Peter Ginna and Susan Day as my editors at Oxford.

Index

8/01

B
Powell
Worster
A river running west

GAYLORD R